Y22998

LONDON BOROUGH OF ENFIELD
LIBRARY SERVICES

This book to be RETURNED on or before the latest date stamped unless a renewal has been obtained by personal call or post, quoting the above number and the date due for return.

(C7-0/P)

Industrial Relations in Context

General Editor: George Sayers Bain

Titles (available or in preparation)

Industrial Relations in Britain
George Sayers Bain (ed.)

Labour Law in Britain
Roy Lewis (ed.)

Personnel Management in Britain
Keith Sisson (ed.)

Labour Law
in Britain

Edited by
Roy Lewis

Basil Blackwell

© Roy Lewis 1986
© Chapter 17 Mary Redmond 1986
© Chapter 20 Paul O'Higgins 1986

First published 1986

Basil Blackwell Ltd
108 Cowley Road, Oxford OX4 1JF, UK

Basil Blackwell Inc.
432 Park Avenue South, Suite 1503,
New York, NY 10016, USA

British Library Cataloguing in Publication Data
Labour law in Britain.
  1. Labor laws and legislation — Great
  Britain
  I. Lewis, Roy
  344.104'1125   KD3009

  ISBN 0–631–13754–8
  ISBN 0–631–13755–6 Pbk

Library of Congress Cataloging in Publication Data
Labour law in Britain.

  (Industrial relations in context)
  Includes bibliographies and index.
  1. Labor laws and legislation—Great Britain.
I. Lewis, Roy.   II. Series.
KD3009.L33   1986   344.41'01   86–6104
ISBN 0–631–13754–8
ISBN 0–631–13755–6 (pbk.)

Typeset by Photo·graphics, Honiton, Devon
Printed in Great Britain by TJ Press Ltd, Padstow

Contents

Contributors

Steven Anderman, Reader in Law, University of Warwick

George Sayers Bain, Professor of Industrial Relations, University of Warwick

Brian Bercusson, Senior Lecturer in Law, Queen Mary College, London

David Cockburn, Solicitor, Pattinson and Brewer, London

Linda Dickens, Lecturer in Industrial Relations, University of Warwick

Brian Doyle, Lecturer in Law, University of Salford

Keith Ewing, Fellow of Trinity Hall and University Assistant Lecturer in Law, Cambridge

Philip James, Research Officer, Industrial Relations Services

Patricia Leighton, Reader in Law, Essex Institute of Higher Education

David Lewis, Principal Lecturer in Law, Middlesex Polytechnic

Roy Lewis, Principal Research Fellow, Industrial Relations Research Unit, University of Warwick

John Mesher, Senior Lecturer in Law, University of Sheffield

Kenneth Miller, Lecturer in Law, University of Strathclyde

Graham Moffat, Lecturer in Law, University of Warwick

Gillian Morris, Senior Lecturer in Law, Polytechnic of North London

Brian Napier, Fellow of Queens' College and University Lecturer in Law, Cambridge

Paul O'Higgins, Regius Professor of Laws, Trinity College, Dublin, and Fellow of Christ's College, Cambridge

Mary Redmond, Solicitor, Dublin

Bob Simpson, Lecturer in Law, London School of Economics and Political Science

Frank Sutcliffe, Lecturer in Law, University of Sheffield

Erika Szyszczak, Lecturer in Law, University of Kent

Sue Ward, Freelance Writer and Researcher

Tables

Foreword

'Industrial Relations in Context' is a new series of books which complements the well-established 'Warwick Studies in Industrial Relations'. The latter continues as a vehicle for disseminating research undertaken at Warwick University's Industrial Relations Research Unit, which includes both teaching staff and the staff of the ESRC-funded Designated Research Centre. The new series is designed for the purposes of teaching and wider dissemination. Its rationale is the need for an analysis of current problems and issues in British industrial relations which is systematically informed by the relevant research and scholarship, and by an awareness of recent trends and developments and the wider social, economic, political and international contexts of industrial relations.

The series began with the publication in 1983 of *Industrial Relations in Britain*, a general text covering trade unions, management, collective bargaining, industrial conflict, the labour market, labour law, and state intervention in industrial relations. It continues with the publication of the present volume, *Labour Law in Britain* edited by Roy Lewis, and a forthcoming volume, *Personnel Management in Britain* edited by Keith Sisson. Further volumes on, among other subjects, industrial sociology and labour economics are planned.

The series aims at providing a clear, comprehensive, authoritative, and up-to-date analysis of the entire field of employment relations. It is intended for students doing diploma, undergraduate, or postgraduate courses in personnel management and industrial relations at colleges, polytechnics, or universities as well as for those studying industrial sociology, labour economics, and labour law. It should also be of interest to those in adult education, to those seeking membership of professional bodies like the Institute of Personnel Management, to industrial relations practitioners in both unions and management, and to the general reader who wants to find out more about industrial relations in Britain today.

The hallmarks of the series are clarity, comprehensiveness, authoritativeness and topicality. Each chapter is an original essay that brings together the relevant theoretical and empirical work. Each is stamped with the views of the authors who are leading experts in the field. Each emphasises analysis and explanation as well as description. Each focuses on trends over the past two or three decades (unless a longer time perspective is required to develop the argument) and says something about likely future developments. And in each case the complete text is welded into a coherent order for teaching purposes by an editor who combines a distinguished research record with a proven ability to communicate to a wide audience.

Labour Law in Britain is an integral and essential part of the series. At Warwick, and at many other institutions of higher and further education, a high priority is placed on teaching and research in labour law. The reason is not hard to find. The last two decades have seen a vast increase in the legal regulation of union organisation, strikes, equal pay, pensions, dismissals, redundancies, and working conditions. The law now exerts a profound influence on personnel management, collective bargaining, and the conduct of industrial disputes. This volume brings together the work of twenty-two experts. Their combined effort constitutes the most comprehensive account available of British labour law and of its fundamental importance for the employment relation.

George Sayers Bain

Preface

Labour law is a practical subject and, at the same time, a focus of public debate and controversy. Its study contributes to the vocational training and liberal education of both lawyers and non-lawyers. Lawyers approach the subject as a legal discipline but their professional expertise is likely to be enhanced by an appreciation of the socio-economic and, where appropriate, international and comparative contexts. Students of management and industrial relations also need to acquire a thorough understanding of labour law if they are to equip themselves for the modern practice of personnel management and trade unionism. The aim of this book is to provide lawyers and non-lawyers with a clear, detailed, and contextual exposition of the entire field of labour law.

There are twenty chapters dealing with, among other things, collective bargaining, industrial democracy, industrial conflict, trade union government and politics, the contract of employment, statutory employment protection, pensions, dismissals, sex and race discrimination, marginal employment, the courts and dispute settlement procedures, and international standards. The order of topics is a matter of convenience rather than doctrine. Some teachers of labour law will for good reasons prefer to start with the contract of employment or strike law or even union government, and it must be admitted that the overview in Chapter 1 is as much a conclusion as an introduction. In any case, the overriding aim is the provision of a comprehensive coverage which takes full account of recent developments.

One of the outstanding features of labour law over the last two decades has been the rapidity of its development. Statutory rights enforceable in the industrial tribunals – particularly the rights concerned with unfair dismissal, redundancy, and discrimination – now rank equally with the more traditional areas of legal regulation such as the contract of employment, strike law, occupational health and safety, and the relation between unions and their members. Another example is provided by the recent development of the right to dissociate from unions, which now has a central place in collective bargaining law. The chapters in this volume reflect the need to take the new areas on board, to reassess the traditional ones, and to elaborate systematically a number of topics which have hitherto been underdeveloped in the literature. These innovative themes include the interaction of employment protection and social security, the labour law framework of occupational pensions, the implications of marginal work, the company law dimension of the employment relation, and the effect of international and European law.

The sheer pace of the subject's development combined with the logistics of editing a large multi-authored work have made it difficult to specify a precise date for the law as stated in this book. Chapters 2 to 20 were finalised between May and July 1985 and only minor modifications were made on proofs in September–October, the period when Chapter 1 was written. In most respects the book conforms to the usual conventions of legal texts, including the provision of a scholarly apparatus of footnotes, tables of cases and statutes, and an index. In addition, each chapter has its own bibliography setting out in full the references to cited works.

Thanks are due to many people who made this book possible: the authors, who went through at least two drafts and generally complied with my incessant and sometimes unreasonable requests; Judith Auty, who undertook the mammoth tasks of copy-editing and preparing the index and tables of cases and statutes; Annemarie Flanders, who ensured the accuracy of the bibliographies; Norma Griffiths, who provided the indispensable secretarial support; and René Olivieri of Basil Blackwell, who gave invaluable advice and encouragement. Finally, I would like to acknowledge the moral support and forbearance of academic colleagues at Warwick University, especially Stephen Evans, with whom I am engaged in joint research.

Roy Lewis

Abbreviations

ACAS	Advisory, Conciliation and Arbitration Service
ACTSS	Association of Clerical, Technical and Supervisory Staffs
ACTT	Association of Cinematograph, Television and Allied Technicians
AEU	Amalgamated Engineering Union
APEX	Association of Professional, Executive, Clerical and Computer Staff
ASLEF	Associated Society of Locomotive Engineers and Firemen
ASRS	Amalgamated Society of Railway Servants
ASTMS	Association of Scientific, Technical and Managerial Staffs
AUEFW	Amalgamated Union of Engineering and Foundry Workers
AUEW	Amalgamated Union of Engineering Workers
AUEW (E)	Amalgamated Union of Engineering Workers (Engineering Section)
AUEW (TASS)	Amalgamated Union of Engineering Workers (Technical and Supervisory Section)
BBC	British Broadcasting Corporation
BIM	British Institute of Management
BISKTA	British Iron, Steel and Kindred Trades' Association
BL	British Leyland
BOAC	British Overseas Airways Corporation
BP	British Petroleum
BRB	British Railways Board
BREL	British Rail Engineering Ltd
BT	British Telecom
CA	Companies Act 1985
CAC	Central Arbitration Committee
CBI	Confederation of British Industry
CC	County Council
CEGB	Central Electricity Generating Board
CIR	Commission on Industrial Relations
CO	Certification Officer
CPAG	Child Poverty Action Group
CPPA	Conspiracy and Protection of Property Act 1875
CPS	Centre for Policy Studies
CRE	Commission for Racial Equality

DC	District Council
DE	Department of Employment
DEP	Department of Employment and Productivity
DHSS	Department of Health and Social Security
DPP	Director of Public Prosecutions
DTI	Department of Trade and Industry
EA 1980	Employment Act 1980
EA 1982	Employment Act 1982
EAT	Employment Appeal Tribunal
EC	European Commission; European Communities
ECJ	European Court of Justice
EEC	European Economic Community
EEF	Engineering Employers' Federation
EETPU	Electrical, Electronic, Telecommunication and Plumbing Union
EIRR	European Industrial Relations Review
EMA	Engineers' and Managers' Association
EMAS	Employment Medical Advisory Service
EOC	Equal Opportunities Commission
EPA	Employment Protection Act 1975
EPCA	Employment Protection (Consolidation) Act 1978
EqPA	Equal Pay Act 1970
EqPAR	Equal Pay (Amendment) Regulations 1983
ESRC	Economic and Social Research Council
ETU	Electrical Trades Union
FA	Finance Act 1970
FAA	Film Artistes' Association
FIS	family income supplement
FPS	Federation of Personnel Services
FWR	Fair Wages Resolution 1946
GAS	General Aviation Services Ltd
GCHQ	Government Communications Headquarters
GMBATU	General, Municipal, Boilermakers and Allied Trades Union
GMP	guaranteed minimum pension
GMWU	General and Municipal Workers' Union
GMWU (MATSA)	General and Municipal Workers' Union (Managerial, Administrative, Technical and Supervisory Association Section)
GOQ	genuine occupational qualification
HA	Health Authority
HC	House of Commons
HL	House of Lords
HMSO	Her Majesty's Stationery Office
HSC	Health and Safety Commission
HSE	Health and Safety Executive
HSIB	Health and Safety Information Bulletin
HSWA	Health and Safety at Work etc. Act 1974

IAB	Industrial Arbitration Board
IDS	Incomes Data Services
ILO	International Labour Office; International Labour Organisation
IIME Committee	OECD Committee on International Investment and Multinational Enterprises
IOD	Institute of Directors
IR	Inland Revenue
IRA	Industrial Relations Act 1971
IRC	Independent Review Committee
IRRR	Industrial Relations Review and Report
IRS	Industrial Relations Services
ITF	International Transport Workers' Federation
JRC	joint representation committee
LBC	London Borough Council
LRD	Labour Research Department
MP	Member of Parliament
MSC	Manpower Services Commission
NACODS	National Association of Colliery Overmen, Deputies and Shotfirers
NALGO	National and Local Government Officers' Association
NAPF	National Association of Pension Funds
NATO	North Atlantic Treaty Organisation
NATSOPA	National Society of Operative Printers' Assistants; National Society of Operative Printers, Graphical and Media Personnel
NCB	National Coal Board
NCCL	National Council for Civil Liberties
NDN	non-discrimination notice
NEDO	National Economic Development Office
NGA	National Graphical Association
NHS	National Health Service
NI	national insurance; Northern Ireland
NIRC	National Industrial Relations Court
NUGMW	National Union of General and Municipal Workers
NUJ	National Union of Journalists
NUM	National Union of Mineworkers
NUPE	National Union of Public Employees
NUR	National Union of Railwaymen
NUS	National Union of Seamen
OECD	Organisation for Economic Co-operation and Development
OJ	Official Journal
OMWP	Office of the Minister without Portfolio
OPB	Occupational Pensions Board
PA	Press Association
PHA	pre-hearing assessment
POEU	Post Office Engineering Union

PSI	Policy Studies Institute
QBD	Queen's Bench Division
RPA	Redundancy Payments Act 1965
RRA	Race Relations Act 1976
SAGA	Staff Association General Accident
SDA	Sex Discrimination Act 1975
SDP	Social Democratic Party
SERPS	state earnings-related pension scheme
SI	Statutory Instrument
SJIC	statutory joint industrial council
SOGAT	Society of Graphical and Allied Trades
SR & O	Statutory Rules and Orders
SRC	Science Research Council
SSA	Social Security Act 1975
SSHBA	Social Security and Housing Benefits Act 1982
SSP	statutory sick pay
SSPA	Social Security Pensions Act 1975
SSRC	Social Science Research Council
TASS	*See* AUEW (TASS) *above*
TDA 1906	Trade Disputes Act 1906
TDA 1965	Trade Disputes Act 1965
TES	Temporary Employment Subsidy
TGWU	Transport and General Workers' Union
TSTWCS	Temporary Short-Time Working Compensation Scheme
TUA 1913	Trade Union Act 1913
TUA 1984	Trade Union Act 1984
TUAC	Trade Union Advisory Committee to the OECD
TUC	Trades Union Congress
TULRA	Trade Union and Labour Relations Acts 1974 and 1976
TULR(A)A	Trade Union and Labour Relations (Amendment) Act 1976
UCATT	Union of Construction, Allied Trades and Technicians
UDC	Urban District Council
UKAPE	United Kingdom Association of Professional Engineers
UMA	union membership agreement
UPW	Union of Post Office Workers
USDAW	Union of Shop, Distributive and Allied Workers
WCA	Wages Councils Act 1979
YOP	Youth Opportunities Programme
YTS	Youth Training Scheme

Table of Statutes

Table of Orders and Regulations

Table of Cases

xxix

PART I
Introduction

1 The Role of the Law in Employment Relations

Roy Lewis*

Labour law affects the working lives of millions of people. For two decades it has also been a major focus of public debate about industrial relations, economic performance, and political ideology. Yet the law is only one aspect of the employment relationship, its role being determined not only by its own rules and institutions but also by its interaction with economic circumstances and social attitudes. Furthermore, the tradition in Britain was to accord legal regulation a secondary role in comparison with voluntary regulation. This normally took the form of collective bargaining between management and trade unions or individual bargaining – often a euphemism for the exercise of managerial power – between employers and employees. The balance between legal and voluntary regulation, whether collective or individual, may shift, however, either generally or in specific areas.

The first clear sign of a general trend towards legal regulation was the development of statutory employment protection through the Contracts of Employment Act 1963, the Redundancy Payments Act 1965, EqPA, and the IRA's provisions on unfair dismissal. But the IRA had a wider significance in that it attempted a general legal regulation of the employment relation and thereby broke with the earlier tradition of non-interventionism. The repeal of the IRA by TULRA in 1974 stemmed the legal tide in relation to strikes, closed shops and the enforceability of collective agreements, though subsequent legislation in the 1970s – EPA, HSWA, SDA and RRA – extended the scope of the law in other areas, notably, employment protection and support for union organisation and collective bargaining. The direction was changed once again by the legislation of the 1980s: EAs 1980 and 1982 and TUA 1984. On the one hand, it provided for more legal regulation of industrial action, trade union government, and the individual freedom to choose between and dissociate from trade unions. On the other hand, it aimed to 'deregulate' as far as aspects of employment protection and support for collective bargaining were concerned.

Nevertheless, the overall growth of legal regulation has continued even in some of the areas singled out for deregulation. This development has

* The author wishes to thank Linda Dickens, Stephen Evans, Bob Simpson and David Winchester for their help in the preparation of this chapter. The author alone is responsible for any errors which remain and for the views expressed.

typically taken the form of statutory intervention, which has often led to secondary waves of judicial intervention. But the sheer growth of labour law gives rise to more contentious questions, which the chapter will also address. How has increasing legal regulation affected the behaviour of employers, workers and trade unions? Does the law's impact amount to a trend towards the 'juridification' of industrial relations and, if so, might this affect the collective as much as the individual employment relation? To what extent is this trend an inevitable or desirable consequence of recent state policies? The answers to these questions may have significant implications for the future development of the role of the law in industrial relations.

GROWTH OF LEGAL REGULATION

Labour law has developed rapidly over the last two decades. Under the previous public policy of non-intervention or abstention by the state, the characteristic features of British industrial relations were voluntary self-regulation by the autonomous social forces of management and labour and the priority of collective bargaining over legal enactment. Consistently, the promotion of voluntarism was seen as one of the underlying rationales of the law.[1] Thus the internal affairs of trade unions were regulated more by the unions' own rule books than by external legal regulation, despite the importance of the Registrar of Friendly Societies and the common law policy of safeguarding the interests of individual union members. Individual choice between and dissociation from unions were not regulated by statutory or common law rules. Nor did the law protect the basic freedoms to join or be active in unions against employers' hostility or interference. Employers were not obliged by law to deal with unions, collective agreements were not directly enforceable as contracts, and the state's occasional interventions in support of collective bargaining – the fair wages policies, state-provided conciliation and arbitration, the wages councils, and the very limited provisions for unilateral arbitration, for example, s.8 of the Terms and Conditions of Employment Act 1959 – were underpinned by indirect sanctions or by none at all. Of fundamental importance was the way in which the state granted the legal freedom to strike: it was embodied not in positive rights but in negatively expressed statutory immunities from common law liabilities. Even legislation for the protection of individual employees was – outside of laws on health and safety and the payment of wages to manual workers – largely conspicuous by its absence. There were of course deviations from the trend, for example, wartime measures of compulsory arbitration and the restrictions on the freedoms to associate and to strike in the Trade Disputes and Trade Unions Act 1927. But the general character of state policy in Britain as compared with other industrialised countries was non-interventionist. What legislation there was (in contrast to some of the

---

[1] On the historical development, see Kahn-Freund (1959; 1983a); Wedderburn (1978; 1980; 1985a); Clark and Wedderburn (1983); Lewis (1976; 1983).

common law) assumed the desirability of voluntary collective regulation. This framework was indicative of the replacement of the Victorian doctrine of individual laissez-faire by what Kahn-Freund (1959:224) described as 'collective laissez-faire'.

Collective laissez-faire is no longer the dominant public policy. Confronted by a persistent economic and social crisis, in which industrial conflict and low productivity were depicted as salient features, or even prime causes, the state devised new industrial relations strategies. These may be broadly described as 'reform' and 'restriction', terms which are discussed later in this chapter. For present purposes the essential point about both these strategies is that they involved a great increase in statutory intervention. At the same time the climate of public opinion influenced the judges, who developed the common law sometimes in response to and sometimes in anticipation of the legislative framework. The non-interventionist character of labour law was thus overwhelmed by successive waves of legislation and common law. By the mid-1970s a 'fundamental and irreversible trend' towards the legal regulation of British industrial relations was discernible (Lewis, 1976:15). Since then the trend has continued, though the focus and pace of further legal regulation has not been uniform. This can be seen from an examination of how the law has sought to regulate collective bargaining, industrial conflict, trade union government, and the rights of individual employees.

Collective Bargaining

While British law does not provide a comprehensive or effective guarantee of the freedom to organise in trade unions, it does offer a series of legal rights enforceable in the industrial tribunals by individual employees: the right not to be dismissed because of membership of or activity in an independent union, the right not to be subject to employer action short of dismissal for such reasons, and the rights to paid and unpaid time off for industrial relations duties and trade union activities.[2] Safety representatives of independent, recognised unions have a somewhat more extensive framework of statutory rights to time off and other facilities.[3] These provisions were originally enacted in the mid-1970s as part of a wider policy for the extension and reform of collective bargaining. Although the election of a Conservative Government in 1979 marked the reversal of that policy, the existence of the 'positive' right supportive of union membership and activity was part of the argument for the introduction of the 'negative' right to dissociate.

Wedderburn (1985b:508) argues that the right to dissociate could have been enacted without the stimulus of the existence of a positive right. While his view is logically correct, in practice the development of the right to dissociate appears to have been intertwined with that of the positive right

[2] EPCA ss.58(1), 23(1), 27–8 respectively; see Chapter 2.
[3] HSWA s.2; Safety Representatives and Safety Committees Regulations SI 1977 No. 500; see Chapter 16.

both in the UK and abroad. The tendency to equate the positive and negative rights is a feature of Continental jurisprudence, which became directly relevant to British labour law as a result of the interpretation of Art.11 of the European Convention on Human Rights in the *British Rail* case.[4] But the equation of the two types of rights in the UK pre-dates this litigation. Thus the right to dissociate in s.5 of the IRA was drafted as a correlative to the positive right and also was not confined to the closed shop. This pattern is repeated in the current provisions (EPCA ss.58(1)(c), 23(1)(c)) introduced by the Employment Acts 1980–82: the rights not to be dismissed because of a refusal to join and not to be subject to action short of dismissal to compel membership of any or a particular union. The correlative principle appears not only in the substantive rights but also in the remedies and procedures. While 'joinder' of a union or other person pressurising an employer is applicable only to the enforcement of the negative right, the interim relief procedure and the same generous sums of compensation are made available to both the union activist and the non-member. ~~£20,000 of £598~~

But the recent development of the right to dissociate, which is reinforced by the special rules applicable where UMAs apply[5] and by the ban on union- and recognition-only practices (EA 1982 ss.12–14), is only one aspect of the way in which the law impinges on collective bargaining. As mentioned above, non-interventionist public policy regarded collective bargaining as the preferred method of settling conditions of employment and provided some unobtrusive support for it. In the mid-1970s this traditional support was extended and reorganised. ACAS took over the state's peacekeeping machinery of conciliation, arbitration and mediation,[6] and the wages councils, which both promoted collective bargaining and employment protection, were empowered to make their own orders instead of having to submit proposals for ministerial approval (see Chapter 4). In addition, legal support was significantly extended not only by individual rights in respect of union membership and activity (see above) but also by collective trade union rights. This development started with the IRA, which permitted registered unions to avail themselves of procedures for disclosure of information (a provision which was not, in fact, brought into force) and the determination of bargaining units and agencies. After the repeal of the IRA, the EPA and other statutes introduced a new set of collective rights. Independent unions could refer a recognition issue to ACAS, and failure by the employer to implement an ACAS recommendation led to the possibility of an arbitration award by the CAC.[7] Independent unions were also given the right to claim arbitration before the CAC on 'recognised' terms and conditions (a continuation of s.8 of the Terms and Conditions of Employment Act 1959) or,

---

[4] *Young, James and Webster v UK* [1981] IRLR 408.

[5] As Chapter 2 explains, these include the requirements on ballots and the special protection of broad categories of employees, including those who genuinely object on grounds of conscience or other deeply held personal conviction to membership of any or a particular union; see *Home Delivery Services v Shackcloth* [1985] ICR 147.

[6] EPA ss.2, 3; see Chapter 19.

[7] EPA ss.11–16; see Chapter 3. For a discussion of the CAC, see Chapter 19.

in the absence of such terms, the 'general level' for comparable workers in the district.[8] The CAC was also involved in an arbitration procedure introduced to make collective agreements conform with the principle of equal pay.[9] In addition, employers were placed under a legal duty to recognised unions to disclose information for collective bargaining,[10] and the final stage of this procedure was, once again, arbitration by the CAC.

In all these jurisdictions the CAC's awards were confined by and large to substantive rather than procedural issues, and were ultimately enforceable only through actions for breach of contract brought by individual employees. These limitations were consistent with the tradition of non-interventionist support for collective bargaining. But sanctions of a different order were envisaged for the legal rights of recognised unions to consultation on industrial safety[11] and proposed redundancies.[12] In theory the duty to consult on safety could have been enforced by 'improvement notices' and criminal prosecutions,[13] though in practice (as Chapter 16 explains) the safety inspectorate prefers to leave this matter to voluntary procedures. The redundancy consultation procedure was unusual in that it gave unions (as opposed to employees) a direct right of complaint to the industrial tribunals, even though the culmination of the procedure was a protective award for individual employees.

Collective bargaining or collective consultation with trade unions was the model of employee participation implicit in these measures. They did not address the problems arising from the legal structure of ownership, in particular, the sparse recognition accorded to employees by company law and the tendency for employers to belong to corporate groups operating on a multi-establishment and multi-national basis.[14] That was the province of the Bullock Report (1977), which recommended a system of union representation at boardroom level (see Chapter 5). The implementation of this recommendation would have involved a major reform of company law and the extension of legal regulation over the procedures of collective industrial relations. Since the Bullock Report, however, public policy has changed. The British government is now in the forefront of opposition to moves by the EEC to finalise the draft directives on company law and on procedures for information and consultation in companies with complex structures (the 'Vredeling' directive).[15]

This is only one aspect of its more general opposition to the principle of legislative support for collective bargaining, an area where the trend towards legal regulation has in important respects been checked. EA 1980 repealed the EPA's procedure for union recognition, a symbolic reversal of public

---

8   EPA Sch.11; see Chapter 4.
9   EqPA s.3; see Chapter 17.
10 EPA ss.17–21; see Chapter 3.
11 See note 3 above.
12 EPA Part IV; see Chapter 15.
13 But disputes over a safety representative's right to paid time off are referable to the industrial tribunals: SI 1977 No.500 reg.11.
14 Cf. the discussion in Chapter 5 of the labour law concept of 'associated' employers.
15 OJ C240/2 9.9.83 and C217/3 12.8.83; DE and DTI (1983); see further Chapters 5 and 20.

policy (see Chapter 3). The 1980 Act also swept away the EPA's provisions on arbitration of terms and conditions of employment, whether 'recognised' or 'general level', even though some variant of the former had existed since 1940. This was followed by the UK's denunciation of ILO Convention No.94 on Labour Clauses in Public Contracts and the rescission, effective from September 1983, of the Fair Wages Resolution 1946. The statutory fair wages clauses were also repealed or rendered obsolescent. In addition, local authorities are to be restrained from operating their equivalent fair wages clauses under proposed legislation to make void contractual conditions not directly related to the required performance of the work (Department of the Environment, 1985:para.16). Finally, after announcing its intention to denounce ILO Convention No.26 concerning minimum wage-fixing, the government proposed to limit the scope of the wages councils' orders and to remove workers under the age of twenty-one from their protection.[16]

Nevertheless, the EPA's disclosure duty was retained and an important new disclosure duty was introduced. It requires trustees and managers of pension funds to disclose information both to individuals and independent, recognised unions.[17] While disputes about whether a union is recognised are referable to the industrial tribunals, the enforcement provisions enable a union to obtain an order in the ordinary courts. Furthermore, though the statutory minimum period for redundancy consultation was reduced,[18] the British government has been constrained by EEC and other pressures from repealing the statutory consultation rights. It has, in fact, supplemented them with the Transfer of Undertakings (Protection of Employment) Regulations,[19] reluctantly enacted after the European Commission threatened legal proceedings against the UK for failure to implement the 1977 Directive on Acquired Rights. The Regulations suffer from numerous limitations, but they are a novel development of British labour law in that they require the automatic transfer of contracts of employment, collective agreements and union recognition, as well as imposing a duty to inform and consult the representatives of recognised trade unions. But perhaps the most innovative of the recent developments in collective consultation arose, ironically, from the government's banning of trade union membership and withdrawal of employees' rights of access to the tribunals at GCHQ. Although the unions lost their case against the government on grounds of national security, the House of Lords elaborated a new legal duty to exercise Crown prerogative fairly – a duty amenable to judicial review in appropriate

---

[16] See generally Chapter 4. On the reform of wages councils, see DE (1985a) and HC Deb. 17 July 1985, 326–9 (Secretary of State).

[17] Social Security Pensions Act 1975 s.56A, inserted by Social Security Act 1985 Sch. 2; see further Chapter 14.

[18] Employment Protection (Handling of Redundancies) Variation Order SI 1979 No.958.

[19] SI 1981 No.1794, discussed from several perspectives in subsequent chapters: collective bargaining (Chapter 4), company law (Chapter 5), contract of employment (Chapter 12), redundancy (Chapter 15), and international obligations (Chapter 20). A further EEC pressure, the need to comply with the EC Directive on Equal Treatment (1976), has prompted the government to propose the amendment of SDA and EqPA so as to make discriminatory terms in collective agreements void: DE (1985c).

cases – which embraces the legitimate expectation of employees and recognised unions to be consulted prior to major alterations in conditions of employment.[20]

Industrial Conflict

The legal regulation of industrial conflict operates in diverse ways. The policy objective is not necessarily to encourage legal actions, though that may occur in practice, but rather to deter strikes and other forms of industrial action and to limit their scale. One method of attempting to achieve this is to deny legal rights to individual strikers. They are liable to summary dismissal under their contracts of employment and are excluded from statutory redundancy pay and social security benefits. Since 1979, as Chapter 9 explains, this legal deterrence has been intensified. The strikers' dependants' entitlement to supplementary benefit was reduced and – under EPCA s.62 as amended – the employer's immunity from liability for the unfair dismissal of strikers was widened. A further legal pressure is the requirement that ballot papers issued under Part II of the TUA 1984, which deprives a union of immunity if it fails to secure a majority in a ballot on official industrial action, must indicate that the action involves the individual in a breach of contract.

Turning to the legal liabilities arising from strikes, the judges traditionally restricted industrial action through the development of common law liabilities, especially the 'economic' torts. The statutory immunities from these liabilities gave only a limited freedom to strike and so preserved an important function for the judges, who could widen the liabilities or narrowly construe the immunities (see generally Chapter 6). Judicial creativity in this area has featured prominently in the legal developments of the last twenty years, for example, the invention of the tort of intimidation,[21] the expansion of liabilities for inducing breach of and interference with commercial contracts,[22] the application of 'economic duress' to industrial action,[23] and the restraint of picketing through a novel liability for unreasonable harassment.[24] Even when the Law Lords upheld a broad interpretation of the phrase 'in contemplation or furtherance of a trade dispute', they condemned the system of immunities and, in effect, invited the legislative restriction of secondary industrial action, which soon materialised in EA 1980 s.17.[25] This statute began perhaps the most decisive stage in the legal regulation of industrial conflict, namely, the legislative (as distinct from the judicial) narrowing of the immunities so as to enlarge the field of application of the common law liabilities.

20 *Council of Civil Service Unions v Minister for the Civil Service* [1985] ICR 14.
21 *Rookes v Barnard* [1964] AC 1129.
22 *Stratford v Lindley* [1965] AC 269; *Torquay Hotel Co. Ltd v Cousins* [1969] 2 Ch. 106.
23 *Universe Tankships Inc. of Monrovia v ITF* [1983] 1 AC 366.
24 *Thomas v NUM (S Wales Area)* [1985] IRLR 136.
25 *NWL Ltd v Woods* [1979] ICR 867; *Express Newspapers Ltd v MacShane* [1980] AC 672; *Duport Steels Ltd v Sirs* [1980] ICR 161. See Wedderburn (1980:325).

Immunities no longer protect against tortious liabilities across a wide range of industrial action:[26] picketing where the pickets venture away from their own place of work (TULRA s.15 as amended); secondary industrial action (EA 1980 s.17), particularly after the case law confirmed the narrowness of the possible exceptions to this loss of immunity;[27] action to uphold union- and recognition-only practices (EA 1982 s.14); and 'official' industrial action which has not been approved by secret ballot (TUA 1984 Part II). The definition of 'trade dispute' (TULRA s.29), on which the immunities depend, was narrowed in several ways: for example, it was confined to disputes between employers and their own workers, and the increasing number of disputes with a significant political as well as industrial content were excluded.[28] Further, EA 1982 s.15 withdrew the blanket immunity in tort previously enjoyed by trade unions and employers' associations, directly exposing unions to injunctions, damages, and contempt of court proceedings.

Tort liability is not the only branch of civil law which regulates industrial conflict. Dissident members of a union may seek to invoke the law against a strike by way of a legal action in contract to enforce the union rule book. Litigation brought by working miners in the strike of 1984–5 was based on the failure of the national and several area unions to hold ballots on industrial action under their rules. This breach of contract allowed the members to obtain remedies restraining the strike, expenditure on it, the description of it as 'official' and, above all, disciplinary action against those who refused to participate in it.[29] Moreover, the Secretary of State's Code on the Closed Shop, which may be taken into account not only in cases to enforce the rule book but also in complaints to a tribunal alleging unreasonable exclusion from membership under EA 1980 s.4, envisages (para.61) a wide variety of circumstances in which a union ought not to take disciplinary action against members who refuse to strike.

It is noteworthy that the ultimate enforcement of the civil law – whether tort or contract – may involve quasi-criminal penalties such as fines and even imprisonment for contempt of court. Chapter 19 discusses the recent developments in court enforcement procedures involving, among other methods, the sequestration of union assets and the appointment of receivers. Criminal penalties may, however, be of more immediate relevance to the legal regulation of industrial action. When picketing takes place, public order is maintained through the exercise of police powers backed by criminal sanctions. The miners' dispute 1984–5 demonstrated that the criminal as well as the civil law may be harnessed in aid of the government's

---

[26] See Chapters 6 and 7 below.
[27] E.g. *Marina Shipping Ltd v Laughton* [1982] ICR 215; *Merkur Island Shipping Corp. v Laughton* [1983] 2 AC 570; *Dimbleby & Sons Ltd v NUJ* [1984] ICR 386.
[28] See *Mercury Communications Ltd v Scott-Garner* [1984] ICR 74.
[29] E.g. *Taylor v NUM (Derbyshire Area)* [1984] IRLR 440; see generally Ewing (1985). Cf. earlier decisions such as *Porter v NUJ* [1980] IRLR 404 discussed in Chapter 10. On the potential of rule book actions for the restraint of criminal and tortious acts: see *Thomas v NUM (S Wales Area)* [1985] IRLR 136.

industrial relations policies, notably the restriction of secondary picketing.[30] The existing powers of the police to control the number and location of pickets are to be enlarged under proposals aimed at bringing 'static' demonstrations within the framework of the Public Order Act (Home and Scottish Offices, 1985). Moreover, the Special Branch of the police not only gathers information on pickets who might pose a threat to public order but also counters 'subversion', the wide definition of which appears to envisage industrial conflict.[31] Finally, as discussed in Chapter 8, a range of both civil and criminal liabilities already exists to ensure the continuance of essential services during industrial disputes.

Trade Union Government

Under non-interventionist legal policy, the primary basis of authority within trade unions was the union rule book. The Registrar of Friendly Societies, a state agency, exercised important functions in relation to union finances, amalgamations, and political funds, but by and large the internal affairs of unions were a matter of self-regulation. In contrast, under the IRA, only registered organisations counted in law as 'trade unions', enjoying legal rights but subject to a degree of control by the Registrar of Trade Unions. After the repeal of the IRA, a modified version of the traditional framework was restored, the supervisory rule being given to the CO (see Chapter 10). The modifications were, however, consistent with more legal regulation. For example, TULRA s.2 confirmed that unions had some of the characteristics of corporate bodies for the purposes of different kinds of proceedings, and the CO's powers included the issuance of certificates of independence, which unions needed in order to assert their new legal rights in respect of disclosure, recognition, consultation, and workplace organisation. More-over, the anti-discrimination laws were applied to unions. SDA s.12 and RRA s.11 prohibited discrimination on grounds of sex, marital status and race in respect of admission to and disciplinary action by unions. This statutory regulation of the member-union relation overlapped with the common law policy, which pre-dated the legislative initiatives of the mid-1970s, of protecting the individual member. With the aid of principles imported from administrative and company law, this policy underpinned the judicial interpretation of the contract of membership contained in the union rule book. Such judicial regulation extended to membership participation, disciplinary action, and expulsion from and – in certain cases of dubious authority – admission to unions.[32] It also had implications for industrial

---

[30] E.g. *Moss v McLachlan* [1985] IRLR 76 (road blocks) and *R v Mansfield Justices ex parte Sharkey* [1984] IRLR 496 (bail conditions); see Chapter 7.

[31] 'Subversive activities are those which threaten the safety or well-being of the state, and which are intended to undermine or overthrow parliamentary democracy by political, industrial or violent means': 'Home Office Guidelines on Work of a Special Branch' set out in HC Home Affairs Committee 1984–85, Fourth Report, 71, p.x.

[32] See Chapter 10 for details, including the development of Lord Denning's notion of the 'right to work' in such cases as *Nagle v Feilden* [1966] 2 QB 633.

conflict. The cases brought by working miners in the 1984–5 coal dispute were a classic illustration of how union members could use legal tactics to frustrate, or even defeat, a strike called in breach of the rule book.[33]

These foundations of legislative and judicial regulation were extensively built on by the provisions introduced in the 1980s. EA 1980 s.4 enacted a legal right not to be unreasonably excluded or expelled from a union where a UMA applied, and specifically required the industrial tribunals not to regard a union as behaving reasonably merely because it acted in accordance with its rules. The legislative target was not only the recruitment policies of unions but also their ability to maintain solidarity in trade disputes. The latter point was clear from paras. 61–2 of the Secretary of State's Closed Shop Code, which (as noted above) condemned as unreasonable the disciplining of members who declined to participate in industrial action in many circumstances, including where the action had not been affirmed in a secret ballot.

The statutory encouragement of ballots proceeded on a 'carrot and stick' basis. The carrot, in EA 1980 ss.1 and 2, comprised a legal right for recognised unions to hold workplace ballots on employers' premises and a financial subsidy, administered by the CO, for certain secret postal ballots. The stick was suggested by the provisions in the Closed Shop Code already mentioned and by the need to hold ballots on the continuance of UMAs, on pain of unfair dismissal liability for employers and, through joinder, of unions as well, though in this instance it was unclear whether the ballot was supposed to be conducted by the employer or the union. But the strongest concept of the mandatory trade union ballot was embodied in the TUA 1984. Part I of this Act (see Chapter 10) requires ballots at least once every five years for the election of principal executive committees, which under union constitutions are usually the sovereign bodies between policy-making conferences. The Act's detailed regimen for balloting – covering voting methods, candidatures, and constituencies, together with a separate duty on unions to maintain a central register of members – overrides union rules and applies to both national and also, perhaps, some branch executive committees.[34] The enforcement procedure gives the individual member rights of complaint to the CO and the courts. An enforcement order issued by a court may require a union to conduct a postal ballot. Under Part II of the Act (discussed in Chapter 6), a trade union proposing to engage in official industrial action loses immunities unless a majority of its affected members vote in favour of the action in a secret ballot. Once again the Act regulates the ballot in considerable detail, in this instance down to the wording on the ballot paper. Part III of the Act (see Chapter 11) requires unions, under the close supervision of the CO, to hold ballots every ten years, in order to confirm the continuance of their political funds. It also broadens the definition of 'political objects', which has the effect of enlarging the potential field of application for the detailed legal and

---

[33] See note 29 above.
[34] Where a branch with negotiating functions falls within the legal definition of a 'trade union' (TULRA s.28); see Wedderburn (1985c:56).

administrative regulation accompanying political expenditure. And it makes employers legally liable for failure to comply promptly to requests from contracted-out members to cease deducting the political levy through the check-off. This combined onslaught from Parliament, the courts, and the CO is a severe challenge to the tradition of rule-book autonomy.

Individual Employment Protection

The rapid development of statutory protection for individual employees over the last twenty years was accompanied by a strengthening of some of the more traditional areas of legal regulation such as wages councils (see above) and the law concerned with health and safety at work. In the latter area, the unceasing stream of claims for damages – a major industry involving lawyers, insurers, and trade unions – continued and, despite its tendency to reduce safety issues to a determination of the employer's legal fault, received the qualified approval of a Royal Commission.[35] In addition, the HSWA rationalised and extended earlier safety legislation, gave the inspectorate important new powers to issue improvement and prohibition notices, and brought several million extra workers within the legislative framework. But the main thrust of recent developments in employment protection was the enactment of individual rights enforceable in the industrial tribunals.

The process began with the Contracts of Employment Act 1963, which specified minimum periods of notice for the termination of contracts of employment and required that employees be given a written statement of particulars of their terms and conditions of employment. This was followed by the Redundancy Payments Act 1965, which gave employees a right to redundancy pay. The right not to be unfairly dismissed, which had been strongly advocated by the Donovan Report (1968), was finally introduced in the one part of the IRA to be re-enacted in 1974 by TULRA. Amended versions of these provisions were later incorporated in the EPCA,[36] which also consolidated a series of other protective measures, including rights to an itemised pay statement (ss.8–10), guarantee pay (ss.12–18), payment for suspension on medical grounds (ss.19–22), time off work for specified purposes (ss.27–30), maternity pay and leave (ss.33–44), a written statement of reasons for dismissal (s.53), and protected wages, holiday pay and certain other statutory pay entitlements in the event of the employer's insolvency (ss.121–7). In addition, the right to equal pay was introduced by the EqPA, and sex and race discrimination against workers and job applicants was prohibited by the SDA and RRA. Finally, the EPA contained a legal right for the individual employee to seek damages for breach of employment

---

[35] Pearson (1978). On compensation and also on the provisions of the HSWA, see Chapter 17.

[36] Written particulars (EPCA ss.1–7) and notice periods (ss.49–52) – discussed in Chapter 12; unfair dismissal (ss.54–80) and redundancy pay (ss.81–120) – discussed in Chapter 15. On the general development of employment protection, see Chapter 13.

contract in the industrial tribunals,[37] though the ministerial order to implement this provision is yet to be made.

An inherent limitation of most of the employment protection rights is that they apply only to employees (those with legally recognised contracts of employment), who have worked for a minimum number of hours and who have a specified length of service with the same employer.[38] Excluded, therefore, are many of the 2.5 million self-employed, 4.5 million part-timers, 660,000 homeworkers, and 600,000 mainly young workers on government-sponsored employment and training schemes. The relentless increase in the numbers of these so-called 'marginal' workers, now approaching a third of the labour force, is related to underlying trends in the labour market, but is also encouraged by the present government, partly because the reduced application of the employment protection laws is consistent with its wider policy of deregulation. This is intended to encourage enterprise and job creation by lifting apparent burdens from business, particularly small firms (OMWP, 1985). As applied to labour law, it has meant the dismantling of some of the legal support for collective bargaining (see above) and a reduction in employment protection.[39]

The main target has been unfair dismissal legislation. Amendments were enacted to increase the number of those who are ineligible to apply to the tribunals, to make it harder to win a case, and to narrow the basis of compensation. The service qualification needed to make an unfair dismissal claim was first doubled from six months to twelve, then extended to two years for firms with twenty or fewer employees, and finally converted into a general two-year qualification for all contracts of employment commencing after 1 June 1985.[40] The minimum length of a fixed term contract, under which an employee may agree to waive the right to claim unfair dismissal, was cut from two years to one (EPCA s.142 as amended). A pre-hearing assessment, an additional stage in the procedure of the tribunals, was introduced in order to identify weak claims and to warn claimants that costs might be awarded against them if they were to lose at the full hearing, the basis for awarding costs being broadened to cover unreasonable claims.[41] The burden of proving the reasonableness of a dismissal – the decisive factor in most unfair dismissal claims – was shifted from the employer, and, in applying the reasonableness test, the tribunals were expressly required to consider the employer's 'size and administrative resources' (EPCA s.57(3) as amended). The 'basic' award component of compensation was restricted for successful claimants (EPCA s.73 as amended), while the unsuccessful could conceivably be discouraged from appealing under the revised regulations allowing the tribunals to give only summary reasons (see Chapter 19).

---

[37] Now EPCA s.131; see Chapter 19.

[38] See Chapter 13, esp. Table 13.1, and Chapter 18.

[39] For a critique of the 1979–80 reductions, see Lewis and Simpson (1981:ch.2). It is noteworthy that 'deregulation' is an international phenomenon: Clark (1985:76–7).

[40] EPCA s.64 as amended by Unfair Dismissal (Variation of Qualifying Period) Order SI 1979 No.959; s.64A (inserted by EA 1980 s.8(1)); and Unfair Dismissal (Variation of Qualifying Period) Order SI 1985 No.782.

[41] See now Industrial Tribunals (Rules of Procedure) Regulations SI 1985 No.16 para. 11.

In addition to these changes in the unfair dismissal provisions, the basis of the entitlement to statutory guarantee pay was somewhat narrowed (EPCA s.15 as amended), and the right to return to work after pregnancy was weakened in various ways, including a complex notification requirement (s.33 as amended) and an exception for small firms (five or fewer employees) which could point to practical difficulties with compliance (s.56A). Employment protection is to be further eroded.[42] Apart from the proposal on wages councils already mentioned, the Truck Acts are to be repealed and replaced by a weaker scheme of protection, the threshold for the small firms' exemption from the HSWA's requirement to issue written safety policies – currently five or fewer employees – is to be raised to twenty, and the Factories Act's limits on women's hours of work are to be repealed. Further implications for flexible working hours may flow from the government's plan to abolish the statutory restrictions on shop opening hours and its pressure for changes in the EEC's regulation of heavy goods and passenger service vehicles.

The tendency of OMWP (1985) to lump these policies, measures and proposals together under the broad heading of 'deregulation', however, may be misleading. Why should reforms designed to make the task of the unfair dismissal claimant more difficult – changing the rules about the burden of proof, adding the pre-hearing assessment to the stages of tribunal procedure, or altering the method of calculating the basic award – be counted as examples of deregulation? Even where workers are more straightforwardly deprived of employment protection, for example, by raising the service qualification for unfair dismissal or excluding young workers from wages councils, the deregulation is strictly relative. As Brown and Hepple (1985:xi) comment, 'an economist who talks of "deregulation" when he means the re-imposition of "common law regulation" would, one hopes, today receive short shrift for having failed to study his law as well as his economics'.

Common law rules may, indeed, regulate the employment relation as much as statutory rules. The case law and the empirical evidence (see Chapter 18) give the impression that a good many lawyers and managers are engaged in devising ever more elaborate schemes of self-employment, or of part-time or temporary work. The object is to enable employers and workers to avoid a range of financial and legal burdens, and in some instances to undermine union organisation. But one consequence of this activity is a stream of litigation – initiated by the Inland Revenue or the DHSS or by individual employees asserting common law and statutory rights – to determine whether particular workers are 'employees' for particular purposes, or are genuinely self-employed. Uncertainty over this issue has not been dispelled by the various tests and criteria developed in the case law. Such are the difficulties – Clark and Wedderburn (1983:151) refer to the 'legal crisis of the contract of employment' – that some of the advice and decisions of the Inland Revenue and the DHSS are in conflict (Leighton, 1984:91–6). While the government has acknowledged this problem, its

---

[42] See DE (1984; 1985a; 1985b); DTI (1985); and especially OMWP (1985).

solution of 'reviewing the guidelines to staff derived from the case law and … improving staff training' (OMWP, 1985: para.4:14) is hardly likely to be effective. For the cases reveal that, despite, or perhaps because of, the complex legal criteria for identifying employee status, the courts can use their discretion to find a contract of employment for workers whose plight they regard with sympathy and to deny it to others.[43] Similarly, the vagaries of judicial decision-making on, for example, continuity of employment may have profound implications for the conditions and rights of temporary and part-time employees.[44] But even the effective exclusion of such workers from statutory protection, whether by means of employers' personnel policies or legislative amendments, serves to underline the importance of the regulatory function of the contract of employment, the supreme example of common law regulation.

This contract, as Chapter 12 makes clear, is complemented not ousted by statutory employment protection. Judicial interpretation of statutory concepts such as dismissal, fairness, redundancy, and continuity of employment has often relied on contractual doctrines, which have been refined and developed in the case law, including the extensive litigation arising from the enforcement of statutory rights. But the point here is that the contract directly regulates the employment relation, especially where the statutory provisions are either not applicable or inadequate. Recent trends in the case law, moreover, show that while the contract of employment – particularly the standard terms implied by the courts – still gives legal legitimacy to the employer's right to manage,[45] that right has to be exercised within certain bounds. Thus the employer's traditional prerogative to command may be subject to his contractual duty to retain the employee's trust and confidence,[46] and the courts are more reluctant than they were in the past to classify disobedience to a command as misconduct justifying summary dismissal.[47] There have even been a few steps, albeit small and faltering, in the direction of applying 'natural justice' and public law remedies to the normal contract of employment.[48] Other recent cases have confirmed the basic regulatory function of the contract of employment: even where employees' contractual rights were acquired through the incorporation of collectively agreed terms into the contract, they were not necessarily lost when either the employer or the union terminated the collective agreement.[49]

[43] See the discussions in Chapters 12 and 18 of cases such as *Nethermere (St Neots) v Taverna and Gardiner* [1984] IRLR 240 and *O'Kelly v Trusthouse Forte Plc* [1983] IRLR 369.

[44] E.g. *Ford v Warwickshire CC* [1983] IRLR 126; *Secretary of State for Employment v Deary* [1984] IRLR 180.

[45] E.g. the right to require a change in working methods in the interests of business efficiency: *Cresswell v Board of Inland Revenue* [1984] IRLR 190. On the extensive case law concerning the flexibility of labour under the contract and its implications for statutory rights, see Chapter 15.

[46] See authorities cited in Hepple and O'Higgins (1981:134–5).

[47] E.g. *Wilson v Racher* [1974] ICR 428.

[48] See the discussion of 'wrongful dismissal' in Chapter 12, and Stokes (1985); on the relevance of the *GCHQ* case (note 20 above) to this issue, see Wade (1985).

[49] *Robertson v British Gas Corporation* [1983] ICR 351. *Gibbons v Associated British Ports* [1985] IRLR 376.

The limits on deregulation in the employment protection sphere are demonstrated, above all, by the fact that a government which has made deregulation a political slogan has itself added further layers of regulation. Two of these measures were reluctantly enacted in order to comply with EEC law: the Transfer of Undertakings (Protection of Employment) Regulations[50] and the Equal Pay (Amendment) Regulations.[51] The Transfer of Undertakings Regulations automatically transfer contracts of employment and accrued periods of continuous employment to the new employer. Although this provision applies only to a minority of takeovers in the UK, it has, at a time of recession and rationalisation, featured in the recent case law concerning dismissal and redundancy (see Chapter 15). Of more general importance perhaps are the Equal Pay Regulations, which introduced a right to equal pay for work of equal value. This is enforceable through a complex procedure, in which an industrial tribunal may require the work to be evaluated by an independent expert from an ACAS panel.

In another measure of major significance the government transferred the cost of administering short-term sickness benefit from the DHSS to employers, who eventually became responsible for the payment of statutory sick pay (SSP) for a period of twenty-eight weeks.[52] In practice, as Chapter 13 explains, while SSP still entailed DHSS responsibilities – for example, monitoring sick pay records and assessing SSP claimants for means-tested benefits – it added to the administrative burden on employers, despite the government's zeal for deregulation.[53] But SSP should not be dismissed merely as a less than successful attempt 'to roll back the frontiers of the state'. It was indicative of a more general recent development, namely, the increasing complexity of the interaction between social security, employment protection, the contract of employment and, if applicable, collective bargaining (see Chapter 13). Thus the enactment of statutory guarantee pay in the mid-1970s was intended to shift some of the cost – in this case economic as well as administrative – of short-term unemployment from the state to the employer. While the individual employee gained only a minor benefit, employers and sometimes union officials had to thread their way through the overlapping rules governing unemployment benefit and employment protection, complexities which became even worse with the introduction of employment subsidies. A similar point concerning the overlap between employment protection and social security could be made about maternity benefits. These benefits, incidentally, include a new regulatory measure, the cost of which was placed on the employer: the right to time off work for ante-natal care.[54]

---

50 SI 1981 No.1794. See note 19 above.
51 SI 1983 No.1794, enacted after it was held that the UK was in breach of European law by failing to comply with Art.1 of the EC Directive on Equal Pay (OJ 1975 L45/19): *Commission of the EC v UK* [1982] ICR 578, ECJ. See Chapter 17.
52 SSP was introduced by the Social Security and Housing Benefits Act 1982 and extended by the Social Security Act 1985.
53 The problem was belatedly recognised with the publication of a consultative document (DHSS, 1985a) on whether employers might be allowed to opt out of SSP.
54 EPCA s.31A, inserted by EA 1980 s.13.

Occupational pension schemes, which for millions of workers are the most important condition of employment after current pay and are, indeed, increasingly regarded as deferred pay, constitute another area where the present government has contributed to the trend towards statutory regulation (see Chapter 14). Although trusts law remains the basic legal framework for occupational pensions, the Social Security Act 1985 provided for disclosure of information to individual scheme members and recognised trade unions (see above), facilitated the transfer of pension entitlement for job changers, and guaranteed a degree of inflation-proofing for preserved pensions. European law has added a further regulatory element in regard to women's rights,[55] notwithstanding the formal exclusion of pension entitlement from the UK's equal pay and sex discrimination legislation. Furthermore, if the proposal to abolish the state earnings-related pension scheme (SERPS) were to be implemented, both occupational and personal pension schemes would have a major role in filling the gap, which would in either case place considerable extra burdens on employers.[56]

These measures on equal pay, transfers of undertakings, statutory sick pay, ante-natal care, and occupational pensions all reflect contemporary socio-economic trends. A further encouragement to legal regulation has been the continuing development of hazardous technologies in, for example, the chemical and nuclear industries, which has led to extensive statutory employment and environmental protection as well as restrictions on the liberties of individual workers and citizens.[57] Another technological stimulus for legal regulation is the widespread computerisation of personnel records. The Data Protection Act 1984, which is being phased in over a three-year period, subjected employers, the 'data users', to extensive legal obligations, including registration with the Data Protection Registrar, in respect of computerised personal data on employees, the 'data subjects'. The latter were given the legal right, subject to qualifications and exemptions, to obtain such data and, in certain circumstances, to have it erased or corrected, under an enforcement procedure involving civil court orders and damages awards or the exercise by the Registrar of his administrative powers backed by criminal sanctions.

Part of the stimulus for the Data Protection Act came from the Council of Europe's Convention for the Protection of Individuals with regard to the Automatic Processing of Data (1981). International pressure for new measures of employment protection is, as Chapter 20 argues, in conflict with the ideology of deregulation. Which force is stronger varies according to subject matter and legal sanctions. As regards ILO Conventions, the UK government has felt free to refuse to ratify,[58] to denounce,[59] and to act in

---

55 *Worringham and Humphreys v Lloyds Bank Ltd* [1981] IRLR 178, ECJ; [1982] IRLR 74, CA; *Garland v British Rail Engineering Ltd* [1982] IRLR 111, ECJ; [1982] IRLR 157, HL.
56 See DHSS (1985b). For this reason it seems unlikely to be implemented.
57 Cf. Clark (1985:83–4) and Wedderburn (1984:83–4). On the nuclear industry, see Lewis (1978).
58 No. 158 on Termination of Employment.
59 No. 94 on Labour Clauses (Public Contracts), No. 95 on Protection of Wages, and – shortly – No. 26 on Minimum Wage Fixing.

flagrant breach of them.[60] But it is not so easy to cast aside the instruments of the Council of Europe,[61] and there is no escape from EEC law. The influence of the latter is seen not only in British legislation based on European Directives, for example, the Transfer of Undertakings and Equal Pay Regulations and the law on redundancy consultation and notification,[62] but also in the fact that Community Law is a separate source of employment protection, which may in certain circumstances be enforced directly in the national courts (see Chapter 20). It is safe to predict that it will continue to stimulate the development of employment protection in the UK.

IMPACT OF THE LAW

The growth of legal regulation can hardly be questioned. A more critical issue is the degree to which the extensive body of law limits the scope of the voluntary employment relation. But this raises a preliminary question concerning the nature of voluntary regulation. Far from being exclusive alternatives, the two principal modes of such regulation – collective and individual – co-exist and overlap. Collective bargaining in Britain does not obliterate the individual employment relation. In practice, union recognition is a matter of degree and of power relations and collective agreements do not normally attempt to provide a comprehensive statement of rights and duties. Collective bargaining, therefore, leaves ample scope for personnel policies to operate at the level of the individual employment relation. Moreover, the individual contract of employment remains the basic legal expression of the employment relation, notwithstanding the negotiation of collective agreements. It is through the individual employment contract, indeed, that collectively agreed terms are given legal effect.

Another aspect of the distinction between the individual and collective relation is that the law may have, or may be intended to have, a greater impact on the one rather than the other. Thus the development of statutory employment protection was intended to bring the individual employment relation within a statutory framework, without disturbing the essential autonomy of the collective parties. This approach assumed that the impact of individual labour law could be largely confined to the individual employment relation (a matter discussed below). It also had a broader implication

---

60 See Chapter 20 on the finding of the ILO's Committee on Freedom of Association (Case No.1261) that by banning union membership at GCHQ the government was in breach of Convention No.87.

61 The government of course did not wish to avoid the finding of the European Court of Human Rights in the *British Rail* case (see note 4 above) that the UK was in breach of Art.11 of the European Convention on Human Rights.

62 EPA Part IV based on EEC Directive on Collective Redundancies (OJ 1975 L48/29). The Draft Directive on Voluntary Part-Time Work (OJ 1982 C62, COM 830 Final) has major implications for British labour law, see HL Select Committee on the European Communities, 1981–82, 19th Report, HL 216. At the time of writing, the government has announced its intention of repealing the small firms exemption (firms with five or fewer employees) in the SDA in order to comply with the EC Directive on Equal Treatment: DE (1985c).

for the role of the law. The greater the scope for the individual employment relation, the greater the potential for legal regulation. Conversely, a system of collective bargaining which effectively determined employment conditions might reduce the potential for legal regulation (cf. Kahn-Freund, 1983a:37). Certainly, the discovery of what Flanders (1970:185) called the 'poverty' of content of collective agreements helped to stimulate the development of statutory employment protection. This occurred during the 1960s and 1970s as part of a wider 'reform' policy, under which collective bargaining was regarded as both widespread and as the preferred method of settling terms and conditions of employment. But in the 1980s not only has public policy changed but also it is at least questionable whether collective bargaining has as much regulatory impact as in the past.

In the late 1970s, probably the high point of collective regulation, it was found that the pay and conditions of about 70 per cent of all full-time employees 'were affected in some way by collective agreements',[63] whereas only 55 per cent of the workforce were members of trade unions. One major explanation for this disparity between union density and the coverage of collective bargaining is that the statistics for the latter included the weakly unionised wages council sector. Also relevant perhaps is the method of giving legal effect to collectively agreed terms: they may be incorporated into the individual contract of employment, irrespective of whether the employee is a union member. In the last few years, however, it is likely that managerial power has been relatively less constrained by collective regulation. This is suggested by the downward spiral of union density to about 45 per cent in the mid-1980s. According to Bain and Price (1983), the decline was associated with unemployment, fundamental changes in technology and in the labour market, particularly the growth of the 'marginal' workforce, and the reversal of the former public policy in favour of collective bargaining.

Although few employers have gone to the length of repudiating the principle of collective bargaining, a number have tried to trim back its coverage.[64] But many employers seem content to continue with the formal structure of joint regulation, which, at a time of recession, may not seriously inhibit their ability to manage individual employees. Moreover, in many of the larger employment units – the traditional heartlands of collective regulation – the emphasis in the mid-1980s appears to be on hiving off activities to sub-contractors and on systematic personnel policies to secure the commitment of the remaining 'core' employees. The techniques include direct communication, merit pay, appraisal systems, quality circles, and training and development programmes geared to individual employees (Purcell and Sisson, 1983:118–20). While certain new developments such as consultative company councils may give opportunities for joint regulation, the 'management of human resources', as currently practised, tends to individualise the employment relation. It points to the intensification of

---

[63] ACAS (1983:para.3.3) citing New Earnings Survey statistics.
[64] About a fifth of firms in one recent survey (Batstone, 1984:257–60) had tried to reduce the role of shop stewards and unions.

managerial control tempered, if at all, by law as much as by the weakened collective forces.

Legal Rights

The introduction of a series of mainly individual legal rights and the development of the industrial tribunals to process them have had profound implications for voluntary regulation. Hepple (1983a:393–4) discerned 'an underlying trend towards the juridification of individual disputes ... Matters which were once entirely within the sphere of managerial prerogatives, or left to collective bargaining, are now directly regulated by positive legal rights and duties'. These sweeping implications did not arise from the effectiveness of the statutory rights from the point of view of individual employees. Research on unfair dismissal legislation indicated a poor success rate in the tribunals, low levels of compensation, a marked reluctance to order reinstatement, and a judicial attitude geared to the needs of managerial efficiency.[65] Yet Hepple was able to cite unfair dismissal as his primary illustration, basically because of its effect on management behaviour, and, through management, on the system as a whole.

The legislation on unfair dismissal stimulated the spread and formalisation of individual grievance and disciplinary procedures. Although the evidence suggests that small firms may have been less prone to such 'proceduralism' (Evans et al., 1985b:38), the law's impact was still widespread and influenced not only the formal procedures but also the way in which management made decisions under them. Employers needed 'adequate factual grounds' on which to make decisions 'after a reasonably careful investigation following a fair procedure' (Hepple, 1983a:411). The unfair dismissal law, according to Wood (1984:41), 'gave to management the necessary discipline, second nature to lawyers, of making important decisions only on ascertained facts and after hearing both sides of the argument. Reasons for action had to be clear; procedures sensible and followed.' Dickens et al. (1985:252) identified the incorporation of natural justice and due process into the procedures and the 'quasi-judicial managerial review of decisions' as signs of 'juridification' (a concept discussed below).

The tribunals played a vital role in this process. It was their interpretation of the statutes and the codes which, under the supervision of the EAT and the appellate courts, developed the prevailing standards of procedural fairness. In fact, over three-quarters of the annual 40,000 or so applications to the tribunals are concerned with unfair dismissal. For various reasons – the dominance of legal chairmen, the frequent use of lawyers as representatives, the complexity of the legal arguments, and the adversarial style of proceedings (see Chapter 19) – the tribunals themselves became increasingly legalistic, which no doubt provided some material benefit to lawyers. At the

---

[65] See Chapters 15 and 19 below, which draw on Dickens et al.(1985). The record on race and sex discrimination and equal pay is even worse, see Chapters 17 and 19, Hepple (1983b), and Lustgarten (1985).

same time, the status of personnel management rose as its practitioners developed their own professionalism in response to the demand for expert knowledge of the statutory provisions and the case law.[66] For similar reasons, legal services became a growth area for employers' associations[67] and, in certain instances, provided a substitute for their diminishing role in pay bargaining. It was professional management as much if not more than workers and unions who espoused the legislative standards. Even where unions formally signed them, most individual grievance and discplinary procedures were management-designed and administered, and drafting of disciplinary rules was a virtual management monopoly (Dickens et al., 1985: 242). Survey evidence confirmed that for many employers the unfair dismissal legislation was not a burden deterring recruitment but a catalyst to improve personnel management, especially in matters of recruitment and discipline.[68] Personnel managers generally saw the more widespread compliance with disciplinary procedures as an enhancement of managerial authority (Daniel and Millward, 1983:170).

The emphasis on management and on individual employees might be thought to have minimised the effect of the unfair dismissal legislation on the collective employment relation. It does indeed appear to be the case that tribunal applicants are drawn disproportionately from non-unionised firms and that collective conflict over disciplinary issues persists. However, some union officials believe that, at a time of high unemployment, the spread of disciplinary procedures has made their members less willing to support calls for collective action on such issues (Evans et al., 1985a:96). In any event, collective bargaining over discipline, where it occurs, can hardly remain immune from the norms and values of the tribunal system (Dickens et al., 1985:252). This effect on the collective relation can only have been enhanced by the fact that the reform and formalisation of disciplinary procedures has been most concentrated in large firms, which are typically unionised (Brown, 1981:44; Daniel and Millward, 1983:160). At the same time the opportunity to negotiate approved collective agreements on dismissals so as to exclude the jurisdiction of the tribunals (under EPCA s.65) was generally not taken up. The result is that the conscious awareness of legal norms and procedures informs disciplinary decisions in the unionised sector. Although unions might still be able to deter employers from such decisions, once dismissal becomes a serious option the unions tend to

[66] For a summary of the considerable survey evidence on this point, see Dickens et al. (1985:264–5).

[67] Brown (1981:22). Doubtless, analogous trends attributable to unfair dismissal and other legislation would have been discernible if there had been surveys of management consultants, organisers of management education, and publishers of management information journals.

[68] Daniel and Stilgoe (1978:74) and Clifton and Tatton-Brown (1979:20). The general absence of a recruitment-deterrent effect even in small firms was confirmed by Evans et al. (1985b), who also found that the 1979–80 amendments had had little impact on personnel policies in either large or small firms. These three surveys carry more weight than the 'research' featured in DTI (1985), which is not to deny that the demands for deregulation by the small firms lobby reflect a genuinely felt grievance or that line managers may take a different view from personnel managers.

acquiesce in the combination of managerial and legal regulation, settling in the main for a representational role within the procedures and the tribunals.

The process of decision-making with reference to legal norms applies not only to disciplinary dismissals but also to dismissals by reason of redundancy.[69] The legal provision of critical importance here is the individual employee's entitlement to statutory redundancy pay. From the mid-1960s this right encouraged the development of 'voluntary' schemes whereby individuals, within categories specified by management, could volunteer for redundancy in return for enhanced severance pay. Even when these schemes were embodied, as they often were, in collective agreements, they were management-designed and implemented, the union role being confined normally to demands for increased compensation and voluntary rather than compulsory redundancies (Daniel, 1985:74). But as the decline of industry deepened, the distinction between voluntary and compulsory redundancies was blurred. This general picture was not substantially altered by the introduction in the mid-1970s of the consultation duty over proposed redundancies. The main impact of this provision appears to have been the incorporation of the 'ninety-day notice' to recognised unions into the standard procedure for managing or threatening workforce reductions. Moreover, virtually no interest has been shown in the possibility of negotiating specially approved and exempted collective agreements on redundancy pay (EPCA s.96) and consultation (EPA s.107) (see Davies and Freedland, 1984:262–7). Thus the 'employment protection' rights – whether the collective right to consultation or the individual right to redundancy pay – appear to have encouraged employee and union acquiescence in management's planning of redundancies. When it comes to the point of redundancy, one question is usually paramount: how much compensation will be paid to the individual employee?

Union membership provides a further dimension to the law regulating the termination of employment. The legal protection from dismissal because of union membership or activity is embodied in an individual legal right, part of the general framework of unfair dismissal law. In practice, it has been so ineffectual – thanks to inherent drafting limitations and narrow judicial interpretation – that it has had little impact on industrial relations, though the dismissal of shop stewards is of course an emotive issue. Nevertheless, it could possibly play a more significant role in the future because of the vast increase in the compensation levels introduced by EA 1982. The rationale for this amendment was the correlative principle as between the positive right to associate and the negative right to dissociate, in particular, the right not to be dismissed because of non-membership of any or a particular union. This right more than any other epitomises the individualist values of the 1980s legislation. It may be qualified only if there is a UMA, which raises the intriguing possibility of the juridification of that traditional pillar of collective autonomy, the closed shop. Even the extremely limited form of protection, applicable between 1976 and 1980, for those who objected to union membership on religious grounds helped to stimulate the formalisa-

[69] See Chapter 15, and Daniel (1985).

tion of UMAs, a development which was necessary from management's point of view in order to minimise the risk of liability for unfair dismissal (Weekes, 1976:217; Dunn and Gennard, 1984:148–9). The potential impact of the current legal framework is of course much greater. Management (and also unions through the 'joinder' provisions) are likely to face legal liabilities, unless UMAs are subjected to a strict legal regimen of ballots.[70]

The impact of individual rights on the employment relation extends beyond the important issue of termination of employment. The employee's entitlement to a statement of written particulars has encouraged the development of employment 'documentation', which is now an important aspect of the personnel management function. It provides a means of direct communication with employees and an opportunity to spell out contractual rights and obligations (see Leighton and Dumville, 1977; Leighton and Doyle, 1982). The law's impact may be further illustrated by the legislation on sex and race discrimination and equal pay. Although this has manifestly failed to eliminate discrimination,[71] it must have had a significant effect – no doubt concentrated in larger employment units – on the practice of personnel management and industrial relations: hence the development of equality policies by employers and the explicit references to eliminating discrimination in collective agreements. It is possible, moreover, that the right to equal pay for work of equal value, introduced by the Equal Pay Regulations and strongly supported by the EOC and the unions, will have far-reaching effects on pay structures (Wainwright, 1983; ACAS, 1985:68). Once again the individual legal right points inexorably towards the collective employment relation. But as already noted in respect of the termination of employment, individual rights seem bound to affect the collective relation, including the activities of trade union representatives. Survey evidence has suggested that the growth in the number of full-time shop stewards was stimulated by the employment legislation of the mid-1970s – a parallel development to the growth of personnel management perhaps – and, specifically, that the time off rights led to an expansion of shop steward training (Daniel and Millward, 1983, 37–9). Furthermore, the introduction of a legal framework for safety representatives encouraged the development of joint safety committees (Brown, 1981:75; Daniel and Millward, 1983:142–4). Was this an example of a legal or a voluntary development or some mixture of the two (cf. Clark and Wedderburn, 1983:186)? Certainly the legislation gave safety representatives legal rights, and joint regulation over the question of safety has to take place within the framework of both the HSWA's regulatory system and extensive litigation based on the employer's common law liabilities.

But other laws in the form of collective trade union rights did not, in practice, appear to have major implications for the voluntarist tradition. The legal procedures for union recognition under the IRA and the EPA may have influenced managerial policy towards the orderly extension of recogni-

---

[70] From November 1984 to September 1985 ACAS monitored 97 closed shop ballots, of which 75 secured the requisite 85 per cent majority: *Daily Telegraph*, 27 September 1985.
[71] See note 65 above.

tion in respect of white-collar workers, but they had little impact on the established pattern of collective bargaining.[72] Arbitration under the Fair Wages Resolution and the EPA's 'recognised' and 'general level' provisions was extensively used as an exception to incomes policies, but it did not – with its very indirect sanction – exert a legalistic grip over collective bargaining. As far as the legal duty to disclose information for collective bargaining was and is concerned, it is not clear that it has had any discernible effect on collective industrial relations (Gospel and Willman, 1981:22). The lack of impact of these provisions underlines some of the limits on the law's regulation of the collective employment relation. However, account must also be taken of the attempt by the 1980s legislation to subject strikes to extensive legal regulation, especially as the right to strike is recognised, even judicially, as 'an essential element in principle of collective bargaining'.[73]

Loss of Legal Immunities

The seemingly obvious place to discern the impact of strike law is in the record of strike statistics. Table 1.1 shows the steep decline – excluding coal mining which drastically affected the 1984 figures – in the number of strikes and days lost through strikes since 1979. Does this mean that the legislation of the 1980s has 'worked', as Conservative politicians frequently claim? Or does it mean that the recession rather than the law has been the most potent factor, bearing in mind the example of the IRA, which Weekes et al. (1975) found to have had virtually no effect on strikes or, for that matter, on collective bargaining, the closed shop, and union administration?

The difficulties of interpreting strike statistics may be illustrated by a disagreement in the academic literature about the significance of an older set of figures concerning the impact of the *Taff Vale* case[73A] and its reversal by the Trade Disputes Act 1906, especially s.4, which gave unions their 'blanket' immunity from liability in tort. This issue has contemporary relevance as one of the central provisions in the 1980s legislation is the removal of the equivalent immunity (EA 1982 s.15 repealing TULRA s.14), a return to the policy of *Taff Vale*, subject to certain limits on damages depending on the size of the union (see Chapter 6). The case for removal was that over a long period of time the blanket immunity had fostered a form of irresponsible trade unionism, allowing union leaders either to abdicate control to local militants or to organise 'official' action without fear of the legal consequences (DE, 1981: paras. 104–37). Such reasoning has been supported by reference to the impact of *Taff Vale* on industrial relations in the early part of the twentieth century. According to Phelps

---

[72] See Chapter 3. Decisions of the Court of Appeal would have required ACAS to take a fragmentary approach to the definition of bargaining units under the EPA's procedure, but prior to repeal these were overruled by the House of Lords: *UKAPE v ACAS* [1980] ICR 201, HL, [1979] ICR 303, CA; *EMA v ACAS* [1980] ICR 215, HL; [1979] ICR 637, CA. See Simpson (1979).
[73] *Crofter Hand Woven Harris Tweed Co. v Veitch* [1942] AC 435, 463 (Lord Wright).
[73A] [1901] AC 426.

TABLE 1.1
STRIKES IN THE UNITED KINGDOM, 1979–84

Year	All Industries				Excluding Coal Mining			
	S	*W*	*D*	*D/W*	*S*	*W*	*D*	*D/W*
1979	2,080	4,608	29,474	6.4	1,782	4,555	29,361	6.4
1980	1,330	834	11,964	14.3	1,028	748	11,812	15.8
1981	1,338	1,513	4,266	2.8	1,036	1,415	4,031	2.8
1982	1,528	2,103	5,313	2.5	1,125	1,878	4,939	2.6
1983	1,352	574	3,754	6.5	997	441	3,270	7.4
1984	1,206	1,464	27,135	18.5	1,128	1,183	4,652	3.9

Source: Edwards (1983:Table 9.1) with data derived for 1982 onwards on a comparable basis by Paul Edwards from the *Employment Gazette*.

Note: S is number of strikes beginning in year. W and D are, respectively, numbers of workers involved and days lost (in thousands) in strikes in progress during year. D/W is the number of days lost per worker involved.

Brown (1983:68, 148) 'the unions were hamstrung' after *Taff Vale* and other leading cases, to which he also attributed the 'bigness of the wage cuts in 1901–2'. In an earlier work (1959:194–5) he described the 'overwhelming' effect of the law: 'the impression was strong and the threat real that any strike would result in the union's funds being mulcted, and there were few strikes'. In contrast, Clegg et al. (1964:ch.9) argued that the period of relative industrial peace – 1899 to 1907 – both pre- and post-dated *Taff Vale* and its statutory reversal, and further, that the decline in strikes was associated with an economic recession and the development of collective bargaining machinery as an alternative to industrial action.

Returning to the current statistics, it may be argued that the decline in the incidence of strikes in the 1980s is more attributable to the recession than to the legislative framework (see, for example, Mayhew, 1985:66). But while it would be rash and almost certainly wrong to suggest that the law was the cause, or even the most important cause, of this decline, it would be equally wrong to dismiss it as irrelevant or unimportant. The impact of the recession, of the law, and of shifts in social attitudes are inextricably linked. Moreover, subject to the inherent difficulty of isolating legal from non-legal factors, the evidence indicates that the role of the law is becoming an increasingly important consideration in the conduct of industrial disputes.

The extent to which legal rights are enforced may be of considerable relevance to their impact on behaviour, especially in the sphere of collective conflict where social consensus is lacking. One of the reasons suggested for the apparent ineffectiveness of the IRA's restrictions on industrial action was that, during a period of a quite high incidence of strikes, relatively few employers applied to the NIRC for restraining orders (Weekes et al., 1975:217). But according to Evans (1985b) and LRD (1985), the relative propensity to go to law appears to have increased in the last couple of years. Evans listed thirty-four cases, mainly applications for interlocutory injunctions, which were heard from September 1980 to April 1984. This was a modest figure, but LRD found an upsurge of litigation to the period ending 31 August 1985, with the total then standing at seventy cases.

These figures are almost certainly underestimates. They are derived essentially from monitoring reports in the national press, which are likely to miss a proportion of cases, especially those occurring outside the newspaper industry itself. Moreover, they refer only to civil litigation brought by employers, and ignore the series of cases arising from the 1984–5 strike brought by working miners against the NUM and its area unions, as well as all the criminal prosecutions. Furthermore, they do not take into account threats of litigation, which, in terms of the law's impact, may be almost as important as the cases. In the research undertaken by Evans (1983; 1985a) into thirty-eight strikes involving picketing, eight disputes were selected for study because injunction proceedings had been commenced and the rest simply because of the presence of picketing. One of those gave rise to legal proceedings, in seven management gave very serious consideration to suing, and in several others it warned the unions that it would do so if picketing persisted.

The available information is, nevertheless, of great interest. The cases were initiated by all types of employers – large and small, public and private sector, those with extensive bargaining arrangements and those without – operating in a wide range of industries, though in 1984–5 the printing and newspaper industries did appear to be exceptionally litigation-prone. Evans found that the majority of plaintiffs were the employers of the defendants, thus confounding earlier predictions by Lewis and Simpson (1981:180), among others, that management would be extremely reluctant to invoke the legislation, except perhaps for the customers and suppliers of employers in dispute. The plaintiffs were almost invariably successful at law, which is hardly surprising given the substance of the legal rules and the nature of interlocutory proceedings.

The impact of the law is, however, measured in qualitative as well as quantitative terms. Evans found many variations between different industries, firms and unions but was still able to provide some general insights into the implications for management and union behaviour stemming from the 1980 Act's restriction of the legal right to picket.[74] As far as employers were concerned, the Act and the controversy which surrounded its introduction increased awareness of the law and the preparedness to use it. This attitude affected personnel and industrial relations specialists, even though they had a vested interest in maintaining good relations with union officials. It also influenced commercial and legal managers, who were sometimes more inclined than personnel specialists to countenance legal tactics in order to

---

[74] This paragraph is based mainly on Evans (1985a). The study of dispute tactics in S Yorks and Humberside in 1980–82 by Kahn et al. (1983) is more difficult to evaluate because of the authors' omission to disclose their data base and their tendency to analyse dispute tactics in the light of the government's ideology rather than the law.

maintain production and competitiveness. On the union side, legal proceedings tended to have the effect of reducing the discretion of shop stewards and of enhancing the role of full-time officers, especially at regional and national level and including specialist legal officers. In one union, experience of litigation led to an insistence that officials referred to the legal officer before initiating or endorsing industrial action likely to attract litigation. Union officers were generally unenthusiastic about taking legal risks, tended to counsel orderly retreats, and in certain instances appeared to be paralysed by fear of injunctions. In virtually all cases, defendant shop stewards and local officials followed the advice of senior officials and lawyers to cease unlawful picketing. In general terms, it appeared that the picketing law had encouraged a shift of power within unions to full-time officials, including legal officers, whose definition of appropriate dispute tactics was likely to be influenced by legal considerations.

Evans's research was based on a series of localised disputes in 1980–81. The subsequent Stockport Messenger dispute of 1983–4 and, above all, the miners' strike of 1984–5 seemed to indicate that the law had failed to suppress secondary picketing and, to that extent, had not influenced behaviour. But this is to ignore the significance of the role of the law in the defeat of these strikes – a combination of criminal and civil law, the latter involving liabilities in tort and contract, and fines for contempt followed by sequestration and, in the case of the miners' dispute, the appointment of a receiver. It is inconceivable that management, unions, and dissenting minorities within unions could pretend that these causes célèbres had not occurred or should not be taken into account. As ACAS (1985:12) commented, one of the legacies of the miners' dispute may be 'the way in which it brought to public attention issues of law and order in the conduct of industrial relations, and the rights and obligations which both older and new legislation confer on the parties'.

The degree of juridification discerned by Evans has probably increased after the Employment Act 1982 and the Trade Union Act 1984. Since the 1982 Act's removal of the unions' blanket immunity, the statistical record shows that most legal actions have been brought against trade unions. This is likely to have enhanced the influence within unions of senior officials, legal officers, and perhaps even union solicitors.[75] Moreover, after the commencement of Part II of the 1984 Act, most of the litigation centred on the failure of unions to hold secret ballots on 'official' industrial action, in the manner prescribed by the Act, on pain of loss of immunities. In many of these cases industrial action was called off either without a ballot or after one, though in some instances ballots strengthened the union's position (see LRD, 1985:261). One of the consequences of Part II of the Act appears to have been a general increase in the number of strike ballots.[76] This

---

[75] By contrast, in the different socio-economic circumstances of the mid-1970s, the vicarious liability of unions under the IRA did not lead to more centralised union structures (Weekes et al., 1975: 113–19).

[76] See *The Times*, 30 August 1985. From the commencement of Part II of the 1984 Act (26 September 1984) to mid-October 1985, ACAS monitored 79 strike ballots: 53 were for strike action, 23 were against, 1 was tied, and the results of 2 were unknown.

demonstrates the potency of the law when it cuts with the popular grain. The encouragement of ballots – like the restriction of secondary picketing – strikes a sympathetic chord among both employers and workers. Ballots under Part II of the 1984 Act also exemplify how a law to influence dispute tactics may also affect, as Martin (1985:72) suggests, 'the process and the outcome of collective bargaining'. Part II of the Act may have had the further effect of shaping internal union democracy, especially if taken in conjunction with Parts I and III. Finally, mandatory or semi-mandatory ballots requiring the individual union member to express a view by marking a piece of paper in secret show how legal regulation and individualisation are mutually reinforcing and may reach into the heart of the collective relation.

LIMITS OF VOLUNTARY REGULATION

The analysis of the law's impact raises the question of how far the legal rules and procedures may be said to shape the content and conduct of the employment relation. The key concept is 'juridification', which was defined by Clark and Wedderburn (1983:188) as the extent to which the behaviour of employers and unions in 'dealing with individual and collective employment issues [is] determined by reference to legal (or what are believed to be legal) norms and procedures, rather than to voluntarily agreed norms and procedures or to "custom and practice"'. A subtle interaction between legal and voluntary regulation is suggested in the formulation of Dickens et al. (1985:252–3): 'voluntarily agreed norms and procedures are not *replaced* necessarily by legal ones, but rather their form and operation may be modified and informed by an awareness of the legal provisions and their operation'. In discussing juridification it is important to note, however, that in origin it is a Germanic concept applicable not merely to employment but to social and economic relations at large. It has been defined by Simitis, an eminent labour lawyer in West Germany, in terms of state intervention – including legislation, case law, administrative measures, and 'indirect steering' – which limits the autonomy of individuals or groups to determine their own affairs.[77] In Simitis's view, the juridification of the employment relation is a trend in all western industrialised countries, to which the British experience is no exception.

Clark and Wedderburn have expressed scepticism about the application of the juridification thesis to the UK.[78] Their analysis distinguished between different types of legal and voluntary regulation. If juridification is discernible in the individual employment relation, it has not taken hold at the collective level, especially in large, unionised workplaces. Although the growth of individual legal rights, especially unfair dismissal, has implications for the conduct of collective bargaining, British labour law does not, in general, structure bargaining or directly influence, still less determine, its outcome on such basic issues as pay levels, hours, and holidays. A further

[77] See Clark (1985), who provides an explanation and critique of Simitis's juridification thesis.
[78] (1983:188 et seq.). See further Clark (1985:85–90) and Wedderburn (1985a, esp.33–4).

strand of this argument is that collective agreements are not normally enforceable as contracts since negotiators are presumed by TULRA s.18, and previously by the common law, not to intend to create legal relations. This presumption is consistent with the fact that collective bargaining, though formalised to some extent since the Donovan Report, remains – in comparison, say, to bargaining in North America – a relatively non-legalistic process, which often fails to make the lawyer's distinction between conflicts of interests and of rights. The panoply of state-sponsored conciliation, arbitration, and mediation for collective disputes is equally non-legalistic. Furthermore, the main threads of this argument are not necessarily undermined by the legislation of the 1980s. Admittedly, this poses a potential threat to the autonomy and effectiveness of the unions and indirectly, therefore, to the future of collective bargaining. But Wedderburn (1985c:59) was still able to conclude that the legislation 'has not suppressed industrial conflict to any degree, nor has it obstructed the continuance and the evolution of voluntary collective bargaining in great measure as the primary source of industrial norms'.

Despite the force of these arguments, this view of juridification is open to question. While it has not gone as far in the UK as, for example, in West Germany (see Kahn-Freund, 1983b), the proposition that there is a trend towards juridification may be supported by the conclusions arising from the analysis of the law's impact. First, the individual legal rights in respect of dismissal, employment documentation and sex and race discrimination, together with the strengthened legal regulation of health and safety, have exercised a powerful influence on the practice of personnel management. Second, while these rights are in the main ostensibly aimed at the individual employment relation, the relative importance of which has probably increased in recent years, the collective relation has also been influenced by the law on vital issues such as discipline, redundancy, union membership and non-membership, and equal pay. Third, the law appears to be having an increasingly significant impact on the conduct of collective industrial disputes. These developments are indicative of a trend towards juridification. Could it be further argued that this trend was an inevitable consequence of the state's strategies – reform and restriction[79] – which stimulated so much of the growth of legal regulation?

Restriction

The restrictive strategy was developed in the IRA, which combined a legalistic version of reform with a strong emphasis on the individual right to dissociate from unions and the legal control of strike action.[80] It also

---

[79] For elaborations of these strategies, which differ somewhat in their interpretation of reform, see Clark and Wedderburn (1983) and Lewis (1983).

[80] See Kahn-Freund (1972; 1974); Wedderburn (1972); McCarthy and Ellis (1973); Simpson and Wood (1973); Weekes et al. (1975); Thomson and Engleman (1975); Moran (1977); and Crouch (1977).

underpins the 1980s legislation, which exemplifies restriction in a pure if not entirely simple form. Its hallmark is the use of the law to restrict trade union power, particularly a union's ability to engage in industrial action and to maintain the infrastructure of collective regulation. The restriction of industrial conflict was also part of traditional non-intervention and the reform strategy, but under the restrictive, or, in this sense, 'ultra-restrictive' strategy it is extended to the point where the systematic enforcement of the law would mean the virtual extinction of the legal freedom to strike. At the same time, the right to dissociate in its various manifestations is designed to undermine the closed shop and the capacity of unions to maintain collectively bargained standards and procedures.

The object is to free the employer from the constraints of union power, to which 'free market' analysis ascribes the blame for inflation, strikes, inefficiency, and unemployment, and further to free the individual employee by neutralising the supposed threat posed by unions to personal liberty. The ideal behind the legislation is the individual bargain determined by the free play of market forces, without the distorting imperfection of trade union power.[81] In practice, however, political and economic realities prevent the full application of market logic. While certain provisions in the 1980s legislation could be used to 'deunionise' the labour force, the central thrust of the legislation is not to eliminate but to constrain trade unions within a complex web of legal liabilities. These have already provided, and were intended to provide, a powerful stimulus to the juridification of collective conflict and, indirectly, of the whole process of collective regulation.

While the logic of the market points to the legal regulation of unions, it requires that the burden of state intervention is lifted from employers. This is to be achieved by a combination of economic and legal policies, including privatisation, the encouragement of sub-contracting and marginal work, low wages for young persons on training schemes, the ban on union- and recognition-only practices and the general dilution of legal support for fair wages, collective bargaining and employment protection. Hence the amendments to make fewer employees eligible to claim unfair dismissal and the proposed removal of young people from the protection of wages councils. Once again, however, practical realities ensure that 'deregulation' means a reduction rather than the elimination of statutory employment protection. The larger part of it stays intact and remains a major force for juridification. Moreover, far from reversing the overall trend towards legal regulation, under pressure from the EEC and unable to escape the basic responsibilities of the modern state, the UK government has actually added new layers of statutory regulation and, to that extent, may have, albeit unwillingly, reinforced the juridification trend. Even in the sphere of legal support for collective bargaining, the government's record is, as argued above, by no means all in the direction of deregulation.

---

[81] On the role of labour law in the present government's overall political and economic strategy, see Moore (1982); Wedderburn (1984); Gregory (1985); and Mayhew (1985).

Reform

The logic underlying the reform strategy is more difficult to define. It is important to do so, however, partly because it is the key to understanding the development of legal policy in the Donovan and Social Contract eras, and partly because reform may supplant restriction at some point in the not too distant future. Donovan's reform strategy, it will be argued, departed from traditional non-intervention by advocating a series of legislative measures and by strongly emphasising the need for managerial and economic efficiency, a strand of industrial relations policy which was closely linked with the requirements of incomes policy. In the Social Contract phase, incomes policy was combined with a major programme of legislation, having the form, though not necessarily the substance, of a great expansion of worker and trade union rights. On closer examination, the legislation was essentially reformist in the Donovan mould, but it was sufficiently extensive to jeopardise the reform strategy's aim of keeping industrial relations out of the courts.

In the 1960s persistent problems over inflation, the balance of payments, and manufacturing industry's competitiveness led to increased state intervention in the labour market through measures such as the Redundancy Payments Act and fairly elaborate incomes policies. This was the background to the Donovan Report (1968), which provided an authoritative prescription for the reform of industrial relations institutions. The central issue for Donovan was how to restore order, peace and efficiency to industrial relations and yet preserve and even extend the voluntarist tradition of collective bargaining. Donovan's commitment to both collective regulation and its reform was stated in its much quoted opinion (1968:para.212) that 'properly conducted, collective bargaining is the most effective means of giving workers the right to representation in decisions affecting their working lives, a right which is or should be the prerogative of every worker in a democratic society'. The significance of the qualification 'properly conducted' was that collective bargaining had to be consistent with what Donovan saw as the national interest in reducing strikes, inefficient working practices, wage drift and inflation. To that end, it advocated, as the centrepiece of its prescription, an employer-initiated reform of industrial relations, under which management and union officials would regain control over the workplace by means of comprehensive collective agreements at plant and company level.

The law was to have an important role within this strategy (Clegg, 1970:425–9). Institutional reform was to be encouraged by a series of legal measures ranging from a right to claim unfair dismissal in an expanded tribunal system to a procedure for union recognition, though in general the intention was to keep collective issues out of the tribunals and the courts. Donovan's reform strategy was, nevertheless, compatible with the function of the law, even under the traditional immunities system, of restricting industrial conflict. Indeed, the Donovan Report proposed a scheme for the selective legal enforceability of disputes procedures if reform failed to cure strike-proneness (para.508), and recommended, albeit by a narrow majority, that unofficial strike organisers should be deprived of immunity from liability in tort (para.801). The Commission thus envisaged that the law's restrictive function could be adapted to promote changes in the pattern of collective conflict as part of the wider reform of industrial relations, a perspective later taken on board in very different ways by the White Paper *In Place of Strife*[82] and by the IRA.

Donovan's reform strategy, including its proposals for an enlarged role for the law, was closely related to the development of incomes policy. The reform of industrial relations and the restraint and rationalisation of the growth of money incomes are of course two separately identifiable heads of public policy, though during the mid- to late-1960s they became increasingly interdependent. Incomes policy was concerned not merely with the economic outcome of bargaining but inevitably with the pay systems and bargaining arrangements which influenced that outcome (Clegg, 1970:441–5). Similarly, there was a 'logical connection', as McCarthy and Ellis (1973:26) called it, between Donovan's prescription for the reform of industrial relations institutions and income policy's concern with inflationary wage bargaining, wage drift, and inefficient working practices. The reform of collective bargaining was in general intended to 'assist an incomes policy to work effectively' (Donovan, 1968: para.207), the proposed registration of collective agreements would, more specifically, 'expose the whole process of pay settlement to the influence of policy' (para.209), and legislation was recommended 'placing on all arbitrators an obligation to take incomes policy into account when making their awards' (para.285). In fact, throughout 1965–8 when the Commission was deliberating, incomes policy was a central preoccupation of government. From the summer of 1966 the policy became statutory under the Prices and Incomes Acts 1966–8. The legislation embodied a novel extension of the law's restrictive function. The 1966 Act's legal orders to delay the implementation of pay awards and its criminal sanctions aimed at those engaged in industrial action in contravention of the orders – sanctions which were not, in practice, ever used – were vividly described by Kahn-Freund (1968:19) as the 'deepest inroad ever made into the freedom of collective bargaining in Britain'.

It has been argued, however, that the exclusively criminal liabilities under both the Prices and Incomes Acts and the later Counter-Inflation Acts 1972–3 were peripheral to labour law and industrial relations and, more fundamentally, that incomes policy, whether statutory or voluntary, was not an integral part of the state's strategy towards industrial relations until the onset of the current round of restrictive legislation. According to Wedderburn (1985a:35), 'liabilities in tort were deliberately excluded from the incomes policy legislation precisely because there was to be no overlap with the industrial relations system, where the rule was "torts with immunities". Labour law was thereby insulated from incomes policy law.'[83] The exclusively

---

82   DEP (1969). See Simpson (1969).
83   See further Wedderburn (1984). Another argument is that awards under measures anciliary to collective bargaining – e.g. the Fair Wages Resolution, Terms and Conditions of Employment Act 1959 s.8 – were often exceptions to pay norms. Cf. Ch. 4 below.

criminal nature of the sanctions was undoubtedly of great significance – it meant that enforcement was at the discretion of the state. It is not clear, however, why labour law should be equated solely with tort liabilities and immunities. Actions in contract to enforce the union rule book, which are not protected by immunities, may have the effect of restricting strikes and, furthermore, criminal liabilities are part of labour law, as may be seen from the law regulating picketing. But the basic point is that, while the tort liabilities were 'insulated', the trade unions and the collective bargaining system were not. The second limb of the argument was summarised by Wedderburn (1984:77) as follows: 'there was between 1948 and 1979 a dichotomy in government policies: anti-wage inflation policy on the one hand, and traditional labour law, or industrial relations, policy on the other'. The dichotomy thesis was in part a response to the argument by Davies and Freedland (1983) that the need to restrain inflation, especially inflation resulting from collective bargaining, was a consistent perspective of the state throughout the post-war period. It found expression, according to Davies and Freedland, in a variety of ways: incomes policies, both statutory and voluntary, which impinged on collective bargaining and conciliation and arbitration; the legislation of the Social Contract era, which in effect was a quid pro quo for wage restraint, the wider ramifications of the Social Contract notwithstanding; and the restrictive legal strategy, a pre-emptive alternative to incomes policy, especially when combined with the abandonment of both full employment and support for collective bargaining. This chapter's gloss on this debate is that during the 1960s the state's industrial relations and labour law policies ceased to be 'traditional' and, as argued above, took on reformist features logically connected with incomes policy, which itself was concerned with industrial relations institutions.

A strong link between the reform strategy and incomes policy was also apparent in the 1970s during the period of the Social Contract.[84] Indeed, pay restraint, or its absence, was widely regarded as the central issue under the Contract. Voluntary incomes policy was the order of the day, though the first effective phase of such policy was agreed with the TUC in July 1975, against the background of a sterling crisis and raging inflation, only after the threat of immediate legislation. Pay restraint was, however, necessarily implicit in the Social Contract, the TUC seeing its co-operation as part of a wider understanding with the Labour Party on policies for a more planned economy and the redistribution of wealth and power. Labour legislation was one element in this package, but since so many of the other elements were watered down or not implemented, it assumed great significance as perhaps the major contribution from the government in the political exchange that facilitated voluntary pay restraint.

The Social Contract labour laws were characterised by a gap between aspiration and reality. They were supposed to be a great extension of worker and trade union rights, which would, nevertheless, not give rise to a legally

---

[84] On the Social Contract, see Clark et al. (1980); and on the legal policy issues arising under it, see Wedderburn (1978); Clark and Wedderburn (1983:184 et seq.); and Lewis (1983:373–81).

regulated system of industrial relations. In practice, these rights secured workers and unions only limited benefits, but they did represent a significant increase in legal regulation and had the effect of encouraging the process of juridification. The ineffectiveness from the worker and union viewpoints was attributable to several causes: the sanctions attached to the rights were generally weak, sometimes deliberately so in order not to jeopardise the integrity of voluntary collective bargaining, and there were inherent drafting defects and, predictably, narrow and legalistic judicial interpretations. Moreover, the senior civil servants responsible for framing the legislation – and perhaps the majority of the Cabinet – were less concerned to redistribute power than to encourage the reform and modernisation of industrial relations. The model of reform was provided by international, especially EEC standards and, of course, the Donovan Report. The most explicitly reformist statement in the legislation was to be found in the EPA's definition of ACAS's powers to provide an advisory service (s.4), to publish inquiries (s.5) and to issue codes of practice (s.6); the spirit of Donovan reformism, has, in fact, strongly influenced ACAS's advisory work and its codes and other publications (Armstrong and Lucas, 1985; Dickens, 1986). A similar rationale could be discerned in the consultation rights for unions and in the EPA's recognition and 'further' recognition procedures, its disclosure duty and the various legal protections for union activity, including the time-off rights. It was also discernible in the expansion of employment protection, which was intended to secure justice for individual employees merely as one of several objects, including British compliance with international standards and improvements in the efficiency of the labour market and personnel management.

But why was the process of juridification encouraged by a legislative programme which was only modestly useful to those who were given legal rights, and which included some decidedly non-interventionist measures, for example, the restoration of the immunities and the presumption about non-enforceable collective agreements? An important factor was the sheer scale of the new framework of rights. The enlargement of employment protection entrenched an interventionist trend in individual regulatory law which was already strong by the mid-1970s. Then there was the enactment of a wide range of positive legal rights in respect of trade union organisation and collective bargaining, a development which would have been even more extensive if legislation had been brought forward to implement the Bullock Report. Prondzynski (1985:179) has suggested that the new collective labour law was just as substantial as the enlargement of employment protection, and, 'provided definite, justifiable principles which were to affect the patterns of industrial relations conduct'. It was the employment protection laws, however, which had the biggest impact on behaviour. As argued above, the statutory norms and procedures were adopted by management with major implications for the collective as well as the individual employment relation.

This experience shows that the analytical distinction between individual and collective, whether in legal intervention or in voluntary regulation, cannot be sustained in practice (cf. Lewis, 1979:218–19; Clark and Wedderburn, 1983:181–3). The breakdown of the individual-collective distinction has been most apparent in the work of the industrial tribunals, which were envisaged as a forum for individual rather than collective issues. Yet the legislation enacted under the reform strategy placed the interpretation of UMAs in the hands of the tribunals, provided a right to organise collectively in the form of a series of individual legal rights enforceable in the tribunals, conferred on the tribunals the task of determining whether or not a union was recognised as a pre-condition for the exercise of numerous statutory rights, and gave the collective entity, the union, a right of complaint to the tribunals under the procedure for redundancy consultation, which was in any case a collective issue. A similar right was provided by the Transfer of Undertakings Regulations, and the Equal Pay Act, as amended by the Equal Pay Regulations, made pay structures a justiciable issue in the tribunals. Perhaps even more important was the role of the tribunals and the appellate courts in interpreting the substantive and sometimes the procedural terms of collective agreements. This arose from the judicial tendency to interpret statutory rights, especially those concerned with redundancy pay and unfair dismissal, by reference to the contract of employment, which in turn often incorporated collectively agreed terms. Finally, the restrictive strategy of the 1980s opened up the tribunals to complaints against trade unions on essentially collective issues: allegations of unreasonable exclusion or expulsion from unions and, under the joinder procedure, of industrial action inducing the employer to contravene the right to dissociate.

Some Implications for a Future Reform Strategy

Proposed alternatives to the prevailing strategy of restriction should recognise the extent to which the present system is legally regulated. The trend towards juridification has become a feature of British industrial relations as a result of both the reform strategy of the 1960s and 1970s and the restrictive strategy of the 1980s. Neither of these experiences can or should be ignored. A future version of the reform strategy would aim to make strike law far less one-sided, but it clearly could not abandon the law's historic function of drawing a line between lawful and unlawful action, or perhaps, in that context, overlook the apparent effectiveness of the recent role of the law in encouraging strike ballots. It would recognise that any major extension of positive legal rights for workers and unions would accelerate the trend towards juridification.

Juridification need not have a pejorative taint. It should be distinguished from unnecessary legalism, as displayed, for example, in long-winded procedures or excessively complex rules. While consideration should be given to proposals to reduce legalism, including radical suggestions for the reform of the tribunals or even their partial replacement by an extended arbitration system (see Chapter 19), it is, nevertheless, likely and, in some instances, desirable that employers and unions will be increasingly influenced by legal norms and procedures. The handling of sex and race discrimination may provide an example. The existing law, the codes of practice, and the work of the EOC and CRE have in a harsh economic climate generally failed to deal effectively with the problems. A strengthened law, in conjunction perhaps with anti-discrimination clauses in public contracts, would aim to have a greater impact on the entire field of personnel management and on pay structures, a traditional area of collective regulation.

If it is accepted that collective issues are frequently dealt with by the tribunals, there seems little point in continuing to argue that they ought not to be. Indeed, the abandonment of that position would open up new possibilities for the reform strategy. Two proposals in particular have been canvassed for some time. First, the Lord Chancellor could exercise the power under EPCA s.131 to give the tribunals jurisdiction – as originally envisaged by the Donovan Report – over complaints of breach of contract of employment. The tribunals ought to be a more suitable forum than the ordinary courts, and the extent to which they already determine collective issues destroys the force of the objection raised in the past by the TUC that the tribunals would be drawn into interpreting collective agreements and ruling on the merits of disputes. Second, the right not to be dismissed unfairly could be fully applied to those dismissed while on strike, whether or not as an element in a wider positive right to strike. The 'non-interventionist' argument against this proposal is that if dismissal during a strike without victimisation (currently defined by EPCA s.62 as amended) were made justiciable, 'the principles by which a strike is to be accounted "reasonable" would be placed squarely into the hands of the tribunals, and before long therefore into the hands of the judges' (Wedderburn, 1985b:517). Again, the view that the tribunals ought not to determine collective issues, when in reality they do, appears as an unnecessary constraint on the development of policy. Furthermore, the question of the unreasonableness of a striker's dismissal may arise under the present law. For those who can show that they are victimised, which is difficult after the 1982 Act, the test which the tribunal applies is not one of automatic liability but is, in fact, the test of reasonableness. In any event, a reform of the law might redefine the fairness of a striker's dismissal in terms other than reasonableness as well as providing a more effective reinstatement remedy.

A more legally regulated system would have major implications for the role of trade unions. What is the point of belonging to a union if conditions of employment are increasingly regulated by legislation? But this formulation of the question tends to exaggerate the law's impact – clearly it would not regulate all issues – and to underestimate the resourcefulness of unions. As Dickens et al. (1985:252–3) have suggested, voluntarily agreed norms and procedures are not necessarily '*replaced* by legal ones, but rather their form and operation may be modified and informed by an awareness of the legal provisions and their operation'. In a more regulated system, a comprehension of legal rights may become increasingly necessary for the conduct of voluntary negotiation, but such negotiation will continue. Part of the attractiveness of union membership is that unions can provide such expertise, whether in negotiation or litigation.[85]

---

[85] Union legal services have, in fact, always been important for the recruitment and maintenance of membership: see Evans et al. (1985a: 106–7); Latta and Lewis (1974:68).

The erosion of union bargaining power by unemployment, the growth of sub-contracting and marginal work, and the individualistic fashion in 'human resource' management all suggest that unions need a more effective framework of legal rights. Certainly, the TUC regularly calls for more legislation.[86] A major extension of individual and collective rights, the latter including legal duties to disclose information and consult with unions over corporate strategy, appears to have become an established part of the programme of the labour and trade union movement. This demand for more legal rights is combined, not illogically, with opposition to the 1980s restrictive legislation. But it has been suggested that the unions' acceptance of the industrial tribunals, and thereby of the role of judicial institutions in industrial relations, may have weakened their ability to mount effective resistance to this legislation (Clark and Wedderburn, 1983:183–4; Dickens et al., 1985:253–5). The TUC's relative lack of success in opposing the 1980s laws – in comparison with its campaign against the IRA – is attributable, however, to many factors, including an unfavourable economic climate and the fact that some of the provisions, such as those designed to encourage balloting, have popular support. Over-reliance on the law weakening the trade unions' ability to resist authoritarian state tendencies is not a realistic prospect in modern Britain.[87] More legislation especially if combined with another attempt at incomes policy and more interventionist economic and industrial policies will undoubtedly have major implications for the future development of voluntary industrial relations. But the issue should be faced with an understanding of the extent to which legal intervention has already juridified the system.

[86] See, e.g., TUC–Labour Party Liaison Committee (1982) and the debates reported in TUC (1986).

[87] Cf. the fate of the trade union movement in Weimar Germany as depicted by Kahn-Freund (1981).

Bibliography

Advisory, Conciliation and Arbitration Service (ACAS). 1983. *Collective Bargaining in Britain: Its Extent and Level*. Discussion Paper no. 2. London: ACAS.

——. 1985. *Annual Report 1984*. London: HMSO.

Armstrong, E., and R. Lucas. 1985. *Improving Industrial Relations: The Advisory Role of ACAS*. London: Croom Helm.

Bain, G.S., and R. Price. 1983. 'Union Growth: Dimensions, Determinants, and Destiny'. *Industrial Relations in Britain*. Ed. G.S. Bain. Oxford: Blackwell, 3–33.

Batstone, E. 1984. *Working Order: Workplace Industrial Relations Over Two Decades*. Oxford: Blackwell.

Brown, W.A. (ed.). 1981. *The Changing Contours of British Industrial Relations: A Survey of Manufacturing Industry*. Oxford: Blackwell.

——, and B. Hepple. 1985. 'Foreword: The Monitoring of Labour Legislation'. *Industrial Relations and the Law in the 1980s: Issues and Future Trends*. Eds. P. Fosh and C. Littler. Aldershot: Gower, iv–xv.

Bullock. 1977. Committee of Inquiry on Industrial Democracy. *Report*. Cmnd 6706. London: HMSO.

Clark, J. 1985. 'The Juridification of Industrial Relations: A Review Article'. *Industrial Law Journal*, 14 (June), 69–90.

——, H. Hartman, C. Lau and D. Winchester. 1980. *Trade Unions, National Politics and Economic Management: A Comparative Study of the TUC and the DGB*. London: Anglo-German Foundation.

——, and *Lord* Wedderburn. 1983. 'Modern Labour Law: Problems, Functions and Policies'. *Labour Law and Industrial Relations: Building on Kahn-Freund*. Eds. *Lord* Wedderburn, R. Lewis and J. Clark. Oxford: Clarendon Press, 127–242.

Clegg, H.A. 1970. *The System of Industrial Relations in Great Britain*. Oxford: Blackwell.

——, A. Fox and A.F. Thompson. 1964. *A History of British Trade Unions Since 1889*. Volume I, 1889–1910. Oxford: Clarendon Press.

Clifton, R., and C. Tatton-Brown. 1979. *Impact of Employment Legislation on Small Firms*. Research Paper no. 6. London: Department of Employment.

Crouch, Colin. 1977. *Class Conflict and the Industrial Relations Crisis: Compromise and Corporatism in the Policies of the British State*. London: Heinemann.

Daniel, W.W. 1985. 'The United Kingdom'. *Managing Workforce Reduction: An International Survey*. Ed. M. Cross. London: Croom Helm, 67–90.

——, and N. Millward. 1983. *Workplace Industrial Relations in Britain: The DE/PSI/SSRC Survey*. London: Heinemann.

——, and E. Stilgoe. 1978. *The Impact of Employment Protection Laws*. London: Policy Studies Institute.

Davies, P., and M. Freedland. 1983. 'Editors' Introduction'. *Labour and the Law*. O. Kahn-Freund. 3rd edn. London: Stevens, 1–11.

——, and M. Freedland. 1984. *Labour Law: Text and Materials*. 2nd edn. London: Weidenfeld & Nicolson.

Department of Employment (DE). 1981. *Trade Union Immunities*. Cmnd 8128. London: HMSO.

——. 1984. *Protection of Wages: Legislative Proposals*. London: DE.

——. 1985a. *Consultative Paper on Wages Councils*. London: DE.

——. 1985b. *Employment: The Challenge for the Nation*. Cmnd 9474. London: HMSO.

——. 1985c. *Sex Discrimination Act 1975 and European Community Legislation: A Consultative Document*. London: DE.

—— and Department of Trade and Industry (DTI). 1983. *Draft European Communities Directive for Informing and Consulting Employees. Draft European Communities Fifth Directive on the Harmonisation of Company Law. A Consultative Document*. London: DE and DTI.

Department of Employment and Productivity (DEP). 1969. *In Place of Strife: A Policy for Industrial Relations*. Cmnd 3888. London: HMSO.

Department of Health and Social Security (DHSS). 1985a. *Reductions of Burdens on Business: Statutory Sick Pay Aspects*. London: DHSS.

——. 1985b. *Reform of Social Security. Vol. 2. Programme for Change*. Cmnd 9518. London: HMSO.

Department of the Environment. 1985. *Competition in the Provision of Local Authority Services*. London: The Department.

Department of Trade and Industry (DTI). 1985. *Burdens on Business: Report of a Scrutiny of Administrative and Legislative Requirements*. London: HMSO.

Dickens, L. 1986. 'Advisory, Conciliation and Arbitration Service: Regulation and Voluntarism in Industrial Relations'. *Regulation and Public Law*. Eds. R. Baldwin and C. McCrudden, London: Weidenfeld & Nicolson.

——, M. Jones, B. Weekes and M. Hart. 1985. *Dismissed: A Study of Unfair Dismissal and the Industrial Tribunal System*. Oxford: Blackwell.

Donovan. 1968. Royal Commission on Trade Unions and Employers' Associations 1965–1968. *Report*. Cmnd 3623. London: HMSO.

Dunn, S., and J. Gennard. 1984. *The Closed Shop in British Industry*. London: Macmillan.

Edwards, P.K. 1983. 'The Pattern of Collective Industrial Action'. *Industrial Relations in Britain*. Ed. G.S. Bain. Oxford: Blackwell, 209–34.

Evans, S. 1983. 'The Labour Injunction Revisited: Picketing, Employers and the Employment Act 1980'. *Industrial Law Journal*, 12 (September), 129–47.

——. 1985a. 'Picketing under the Employment Acts'. *Industrial Relations and the Law in the 1980s: Issues and Future Trends*. Eds. P. Fosh and C. Littler. Aldershot: Gower, 118–52.

——. 1985b. 'The Use of Injunctions in Industrial Disputes'. *British Journal of Industrial Relations*, 23 (March), 133–7.

——, J. Goodman and L. Hargreaves. 1985a. 'Unfair Dismissal Law and Changes in the Role of Trade Unions and Employers' Associations'. *Industrial Law Journal*, 14 (June), 91–108.

——, J. Goodman and L. Hargreaves. 1985b. *Unfair Dismissal Law and Employment Practice in the 1980s*. Research Paper no. 53. London: Department of Employment.

Ewing, K.D. 1985. 'The Strike, the Courts and the Rule-Books'. *Industrial Law Journal*, 14 (September), 160–75.

Flanders, Allan D. 1970. *Management and Unions: The Theory and Reform of Industrial Relations*. London: Faber.

Gospel, Howard, and Paul Willman. 1981. 'Disclosure of Information: The CAC Approach'. *Industrial Law Journal*, 10 (March), 10–22.

Gregory, R. 1985. 'Industrial Relations, the Law and Government Strategy'. *Political Quarterly*, 56 (January–March), 23–32.

Hepple, B. 1983a. 'Individual Labour Law'. *Industrial Relations in Britain*. Ed. G.S. Bain. Oxford: Blackwell, 393–418.

——. 1983b. 'Judging Equal Rights'. *Current Legal Problems*, vol. 36, 71–90.

——, and P. O'Higgins. 1981. *Employment Law*. 4th edn. B.A. Hepple. London: Sweet & Maxwell.

Home and Scottish Offices. 1985. *Review of Public Order Law*. Cmnd 9510. London: HMSO.

Kahn, P., N. Lewis, R. Livock and P. Wiles. 1983. *Picketing – Industrial Disputes, Tactics and the Law*. London: Routledge & Kegan Paul.

Kahn-Freund, Otto. 1959. 'Labour Law'. *Law and Opinion in England in the 20th Century*. Ed. M. Ginsberg. London: Stevens, 215–63.

——. 1968. *Labour Law: Old Traditions and New Developments*. Toronto: Clark Irwin.

——. 1972. *Labour and the Law*. London: Stevens.

——. 1974. 'The Industrial Relations Act 1971 – Some Retrospective Reflections'. *Industrial Law Journal*, 3 (December), 186–200.

——. 1981. *Labour Law and Politics in the Weimar Republic*. Ed. and intr. by R. Lewis and J. Clark. Oxford: Blackwell.

——. 1983a. *Labour and the Law*. 3rd edn. Ed. and intr. by P. Davies and M. Freedland. London: Stevens.

——. 1983b. 'Labour Law and Industrial Relations in Great Britain and West Germany'. *Labour Law and Industrial Relations: Building on Kahn-Freund*. Eds. *Lord* Wedderburn, R. Lewis and J. Clark. Oxford: Clarendon Press, 1–13.

Labour Research Department (LRD). 1985. 'Rise in Legal Actions Against Unions'. *Labour Research*, 74 (October), 259–61.

Latta, G., and R. Lewis. 1974. 'Trade Union Legal Services'. *British Journal of Industrial Relations*, 12 (March), 56–70.

Leighton, P. 1984. 'Observing Employment Contracts'. *Industrial Law Journal*, 13 (June), 86–106.

——, and B. Doyle. 1982. 'Making and Varying Contracts of Employment'. London: Polytechnic of North London. (Mimeographed.)

——, and S. Dumville. 1977. 'From Statement to Contract: Some Effects of the Contract of Employment Act 1972'. *Industrial Law Journal*, 6 (September), 133–48.

Lewis, R. 1976. 'The Historical Development of Labour Law'. *British Journal of Industrial Relations*, 14 (March), 1–17.

——. 1978. 'Nuclear Power and Employment Rights'. *Industrial Law Journal*, 7 (March), 1–15.

——. 1979. 'Kahn-Freund and Labour Law: An Outline Critique'. *Industrial Law Journal*, 8 (December), 202–21.

——. 1983. 'Collective Labour Law'. *Industrial Relations in Britain*. Ed. G.S. Bain. Oxford: Blackwell, 361–92.

——, and Bob Simpson. 1981. *Striking a Balance? Employment Law after the 1980 Act*. Oxford: Martin Robertson.

Lustgarten, L. 1985. 'Racial Inequality and the Limits of Law'. Coventry: University of Warwick, School of Law. (Mimeographed.)

McCarthy, W.E.J., and N. Ellis. 1973. *Management by Agreement: An Alternative to the Industrial Relations Act*. London: Hutchinson.

Martin, R. 1985. 'Ballots and Trade Union Democracy: The Role of Government'. *Industrial Relations and the Law in the 1980s: Issues and Future Trends*. Eds. P. Fosh and C. Littler. Aldershot: Gower, 66–81.

Mayhew, K. 1985. 'Reforming the Labour Market'. *Oxford Review of Economic Policy*, 1 (Summer), 60–79.

Moore, R. 1982. 'Free Market Economics, Trade Union Law and the Labour Market'. *Cambridge Journal of Economics*, 6 (September), 297–315.

Moran, M. 1977. *The Politics of Industrial Relations*. London: Macmillan.

Office of the Minister without Portfolio (OMWP). 1985. *Lifting the Burden*. Cmnd 9571. London: HMSO.

Pearson. 1978. Royal Commission on Civil Liability and Compensation for Personal Injury. *Report*. Cmnd 7054. 3 vols. London: HMSO.

Phelps Brown, E.H. 1959. *The Growth of British Industrial Relations: A Study from the Standpoint of 1906–14*. London: Macmillan.

——. 1983. *The Origins of Trade Union Power*. Oxford: Clarendon Press.

Prondzynski, F. von. 1985. 'Conclusions: The Changing Functions of Labour Law'. *Industrial Relations and the Law in the 1980s: Issues and Future Trends*. Eds. P. Fosh and C. Littler. Aldershot: Gower, 176–93.

Purcell, J., and K. Sisson. 1983. 'Strategies and Practice in the Management of Industrial Relations'. *Industrial Relations in Britain*. Ed. G.S. Bain. Oxford: Blackwell, 95–120.

Simpson, Bob. 1969. 'In Place of Strife: A Policy for Industrial Relations'. *Modern Law Review*, 32 (July), 420–26.

——. 1979. 'Judicial Control of ACAS'. *Industrial Law Journal*, 8 (June), 69–84.

——, and J. Wood. 1973. *Industrial Relations and the 1971 Act*. London: Pitman.

Stokes, M. 1985. 'Public Law Remedies for Dismissal'. *Industrial Law Journal*, 14 (June), 117–21.

Thomson, Andrew, and S. Engleman. 1975. *The Industrial Relations Act: A Review and Analysis*. London: Martin Robertson.

Trades Union Congress (TUC). 1986. *Annual Report 1985*. London: TUC.

TUC-Labour Party Liaison Committee. 1982. *Economic Planning and Industrial Democracy: The Framework for Full Employment*. London: TUC.

Wade, H.W.R. 1985. 'Procedure and Prerogative in Public Law'. *Law Quarterly Review*, 101 (April), 180–99.

Wainwright, D. 1983. 'Why Equal Value is Dynamite for Pay Structures'. *Personnel Management* (October), 51–3.

Wedderburn, K.W. (*Lord*). 1972. 'Labour Law and Labour Relations in Britain'. *British Journal of Industrial Relations*, 10 (July), 270–90.

——. 1978. 'The New Structure of Labour Law in Britain'. *Israel Law Review*, 13 (October), 435–58.

——. 1980. 'Industrial Relations and the Courts'. *Industrial Law Journal*, 9 (June), 65–94.

——. 1984. 'Labour Law Now: A Hold and a Nudge'. *Industrial Law Journal*, 13 (June), 73–85.

——. 1985a. 'The New Policies in Industrial Relations Law'. *Industrial Relations and the Law in the 1980s: Issues and Future Trends*. Eds. P. Fosh and C. Littler. Aldershot: Gower, 22–65.

——. 1985b. 'The New Politics of Labour Law'. *Trade Unions*. 2nd edn. Ed. W.E.J. McCarthy. Harmondsworth: Penguin, 497–532.

——. 1985c. 'The New Industrial Relations Laws in Great Britain'. *Labour and Society*, 10 (January), 45–61.

Weekes, Brian. 1976. 'Law and the Practice of the Closed Shop'. *Industrial Law Journal*, 5 (December), 211–22.

——, M. Mellish, L. Dickens and J. Lloyd. 1975. *Industrial Relations and the Limits of Law: The Industrial Effects of the Industrial Relations Act 1971*. Oxford: Blackwell.

Wood, John. 1984. 'The Law and Industrial Relations: 1909–1984 and Back?' *75 Years of Law at Sheffield: The Edward Bramley and Jubilee Lectures*. Ed. D.C. Hoath. Sheffield: University of Sheffield, 37–48.

PART II
Collective Bargaining and Industrial Democracy

2 The Right to Associate

Roy Lewis and Bob Simpson

The right to associate, if broadly defined, may cover almost every aspect of industrial relations, including collective bargaining, the withdrawal of labour, and the independence of unions from employers and the state. It may also cover a worker's rights enforceable against a union to become or remain a member and to participate as a member in union affairs. All these aspects of association are dealt with in Parts II to IV of this volume. This chapter focuses on a more narrowly defined area: the 'positive' right enforceable against an employer to join and be active in a union; the 'negative' right to abstain from membership, or, as it is also called, the right to dissociate; and the right to choose between unions. The right to associate in these three senses was traditionally enforced through social rather than legal sanctions, but is now firmly embodied in the legal framework of British industrial relations. This development has occurred with little public debate about freedom of association, except on the one issue of the closed shop.

INTERNATIONAL AND COMPARATIVE ASPECTS

A variety of international measures aim to protect freedom of association, viewing it either as a basic human freedom or as good industrial relations. The most generally influential standards are those of the ILO.[1] These are important for British labour law and industrial relations in at least two ways. First, they may sometimes feature in particular disputes as exemplified by the ILO's finding that the ban on union membership at Government Communications Headquarters (GCHQ) contravened ILO provisions (see Chapter 20 below). Second, they have influenced the drafting of the laws which protect the positive right to associate in the UK.

The principal ILO Conventions are No.87 on Freedom of Association and Protection of the Right to Organise, which was adopted by the ILO in 1948 and ratified by the UK in 1949, and No.98 on the Right to Organise and to Bargain Collectively, which was adopted in 1949 and ratified by the UK in 1950. The former provides that workers and employers have the right to establish and join organisations of their own choosing without previous

---

[1] See Valticos (1979); Pankert (1982). The legal effect of ILO Conventions and other international measures is explained below in Chapter 20.

authorisation. The latter protects workers from anti-union discrimination: it prohibits the making of non-membership of a union a condition of employment, and bans dismissals and other prejudicial acts where the reason is union membership or participation in union activities outside working hours, or, with the employer's consent, within working hours. In 1971 the ILO adopted Convention No.135 (ratified by the UK in 1973) and Recommendation No.143 on Protection and Facilities for Workers' Representatives in the Undertaking. These aim to safeguard representatives from prejudicial acts, including dismissal, because of union membership or activities, and to give them appropriate facilities such as a reasonable amount of paid time off. More recent ILO measures deal with freedom of association for rural workers and public servants, and with the promotion of collective bargaining.[2] Finally, in 1982 the ILO replaced the famous Recommendation No.119 of 1963 on Termination of Employment with Convention No.158 and Recommendation No.166.[3] The new instruments re-state that union membership and activities are invalid reasons for dismissal.

Only the positive right to associate is expressly protected by the ILO Conventions. Employers' representatives tried without success to amend the recent draft instruments on Termination of Employment so as to extend equal protection to the negative right, or right to dissociate (Napier, 1983). ILO conferences have consistently rejected protection of the negative right. Express protection of this right is, moreover, absent from other international measures dealing with industrial relations,[4] including Art. 5 of the European Social Charter and Art. 11(1) of the European Convention for the Protection of Human Rights and Fundamental Freedoms.[5] The latter provision states that 'everyone has the right ... to freedom of association with others, including the right to form and to join trade unions for the protection of his interests'. Thus the Article expressly protects only the positive right, but it has nevertheless featured in the development of the legal right to dissociate in Britain as a result of the *British Rail* case.[6]

In the mid-1970s union membership was made a condition of employment for British Rail employees in accordance with a union membership agree-

---

[2] Convention No. 141 and Recommendation No. 149 on Organisations of Rural Workers (1975); Convention No. 151 and Recommendation No. 159 on Protection of the Right to Organise and Procedures for Determining Conditions of Employment in the Public Service (1978); and Convention No. 154 and Recommendation No. 163 on the Promotion of Collective Bargaining (1981). The UK ratified Convention No. 141 in 1977 and No. 151 in 1980. In 1982 it announced that it would not ratify Convention No. 154 or adopt Recommendation No. 163: DE, 1982. Texts of ILO provisions are set out in ILO, 1982.

[3] The UK has refused to ratify Convention No. 158 because of alleged extra burdens it would impose on employers: DE, 1983.

[4] Though Art.20(2) of the United Nations' Universal Declaration of Human Rights (1948) provides that 'no one may be compelled to belong to an association'.

[5] Both the Charter and Convention are instruments of the Council of Europe, see Chapter 20 below.

[6] Opinion of the Commission on Human Rights, Application Nos. 7601/76 and 7806/77; *Young, James and Webster v UK* [1981] IRLR 408; Series A, Vol. 44 4 *European Human Rights Reports* 39 (1982). See O'Higgins (1981); Forde (1982; 1983); Prondzynski (1982a); Davies and Freedland (1984:655–67).

ment (UMA). From 1976 to 1980 the law provided that where the practice of a UMA existed it was fair to dismiss an employee for refusing to join a union, unless the employee objected to membership on grounds of religious belief. The three former British Rail employees who invoked the European Convention had been dismissed for refusing to join on grounds which did not encompass religious belief. They claimed that the legislative framework permitting their dismissal put the United Kingdom in breach of Art. 11(1) of the European Convention. When the case was finally determined by the European Court of Human Rights, it was held by a majority of eighteen to three that the UK was in breach of the Article. But most of the majority judges fell short of implying into the Convention a full negative right on an equal footing with the express positive right. Instead they emphasised the special features of the case which justified some degree of protection for the negative right: all three applicants were existing employees at the time when the UMA was introduced, two of the three objected on grounds of strong personal opinions to joining a union, and the UMA's particular constraints on the individuals were so severe as to be inconsistent with any freedom of choice. In a concurring judgment, some of the majority of judges went further by holding that the negative right was a full correlative of and inseparable from the positive right. For these judges freedom of association as embodied in Art. 11 meant an unqualified right to join or not to join, and if to join, to choose freely between unions.

The international provisions and case law tend to reflect the statutes, constitutions and jurisprudence of countries where the legal right to associate is typically more explicit, more comprehensive and of longer standing than the UK equivalent.[7] As regards the positive right, Kahn-Freund (1983:205–8) quoted the examples of the USA, Sweden and Italy. In the USA, the National Labor Relations (Wagner) Act 1935 s.8(a)(1) proscribes as 'unfair labor practices' various employers' acts which encroach on freedom of organisation. These include acts to 'interfere with, restrain or coerce employees' in the exercise of their rights to form, join or assist unions, to bargain collectively through representatives of their own choosing, and to engage in concerted activities for the purpose of collective bargaining or other mutual aid or protection. It also proscribes 'discrimination in regard to hire or tenure of employment or any term or condition of employment to encourage or discourage membership in any labor organisation'. The National Labor Relations Board may make orders on employers to cease and desist and to take affirmative action including reinstatement; ultimately it can seek injunctions to enforce its orders. In Sweden even broader substantive provisions in the Joint Regulation of Working Life Act 1976 are enforced directly through the civil courts, and a union may act as plaintiff (Schmidt, 1977:62–77). The Italian Workers' Statute (*Statuto dei Lavoratori*) 1970[8] prohibits the employer from dismissing or discriminating

---

[7] For a comparative legal survey of France, Italy, West Germany, Sweden, the USA and Britain, see Wedderburn (1978). For a comparison of Britain, Ireland and West Germany, see Prondzynski (1982b).

[8] ILO *Legislative Series 1970*. For a socio-legal analysis of its operation, see Treu (1975).

against a worker because of union membership or activity or participation in a strike. The Statute provides workers and unions with a range of remedies, including reinstatement, and there is a specially expedited injunction procedure to restrain dismissals for union activity. Another instructive example is provided by the French Law on Staff Representation 1982, which strengthens the statutory powers and protections from dismissal of union representatives, workers' delegates and works committee members.[9] These measures show that the law can provide effective remedies. Thus, if an Italian or American worker is dismissed for union membership or activity, there is a remedy of mandatory reinstatement. In contrast to the British experience, moreover, some of the foreign provisions have been broadly interpreted by the courts.[10]

Legal protection for the right to dissociate exists in virtually all countries with industrialised market economies.[11] The form and extent of this right are the product of specific historical circumstances, but a few generalisations may be made in order to provide a critical perspective on the current state of the law in Britain. First, it is not necessarily logical to regard the negative and positive rights as correlatives. In the *British Rail* case the dissenting minority of three Scandinavian judges argued that the negative right protected a purely individual freedom, whereas the positive right was a collective right in so far as it could be exercised only jointly by a plurality of individuals. If the positive right is viewed as an aspect of collective bargaining rather than as an individual human right, the negative and positive aspects appear logically to be opposites rather than correlatives (cf. Davies and Freedland, 1984:651). This was the logic behind the Donovan Commission's much quoted statement (1968:para.599) that 'the two [negative and positive rights] are not truly comparable. The former condition is designed to frustrate the development of collective bargaining, which it is public policy to promote, whereas no such objection applies to the latter'. Second, the idea that freedom of association entails the rights to choose a particular union and to stand apart from any union is understandable on grounds of policy in those countries where a union movement is, as in Italy and France, or was, as in West Germany and Ireland, divided on ideological or religious grounds. Such ideological pluralism is in marked contrast to the British traditions of the closed shop, trade union support for the Labour Party, and the protection of the individual through 'contracting-out' (Kahn-Freund, 1983:247–8; see further Chapter 11 below). Third, in a number of countries, notably Sweden and to a lesser extent the USA, the principle of freedom of choice is in various ways circumscribed in order to limit inter-union rivalry, facilitate collective bargaining, and enable employers to standardise terms and conditions of employment (Summers, 1964). Whether or not the positive and negative aspects take the legal form

---

9   *European Industrial Relations Review*, 1983, nos. 118, 119, 121 and 122 (English translation of the revised law).
10 Wedderburn (1978: 382–3, 387) cites the judicial interpretation of union activities under the Italian Workers' Statute, and 'concerted activities' under the Wagner Act (but for important detail and qualifications, see Gorman, 1976: 296–325).
11 See note 7 above, and Kahn-Freund (1983:236–70).

of correlatives, a limited negative right may operate within a labour law system which reflects an overall public policy in favour of collective regulation. But in Britain the emergence of the right to dissociate marked the reversal of the policy of support for collective bargaining which had hitherto prevailed.

HISTORICAL DEVELOPMENT IN BRITAIN

In 1824 the major statutory criminal restraints on union organisation per se were repealed by the Combination Laws Repeal Act, and half a century later trade unions were granted immunity from the highly restrictive common law doctrine of restraint of trade.[12] But no enforceable right to associate existed for a further century. Only the now rescinded Fair Wages Resolution, which was not 'law' as such (see Chapter 4 below), required a government contractor to 'recognise the freedom of his workpeople to be members of trade unions' and to ensure that the same principle was observed by sub-contractors. Apart from this Resolution, and notwithstanding the UK's ratification of the relevant ILO Conventions, legal protection for the right to organise was considered to be unnecessary. This was part of the tradition of legal non-intervention in British industrial relations. It was also part of that tradition that there was little or no recognition of freedom of choice or of dissociation. Although a few common law precedents of dubious authority cast doubt on the legality of arbitrary exclusion from trade union membership,[13] the closed shop was regarded as a lawful objective.[14]

The turning point was the IRA. This proclaimed in s.1(1)(c) 'the principle of free association of workers in independent trade unions, and of employers in employers' associations, so organised as to be representative, responsible and effective bodies for regulating relations between employers and workers'. More important, s.5 gave every worker the right to be a member of the registered trade union of his or her choice, to take part in its activities at an appropriate time, and not to be a member of any or a particular organisation of workers whether registered or not.[15] Thus s.5 embodied a right to dissociate, which was drafted as a correlative to the positive right and was not confined to the closed shop. The remedy lay only against the employer who in turn could claim against a union exerting direct industrial pressure.[16]

[12] Trade Union Act 1871 s.3, a protection which is currently embodied in TULRA s.2(5).
[13] See the development of Lord Denning's views from *Lee v Showmen's Guild* [1952] 2 QB 329, through *Nagle v Feilden* [1966] QB 633, to their high point in *Edwards v SOGAT* [1971] Ch 354, 376. They are inconsistent with the House of Lords decision in *Faramus v Film Artistes' Association* [1964] AC 925. Cf. also *McInnes v Onslow-Fane* [1978] 1 WLR 1520. Unreasonable exclusion is now the subject of limited statutory regulation, see Chapter 10.
[14] *Reynolds v Shipping Federation* [1924] Ch 28; *Crofter Hand Woven Harris Tweed v Veitch* [1942] AC 435.
[15] See Kahn-Freund (1972: 179–82, 206–10); Wedderburn (1972); Simpson and Wood (1973: 102–6, 324–8).
[16] Cf. the exceptional case where a non-unionist obtained a direct remedy, though no compensation, against the union which induced his employers to suspend him on full pay: *Langston v AUEW (No.2)* [1974] ICR 510. See Kahn-Freund (1974); Hepple (1974).

Clearly, the closed shop was in legal jeopardy, especially as the provisions permitting registered unions the privilege of an 'agency' shop or an 'approved closed shop' were frustrated by the refusal of most unions to register. In practice the closed shop was not seriously affected by the legislation basically because management as well as unions wished to preserve it. But inter-union rivalry was exacerbated as a result of the enforcement of s.5 rights by members of splinter organisations which were registered under the Act but not recognised for bargaining by employers (Weekes et al., 1975:42, 295–303).

After the repeal of the 1971 Act, the legislation of the 'Social Contract' era introduced a range of measures to support collective bargaining, including protection of the positive right to organise. There was not an explicit or comprehensive legal guarantee of freedom of association, rather there were (and still are) a series of individual legal rights to safeguard union membership and activity at the workplace. British law was, as Wedderburn (1976:169) has stated, 'building a collective "right to associate" out of the bricks of certain "individual" employment rights'. The relevant measures – which are now consolidated in the EPCA – are: the right not to be dismissed because of membership of or activity in an independent union (s.58(1)(a)(b)); the right not to be subject to employer action short of dismissal for such reasons (s.23(1)(a)(b)); and the rights to paid and unpaid time off for industrial relations duties and trade union activities (ss.27–8). Safety representatives of independent recognised trade unions have also been provided with a framework of statutory rights to time off and requisite facilities.[17]

The Employment Acts of 1980 and 1982 amended the EPCA in order to introduce general dissociation rights in the form of correlatives to the positive rights. These are the rights not to be dismissed because of a refusal to join any or a particular trade union (s.58(1)(c)), and not to be subject to employer action short of dismissal to compel membership of any or a particular union (s.23(1)(c)). They are enforceable whether or not there is a closed shop, though special rules apply if there is the practice of a UMA. In addition, requirements on contractors to employ union-only labour or to recognise or consult with unions are outlawed by EA 1982 ss.12–14. The rest of this chapter will expand on these provisions and touch on other areas of law where the concept of freedom of association has become important.

THE POSITIVE RIGHT TO ASSOCIATE

The case for legal protection of the positive right to associate in Britain was made by the Donovan Commission in terms of the reform and extension of collective bargaining. In addition to proposing a union recognition procedure (see Chapter 3 below), it recommended that any condition in a contract of employment prohibiting union membership should be made void, and

---

[17] HSWA s.2; Safety Representatives and Safety Committees Regulations SI 1977 No. 500. See Chapter 16 below.

that dismissal for union membership or activity should be deemed to be unfair (1968:paras. 244,545). The reform and extension of collective bargaining were also among the objectives of the IRA, and the Social Contract package of labour legislation (Lewis, 1983:368–81). Thus, in the decade after the Donovan Report, public policy encouraged relatively formal and comprehensive collective agreements with single employers, a form of bargaining which in fact became widespread (Brown:1981).

One of the essential elements in this employer-initiated reform was the formalisation of workplace representation. Union representatives and, in particular, shop stewards needed time off, training, and facilities in order to participate in the new type of collective bargaining. Such developments were promoted by the law and by the publication in 1978 of an ACAS Code of Practice – *Time Off for Trade Union Duties and Activities*. The Code (paras.13–20) envisages an extension of the rights of union representatives within a framework agreed by management and unions: representatives should be allowed paid time off for a variety of purposes including collective bargaining at the appropriate level, report-back meetings with members, meetings with other union officials, grievance handling, tribunal representation, induction procedures and training courses. The Code goes further than the express provisions of the Act by recommending (para.24) that representatives should be accorded necessary facilities such as 'accommodation for meetings, access to a telephone, notice boards and, where the volume of the official's work justifies it, the use of office facilities'.[18] Agreements on time off, training and facilities should be consistent with wider procedural arrangements, 'which should deal with such matters of workplace representation as constituencies, number of representatives and the form of any joint credentials' (para.12). Joint regulation of these items shows how far the reform policy concerned itself with the problems of social control within organisations.

Whatever the precise nuances of the policy, however, its broad impact was to encourage the development of workplace representation. By the late 1970s the number of shop stewards had increased to an estimated quarter of a million (Clegg, 1979:51–3), of whom up to 10,000 spent all their working time on industrial relations duties (Terry, 1983:70). Survey evidence suggests that this growth in the number of full-time stewards was stimulated by the employment legislation of the mid-1970s, and specifically that the time-off rights led to an expansion of shop stewards' training. The legal rights of safety representatives also had a positive impact on the parallel development of joint safety committees (Daniel and Millward, 1983:37–9, 142–4; Brown, 1981:75).

The reform and extension of collective bargaining implied an increase in the 'depth of union participation in areas where union recognition had been conceded many years earlier' (Bain and Price, 1983:21). Indeed, the time-off rights and the statutory framework for safety representation only apply where a union is already recognised for collective bargaining. But the

---

[18] The Code treats facilities as part of the reasonable conditions for the exercise of time-off rights under EPCA s.27(2). On shop stewards' facilities, see CIR (1971).

rights not to be dismissed or subject to action short of dismissal because of union membership or activity – the basic planks of the positive right – apply irrespective of whether a union is recognised. An employer who formally recognises unions may nevertheless withdraw facilities and dismiss shop stewards. Such dismissals may lead to strikes. Between 1966 and 1976 'trade union' issues accounted for an annual average of 4 per cent of working days lost and 8 per cent of stoppages. Of these stoppages, about one third concerned the status of workplace representatives, and a further third concerned union recognition and other disputes about union membership (Smith et al., 1978:45–6). Dismissals are just one example of a wide range of techniques by which union organisation can be weakened, destroyed or prevented. One of the most common is the blacklist or refusal to hire known trade unionists. In recent years some employers have reduced the number of full-time shop stewards, restricted the mobility of others, and by-passed them by obtaining workforce consent directly through ballots, or by unilaterally imposed changes in conditions, or by making extensive use of sub-contractors (Terry, 1983:90–91). A climate of growing hostility to unions can only have been encouraged by the government's withdrawal of union membership rights at GCHQ, and by its legislative changes, including the introduction of general rights to dissociate from trade unions. Although the decline in union membership from about 55 per cent of the employed workforce in 1979 to 47 per cent in 1983 is attributable to a host of economic, industrial and technological factors, the abandonment of the Donovan policy by the government and by some employers may also have been a contributory factor (Bain and Price, 1983:31–3). Against this background, the legal support for the positive right to associate has a significance which could not have been anticipated in the mid-1970s.

Scope of Protection

The rights to time off and not to be dismissed or subjected to action short of dismissal for union membership or activity only apply to those who fall within the statutory definition of 'employee', that is, individuals who work or worked under a 'contract of employment' (EPCA s.153(1), HSWA s.53(1)). The many workers who fall outside this definition (see Chapters 12 and 18) are unprotected. There are, however, precedents for not confining rights intended to provide protection against discrimination to 'employees'. The IRA's provision on the right to associate, s.5, applied to all 'workers', workers being defined in the same terms as the current definition in TULRA s.30 to include those who work under contracts personally to perform work or services as well as employees. Similarly, the legislative protection from sex and race discrimination covers contracts to execute personally any work or labour as well as contracts of employment (see Chapter 17 below).

    There is no upper age limit at which employees are excluded from any of these rights, but employees who normally work less than sixteen hours a week, or eight hours a week after five years' continuous employment, are excluded from the time-off rights (EPCA s.146). Excluded from all rights under the EPCA are the police and the armed services. But Crown employees are protected by virtue of EPCA s.138. This section and the parallel provision in EPA s.121 are crucial for civil servants. Without them, they would be denied the benefit of the whole range of employment protection rights.[19]

The government may, however, withdraw these rights from specified work or individuals 'for the purpose of safeguarding national security' (EPCA s.138(4), EPA s.121(4)). At the beginning of 1984 certificates under these provisions were issued in order to take away the legal rights of workers employed at GCHQ, including the rights to complain of dismissal or action short of dismissal because of union membership or activity. The certificates were accompanied by an instruction from the Prime Minister, as Minister for the Civil Service, that the conditions of service at GCHQ should be amended to include a requirement of non-membership of trade unions. The civil service unions challenged the validity of this instruction (but not, ultimately, the certificates) principally on the ground of the government's failure to consult them before issuing it. The House of Lords ruled that the unions did have a legitimate expectation that consultation would occur before any such instruction was issued, but that where ministers provided evidence that considerations of national security prevented them from fulfilling such expectations, the matter fell outside the courts' powers of judicial review. The Law Lords were satisfied that alleged fears that prior consultation might have provoked industrial action – which it was the purpose of the instruction to prevent – was sufficient evidence to this end.[20] In this respect trade union membership rights of civil servants have no more legal protection than those of other workers, since the government can take away the legal protection for the right to belong and take part in union activities from *any* worker by a certificate, issued under EPCA s.128(3) and Sch.9 para.2, to the effect that the particular dismissal or action short of dismissal was in the interests of national security. In this event the tribunal must dismiss the complaint.

Perhaps the most surprising limitation is the failure to extend the positive right to those seeking jobs, even though IRA s.5(1)(a) and the anti-discrimination statutes (SDA s.6(1) and RRA s.4(1)) provide precedents for attempting to protect the rights of job seekers. The *Beyer* case[21] demonstrates both the existence of anti-union discrimination by employers at the point of recruitment and the failure of the legislation to prevent it. Beyer was blacklisted by large building employers in the Birmingham area because of his activities as a member of UCATT. Although he managed to get taken on at a place where he was not known by the site agent, his employment only

---

[19] The right to time off for safety representatives applies to Crown employment, but the legal sanctions for non-compliance do not: HSWA s.48.
[20] *Council of Civil Service Unions v Minister for the Civil Service* [1985] ICR 14.
[21] *City of Birmingham District Council v Beyer* [1977] IRLR 210.

lasted until his true identity became known to management a couple of hours later. The tribunal found the positive right did protect him because he had been dismissed for taking part in union activities. But the EAT reversed this decision on the ground that the legal protection did not extend to activities before the employment in question began.

Time Off Work

Section 27 of the EPCA gives employees who are 'officials' of 'independent' 'recognised' unions the right to paid time off to enable them to carry out certain industrial relations duties or undergo training, which is both relevant to those duties and approved either by their union or the TUC.[22] This right covers duties which are concerned with industrial relations between the official's employer and any associated employers[23] and their employees. While exercising the right, officials are entitled to the pay they would have received had they been at work. Section 28 of the EPCA provides members of 'appropriate', that is, recognised unions with a right to unpaid time off to take part in union activities. These expressly include activities where the employee is acting as a representative of the union and exclude industrial action. The amount of time off and the purposes and conditions subject to which it may be taken are those that are reasonable in the circumstances, having regard to the ACAS Code of Practice discussed above. The enforcement procedure is by way of complaint to an industrial tribunal within the three months' time limit applicable to most of the individual employment protection rights. Where a complaint is upheld, the tribunal may award compensation which it considers to be just and equitable in the circumstances and, on a complaint of failure to pay for time off under s.27, must order the employer to pay the amount due.

The EAT and Court of Appeal have had to consider some important aspects of the right to paid time off, notably the scope of industrial relations duties within s.27(1)(a) and the application of the reasonableness qualification in s.27(2). But the case law has not created a satisfactory or coherent body of principles.

Industrial relations duties. The courts have taken an apparently liberal approach to the meaning of 'industrial relations duties', refusing to limit the right to time off by reference to the statutory definition of recognition or the industrial relations structure laid down by the employer. In the leading case of *Beal v Beacham Group Ltd*,[24] it was held that union representatives were

---

22 Officials are defined by TULRA s.30(1) to include shop stewards. On recognition, see Chapter 3, and on independence, see Chapter 10 below.

23 Two employers are associated if one is a company of which the other (directly or indirectly) has control, or if both are companies of which a third person (directly or indirectly) has control: EPCA s.153(4). See further Chapter 5 below.

24 [1982] ICR 460. Both in *Beal* and *Allen v Thomas Scott Ltd* [1983] IRLR 329 the Court of Appeal endorsed the approach of the EAT in *Sood v GEC Elliott Process Automation Ltd* [1980] ICR 1. See too *RHP Bearings Ltd v Brookes* [1979] IRLR 452; *Depledge v Pye*

entitled to paid time off to attend a union national advisory committee meeting to discuss co-ordination of forthcoming pay claims in the two sub-groups of the employer's business. But meetings of unofficial union committees such as a shop stewards' combine operating outside union rules and formal procedures are always excluded. The cases also suggest that for meetings between officials employed by associated employers, those attending must have a pre-existing problem with their own employer before their attendance can qualify, a restriction which may be hard to justify on industrial relations grounds (see Fitzpatrick, 1983:259). Where only part of the business of an internal union meeting qualifies for paid time off, tribunals may find that only part of the time off to attend should be paid, but such apportionment is not always necessary. In one case where the question arose of what training could be relevant to an official's industrial relations duties, the EAT took a broad approach in holding that it included attendance at a course on pensions and participation, even though the employer's current pension scheme did not permit workers to have any direct say in its administration.[25]

Reasonableness limitation. The Court of Appeal's decision in *Allen v Thomas Scott* asserted a very high degree of tribunal autonomy in deciding whether a claim for paid time off was in the circumstances reasonable. It held that the EAT could not overturn a tribunal's decision on this issue unless it was shown that erroneous factors had been taken into account. While this is consistent with the general role of industrial tribunals as 'industrial juries' bringing the expertise of the lay members to bear on the facts of each case, it makes it difficult for management and unions to know where the law stands. On a particular point of some importance, it is not clear whether an employer who is prepared to give unpaid time off for industrial relations duties can argue that it was unreasonable for it to be paid.[26]

The principle of tribunal autonomy was also decisive in *Ashley v Ministry of Defence*. AUEW shop stewards claimed time off with pay at average rates to attend meetings in preparation for negotiations with management under established procedures. The employers were prepared to grant time off either without pay or paid at basic rates in accordance with a Ministry of Defence manual. The tribunal found that neither of the two meetings in question came within the scope of industrial relations duties under the statute. Even though the EAT did not agree with this in respect of one of the

---

Communications Ltd [1981] ICR 82; *Beal v Beecham Group Ltd (No.2)* [1983] IRLR 317; and *Ashley v Ministry of Defence* [1984] ICR 298. For critical appraisals of the case law see Bowers and Clarke (1980); Fitzpatrick (1983).

25 *Young v Carr Fasteners Ltd* [1979] ICR 844. Contrast *Menzies v Smith and McLaurin Ltd* [1980] IRLR 180, where the EAT in Scotland excluded attendance at a course on job security on the ground that the syllabus was too wide and general.

26 In *Beal v Beecham (No.2)* the EAT held that he could not; in *Allen v Thomas Scott* the Court of Appeal found that he could. In deciding whether a claim is reasonable under EPCA ss.27 and 28 a tribunal is entitled to have regard to the amount of time off taken for other purposes: *Wigley v British Gas Corporation* [1984] ICR 716.

meetings, cautioned by the Court of Appeal's views on tribunal autonomy in *Allen*, it held that the decision could not be overturned since no erroneous considerations had been taken into account. Thus, not only the reasonableness of the claim but the question of whether it relates to industrial relations duties are both apparently matters for the tribunals to decide on the facts of each case.

Ashley also raised another issue. Can a worker whose job is governed by an agreement on time off take advantage of the statutory right where the latter is more favourable? In the EAT's view this would be undesirable; it was improbable that tribunals would regard statutory claims by workers with separate agreed rights as reasonable, especially as the Time Off Code encouraged agreement between employers and unions. The EAT omitted to consider the effect of EPCA s.140, which renders void agreements excluding or limiting statutory rights. If its view is correct, however, it means that union officials will not be able to combine statutory and contractual rights to their advantage. This contrasts with the position under other employment protection provisions such as the right to return to work after maternity leave (EPCA s.48).

Comparison with safety representatives. These time-off rights as judicially interpreted may be compared with the rights of safety representatives under the Safety Representatives and Safety Committees Regulations (see note 17 above). In one respect the position of safety representatives is more favourable. Regulation 4(2)(a) requires employers to give them time off with pay 'as shall be necessary for the purpose of performing [their] functions'. Unlike union officials' right to time off to carry out their duties, this is not qualified by the 'reasonable in all the circumstances' criterion limiting, among other things, the amount of time off. But reasonableness does limit the right to time off to undergo training as a safety representative (reg.4(2)(b)), and guidance on what training is 'reasonable in all the circumstances' is provided in a Code of Practice (HSC, 1978).

In another respect, however, the legal position of safety representatives is less favourable than that of union officials. EPCA s.27 requires training to be approved by the trade union or the TUC. A similar provision is made on training for safety representatives, but it is contained only in the HSC's Code rather than the regulations and, therefore, lacks the force of law. This difference was held by the EAT to justify a tribunal decision that an employer who provided his own safety training had discharged his legal obligation to permit time off, even though the training in question did not have the support of either the TUC or the safety representative's union.[27]

---

[27]   *White v Pressed Steel Fisher* [1980] IRLR 176 (noted by McIlroy, 1981). But a tribunal has held that a statutory safety representative may be a trade union official entitled to time off under EPCA s.27: *Little v Haringey LBC* (1983) 88 HSIB, 5 April.

Trade Union Membership and Activity

The reported cases on the rights not to be dismissed or subjected to action short of dismissal have concerned participation in union activities rather than membership. Two key issues of interpretation have emerged. First, were the acts in question 'activities of an independent trade union' and was the employee dismissed or subjected to action short of dismissal for taking part in them? Second, was he or she taking part in them at an 'appropriate time'?

Appropriate time. This is defined as *either* outside working hours *or* at a time within working hours at which, in accordance with arrangements agreed with or consent given by the employer, it is permissible to take part in those activities (EPCA ss.23(2) and 58(2)). This definition is the same as that used in IRA s.5(5). It was acceptable to the government at the time of enactment because of the way it had been interpreted by the House of Lords in the *Post Office* case.[28] This was one of a series of legal actions brought by officials of the unrecognised Telecommunications Staff Association over the Post Office's refusal to provide facilities for recruitment, collection of subscriptions, meetings, etc., and over threats of disciplinary action against them for carrying on these activities during meal breaks. The case dealt only with the first part of the definition of appropriate time: outside working hours. The Law Lords opted for a broad interpretation. Since working hours are defined as any time when employees are required to be at work in accordance with their contracts of employment, they concluded that times when the employee is entitled to be on the employer's premises but not required to be working were outside working hours. Thus meal breaks were outside working hours and a similar principle has been applied to tea breaks.[29]

The meaning of the other limb of the definition is arguably more important. On this issue the judicial approach has been more restrictive. In the leading case of *Marley Tile Co. Ltd v Shaw*[30] it was decided that in principle the employer's consent to taking part in union activities during working hours need not be express but could be implied. Thus the EAT had held that in the absence of an express prohibition there was implied consent to an employee talking to her fellow workers about union affairs while working.[31] But in *Shaw* the Court of Appeal, despite its policy of tribunal autonomy on factual questions, reversed the tribunal finding (which the EAT had upheld) of implied consent to a shop steward calling a meeting of members in working hours after management had refused to accept his status as a steward. As the EAT had observed, limiting consent and agreed arrangements to express agreements would effectively confine the protec-

---

[28] *Post Office v UPW* [1974] ICR 378. See HC Standing Committee F, 26 June 1975, 846, 849–51 (Minister of State for Employment).
[29] *Zucker v Astrid Jewels Ltd* [1978] ICR 1088.
[30] [1979] ICR 828, EAT, reversed [1980] ICR 72, CA.
[31] *Zucker v Astrid Jewels Ltd* [1978] ICR 1088.

tion for taking part in union activities in working hours to members of recognised unions, which is not a statutory requirement. But the Court of Appeal decision leaves it unclear how much wider the protection in fact goes.[32]

Union activities. The scope of union activities in the EPCA was intended to be similar to that of the equivalent phrase in IRA s.5(1)(c).[33] This was interpreted by the House of Lords in the *Post Office* case to mean activities not requiring the employer's assistance by providing facilities, or only requiring facilities normally available to employees, or requiring the employer to submit to only trifling inconvenience. Subject to this guidance, the question was said to be one of fact for the tribunals to resolve on a case-by-case basis. This approach excludes activities which impose anything beyond the most minimal constraints on management by way of necessary co-operation. For example, in the *Post Office* case itself, use of a canteen table for recruiting and collecting subscriptions in a way that did not hinder people using the canteen for other purposes was held to fall within the range of protected activities while notice board facilities fell outside.

Subsequent decisions have not created a coherent body of law. In *Dixon v West Ella Developments Ltd*,[34] the EAT said that union activities were not confined to meetings of members and other activities involving the status of employees as trade unionists. They could include asking a shop steward for advice, seeking to apply approved union practice and contacting a union about working conditions. In marked contrast is *Chant v Aquaboats Ltd*[35] where the EAT decided that drawing up a petition about safety at work, which was vetted by the union before being presented to management, fell outside the statute. Kilner Brown J distinguished 'activities of an independent trade union', which were protected, from the activities of a trade unionist, which were not.

The uncertainty created by these different approaches limits the potential effectiveness of the law. But a more far-reaching limitation was exposed by the Court of Appeal decision in *Carrington v Therm-A-Stor*.[36] There it was found that the employer's decision to make twenty of his approximately seventy workers redundant was a direct response to the TGWU's request for recognition, after most of the workforce had joined the union. As construed by the Court of Appeal, the protection for the individual employee in s.58(1)(a) and (b) does not extend to situations where dismissal is the

---

[32] Cf. the decision of the Northern Ireland Court of Appeal on the equivalent provision of the Industrial Relations (No.1) Order SI 1976 No. 1043 in *Eastern Health and Social Services Board v Deeds* (1984) 256 IRLIB, 8 May: consent to a union meeting in working hours could be implied from the personnel officer having telephoned a full-time union officer and given her half an hour to get the workers to abandon their refusal to provide lunches for a management meeting.

[33] See note 28 above.

[34] [1978] ICR 856. See too *British Airways Engine Overhaul Ltd v Francis* [1981] ICR 278 where criticism of official union bodies was held to be taking part in union activities.

[35] [1978] ICR 643.

[36] [1982] ICR 8, EAT, reversed [1983] ICR 208, CA.

employer's response to action taken by the union. The courts have thus excluded employees from protection both where the employer's action was directed at the *collective* activity of the union (*Therm-A-Stor*), and where it was directed at the activities of the *individual* trade unionist (*Chant*).

A similar contradiction is evident in the exclusion of industrial action from the ambit of union activities. Although there is no express stipulation to this effect, it is clear from EAT decisions that this exclusion applies on the reasoning that dismissal while taking part in industrial action is the subject of separate provision in what is now EPCA s.62.[37] When the employment legislation of the mid-1970s was formulated, this issue presented a conflict between two different strands of policy: legal protection for the positive right to organise, and exclusion of courts and tribunals from jurisdiction over the merits of industrial disputes. The EAT no doubt correctly discerned the legislative intention in holding that the latter policy prevailed. In the light of the judicial interpretation of s.62 and the amendments made to it by EA 1982 (discussed in Chapter 9), however, support for the positive right gives way to a policy not of neutrality in industrial disputes but to discriminatory dismissal of trade union activists.

Action Short of Dismissal

The rights in EPCA s.23(1)(a) and (b) provide redress for 'action short of dismissal' taken against an employee 'as an individual' for the purpose of 'preventing or deterring' him or her from being or seeking to become a member of an independent trade union or taking part in the activities of an independent union at an appropriate time, or 'penalising' him or her for doing either of these things. The meaning of these provisions is far from clear. The EAT has accepted that 'action short of dismissal' covers transferring a shop steward to less desirable work where he had fewer contacts with fellow workers.[38] It also covers disciplinary action.[39] Whether it covers a threat of action as distinct from the action itself was questioned by the EAT in *Brassington v Cauldron Wholesale Ltd*,[40] where the employer had informed his workforce that the business would close if he was required to recognise the TGWU. Since the status of a threat was not appealed the EAT accepted that this was action short of dismissal for the purpose of preventing or deterring the applicants from belonging to the union.

The circumstances when action is not taken against an employee 'as an individual' are equally hard to identify (see Lewis and Simpson, 1981:68). A further condition which may also cause difficulty is that the employee must be prevented or deterred or penalised,[41] which are issues of fact essentially

---

[37] *Winnett v Seamarks Ltd* [1978] ICR 1240 and *Drew v St Edmundsbury Borough Council* [1980] ICR 513.
[38] *Robb v Leon Motor Services Ltd* [1978] ICR 506.
[39] *British Airways Engine Overhaul Ltd v Francis* [1981] ICR 278.
[40] [1978] ICR 405. Cf. *Grogan v British Railways Board*, an unreported EAT decision on 17 January, 1978, where it was held that s.23 did cover a threat.
[41] See *Carlson v Post Office* [1981] ICR 343.

turning on the burden of proof. While the onus is on the employer to show the purpose for which the action was taken (EPCA s.25(1)), the burden of proving that 'action was taken against him as an individual' remains on the employee. It will often be an insuperable hurdle, as in the comparable area of sex and race discrimination. The extent to which employees can obtain disclosure of documents to assist in such claims was dealt with by the House of Lords in *SRC v Nassé*,[42] where Mrs Nassé alleged that she was being penalised for her union activities contrary to s.23(1)(b), as well as being the victim of sex discrimination. It was held that disclosure of confidential documents could be ordered if necessary for the fair disposal of the proceedings, a criterion which provides only limited encouragement to applicants.

Where a complaint is upheld, the tribunal makes a declaration to that effect and may award compensation (EPCA s.24(3)). The amount of compensation is that which the tribunal considers just and equitable, having regard to the infringement of the right by the employer's action and the employee's loss attributable to it, including consequential expenses and loss of benefits which the employee might reasonably be expected to have had but for the employer's action (s.26(1)(c)). The original proposals in the Employment Protection Bill specified other losses: less favourable terms and conditions, loss of union advice in dealings with the employer, loss of opportunities for training and education and other benefits, and handicaps which might reasonably be expected in seeking future employment.[43] These matters could still presumably be taken into account. In the *Brassington* case the EAT found that the tribunal had been wrong to limit the amount of compensation to the assumed loss of one day's pay through attending the hearing. It set out other wider heads of potential loss: damage to the employee's health caused by stress, compensation for frustration of a deep and sincere wish to join the union, and loss resulting from the failure of a recognition reference under the now repealed EPA procedure. But it expressly rejected the inclusion of any penal element in an award, which provides a marked contrast with the compensation available for unfair dismissal after the 1982 amendments.

Unfair Dismissal

Under EPCA s.58(1)(a) and (b) a dismissal is automatically unfair where the reason or principal reason for it was that the employee was or proposed to become a member of an independent trade union, or had taken part or proposed to take part at an appropriate time in the activities of an independent union. Section 59(a) extends this principle to unfair selection for redundancy: where redundancy is the reason for dismissal and other employees in similar positions in the undertaking were not dismissed, the

---

[42] [1980] AC 1208. See Chapter 17 below.
[43] HC Bill 1974–75 [119], cl.50.

dismissal is automatically unfair if the reason that the dismissed employee was selected for redundancy was union membership or activities.

The right not to be unfairly dismissed generally protects only those employees who have been continuously employed for two years. This qualifying period of employment does not apply in cases of unfair dismissal for trade union membership reasons. Employees who lack the qualifying period are, however, at a disadvantage as regards the burden of proof. The general rule is that while it is for the employee to prove that he or she has been dismissed,[44] it is for the employer to prove the reason for the dismissal. The Court of Appeal has held that this does not apply to claims of unfair dismissal for union membership reasons by individuals who were employed for less than two years before dismissal; they must prove that their dismissal was for the union membership reason alleged.[45]

The inability of the law to provide a speedy and effective mechanism for resolving unfair dismissal claims (see Chapters 15 and 19) poses a special problem where the positive right can only be upheld if effective reinstatement occurs. Hence the provision of the 'interim relief' procedure as a means to secure the position of employees until the full tribunal hearing. An employee who alleges that his or her dismissal was unfair because the reason for it was union membership or activities can apply to a tribunal under EPCA s.77 for interim relief in advance of the full hearing of the case, though the procedure is not available in cases of alleged unfair selection for redundancy. The application must be made within seven days of the dismissal and be accompanied by a certificate from an authorised union official stating that the applicant was or proposed to become a union member, and that there appeared to be reasonable grounds for saying that the reason for the dismissal was the one alleged in the complaint. Where the tribunal finds that this is 'likely' it will make an order for the continuation of employment, if agreement on reinstatement or re-engagement pending determination of the complaint cannot be reached.

Difficulties concerning the certificate from an authorised union official have been revealed by the case law. The EAT has consistently stated that what is required is substantial rather than technical compliance with the statutory detail on this point.[46] But it has also held that, while a union official's authority to provide the certificate may be implied from his or her general functions, evidence of authority must be produced if it is challenged by the employer.[47] There appears, moreover, to be a general reluctance on the part of tribunals to make interim relief orders. In *Taplin v Shippam*

---

[44] On the definition of dismissal, see Chapter 15 below.
[45] *Smith v Hayle Town Council* [1978] ICR 996. Cf. claims by employees who do have the qualifying period of employment when the onus is on the employer to prove that the reason for the dismissal was one other than union membership or activity: *Maund v Penwith District Council* [1984] ICR 143. Where the reason proved is redundancy, the onus of proof of unfair selection is on the employee, see e.g. *Taylor v Butler Machine Tool Co. Ltd* [1976] IRLR 113.
[46] E.g. *Bradley v Edward Ryde & Sons* [1979] ICR 488.
[47] *Sulemany v Habib Bank* [1983] ICR 60.

Ltd[48] the EAT upheld the tribunal's refusal of an order on the basis that 'likely' meant nearer certainty than probability. The EAT suggested that the correct approach was to ask whether the employee had a 'pretty good chance of success'. In any event an order for continuation of employment does not oblige the employer to permit the dismissed employee to return to work, but only requires him to treat the employee as still employed for purposes of pay and other benefits.

Although tribunals have since 1976 been able to make orders rather than the previous recommendations for reinstatement or re-engagement of unfairly dismissed employees, partial or total non-compliance by an employer can only lead to the penalty of extra compensation. Up to 1982 the penalty for total non-compliance with an order for the reinstatement or re-engagement of an employee dismissed on grounds of union membership or activity was an 'additional award' of between twenty-six and fifty-two weeks' pay. The 1982 Act replaced the additional award in cases of unfair dismissal for union membership reasons with a 'special award', which applies to dismissals infringing both the positive and negative aspects of the right to associate. It is primarily aimed at the latter, however, and is discussed below as part of the analysis of the negative right.

RIGHT TO DISSOCIATE

General Dissociation Rights

The aim of the 'step-by-step' legislative policy embodied in the Acts of 1980 and 1982 is to develop an 'absolute right not to be a trade union member even where there is no closed shop'.[49] Two general dissociation rights exist in the form of protection from unfair dismissal and action short of dismissal. First, it is unfair to dismiss an employee because he 'was not a member of any trade union, or of a particular trade union, or one of a number of particular trade unions, or had refused or proposed to refuse, to become or remain a member' (EPCA s.58(1)(c)). It is also unfair to select an employee for dismissal by reason of redundancy because he was not a member of any or a particular union (s.59(a)). Second, every employee has the 'right not to have action (short of dismissal) taken against him as an individual by his employer for the purpose of compelling him to be or become a member of any trade union or a particular trade union, or one of a number of particular trade unions' (s.23(1)(c)). Moreover, the dismissal of a non-member who refuses to make payments in lieu of membership (normally to a charity) is treated as dismissal because of non-membership (s.58(13)), and there is a parallel right not to be subjected to action short of dismissal for the purpose of enforcing any such payment (s.23(1A)(1B)).

---

[48] [1978] ICR 1068.
[49] HC Standing Committee G, 23 March 1982, 653 (Under Secretary of State for Employment). On the 1980s legislative developments, see Lewis and Simpson (1981: 60–98; 1982); Davies and Freedland (1984: 636–55).

In legal analysis the general dissociation rights are similar to the equivalent positive rights. Thus a complaint may be made to the tribunal irrespective of the employee's length of service, age or working hours. As regards unfair dismissal, the complainant must show that he has been dismissed, and, if the normal service qualification is lacking, that the reason or principal reason for dismissal was non-membership of any or a particular union. A dismissal for this reason 'shall be regarded ... as having been unfair' (s.58(1)), that is, liability is automatic and the tribunal need not consider the reasonableness of the employer's conduct. As regards action short of dismissal, the employer has to show the purpose for which the action was taken (s.25(1)). As indicated above, there is no statutory definition of the basic concept of action short of dismissal. Additional legal uncertainties may arise over whether action is taken *against* an employee *as an individual* and whether the employer's purpose was to *compel* membership of any or a particular union.[50] Subject to these important legal technicalities, s.23(1)(c) might cover the following actions: the offer or imposition of inferior terms of employment; the denial of opportunities for bonus earnings, overtime, training or promotion; transfer to less desirable work; and refusal of access to collectively agreed grievance procedures or improvements in substantive terms, for example, a negotiated pay increase. A statement in the written particulars of employment or a collective agreement to the effect that employees are encouraged to join appropriate unions probably does not constitute unlawful compulsion.

Violations of the general dissociation rights lead to similar legal remedies and procedures as apply to the positive rights. As explained above, if a tribunal upholds a complaint of action short of dismissal it makes a declaration and may award compensation. Although the compensation may take account of an employee's desire to join[51] and therefore by implication not to join a union, it does not involve any penal element or quasi-fine on the employer. The modest compensation for action short of dismissal may encourage complaints of constructive dismissal, which offer the prospect of interim relief and generous compensation in default of reinstatement.

The 1982 Act amended EPCA s.77(1) to make the interim relief procedure available to those dismissed for non-membership. Interim relief may reinforce the negative right more effectively than the positive right,[52] especially as the non-unionist does not have to overcome the technical obstacle of a correctly authorised certificate (s.77(2)(b)). Apart from the interim relief procedure, the usual remedies of a reinstatement or re-engagement order or compensation are available.

Compensation for those dismissed for non-membership and (following the correlative principle) for union membership and activity was increased

---

[50] See *Sakals v United Counties Omnibus Co. Ltd* [1984] IRLR 474; Lewis and Simpson (1981: 67–9).

[51] *Brassington v Cauldron Wholesale Ltd* [1978] ICR 405.

[52] The first interim relief order awarded to a non-unionist was in favour of a worker represented by the Freedom Association. His employer, Vauxhall Motors, subsequently re-instated him notwithstanding a closed shop: *Financial Times*, 20 December 1983; *The Guardian*, 17 February 1984.

dramatically by the 1982 Act's amendments to the EPCA. A compensation award comprises three elements. First, there is a 'basic' award; this is (as of April 1985) a minimum of £2,100 (s.73). Second, if the applicant requests an order of reinstatement or re-engagement, the tribunal may make a 'special' award. If the tribunal decides not to make a reinstatement order, which is quite likely to be the case,[53] the special award is the greater of £10,500 or 104 weeks' pay, subject to a maximum of £21,000. Where an order is made but is not obeyed by the employer, then, unless the employer is able to satisfy the tribunal that compliance was not practicable, the special award is the greater of £15,750 or 156 weeks' pay with no upper limit. Third, assuming any actual loss has been incurred, a 'compensatory' award is calculated in the usual way for unfair dismissal claims. The basic and special awards represent a stark contrast with the low level of awards in the general run of unfair dismissal cases (see Chapters 15 and 19).

Tribunals have a discretion to reduce the compensatory award for conduct which caused or contributed to the dismissal. They may reduce the basic and special awards as they consider just and equitable both for unreasonably refusing an offer of reinstatement and for any conduct of the employee before dismissal. They are, however, specifically prohibited from reducing any part of the compensation on the grounds of breach of a requirement to be or not to be a union member, or not to take part in union activities, or a refusal to comply with or an objection to a requirement to pay money in lieu of union membership (EPCA s.72A). This limitation on tribunals' discretion is likely to be more helpful to the non-unionist than the union activist. If a tribunal finds that the employee is at fault in not belonging to a union it will – in contrast to its discretion prior to the 1982 Act[54] – be unable to make a reduction. But if union activity is the reason for dismissal the employer will still be able to argue that any alleged disruption caused by this activity is a ground for reducing the compensation. It is clear that the non-unionist is the intended beneficiary of a compensation regime which has been widely described as a 'bounty hunter's charter'.

Punitive compensation might in theory deter the employer from a dismissal. But the employer may not have to pay for violating the dissociation rights because of the 'joinder' procedure. At this point the formal equality between the negative and positive rights breaks down as there is no equivalent of joinder at the option of those dismissed or discriminated against because of their union membership or activity. If, however, a dismissal for non-membership is induced by pressure from actual or threatened industrial action, the 'trade union or other person' exercising the pressure may be joined (or in Scotland 'sisted') to the tribunal proceedings, and may be ordered to pay all or part of the compensation (EPCA s.76A). The complainant as well as the employer may initiate joinder before a tribunal hearing begins or, at the tribunal's discretion, even after a hearing

---

[53] Predictable industrial strife was upheld as a legitimate consideration in refusing to recommend re-engagement under the IRA's equivalent provisions: *Coleman v Magnet Joinery Ltd* [1975] ICR 46.

[54] E.g. *Sulemanji v Toughened Glass Ltd* [1979] ICR 799.

has started. The compensation is recoverable directly from the party joined, a rule which may in some circumstances make the employer's role in litigation purely nominal. The financial liability of the union raises all the difficult questions of an organisation's vicarious responsibility for its members.[55] The liability of other persons implies the possibility of severe financial burdens being placed on named union activists. Joinder is also available in similar circumstances in hearings to determine whether action short of dismissal has been taken to compel union membership (s.26A).

The joinder procedure is difficult to reconcile with certain other sections of the EPCA. These provide that pressure from industrial action or the threat of it must be ignored in determining both the purpose of the employer's action short of dismissal (s.25(2)) and, in unfair dismissal complaints, the reason for dismissal and whether the employer acted reasonably in dismissing (s.63), although reasonableness is not an issue in claims under s.58. This requirement is reiterated for the purposes of assessing compensation for action short of dismissal (s.26(4)), and the compensatory award in unfair dismissal cases (s.74(5)). The tribunals are therefore in the bizarre position of having to determine the substance of complaints and, where necessary, assess compensation against the employer without regard to any pressure from industrial action, and then to determine the amount of any contribution to the compensation solely on the basis of such pressure. Needless to say, the joinder procedure is also inconsistent with the principle that the tribunals ought not to be required to pronounce on the merits of industrial action or collective disputes at large.

The general dissociation rights and concomitant legal procedures and remedies apply regardless of whether a closed shop exists. It may indeed be misleading to lump the analysis of these provisions under an overall 'closed shop' heading. They have a significance independent from the operation or enforcement of the closed shop. The right not to be subject to action short of dismissal to compel union membership, for example, may, if taken in conjunction with the positive rights to organise, have profound implications for collective bargaining procedures, union recognition and inter-union conflict (see below). Nevertheless, the closed shop context is fundamental to the 1980–82 legislation, which enacts a series of special rules applicable to the closed shop in addition to the general dissociation rights.

Closed Shop

In a closed shop the general dissociation rights may be negatived under complex legal rules, which are explicable in terms of their historical development. Under the IRA, which introduced the unfair dismissal right, dismissal because of non-membership of a union was automatically unfair, except where there was an agency or approved closed shop in which only conscientious objectors or, in agency shops, contributing non-members were

---

[55] Though without the guidance of EA 1982 s.15, which applies only to liability for economic torts, see Chapter 6.

protected. In 1974 TULRA amended the unfair dismissal law with the intention, though not necessarily the effect, of making the legal regulation of the closed shop less restrictive. A dismissal was fair if it was the practice under a UMA for all relevant employees to belong to a specified trade union and the reason for dismissal was refusal to join, unless the employee objected on grounds of religious belief to being a member of any union whatsoever, or objected on any reasonable grounds to joining a particular union. In addition, the legal definition of a UMA required union membership to be a condition of employment for *all* relevant employees. These measures gave rise to problems for management, unions, and the tribunals (Weekes, 1976). In the 'Ferrybridge Six' case,[56] the employer was unable to rely on the fair dismissal provision because the practice of membership of one of the four closed shop unions could not be established in the face of evidence that some 1,000 out of 39,000 employees did not belong. The selective dismissals of activists in the breakaway Electricity Supply Union was not therefore automatically fair, and was indeed found to be unfair because the employer had acted unreasonably. Thus the tribunal did not have to define the legal basis of a reasonable objection to a particular union, which would have been necessary had there been a practice of a UMA.

The Amendment Act of 1976 aimed to resolve such difficulties. It revised the definition of UMA in TULRA s.30(1), and this has been left untouched by the Acts of 1980 and 1982. A UMA is defined as an agreement or a more informal arrangement between independent unions and one or more employers or employers' associations concerning the union membership of employees of an identifiable class. A class of employees may be identified 'by reference to any characteristics or circumstances whatsoever', which allows individuals or groups of employees to be expressly excluded.[57] The effect in practice of the agreement or arrangements must be to require employees to belong to a union specified in the UMA or accepted as equivalent to a union so specified. In contrast to the earlier definition, this requirement need not be a formal condition in employment contracts and it need not apply to every employee. The courts have since confirmed that 'practice' is a matter of fact or degree and does not imply any particular percentage of membership.[58] A further point of judicial interpretation is that where a UMA contains a procedure for processing disputed cases of individuals who refuse to join or who lose their membership, the employer must observe all the procedural stages, unless the deviations were insignificant or unless it was for the employee to initiate the procedure and he failed to do so.[59]

---

[56] *Sarvant v CEGB* [1976] IRLR 66.
[57] The amendment was partly a response to fears that UMA provisions threatened press freedom. This issue was dealt with by TULRA s.1A (see England and Rees, 1976), which was then repealed by EA 1980 and replaced by paras. 63–8 of the Secretary of State's Closed Shop Code. References to the Code are to the 1983 revision.
[58] *Taylor v Co-operative Retail Services Ltd* [1982] ICR 600.
[59] *Jeffrey v Lawrence Scott* [1977] IRLR 466; *Curry v Harlow DC* [1979] ICR 769. See too Closed Shop Code, para. 51. Cf. Chapter 15 below on the normal standard of procedural fairness in unfair dismissal cases.

Apart from re-defining a UMA, the 1976 Amendment Act removed protection from those with a reasonable objection to membership of a particular union. As re-enacted by EPCA s.58(3), dismissal for non-membership was fair if there was the practice of membership in accordance with a UMA, unless the dismissed employee genuinely objected on grounds of religious belief to membership of any union.[60] The legislation of 1980–82 retained s.58(3), but only as an exception to the general dissociation right in s.58(1)(c). After the 1982 Act, the legal right not to be dismissed because of non-membership is displaced by a presumption of fair dismissal if there is the practice, in accordance with a UMA, for employees to belong to an independent union; the reason for the dismissal was that the employee was not or had refused or proposed to refuse to become or remain a member; and the UMA had been approved by ballot within the previous five years. But even if these three conditions are satisfied the dismissal is still unfair if the employee falls within one of the categories of specially protected employees as defined by statute (s.58(4)–(8)). Similarly, the right not to be subject to action short of dismissal to compel union membership is qualified if there is a practice of union membership in accordance with a UMA, the reason for the action was non-membership, and the UMA was approved by ballot. Again, however, the right not to be subject to action short of dismissal applies if the employee comes within one of the specially protected categories (s.23(2A)). Assuming that a practice of membership exists and that the dismissal or action short of dismissal is because of non-membership,[61] the limitations on the general rights to dissociate turn on two basic questions: was the UMA approved by ballot and, if so, was the dismissed or discriminated against employee within one of the specially protected categories?

Ballots. The rule that the fair dismissal presumption is conditional on the UMA being approved within five years preceding the dismissal requires not a 'once and for all' but a periodic ballot at least once every five years. The statutory requirements are set out in s.58A. If the UMA took effect after 14 August 1980 (the date EA 1980 came into force) the first ballot must produce a majority of at least 80 per cent of those entitled to vote. For a UMA which pre-dates 14 August 1980[62] – a category covering the large majority of UMAs – the requisite majority is either 80 per cent of those entitled to vote or 85 per cent of those voting. The alternative majorities apply in second and subsequent ballots in respect of either category of UMAs. The balloting constituency to whom a UMA may apply consists of a class of employees of an employer, but a class may not be defined for

---

[60] This could be based on a personal interpretation of a religious creed even though the creed did not of itself preclude union membership: *Saggers v British Railways Board* [1977] ICR 809; *(No.2)* [1978] ICR 1111.

[61] This may give rise to evidential difficulties over the employer's belief in the fact of non-membership: *Gayle v John Wilkinson* [1978] ICR 154; cf. *Leyland Vehicles v Jones* [1981] ICR 428.

[62] In respect of which the balloting requirements came into force on 1 November 1984: EA 1982 (Commencement) Order SI 1982 No.1656 Sch.2.

balloting purposes by reference to union membership or objection to it. The ballot, which may be held on more than one day, must be conducted in such a way as to ensure that 'so far as is reasonably practicable' all those entitled to vote have the opportunity of voting and of doing so in secret.

These statutory rules are supplemented by the Secretary of State's Code *Closed Shop Agreements and Arrangements*. While breach of the Code does not of itself render a person legally liable, it is admissible in evidence in legal proceedings and relevant provisions are taken into account (EA 1980 s.3(8)). An important section in the Code (para.47(v)) states that the statutory balloting requirements may be met by either a workplace or a postal ballot, but the general inadequacies of the Code's advice may give rise to difficulties which are compounded by its ambiguous legal effect (Lewis and Simpson, 1981:94–7). For example, para. 47(iv) suggests that the ballot form ought to be confined to the single question of whether the UMA should apply. Would the presence of other questions invalidate the ballot? According to the Code, employees ought to be made aware of the intention to hold a ballot, the terms of the UMA, and 'any other relevant information' (para.47(iii)). Is this supposed to include a statement of the case for or against a UMA? The Code like the statute does not say who is supposed to be responsible for a ballot, though it does limply suggest (para.47(vi)) that 'greater confidence will result if the ballot is independently conducted'. Generally, neither Code nor statute provides the detailed rules necessary for the wholesale regulation of UMAs by ballots.

Excepted categories. Notwithstanding valid approval by ballot, the fair dismissal presumption is inapplicable if the dismissed employee comes within one of five specially protected categories. The first category covers an employee who 'genuinely objects on grounds of conscience or other deeply-held personal conviction to being a member of any trade union whatsoever or of a particular trade union' (EPCA s.58(4)). This replaces the religious objection category but is clearly much wider. Although 'conscience' might be linked to an objective standard such as a religious creed,[63] the phrase 'other deeply-held personal conviction' implies an open-ended and purely subjective test. It would arguably encompass objection to a particular union's industrial or political policies. The EAT has rejected the suggestion that it necessarily involves any question of principle or moral considerations; a worker's deeply-held personal belief that the union had failed to look after his interests was within the provision.[64] But in another case the EAT recognised that it has at least one limit: it does not cover a worker who had no objection to membership as such but protested only against compulsion to join.[65]

The second category covers an employee who was in the relevant employment before the UMA took effect and has not subsequently joined a

---

[63] Under the IRA's provisions 'conscience' was equated with religious belief: *Hynds v Spillers-French Baking Ltd* [1974] ITR 261.

[64] *Home Delivery Services Ltd v Shackcloth* [1985] ICR 147.

[65] *Sakals v United Counties Omnibus Co. Ltd* [1984] IRLR 474.

union – an 'existing non-member', as exemplified by the applicants in the *British Rail* case. The third category covers an employee who was entitled to vote in a ballot which approved a UMA after 14 August 1980 and who has not since the day of the ballot become a member, even if he or she was a member after the UMA took effect but prior to the ballot. The fourth category protects an employee who is prepared to be a union member but has been excluded or expelled from membership. It applies where at the time of the dismissal the employee had obtained or was seeking a declaration that the exclusion or expulsion from membership contravened EA 1980 s.4, unless, in the period between making a s.4 complaint and the effective date of termination, the employee has become a union member or failed to apply (or re-apply) for or to accept an offer of membership. The fifth category envisages that an employee – perhaps a 'professional' employee though the statute does not use that terminology – is subject to a written code of conduct associated with his or her relevant job qualifications. It covers an employee who has been expelled from a union for refusing to take part in industrial action in breach of the written code, or who has refused to join a union because membership would require participation in industrial action contrary to the code.[66]

The categories of specially protected employees and the majorities required in ballots, which are far more stringent than those of the 1971 Act,[67] are intended to emasculate the closed shop by giving full rein to the general dissociation rights. Perhaps the most explicit indications of this policy are to be found in the Closed Shop Code, which is less a source of practical guidance than an anti-closed shop manifesto (cf. McCarthy, 1980). A few examples must suffice. The Code advises employers that they need not accept a UMA even if it has been approved by ballot (para.27); that they should consider whether a closed shop might force unwilling employees to take industrial action (para.32); that they may wish to insist on a ballot majority even higher than 80 or 85 per cent (para.48); and that they ought to inform potential employees of their dissociation rights (para.50), though there is no legal requirement to that effect.

Two further closed shop provisions are noteworthy in this context. First, the Secretary of State was empowered under EA 1982 Sch.1 to pay retrospective compensation from state funds to those who were dismissed for non-membership between 1974 and 1980, provided that they would have been able to bring a successful unfair dismissal case under the provisions of the 1980 Act (see Ewing and Rees, 1983). Second, under EA 1980 ss.4 and 5, where there is the practice of union membership in accordance with a UMA, every person who is or is seeking to be in employment has the right not to be unreasonably excluded or expelled from a union (see below, and further Chapter 10).

Underpinning this entire legislative initiative is the belief that the closed shop is an unreasonable limitation on individual liberty, and a reinforcement

---

[66] Cf. Closed Shop Code, para. 61(b), and facts of *Partington v NALGO* [1981] IRLR 537.
[67] These were a majority of those eligible to vote or two-thirds of those actually voting in ballots on agency (IRA s.13) and approved closed shops (IRA Sch.1, para.14).

of restrictive practices and the 'monopoly' power of trade unions. Research indicates that this problem can be overstated.[68] Closed shops normally develop out of high levels of voluntary membership. Formal UMAs often contain special procedures for the resolution of individual grievances, and exceptions for categories such as conscientious objectors and existing non-members. There appears to be no general link between the closed shop in its usual post-entry form and restrictive practices, or indeed union bargaining power. The closed shop, moreover, is conducive to orderly inter- and intra-union relations and, though it may not significantly reduce unconstitutional strikes, it consolidates the whole system of joint regulation. The growth of the formal UMA was, in fact, an integral part of the management-initiated reform of collective bargaining in the 1970s.

Notwithstanding the current legal rights to dissociate, many employers and unions may wish to continue their closed shop arrangements. Employers are still legally free to refuse to hire individuals who are unlikely to join or remain in a union. Non-unionists may be 'red-circled' so that they are left in employment rather than dismissed. If they are dismissed it may be possible to point to reasons other than their non-membership. Despite the stringent legal requirements and the TUC's policy of boycotting UMA ballots (TUC, 1982), instances of ballots where 85 per cent of those voting approved the UMA are not unusual. Nevertheless, the financial incentive to assert the dissociation rights is strong, and the prevailing economic circumstances as well as the legislation have prompted some employers to withdraw or at least not to enforce the closed shop. Whether it will remain a central institution of British industrial relations is difficult to predict.

Union-Only and Recognition-Only Practices

Stipulations that work should be performed only by union members, or only by the employees of firms which recognise unions, appear to be widespread. Such requirements may be embodied in union 'fair lists', collective agreements, or commercial contracts with suppliers of goods and services. Workplace enforcement is suggested by 'card checks' on outside workers who install or service equipment or on drivers who deliver goods, or by the insistence that material brought in from elsewhere is produced by firms which operate closed shops or at least recognise unions. In some industries, elaborate systems of interlocking commercial contracts and collective agreements have been developed in order to minimise self-employment (building and contract drawing), or regulate the terms and conditions of self-employed workers (acting), and in either situation to ensure that everyone is in a union. The government and some but by no means all employers regard such practices as anti-competitive, and as an infringement of the liberty of

---

[68] Gennard et al. (1979; 1980); Dunn (1981; 1985); Brown (1981: 54–8); Dunn and Gennard (1984); Daniel and Millward (1983: 60–81, 280–84). For the earlier classic work, see McCarthy (1964).

suppliers and their employees, who should be free respectively to choose whether or not to recognise or join unions.

The 1980 Act contained two relevant measures. Under a 'double' joinder procedure, a sub-contractor who dismissed a non-unionist in accordance with a union-only requirement could join and be indemnified by a main contractor, who could in turn join a union or other person exerting industrial pressure. In addition, immunity was withdrawn from persons organising industrial action intended to compel into union membership workers employed by a different employer at different premises from those taking the action. This was ostensibly to deter coercive union recruitment practices on the fringes of the printing industry (Leggatt, 1979). The 1982 Act repealed these measures and replaced them with far more sweeping provisions. Section 12 defines liabilities arising from the insistence on either union-only practices or, for the sake of a purely formal equality, practices requiring work to be performed by non-union labour. Section 13 operates against recognition-only practices, though in this case the statute does not bother to go through the motions of prohibiting practices requiring suppliers not to recognise unions. Section 14, which is discussed in Chapter 6, removes immunity from those who take industrial action to uphold union- and recognition-only practices.

Sections 12 and 13 mount a two-pronged attack on such practices. First, a clause imposing either requirement is made 'void' in 'a contract for the supply of goods or services' (ss.12(1), 13(1)). This covers commercial contracts and also contracts for services of workers who are, legally, self-employed. If a supplier fails to observe a void union- or recognition-only requirement, he would not be open to an action for damages for breach of contract, and the party who imposes the requirement could not on grounds of its breach lawfully refuse to perform his side of the bargain. The voiding of the union- or recognition-only requirement would not normally affect the enforceability of the rest of the contract.

Second, a right to sue for breach of statutory duty is created. It arises where any of the following actions is taken on grounds of 'union membership' or 'union exclusion': failing to include a person on a list of suppliers; terminating a supply contract; excluding a person from those from whom tenders are invited, failing to permit him to tender or otherwise determining not to enter into a supply contract with him (ss.12(2) and (7), 13(2) and (4)). 'Union membership' grounds are defined to include all circumstances where one of the reasons for the action was that work done or to be done under the contract has been or is likely to be performed by non-unionists (or unionists) or non-members (or members) of a particular union (s.12(4)–(6)). 'Union exclusion' means that one of the grounds for the action is that the person against whom it was taken does not or is not likely to recognise or negotiate or consult with unions or union officials (s.13(3)).[69] The statutory duties are owed not only to specified persons such as the supplier excluded from the list or the person not permitted to tender, but to 'any other person who may be

---

[69] 'Recognise', 'negotiate' and 'consult' are not defined for the purposes of s.13. Cf. definition of recognition in EPA s.126(1) discussed in Chapter 3.

adversely affected' (ss.12(7)(d), 13(4)(b)). This formulation would arguably cover a sub-contractor adversely affected because the supplier lost or was denied the contract on grounds of union membership or exclusion, an employee made redundant in consequence of such loss, and, subject to questions of remoteness and causation, a range of other potential loss sufferers. The problem of who may sue is but one of the 'defences and other incidents applying to actions for breach of statutory duty' to which the statute refers (ss.12(7), 13(4)). But plaintiffs are assisted by the fact that a breach of duty arises even where 'union membership' or 'union exclusion' is only *one* of the grounds for the defendant's acts.

The ban on union-only practices might be portrayed as an extension of the anti-closed shop policy, but the ban on recognition-only is indicative of a more fundamental hostility towards union recognition and collective bargaining. This attitude was implicit in the rescission of the Fair Wages Resolution and the repeal of the statutory supports for collective bargaining, notably the EPA's procedures for union recognition and arbitration of claims for 'recognised' or 'general level' terms and conditions (see Chapters 3 and 4). The 1982 Act goes further by interfering with private contracting power where it is used in support of collective standards. It might be contended that this overstates the effect of s.13 since a commercial contract may lawfully require a supplier to pay the recognised (collectively negotiated) rate, provided it does not also require him to recognise a union. The distinction is, however, difficult to sustain. Some commercial contracts stipulate that the supplier should observe the terms of collective agreements. In so far as these include union recognition and other procedural items, the stipulation would clearly contravene the 1982 Act. Support for consultation – a weaker concept than negotiation – is also legally hazardous, even in respect of statutory consultation duties. Employers are under a statutory duty to consult with representatives of recognised trade unions on redundancies (EPA s.99), transfers of businesses (Transfer of Undertakings (Protection of Employment) Regulations 1981), safety (HSWA s.2(6)), and pensions (Social Security Pensions Act 1975 s.31(5)). But to deny a contract to a supplier because he has not complied with these legal obligations would apparently be a breach of statutory duty under the 1982 Act.

DISORGANISING INDUSTRIAL RELATIONS

Legal support for the positive right to organise encouraged the development of trade union representation at the workplace, but has proved ineffective where the employer resists union organisation. The statutory provisions, which have been on the whole narrowly interpreted by the judges, are marred by inherent defects such as the absence of an effective reinstatement remedy or of protection for job seekers who are blacklisted. Not surprisingly, employers tend to win unfair dismissal cases where union membership or activities is the alleged reason for dismissal: between 1979 and 1982 an average of less than 15 per cent of such tribunal decisions went in favour of employees (Dickens et al., 1985:245–7).

But even weak legal support for the positive right facilitates some freedom of choice of union, and may, to that extent, undermine exclusive recognition arrangements in favour of established unions. The *Post Office* and other IRA cases demonstrated how the enforcement of membership and participation rights could promote the cause of unrecognised unions. This difficulty persists under the current legal support for the positive right which dates back to the Social Contract period. For example, employers infringe EPCA s.23 if they refuse to make available to members of unrecognised unions who wish to commence organising activities 'facilities which are normally available to the employer's workers'.[70] Clearly the inter-union dimension has major implications for employers' recognition policies and for the TUC's arrangements (explained in Chapter 10 below), notably, the 'Bridlington' Disputes Principles and Procedures and the Independent Review Committee, which determines issues about the exclusion of workers from union membership in closed shops. Mindful of the experience of the IRA, the draftsmen of the Social Contract legislation tried in two ways to mitigate the problem, though their efforts have since been nullified by the legislation of 1980–82.

First, protection against action short of dismissal for taking part in union activities *on the employer's premises* was confined, where employment was subject to a UMA, to the activities of unions specified in the UMA or accepted as such. The limits of this provision were illustrated by a tribunal decision, *Cheall v Vauxhall Motors Ltd.*[71] An inter-union dispute arose when APEX accepted into membership some Vauxhall workers who had left the TGWU. After a TUC Disputes Committee decision that APEX had infringed the Bridlington principles, Vauxhall refused to allow an APEX official to represent one of these workers in presenting a grievance. He made a successful complaint that Vauxhall had thereby infringed his rights under EPCA s.23(1)(a). Not only did no UMA cover his employment, but the complaint related to his right to membership of APEX rather than to union activities on the employer's premises. The employer's premises limitation was thus ineffectual, but it has now been emasculated by the amendments made to s.23 by the 1980 and 1982 Acts. While the provision remains, in s.23(2A)(a), it is both conditional on the approval of the UMA by ballot and inapplicable to the excepted categories of employees, including those who genuinely object to membership of a particular union – one specified in a UMA perhaps – on grounds of deeply-held personal conviction. Furthermore, the facts of *Cheall v Vauxhall Motors* might now give rise to a claim not to be subject to action short of dismissal to compel membership of a particular union.

Second, under the Social Contract legislation, there was no automatic liability if an individual was dismissed for a refusal to join a particular union. For instance, the EAT held in *Rath v Cruden Construction*[72] that a

---

[70] Lord Reid in *Post Office v UPW* [1974] ICR 378, 400, applied by a tribunal to this effect in *Carter v Wiltshire County Council* [1979] IRLR 331. Contrast Davies and Freedland (1984: 194).
[71] [1979] IRLR 235.
[72] [1982] ICR 60.

plasterer's dismissal for refusing to transfer his membership to the TGWU from UCATT was fair. It was not to be equated with dismissal because of his membership of UCATT, which would have been automatically unfair by virtue of EPCA s.58(1)(a). The object of this section, according to the EAT, was protection against an employer who objected to membership of independent unions among his workforce. It was not directed to inter-union disputes. This policy was, however, reversed by the Acts of 1980 and 1982. Workers who wish to belong to unrecognised unions can now assert their general right to refuse to join a particular recognised union. A case like *Rath v Cruden Construction* would produce the opposite result.

This raises the issue of the lawfulness of Disputes Committee rulings under Bridlington, which sometimes require workers to belong to unions other than those of their current choice. Dismissal of and action short of dismissal against workers who refuse to accept these rulings are likely to be unlawful, and the joinder procedure makes the union rather than the employer the primary target for compensation. Moreover, despite the Closed Shop Code's acknowledgment (para.56) of the need to observe Bridlington, a union's expulsion of members in accordance with a Dispute Committee's ruling could violate the legal protection of those in or seeking to be in UMA employment, that is, the right enshrined in s.4 of the 1980 Act not to be unreasonably expelled. Such expulsions have led to a series of common law cases (see Chapter 10 below), one of which explicitly raised the question of freedom of association. In *Cheall v APEX*[73] it was argued that Cheall's expulsion by APEX in order to comply with a Disputes Committee ruling infringed his right to freedom of association by denying him the right to choose which union to join. This freedom of choice allegedly derived from 'the right to form and join trade unions' in Art.11 of the European Convention on Human Rights. It was endorsed only by Lord Denning in the Court of Appeal.[74] The House of Lords met this argument with the response that 'freedom of association can only be mutual';[75] it was not infringed when a union excluded those with whom its members did not wish to associate.

The legal rights whether or not to join a union, and if to join, to choose between unions are designed – like the balloting provisions discussed in Chapters 6 and 10 – to undermine collective strength by promoting sectionalism within the workforce. While recognition of the interests of dissenting individuals and minority groups is compatible with the overall primacy of collective regulation, the 1980s legislation and in particular the right to dissociate represent a rampant individualism, to which all collective interests are to be subordinated. The new policy has been aptly described (Clark and Wedderburn, 1983:143) as a 'preference for non-unionism'. Its ideological and symbolic importance can hardly be overstated, though its practical impact remains uncertain.

---

[73] [1983] ICR 398.
[74] [1982] ICR 543, 553–5. This is part of Lord Denning's idiosyncratic views on both the meaning of Art.11 and its impact in English law. See too *UKAPE v ACAS* [1979] ICR 303, 316–17 (contrast Lord Scarman in the House of Lords in the same case [1980] ICR 201, 214), and *Taylor v Co-operative Retail Services Ltd* [1982] ICR 600, 608–10.
[75] [1983] ICR 398, 405.

Bibliography

Bain, G.S., and R. Price. 1983. 'Union Growth: Dimensions, Determinants, and Destiny'. *Industrial Relations in Britain*. Ed. G.S. Bain. Oxford: Blackwell, 3–33.

Bowers, J., and A. Clarke. 1980. 'Time Off: Time Off for Trade Union Duties'. *Industrial Law Journal*, 9 (March), 56–9.

Brown, W.A. (ed.). 1981. *The Changing Contours of British Industrial Relations: A Survey of Manufacturing Industry*. Oxford: Blackwell.

Clark, J., and Lord Wedderburn. 1983. 'Modern Labour Law: Problems, Functions and Policies'. *Labour Law and Industrial Relations: Building on Kahn-Freund*. Eds. Lord Wedderburn, R. Lewis and J. Clark. Oxford: Clarendon Press, 127–242.

Clegg, H.A. 1979. *The Changing System of Industrial Relations in Great Britain*. Oxford: Blackwell.

Commission on Industrial Relations (CIR). 1971. *Facilities Afforded to Shop Stewards*. Report 17. Cmnd 4668. London: HMSO.

Daniel, W.W., and N. Millward. 1983. *Workplace Industrial Relations in Britain: The DE/PSI/SSRC Survey*. London: Heinemann.

Davies, P., and M. Freedland. 1984. *Labour Law: Text and Materials*. 2nd edn. London: Weidenfeld & Nicolson.

Department of Employment (DE). 1982. *International Labour Conference*. Cmnd 8773. London: HMSO.

——. 1983. *International Labour Conference*. Cmnd 9078. London: HMSO.

Dickens, L., M. Jones, B. Weekes and M. Hart. 1985. *Dismissed: A Study of Unfair Dismissal and the Industrial Tribunal System*. Oxford: Blackwell.

Donovan. 1968. Royal Commission on Trade Unions and Employers' Associations 1965–1968. *Report*. Cmnd 3623. London: HMSO.

Dunn, S. 1981. 'The Growth of the Post-Entry Closed Shop in Britain since the 1960s: Some Theoretical Considerations'. *British Journal of Industrial Relations*, 19 (November), 275–96.

——. 1985. 'The Law and the Decline of the Closed Shop in the 1980s'. *Industrial Relations and the Law in the 1980s: Issues and Future Trends*. Eds. P. Fosh and C. Littler. Aldershot: Gower.

——, and J. Gennard. 1984. *The Closed Shop in British Industry*. London: Macmillan.

England, G., and W.M. Rees. 1976. 'Trade Union and Labour Relations (Amendment) Act 1976'. *Modern Law Review*, 39 (November), 698–706.

Ewing, K.D., and W.M. Rees. 1983. 'Closed Shop Dismissals 1974–80: A Study of the Retroactive Compensation Scheme'. *Industrial Law Journal*, 12 (September), 148–56.

Fitzpatrick, B. 1983. 'Time Off: Recent Developments in the Court of Appeal'. *Industrial Law Journal*, 12 (December), 258–61.

Forde, M. 1982. 'The "Closed Shop" Case'. *Industrial Law Journal*, 11 (March), 1–15.

——. 1983. 'The European Convention on Human Rights and Labor Law'. *American Journal of Comparative Law*, 31 (Spring), 301–32.

Gennard, J., S. Dunn and M. Wright. 1979. 'The Content of British Closed Shop Agreements'. *Employment Gazette*, 87 (November), 1088–92.

——, S. Dunn and M. Wright. 1980. 'The Extent of Closed Shop Arrangements in British Industry'. *Employment Gazette*, 88 (January), 16–22.

Gorman, R.A. 1976. *Basic Text on Labor Law: Unionization and Collective Bargaining*. St Paul, Minnesota: West Publishing Company.

Health and Safety Commission (HSC). 1978. *Code of Practice on Time Off for the Training of Safety Representatives*. London: HSC.

Hepple, B.A. 1974. 'The Right to Work on One's Job'. *Modern Law Review*, 37 (November), 681–5.

International Labour Organisation (ILO). 1982. *ILO Conventions and Recommendations 1919–1981*. Geneva: ILO.

Kahn-Freund, O. 1972. *Labour and the Law*. London: Stevens.

——. 1974. 'The Industrial Relations Act 1971 – Some Retrospective Reflections'. *Industrial Law Journal*, 3 (December), 186–200.

——. 1983. *Labour and the Law*. 3rd edn. Ed. and intr. by P. Davies and M. Freedland. London: Stevens.

Leggatt, A. 1979. *Report of Inquiry into Certain Trade Union Recruitment Activities*. Cmnd 7706. London: HMSO.

Lewis, R. 1983. 'Collective Labour Law'. *Industrial Relations in Britain*. Ed. G.S. Bain. Oxford: Blackwell, 361–92.

——, and Bob Simpson. 1981. *Striking a Balance? Employment Law After the 1980 Act*. Oxford: Martin Robertson.

——, and Bob Simpson. 1982. 'Disorganising Industrial Relations: An Analysis of Sections 2–8 and 10–14 of the Employment Act 1982'. *Industrial Law Journal*, 11 (December), 227–44.

McCarthy, W.E.J. 1964. *The Closed Shop in Britain*. Oxford: Blackwell.

——. 1980. 'Closed Minds and Closed Shops'. *Federation News*, 30 (October), 145–51.

McIlroy, J. 1981. 'Safety at Work: Time Off for Safety Representatives'. *Industrial Law Journal*, 10 (March), 58–61.

Napier, B. 1983. 'Dismissals – the New ILO Standards'. *Industrial Law Journal*, 12 (March), 17–27.

O'Higgins, P. 1981. 'The Closed Shop and the European Convention on Human Rights'. *Human Rights Review*, 6 (Spring), 22–7.

Pankert, A. 1982. 'Freedom of Association'. *Comparative Labour Law and Industrial Relations*. Ed. R. Blanpain. Deventer: Kluwer, 146–65.

Prondzynski, F. von. 1982a. 'Freedom of Association and the Closed Shop'. *Cambridge Law Journal*, 41 (November), 256–72.

——. 1982b. 'Freedom of Association and Industrial Relations: A Comparative Study'. PhD thesis, University of Cambridge.

Schmidt, Folke. 1977. *Law and Industrial Relations in Sweden*. Stockholm: Almquist & Wiksell.

Simpson, Bob, and J. Wood. 1973. *Industrial Relations and the 1971 Act*. London: Pitman.

Smith, C.T.B., R. Clifton, P. Makeham, S.W. Creigh and R.V. Burn. 1978. *Strikes in Britain: A Research Study of Industrial Stoppages in the United Kingdom*. Department of Employment, Manpower Papers 15. London: HMSO.

Summers, C.W. 1964. 'Freedom of Association and Compulsory Unionism in Sweden and the United States'. *University of Pennsylvania Law Review*, 62 (March), 647–96.

Terry, M. 1983. 'Shop Steward Development and Managerial Strategies'. *Industrial Relations in Britain*. Ed. G.S. Bain. Oxford: Blackwell, 67–91.

Trades Union Congress (TUC). 1983. *Annual Report 1982*. London: TUC.

Treu, T. (ed.). 1975–76. *Sindacato e Magistratura nei Conflitti di Lavoro*. Bologna: Il Mulino. 2 vols.

Valticos, N. 1979. *International Labour Law*. Deventer: Kluwer.

Wedderburn, K.W. (*Lord*). 1972. 'Labour Law and Labour Relations in Britain'. *British Journal of Industrial Relations*, 10 (July), 270–90.

——. 1976. 'The Employment Protection Act 1975: Collective Aspects'. *Modern Law Review*, 39 (March), 168–83.

——. 1978. 'Discrimination in the Right to Organise and the Right to be a Non-Unionist'. *Discrimination in Employment*. Ed. Folke Schmidt. Stockholm: Almquist & Wiksell, 367–487.

Weekes, Brian. 1976. 'Law and the Practice of the Closed Shop'. *Industrial Law Journal*, 5 (December), 211–22.

——, M. Mellish, L. Dickens and J. Lloyd. 1975. *Industrial Relations and the Limits of Law: The Industrial Effects of the Industrial Relations Act 1971*. Oxford: Blackwell.

3 A Duty to Bargain?
Union Recognition and
Information Disclosure

Linda Dickens and
George Sayers Bain

In Britain, as in most other countries that enjoy freedom of association, collective bargaining is one of the most important forms of job regulation. A necessary, indeed sufficient, condition for its existence is that employers negotiate collective agreements with trade unions. In an attempt to promote collective bargaining, some countries have given legal force to this condition by creating, as in Sweden, 'a right to negotiate' or, as in the United States, 'a duty to bargain' (Gospel, 1983).

The closest Britain has come to following this approach is the legal duty placed on some of the public corporations that administer nationalised industries 'to enter into' or 'to seek' consultation with a view to establishing machinery for collective bargaining and for joint consultation.[1] But 'the industries in question have all been so well organised for many years that the vague legal formulas (scarcely open to enforcement in court since they always leave the choice of appropriate unions to the employer) have not, in the opinion of the corporations concerned, added anything to the practice' of collective bargaining (Wedderburn and Davies, 1969:58). This view is supported by cases in which the courts upheld the statutory discretion of the Post Office with regard to union recognition.[2] In short, as Kahn-Freund (1954:54) pointed out many years ago, 'these provisions in the nationalization statutes are more significant as expressions of a policy than as a basis of enforceable legal obligations'.

Although Britain has not created a general legal duty to bargain, it has offered considerable public support for two of the elements of any such duty: union recognition and information disclosure for collective bargaining. This chapter describes the nature of this support, analyses some of the

---

[1] These corporations include those administering the following industries: coal mining, iron and steel, road transport, railways, civil air transport, electricity, gas, shipbuilding, and the post office. For further detail, see Elias et al. (1980:106–8) and Kahn-Freund (1983:89–90).

[2] *Gallagher v Post Office* [1970] 3 All ER 712, and *ASTMS (Telephone Contracts Officers' Section) v Post Office* [1980] IRLR 475.

questions it has given rise to and the way they have been addressed, and discusses some of the problems that have arisen.

UNION RECOGNITION

Union recognition in practice is a relative concept. What employers concede varies from the right to represent the individual interests of employees under a grievance procedure, through the right to consultation on their collective interests, to the right to negotiate collective agreements. Even when employers agree to collective negotiations, union recognition still remains a relative matter, because employers vary greatly in the number of subjects they are willing to negotiate and in the amount of information they are prepared to disclose to enable unions to bargain effectively.

Regardless of how narrowly union recognition is defined, employers are usually opposed to conceding it, because unions tend to constrain them in various ways. In attempting to use their own strength to overcome employer opposition to recognition, unions are caught in a vicious circle because, as Bain (1970:ch. 8) has demonstrated, the absence of recognition is one of the major factors impeding the development of their strength. Unions nevertheless have been able to coerce employers into conceding recognition by engaging in strikes and other forms of industrial warfare and, as Flanders (1974:355–6) has noted, to induce them into doing so by assisting in market and managerial control. In seeking recognition from employers, however, unions have not had to rely entirely upon their own strength; they have also received considerable public support.

This support has been both social – the pressures of public opinion – and legal. A good example of the force of social support in promoting union recognition and collective bargaining is provided by the climate of opinion created by the reports of the Whitley Committee towards the end of World War I. Similar examples can be extracted from the industrial history of World War II: the reports of various Courts of Inquiry which found in favour of recognising unions; the informal pressures exerted upon employers by the Minister of Labour, Ernest Bevin; and, more generally, the favourable social climate created by the war (Bain, 1970:142–75). More recent examples are provided by the report of the Donovan Commission (1968) and the White Paper *In Place of Strife* (DEP, 1969) – which both affirmed the principles of freedom of association and union recognition – and by the Commission on Industrial Relations, which during 1969–71 existed on a voluntary basis and strongly reaffirmed these principles in a series of reports recommending the recognition of unions and the development of collective bargaining (Bain and Price, 1972:375–7).

Legal support for union recognition can be classified according to its point of application as either direct or indirect. Indirect legal methods, which are discussed in detail in Chapter 4, help unions to obtain and maintain recognition by facilitating the enforcement of collective standards or by extending their coverage to employers who are not parties to them. A current example of such methods is the system of statutory wage regulation initially established in 1909 not only to bring to unorganised workers some of the advantages of collective bargaining but also 'to promote the willingness to, and create the habit of, collective bargaining' (Kahn-Freund, 1965:25). Other examples – all now rescinded or repealed – are provided by the following: the House of Commons Fair Wages Resolution which required government contractors to recognise the right of their employees to belong to a trade union and to observe the terms and conditions of employment generally recognised in the industry concerned by representative unions and employers' organisations; the various Essential Works Orders passed during World War II which required firms to have 'recognised' conditions of employment before they could be scheduled as essential and their employees prohibited from quitting; the Conditions of Employment and National Arbitration Order 1940 (No. 1305) and the Industrial Disputes Order 1951 (No. 1376), which enabled unions unilaterally to refer employers to a tribunal for a binding award on wages and working conditions; and s.8 of the Terms and Conditions of Employment Act 1959 and Sch.11 of the EPA, which enabled unions to require employers to observe collectively agreed terms and conditions of employment.[3]

The only example outside the nationalised industries of the state using the law directly to promote union recognition in Britain – and that which is the focus of the following discussion – is the compulsory recognition procedures which existed between 1972 and 1980. These procedures developed out of the work of the Donovan Commission. After commissioning research on union growth and recognition (Bain, 1967) and taking evidence from various individuals and organisations, it concluded (1968:para.224) that

> there is now a dilemma for public policy. Collective bargaining is recognised as the best way of conducting industrial relations and as depending on strong trade union organisation. The proportion of employees who are organised has however been declining. Employment is increasing in areas which have proved difficult to organise, so that the effect of obstacles to the development and recognition of unions in these areas is assuming greater importance for the future of collective bargaining. The evidence is that if these obstacles are to be surmounted more effective means of dealing with problems of trade union recognition are needed.

The Commission dealt with this dilemma by recommending that the government adopt Flanders's (1967:39–44) proposal that an independent tribunal be established to handle recognition disputes. The Labour Government ment accepted this recommendation and, in 1969 in anticipation of legislation, it used a Royal Warrant to establish the Commission on Industrial

---

[3] For the details of how these indirect methods may encourage union recognition see Bain (1967:ch. 6; 1970:ch. 9); Bercusson (1978:342–53); and Dickens et al. (1979:50–60). In addition, see Flanders (1974:356) for two industry-specific examples of such methods: the Railways Act 1921 which, among other things, gave legal backing to the industry's wage negotiation and disputes procedure, and the Cotton Manufacturing Industry (Temporary Provisions) Act 1934 which enabled the Minister of Labour to make the wages provisions of the relevant agreements compulsory.

Relations (CIR) on a voluntary basis with the power, among other things, to hear recognition disputes and to make recommendations for their settlement.

The voluntary period of the CIR's existence ended in 1971 with the enactment by a Conservative Government of the IRA. The Act (ss.45–55) enabled the Secretary of State, an employer, a registered union, or the last two jointly to request the National Industrial Relations Court (NIRC) to refer a recognition dispute to the CIR. If certain conditions were met, the NIRC instructed the CIR to undertake an investigation and, if the matter was not settled, to issue a report. If the CIR's report recommended recognition, the NIRC could render the recommendation binding if a ballot showed that a majority of the employees concerned were in favour. If the employer still refused to concede recognition, then a registered union could present a claim to the Industrial Arbitration Board for improved terms and conditions of employment, and its award would become an implied term in the individual employees' contracts of employment. Finally, where a union – whether registered or not – lost the support of the employees it had been representing, the Act provided for the withdrawal of recognition.

The return of a Labour Government, with the consequent repeal of the IRA in 1974 and the passage of the EPA in 1975, created a new statutory framework for union recognition which, as Davies and Freedland (1979:66) note, was 'in effect, half way between the purely voluntary approach of the CIR in its early days and the highly regulated procedure of the IRA'. Section 2(1) of the EPA enables ACAS to provide conciliation in recognition disputes. Sections 11–16 of the Act supplemented this voluntary provision, which had been enshrined in statute since the Conciliation Act 1896, with a compulsory procedure enabling an independent union to refer a recognition issue to ACAS. If ACAS failed to settle the issue by conciliation, it had to conduct an inquiry and, if the issue was not settled or withdrawn, to prepare a report giving its findings and stating whether or not it recommended recognition. If an employer failed to comply with a recommendation for recognition, then the union could, after further conciliation by ACAS, refer the issue to the CAC; the CAC could award terms and conditions of employment which became part of the individual employees' contracts of employment. This compulsory procedure was repealed in 1980 by the Employment Act of that year; the voluntary provision continues to operate.

The union recognition procedures which existed in Britain between 1972 and 1980 were compulsory in at least two respects: employers involved in recognition disputes could be referred against their will to an independent body and, if it recommended recognition, a sanction could be imposed for failure to comply. Although the statutory framework surrounding these procedures and the institutions established to administer them differed in significant ways, a basic similarity exists between the work of the CIR – not only in its compulsory phase but also in its voluntary phase – and that of ACAS. One reason for this similarity is that regardless of which statutory provisions were in force, both the CIR and ACAS strongly emphasised the value of voluntary agreement between the parties and relied heavily upon the techniques of persuasion and conciliation. Another reason, as James

(1977:29) has pointed out, is 'the universal and enduring nature of the problems which tend to arise in recognition disputes and which condition the methods of bodies handling those disputes'. These problems can be expressed as a series of questions: who is to have access to, and benefit from, the procedure; by what method, and according to which criteria, is the recognition issue to be determined; how is recognition to be defined; and how are decisions on recognition, once made, to be enforced. The following discussion shows how the CIR and the NIRC under the IRA and, in particular, ACAS and the CAC under the EPA answered these questions.

Access

The IRA and EPA procedures were intended to promote collective bargaining by encouraging the recognition and growth of certain kinds of organisation. The IRA procedure was also seen as a means of reforming union structures and bargaining structures (Weekes et al., 1975:ch. 6), and, like the American legislation on which it was based, it allowed employers to refer inter-union disputes to the CIR. Relatively few employers used the IRA procedure, however, and those who did were often motivated less by its potential for structural reform than by s.54 of the Act, which provided that once notice was given that an application was to be made it was an unfair industrial practice for a union to take or threaten industrial action (Weekes et al., 1975:132–3). In contrast, the EPA placed no such restriction on industrial action. Nor did it give employers the right of access to its recognition procedure.

As the furtherance of sham unions controlled by employers would have been contrary to the legislative intention to promote union growth and effective collective bargaining, trade union independence was a key to access to the recognition procedures of both the IRA and the EPA.[4] Independence was a prerequisite of registration as a trade union under the IRA, and the Registrar of Trade Unions had to determine whether an organisation was 'under the domination or control' of an employer (s.167). Both the definition of independence and the Registrar's approach were criticised as inadequate to distinguish bona fide from other organisations (Mellish and Dickens, 1972:235–6; Weekes et al., 1975: 304–28). The definition of independence for the purposes of the recognition procedure under the EPA was more rigorous; it covered not only employer control but also liability to interference by the employer tending towards control.[5]

Non-TUC organisations – notably one-company staff associations and 'professional' organisations – which used their independent status to gain

---

4   Independence is still a key to access to other statutory provisions: disclosure of information (EPA s.17), consultation over redundancy (EPA s.99), and time off for union officials (EPCA ss.27–8). It also affects the rights in respect of union membership and activities (EPCA ss.23, 58) and to appoint safety representatives (HSWA s.2(4)). Furthermore, only an independent union can be a party to a UMA (TULRA s.30(1)), obtain refunds from the CO for the cost of postal ballots (EA 1980 s.1), and use the employer's facilities for secret ballots (EA 1980 s.2).
5   TULRA s.30(1). This is the current definition for other purposes and is discussed in detail, in the context of the CO's role, in Chapter 10.

access to the recognition procedure generally did not succeed in obtaining recommendations for recognition from either the CIR or ACAS. Under the IRA, for example, staff associations generally failed to satisfy the CIR of their 'effectiveness' (Weekes et al., 1975:139–41). But several of these associations considered that registration under the IRA of itself was 'a seal of approval' with a beneficial effect on membership and recruitment (Dickens, 1975:33).

A union's independent status was not the only formal gateway to access to the IRA procedure. Under s.46(1)(b) of the Act, the NIRC could refuse to refer a recognition issue to the CIR if the parties had not made adequate use of any facilities for conciliation available to them. It also had to be satisfied, under s.46(1)(c), that reference to the CIR was necessary to promote a 'satisfactory and lasting settlement' of the recognition issue. It used this provision, until curbed by the Court of Appeal,[6] to develop a significant screening role for itself. The TUC feared that in allowing access to employers the IRA procedure would threaten the 'Bridlington' arrangements (discussed in detail in Chapter 10) for settling disputes between TUC affiliates. The problem did not actually arise in practice, but, if it had, these provisions conceivably could have been used to ensure that primacy was given to the TUC's own procedures.

In contrast, although the EPA procedure denied access to the employer, the willingness of certain unions to use the EPA procedure to gain recognition in areas where the TUC had recognised the interests of other unions did threaten Bridlington. For example, in the *EMA* case,[7] ACAS was used in effect as an appeal body against the decision of a TUC Disputes Committee (Ball, 1980:21–3). Because unions attempted to pursue claims which might not be acceptable under Bridlington, in 1979 the TUC revised its rules to impose its own access barrier, requiring notification by an affiliate before it made a reference under s.11 of the Act. About 10 per cent of the recognition references that ACAS concluded and about 25 per cent of those that were outstanding when the EPA procedure was repealed had run into inter-union difficulties (ACAS, 1981:73). Although the Lords in the *EMA* case finally upheld ACAS's discretion not to proceed with a case, ACAS, unlike its Northern Ireland counterpart (Sholl, 1980:chs. 3–4; Beaumont, 1984b), still lacked total discretion to refuse to proceed with a reference where it considered this would be contrary – whether because of Bridlington or other considerations – to the interests of good industrial relations.

Determining the Recognition Issue

Method. Both the CIR and ACAS adopted a conciliatory approach, seeking where possible to achieve an agreed settlement. This approach,

---

[6] *Telecommunications Staff Association v Post Office* [1974] ICR 97.
[7] *Engineers' and Managers' Association v ACAS* [1980] IRLR 164, HL and [1979] IRLR 246, CA.

required of ACAS by the EPA s.12(3)(a), achieved some success where unwillingness to recognise was based on beliefs (for example, concerning employees' lack of desire for collective representation) which during conciliation or inquiry could be shown to be unfounded, or where use of the procedure in effect acted as a catalyst by bringing the parties together (ACAS, 1981:99). In such situations the reference was likely to be withdrawn before the final report stage. Of the 1,610 references made to ACAS under the EPA procedure, 1,115 were withdrawn; in 518 (46 per cent) of the withdrawn references ACAS reported that the union was fully or partially successful in securing recognition (1981:117).

Withdrawal because of a willingness to recognise was far less likely, however, where the employer was opposed in principle to union recognition, as was often the case in small single-establishment companies which were the subject of references by various manual unions, or where opposition was based on an alternative perception of preferable personnel structures and policies, as was often the case in white-collar recognition claims. But even in these cases ACAS attempted to get agreement on the scope and nature of the inquiry. The emphasis on consultation and conciliation built in delay and provided opportunities for employers to seek to frustrate union attempts to gain recognition. References took over a year on average to reach the final report stage; over one-fifth took eighteen months or more (ACAS, 1981:80). The longer the elapse of time before workers' opinions are surveyed, the more support for the union is likely to wane as they become exasperated with the lack of results or are subjected to anti-union pressures from the employer (Dickens, 1978:168; Beaumont, 1981a; 1981b).

Unlike American legislation which regulates 'campaigning' tactics while a recognition issue is being determined (Hart, 1978:208), the EPA did not prevent employer or union action to influence the way workers replied to the questions in an ACAS inquiry. ACAS identified several employer tactics designed to reduce support for the applicant union and, where these were blatant, it attempted to take account of them in interpreting the results of its inquiries.[8] The law in practice affords little protection to employees who are victimised because of their union membership or activities (see Chapters 2 and 9), and under EPCA s.62 workers on strike for recognition can be dismissed lawfully as, for example, happened during the union recognition dispute at Grunwick's.[9] ACAS was held to be correct in this case,[10] however, in including dismissed workers still available for employment among those affected by the reference whose opinions had to be ascertained.

---

[8] See, for example, Report 34, *Playboy Club of London Ltd and the ACTSS Group of the TGWU*. ACAS withdrew this report following the decision in *Powley v ACAS* [1977] IRLR 190.

[9] For full details, see Scarman (1977), Rogaly (1977), Dromey and Taylor (1978), and Ward (1977).

[10] *ACAS v Grunwick Processing Laboratories Ltd* [1978] IRLR 38. See James and Simpson (1978).

EPA s.12 (1) required ACAS to 'make such inquiries as it thinks fit', including ascertaining 'the opinions of workers to whom the issue relates by any means it thinks fit' (s.14(1)), which might have included a formal ballot. That the statute did allow ACAS considerable discretion in making its inquiries was confirmed by the House of Lords as the procedure was being repealed,[11] but during the life of the procedure the way ACAS exercised its discretion was challenged in the courts on a number of grounds, including the method and scope of its inquiries. As the EPA provided no right of appeal from ACAS decisions, the legal challenges came through the power of judicial review which enables the courts to examine the action, or lack of action, of a public body in order to determine whether it has complied with its legal powers.[12] CIR decisions could have been subjected to judicial review but were not, perhaps reflecting the more limited use of the IRA procedures, with the TUC unions boycotting the Act, as well as the prior involvement of the NIRC (Simpson, 1979:72).

ACAS usually sought to ascertain the opinions of the workers concerned by the use of a questionnaire that conformed to a standard pattern, asking about actual and, often, potential union membership, support for collective bargaining in general, and support for collective representation by the applicant union and, where relevant, by other unions (Dickens, 1978). Employers tried to widen the scope of the opinion surveys to canvass views, not only about the applicant union, but also more generally about other organisations, existing methods of handling industrial relations, and possible alternatives to collective bargaining. Court decisions meant ACAS finally had to seek opinions regarding organisations other than the applicant union,[13] but only where they had members and wished to be included.[14] A further legal challenge on the grounds that the form and presentation of questions on the ACAS questionnaire encouraged 'yes' answers favourable to the applicant union failed.[15] But many employers objected to the inclusion of 'hypothetical questions' designed to ascertain potential support for the applicant union. One question normally took the following form: 'if the [specified] union were recognised by the company to negotiate on your behalf, would you join it?' The question acknowledged the importance of the 'vicious circle' argument noted above and reflected the view of ACAS, echoing that of the CIR (1974:68), that actual membership alone need not determine the recognition issue; potential membership was also important. Although this question was sometimes dropped to gain employer co-operation (ACAS, 1981:78), there was always a question concerning employee support for collective bargaining by the applicant union as well as a question on present union membership.

The questionnaire survey, administered at the workplace or by post, was ACAS's preferred method of ascertaining workers' opinions, but its use

---

[11] *ACAS v UKAPE* [1980] IRLR 124.
[12] The classic case on the scope of judicial review is *Associated Provincial Picture Houses Ltd v Wednesbury Corporation* [1948] 1 KB 223.
[13] *Powley v ACAS* [1978] ICR 123.
[14] *National Employers Life Assurance Co. Ltd v ACAS and ASTMS* [1979] IRLR 282.
[15] ibid.

depended upon employer co-operation. Although ACAS's statutory duty under s.14(1) was held to require it to 'ascertain and take into consideration the opinions ... that are held by every group of workers of any significant size that forms part of the work force that would be affected by the recommendation',[16] employers could lawfully refuse access to their employees or to their names and addresses. Following the *Grunwick* case, ACAS felt debarred from making a recommendation in six cases which reached the report stage because it had not secured an adequate response from workers, and in another five cases it decided that attempts to ascertain opinions other than through employer co-operation were impracticable and so was unable to carry out its statutory duty (ACAS, 1981:77).

Criteria. Little explicit guidance was given in the statutes, particularly the EPA, as to the criteria to be adopted in determining the boundaries of a bargaining group or the level of membership or support for a union which should be considered appropriate in recommending recognition. ACAS, which inherited some staff from the CIR, consciously built upon the CIR's experience of recognition (ACAS, 1981:81; CIR, 1974) and both agencies had the guidance of the same Industrial Relations Code of Practice (DE, 1972), which outlined several factors to be taken into account in determining a bargaining unit or, in ACAS's terminology, a negotiating group. But while an examination of the recognition reports published by the CIR and ACAS provides a post hoc indication of which factors were important in particular references (CIR, 1974), it provides no prescriptive general principles. The lack of such principles reflects the practice of industrial relations in Britain: union jurisdiction follows no neat nor necessarily agreed pattern, bargaining occurs at various levels, and recognition may be granted to a union with anything from 100 per cent membership to none. It also reflects the different views held by the TUC and the CBI members of ACAS's Council; agreement on union recognition cases became increasingly difficult to reach and consensus decision-making was replaced by vote-taking (ACAS, 1981:86–7).

In some countries, such as the USA, recognition issues are determined on the principle of majority decision by employees. The CIR and ACAS were not simply balloting agencies, however, and they brought to bear a range of factors in deciding whether or not to recommend recognition. This approach led to the CIR recommending recognition despite only minority support for the union recommended as the bargaining agent (CIR, 1974:53); to ACAS recommending recognition in twenty-three cases where support was below 50 per cent and in thirteen cases where it was below 40 per cent; and to ACAS not recommending recognition in nineteen cases even though there was majority support in the area defined by the applicant union (ACAS, 1981:83).

This discretion to find against the majority was challenged in the courts. It was finally upheld by the House of Lords, which accepted that s.1 of the EPA did not give priority to the duty to encourage the extension of

16   *ACAS v Grunwick Processing Laboratories Ltd* [1978] IRLR 38, 41 (per Lord Diplock).

collective bargaining where ACAS was faced with a conflict between that duty and the duty – also specified in s.1 – of promoting the improvement of industrial relations. Although the applicant union had 79 per cent support in the negotiating group it defined, the Lords held that ACAS had acted appropriately in deciding not to recommend it for recognition after considering the existing arrangements in the industry and the threat of industrial strife.[17] In other words, stable industrial relations may demand that, to take Lord Denning's analogy, the 'Goliath' of established unions wins over the 'Davids' of breakaway groups, new organisations, and individual interests (Robinson, 1979). This perspective, which informed the work of ACAS and that of the CIR before it, was not readily accepted by the judges whose approach generally was individualistic and legalistic (Simpson, 1979:78). Although the House of Lords judgments finally appeared to allow ACAS sufficient discretion to continue, Elliott (1980:585–6) argued that the 'courts did not establish for all time a set of discretions that ACAS could operate sensibly. They simply granted some discretion to ACAS in language that enables this discretion to be legitimately removed if fashions change.'

Defining Union Recognition

Unions often regard the right to represent the individual interests of their members under a grievance procedure as an early stage in the recognition process, as part of establishing a bargaining relationship with an employer. Although ACAS sometimes advised the granting of individual representational rights to unions, it took the view (ACAS, 1981:71) that such rights did not constitute 'recognition' as defined by s.126 (1) of the EPA: 'the recognition of the union by an employer, or two or more associated employers, to any extent, for the purpose of collective bargaining', that is, for the 'purpose of negotiations related to or connected with one or more of the matters specified in' TULRA s.29 (1).[18] This distinction between representational rights and negotiating rights was in keeping with decisions made in relation to s.5 of the IRA,[19] and was followed by the CAC in enforcing recognition under s.16 of the EPA. As is indicated below, the CAC would not award 'recognition', but it was prepared to include representational rights as an element in an arbitration award on terms and conditions of employment.[20]

---

[17] *ACAS v UKAPE* [1980] IRLR 124. The Lords decision overruled the Court of Appeal ([1979] IRLR 68), which had upheld the High Court decision ([1978] IRLR 336) declaring the report a nullity.

[18] The matters specified in TULRA s.29 (1) – the definition of a trade dispute – are terms and conditions of employment, physical conditions, engagement, non-engagement, termination or suspension of employment, allocation of work, discipline, membership or non-membership of a trade union, facilities for union officials, machinery for negotiation or consultation, and other procedures relating to any of these matters. See Chapter 6.

[19] *Howle v GEC Power Engineering Ltd* [1974] ICR 13; see Weekes et al. (1975:App. VIII).

[20] E.g. *Uniroyal Ltd and ASTMS*, CAC Award 79/27. Initially, however, the CAC did not distinguish between representational rights and negotiating rights: *Commodore Business Machines (UK) Ltd and EETPU*, CAC Award 78/339.

The question of what constitutes recognition within this definition arises under other provisions which make statutory rights available only to recognised trade unions or their members. Under EPA s.17, discussed later in this chapter, employers must disclose information to unions about matters for which they are recognised, and the CAC plays an enforcement role similar to that under the recognition procedure. In contrast to its decisions under that procedure, in some information disclosure awards the CAC treated a union as recognised where it only had representational rights,[21] but that approach was in effect overruled by the High Court.[22] Under s.99 of the EPA employers are legally obliged to consult with recognised unions on proposed redundancies (see Chapter 15). The issue of whether or not a union was recognised has arisen on several occasions. In one case the EAT rejected the contention that the distinction between recognition for representational purposes and recognition for negotiation purposes is artificial and unworkable,[23] and from several others[24] has emerged the need to show sufficiently 'clear and unequivocal' evidence of actions involving recognition and a positive mental decision on the part of the employer to enter into negotiations. These cases make clear that an unwilling employer does not in law recognise a union simply by virtue of membership of an employers' association which does negotiate with unions, or as a result of a minister giving a particular union a right of representation on the teachers' national negotiating body.[25] The need to define union recognition may similarly arise under other legislation concerning time off for the representatives of recognised unions, and consultation with recognised unions over safety, pensions, and transfers of undertakings.[26]

In the contexts discussed above, the focus is on defining a minimum standard of recognition. But in keeping with the relative nature of union recognition, as described earlier in this chapter, the EPA enabled a union that was recognised to some degree to extend either the scope or depth of that recognition – that is, to extend its negotiating rights to additional workers or additional subjects – by seeking 'further recognition' under s.11 (3). But only a handful of 'further recognition' claims were made. These typically concerned union attempts to bargain over pensions, and all were withdrawn before they reached the report stage usually on the basis of a compromise which fell short of collective bargaining (ACAS, 1981:100). Thus the further-recognition provision was not used to improve what

21 E.g. *GKN Sankey Ltd and ASTMS*, CAC Award 78/708.
22 *R v CAC ex parte BTP Tioxide* [1982] IRLR 60.
23 *USDAW v Sketchley Ltd* [1981] IRLR 291.
24 E.g. *Joshua Wilson & Bros Ltd v USDAW* [1978] IRLR 120; *National Union of Gold, Silver and Allied Trades v Albury Bros Ltd* [1978] IRLR 504. See Neal, 1979.
25 *Cleveland County Council v Springett* [1985] IRLR 131, a case where the EAT affirmed that, despite a minor variation in wording, recognition for the purposes of statutory safety representation has the same meaning as in other branches of employment law.
26 See Chapter 2 below on EPCA ss.27, 28; Chapter 16 on HSWA s.2(4)(6) and SI 1977 No. 500; Chapter 14 on Social Security Pensions Act 1975 s.31 (5) and SI 1978 No. 1089; and Chapter 15 on the Transfer of Undertakings (Protection of Employment) Regulations SI 1981 No. 1794.

Flanders (1967:15) described as the 'poverty' of the content of British collective agreements compared with that of their American counterparts. The rarity of further-recognition claims also meant that ACAS was spared the job of determining what in the United States are termed 'mandatory' subjects for bargaining (Gospel, 1983:344–5).

Enforcement

Although a CIR recommendation for recognition could be made binding if a ballot showed that a majority of the employees concerned were in favour, the IRA procedure operated in effect without sanctions. Only two ballots were held under the first stage of the enforcement procedure, to see if the CIR recommendation should be made binding (Weekes et al., 1975:146), and the second stage, recourse to arbitration where the employer withheld recognition after the recommendation had been made binding, was never used. Over half (fourteen out of twenty-three) of the recommendations to recognise made by the CIR were implemented despite the absence of an effective sanction (James, 1977:40).

Recommendations for recognition were made in 158 of the 247 cases which resulted in reports under the EPA procedure. Only 55 of the 158 were known by ACAS to have been implemented by the end of October 1980 (ACAS, 1981:92). Where the employer refused to comply with a recommendation, then the union could, after further conciliation by ACAS, refer the matter to the CAC, and it could under EPA s.16 award terms and conditions of employment which became part of the individual employees' contracts of employment. Fifty complaints of non-compliance were made; after conciliation eight of these led to recognition agreements. Of the twenty-nine cases which went to the CAC, twenty-two led to declarations that the employer was not complying with a recommendation and in eighteen cases a terms and conditions award was made (ACAS, 1981:90).

The CAC had no problem in determining non-compliance as defined in EPA s.15(2) because employers admitted the fact (Doyle, 1980:156). In some cases they continued to make the same arguments against recognition that they had made unsuccessfully to ACAS; in others they claimed circumstances had changed.[27] Thus the CAC did not have to determine what an employer would need to do to demonstrate a willingness to bargain, a question of importance in the United States where the National Labor Relations Act s.8(a)(5) requires employers to bargain with union representatives in 'good faith' (Bragg, 1976:147–8). Rather, the CAC concentrated on the appropriate scope and nature of the terms and conditions award under s.16.

The CAC soon disappointed those who hoped that it would enforce ACAS recommendations either by incorporating them into its awards or by

---

[27] Some employers applied under EPA s.13 for a variation or revocation of the recognition recommendation, though with desultory results (ACAS, 1981:91–2).

penalising recalcitrant employers. Instead, it saw its 'role as fulfilling the negotiating function which the company, by its refusal to recognise the union, is failing to undertake' (Award 80/15). Thus s.16 was 'the substitute for a hard bargain which recognition, had it been granted, would have provided' (Award 78/808). In practice, however, the CAC posed little threat to the non-compliant employer who was already providing reasonable or 'general level' terms and conditions (Doyle, 1980:158).

Even if the CAC had taken what Davies (1979:56) has called an 'inducement to compliance' or a penal approach to arbitration by awarding superior terms and conditions, the subject matter of the award would still have been the substantive terms and conditions of employment such as pay, hours, and holidays. As McIlroy (1979:14) noted, 'if only "individual" matters such as money or hours can be incorporated into an individual's contract of employment then the only remedy is a rather narrow compulsory arbitration, and an employer can stall a union all the way through this lengthy procedure and in the end concede not one jot of the real *substance* of recognition – the day to day control trade unionism can exert on the business'. The loss of employer autonomy, the sanction behind unilateral arbitration, might have been felt more keenly, and hence have been more effective against non-compliance, in claims seeking to extend the subject matter of bargaining, but no recommendations for further recognition came to the CAC.

Davies (1979:57–8) has argued that the statute did not preclude the CAC taking a different approach since 'nearly all collective obligations can be meaningfully expressed as obligations in the individual contract'. Various factors can be pointed to which might help account for the CAC's reluctance to 'award recognition', including the problems which could face the ordinary courts if asked to enforce an employee's contract. The factor emphasised by the CAC itself, however, was that Parliament had not intended to introduce an enforceable 'right to be recognised'. Indeed, Wedderburn (1976:183) suggested that the choice of a weak sanction was perhaps 'not too high a price to be paid for the maintenance of what will still be fundamentally a voluntary system of collective labour relations'. Although the sanction was weak in intention, and weaker still in operation, it was perceived differently by the judges. They compared it with the powers of compulsory acquisition of property[28] and described it as 'an interference with individual liberty', which 'could hardly be tolerated in a free society unless there were safeguards against abuse'.[29]

Impact

The compulsory recognition procedures had little direct impact upon the extent of union recognition. The lack of impact of the IRA procedure is not surprising: only registered unions could use it and most TUC unions refused

[28] *Powley v ACAS* [1977] IRLR 190, 195.
[29] Lord Salmon, approving the view of Lord Denning, *ACAS v Grunwick Processing Laboratories Ltd* [1978] IRLR 38, 44.

to register (Weekes et al., 1975:252–6). More surprising perhaps is ACAS's conclusion that the direct impact of the EPA procedure had been 'marginal' except in one or two sectors of industry. Of the 1,610 cases handled under the EPA's compulsory procedure, some form of recognition was established in only 573 or 36 per cent of the cases, covering 65,000 employees (1981:92, 99–100).

But the indirect impact of these procedures, their tendency to engender a climate of opinion which encourages the voluntary recognition of unions, must also be taken into account. Although the CIR did not have the power during its voluntary phase of 1969–71 to enforce its recommendations, and many of the firms to which they were directed ignored them, Bain and Price (1972:375–7) have argued that the CIR and the prospect of a compulsory recognition procedure encouraged employers to view the growth of union organisation as virtually 'inevitable' and to recognise unions as part of a more general restructuring of industrial relations within their firms and industries.

However favourable the climate for union recognition was during the CIR's voluntary phase, it became less favourable with the passage of the IRA in 1971. The whole tenor of the legislation was restrictive rather than permissive. At no point did the Act or its accompanying Code of Practice stress the desirability of extending union recognition. Not surprisingly, therefore, a comprehensive analysis of the operation of the IRA came to the conclusion that 'the growth of traditional unions through voluntary recognition does not appear to have been positively influenced by the Act' (Weekes et al., 1975:130). But the IRA did have an impact upon the voluntary recognition of non-TUC organisations. Some employees and employers feared that the Act's compulsory procedure would promote the growth of TUC unions, and they formed and recognised 'staff associations' and 'professional associations' in an attempt to provide an alternative form of organisation. Although eighty-six non-TUC unions were formed during 1971–4, however, most of them were very small; their membership in 1974 was only 0.64 per cent of total union membership (Price and Bain, 1976:352–3).

ACAS under the EPA, like the CIR during its voluntary phase, embodied a public policy favourable to union organisation and collective bargaining. ACAS believes that this policy indirectly promoted union recognition not only by making employees more aware of the feasibility of collective representation, but also by encouraging employers to recognise unions voluntarily in order to obtain orderly bargaining structures and to avoid the public scrutiny which would result from a reference under the statutory procedure. Hence many recognition issues were settled either without ACAS involvement or under the voluntary conciliation machinery provided by s.2 of the EPA. Of the 2,292 cases completed under s.2 during the period when the compulsory procedure was in force, some form of recognition was established in 981 or 43 per cent of the cases, covering approximately 77,500 employees (ACAS, 1981:65). The number of cases, the proportion won by unions, and the number of employees covered were greater under s.2 than under ss.11–16.

The relative success of the voluntary conciliation route to recognition was achieved, however, in the context of the compulsory procedure. As Dickens et al. (1979:37) noted just before this procedure was repealed, there was 'no guarantee that similar success would be obtained by conciliation in the absence of statutory provisions'. This assessment appears to have been borne out by the subsequent experience of s.2; Beaumont (1984a), using Scottish data, found that both the number of recognition cases and the proportion resulting in union recognition have declined dramatically since 1979. Indeed, any indirect impact which the compulsory procedure had upon union recognition was probably largely spent even before it was repealed. The process of judicial review had revealed to employers that they could successfully obstruct ACAS and avoid a recognition recommendation, and the CAC had shown that employers ultimately could not be forced to recognise unions.

DISCLOSURE OF INFORMATION

'Negotiation', as Kahn-Freund (1983:110) has noted, 'does not deserve its name if one of the negotiating partners is kept in the dark about matters within the exclusive knowledge of the other which are relevant to an agreement'. Disclosure of information is thus an important aspect of collective bargaining.

The EPA ss.17–21 spells out the general duty of employers to disclose information to representatives of an independent, recognised trade union for the purposes of all stages of collective bargaining provided certain tests are met and specified exemptions do not apply. The Act does not indicate the information which should be disclosed. If a union requests information which is refused, it may complain to the CAC which, if it finds the complaint well founded, will order disclosure. Should a disclosure award not be complied with, a further complaint, together with a written claim regarding the terms and conditions of specified employees, may be made to the CAC. As with the enforcement mechanism of the EPA's recognition procedure, any terms and conditions awarded by the CAC become part of the employees' contracts of employment and cannot be adversely varied by individual bargaining.[30]

These provisions reflect the view that there is a distinction between information required for collective bargaining and that which may be given to employees generally, and that although some information is available from a variety of sources – for example, shareholder reports and company accounts – trade unions have special requirements in respect of

---

[30] EPA s.99 and the Transfer of Undertakings Regulations (see above note 26) contain further provisions for disclosure of information regarding redundancy and transfer of undertakings (see Chapter 15), and the Regulations accompanying the HSWA 1974 also provide for information to be made available to safety representatives (see Chapter 16). Disclosure in company reports to shareholders is discussed in Chapter 5.

information.[31] The British approach resembles that of the United States where the employer's duty to disclose arises from the statutory duty to bargain (Bellace and Gospel, 1983:61). It differs considerably from the approach adopted by some European countries where employers have a duty to disclose specified information on a regular basis, but not necessarily to trade unions. The emphasis in such countries as Germany (Blanpain, 1982:212) and Belgium (Smith, 1977) is on collaborative disclosure and consensus-building consultation, with information given to works councils which contain employer as well as employee representatives, rather than on information to improve the conduct of bargaining. The two-channel system of works councils and trade unions was explicitly rejected by British trade unions at the time of the Bullock Committee on Industrial Democracy (see Chapter 5), and the disclosure provisions in the EPA, like the amended health and safety consultation provisions (HSWA s.2), reflect the unions' claim to be the single channel in the enterprise for communication and contact between employer and employee.

Disclosure of information to unions can be seen as part of the process of extending collective bargaining towards 'industrial democracy' (Basnett, 1971:116–19), but the EPA's disclosure duty is limited by the extent of prior recognition for bargaining. The statutory provisions cannot be used to extend either the scope or the depth of bargaining; s.17(2) requires that the collective bargaining in relation to which the information is sought concerns workers and matters in respect of which the union is recognised by the employer. A possible way round this restriction, as Wedderburn (1976:178) has noted, would have been to use the provisions on information disclosure in conjunction with the recognition procedure by seeking a recommendation for further recognition and then claiming disclosure in respect of that area, although the statutory definition of collective bargaining might ultimately have limited the subjects which could have been covered in this way.[32] This combined approach to extending the range of collective bargaining was not tried, though some unions awarded first-time recognition by ACAS used the disclosure provisions to aid recognition struggles.[33] The 'recognised union' status conferred by an ACAS recommendation enabled the disclosure provisions under s.17(2)(b) to be used to put more pressure on the employer. Attempts to use the disclosure provisions to help in other areas – for example, in the preparation of a claim under the Fair Wages Resolution – have been unsuccessful (Doyle, 1980:164).

As the Consultative Document on the Employment Protection Bill (DE, 1974:paras. 49–51) made clear, the disclosure provisions were meant to affect the quality rather than the extent of bargaining. Certainly, some employers see an advantage of information disclosure being 'better bargain-

---

[31] The unimplemented disclosure provisions of the IRA (ss.56–7) covered disclosure to trade unions in similar terms to the EPA, but also required undertakings with more than 350 employees to issue a financial statement to all employees.

[32] E.g., it arguably does not cover investment planning; see TULRA s.29 (1) and note 18 above.

[33] E.g. ASTMS's claims against *Holo-Krome Ltd*, Award 78/626, and *Uniroyal Ltd*, Award 79/27.

ing', by which they usually mean more 'realistic' demands resulting from unions obtaining a better understanding of the business or of management problems (Dickens, 1980a:29). Alternatively, or additionally, 'better bargaining' might mean the achievement of greater equality in the bargaining relationship by allowing unions access to information which only the employer possesses. The usefulness of the disclosure provisions in redressing this information inequality, however, is reduced under s.18 because they do not allow unions access to original documents, and employers can argue excessive time or cost as well as any of six listed exemptions to avoid having to disclose.

Disclosure Hurdles

Under the EPA a union which is recognised by the employer is entitled to 'all such information relating to his undertaking as is in his possession, or that of an associated employer' in any stage of collective bargaining, and which it 'would be in accordance with good industrial relations practice' to disclose (s.17(1)). This formulation contains difficult hurdles for a claimant union to surmount.

The defence that the information is not collected and not in the employer's possession has not been significant in thwarting union requests; the claim that the union is not recognised has been. Initially, the CAC took a wide view of what constitutes union recognition for disclosure purposes. Given the diverse nature of union recognition in Britain, which depends not on a written agreement or a legal certificate but rather on established practice, this was a realistic approach. In one case, for instance, the CAC saw the distinction between consultation and negotiation in this context as 'insupportable legalism' (Award 80/65), and its early interpretation of what constituted recognition included individual representational rights. As noted earlier in this chapter, however, this interpretation was overruled by the courts.[34]

The CAC interprets 'all stages of collective bargaining' to include the formulation of a claim and not just its preparation and pursuance as well as the preparation of a claim in a currently 'dormant' area of bargaining. But where an employer argues that no recognition is accorded for a particular matter and no bargaining on it is anticipated, then the area is put out of reach of the disclosure provisions. When British Leyland decided to close the MG plant at Abingdon, management declined to negotiate on this issue with the local unions, although it was prepared to negotiate on the consequences of the closure. The claim for disclosure of information relating to the actual closure therefore failed, with the CAC noting that the refusal to bargain in an area where it felt the company was morally obliged to do so effectively frustrated the statutory right to information (Award 80/65).

Since unions are confined to 'the parameters of their bargaining table' (Award 78/353), most of the forty-six awards made by the CAC between

---

[34]   *R v CAC ex parte BTP Tioxide* [1982] IRLR 60.

1978 and 1983 concerned claims for information relating to the 'core areas' of recognition and negotiation such as earnings, pay scales and pay systems, job evaluation and grading (Dickens, 1980a:12; Gospel and Willman, 1981:15). The provisions generally appear to have functioned to allow white-collar unions (the most frequent applicants) to obtain information of a kind generally disclosed to manual unions. The statutory provisions are most likely to be used successfully on topics where employers are already fairly open and to prove ineffective on those topics, such as certain financial matters and future planning, where information disclosure is rare (Dickens, 1980a:30,48; Smith, 1975:9; CIR, 1972). The CAC does not see its remit as allowing it to set new standards or to blaze a trail for greater disclosure. Wide-ranging claims, which the CAC has described as more suitable to the negotiation of a planning agreement than the basis of collective bargaining, have not succeeded. Nor, at the other extreme, have claims too narrowly focused on information necessary to process an individual grievance where no wider bargaining issue was involved; in such cases the CAC considered the disclosure provisions were being used as a 'discovery of documents procedure' (CAC, 1978:16).

If the disclosure claim relates to the terms and conditions of workers outside the claimant union's negotiating sphere, the information has to be shown to be relevant to bargaining on behalf of workers who are covered by the claimant union because s.17(2) refers to collective bargaining in 'relation to the descriptions of workers' for which the union is recognised. Since the other workers may be covered by other unions (as in Award 78/353), such claims may raise sensitive issues and call for attention to 'good industrial relations'. Guidance has to be sought (s.17(4)) from the ACAS Code *Disclosure of Information to Trade Unions for Collective Bargaining Purposes* (1977). This Code, like the CIR report (1972) which was to provide guidance for the disclosure provisions of the IRA, gives examples of information which 'could be relevant in certain collective bargaining situations' (1977:paras. 11–12), but it fails, as did the CIR report, to address itself specifically to what good industrial relations practice in this area might be. ACAS codes need to be approved by the Service's tripartite Council and Gospel (1976) has suggested that the weakness of the Code stems from its attempting to steer a middle course between the views of the CBI and the TUC. The CAC itself (1979:15) has noted the lack of consensus on good practice in this area and has found the Code of little assistance to it (Award 78/353; Gospel and Willman, 1983).

The CAC's general view appears to be that disclosure is normally in the interests of good industrial relations (for example, Award 78/711). It has noted, however, that it 'sometimes finds itself in a position where its statutory obligations preclude a decision based on good industrial relations practice' (1979:15). Similarly, although it may be in the interests of good industrial relations for the CAC to indicate what the employer might disclose in the future, to do so is outside its power.[35]

---

[35] ibid.

Part of the CAC's statutory obligation is to award disclosure only if the union is materially impeded by the lack of it. Many union claims have fallen at this hurdle (Dickens, 1980b:14; Gospel and Willman, 1981:16). The duty to disclose was intended, as indicated above, to affect the quality of bargaining. The application of the 'material impediment' test, however, focuses attention not on the nature of the bargaining that disclosure might facilitate but, rather, on whether bargaining can take place at all without disclosure. The material impediment test centres attention not on the relevance of information, as in the United States, but on the narrower concept of importance (Award 78/353). Where a union has concluded agreements in the past in respect of a matter about which it then seeks disclosure under s.17, it will have difficulty in showing a material impediment (Award 84/15). Similarly, where unions have reasonable alternative means of obtaining the information sought from an employer, they will fail the material impediment test (Award 78/277). Legal problems, such as breach of a fiduciary duty, may arise, however, where unions seek to use their individual members as sources of information about their employing companies.[36]

Lack of material impediment has been a major plank in employer arguments against disclosure claims (Gospel and Willman, 1981:16) and the courts have taken a narrower view than the CAC.[37] Where the union surmounts this hurdle, however, the employer may succeed in arguing a s.18 exemption. Under s.18(1) an employer can avoid disclosure if it would be against the interests of national security or would contravene a prohibition imposed by or under an enactment; or if the information has been communicated to the employer in confidence or has been otherwise obtained in consequence of the confidence imposed in the employer by another person; or is information relating to an individual unless he or she has consented to it being disclosed; or is information 'the disclosure of which would cause substantial injury to the employer's undertaking for reasons other than its effect on collective bargaining'; or is information obtained by the employer for the purpose of bringing, prosecuting, or defending legal proceedings.

The main exemption in s.18(1) which has prevented disclosure awards is that covering information which would cause substantial injury to the employer's undertaking (s.18(1)(e)), although, as Dickens (1980b:14.16) notes, other exemptions might have been used more frequently to frustrate claims if the prior tests of s.17 had not eliminated certain cases. The 'substantial injury' exemption has applied, for example, where business contracts were obtained by competitive tender and the information requested by the union regarding profits on a contract coming up for renewal was argued likely to jeopardise the company's chance of renewal should it fall into the hands of a competitor. In this case (Award 78/584) the union had given an assurance of confidentiality. Management often provides information to union representatives on a confidential basis (Knight, 1979),

---

[36] *Bents' Brewery v Hogan* [1945] 2 All ER 570; see Elias et al. (1980:146–7).
[37] *Civil Service Union v CAC* [1980] IRLR 274.

but the CAC in another case (Award 78/711) has held that disclosure in confidence does not constitute disclosure under the Act.

Employer defences based on substantial injury convey the view of the union as an outsider, although in at least one case (Award 79/337) the union argued that a distinction should be drawn between disclosure of commercially sensitive information to a competitor and disclosure of such information to a trade union. In Sweden, where the notion of the union as an outsider is regarded as antiquated and incorrect (Schmidt, 1977:116), the Joint Regulation Act 1976 provides that the employer must furnish the union with an opportunity to examine books, accounts, and other documents and assist with the investigatory work. The employer may impose a duty of confidentiality on the union, but the information nevertheless may be conveyed to the members of the appropriate union branch committee. These legislative provisions have been extended by voluntary agreements giving unions the right to send their own experts into the firm to examine the books. As noted earlier, there is no question of 'opening the books' under the British statutory provision; in fact, s.18(2), exempting the production of original documentation and allowing a defence of disproportionate work, has been used to dispose of a number of union claims (Gospel and Willman, 1981:17).

Although substantial injury defences usually involve claims of confidentiality of information to the company, s.18(1)(c) provides a specific defence which precludes disclosure of information provided to the employer in confidence. This provision was held by the High Court to cover information relating to the costs of cleaning supplied in a tender in a case concerning proposals to change from direct labour to contract labour with consequent redundancies.[38] This decision clearly limits the utility of the EPA disclosure provisions to unions seeking to protect members' interests by arguing against privatisation or the sub-contracting of work.

Enforcement and Impact

In the event of non-compliance, the employer may be exposed to the same indirect sanction as existed under s.16 of the recognition procedure. The limitation for the union, therefore, is the same: ultimately it does not get that to which it is lawfully entitled. In the only award made under s.21 (Award 79/451), the CAC did provide for some information disclosure in its terms and conditions award but it noted that 'there can be important differences between information necessary for collective bargaining and information suitable for inclusion in an individual's contract of employment'. While the range of possible alternative sanctions may be wider than in the case of non-compliance with a recognition award (Dickens, 1980b:18), there has been little pressure to explore them, with only three applications for enforcement under ss.20–21.

The lack of applications for enforcement largely reflects the lack of applications for disclosure. From the time the provisions came into effect

[38] ibid.

until the end of 1983 fewer than two hundred complaints of failure to disclose were made (the majority of applications coming in the first three years, before 1980) and only forty-six awards have been issued (CAC, 1978–84). Slightly less than half (47 per cent) of the awards were for full or partial disclosure as claimed by the union. The problem for unions with the EPA duty to disclose lies less in the nature of the enforcement mechanism than in the restricted scope for disclosure to be awarded. Growing awareness of this problem may underlie the declining use of the provisions.

To assess the impact of the information-disclosure provisions in terms only of published awards is misleading; the agreed outcomes achieved at earlier stages also need to be taken into account (CAC, 1983:21). The CAC holds informal meetings, with an ACAS conciliation officer present, to explore whether 'the complaint is reasonably likely to be settled by conciliation' (s.19(2)). The majority of cases are in fact disposed of without a hearing and the CAC's reports show two-thirds of all cases withdrawn between 1977 and 1983 as resulting in full or partial disclosure.

Additionally, as with union recognition, the statutory duty to disclose may have an indirect impact. As Dickens (1980b:20) has noted, 'the provisions do at least symbolise or sanction that disclosure of information to trade unions is seen as desirable', and the CAC (1981:16) has suggested that lack of applications for information disclosure may reflect more widespread good practice in disclosure, obviating the need to use the statutory procedure. In fact, research (Mitchell et al., 1980:55; Gospel and Willman, 1983:78) has found that the legislation and its accompanying Code of Practice have had little impact on company disclosure policies and practices. But the impact of legislation, as Kynaston-Reeves (1980:5) has observed, may be quite diffuse and consequently go unacknowledged or unrecognised.

Although some unions, such as the GMBATU, have produced model 'information agreements' to guide negotiators (Kynaston-Reeves, 1980:24–5), few such agreements have been concluded and most unions have not been very active in pressing for greater disclosure (Dair and Reeves, 1979). Explanations for their lack of interest are to be found not only in the limitations of the statutory procedure described above but also in an understanding of the factors which constrain the acquisition and use of company information. Such factors include the industrial relations structure and policies of the company, the nature of union organisation, and the pattern, content and traditions of British collective bargaining.[39]

The nature of information itself is also relevant. Facts are not neutral and information disclosure need not necessarily result in more 'effective' or 'scientific' bargaining as the legislation appears to assume (Marsh and Rosewell, 1976:10) and as the CAC has sometimes supposed (for example, Award 78/353). The disclosure of financial and economic information, as Foley and Maunders (1977:42) have argued, may help define a central area within which any settlement may fall, but information does not arise, nor does it operate, in a vacuum. Information is often intentionally or uninten-

---

[39]   See Gold et al. (1979:71–81); Dickens (1980b:25–7); Gospel (1978); Jenkins (1982); Marsh and Hussey (1979:9); and Owen and Broad (1983).

tionally geared to specific ends, to favour particular courses of action. Indeed, 'in reality, information is so much a tool of management that its formulation is incorporated into the organisation of a company' (Gold et al., 1979:98). Thus trade unions need a knowledge of the company's information system in order to understand the limits within which decisions are made. In addition, although information may be power, the power of information cannot be divorced easily from the power of whoever seeks to use it. The importance of particular facts in reaching a decision may depend less on the nature of the facts than on the power position of the person forwarding them.

Finally, information disclosure cannot be isolated from its industrial relations context. The context in which negotiations have taken place since 1979 is such that unions are now less likely to be pushing for a wider range of company information than for more detailed information in areas such as staffing and pay and conditions where employers are comparatively open. In the future pressures from unions for greater disclosure of company information may result from the development of union policies, priorities, and strategies that create a need for information, that is, a 'decision-oriented' (Gospel, 1978:21) or a 'user' (Gold et al., 1979:29–30) approach; from the acquisition of new functions (perhaps in participation schemes); or from the unions' entry into areas of decision-making at present the prerogative of management (Dickens, 1980b:27). If such pressures develop, however, the experience to date suggests that the statutory disclosure provisions will offer little assistance to unions in the face of management reluctance to disclose.

CONCLUSION

Although union growth and recognition expanded greatly in Britain during the 1970s (Price and Bain, 1983), many employers in the private sector still do not recognise unions. A recent survey (Daniel and Millward, 1983:18) found that 32 per cent of establishments in private-sector manufacturing and 58 per cent in private services recognise neither manual nor non-manual unions. Both manual and non-manual unions were recognised by 31 per cent of establishments in private manufacturing and by only 18 per cent of those in private services. This contrasts with 88 per cent of establishments in nationalised industries and 65 per cent in public administration recognising both types of union. Obviously, therefore, there is still potential for an extension of collective bargaining in the private sector.

The flow of company information probably has increased recently in line with such developments as the resurgence of joint consultation (Daniel and Millward, 1983:133) and communication-based employee participation strategies, stimulated by pressure emanating from the European Economic Community (see Chapter 5). But this is not information disclosed primarily for the purposes of collective bargaining. Indeed, some communication-consultation schemes act as a substitute for joint regulation; others undermine the status of the union as the single channel for contact between employees and their employer. All information disclosed may feed into bargaining, however, if the union is recognised.

Recognition is the key to the 'duty to bargain'. As unions still have a 'recognition problem' in the private sector, they are likely to continue the search for legislative solutions. The lessons of the legislative experience of the 1970s, therefore, need to be understood. This chapter has shown that the main problems encountered by the EPA recognition procedure were those arising from judicial review – which, among other things, highlighted the lack of agreed recognition criteria – and the absence of an effective sanction.

Although the EPA allowed ACAS a very wide discretion and provided no right of appeal against its decisions, ACAS was challenged in the courts over its method and scope of enquiry, its ability to delay proceedings, and the criteria by which it decided whether or not to recommend recognition (Miller, 1979). The effect of this judicial review was to leave ACAS with a statutory function it felt unable to perform (1981:138). Although in some of these cases the House of Lords eventually held that ACAS had not wrongly exercised its discretion, it was, as Townshend-Smith (1981:208) has noted, 'something of a Pyrrhic victory if ACAS had to fight a case to the highest court to escape the clutches of interventionist judges, and only served to show that the inherent judicial power to control the operation of bodies such as ACAS is such that their usefulness is likely to be significantly hamstrung unless judges are sympathetic to the aims and methods adopted'.

A problem highlighted by judicial review was the lack of agreed criteria for determining bargaining units and for choosing bargaining agents, reflecting the fact that union organisation in Britain follows no predetermined plan but is governed, if anything, by a series of ad hoc 'sphere of influence' agreements and the Bridlington procedure. This feature of British industrial relations would pose problems for any legislative attempt to stimulate recognition of trade unions. For example, an alternative legal approach to a statutory procedure might be to build upon the individual right to associate (see Chapter 2) and the model provided by the consultation provisions.[40] Such an approach might give a right to consultation, which was not dependent on prior recognition, to a union with members in a particular company. If established bargaining arrangements were to be preserved and inter-union conflict and multi-unionism avoided, however, decisions still would be required on which unions were appropriate and when the right might be claimed, and such decisions would require appropriate criteria to be formulated.

The EPA did not provide recognition criteria and ACAS Council failed to fill the vacuum. It is a moot point whether ACAS would have fared better at the hands of the courts if it had grasped this particular nettle. What is clear is that, even if criteria could have been agreed and the courts had left ACAS free to exercise its discretion in applying them, there would still have been the problem of enforcement. The success of an indirect sanction of unilateral arbitration rather than, say, mandatory court injunctions as in the United

[40] EPA s.99(1); HSWA s.2(4); Transfer of Undertakings Regulations 1981 regs. 10 and 11.

States rested on the assumption that employers would prefer to bargain over the terms and conditions of their employees than have them determined by a third party. In practice, however, arbitration contained no threat where the employer was already providing reasonable terms and conditions. Even if arbitration had penalised non-compliant employers by requiring them to provide superior terms and conditions, it would still not necessarily have resulted in union recognition.

If Parliament had wished to adopt a different approach, it is not clear what type of enforcement mechanism would have been effective. The American experience shows that determined employers will not concede recognition even when repeatedly fined (Townshend-Smith, 1981:204; Hart, 1978:210–11) and it is doubtful whether any weapon in the legal armoury would bring about bargaining in situations such as Grunwick. The root of the problem is that recognition is not a discrete phenomenon but a continuous process, a relationship which by its very nature depends on the co-operation and mutual accommodation of unions and employers. Thus union recognition is not something which can be granted by a third party; it is not a once and for all event which can be imposed by recommendations and legal sanctions, although these can play a part in creating a context in which the balance of advantage tilts towards the granting of recognition.

Stronger economic sanctions against employers might have helped tilt the balance in favour of conceding recognition. Compensation to the union denied recommended bargaining rights, or withdrawal of government assistance and public contracts from companies refusing to comply with recommendations, in addition to 'substitute bargaining' arbitration awards, might have been more effective in gaining compliance with recommendations. But stronger sanctions may also have led to more legal challenges to recommendations, increasing the emphasis on legalistic rather than industrial relations concerns. They may also have made the recognition function of ACAS even more controversial and adversely affected its other, voluntary third-party functions – conciliation, arbitration, and advice – which depend on its acceptability to both employers and unions (ACAS, 1979:30). Finally, stronger economic sanctions might have damaged the viability of the company concerned which, as Bain (1967:103–4) noted with other suggestions canvassed at the time of Donovan, is not the most obvious way of furthering the employees' interests.

Given the difficulties posed by unsympathetic judicial review and the problem of enforcement – which can be ameliorated but not overcome completely – the question arises whether the search should continue for legislative solutions to the unions' recognition problem. The answer, even for those who support trade unionism and the collective bargaining which it makes possible, is not straightforward. Hart (1978:215) has argued that dependence on statutory arrangements for securing recognition can have a debilitating effect on trade union strength, especially when such arrangements are inadequate and open to abuse, because they may make union members more reluctant 'to mobilise independent collective action to achieve objectives for which statutory arrangements offer some hope of attainment'. This assumes, however, that the mobilisation of collective action is possible whereas it is largely the difficulty of this in particular contexts which stimulates union demands for legislative support. Certainly the present economic climate does not favour such mobilisation. It is the case, however, that statutory provisions designed to promote a duty to bargain may be double-edged. For example, employers may treat recognition in legalistic terms rather than allowing the gradual evolution of trade union organisation and relationships with management (Dickens et al., 1979:39). Similarly, statutory provisions on disclosure might be seen by employers as setting maximum entitlements to the detriment of a flexible approach suitable to the nature and needs of the bargaining relationship (Dickens, 1980b:19–20).

These potential disadvantages will need to be weighed against the gains which may be achieved by the actual operation of any legal provisions and through their symbolic and indirect effects. These are primarily gains for trade unions and their members but may be seen as gains also by those who do not wish to have industrial action as the only sanction open to a union denied recognition.

Perhaps the major lesson which emerges from the experience of the 1970s is not to entertain too high expectations of what legislation can achieve in this area. Legislative procedures cannot substitute for union organising and recruitment activity. Many of the largest groups referred under the EPA procedure were not the subject of recognition agreements or recommendations, as ACAS (1981:100) has pointed out, because of low support for the applicant unions. Statutory provisions cannot conjure up union support among workers who are not persuaded that their interests are best served by combination. They can consolidate such support and bring pressure upon employers to induce them to negotiate but, ultimately, they cannot by themselves deliver a phenomenon as intangible as union recognition.

Bibliography

Advisory, Conciliation and Arbitration Service (ACAS). 1977. *Disclosure of Information for Collective Bargaining Purposes*. Code of Practice 2. London: HMSO.

———. 1979. *Annual Report 1978*. London: HMSO.

———. 1981. *Annual Report 1980*. London: HMSO.

Bain, G.S. 1967. *Trade Union Growth and Recognition*. Research Paper 6, Royal Commission on Trade Unions and Employers' Associations. London: HMSO.

———. 1970. *The Growth of White-Collar Unionism*. Oxford: Clarendon Press.

———, and Robert Price. 1972. 'Union Growth and Employment Trends in the U.K., 1964–70'. *British Journal of Industrial Relations*, 10 (November), 366–81.

Ball, C. 1980. 'The Resolution of Inter-Union Conflict: The T.U.C.'s Reaction to Legal Intervention'. *Industrial Law Journal*, 9 (March), 13–27.

Basnett, D. 1971. 'Disclosure of Information: A Union View'. *Conflict at Work*. Eds. S. Kessler and B. Weekes. London: BBC Publications, 115–23.

Beaumont, P.B. 1981a. 'Time Delays, Employer Opposition and White Collar Recognition Claims: The Section 12 Results'. *British Journal of Industrial Relations*, 19 (July), 238–42.

———. 1981b. 'Worker Support and Union Recognition in Britain'. *Industrial Relations Journal*, 12 (May-June), 58–64.

———. 1984a. 'Trade Union Recognition and Public Policy in the UK since 1980'. Unpublished paper.

———. 1984b. 'Trade Union Recognition in Northern Ireland'. *British Journal of Industrial Relations*, 22 (November), 364–71.

Bellace, J., and H. Gospel. 1983. 'Disclosure of Information to Trade Unions: A Comparative Perspective'. *International Labour Review*, 122 (January–February), 57–74.

Bercusson, Brian. 1978. *Fair Wages Resolutions*. London: Mansell.

Blanpain, R. 1982. 'Information and Consultation'. *Comparative Labour Law and Industrial Relations*. Ed. R. Blanpain. Deventer: Kluwer, 208–19.

Bragg, Richard J. 1976. 'Recognition and Legal Procedures'. *Studies in Labour Law*. Ed. J.R. Carby-Hall. Bradford: MCB Books, 119–59.

Central Arbitration Committee (CAC). 1978–84. *Annual Reports 1977–83*. London: HMSO.

Commission on Industrial Relations (CIR). 1972. *Disclosure of Information*. Report 31. London: HMSO.

———. 1974. *Trade Union Recognition: CIR Experience*. Study 5. London: HMSO.

Dair, P., and T.K. Reeves. 1979. 'Why Disclosure Could be a Non-Event'. *Personnel Management* (January), 24–39.

Daniel, W.W., and N. Millward. 1983. *Workplace Industrial Relations in Britain: The DE/PSI/SSRC Survey*. London: Heinemann.

Davies, P.L. 1979. 'Failure to Comply with Recognition Recommendation'. *Industrial Law Journal*, 8 (March), 55–60.

——, and Mark Freedland. 1979. *Labour Law: Text and Materials*. London: Weidenfeld & Nicolson.

Department of Employment (DE). 1972. *Industrial Relations Code of Practice*. London: HMSO.

——. 1974. *Employment Protection Bill: Consultative Document*. London: DE.

Department of Employment and Productivity (DEP). 1969. *In Place of Strife: A Policy for Industrial Relations*. Cmnd 3888. London: HMSO.

Dickens, L. 1975. 'Staff Associations and the Industrial Relations Act: The Effect on Union Growth'. *Industrial Relations Journal*, 6 (Autumn), 29–41.

——. 1978. 'ACAS and the Union Recognition Procedure'. *Industrial Law Journal*, 7 (September), 160–77.

——. 1980a. 'What are Companies Disclosing for the 1980s?'. *Personnel Management* (April), 28–30, 48.

——. 1980b. *Disclosure of Information to Trade Unions in Britain*. Ottawa: Labour Canada.

——, M. Hart, M. Jones and B. Weekes. 1979. 'A Response to the Government Working Papers on Amendments to Employment Protection Legislation'. Discussion Paper. Coventry: SSRC Industrial Relations Research Unit, University of Warwick.

Donovan. 1968. Royal Commission on Trade Unions and Employers' Associations 1965–1968. *Report*. Cmnd 3623. London: HMSO.

Doyle, B. 1980. 'A Substitute for Collective Bargaining? The Central Arbitration Committee's Approach to Section 16 of the Employment Protection Act 1975'. *Industrial Law Journal*, 9 (September), 154–66.

Dromey, Jack, and Graham Taylor. 1978. *Grunwick: The Workers' Story*. London: Lawrence & Wishart.

Elias, P., B. Napier and P. Wallington. 1980. *Labour Law Cases and Materials*. London: Butterworths.

Elliott, M. 1980. 'ACAS and Judicial Review'. *Modern Law Review*, 43 (September), 580–86.

Flanders, A.D. 1967. *Collective Bargaining: Prescription for Change*. London: Faber.

——. 1974. 'The Tradition of Voluntarism'. *British Journal of Industrial Relations*, 12 (November), 352–70.

Foley, B.J., and K.T. Maunders. 1977. *Accounting Information Disclosure and Collective Bargaining*. London: Macmillan.

Gold, M., H. Levie and R. Moore. 1979. *The Shop Stewards' Guide to the Use of Company Information*. Nottingham: Spokesman Books.

Gospel, H. 1976. 'Disclosure of Information to Trade Unions'. *Industrial Law Journal*, 5 (December), 223–36.

——. 1978. 'The Disclosure of Information to Trade Unions: Approaches and Problems'. *Industrial Relations Journal*, 9 (Autumn), 18–26.

——. 1983. 'Trade Unions and the Legal Obligation to Bargain: An American, Swedish and British Comparison'. *British Journal of Industrial Relations*, 21 (November), 343–57.

——, and P. Willman. 1981. 'Disclosure of Information: The CAC Approach'. *Industrial Law Journal*, 10 (March), 10–22.

——, and P. Willman. 1983. 'The Role of Codes in Labour Relations: The Case of Disclosure'. *Industrial Relations Journal*, 14 (Winter), 76–82.

Hart, M. 1978. 'Union Recognition in America: The Legislative Snare'. *Industrial Law Journal*, 7 (December), 201–15.

James, Bernard. 1977. 'Third Party Intervention in Recognition Disputes: The Role of the Commission on Industrial Relations'. *Industrial Relations Journal*, 8 (Summer), 29–40.

——, and R.C. Simpson. 1978. 'Grunwick v. ACAS'. *Modern Law Review*, 41 (September), 572–81.

Jenkins, G. 1982. 'Disclosure of Information, Stratification and Collective Bargaining'. *Industrial Relations Journal*, 13 (Autumn), 57–62.

Kahn-Freund, Otto. 1954. 'Legal Framework'. *The System of Industrial Relations in Great Britain*. Eds. A.D. Flanders and H.A. Clegg. Oxford: Blackwell, 42–127.

——. 1965. 'Report on the Legal Status of Collective Bargaining and Collective Agreements in Great Britain'. *Labour Relations and the Law: A Comparative Study*. Ed. O. Kahn-Freund. London: Stevens, 21–39.

——. 1983. *Labour and the Law*. 3rd edn. Ed. and intr. by P. Davies and M. Freedland. London: Stevens.

Knight, I.B. 1979. *Company Organisation and Worker Participation*. London: HMSO.

Kynaston-Reeves, T. 1980. *Information Disclosure in Europe*. Bradford: MCB Publications.

McIlroy, John. 1979. *Trade Union Recognition: The Limitations of Law*. Studies for Trade Unionists. London: WEA.

Marsh, A., and R. Hussey. 1979. *Disclosure to Unions – How the Law is Working*. London and Oxford: Touche Ross & Co. and St Edmund Hall Industrial Relations Annexe.

——, and R. Rosewell. 1976. 'A Question of Disclosure'. *Industrial Relations Journal*, 7 (Summer), 4–16.

Mellish, M., and L. Dickens. 1972. 'Recognition Problems under the Industrial Relations Act'. *Industrial Law Journal*, 1 (December), 229–41.

Miller, K. 1979. 'Trade Union Recognition: ACAS and the Courts'. *Journal of the Law Society of Scotland*, 24 (May), 185–9.

Mitchell, F., I. Sams, D. Tweedie and P. White. 1980. 'Disclosure of Information: Some Evidence from Case Studies'. *Industrial Relations Journal*, 11 (November-December), 53–62.

Neal, A. 1979. 'Trade Union Recognition for the Purposes of the Consultative Requirements of Part IV of the Employment Protection Act 1975'. *Industrial Law Journal*, 8 (March), 37–40.

Owen, D., and G. Broad. 1983. 'Information Disclosure: Views from the Shop Floor'. *Employee Relations*, 5 (6), 28–32.

Price, R.J., and G.S. Bain. 1976. 'Union Growth Revisited: 1948–1974 in Perspective'. *British Journal of Industrial Relations*, 14 (November), 339–55.

——, and G.S. Bain. 1983. 'Union Growth in Britain: Retrospect and Prospect'. *British Journal of Industrial Relations*, 21 (March), 46–68.

Robinson, D. 1979. 'Trade Union Recognition and the Case for Goliath'. *Personnel Management*, (August), 29, 35.

Rogaly, J. 1977. *Grunwick*. Harmondsworth: Penguin.

Scarman. 1977. *Report of a Court of Inquiry under the Rt Hon Lord Justice Scarman, OBE into a Dispute between Grunwick Processing Laboratories Limited and Members of the Association of Professional, Executive, Clerical and Computer Staff*. Cmnd 6922. London: HMSO.

Schmidt, F. 1977. *Law and Industrial Relations in Sweden*. Stockholm: Almquist & Wiksell International.

Sholl, R.K. 1980. 'An Analysis of the Northern Ireland Statutory Recognition Procedure'. MA dissertation, University of Warwick.

Simpson, Bob. 1979. 'Judicial Control of ACAS'. *Industrial Law Journal*, 8 (June), 69–84.

Smith, Robin. 1975. *Keeping Employees Informed*. BIM Management Survey, Report 31. London: BIM.

——. 1977. 'Disclosure of Information: Can Britain Learn from Belgium?'. *Personnel Management* (July), 20–24.

Townshend-Smith, R. 1981. 'Trade Union Recognition Legislation – Britain and America Compared'. *Legal Studies*, 1 (July), 190–212.

Ward, G. 1977. *Fort Grunwick*. London: Temple Smith.

Wedderburn, K.W. (*Lord*). 1976. 'The Employment Protection Act 1975: Collective Aspects'. *Modern Law Review*, 39 (March), 169–83.

——, and P.L. Davies. 1969. *Employment Grievances and Disputes Procedures in Britain*. Berkeley and Los Angeles: University of California Press.

Weekes, B., M. Mellish, L. Dickens and J. Lloyd. 1975. *Industrial Relations and the Limits of Law: The Industrial Effects of the Industrial Relations Act, 1971*. Oxford: Blackwell.

4 Legal Regulation of Collective Bargaining

Brian Doyle

Collective bargaining is the central institution of the British system of industrial relations. Yet, as will be seen, the title of this chapter contains an apparent paradox. British labour lawyers cannot speak accurately of the legal regulation of collective bargaining. The law does not trigger the bargaining process nor regulate the methods of bargaining. Frequently, collective bargaining and legal regulation have been mutually exclusive forces. Nevertheless, a body of law has evolved and is evolving which impinges upon the conduct of collective bargaining, while the growth of collective bargaining since 1945 has been accompanied by an increasing clamour for its reform by legal initiatives. This chapter will attempt to describe and to analyse those aspects of labour law which have an effect upon the structure and process of collective bargaining and to assess the role of legal intervention therein.

The chapter begins by defining its subject area and there follows a brief account of the historical and theoretical development of the legal regulation of collective bargaining. Next an analysis of the legal status and effect of collective agreements prefaces an examination of the function of labour law in the development and extension of collectively bargained standards. In the penultimate section the influence of labour law and economic policy upon collective bargaining is considered before drawing the chapter to a conclusion.

COLLECTIVE BARGAINING AND LABOUR LAW

Widespread collective bargaining is the distinguishing feature of British industrial relations. Upon one recent estimate (Palmer, 1983:149), some 70 per cent of all full-time workers have their basic terms and conditions of employment directly or indirectly determined by collective bargaining. The Donovan Commission (1968:para. 212) stated: 'properly conducted, collective bargaining is the most effective means of giving workers the right to representation in decisions affecting their working lives, a right which is or should be the prerogative of every worker in a democratic society'. That is a view which appears to have international recognition (ILO, 1978) and to some extent corresponds with the experience of comparable societies

(Cordova, 1978). Collective bargaining may be defined as a voluntary process for reconciling the conflicting interests and aspirations of management and labour through the joint regulation of terms and conditions of employment. This narrowly drawn definition (cf. Flanders, 1970b; Clegg, 1976; Kahn-Freund, 1983:65–70) accepts the assumption that industrial and economic conflict is inevitable in the labour-management relationship and that such conflict is soluble within the institutions and procedures of collective bargaining. In Dubin's words (1954:44), collective bargaining is 'the great social invention that has institutionalised industrial conflict' and 'created a stable means for resolving it'. Although this assumption is open to challenge, the definition indicates the multifaceted role of collective bargaining.[1] It functions as a device for dispute settlement, regulates the individual employment relationship, establishes social and economic standards of wider application and orders relations between management and trade unions (Cordova, 1982). Furthermore, collective bargaining is a multilateral source of regulation distinguishable from unilateral rule-making by managerial (or trade union) prerogative. It is an expression of collective authority in which individual values are assumed to be either identical with or subordinate to collective objectives. The definition does not expressly countenance rule-making and dispute settlement through the various forms of joint consultation and employee participation outside the single channel of trade union representation (see Chapter 5). Finally, and significantly, defining collective bargaining as a voluntary source of rule-making distances it from the compulsory or automatic imposition of norms by administrative, statutory or common law regulation.

The classical critique of the role of labour law in collective bargaining in Britain is that of Flanders and Kahn-Freund.[2] Flanders (1974) described what had occurred as a 'tradition of voluntarism' in which management and labour subscribed to the primacy of voluntary action. Within the mature system of collective bargaining industrial relations issues were the subject of self-regulation, the internal resolution of conflict was preferred and industrial peace was sought through collective agreement. In the voluntarist system the state remained aloof from collective bargaining and industrial conflict while labour law was accorded only a marginal role. Kahn-Freund (1983:14) described law as 'a technique for the regulation of social power' but recognised that 'the law is not the principal source of social power'. In a neat rationalisation of labour history Kahn-Freund constructed a theory of collective bargaining founded upon the principle of legal abstention or non-intervention. Strong collective organisation emerged despite early legal restriction and without direct political support, while the evolution of collective bargaining occurred largely in the absence of state aid or legal prescription (Lewis, 1976; Wedderburn, 1980). According to Kahn-Freund (1954b:66), labour legislation was 'in a sense a gloss or a footnote to

---

[1] For the theoretical debate on the role of collective bargaining, see: Fox (1966; 1973; 1974:248–96); Clegg (1975); Hyman (1978); Crouch (1977; 1982).

[2] See: Flanders (1965; 1967; 1970a; 1970b; 1974); Kahn-Freund (1948; 1954b; 1959; 1968; 1972; 1977; 1983).

collective bargaining', although later he added (1983:15, 291) that the role of labour law was 'to regulate, to support and to restrain the power of management and the power of organised labour' and 'to redress any disequilibrium of power'.[3] Apart from the laws designed to restrict industrial conflict, labour legislation could be described as being either 'regulatory' or 'auxiliary'. Regulatory legislation, as exemplified by laws on safety, wages and individual employment rights, acted as a brake upon managerial prerogative and provided minimum labour standards, subject to improvement by collective bargaining but available to all employees regardless of collective strength. Auxiliary legislation, of which state-sponsored dispute settlement machinery and statutory procedures achieving the limited extension of collectively agreed terms were early examples, accepted the primacy of voluntary action but also served to encourage the development of joint regulation.

In the 1960s the classical analysis was modified in the light of the movement for the reform of collective bargaining. The protagonists of an interventionist policy in industrial relations (for example, Conservative Party, 1968) had sought to equate Britain's economic decline with the uncontrolled growth of the voluntary system and prescribed a comprehensive framework for the legal regulation of collective bargaining. Indeed, when the Donovan Commission reported in 1968 the voluntarist tradition was not given a complete bill of health. The Commission (1968:paras. 46–74) described the inherent tensions of Britain's formal and informal systems of industrial relations, in which the power of workplace or plant bargaining had waxed as the influence of industry-wide or national bargaining had waned. The decentralisation of bargaining structures had produced fragmented, outdated and conflicting agreements in which the regulation gap was often filled by informal and unwritten practices. It was this 'disorder' which the Commission viewed as the 'central defect' of the British system of industrial relations from which all other symptoms of industrial conflict derived (para. 162). The Donovan prescription for the reform of collective bargaining, however, was not the abandonment of the autonomous system but rather its reform and extension. First, the decentralisation of bargaining was to be encouraged and the scope and content of plant (or company) agreements were to be expanded and formalised (paras. 162–80). Second, the growth of collective bargaining into areas of employment not previously the subject of joint regulation was to be pursued (paras. 213–75). While this latter objective was to be promoted by limited legal intervention, the former goal would be achieved by voluntary reform, aided by a standing Industrial Relations Commission, with the selective use of legislation being envisaged only as a last resort (paras. 181–206).

As Fox and Flanders (1969) have noted, the Donovan analysis represented a crystallisation of views which had been developing since the 1940s but it was not an analysis which was readily understood nor easily accepted in all quarters (Sisson and Brown, 1983; Batstone, 1984:1–32). Within a year

---

[3] For a critique of this analysis see: Lewis (1979b); Clegg (1983); Wedderburn (1983); Davies and Freedland (1983).

the Labour Government had produced proposals for a more interventionist strategy of collective bargaining reform (Department of Employment and Productivity, 1969). Events overtook this initiative and in 1971 the newly-elected Conservative Government secured the passage of the IRA, which represented an attempt to construct a comprehensive legal framework for the regulation of collective bargaining.[4] Thomson and Engleman (1975:126–7) have observed that the Act was replete with competing philosophies but that, in particular, 'it was hoped that the legislation would contribute to the restructuring and decentralisation of industrial relations, much as recommended by the Donovan Commission, but with a stronger legal and contractual basis to the relationship'. Thus the IRA attempted to effect structural changes in collective bargaining by establishing legal procedures for the determination of recognition issues (ss.44–55), which procedures have been discussed in Chapter 3. Furthermore, the legislation sought to foster the development of comprehensive collective agreements: principally by introducing the presumption that the parties to joint regulation were legally bound by their agreements (ss.34–6), by constructing machinery for remedying non-existent or defective procedure agreements (ss.37–43) and by providing for the registration of procedure agreements (ss.58–9). The Act lent heavily upon concepts borrowed from American legislative experience and illustrated the dangers, highlighted by Kahn-Freund (1974) and Whelan (1982), of transplanting legal organs without considering the perils of rejection. The unashamedly interventionist thrust of the Act met the defence mechanisms of the voluntarist tradition head on and, as Weekes et al. (1975) record, in both industrial relations and legal terms the Act was a failure.

The inevitable repeal of the IRA upon the return to office of a Labour Government was achieved by TULRA which restored the non-interventionist basis of the relationship between collective bargaining and labour law. A combination of the need to modernise that relationship, to redress the imbalance of power between management and labour so recently exposed by the IRA, and to secure trade union co-operation in a policy of voluntary wage restraint, however, led to the enactment of the EPA. The Act had immediate repercussions for the traditional analysis of the role of law in collective bargaining (cf. Wedderburn, 1978:447–58).

First, by expanding the floor of individual rights for employees, the Act invited collective bargaining to improve upon these newly created standards. These rights are now to be found in the EPCA, and include the right to guaranteed payments (ss.12–18), the rights in connection with pregnancy and maternity (ss.33–48) and the strengthened rights of protection from dismissal (ss.49–80). Second, the legislation provided a number of rights which, although 'individual to each employee', obtained 'true significance ... in the organisational strength of the union at collective level' (Wedderburn, 1978:443). In particular, employees enjoy the right not to be dismissed or discriminated against on the grounds of trade union membership or activities (EPCA ss.23–26A and 58–58A); union members have the right as em-

---

[4]   See: Wedderburn (1972); Thomson and Engleman (1975); Weekes et al. (1975).

ployees to reasonable time off to take part in trade union activities (s.28); and employees who hold trade union office (which will include shop stewards) are entitled to reasonable time off with pay to carry out trade union duties and to undergo training in connection therewith (s.27). Together with the rights to time off enjoyed by the health and safety representatives of recognised trade unions under the HSWA, these provisions to some extent protect and encourage workplace union organisation (see Chapter 2). Third, the EPA intervened directly in collective labour relations by constructing machinery and procedures for handling issues at the heart of the collective bargaining relationship. Of greatest significance for this account were the statutory procedures (ss.11–16) for the reference of recognition disputes to ACAS, and the right of recognised trade unions to seek disclosure of information for the purpose of collective bargaining (ss.17–21), which provisions are discussed in Chapter 3. The EPA Sch.11, described below, also expanded the pre-existing machinery by which the extension of collectively agreed terms had been promoted. Finally, the Act required employers to consult with the representatives of recognised trade unions in advance of redundancies (ss.99–107). Although a legal duty to consult trade unions falls short of a duty to bargain,[5] there is evidence (Brown, 1981:75–8; Daniel and Millward, 1983:129–48) that in practice there is a considerable overlap between consultation and negotiation.

Whereas the latter part of the 1970s saw the development of legislation supporting and encouraging collective bargaining, the 1980s saw a new emphasis on restriction rather than reform (Clark and Wedderburn, 1983; Lewis, 1983). In particular, the most recent legislation has dismantled much of the statutory support for collective bargaining, weakened the framework of employment protection rights and, as Batstone (1984:314) has argued, aims 'to reduce labour market rigidities through the imposition of constraints upon union action'. These constraints include legal restrictions to weaken (rather than, as traditionally, to strengthen) union organisation at the workplace and are exemplified by the ban on union-only and recognition-only practices in EA 1982 ss.12–14. Moreover, the 'individualism' of this legislation serves to limit the extent of the collective regulation of employment relations (Wedderburn, 1984:78–84). No less important in this context is the government's denationalisation and privatisation policies, which aim to enforce the structural reform of public sector bargaining through the weakening of the unions (Heald and Morris, 1984: 33–4; Heald, 1983:227–33). Finally, the new policy conflicts with internationally established labour standards which support collective bargaining. Thus, the threat to minimum wage-fixing machinery and the rescission of fair wages provisions, discussed below, involve the disavowal of international standards, while new EEC proposals strengthening collective employment rights and

---

5 Note also the requirement to consult recognised trade unions in respect of health and safety matters, occupational pension schemes and proposed transfers of undertakings: HSWA s.2(4)(6); Occupational Pension Schemes (Certification of Employments) Regulations SI 1975 No. 1927 reg.4 and Contracted-Out and Preservation (Further Provisions) Regulations SI 1978 No. 1089 reg. 4; and Transfer of Undertakings (Protection of Employment) Regulations SI 1981 No. 1794 regs.10–11.

extending the principle of joint regulation are unlikely to receive a warm welcome (cf. Clark and Wedderburn, 1983:209–11 and Chapter 20 below).

COLLECTIVE AGREEMENTS

The collective agreement has been described by Kahn-Freund (1983:154) as 'an industrial peace treaty' and as 'a source of rules for terms and conditions of employment, for the distribution of work and for the stability of jobs'. It represents the conclusion of the joint regulation of 'market relations' and 'managerial relations' (Flanders, 1965:13) between the collective parties. Bargaining over 'market relations' is concerned primarily with pay and pay-related issues such as holiday entitlement or working hours. The outcome of such bargaining is reflected in the substantive terms of the collective agreement. Such terms deal with internal job regulation and the employer-employee relationship. Bargaining over 'managerial relations', in contrast, is designed to regulate the rights and duties of employers and trade unions in the context of a continuing bargaining relationship. It addresses matters such as bargaining rights, negotiating procedures, dispute and grievance resolution, shop steward facilities and like matters. These collective rights and duties are recorded in the procedural terms of the collective bargain or in a separate procedure agreement. The collective agreement is a memorandum or formula for the future conduct of management and labour relations in the enterprise or industry to which it refers. Although modern bargaining practice has increased the number of formalised and written agreements (Brown, 1981), the collective agreement is rarely a comprehensive and authoritative statement of negotiated consensus. Matters of importance may still be determined by informal 'understandings' or left to future interpretation through 'custom and practice' (Brown, 1972). Thus the collective agreement is only one element of evolving industrial relations, subject to existing workplace precedents and future renegotiation.

Are Collective Agreements Legally Enforceable?

The answer to this question, quite exceptionally in British labour law, has been strongly influenced by academic opinion. The proposition that collective agreements were not legally enforceable as contracts was advanced by Kahn-Freund. He considered (1954b; 1959; 1983:158–66) that the parties to the collective bargain normally did not intend legal consequences and viewed their agreement as being binding in honour only. The non-legalistic style of collective bargaining and the vague content of collective agreements, taken with the voluntary nature of the British industrial relations system as a whole, made such reasoning irresistible (cf. Lewis, 1979a; Wedderburn, 1983; Wilson, 1984). Kahn-Freund's analysis was accepted by the Donovan Commission (1968:paras. 470–74) and played an influential part in the leading case on the legal enforceability of collective agreements: *Ford Motor Co. Ltd v AUEFW*.[6]

The facts of the case illustrated the difficulties associated with subjecting collective agreements to legal analysis. The central issue concerned the status of agreements made by a joint negotiating committee which settled the terms and conditions of a workforce represented by some fifteen unions at Fords. Did such agreements, including one which required notice of industrial action to be given and penalised individual workers who took industrial action in breach of procedure, contractually bind the unions who were party to them? The issue was tested when two unions, represented on the committee but opposed to the changes in conditions accepted by a majority of the unions, gave official support to industrial action taken by their members allegedly in breach of agreement. The company sued the unions for breach of contract and sought injunctive relief. The court took the view that the unions could not be automatically bound by the agreements in question, but also ruled that the parties had not intended their agreements to have legal consequences. This ruling derived in part from the few legal precedents on the issue of contractual enforceability but, more significantly, the court received evidence, including that represented by Kahn-Freund's writings and the Donovan Commission's conclusions, which showed that the climate of industrial relations opinion did not favour the argument that collective agreements generally were intended to be contractually binding. The court was unable to find an express or implied intention on the part of Ford's management and unions to indicate that they regarded their agreements as anything more than binding in honour only. In addition, as the agreements were couched in vague and aspirational terms, they were hardly amenable to legal enforcement.

The *Ford* case, as a first instance decision upon particular facts, should not be viewed as a universal precedent, but the ruling that the collective agreement in question was not contractually enforceable was nevertheless judicial recognition that the parties to collective bargaining generally did not intend their agreements to be legally binding (Lewis, 1970; Wedderburn, 1971:171–85). Although the theory of non-enforceability and its implications may be criticised (Hepple, 1970; Wilson, 1984), the principle of the *Ford* case is now entrenched in TULRA s.18(1). This raises a rebuttable presumption that the parties to collective bargaining do not intend their agreements to have the force of contract. There is nothing to prevent employers and unions concluding contractual agreements, and s.18(1) countenances this where provision for contractual intention is made, 'however expressed', within a written collective agreement. In practice such provision is rare, although Lewis (1979a:622) has suggested that agreements which are exceptionally detailed and legalistic may give rise to an implication of contractual intention sufficient to satisfy the statutory proviso.

While collective agreements are generally unenforceable under British labour law, nevertheless they may have some legal consequences or effect.

[6] [1969] 2 QB 303. See also: *Monterosso Shipping Co. Ltd v ITF* [1982] IRLR 468, CA.

The substantive terms of collective agreements are frequently indirectly enforceable through the conduit of the individual employment contract (see Chapter 12). In addition, the individuation by force of law of the orders of wages councils (discussed below) and of the awards of the CAC when acting under a statutory jurisdiction, such as EPA s.21, exemplify a process analogous to incorporation of collectively agreed terms into the contract of employment. Although the device of incorporation into the individual employment contract is the most frequent way in which legal effect is given to collective agreements, a variety of other provisions and techniques are of relevance.

The Transfer of Undertakings (Protection of Employment) Regulations 1981 (cited above) provide for the automatic continuity of collective agreements where the employer's business is transferred, in relevant circumstances, to a new employer (reg.6). Given that the collective agreements are unlikely to be legally enforceable, it is difficult to see what is the purpose of this provision. Hepple (1982:36) points out that the effect of this rule is limited and falls short of promoting a concept of legally enforceable agreements (cf. Chapter 20 below). As Davies and Freedland (1982) explain, however, the simple significance of this provision is probably to ensure that in the employment contracts of employees affected by the transfer references to a collective agreement concluded by the transferor employer are read as if the transferee employer had been a party thereto. As those employment contracts continue in force after the transfer (reg.5), any doubt about the status of substantive terms derived from the collective agreement is avoided. In respect of procedural terms, the transferee employer is free to renegotiate the collective agreement or, subject only to the rare case where the original parties had intended their agreement to be legally binding, to cease to observe those terms.

Finally, employment protection legislation expressly anticipates that collective bargaining may already provide more appropriate safeguards for the individual employee. The standards established by a relevant collective agreement within a particular industry or enterprise may by order of the Secretary of State, upon the application of the parties, supersede those framed by regulatory legislation. The power to confer exemption from legislative provisions in respect of jointly negotiated arrangements may be exercised in relation to redundancy procedure agreements (EPA s.107), guaranteed payment arrangements (EPCA s.18), dismissal procedure agreements (EPCA s.65) and redundancy payment agreements (EPCA s.96).[7] But Bourn (1979) and Davies and Freedland (1984:262–7) show that, as a stimulus to the improvement of standards through collective bargaining, these devices have not proved to be successful. Only the exemption facility in respect of guaranteed payment rights has been used to any significant extent, reflecting that this is an area where joint regulation often provides more generous standards than the statutory minimum payments (see Chapter 13). Otherwise the tendency seems to be that collective bargaining

---

[7] Cf. EPA ss.21(6), 118 and EPCA s.140 (restrictions on contracting out). On the legal regulation of union membership agreements, see Chapter 2 above.

has acted to supplement the statutory provisions rather than to replace them. Such legislation remains in effect regulatory in character rather than auxiliary to collective bargaining.

Collective Agreements and Industrial Relations Reform

The non-contractual status of collective agreements was consistent with the nature of British collective bargaining. The characteristic focus upon the institutions and procedures of joint regulation, rather than upon the substantive rules which were thereby produced, resulted in a system of informal and flexible bargaining with open-ended agreements in which the distinction between enforcing existing standards ('conflicts of right') and creating new ones ('conflicts of interest') was unimportant (Kahn-Freund, 1954a:202–9; 1983:70–74). This description must be qualified today in the light of evidence (Brown, 1981; Daniel and Millward, 1983) pointing to the growth of formalisation in collective bargaining, but the distinction between conflicts of right and conflicts of interest, which in continental systems determines the forum and methodology of dispute settlement (see Aaron, 1982; Goldman, 1982 and Chapter 19 below), remains of relatively little significance (Kahn-Freund, 1983:70–74). Disputes of right and disputes of interest, whether collective or individual in nature, are equally amenable to resolution through the machinery of collective bargaining.

The resolution of industrial disputes in Britain is buttressed by two traditions which have grown side by side (Kessler, 1980). The first is reflected in the preference for settling disputes within the parties' own voluntary autonomous machinery and in the rejection of compulsory and binding dispute resolution methods. The second tradition, of equal pedigree, lies in the provision of state-aided machinery, established upon a statutory basis, to assist the process of dispute settlement (see Chapter 19). An 'autonomous system of collective bargaining presupposes that the parties to the bargaining will have access to autonomous social sanctions in order to secure and enforce agreements' (Davies and Freedland, 1984:138). Thus an increase in strike activity may be explicable by the failure or inability of collective bargaining to contain conflict within the procedures of joint regulation. The Donovan Commission (1968), reporting against the background of Britain's controversial post-war strike record, implicitly accepted the supposed association between a fragmented, informal system of bargaining and a rise in industrial action. Although this analysis is open to question (Edwards, 1983:212–14), it forms the assumptive basis from which the debate upon the legal enforcement of collective agreements has proceeded. Two major objectives are discernible in this debate: the pursuit of procedural reform in collective bargaining and the promotion of a 'peace obligation' enforceable at law.

The idea that legally enforceable collective agreements would automatically produce more formal procedures and less strike activity was not accepted by the Donovan Commission. Donovan counselled the voluntary reform of collective agreements as a necessary step towards the reduction of conflict and saw no role for legal enforcement so long as agreements remained unreformed. The selective enforcement of agreements was foreseen as necessary, however, if industrial action in breach of procedure persisted within a reformed system (Donovan, 1968:paras. 475–519). The IRA tackled the question of procedural reform on two fronts. The broad strategy was contained in ss.34–5 which enacted a presumption of legally enforceable collective agreements, which was neutralised in practice by the insertion of disclaimer clauses by the collective parties (Weekes et al., 1975:156–61). The potentially more incisive strategy was contained in ss.37–43 providing for the compulsory imposition of legally enforceable procedure agreements where such agreements were non-existent or defective. These provisions were almost totally unused (Thomson and Engelman, 1975: 119), and the Act appeared to exercise little practical influence upon procedural reform (Weekes et al., 1975:169–85). In the post-IRA period the issue of reform was removed from the legal arena and restored to the hands of the collective parties, aided by ACAS acting in an advisory or inquiring capacity under EPA ss.1(2), 4 and 5 (ACAS, 1980a:57–79; Armstrong and Lucas, 1984). A recent Green Paper (DE, 1981) returns to the question of legally enforceable collective agreements, but appears to accept the futility of using the law as the primary tool of procedural reform (para. 243).

A 'peace obligation' is an express or implied undertaking by one or both parties to a collective agreement not to take industrial action in breach of the agreement (or, sometimes, at all) during the currency of the agreement (Giugni, 1972:128–30; Cordova, 1982:235). Procedural agreements also frequently contain 'status quo' clauses which limit the freedom of the collective parties to take unilateral action in pursuit of an issue which is subject to domestic dispute resolution machinery (Hyman, 1972; Anderman, 1975; Thomson and Murray, 1976). In Britain, as a general rule, the non-contractual status of collective agreements denies such peace obligations legal significance.[8] The IRA s.36 attempted to impose a far-reaching peace obligation upon trade union parties to collective agreements, including a duty to prevent its officials and members from acting in breach of agreement, which obligation could be ignored only at the risk of damages or injunctive relief. The effect of this provision was largely nugatory because it relied for its strength upon the presumption of legal enforceability of collective agreements contained in ss.34–5 which, as has been seen, was negated by the parties themselves.

Contemporary government thinking (DE,1981), drawing upon the lessons of this experiment, suggests a novel approach to the construction of a peace obligation. The withdrawal of immunity is considered where industrial action is taken either during the currency of a collective agreement or before agreed procedures have been exhausted (para. 220). This formula avoids only some of the pitfalls of making collective agreements legally binding and does not address some of the issues touched upon by the *Ford* case: for example, what constitutes a current agreement, who are the parties to an

---

[8] By virtue of TULRA s.18(1). See Chapter 9 below on the effect of s.18(4) in relation to peace obligations and the individual employee.

agreed procedure, what action would amount to a breach of agreement, how is the exhaustion of procedure to be defined and so on? As a logical extension of the mechanisms for the control of industrial action contained in the Acts of 1980, 1982 and 1984, discussed in Chapter 6, it is further envisaged that a trade union could be made vicariously liable for breaches of agreement committed by its officials or members (paras. 236–8). Taken together, the effect of these proposals would be to produce collective agreements 'enforceable' at several removes from the bargaining process, with an obligation to observe the agreement placed upon labour without a concurrent duty upon management to give effect to the code of terms and conditions contained in the collective bargain.

Britain is not unique in regarding the collective bargain as being subject to social rather than legal sanctions, but a number of countries, including France and West Germany, do treat the collective agreement as being contractually binding (Kahn-Freund, 1983:161–2). In the British context, the non-contractual status of collective agreements and the absence of a peace obligation enforceable at law are consistent with the state's refusal to place upon the parties a duty to negotiate and to reach agreement. Despite inroads into the voluntarist principle, management and unions remain suspicious of legal incursions into the bargaining process. As the Green Paper (DE, 1981:paras. 239–41) acknowledges, the potential success of a legislative provision designed to promote the observance of agreements and procedures must be measured by the willingness of the industrial parties to embrace new attitudes and practices. Despite greater sophistication in pay bargaining, bargaining over managerial relations at the workplace remains largely unreformed and informal (Sisson and Brown, 1983). This state of affairs may underline the case for legal reform, but equally, may short-circuit any attempts to impose a legal solution. Furthermore, many countries which regard the collective agreement as being of contractual effect also accept the logic of treating it as a compulsory and automatic code of employment terms (Kahn-Freund, 1983:177–80). In current British labour law, while the observance of the collective agreement as a contract depends upon the ability and willingness of the parties to negotiate agreement and to abide by its results, the observance of the collective agreement as a code is determined by whether or not its substantive terms become incorporated in the individual employment contract. As Davies and Freedland (1984:281–97) demonstrate, there are difficulties of principle and practice in attempting to construct a general theory of the individuation of the results of collective bargaining. This particular nettle has yet to be grasped by the protagonists of the legal reform of collective bargaining. A number of instruments having the effect of enforcing and extending collectively agreed standards exist, however, and these are examined next.

LABOUR STANDARDS AND THE LAW

Thus far collective bargaining has been explained as a source of rule-making, a technique for the ordering of collective and individual relations at the workplace and an institution of conflict resolution. Collective bargaining may also be understood as a source of socio-economic norms: augmenting, surpassing or anticipating labour standards established by legislation. The question now posed is how can law assist collective bargaining in the maintenance and extension of collective labour standards?

Fair Wages Policies

Since 1891 and until quite recently a combination of administrative and legislative action has supported the observance and extension of collectively agreed or recognised terms and conditions through a series of fair wages policies (see Bercusson, 1978; Davies and Freedland, 1984:154–63). At least two objectives were discernible in these policies: the need to encourage and maintain acceptable labour standards under government contracts, and the concern to ensure industrial peace through the provision of machinery promoting the observance of the code of terms contained in collective agreements. The first objective was represented by the Fair Wages Resolution 1946 (FWR) and the second ran through a series of enactments culminating in Sch.11 to the EPA.

The FWR, as a resolution of the House of Commons, was a socio-political, rather than legal, instrument. It was reflected in and was a model for the international standards set by ILO Convention No. 94 concerning Labour Clauses in Public Contracts. The effect of the FWR was to require government departments to insist that contractors and sub-contractors dealing with central government should observe fair labour standards in respect of their employees. In practice, this requirement was complied with by the insertion of a clause giving expression to the FWR into the commercial contracts concluded by government departments. Local authorities and nationalised industries of their own volition frequently required parties entering into commercial contracts with them to accept, either expressly or by reference, the standards set by the FWR and, in a few cases, the FWR model was placed upon a statutory basis.[9] A failure to observe the standards enshrined in the clause was, in legal terms, a breach of commercial contract, entitling the government department (or the public authority in question) to exercise the legal and commercial sanctions which are usually available to the innocent victim of a contractual breach (Kahn-Freund, 1948). The employees of an employer party to a commercial contract governed by the FWR enjoyed no direct rights deriving from the Resolution under their employment contracts.[10] The FWR, however, contained an arbitration clause under which a complaint that a contractor was failing to meet the due labour standards could be referred to the CAC (and its

---

[9] E.g. Road Haulage Wages Act 1938 s.4. Some statutes incorporated the FWR standards by referring to 'any resolution of the House of Commons for the time being in force': e.g. Films Act 1960 s.42; Road Traffic Act 1960 s.152; Public Passenger Vehicle Act 1981 s.28; Broadcasting Act 1982 s.25.

[10] *Simpson v Kodak Ltd* [1948] 2 KB 184.

predecessors) acting as a non-statutory, independent tribunal (CAC, 1979:paras. 4.15–4.18). An award of the CAC in favour of an employee did not become an automatically enforceable term of the employment contract but could become so, on general principles, if the employer accepted and implemented the award's implications.

The FWR laid down two criteria defining fair wages or standards. The first criterion required the contractor to pay wages and to observe working conditions not less favourable than those 'established' by multi-employer collective bargaining in the trade or industry in question. In the absence of such 'established' terms the second criterion would apply: namely, the 'general level' of standards observed by comparable employers in similar circumstances. With the devolution of pay bargaining from industry-level to plant-level the standards set by the first criterion were likely to be minimum standards, but the Industrial Arbitration Board (IAB), a forerunner of the CAC, refused to be shackled by a device which had been overtaken by events. In its award in *Crittall-Hope Ltd and Pay Board*[11] the IAB interpreted the FWR so as to give preference to the 'general level' standard wherever the nationally agreed minimum had been surpassed by the prevailing rate. As Beaumont (1977:38) records, this interpretation 'deliberately sought to maintain the long-term relevance of the resolution in an institutional context in which shop-floor negotiations were an all-important fact of industrial life'.

In contrast to the FWR, Sch.11 and its predecessors were legislative devices. Developing from the prototype of war-time procedures for the enforcement of collectively agreed terms, Sch.11 could be seen as the refinement of a model for the legal extension of collective bargaining.[12] The impact of earlier models had been limited because of the exclusive emphasis upon national and industry-wide agreements (Latta, 1974). Schedule 11, however, adopted the 'general level' criterion of the FWR in addition to a 'recognised terms' standard which approximated to the FWR's 'established terms' criterion. The new machinery was welcomed as a reproduction of fair wages policy applicable beyond government contracts (Bercusson, 1976), but whereas the two standards of the FWR had been interpreted as alternatives, the legalistic drafting of Sch.11 suggested that the 'recognised terms' standard would predominate over the 'general level' standard where a national or industry-wide agreement was extant (Wood, 1978:67–73). The measure of 'recognised terms' established by multi-employer, national or industry-wide agreements was that of minimum or basic rates, whereas the actual level of wages (and thus the more realistic measure) was that generated by single-employer bargaining at the level of the firm. Recognising that the 'general level' standard was often the more appropriate basis upon which to treat a Sch.11 claim, the CAC adopted a flexible approach by

---

[11] (1974) IAB Award 1974/3290. The contrary view taken by the High Court in *Racal Communications Ltd v Pay Board* [1974] ICR 590 did not disturb the reasoned approach of the IAB and the CAC to the FWR.

[12] The recent pedigree of Sch.11 may be traced from the following enactments: Conditions of Employment and National Arbitration Order SR & O 1940 No. 1305; Industrial Disputes Order SI 1951 No. 1376; Terms and Conditions of Employment Act 1959 s.8.

looking beyond the level of wages established by a national agreement where that level had been supplemented by plant bargaining. Although this approach was rejected emphatically by the High Court in *R v CAC ex parte Deltaflow Ltd*,[13] Sch.11 was heavily subscribed to during its existence. As Jones (1980) pointed out, this reflected the gradual supersession of national agreements by local bargaining and the willingness of trade unions, often with the collusion of employers (Beaumont, 1979b), to use machinery which constituted an express exception to incomes policy.

Both the FWR and Sch.11 were used in fact to circumvent incomes policies during the latter part of the 1970s and, as Lewis and Simpson (1981:147–52) record, inflationary tendencies were attributed to them. Davies and Freedland (1984:161) note that the destiny of the fair wages principle and devices for the enforcement of recognised terms became 'inextricably entwined' in the late 1970s. Schedule 11 was repealed by the EA 1980 and the FWR was rescinded with effect from September 1983, in both cases a reflection of changing public policy towards collective bargaining. Those cases where fair wages policy had been placed upon a statutory footing have either been repealed or have become obsolescent by virtue of the rescission of the FWR.[14] The continuing relevance of fair wages clauses elsewhere will depend upon the language of their drafting and the determination of local and public authorities to insist upon their inclusion in commercial contracts.[15]

Minimum Wage Standards and the Law

The instruments of fair wages policy underpinned collective bargaining arrangements. As a general rule, however, British labour law has been unable or unwilling to influence directly the structure and agenda of joint regulation. An exception to this rule is to be found in the wages councils legislation. Since 1909 legislation has provided a surrogate framework of collective bargaining in industries associated with poor union organisation, inadequate bargaining arrangements and low pay (Bayliss, 1962; Pond, 1984). The present source of this provision is the Wages Councils Act 1979 (WCA) under which 26 wages councils give direct coverage to an estimated 2.75 million workers in 391,000 establishments. Separate but similar provision for agricultural workers is made by the agricultural wages boards established under the Agricultural Wages Act 1948. The underlying purpose

13 [1977] IRLR 486, reviewing the reasoning of the CAC in Award 1977/236 *TGWU and Deltaflow Ltd*. See Wood (1978: 70–72).
14 The Road Haulage Wages Act 1938 was repealed by EA 1980 s.19 and the Broadcasting Act 1981 s.25 was repealed by the Cable and Broadcasting Act 1984 s.50. The other examples cited at note 9 above are now devoid of meaning.
15 In *NUPE and Exclusive Cleaning Services* (Award 1984/13) the CAC upheld a fair wages clause in a local authority contract. Although the clause had adopted the FWR by reference, there was no indication that it was to be interpreted as losing validity upon the rescission of the FWR. See further IRS (1985).

of the legislation is the maintenance of minimum wage standards and the encouragement of voluntary collective bargaining. To a lesser extent the legislation also acts as a palliative to the problem of low pay. The British statutory scheme was influential upon the authors of ILO Convention No. 26, the international provision on minimum wage-fixing machinery.

A wages council may be established by order of the Secretary of State where no adequate wage-fixing machinery exists for a group of workers and where the level of remuneration of such workers points to the necessity of providing statutory machinery (WCA s.1). The initiative for the establishment of a wages council will usually come from an existing joint industrial council (or similar body) or by a joint application from trade unions and employers' associations already engaged in the regulation of terms and conditions in the industry. The grounds for the application must indicate that existing machinery is likely to cease to exist or to be adequate (s.2(1)). In the normal course of events the issue is referred to ACAS for consideration, inquiry and report (ss.2–3). Although the extension of the system has been proposed on occasion (for example, ACAS, 1980c), no new wages councils have been founded in recent years. Once established, wages councils replicate autonomous bargaining arrangements with a notable distinction: they are tripartite bodies containing up to three independent members who act in a quasi-conciliatory role with the ultimate power to break a deadlock between the industrial sides. The power of wages councils to fix the terms of employment of workers within their scope includes the setting of the minimum rate, the definition of holiday entitlements, and the determination of other substantive items (s.14).

Since 1975 wages councils have issued their own orders dealing with these terms without the need to refer them to the Secretary of State. Such an order has direct effect upon the employment contract of a worker within its ambit in substitution for any less favourable terms and conditions therein (s.15(1)(2)). Thus the standards set by wages councils are contractually enforceable by the individual worker. In addition, an employer who ignores the provisions of an order in respect of minimum remuneration and holiday pay or allowances commits a criminal offence. Such an employer may be fined and ordered to make payment of due arrears (s.15(3)(4)). The enforcement of wages councils' orders is overseen by the DE's Wages Inspectorate by means of random checks of establishments covered by the legislation.

Wages councils are a substitute for collective bargaining. Wedderburn (1971:210) has commented that 'the first objective of any Wages Council should be to commit suicide' by transmogrification into a voluntary institution of joint regulation. Although, in a period when the future of the wages council system is under threat, such a statement must be open to doubt, attention naturally focuses upon the power of the Secretary of State to abolish individual wages councils or vary their fields of operation (s.4). An application for the abolition of a wages council may originate in a joint application but, in addition, a trade union representing a substantial proportion of workers covered by the wages council may make a unilateral application for abolition (s.5(1)). Significantly, it is not an express precondition for the abolition of a wages council that adequate collective bargaining machinery exists but merely that its continuation is no longer necessary for the maintenance of a reasonable standard of remuneration (s.5(2)). In practice ACAS, to which an abolition or variation question is referred (s.6), has taken both criteria into account. As an alternative to abolition a wages council may be converted into a statutory joint industrial council (SJIC), which is envisaged as a bipartite body but still wedded to the statutory enforcement procedures. The abolition of a number of wages councils occurred in the period 1969–76 and since then the emphasis has been upon rationalisation of the system (Craig et al., 1982:14–21). While the establishment of SJICs has been periodically considered (ACAS, 1978b; 1980b; 1980c), none have been founded. As Pond (1983:198) remarks, critics of the wages councils system have frequently argued that it has actively discouraged the growth of voluntary collective bargaining. The impressive evidence of empirical studies (Craig et al., 1982) in industries where wages councils have been abolished, however, points to the conclusion that abolition has not fostered the development of effective joint regulation in place of the legislative machinery, and that the retention of minimum wage legislation is a necessary safety net.

The wages councils legislation is a limited attempt to confront the problem of low pay and wage inequality. Yet Pond (1983), reviewing the nature, causes and extent of low pay in Britain, provides evidence that it is a phenomenon heavily concentrated in the largely non-unionised wages councils sector. Low pay is not merely a sectoral problem, however, as pockets of low pay exist in areas where union density is high or where the general level of wages is above average (Craig et al., 1982; Low Pay Unit, 1983; Byrne, 1983). Thus the wages councils have failed to overcome the influence of industrial structure, union density and labour force characteristics upon the low pay equation (Pond, 1983: 200–204).

Three major criticisms of the wages councils machinery may be made. First, the WCA 1979 requires statutory minimum remuneration to be fixed at a 'reasonable' level, but makes no attempt to define such a standard. When the legal minima are compared with average earnings (Bissett and MacLennan, 1984) or against some other measure of the wage income threshold (Low Pay Unit, 1983), the consequences of such omission become obvious. During the 1970s wages councils rates fell significantly against minimum rates set by collective bargaining and, although the 1980s have seen a comparative strengthening of statutory minimum rates, they remain low relative to average earnings (Steele, 1979; IRS, 1983). Thus the wages councils legislation has failed both to improve internal wage anomalies in the particular industries within its scope or to advance the level of earnings in the wages councils sector relative to other industries.

Second, the establishment of a statutory rate of minimum remuneration is not a guarantee of its observance. In 1983 the Wages Inspectorate checked the pay of workers at 11 per cent of establishments registered as covered by current wages councils orders and found that only 6 per cent of workers were not receiving the due rate (DE, 1984). The resources of the Inspectorate, however, are not sufficient to undertake comprehensive policing of employers covered by the legislation and diverse evidence — for example ACAS (1978a); Winyard (1982); Low Pay Unit (1983) — suggests that as many as 40 per cent of employers are underpaying about 16 per cent of workers entitled under the WCA. Commentators (Beaumont, 1979a; Pond, 1983:196–7, 205) frequently make the case for reforming the administrative and enforcement structures of the Act.

Third, as the legislation only provides a *selective* form of minimum wage machinery it is clearly incapable of dealing with the overall problem of low pay or of tackling hidden pockets of wage inequality (Starr, 1981a; Pond, 1984). Starr (1981b:548–9) categorises the British legislation alongside international examples of machinery whose role is designed to provide 'a "second best" alternative' to collective bargaining and which appears 'to presume, implicitly if not explicitly, that there is only limited scope for achieving improvements in the relative position of low-paid workers through statutory regulation without causing unacceptable economic repercussions'. Although the orthodox view is that statutory minimum wage machinery is designed to provide relief to the low paid while encouraging the development of voluntary collective bargaining, the experience of the British wages councils may suggest that such machinery can do no more than provide minimum protection to groups of workers whose vulnerability is expressed in a vicious circle of low pay and collective weakness. The victims of such low pay and wage inequality must look to other forms of legal regulation for protection.

Arguably, the instruments of fair wages policy have been of greater significance in this respect. Pond and Winyard (1983:28) described Sch.11 and the FWR as 'mechanisms for securing improvements in the position of the low paid', citing evidence (Dickens et al., 1979) that some 90 per cent of successful claims under Sch.11 were to the benefit of workers with below average earnings. Although the effectiveness of these measures as a means of combating low pay was limited, their abandonment reverses the public policy of tackling low pay through legislative devices supportive of collective bargaining. More recently, the adherents of neo-classical 'free market' economic philosophy – for example, Hayek (1984); Forrest (1984) – have begun to question any artificial restraint upon the downward adjustment of wages as a negative influence upon the competitiveness of the labour market. It is against this background that the government appears ready to rescind Britain's commitment to the principle, represented by ILO Convention No. 26, of maintaining minimum wage-fixing machinery under statute. The future reform of the WCA has been placed upon the legislative agenda.[16]

Looking beyond the simple expedient of abolishing legal minimum wage standards, a number of proposals for constructive reform have been canvassed. Pond (1983:200) states that 'the only effective long-term solution to low pay' lies with the development and extension of collective bargaining. Labour law can assist the achievement of this goal through measures

---

[16]   DE (1985); HC Employment Committee, 1984–85, 5th Report, 254; 83 HC Deb, 17 July 1985, 326–39.

designed to guarantee collective rights of association, recognition and bargaining. Similarly, the reintroduction of a fair wages policy backed by law would represent 'an advance', but 'it should not be expected on its own to tackle the fundamental problem of low pay' (Pond and Winyard, 1983:29). Furthermore, as Craig et al. (1982:96–130) have argued, existing collective bargaining arrangements combined with the present limitations of selective legal minimum wage standards have failed to provide a comprehensive structure of wage protection. Their proposals for the urgent reform of the system would require the expansion, rather than the contraction, of the wages councils framework and, in addition, the achievement of universal, as opposed to selective, minimum wage control. The result would be the foundation of a *national minimum wage* by 'the establishment of a basic floor to the wage structure' (Starr, 1981b:554).

The adoption of a general or national minimum wage standard under legal regulation has occurred in a number of advanced industrial countries (see generally Starr, 1981a; Field, 1984a), such as France (Sandoval, 1984), the United States (Eccles, 1984) and Australia (Macdonald, 1984). In contrast, some countries, of which Belgium is the leading example (Pond and Winyard, 1983:44–5), have achieved the same objective through national collective wage bargaining. In Britain, the debate upon a national minimum wage has recently been revivified by renewed enthusiasm for the subject among trade unions who had previously resisted any form of state intervention in wage determination (cf. Pond, 1983:206; Pond and Winyard, 1983:34–8). Although the question of a *statutory* national minimum wage remains controversial in trade union circles, and may prove unpalatable to employers and government alike (Dennison, 1984), it is now a live issue. If a national minimum wage is to be shaped in the forge of labour law, rather than in the forge of social security and taxation law (Field, 1984b), this will alter the relationship between law and collective bargaining. Recognition of this is already apparent in the blueprints of reform offered by the supporters of a national minimum wage (Craig et al., 1982:141; Pond and Winyard, 1983:45) who acknowledge that it must be an extension of collective bargaining and not merely a substitute for or usurper of the function of joint wages determination. In the final analysis, however, the future of minimum wage standards will rely not upon the influence of collective bargaining or the regulation of labour law but upon the dictation of economic policy. The interrelationship between collective bargaining, labour law and economic policy is next considered.

ECONOMIC POLICY AND COLLECTIVE BARGAINING LAW

The major economic concerns of governments, at least until 1979, were the maintenance of high levels of employment and the control of inflation. The wage-push inflationary effects of collective bargaining periodically threatened the balance of these objectives. Economic policy attempted to neutralise these effects through various policies of incomes control which became, in Davies's analysis (1983:419), 'a more or less permanent feature' of the British economy in the 1960s and 1970s. In so far as incomes policies restrained pay they were a form of state interventionism in collective bargaining. Apart from the periods 1966–9 and 1972–3, however, when incomes policy rested upon a statutory basis and relied ultimately upon sanctions of criminal law,[17] economic policy has been generally associated with voluntary restraint rather than with legal control. As Wedderburn (1984:73–7) observed, even statutory forms of incomes policy have been isolated from 'traditional' labour law, at least in the sense that the trade union immunities, the auxiliary legislation and the autonomy of the contract of employment remained undisturbed. But Davies and Freedland (1983:6– 7) have argued, echoing Kahn-Freund (1968:19), that as an encroachment 'directly upon the autonomy of collective bargaining and the whole voluntarist stance', incomes policy has 'gone to the heart of labour law'. In Lewis's words (1983:369), incomes policy and industrial relations reform can be seen 'as two sides of the same coin'.

Whatever the merits of that argument, the experience of incomes policies points to their transient nature and their ultimate failure to 'obliterate the fundamental market (and bargaining) forces leading to pressure for higher pay' (Crouch, 1982:55). It is the recognition of this, perhaps, which informs the economic policy in the 1980s. During the previous two decades incomes policy generally sought to place a ceiling upon the level of wage settlements and established machinery or made provision for the adjustment of anomalies which the policy inevitably created. The auxiliary devices of labour law which underpinned collective bargaining constituted exceptions to incomes policies and employers and unions frequently used such devices to circumvent wage restraints. The repeal of Sch.11 and the fair wages instruments can be partly explained as a reaction to such tactics. In the 1980s, however, incomes policy assumes a different guise. In the public sector, cash limits serve as a wage-deflation mechanism without the need to provide statutory or administrative enforcement procedures (Pliatzky, 1982; Winchester, 1983:168–76). Furthermore, throughout the whole economy, as Wedderburn (1984) has argued, the major thrust of wage-inflation control is felt through a combination of legal restriction and the release of free market forces producing a readjustment of the bargaining strength of the collective parties. The restrictive provisions of the EAs 1980–82 and the TUA curtail the legal freedom of trade unions to deploy industrial tactics in support of bargaining and thus weaken their negotiating position. The commitment to maintain high levels of employment is abandoned, unleashing the uncontrolled vagaries of the labour market to exercise a regulating influence upon pay bargaining. For Davies and Freedland (1983:9) the centre of gravity in incomes policy is moved from 'the level of the collectively agreed settlement' to the 'prior level of the ability of unions to apply the sort of pressure that is likely to result in a high level of settlement'.

The burden of this chapter has been to expand upon the 'footnotes' to collective bargaining by describing the various ways in which labour law

---

[17] Prices and Incomes Act 1966; Counter-Inflation (Temporary Provisions) Act 1972 and Counter-Inflation Act 1973.

impinges upon the structure and process of joint regulation. For the best part of this century, so long as public policy was favourable to the development and extension of collective bargaining, the role of labour law has been to nurture and to sustain the principle of joint regulation in industrial relations. If this role has been a selective one, this underscores the fact that there are other forces — economic, social and political — at work in industrial society which are more powerful and influential than law. Students of labour law come to recognise at first hand that law is but a tool of policy and that the 'legal regulation' of collective bargaining is shaped and directed by the wider considerations of socio-economic policy. The relationship between collective bargaining and the law is not a constant and its values are derived from the prevailing policies of state and government. At least until the 1970s that relationship rested upon a political consensus which advanced, or at least did not disturb, the liberal-collectivist values of voluntary collective bargaining. The labour legislation of the 1970s did not abandon those values although it did represent a readjustment of the relationship between collective bargaining and the law (cf. Crouch, 1977 and 1982; Clark and Wedderburn, 1983; Lewis, 1983). In the 1980s, however, a new era of restriction and radicalism has replaced the political consensus and traditional values of the voluntary system and anticipates a new role for legal regulation, challenging the autonomy of collective bargaining. In this new role labour law is recruited to the service of economic policy while the die of industrial relations policy is recast.

Bibliography

Aaron, B. 1982. 'Settlement of Disputes over Rights'. *Comparative Labour Law and Industrial Relations*. Ed. R. Blanpain. Deventer: Kluwer, 260–79.

Advisory, Conciliation and Arbitration Service (ACAS). 1978a. *Button Manufacturing Wages Council*. Report 11. London: ACAS.

——. 1978b. *Toy Manufacturing Wages Council*. Report 13. London: ACAS.

——. 1980a. *Annual Report 1979*. London: ACAS.

——. 1980b. *Licensed Residential Establishment and Licensed Restaurant Wages Council*. Report 18. London: ACAS.

——. 1980c. *The Contract Cleaning Industry*. Report 20. London: ACAS.

Anderman, S.D. 1975. 'The "Status Quo" Issue and Industrial Disputes Procedures: Some Implications for Labour Law'. *Industrial Law Journal*, 15 (September), 131–54.

Armstrong, Eric, and Rosemary Lucas. 1984. 'The Advisory Function of ACAS: A Preliminary Appraisal of the Advisory Visit'. *Industrial Relations Journal*, 15 (Spring), 17–28.

Batstone, Eric. 1984. *Working Order: Workplace Industrial Relations over Two Decades*. Oxford: Blackwell.

Bayliss, F.J. 1962. *British Wages Councils*. Oxford: Blackwell.

Beaumont, P.B. 1977. 'Experience under the Fair Wages Resolution of 1946'. *Industrial Relations Journal*, 8 (Autumn), 24–42.

——. 1979a. 'The Limits of Inspection'. *Public Administration*, 57 (Summer), 203–17.

——. 1979b. 'Research Note: Union–Management Collusion and Schedule 11 Awards'. *Industrial Relations Journal*, 10 (Spring), 66–8.

Bercusson, Brian. 1976. 'The New Fair Wages Policy: Schedule 11 to the Employment Protection Act'. *Industrial Law Journal*, 5 (September), 129–47.

——. 1978. *Fair Wages Resolutions*. London: Mansell.

Bissett, L., and E. MacLennan. 1984. 'Britain's Minimum Wage System: The Wages Councils'. *Policies Against Low Pay: An International Perspective*. Ed. F. Field. London: Policy Studies Institute, 15–33.

Bourn, Colin. 1979. 'Statutory Exemptions for Collective Agreements'. *Industrial Law Journal*, 8 (June), 85–99.

Brown, William. 1972. 'A Consideration of "Custom and Practice"'. *British Journal of Industrial Relations*, 10 (March), 42–61.

—— (ed.). 1981. *The Changing Contours of British Industrial Relations: A Survey of Manufacturing Industry*. Oxford: Blackwell.

Byrne, Dominic. 1983. *Making Ends Meet: Working for Low Wages in the Civil Service*. Low Pay Pamphlet no. 26. London: Low Pay Unit.

Central Arbitration Committee (CAC). 1979. *Annual Report 1978*. London: CAC.

Clark, Jon, and *Lord* Wedderburn. 1983. 'Modern Labour Law: Problems, Functions and Policies'. *Labour Law and Industrial Relations: Building on Kahn-*

Freund. Eds. *Lord* Wedderburn, R. Lewis and J. Clark. Oxford: Clarendon Press, 127–242.

Clegg, H.A. 1975. 'Pluralism in Industrial Relations'. *British Journal of Industrial Relations*, 13 (November), 309–16.

——. 1976. *Trade Unionism Under Collective Bargaining: A Theory Based on Comparisons of Six Countries*. Oxford: Blackwell.

——. 1983. 'Otto Kahn-Freund and British Industrial Relations'. *Labour Law and Industrial Relations: Building on Kahn-Freund*. Eds. *Lord* Wedderburn, R. Lewis and J. Clark. Oxford: Clarendon Press, 14–28.

Conservative Party. 1968. *Fair Deal at Work: The Conservative Approach to Modern Industrial Relations*. London: Conservative Political Centre.

Cordova, Efren. 1978. 'A Comparative View of Collective Bargaining in Industrialised Countries'. *International Labour Review*, 117 (July–August), 423–39.

——. 1982. 'Collective Bargaining'. *Comparative Labour Law and Industrial Relations*. Ed. R. Blanpain. Deventer: Kluwer, 220–42.

Craig, C., J. Rubery, R. Tarling and F. Wilkinson. 1982. *Labour Market Structure, Industrial Organisation and Low Pay*. Cambridge: Cambridge University Press.

Crouch, Colin. 1977. *Class Conflict and the Industrial Relations Crisis: Compromise and Corporatism in the Policies of the British State*. London: Heinemann.

——. 1982. *The Politics of Industrial Relations*. 2nd edn. London: Fontana.

Daniel, W.W., and N. Millward. 1983. *Workplace Industrial Relations in Britain: The DE/PSI/ESRC Survey*. London: Heinemann.

Davies, Paul, and Mark Freedland. 1982. *The Transfer of Undertakings (Protection of Employment) Regulations with Annotations*. London: Sweet & Maxwell.

——, and M. Freedland. 1983. 'Editors' Introduction'. *Labour and the Law*. O. Kahn-Freund. 3rd edn. London: Stevens, 1–11.

——, and M. Freedland. 1984. *Labour Law: Text and Materials*. 2nd edn. London: Weidenfeld & Nicolson.

Davies, R.J. 1983. 'Incomes and Anti-Inflation Policy'. *Industrial Relations in Britain*. Ed. G.S. Bain. Oxford: Blackwell, 419–52.

Dennison, S.R. 1984. 'Economics Without Prices: A Critique of the Low Pay Unit'. *Low Pay or No Pay? A Review of the Theory and Practice of Minimum-Wage Laws*. Ed. D. Forrest. Hobart Paper no. 101. London: Institute of Economic Affairs, 61–86.

Department of Employment (DE). 1981. *Trade Union Immunities*. Cmnd 8128. London: HMSO.

——. 1983. *Democracy in Trade Unions*. Cmnd 8778. London: HMSO.

——. 1984. 'Statutory Wage Regulation in 1983'. *Employment Gazette*, 92 (October), 451–2.

——. 1985. *Consultative Paper on Wages Councils*. London: DE.

Department of Employment and Productivity (DEP). 1969. *In Place of Strife: A Policy for Industrial Relations*. Cmnd 3888. London: HMSO.

Dickens, L., M. Hart, M. Jones and B. Weekes. 1979. 'A Response to the Government Working Papers on Amendments to Employment Protection Legislation'. Discussion Paper. Coventry: SSRC Industrial Relations Research Unit, University of Warwick.

Donovan. 1968. Royal Commission on Trade Unions and Employers' Associations 1965–1968. *Report*. Cmnd 3623. London: HMSO.

Dubin, R. 1954. 'Constructive Aspects of Industrial Conflict'. *Industrial Conflict*. Eds. A. Kornhauser, R. Dubin and A.M. Ross. New York: McGraw-Hill, 37–47.

Eccles, Mary. 1984. 'Minimum Wage Policy in the United States'. *Policies Against Low Pay: An International Perspective*. Ed. F. Field. London: Policy Studies Institute, 67–95.

Edwards, P.K. 1983. 'The Pattern of Collective Industrial Action'. *Industrial Relations in Britain*. Ed. G.S. Bain. Oxford: Blackwell, 209–34.

Field, Frank (ed.). 1984a. *Policies Against Low Pay: An International Perspective*. London: Policy Studies Institute.

——. 1984b. *The Minimum Wage: Its Potential and Dangers*. London: Policy Studies Institute/Heinemann.

Flanders, Allan D. 1965. *Industrial Relations: What is Wrong with the System?* London: Faber.

——. 1967. *Collective Bargaining: Prescription for Change*. London: Faber.

——. 1970a. *Management and Unions: The Theory and Reform of Industrial Relations*. London: Faber.

——. 1970b. 'Collective Bargaining: A Theoretical Analysis'. *Management and Unions*, 213–40.

——. 1974. 'The Tradition of Voluntarism'. *British Journal of Industrial Relations*, 12 (November), 352–70.

Forrest, David (ed.). 1984. *Low Pay or No Pay? A Review of the Theory and Practice of Minimum-Wage Laws*. Hobart Paper no. 101. London: Institute of Economic Affairs.

Fox, Alan. 1966. *Industrial Sociology and Industrial Relations*. Research Paper 3, Royal Commission on Trade Unions and Employers' Associations. London: HMSO.

——. 1973. 'Industrial Relations: A Social Critique of Pluralist Ideology'. *Man and Organisation*. Ed. J. Child. London: Allen & Unwin, 185–234.

——. 1974. *Beyond Contract: Work, Power and Trust Relations*. London: Faber.

——, and A.D. Flanders. 1969. 'The Reform of Collective Bargaining: From Donovan to Durkheim'. *British Journal of Industrial Relations*, 7 (July) 151–74.

Giugni, Gino. 1972. 'The Peace Obligation'. *Industrial Conflict: A Comparative Legal Survey*. Eds. B. Aaron and K.W. Wedderburn. London: Longman, 127–74.

Goldman, A. 1982. 'Settlement of Disputes over Interests'. *Comparative Labour Law and Industrial Relations*. Ed. R. Blanpain. Deventer: Kluwer, 280–97.

Hayek, F.A. 1984. *1980s Unemployment and the Unions*. 2nd edn. London: Institute of Economic Affairs.

Heald, D.A. 1983. *Public Expenditure: Its Defence and Reform*. Oxford: Martin Robertson.

——, and G.S. Morris. 1984. 'Why Public Sector Unions are on the Defensive'. *Personnel Management*, 16 (May), 30–34.

Hepple, B.A. 1970. 'Intention to Create Legal Relations'. *Cambridge Law Journal*, 28 (April), 122–37.

——. 1982. 'The Transfer of Undertakings (Protection of Employment) Regulations'. *Industrial Law Journal*, 11 (March), 29–40.

Hyman, Richard. 1972. *Disputes Procedure in Action*. London: Heinemann.

——. 1978. 'Pluralism, Procedural Consensus and Collective Bargaining'. *British Journal of Industrial Relations*, 16 (March), 16–40.

Industrial Relations Services (IRS). 1983. 'Wages Councils 2: Views on Reform'. *Industrial Relations Review and Report*, no. 290 (February), 8–15.

——. 1985. 'Fair Wages Clauses'. *Industrial Relations Review and Report*, no. 342 (April), 2–6.

International Labour Office (ILO). 1978. *Collective Bargaining in Industrialised Countries*. Labour-Management Relations Series no. 5. Geneva: ILO.

Jones, Michael. 1980. 'CAC and Schedule 11: The Experience of Two Years'. *Industrial Law Journal*, 9 (March), 28–44.

Kahn-Freund, Otto. 1948. 'Legislation through Adjudication: The Legal Aspect of Fair Wages Clauses and Recognised Conditions'. *Modern Law Review*, 11 (July),

269–89 and (October), 429–48.

——. 1954a. 'Intergroup Conflicts and their Settlement'. *British Journal of Sociology*, 5 (September), 193–227.

——. 1954b. 'Legal Framework'. *The System of Industrial Relations in Great Britain*. Eds. A.D. Flanders and H.A. Clegg. Oxford: Blackwell, 42–127.

——. 1959. 'Labour Law'. *Law and Opinion in England in the 20th Century*. Ed. M. Ginsberg. London: Stevens, 215–63.

——. 1968. *Labour Law: Old Traditions and New Developments*. Toronto: Clark, Irwin.

——. 1972. *Labour and the Law*. London: Stevens.

——. 1974. 'On Uses and Misuses of Comparative Law'. *Modern Law Review*, 27 (January), 1–27.

——. 1977. *Labour and the Law*. 2nd edn. London: Stevens.

——. 1983. *Labour and the Law*. 3rd edn. Ed. and intr. by Paul Davies and Mark Freedland. London: Stevens.

Kessler, Sid. 1980. 'The Prevention and Settlement of Collective Labour Disputes in the United Kingdom'. *Industrial Relations Journal*, 11 (March-April), 5–31.

Latta, Geoff. 1974. 'The Legal Extension of Collective Bargaining: A Study of Section 8 of the Terms and Conditions of Employment Act 1959'. *Industrial Law Journal*, 3 (December), 215–33.

Lewis, Roy. 1970. 'The Legal Enforceability of Collective Agreements'. *British Journal of Industrial Relations*, 8 (November), 313–33.

——. 1976. 'The Historical Development of Labour Law'. *British Journal of Industrial Relations*, 14 (March), 1–17.

——. 1979a. 'Collective Agreements: The Kahn-Freund Legacy'. *Modern Law Review*, 42 (November), 613–22.

——. 1979b. 'Kahn-Freund and Labour Law: An Outline Critique'. *Industrial Law Journal*, 8 (December), 202–21.

——. 1983. 'Collective Labour Law'. *Industrial Relations in Britain*. Ed. G.S. Bain. Oxford: Blackwell, 361–92.

——, and Bob Simpson. 1981. *Striking a Balance? Employment Law after the 1980 Act*. Oxford: Martin Robertson.

Low Pay Unit. 1983. *Who Needs the Wages Councils?* Low Pay Pamphlet no. 24. London: Low Pay Unit.

Macdonald, Duncan. 1984. 'Minimum Wage Policy in Australia'. *Policies Against Low Pay: An International Perspective*. Ed. F. Field. London: Policy Studies Institute, 107–34.

Palmer, Gill. 1983. *British Industrial Relations*. London: Allen & Unwin.

Pliatzky, Leo. 1982. 'Cash Limits and Pay Policy'. *Political Quarterly*, 53 (January–March), 16–23.

Pond, Chris. 1983. 'Wages Councils, the Unorganised and the Low Paid'. *Industrial Relations in Britain*. Ed. G.S. Bain. Oxford: Blackwell, 179–208.

——. 1984. 'Selective, Industry-Based Minimum Wages: The Experience of the United Kingdom and Ireland'. *Policies Against Low Pay: An International Perspective*. Ed. F. Field. London: Policy Studies Institute, 44–62.

——, and Steve Winyard. 1983. *The Case for a National Minimum Wage*. Low Pay Pamphlet no. 23. London: Low Pay Unit.

Sandoval, Veronique. 1984. 'Minimum Wage Policy in France'. *Policies Against Low Pay: An International Perspective*. Ed. F. Field. London: Policy Studies Institute, 96–106.

Sisson, Keith, and William Brown. 1983. 'Industrial Relations in the Private Sector: Donovan Re-visited'. *Industrial Relations in Britain*. Ed. G.S. Bain. Oxford: Blackwell, 137–54.

Starr, Gerald. 1981a. *Minimum Wage Fixing: An International Review of Practices and Problems*. Geneva: International Labour Office.

——. 1981b. 'Minimum Wage Fixing: International Experience with Alternative Roles'. *International Labour Review*, 120 (September–October), 545–62.

Steele, R. 1979. 'The Relative Performance of the Wages Council and Non-Wages Council Sectors and the Impact of Incomes Policy'. *British Journal of Industrial Relations*, 17 (July), 224–34.

Thomson, A.W.J., and S. Engleman. 1975. *The Industrial Relations Act: A Review and Analysis*. London: Martin Robertson.

——, and V.V. Murray. 1976. *Grievance Procedures*. Farnborough: Saxon House.

Wedderburn, K.W. (*Lord*). 1971. *The Worker and the Law*. 2nd edn. Harmondsworth: Penguin.

——. 1972. 'Labour Law and Labour Relations in Britain'. *British Journal of Industrial Relations*, 10 (July), 270–90.

——. 1978. 'The New Structure of Labour Law in Britain'. *Israel Law Review*, 13 (October), 435–58.

——. 1980. 'Industrial Relations and the Courts'. *Industrial Law Journal*, 9 (June), 65–94.

——. 1983. 'Otto Kahn-Freund and British Labour Law'. *Labour Law and Industrial Relations: Building on Kahn-Freund*. Eds. *Lord* Wedderburn, R. Lewis and J. Clark. Oxford: Clarendon Press, 29–80.

——. 1984. 'Labour Law Now: A Hold and a Nudge'. *Industrial Law Journal*, 13 (June), 73–85.

Weekes, B., M. Mellish, L. Dickens and J. Lloyd. 1975. *Industrial Relations and the Limits of Law: The Industrial Effects of the Industrial Relations Act, 1971*. Oxford: Blackwell.

Whelan, J.C. 1982. 'On Uses and Misuses of Comparative Labour Law: A Case Study'. *Modern Law Review*, 45 (May), 285–300.

Wilson, Andrew. 1984. 'Contract and Prerogative: A Reconsideration of the Legal Enforcement of Collective Agreements'. *Industrial Law Journal*, 13 (March), 1–24.

Winchester, David. 1983. 'Industrial Relations in the Public Sector'. *Industrial Relations in Britain*. Ed. G.S. Bain. Oxford: Blackwell, 155–78.

Winyard, Steve. 1982. *Fair Remuneration?*. Low Pay Report no. 11. London: Low Pay Unit.

Wood, Penny. 1978. 'The Central Arbitration Committee's Approach to Schedule 11 to the Employment Protection Act 1975 and the Fair Wages Resolution 1946'. *Industrial Law Journal*, 7 (June), 65–83.

5 Workers, Corporate Enterprise and the Law

Brian Bercusson

This chapter examines some central doctrines of company law which have important implications for workers and for employment relations. A few provisions of company law explicitly purport to recognise and provide for the interests of employees in their company, and these will be examined, along with proposals which seek to reshape the company in order to enhance the position of its employees. Labour law also occasionally and to a limited extent recognises the special position of employers who adopt the corporate form, and the problems posed by companies for labour law are explored. The concluding section assesses the potential of labour law and company law to accommodate the position of workers where their employer is a company.

COMPANY LAW DOCTRINES

Collective Capital as a Separate Legal Person

The company is a separate legal entity, but not a human being. It may be allowed to engage in activities or have rights or obligations as if it was a human being. But decisions as to what a company may or may not do are made using the analogy with human persons. So a company is spoken of as an artificial person and is said to have a legal personality. This means that it is a legal entity separate from those who own it (shareholders), work for it (employees), run it (directors and senior management), and do business with it (customers and suppliers).

A key question is how the law should treat these artificial entities. This is, as Wedderburn (1965:71) has said, 'a serious and fundamental decision of policy, a judgment of value that cannot be derived from the nature of things'. Should the duties of companies towards their employees, the consumers of their products and services, and the community at large be extended? Should they — as Pickering (1968:510) has asked — be the same or different from those of any other employer, producer or association? The questions of policy implicit in the existence of companies cannot be avoided.

The company is a 'person' which comes into existence when certain formalities required by the Companies Act 1985 (CA) have been completed.[1] Thus various documents have to be deposited with the Registrar of Companies, notably, the memorandum of association setting out, among other things, the name, capital and objects of the company (CA s.2), and, normally, the articles of association which describe the company's constitution, for example, the functions and powers of the shareholders' meeting, the board of directors, and so on.[2] When the requisite procedures have been complied with, the new legal person, the company, can do many of the things people can do — own property, employ workers, buy and sell goods.

The company is thus a convenient device available to owners of capital who wish to combine some of their property in a business venture. Instead of the business being owned directly and jointly by each and all of the participants, the law allows for the creation of an abstract entity, the company. Each of the participants has a share (or shares) in the company, but they are distanced at one remove from the operation of the business.

The rule that a company is a separate legal entity was settled firmly by the House of Lords in *Salomon v Salomon & Co.*, where creditors were not allowed to claim payment from the owner of 99 per cent of the shares in a company which went bankrupt.[3] A modern illustration is a case where a Mr Lee formed a company to carry on his business of spreading fertilisers from the air. Lee held 2,999 of its 3,000 shares and was by its articles of association appointed sole governing director. One of his first acts was to employ himself at a salary as the company's chief pilot. He was killed in a crash while flying for the company. If he was an employee, then his widow was entitled to be paid compensation by his employer. A lower court ruled that Lee could not be an employee when he was in effect also the employer. But the Privy Council allowed the appeal. Lord Morris held that the 'relationship came about because the deceased as one legal person was willing to work for and to make a contract with the company which was another legal entity.[4]

This legal creation of a collective united entity of capital with many of the rights and powers of human beings affects the balance of power between employer and employee. Workers in the UK are given no equivalent legal status as a collectivity within the business enterprise. Contrast may be made with legally recognised and supported company works councils in the Federal Republic of Germany (Richardi, 1982:34; Streeck, 1984:23) and enterprise committees in France (Forde, 1984:149; Glendon, 1984:462).

This notion of a non-human entity which owns and operates the business using the labour of its employees and the capital of its shareholders is

---

[1]   The CA 1985 consolidated the earlier company law provisions including those of particular relevance to this chapter – Companies Acts 1948, 1967, 1976 and 1980. References in this chapter are to the 1985 Act, except where the context requires mention of the previous Acts.

[2]   Table A of the First Sch. to the Companies Act 1948 was a model of a company's articles of association. See now its replacement in Table A of the Companies (Tables A-F) Regulations SI 1985 No. 805.

[3]   [1897] AC 22, HL.

[4]   *Lee v Lee's Air Farming Ltd* [1961] AC 12, at 25, PC. The exceptional cases where the corporate 'veil' is lifted are described in Gower (1979:112).

company law's contribution to societal alienation. The worker does not work for some human person, and certainly not for himself. The shareholders are removed from the production process and share ownership may become a matter of financial speculation.[5] Managers run the business but are themselves only appointed to work on behalf of the company's shareholders, a 'psychologically peculiar position' in a capitalist society where people work for their own wealth (Beck, 1973:197).

The company is the vehicle by which the law gives recognition to collective capital. This recognition is, in theory, subject to rules and regulations provided in common law, the Companies Act, and other legislation. But a sharp contrast exists between the theory of the company as an organisation of capital controlled by legal rules and the reality of owners of capital shaping the company to fit their own purposes.

For example, the CA s.2(1)(c) requires the company's memorandum of association to set out the objects (vires) of the company. At common law the business activities of the company must fall within the stated objects, otherwise they are ultra vires and have no legal effect. In theory, therefore, the legal capacity of the company is publicly stated and limited. In practice most modern company memoranda are drawn so widely, and the number of objects specified has so proliferated, that a company can carry on any business it likes within the extremely wide boundaries set by the shareholders. It has even become common to include a general discretionary clause which provides that the company may carry on any activities which its directors consider may be profitably combined with its existing operations.[6]

Another illustration of ownership flexibility is the law concerning the constitution of the company. The articles of association regulate the affairs of the company — external as regards business activity, internal as regards corporate governance. Despite the legislative policy recommending what was Table A of Sch.1 to the Companies Act 1948 as a model constitution,[7] the company can easily exclude this model by express words to that effect in its articles. The contents of the articles of different companies can thus vary substantially. An illustration of the extreme flexibility allowed and the lack of effective controls is the case of *Bushell v Faith*.[8] The CA s.303(1) provides that 'a company may by ordinary resolution (requiring a simple majority of shareholders) remove a director before the expiration of his period of office, notwithstanding anything in its articles or in any agreement between it and him'. The company in this case had articles which provided that in any motion for the removal of a director, shares held by that director should carry three votes per share. This effectively enabled the directors to outvote the other shareholders. The majority of the House of Lords held that there was nothing to prevent the creation of multiple voting rights for this purpose.

---

[5] Cf. the attempt to distinguish 'legitimate investments (in companies) from illegitimate wagers' in Gower (1984:para.4.04).

[6] Such a clause was upheld as valid in *Bell Houses Ltd v City Wall Properties Ltd* [1966] 2 QB 656. See the critical notes by Wedderburn (1966; 1983).

[7] See note 2.

[8] [1970] AC 1099, HL; but see the dissenting opinion of Lord Morris.

This flexibility allowed by law to organisations of capital contrasts with the increasing legal intervention in the internal affairs of trade unions (see Chapters 10 and 11). Furthermore, examples of such company law restrictions on flexibility as do exist protect mainly minority shareholders (CA s.459), investors (CA s.67), creditors (CA s.630), and officers of the company (the common law rules precluding shareholders interfering with the functions of the board of directors, as reflected in the model articles of association: Art. 70 of the new Table A). The interests of workers in a company would seem to require some restraint on the flexibility of capital owners to engage in or change to any business activity the company chooses, or to organise the company's internal administration and government with little regard to employees' interests let alone any form of democratic control. Hence the Bullock Report (1977:78–83) proposed that the board of directors (including worker directors) should have the exclusive and non-delegable power to propose changes in the company's memorandum and articles of association. The limited ways in which company law does seek to take workers' interests into account are examined below. In practice, however, workers' influence over capital comes not from company law, but from the power of autonomous workers' organisations.

Corporate Government

The gap between the theory and practice of company law looms large in the area of corporate government. The company's governing structure in theory takes the form of a pyramid, with shareholders at the base electing a board of directors which in turn appoints the managing director. The shareholders' meeting has the formal power to remove directors, to direct them to take certain decisions, to alter the objects of the company, and so on. Reality, however, as Prentice (1978:277–8) notes:

> belies this theory and, in the large public company, the shareholders, except perhaps in a crisis situation, do not exercise any meaningful ownership powers ... The underlying reasons for this shareholder apathy are, of course, not difficult to unearth: (i) holdings are widely dispersed, something which makes concerted shareholder action difficult; (ii) shareholders are relatively ignorant and on the whole lack the necessary skills and aptitudes to scrutinize management performance; (iii) management enjoys liberal access to corporate proxy machinery while the access of shareholders is limited and, unless the company decides otherwise, expensive; (iv) shareholders who are discontented with corporate management will vote with their feet and sell their shares; (v) lastly, a lack of active shareholder involvement in corporate affairs may possibly be explained on the ground that, on the whole, directors manage companies in the economic interests of the shareholders.

Many of these points do not apply, of course, where share ownership is centralised, and the trend in share ownership in the UK has been towards the accumulation of a large proportion of shareholdings in institutional hands. Combined institutional investors increased their equity market share from 17.9 per cent in 1957 to 54.1 per cent in 1981, and are acquiring about 2 per cent of the equity market in the UK each year — by the turn of the century it is estimated they will hold 69–84 per cent. Such proportions are more than adequate to ensure de facto control and even de jure control (50 per cent plus) over companies. Yet a recent review concludes that 'there is little evidence that such power has been exercised in any significant way' (Farrar and Russell, 1984:108). Institutional investors seek maximum investment performance, but their attitude to decision-making in the company is one of abstention. If things go wrong their response is not to intervene but to sell out. So institutional shareholding does not seem to have altered the disengagement of shareholders from control of companies.

More significantly, even where the institutions do take a more active role, their institutional structures provide a barrier to democratic control. The insured person and the employee in a pension scheme have — as explained below in Chapter 14 — virtually no control over the investments of the insurance company or the pension fund manager. Unit or investment trust holders and bank customers similarly have little or no influence over portfolios. 'The dominant issue (as stated by Farrar and Russell (1984:115)) is control of portfolio companies. Who is to control them and who is to control the controllers?

If shareholders do not control the company, who does? The answer to the question depends on the type of economic unit which has assumed the legal form of a company. For example, Hadden (1977:41) distinguishes the small private business in which the proprietors are all directly involved in the day-to-day management of the business; the larger family company in which there is a clear separation between the interests of internal directors and managers and external shareholders; and the quoted public company in which there is a greater degree of public participation through the stock market system. Control in each of these companies is very differently structured, and in the last category there is a wide variety of decision-making structures.

A study of corporate power in the United States developed a concept of 'strategic position' — the occupancy of top positions in large companies with diffused ownership — as the basis of control of the corporation. Top managers (some of whom are usually also company directors), by virtue of their 'authority and dominance over day-to-day operations, the disposition of company resources, and the planning and long-term decisions of the company' have effective power. This includes control over the selection of the board and over decision-making, reinforced by the use of proxy machinery to harness the diffused voting power of shareholders to management objectives (Herman, 1982:28).

The Bullock Committee was well aware of the directors' usurpation of shareholders' functions, and also of the further development of the power of senior management. It treated senior management almost as if it were in effect an organ of corporate government, though company law does not recognise any such organ as separate from the board. Proposals to put worker directors on the board are much affected by the division of functions between the board and senior management. The tendency of company boards today, especially in large companies, to become in practice passive supervisory instruments (whatever their superior status in law) would serve to diminish the power of worker directors.

The significance of the question of corporate control for industrial relations is that neither in the legal model nor in practical reality do workers intrude as participants in corporate government. The problem of grappling with company law concepts of corporate government, while recognising that these concepts do not reflect the reality of power within the company, is a major difficulty for those whose aim is workers' participation within corporate structures. Other attempts to control corporate decision-making have recognised these limitations, the most important of which are, as Hadden (1983:5) argues, 'the very great flexibility which large groups are permitted in the organisation of their affairs and the extent to which their formal legal structures differ from their practical managerial organisation'. The involvement of workers in corporate government requires the updating of company law's conceptual equipment to accord with reality, though other difficulties of inserting workers into the corporate framework would remain.

The legal concept of a member of or shareholder in a company can be contrasted with that of an employee of the company. Shareholders or members of the company are defined as persons who have agreed to be registered as members (CA s.22), the register giving particulars of the shares held by each member (CA s.352). Company law deals in detail with the rights and responsibilities attached to membership of the company: voting rights, dividends, transfers, procedure of shareholders' meetings, control of directors and other officers, special protection for minority shareholders, and so on. These provisions relate to a person who has either initially put some capital into the company, or subsequently purchased, been given or inherited shares. The shareholders' active contact with the business activity carried on by the company is usually limited to receiving information and dividends where paid. Exceptionally, the shareholder may take part in a meeting, but usually only to vote and not to take any initiative relating to the company's activity.

Employees of the company are not treated at all in like manner by company law. Such provisions as exist are exceptional. In company law the employee is an outsider — a contract worker — in contrast to the shareholder who is an insider-member. The worker's only legal relation to the company is through a contract of employment whereby he provides labour for a wage. He is just another and, individually, a very minor creditor. In short, company law regards as an outsider someone who may have worked a lifetime for a company and is an integral part of its activities, while it regards as an insider with the rights and powers of a member someone who has perhaps picked up a few shares without any other involvement. Hence the arguments for reform.

WORKERS AND COMPANY LAW

Despite its fundamental doctrines excluding workers from consideration, company law includes some provisions referring specifically to employees of the company. An example of exceptional provision is the preferential right granted to employees as creditors of an insolvent company. Where a company is wound up, unpaid wages owing during the previous four months (up to a maximum of £800) are to be paid in priority to debts owed to many other (but not all) creditors (CA s.614, Sch.19, para.9). 'Wages' include amounts owed as statutory guarantee payments, remuneration on suspension on medical grounds, payment for time off, statutory sick pay, and remuneration under a protective award for failure to consult over redundancy (CA Sch.19, para.11).[9]

Another example is that companies are normally prohibited from giving financial assistance towards the purchase of their own shares, but this does not apply to money used in connection with an employees' share scheme (CA ss.151(1), 153(4)(b)). Statutory provisions contain incentives for companies to make their employees shareholders (Finance Acts 1978 Sch.9; 1980 s.84; 1984 Sch.10). For the most part these provisions have merely enabled some groups of managers to buy out their companies. One major obstacle to genuine work-force buy-outs is in the guidelines issued by the investment protection committees of the pension fund managers and insurance companies. These stipulate that companies in which the institutions are investors should not allocate to their employees in any one year more than 5 per cent of pre-tax profits or an aggregate of shares in excess of 1 per cent of their issued share capital under an approved scheme. Oakeshott (1985:41) states of these guidelines that 'they do not have the force of law. But companies which break them clearly expose themselves to the risk of institutional disinvestment'.[10]

Disclosure of Information

Various provisions in company law require that certain information of interest to employees should be disclosed in company reports. Directors' annual reports must state the average weekly number of employees and the annual amount of their wages (CA s.261(6), Sch.10, paras.5–8). Particulars in the company's accounts are required of employees receiving more than £30,000 a year (CA s.231 and Sch.5, para.35). The HSWA s.79 amended the Companies Act 1967 s.16 (now CA Sch.7, para.10) to require that specified companies disclose information about arrangements for securing the health, safety and welfare of employees, a provision which may be activated under CA s.235(5) but has not been. Companies employing on average 250 employees throughout the year must disclose in the directors' report

9   Employees of *all* employers, not only companies, are entitled to some protection of wages and some other benefits in the event of insolvency of their employer by virtue of EPCA ss.121–7. As to maternity pay, see EPCA s.40(1)(b). See generally Davies and Freedland (1980).

10   Cf. in Sweden, under the so-called Meidner Plan for allocating company profits to wage-earner funds under trade union control to purchase shares in companies, it was estimated that it would take about thirty-six years to accumulate a majority holding in a company, assuming an allocation of 20 per cent of a pre-tax rate of return on equity averaging 10 per cent (Martin, 1984:278).

information as to the steps taken towards employee involvement (for example, as regards provision of information, consultation, and share schemes (CA Sch.7, para.11). This miscellany of provisions in company law does not as yet approach the relative comprehensiveness of the obligations in labour law of employers (including companies) to disclose to representatives of recognised trade unions information for collective bargaining purposes (EPA 1975 s.17), or that connected with proposed redundancies (EPA s.99), or that relating to transfers of all or part of the undertaking (Transfer of Undertakings (Protection of Employment) Regulations 1981 reg.10).

Encouragement of a more comprehensive disclosure of information by companies to employees is found in the draft European Communities (EC) Directive on procedures for informing and consulting employees (the Vredeling Directive) first published in 1980.[11] The draft Directive proposes that the head offices of companies should be required to inform and consult employees in subsidiaries or separate establishments through local management. Undertakings employing a thousand or more workers in more than one establishment are covered. The provisions on disclosure of information state that the parent undertaking is required to furnish annually to each of its subsidiaries general information as to the activities of the group as a whole and specific information on the activity of the subsidiary. Matters relating to the undertaking's structure include the economic and financial situation, the probable development of the business and of production and sales, the employment situation and probable trends, and investment prospects. The management of the subsidiaries receiving this information is obliged to communicate it to employee representatives 'without delay', and further to provide oral explanation if the representatives so request. Failure by local management to do so allows for the 'by-pass' provision whereby employee representatives make their request in writing to the parent undertaking.

The provisions concerning consultation require the management of the parent company to communicate 'precise' information to managements of subsidiaries when there is a decision to be made 'concerning the whole or a major part of the parent undertaking or of a subsidiary in the Community which [decision] is liable to have serious consequences for the interests of the employees of its subsidiaries in the Community' (Art.4(1) of the revised draft Directive). Local management must communicate this information to employee representatives, who then have thirty days to express opinions and hold consultations with local management 'with a view to attempting to reach agreement on the measures planned in respect of employees'.

The substance of the draft Directive raises a host of issues and problems (see IRRR, 1984). One problem, however, illustrates the difficulties which company structures pose for workers and their organisations, namely, the growth of 'groups' of companies. As Hadden (1983:1–2) explains:

---

[11] Draft Directive on Employee Information and Consultation Procedures (OJ C297/3, 15.11.80). The draft Directive was subsequently revised (OJ C217/3, 12.8.83) and forwarded for consideration to the Council of Ministers.

The complex corporate group is now the typical form of business organisation. The largest commercial and industrial companies in the west have literally hundreds of subsidiaries scattered throughout the world. Even in the case of much smaller local enterprises it is quite common for trading operations to be split up between a number of holding and subsidiary companies. Only for the smallest private business is the single independent operating company the typical form of organisation ... no attempt has been made to define more precisely or to control the relationship between holding and subsidiary companies in large groups nor to regulate the freedom of corporate groups to structure their affairs as they wish ... the judges give the impression of struggling to apply to complex group structures established principles of law developed for use within individual companies rather than of succeeding in creating anything which could reasonably be called a law for corporate groups.

Increasingly sophisticated legal structures of business organisation make it difficult to identify and make responsible the persons or part of the employer's organisational structure which are obliged to inform or consult. One solution adopted by the draft Directive was to impose the obligation not only on subsidiaries but also on separate establishments. An establishment was defined as 'an entity geographically separate from, but not legally independent of the undertaking of which it is part'. This is designed to prevent groups of companies from reducing their subsidiaries to a single company which then alone is liable to provide information. But it also raises the question whether geography alone is an adequate basis for determining employer responsibility, for example, where industrial relations structures and practice have a non-geographical rationale.

Again, the draft Directive provides that only decisions by parent undertakings are to be the subject of consultation. Moreover, the 'decision-making centre' is defined as the place where the undertaking has its central administration. The origin of decisions in complex organisations is by no means always the central administration, given the delegation of authority on many issues. The question of whether the draft Directive might require consultation depends on arguments as to where the decision in question was taken — locally, or by the parent company. A recent study of labour relations decision-making within multinational corporations found that certain types of decisions were much more centralised than others, but that the locus of decision-making varied considerably among firms (Hamill, 1984:30).

'Interests of the Company'

At common law directors of a company must act in the interests of the company. Although the company is a legal entity separate from its shareholders, the common law has traditionally taken the view that the interests of the company are the same as the interests of the shareholders. In one case where the directors of a company proposed to distribute monies to redundant employees, a shareholder's objection was upheld by the court. The directors, said Plowman J:

were prompted by motives which, however laudable, and however enlightened from the point of view of industrial relations, were such as the law does not recognise as a sufficient justification. Stripped of all its side issues, the essence of the matter is this, that the directors of the defendant company are proposing that a very large part of its funds should be given to its former employees in order to benefit those employees rather than the company, and that is an application of the company's funds which the law, as I understand it, will not allow.[12]

Subsequently the law was changed (CA s.719) so as to permit a company to provide for employees on the cessation or transfer of business, 'notwithstanding that [this] is not in the best interests of the company' (s.719(2)). While characterising the common law as 'increasingly anachronistic', a leading text (Gower, 1979:578) was constrained to state that 'it is apparently only the interests of the members and, presumably, creditors, present and future, to which [directors] are entitled to have regard; the interests of the consumers of the company's products, the nation as a whole and even (at present) the employees are legally irrelevant'.

The common law position was further modified by CA s.309(1) which provides that the 'matters to which the directors of a company are to have regard in the performance of their functions include the interests of the company's employees in general, as well as the interests of its members'. The implications of this provision are difficult to assess. Considering a proposal for a similarly worded provision, the Bullock Committee (1977:85) concluded that the directors' job would be 'to weigh up the differing and conflicting interests in the company in order to reach decisions which they genuinely believe to be in the company's overall best interest'. The Committee was criticised by Kahn-Freund (1977:76) for assuming the existence of 'a self-perpetuating entity, the company or the enterprise, whose "interests" transcend those of any of its component elements ... The so-called "interest of the company" is always identical with an interest of its shareholders'. Replying to Kahn-Freund, Davies and Wedderburn (a member of the Bullock Committee) argued (1977:202):

> the point of substance at issue between Kahn-Freund and the majority of Bullock seems not to be the report's incipient tendency to reification of 'the company's interests' but rather a conflict between Kahn-Freund's (implied) assumption that profit maximisation is the dominant objective of corporate activity and the report's (implied) assumption that companies pursue a range of goals, of which making profits is only one ... When a company may pursue a range of goals, attempting to hold a balance among profit, growth, size, employment opportunities etc., then no particular group interested in the company can claim permanent identification of the company's interests with its interests. The crucial question becomes one of how the balance is to be struck. That is the political/business decision which the board has to make. The legal definition of 'the company's interests' serves only to mark out the range of interests that the board may legitimately pursue.

The issue posed is one of substance and procedure. The question of substance is whether it is possible to define the 'interests of the company' as

[12] *Parke v Daily News Ltd* [1962] Ch 927, at 963.

including conflicting interests — for example, of employees and shareholders — and still make it operationally effective. Can directors in practice reconcile these conflicting interests and call the result the interests of the company? Are company directors today sufficiently relieved of what Davies and Wedderburn term the nineteenth century discipline of profit maximisation to be able to give equal or even similar weight to other policy objectives? This is in part a function of the training and ideological orientation of directors and managers. It is also an issue that goes to the heart of the economic system. It does involve — with due respect to Davies and Wedderburn (1977:201) — an 'overall explanation of corporate behaviour' because, even if there is 'no mechanism that will guarantee continuous profit-maximising behaviour on the part of controllers of large companies', such behaviour is arguably the norm and, more important, the promotion of competing interests, certainly those of employees, scarcely intrudes upon the list of corporate priorities. As Herman (1982:15) remarks, 'the profit motive has suffered no discernible eclipse as a result of the rise of management control'.

This makes the focus of CA s.309 essentially procedural. The directors are obliged to *have regard* to the conflicting interests, but having given due consideration, they may then decide 'in the interests of the company' that one or the other prevails. Boyle and Birds (1983:576) argue that s.309 does not alter the common law meaning of 'interests of the company':

> a board might be faced with a decision whether or not to close down a factory that is unprofitable but employs a considerable number of people who would lose their jobs if the decision to close were taken. Provided that the directors considered this latter point, it is submitted that they would not be in breach of [s.309] if they decided to close the factory. Indeed if they did not so decide they might be liable for not acting bona fide in the interests of the company, if it could clearly be shown that they had acted against the interests of the shareholders.

The view that shareholders' interests are still paramount receives indirect support from s.309(2) which provides that 'the duty imposed by this section on the directors is owed by them to the company (and the company alone) and is enforceable in the same way as any other fiduciary duty owed to a company by its directors'. In law, fiduciary duties owed by the directors to the company can be enforced only by shareholders. Hence employees cannot as such compel the directors to observe the provisions in s.309(1). Even if some employees were also shareholders, the law concerning enforcement of directors' duties raises almost insuperable obstacles to a small minority group of employee shareholders attempting to force the directors to do their duty.

Worker Directors

The origins of the recent debates on worker directors lie in the draft Fifth Directive of the European Communities on the structure of public limited companies put forward by the European Commission in December

1972.[13] This included provision for the representation of employees on the executive organs of joint stock companies. Such a Directive would require member states to implement the policy through national legislation. The policy proposed was for companies to have a mandatory two-tier board structure (as in the German and Dutch systems of company law) with employee participation on the supervisory board in firms employing a minimum of five hundred workers. The accession in 1973 of new member states including the UK led to further discussion, reports, opinions and plans culminating most recently with the Commission's final revised proposals submitted to the EC Council of Ministers in 1983.[14] This would apply the requirements only to companies with at least a thousand workers, and allow member states to opt for either a mandatory two-tier board structure or a single board structure and four alternative forms of participation. The UK government published a highly critical consultative document on the proposed new Directive (DE and DTI, 1983). It is expected that the Council of Ministers' Working Group may take a number of years to consider the latest proposals.

One consequence of the EC initiative was the appointment by the then Labour Government of the Bullock Committee of Inquiry on Industrial Democracy, which reported in January 1977. The Report throws considerable light on the legal structure of companies and the implications of industrial democracy for these structures. The majority of the Committee decided that employee representation should be effected through the unitary board of directors, which is the traditional structure of English company law. The formula was to be parity between worker and shareholder directors, with a third group of independents. But major changes in directors' powers were needed if worker directors were not to be outflanked by shareholders. The power of shareholders to remove directors, to alter the objects of the company, and so on would have to be curtailed. The Report recommended that the board of directors have a number of functions attributed to it by law. It would have the exclusive non-delegable power of submitting resolutions to the shareholders' meeting for the winding up of the company, for changes in the memorandum or articles, for the payment or non-payment of dividends, for changes in the capital structure or in the relation between the board, the general meeting of shareholders and the senior management, and for the disposal of a substantial part of the undertaking. It would also have the ultimate responsibility for the allocation and disposition of resources not constituting a substantial part of the undertaking, though it could delegate this power. It would be given the non-delegable power to appoint, remove or control managerial employees and determine their remuneration.

What the Report proposed was a fundamental shift in legal control from the shareholders in general meeting to the board of directors. The general meeting would retain the power to decide upon resolutions dealing with dividends, winding up, and changes in objects, if the board chose to put

13 OJ C131/44, 13.12.72.
14 OJ C240/2, 9.9.83.

these questions to it. The board could run the company; the shareholders had the power to veto anything proposed by the board. But an unrestrained exercise of that veto power would paralyse the company. Eventually they would have to reach a compromise, since the shareholders could not themselves initiate policy. Only the board had that power. There would be hard bargaining between the representatives of the shareholders' interests and those of the board, which would include employee representatives. The formula for representation was summarised as '2 X plus Y', where X was the number of board members representing employees and shareholders — the parity issue was considered crucial — and Y was a co-opted third group of 'independent' or 'expert' members.

The employee representatives were to be based on trade union machinery. A Joint Representation Committee (JRC) was to be formed by shop stewards or other workers' representatives at plant and enterprise level. As the degree of union organisation in enterprises to be affected by the Report's recommendations was estimated to be generally in excess of 70 per cent, these representatives would normally be union members. The JRC, composed of these shop stewards, would select the worker directors, who would in turn report back to the JRC.

One of the critical issues was how such re-cast company structures would fit with industrial relations patterns. As analysed by the Report, collective bargaining at local and national levels missed the vital company level of decision-making, where major decisions on investment, closures, mergers, product specialisation and so on were made. The Report saw worker directors on the board as the catalyst or stimulus for collective bargaining at company level. It analysed at length how it saw board representation and collective bargaining as interdependent. First, worker representation on boards would require a supporting structure. Second, to prevent itself being flooded, the board would have to refer issues down, which would lead to the creation of bargaining machinery at company level to deal with these issues. Third, the fact of board representation would stimulate greater co-operation, more commitment and less apathy. Indeed, the Report (1977:46) saw as the 'main argument' for its proposals that it was 'likely simultaneously to strengthen existing forms of industrial democracy below board level and to extend these structures to the highest levels of decision-making within the company'.

The key machinery for reconciling collective bargaining and board representation was thus the JRC. It would select the workers' board representatives, usually shop stewards; it would be the body to which the worker directors reported back, and would funnel the information further down; it would co-ordinate union policy at board level and in collective bargaining. The JRC would, according to the Report (1977:118) 'need to provide the continuing support for board representation and its interface with collective bargaining'.

The interface of collective bargaining and company board structures demonstrates the problems inherent in the use of company law concepts. Directors in company law are deemed to work co-operatively and collaborate in promoting the interests of the company. Can the board of directors take up the function of dealing with issues neglected by existing collective bargaining machinery? Collective bargaining is a very different process from board level decision-making. It is much more open and exposed to democratic and social pressures. If collective bargaining was not properly carried out in the board, policies would then have to be renegotiated below board level, and workers' representatives on the board would be regarded as compromised if they were seen to be part of the board representing management policy (Coates and Topham, 1977:36,47).

The very idea of collective bargaining in a company board with worker directors is fraught with problems. The Report (1977:125–6) suggested solutions to some of these problems: worker directors could not require senior management to reveal bargaining strategy and positions; where there was an actual or potential industrial dispute, the management's negotiating position was not to be subject to detailed and practical consideration by the board; worker directors mandated to industrial action should declare this and abstain from voting on relevant issues, but they would still be given the right to participate in matters concerned with collective bargaining and industrial relations.

The problem of using the company board as the instrument for expanding industrial democracy is that the board itself does not adequately reflect the realities of corporate government, and in particular, the role of senior managers. The Report (1977:79) acknowledged that 'because of their involvement in the detailed business of the company [senior managers would] continue to exercise enormous influence over all aspects of its affairs from the board downwards'. This perspective led Kahn-Freund (1977:80) to conclude that 'probably the Committee's board would become in fact a supervisory board restricted to its "attributed" functions and delegating to "senior management" those matters which affect the employees most particularly'. The need is, then, to find a counter-balance to the company's senior management. And here the Report's proposals as regards the JRC are very pertinent. If these proposals had been implemented, the legacy in terms of company-wide shop stewards' structures might have been more important than boardroom representation.

The Bullock Report provides an object lesson in the limitations of company law in the achievement of industrial democracy or worker participation. Company law structures are the outcome of a process of historical evolution very different from either trade union or industrial relations structures. With immense ingenuity the Bullock Report attempted to marry the two. But it was compromised from the start by a set of company law doctrines which were already inadequate as a depiction of real power within business organisations.

The options available for EC member states under the draft Fifth Directive revive the issues raised by the Bullock Report. The first two participation options involve representation on a supervisory board. The third participation option involves employees' representative bodies at company level but outside company boards. Under this option bodies, composed solely of employee representatives, would have to be given consultation and information rights closely aligned to those of the company's supervisory board, though they would not have veto rights over management decisions. The fourth option involves participation through collectively agreed procedures. These agreements would have to produce results corresponding to the principles of the other three models, but would allow for flexibility to match the circumstances of the particular company. In order to avoid the use of this fourth option as a delaying tactic, the draft Directive provides that where collective agreements are not concluded within one year of the commencement of national implementing legislation, member states must provide for employee participation by one of the other three legally-based options to be applied automatically.

Experiments with worker directors have not been a uniformly successful experience either in the UK or abroad. A study of the two-year experiment with worker directors at the Post Office (Batstone et al., 1983) concluded that the representatives had relatively little impact upon the outcome of company board discussions. Another study of worker directors in the British Steel Corporation (Brannen, 1983:137) concluded that 'this form of worker participation will not transform the management structure in which it is inserted, nor will it lead to radical changes in management behaviour'. Chell (1983) came to a similar conclusion after analysing seven private sector companies with workers directors.

It is problematical to draw conclusions for the UK from foreign experience because different systems of company law and industrial relations make comparisons difficult. Hadden's evaluation of the West German model highlighted that system's 'complex balance between collective bargaining, with nationally organised trade unions, company-based participation at supervisory board level and plant-based participation on works councils'. But it did conclude (1982:256) that:

> the German systems of participation at company and plant level, which must be seen as complementary to each other, appear to have succeeded in gaining acceptance for the principle that managerial authority on a wide range of issues of direct concern to employees can be subjected to a legal veto by employee representatives without threatening the viability of the enterprise affected. They have not yet gained acceptance for a similar principle in respect of major economic decisions.

COMPANIES AND LABOUR LAW

The primary focus of attention in labour law is the employer–employee relationship. The 'employer', however, is the subject of little further definition, in contrast to the complex case law as to the criteria for defining 'employees' (see Chapter 12). Where the employer is as in most cases a company, which is in turn likely to be part of a wider corporate grouping, the law acknowledges this only to the extent that various provisions refer to 'associated employers'. In many instances the fact of the economic integration of employers is ignored or insufficiently recognised by labour law.

Associated Employers

'Any two employers are to be treated as associated if one is a company of which the other (directly or indirectly) has control, or if both are companies of which a third person (directly or indirectly) has control'.[15] Although a worker's legal claim is formally against one legal person, his employer, the fact that the employer is a company, and is linked with another company, may allow the claim to extend to those other 'associated' employers. Up until TULRA the phrase used in labour law was not 'associated employer' but 'associated *company*', which meant a subsidiary company as defined by what is now CA s.736. The 1974 Act diluted the pure company law test by inserting the word 'employer' for 'company' and substituting the 'control' test. Although it is still essential that *one* of the associated employers is a company, to be 'associated' a company need not be linked via a parent-subsidiary relationship to the other employer (which can but need not be a company).

The essence, however, of the company law concept of parent-subsidiary is retained; the holding company either controls the composition of the board of the subsidiary, or holds more than half the equity share capital in the subsidiary. Thus an 'associated employer' exists in labour law if one of the employers is a company *and* 'it is shown that in fact one person has control, or that a group of persons acting together, if that be the case, have control'.[16] The labour law notion of 'control' is a practical one which differs from the more formal company law test. The latter is both too narrow, as a majority shareholding need not confer control due to weighted voting, and too wide, as control may be obtained without a majority shareholding (Gower, 1979:118). It is interesting that the Court of Appeal has explicitly rejected a 'de facto' test of control as impractical in a company law context.[17]

It is possible, therefore, in certain cases to extend a worker's rights against his employer to others who are economically linked to the employer through control or common subjection to a third party, provided one — either the employer or one of the others — is a company. None the less, the anomaly remains that the links of economic integration are recognised only where limited companies are involved, though in practice economic integration may be achieved with or without the use of the limited company form. The

---

[15] EPCA s.153(4). See similarly TULRA s.30(5), SDA s.82(2) and EqPA s.1(6)(c).

[16] *Zarb & Samuels v British and Brazilian Produce Co. (Sales) Ltd* [1978] IRLR 75, at 80, EAT, where two people owning between them over 50 per cent of the shares in two companies were said to raise the possibility that they were acting together to control the two companies and thus the two companies might be 'associated'.

[17] *Prudential Assurance Co. Ltd v Newman Industries (No. 2)* [1982] Ch 204, CA; see Boyle (1981).

anomaly is highlighted by the changes in 1974 which, by dropping 'associated company' for 'associated employer', also dropped the definition of a company as including any body corporate. The result was that where an employee with a twelve-year career in local government service had worked for four different local authorities in that period, his employment was held not to be continuous as the local authorities, while bodies corporate, were not limited companies.[18] The Court of Appeal did recognise that employers could be 'associated' in several ways: 'associated for a common purpose, or associated through a common element of control, or associated through a common interest, or associated through membership of some trade organisation or associated through negotiation with a trade union'.[19] But it was the very multiplicity of possible links between employers which led to the judicial rejection of a broad interpretation of 'associated employer'.

Workers' rights and obligations extend to employers 'associated' with their own in the following instances:

(a) Provisions dealing with the re-employment of a woman absent on maternity leave cover both her employer and associated employers (EPCA ss.45(3), 56A). In contrast, EPCA s.60(2) allows for dismissal of a pregnant employee where the employer has no suitable available vacancy, but fails to advert to the possibility of an associated employer with such a vacancy (Drake and Bercusson, 1981: note to s.45(3)).

(b) From 1980 to 1985 two years' continuous service was required for unfair dismissal claims where the number of employees of the employer and any associated employer did not exceed twenty.[20]

(c) The remedy of re-engagement for unfairly dismissed employees may be applied both to the employer dismissing and any associated employer (EPCA s.69(4)), though the enforcement provisions (s.71) do not address the problem of an associated employer refusing an order for re-engagement.

(d) Offers to redundant employees of re-engagement in suitable employment, which if refused cause the employee to lose the entitlement to a redundancy payment, may be made by associated employers (EPCA s.82(7)).

(e) An employer must disclose relevant information relating to his undertaking as is in his possession or that of any associated employer (EPA s.17(1)). The sanction for failure to disclose, however, only lies against the employer.

(f) Secondary action may be lawful if it disrupts supplies to or from an associated employer of an employer party to the dispute, given such supplies are substitutes for those which would have been to or from the employer in dispute (EA 1980 s.17(4)).

[18] *Gardiner v London Borough of Merton* [1980] IRLR 472, CA, overruling the EAT's contrary decision in *Hillingdon Area Health Authority v Kauders* [1979] IRLR 197. But continuity for the purposes of statutory redundancy pay is now preserved when an employee moves from one employer to another in local government and related bodies: Redundancy Payments (Local Government) (Modification) Order SI 1983 No. 1160.

[19] [1980] IRLR 472, at 474 (per Griffiths LJ).

[20] EPCA s.64A. See also the SDA s.6(3)(b).

(g) Claims for equal pay may be made with men in the same establishment, regardless of whether they are employed by the same or an associated employer (EqPA s.1(6)).

(h) If an employee is taken into the employment of an associated employer of his employer, the change may not break the continuity of his period of employment (EPCA Sch.13, para.18).

(i) An employee who is a trade union official is entitled to time off to carry out duties concerned with industrial relations between his employer and associated employers and their employees, and undergo training relevant to such duties (EPCA s.27(1)).

(j) An employee's entitlement to statutory guarantee pay is lost if he is laid off due to a trade dispute involving any employee of his employer or of an associated employer (EPCA s.13(1)).

It is questionable whether this hodgepodge of references to 'associated employers' adequately addresses the problem of employers whose economic integration is masked under a variety of legal forms. This may be contrasted with the concern expressed by the Cork Report (1982) about the position of creditors of insolvent subsidiaries. The Report (para.1952) regarded the need for reforming legislation as 'a matter of urgency'.

Transfer of Undertakings

The Transfer of Undertakings (Protection of Employment) Regulations 1981[21] are concerned with the safeguarding of employees' rights in the event of transfer of undertakings, businesses and parts of businesses. Thus they purport to ensure that all the rights and obligations of employees arising from the contract of employment or the employment relationship are transferred automatically (reg.5), that unions recognised by the transferor are deemed to be recognised by the transferee (reg.9), and that recognised unions are informed or consulted. But the regulations apply only where the *undertaking* is transferred 'from one person to another' (reg.3(1)). This means that where a company's *shares* are purchased by another person, that is, ownership of the company is effectively transferred, the regulations do not apply to protect employees from the new owner; it is the shareholding not the undertaking which is being transferred. 'From one person to another', in the words of Davies and Freedland (1982: note to reg.3(1))

> is the most important phrase in the regulations. It emasculates, for example, the provisions imposing a duty to inform and consult trade union representatives by ensuring that they do not apply to the vast majority of takeover transactions, taking the form as they do of changes in share control rather than change of proprietor of the undertaking itself ... It would seem that this limitation is particularly restrictive when applied in the British context, given the special preponderance of share takeovers over asset takeovers in the United Kingdom.

Moreover, the practice of 'hiving-down', whereby viable parts of an insolvent company are transferred to a subsidiary, is not affected by the

[21] SI 1981 No. 1794.

safeguards. Employees of the subsidiary do not benefit from the protection until the newly formed subsidiary is actually sold off. This allows receivers of insolvent companies to transfer employees without any obligations as regards employees or recognised trade unions who may have vital interests to be considered in the hiving-down process itself (Davies and Freedland, 1982: note to reg. 4(1)). Conversely to the case where the law extends employers' obligations to legal persons other than the employer because they are associated employers, here the law has released an employer (in effect the receiver) from his legal obligations because of his association with the subsidiary.

Labour Relations and Corporate Groups

When enterprises take the form of a number of separate legal persons — each of them the 'employer' of a group of workers in the enterprise — the enforcement of legal rights is greatly complicated. The problem of enforcing the duty on employers to disclose all relevant information in their possession or that of an associated employer has already been mentioned. A second illustration is that of the requirement that employers consult trade unions over proposed redundancies. In groups of companies it is often the parent company which makes the decision leading to redundancies. But proposals for redundancies formulated by a parent company and notified to its subsidiary, the employer, do not trigger the need to commence consultation at the earliest opportunity.[22] A third example occurs when shop stewards representing workers employed by the different companies of a group seek to meet to discuss matters of common interest. EPCA s.27(1)(a), which is analysed in Chapter 2, allows a union official time off for duties concerned with industrial relations 'between his employer and any associated employer, and their employees'. Two cases illustrate the potential problems. In the first case, the EAT rejected a union official's complaint when he was refused time off, stating 'we do not consider that the mere exchange of information between the trade union officials themselves necessarily qualifies, even if those officials represent workers in a particular group of companies'.[23] But in the second case, the Court of Appeal held that attendance at a union national group advisory committee was an industrial relations duty for the purposes of paid time off.[24]

The final example is that of secondary industrial action. This is defined as industrial action involving an employer who 'is not a party to the trade dispute' (EA 1980 s.17(2)). The immunities in TULRA s.13(1) are withdrawn from certain industrial action involving a secondary employer which interferes with his commercial contracts. But, as Chapter 6 explains in detail, not all secondary action is unlawful. It is legitimate when the criteria in s.17(3)–(5) are satisfied. In essence these criteria envisage the relationships of the employer in dispute with his customers and suppliers or

[22] *NALGO v National Travel (Midland) Ltd* [1978] ICR 598, EAT.
[23] *Sood v GEC Elliott Process Automation Ltd* [1979] IRLR 416 at 420 (per Slynn J).
[24] *Beal v Beecham Group Ltd* [1982] IRLR 192.

associated employers substituting for the employer in dispute. These categories are easily circumvented. An example is *Dimbleby & Sons Ltd v NUJ*[25] where a printing subsidiary (TBF) of a newspaper group (T Bailey Forman Ltd), which was in dispute with the NUJ, was said to be a secondary employer, although, as put by Griffiths LJ in the Court of Appeal: 'the companies were run by the same people from the same office and with the same ethos — they did not use union labour ... if T Bailey Forman Ltd had produced their papers on their own presses, the union's action would have been protected but, because the owner of the business chooses to operate through associated companies, the union is unprotected'.[26] In the House of Lords it was again argued that the 'corporate veil' of the printing company which separated it, as a legal person, from the parent company in dispute should be pierced, and further that TBF was an employer who was a party to the dispute between the NUJ and T Bailey Forman. But this argument was rejected as unsustainable.

Here the courts denied the link between associated employers apparently envisaged in EA 1980 s.17(4). The fact of economic integration is, however, used against the interests of employees in similar circumstances of industrial conflict. An employee laid off because of a dispute involving employees of an associated employer is denied a statutory guarantee payment (Bercusson, 1979: note to EPCA s.13(1)). Employees linked with the employer in dispute via an associated company are penalised even though they may have nothing to do with the dispute. But employers linked with the employer in dispute via an associated company are protected in the case of secondary action even though they are closely involved in the dispute. The double standard needs no emphasis.

LABOUR LAW AND COMPANY LAW

Companies pose a problem for labour law because the legal concept of the employer has not been adequately developed to match the size and complexity of companies and corporate groups. Labour law has not challenged the flexibility and economic power of unified capital. The problem of companies for modern labour law goes deeper. It lies in the tendency to identify labour law with regulation of the employment relationship. This focuses attention on employers and workers instead of on workers and their problems. In particular, there is insufficient emphasis on workers' relations with each other — not only within trade unions, but on workers' relations with other workers within the enterprise, within the industry and within the working class.

The solution to the problems posed by companies is, in part, to develop a framework of labour law which circumscribes and limits management's control of the enterprise, having regard to the use made of corporate forms as an instrument of management control. At a minimum, workers' rights in

[25] [1984] IRLR 161, HL.
[26] [1984] IRLR 67, at 72.

present labour law should not be constrained by allowing enterprises to invoke company law doctrines to disguise formally an economic communality of interest between companies (as in the problems of 'associated' employers or labour relations in corporate groups) and between shareholders (as in transfers of undertakings).

The framework of labour law should, moreover, promote workers' organisations which counter the challenge of corporate enterprise. A parallel structure of workers' organisations is needed which mirrors the organisational structure of economic enterprises, and which allows for the development of the expertise and the democratic control mechanisms to enable workers to curb and, perhaps, eventually to replace owners' control. The Bullock Report's proposed JRCs might have had some potential in this respect. A report by the TUC-Labour Party Liaison Committee (1982:paras.14.1–6) similarly proposed joint trade union machinery composed of a mixture of full-time officers and lay members, which should have representation rights at all levels of decision-making in the enterprise up to and including board level, including subsidiary and divisional boards.

The problem for workers of contemporary company law is that employees are perceived as an externality. Company law is viewed as the means whereby owners of capital are enabled to engage in business activities with a maximum of freedom, though with some regard to the interests of employees, creditors, and consumers. An alternative view of company law sees it as the means whereby economic organisations are controlled in the interests of various constituencies — creditors, employees, investors, consumers, and the public. Debates over the nature of corporate responsibility have been extensive (see Hopt and Teubner, 1984).

Can company law be integrated into labour law so that employees become a central concern of the law governing the enterprise? Could the functioning of enterprises become dependent on compliance with standards and procedures laid down by labour law? So long as the two spheres of company and labour law are kept distinct, 'one is necessarily led' in the words of an eminent French labour lawyer (Lyon-Caen, 1983:301–2) 'to the conclusion that non-compliance with a labour law obligation [will] not affect the validity of a transaction in commercial law ... the spirit of French law is not to make the functioning of companies subject to a respect for labour law'.

Is British company law any more susceptible? This depends on the role which company law is perceived as playing within capitalism. On the one hand, Gower (1979:49) argues that legislative intervention in the mid-nineteenth century allowing for incorporation with limited liability by simple registration 'finally established companies as the major instrument in economic development'. One problem with this approach to the role of law in the economy is that by the mid-nineteenth century much of the industrial revolution was already coming to an end. As an institution the joint-stock company did not become of any significance until the latter part of the nineteenth century.[27]

---

[27] Hobsbawm (1976:215); Kempner et al. (1976:32). For further argument on these lines, see Sugarman (1983); Ireland (1983); Anderson and Tollinson (1983).

An historical perspective thus raises the issue of just how important company law is to the regulation of economic activity. Are the rules, doctrines and principles of company law empty forms, used only for convenience? The history of economic development indicates that company law may not have been a decisive instrument of economic or political change. Company law seems an unlikely resource for promotion or even recognition of workers' interests. But if labour law develops to embrace the organisation of workers and of work within the enterprise, the boundaries between company law and labour law may begin to fade.

Bibliography

Anderson, G.M., and R.D. Tollinson. 1983. 'The Myth of the Corporation as a Creation of the State'. *International Review of Law and Economics*, 3 (December), 107–20.

Batstone, E., A. Ferner and M. Terry. 1983. *Unions on the Board: An Experiment in Industrial Democracy*. Oxford: Blackwell.

Beck, S.M. 1973. 'Corporate Opportunity Revisited'. *Studies in Canadian Company Law*. Vol.2. Ed. J.S. Ziegel. Toronto: Butterworths, 193–238.

Bercusson, B. 1979. Annotations to the Employment Protection (Consolidation) Act 1978. *Encyclopedia of Labour Relations Law*. Eds. B.A. Hepple and P. O'Higgins. London: Sweet & Maxwell, paras. 2–1778 – 2–1999.

Boyle, A.J. 1981. 'The Prudential, the Court of Appeal and *Foss v Harbottle*'. *Company Lawyer*, 2 (November), 264–6.

——, and J. Birds. 1983. *Company Law*. London: Jordans.

Brannen, P. 1983. 'Worker Directors – An Approach to Analysis: The Case of the BSC'. *Organisational Democracy and Political Processes*. Vol. 1 of *International Yearbook of Organisational Democracy*. Eds. C. Crouch and F. Heller. Chichester: Wiley, 121–38.

Bullock. 1977. Committee of Inquiry on Industrial Democracy. *Report*. Cmnd 6706. London: HMSO.

Chell, E. 1983. 'Political Perspectives and Worker Participation at Board Level: The British Experience'. *Organisational Democracy and Political Processes*. Vol. 1 of *International Yearbook of Organisational Democracy*. Eds. C. Crouch and F. Heller. Chichester: Wiley, 487–504.

Coates, K., and T. Topham. 1977. *The Shop Steward's Guide to the Bullock Report*. Nottingham: Spokesman.

Cork. 1982. *Insolvency Law and Practice: Report of the Review Committee*. Cmnd 8558. London: HMSO.

Davies, P., and M. Freedland. 1980. 'The Effects of Receiverships upon Employees of Companies'. *Industrial Law Journal*, 9 (June), 95–113.

——, and M. Freedland. 1982. *Transfer of Employment*. London: Sweet & Maxwell.

——, and *Lord* Wedderburn. 1977. 'The Land of Industrial Democracy'. *Industrial Law Journal*, 6 (December), 197–211.

Department of Employment (DE) and Department of Trade and Industry (DTI). 1983. *Draft European Communities Directive for Informing and Consulting Employees. Draft European Communities Fifth Directive on the Harmonisation of Company Law. A Consultative Document*. London: DE and DTI.

Drake, C.D., and B. Bercusson. 1981. *The Employment Acts 1974–1980*. London: Sweet & Maxwell.

Farrar, J., and M. Russell. 1984. 'The Impact of Institutional Investment on Company Law'. *Company Lawyer*, 5 (May), 107–16.

Forde, M. 1984. 'Trade Union Pluralism and Labour Law in France'. *International and Comparative Law Quarterly*, 33 (January), 134–57.

Glendon, M.A. 1984. 'French Labor Law Reform 1982–83: The Struggle for Collective Bargaining'. *American Journal of Comparative Law*, 32 (Summer), 449–91.

Gower. 1984. *Review of Investor Protection. Report: Part I*. Cmnd 9125. London: HMSO.

Gower, L.C.B. 1979. *Principles of Modern Company Law*. 4th edn. London: Stevens.

Hadden, T. 1977. *Company Law and Capitalism*. 2nd edn. London: Weidenfeld & Nicolson.

——. 1982. 'Employee Participation – What Future for the German Model?' *Company Lawyer*, 3 (November), 250–57.

——. 1983. *The Control of Corporate Groups*. London: Institute of Advanced Legal Studies.

Hamill, J. 1984. 'Labour Relations Decision Making within Multinational Corporations'. *Industrial Relations Journal*, 15 (Summer), 30–34.

Herman, E.H. 1982. *Corporate Control, Corporate Power*. Cambridge: Cambridge University Press.

Hobsbawm, E.J. 1976. *Industry and Empire*. Harmondsworth: Penguin.

Hopt, K., and G. Teubner (eds.). 1985. *Corporate Governance and Directors' Liabilities*. Berlin: Walter de Gruyter.

Industrial Relations Review and Report (IRRR). 1984. 'EEC Proposals on Employee Involvement: Part 1'. *Industrial Relations Review and Report*, no. 318 (April), 2–8.

Ireland, P. 1983. 'The Triumph of the Company Legal Form, 1856–1914'. *Essays for Clive Schmitthoff*. Ed. J. Adams. Abingdon: Professional Books, 29–58.

Kahn-Freund, Otto. 1977. 'Industrial Democracy'. *Industrial Law Journal*, 6 (June), 65–84.

Kempner, T., K. MacMillan and K.H. Hawkins. 1976. *Business and Society*. Harmondsworth: Penguin.

Lyon-Caen, G. 1983. 'La Concentration du Capital et le Droit du Travail'. *Droit Social* (May), 287–303.

Martin, A. 1984. 'Trade Unions in Sweden: Strategic Responses to Change and Crisis'. *Unions and Economic Crisis: Britain, West Germany and Sweden*. Eds. P. Gourevitch, A. Martin, G. Ross, S. Bornstein, A. Markovits and C. Allen. London: Allen & Unwin, 189–359.

Oakeshott, R. 1985. 'The Beginnings of an Employee Owned Sector'. *Lloyds Bank Review*, 155 (January), 32–44.

Pickering, M.A. 1968. 'The Company as a Separate Legal Entity'. *Modern Law Review*, 31 (September), 481–511.

Prentice, D.D. 1978. 'Employee Participation in Corporate Government – A Critique of the Bullock Report'. *Canadian Bar Review*, 56 (June), 277–304.

Richardi, R. 1982. 'Worker Participation in Decisions within Undertakings in the Federal Republic of Germany'. *Comparative Labor Law*, 5 (Winter), 23–50.

Streeck, W. 1984. *Industrial Relations in West Germany: A Case Study of the Car Industry*. London: Policy Studies Institute.

Sugarman, D. 1983. 'Law, Economy and the State in England, 1750–1914: Some Major Issues'. *Legality, Ideology and the State*. Ed. D. Sugarman. London: Academic Press, 213–66.

TUC–Labour Party Liaison Committee. 1982. *Economic Planning and Industrial Democracy*. London: TUC.

Wedderburn, K.W. (*Lord*) 1965. 'Corporate Personality and Social Policy: The Problem of the Quasi-Corporation'. *Modern Law Review*, 28 (January), 62–71.
——. 1966. 'The Death of Ultra Vires'. *Modern Law Review*, 29 (November), 673–6.
——. 1983. 'Ultra Vires in Modern Company Law'. *Modern Law Review*, 46 (March), 204–13.

PART III
Industrial Conflict

6 Trade Union Immunities

Bob Simpson

Industrial action, which involves disruption of normal working, can take many forms. On the employer's side the best known is the lock-out or closure of the workplace. Other forms of industrial action that may be open to employers receive less publicity. They include withdrawal of recognition or facilities from unions and shop stewards, unilaterally altering working arrangements, transferring workers to less pleasant jobs, withdrawal of bonuses or reduction of overtime. All these actions may be in breach of agreed procedures or legal obligations. The law has a far greater impact however on industrial action taken by workers. The strike is the most important and receives the most attention. But other action including go-slows, working to rule, overtime bans, working without enthusiasm, non-co-operation, and workplace occupations may be equally effective in particular circumstances. Indeed, recent research indicates that non-manual workers take 'non-strike industrial action' more often than they go on strike (Daniel and Millward, 1983:214).

In Britain there is no comprehensive labour code which determines the legality of calling and taking part in industrial action and its consequences. Instead, the law attempts to regulate industrial conflict in various ways through a combination of judge-made law, both criminal and civil, and legislation. First, it seeks to impose limits on physical manifestations such as picketing and workplace occupations. This is covered in Chapter 7. Second, industrial action affects the legal rights and obligations of employer and employee in the context of the individual labour relationship. These, together with social security rights, are dealt with in Chapter 9. Third, trade unions and individuals who organise and take part in industrial action may be made liable for certain torts (civil wrongs) in circumstances where they are not entitled to claim the benefit of statutory 'immunities'. This area of law is the subject of this chapter. Finally there are special provisions in respect of emergencies and particular groups of workers, which are discussed in Chapter 8.

In an often quoted passage from the *Crofter* case, Lord Wright recognised that 'the right of workmen to strike is an essential element in the principle of collective bargaining'.[1] But the courts have not been able to translate this social right into a legal right recognised by common law. In fact they have

---

[1] *Crofter Hand Woven Harris Tweed Co. v Veitch* [1942] AC 435, 463.

rarely tried to do so. The common law has not recognised any general right or freedom of workers to take industrial action without breaking their contracts of employment. Subject to possible exceptions for bans on purely voluntary overtime and industrial action taken after full notice, all industrial action involves breaches of contract which entitle the employer to dismiss without notice the workers who take part (see Chapter 9).

For over a hundred years, however, the judge-made common law has mainly focused not on those who take part in industrial action, but on those who organise it. Before 1875 they could be prosecuted for criminal conspiracy where two or more of them acted together. The Conspiracy and Protection of Property Act 1875 (CPPA) provided an 'immunity' against this liability for acts done in contemplation or furtherance of a trade dispute. Since then attention has shifted to the civil liabilities known as 'economic torts'. Liability for acting in combination with others was developed as part of the civil law to become the tort of 'conspiracy'. The courts also established that it was a civil wrong for one person to 'induce' another to break a contract. Since workers who take part in industrial action are almost invariably breaking their contracts, this tort of 'inducing breach of contract' could be readily invoked by employers — the other party to the broken employment contracts — against strike organisers. More recently in 1964 the House of Lords resurrected the old tort of 'intimidation' which is committed when someone suffers loss as a result of his (or some other person's) giving in to unlawful threats such as a threat to call a strike.

These torts would provide the means for employers to seek injunctions to restrain unions and individuals from organising industrial action and damages to compensate them for losses incurred as a consequence of such action. It was clear at the beginning of this century that if the unions were to be able to function effectively legislation was necessary to protect strike organisers against these liabilities. After the House of Lords held in the *Taff Vale* case[2] that unions as such could be sued and awards of damages made against their funds, their very existence was put at risk. For these reasons the Trade Disputes Act 1906 (TDA 1906), later supplemented by the 1965 Act (TDA 1965), provided immunities against civil liabilities to complement the immunity against criminal conspiracy provided in 1875. For trade unions, the immunity against civil liability in tort was complete. For individuals it was qualified and, like the immunity in the CPPA, applied only to acts done 'in contemplation or furtherance of a trade dispute'.

The point has often been made that these immunities from judge-made liabilities are part of the peculiarly British way of recognising rights essential to the functioning of a system of collective bargaining (Wedderburn, 1971:400; DE, 1981:para.34). In 1971 the Industrial Relations Act (IRA) attempted, in effect, to replace the system of immunities with a separate body of statutory liabilities called 'unfair industrial practices'. But on its repeal in 1974 the immunities of the Trade Disputes Acts were re-enacted in the Trade Union and Labour Relations Acts 1974 and 1976 (TULRA) so that, in Lord Scarman's words: 'briefly put, the law is now back to what

---

[2]   *Taff Vale Railway Co. v Amalgamated Society of Railway Servants* [1901] AC 426.

Parliament intended when it enacted the Act of 1906 — but stronger and clearer than it was then'.[3] It was stronger and clearer in an attempt to meet recent judicial development of the common law liabilities and restrictive construction of the immunities.

In the 1980s, this pattern of judicial expansion of the liabilities followed by corresponding legislative extension of the immunities has come to a halt. The ambit of the liabilities has certainly been increased and remains unclear at the edges. More important is the reduction and qualification of the immunities, so far in three instalments in the Employment Acts of 1980 and 1982 and the Trade Union Act 1984. Analysis of the legality of organising industrial action is now therefore a three-stage process: has one or more of the common law tort liabilities been committed; if so, are the unions or individuals concerned entitled to claim immunity from liability under TULRA; if so, is this immunity lost by virtue of the 1980, 1982 or 1984 Acts? For a complete understanding of the law in this area it is also necessary to appreciate the complexities of legal procedure, in particular on applications for labour injunctions. These are discussed in Chapter 19.

COMMON LAW LIABILITIES

Civil Conspiracy

This tort has two forms: simple conspiracy or conspiracy to injure, and conspiracy to commit an unlawful act. Conspiracy to injure was the form in which the tort originally developed. It can be defined as a combination of two or more persons which intentionally causes economic loss to another by use of means which are lawful in themselves, provided the combiners have a predominant purpose other than that of furthering their own legitimate interests. Where two or more persons in combination cause loss through means in themselves unlawful, there is a conspiracy to commit an unlawful act. Before there can be liability in either form of the tort it must be proved that there was a combination or agreement between two or more persons, one of whom may be a trade union, and that the person bringing the action suffered intended loss or damage as a result of the combiners' acts.

Conspiracy to injure. The essence of this form of the tort lies in the motive or purpose of the combiners. If their predominant purpose was to damage another, then they can be made liable to that person. If it was to further their own legitimate interests, however, there is no liability. While pursuit of commercial goals has always been recognised as legitimate by the courts, it was not until the *Crofter* case in 1942[4] that the House of Lords established that the interests of labour are also acceptable objectives. There an agreement between union officials and employers not to handle supplies for the employers' trade rivals was held to be lawful, since no unlawful

---

[3] *NWL Ltd v Woods* [1979] ICR 867, 886.
[4] *Crofter Hand Woven Harris Tweed Co. v Veitch* [1942] AC 435.

means were employed. The officials were pursuing the legitimate goal of better terms and conditions for their members working for the employers with whom they combined. Moreover, the range of judicially recognised labour interests extends beyond substantive conditions of employment. In the 1950s, officials of the Musicians' Union organised a boycott of a dance hall which operated a colour bar on the dance floor. This was held not to be an actionable conspiracy because it was legitimate to oppose the insidious effects of the colour bar on the union's members, some of whom were coloured, who could not insulate themselves from their audience.[5] But pursuit of a personal grudge against an employer or another worker is not acceptable. Where the evidence discloses such motivation for the combiners' acts as well as a recognised labour interest, their predominant purpose is a question of fact. Only if the legitimate interest was predominant will they escape liability for conspiracy.[6]

In the *Lonrho* case, Lord Diplock described the tort of conspiracy as 'highly anomalous' and gave judicial recognition to the obvious flaw in the rationale for imposing liability for acts done by a combination which would not be unlawful if done by one person alone. In the days of multinational conglomerates it is naive to suggest that individual legal entities lack the power to inflict the same amount of harm as that caused by a combination of, for example, two union officials. Nevertheless, the Law Lords felt that the tort was too well-established to be discarded.[7]

Conspiracy to commit an unlawful act. The *Lonrho* decision does suggest, however, that it is essential in both forms of the tort to establish that the combiners' predominant purpose was to injure the person bringing the action.[8] Liability for conspiracy to commit an unlawful act is relatively straightforward where the unlawful act in question is a separate tort for which the person suing for conspiracy can also sue. For example, the important case of *Rookes v Barnard* in 1964 was an action for conspiracy to commit the tort of intimidation. In such cases an allegation of conspiracy may be added to the other tort in order to make the granting of an interim injunction more likely, or enhance a claim for aggravated damages.

It is less clear which other acts are unlawful for the purposes of this tort. In the *Lonrho* case, the House of Lords refused to extend this 'anomalous' liability to conspiracy to commit acts which were criminal by virtue of legislation which did not provide a civil remedy for those adversely affected. Whether it is possible to sue for conspiracy to commit other criminal acts or other breaches of a statute remains uncertain. Similarly, after *Rookes v Barnard*, where it was held that breach of contract was an unlawful act for the purposes of the tort of intimidation, it has been an unresolved question whether there can be liability for conspiracy to break a contract, a point

---

5   *Scala Ballroom (Wolverhampton) Ltd v Ratcliffe* [1958] 1 WLR 1057.
6   *Quinn v Leathem* [1901] AC 495, where the then prevalent antipathy to basic trade union aims dominated the Law Lords' approach; *Huntley v Thornton* [1957] 1 WLR 321.
7   *Lonrho Ltd v Shell Petroleum Co. Ltd (No.2)* [1982] AC 173, 188–9.
8   See Wedderburn (1982a, the most comprehensive account of this area of the law, paras. 15–23).

expressly left open by Lord Devlin in that case.[9] If there can, almost all industrial action could amount to civil conspiracies for which at least the employers of the workers concerned and possibly others could sue. Most of these economic tort liabilities turn on whether the defendants have committed an unlawful act or used unlawful means, and this issue is discussed further below. But it has to be remembered that what is an unlawful act for the purposes of one tort will not necessarily be held to be unlawful in the context of a different tort liability.

Intimidation

The modern form of the civil liability for intimidation derives from the House of Lords' decision in *Rookes v Barnard*. In that case it was held that a threat by two shop stewards and a full-time union officer that draughtsmen employed by BOAC would go on strike, in breach of their contracts of employment, unless Rookes, a non-unionist, was dismissed, amounted to the tort of intimidation. The three officials were liable to Rookes once BOAC complied with their wishes and dismissed him. The essence of the liability is an unlawful threat against another to compel him to act in a way which causes damage either to himself, or to a third party. 'Two-party' intimidation occurs where compliance with the threateners' wishes causes damage to the person threatened; 'three-party' intimidation occurs where the damage is caused to a third party, as in *Rookes v Barnard*.

The elements of the tort in either form are thus an unlawful threat, compliance with the threatener's wishes by the person threatened, and damage suffered by the person bringing the action as a result of this compliance. There may be problems in distinguishing a threat from merely conveying information, but in most cases the courts would probably construe information about possible industrial action as a thinly-veiled threat. The chief difficulty is in distinguishing lawful threats from unlawful threats. It seems clear that a threat can only be unlawful if an unlawful act is threatened. Thus a threat to commit another tort — to induce workers to break their contracts by going on strike for example – is clearly unlawful. So are threats to commit crimes in many cases. But after the *Lonrho* case it is doubtul whether it is unlawful to threaten to commit acts which are criminal by virtue only of legislation which does not create a civil remedy for those suffering loss. The novelty of the Law Lords' decision in *Rookes v Barnard* lay in their finding that a threat of breach of contract was an unlawful threat which could amount to tortious intimidation. A strike threat is therefore a threat of an unlawful act which becomes the tort of intimidation if it is effective in securing compliance with the wishes of those who make it, and the employer or some third party suffers intended damage as a result.

Although there has been little development of the tort of intimidation since 1964, in 1982 the House of Lords extended a similar doctrine into labour relations: the right to 'restitution' or recovery of money paid under

[9] [1964] AC 1129 at 1210.

'economic duress'. In the *Universe Tankships* case,[10] the ITF blacked a ship flying a flag of convenience until the owners agreed to make payments of back pay to the crew and a contribution to the ITF's Welfare Fund. It was conceded that this amounted to economic duress. In this context duress meant economic pressure vitiating the owner's consent to the ITF's usual collective agreements and payments, brought about by 'coercing their will'. Although the blacking of services for the ship while in port probably involved the torts of either intimidation or inducing breaches of contracts of employment, economic duress is not a tort. There was therefore no statutory immunity preventing recovery of money paid. But the courts nevertheless accepted that if the ITF had been acting in contemplation or furtherance of a trade dispute, the pressure which it brought to bear on the shipowners would have been legitimate and no recovery of money for economic duress possible. In this case though, a majority of the Law Lords surprisingly found that there was no trade dispute. It is clear that facts which constitute intimidation may well also be construed as economic duress. Money paid to the threatener, such as the contribution to the ITF's Welfare Fund in the *Universe Tankships* case, will therefore be recoverable.

Inducing Breach of Contract

In the second half of the nineteenth century the courts established that it was a tort to induce or procure a person to break a contract to which he or she is party. Since almost all industrial action by workers involves them breaking their contracts of employment, those who call on workers to take industrial action are committing the tort of inducing them to break their contracts. Even before the considerable extension of this liability in the last twenty years its application in labour disputes was very complex. The leading case was *Thomson v Deakin*[11] where the Court of Appeal held that the plaintiffs would have to establish that the defendant had sufficient knowledge of the contract and intended to cause breach of it, that it was broken, and that they had suffered damage in consequence. Where the relevant contracts are contracts of employment, these requirements are fairly easy to establish against a defendant who had called on workers to breach their contracts by taking strike action. Where they are commercial contracts the position, at least up to the 1960s, was different. Defendant union officials might have successfully argued that they had insufficient knowledge of these contracts or intended they should be lawfully terminated rather than broken.

If they can establish these four fundamental requirements — *knowledge* of the contract, *intention* to cause its breach, *breach* of the contract, and *damage* to themselves — the plaintiffs must then show that the defendant induced or procured the breach. There are essentially two ways in which this can be done in industrial disputes. The first is by *directly* inducing breach by persuading one of the parties to the contract to break it, for example,

---

[10]   *Universe Tankships Inc. of Monrovia v ITF* [1983] 1 AC 366. See Wedderburn (1982b).
[11]   [1952] Ch 646.

persuading workers to come out on strike. In *Thomson v Deakin* a distinction was drawn between persuasion and merely providing information. Although this distinction has been applied in one case where it was unsuccessfully alleged that union officials had induced workers to break their contracts,[12] the decision is exceptional. Normally the acts of those who organise industrial action will be seen as persuading and therefore inducing workers to break their contracts of employment. The second way in which the tort can be committed is by *indirectly* procuring breach by using unlawful means which render performance of the contract by one of the parties impossible. This is the form usually alleged where the contracts are commercial ones between employers and their customers or suppliers.

Apart from the statutory immunities discussed below there is a common law defence to this tort, namely 'justification'. But it is of limited if any significance in labour disputes. Although it was once held that representatives of an actors' association were justified in inducing chorus girls to break their contracts because their wages were so low that they had to resort to prostitution,[13] trying to secure better pay or conditions of work is of itself no justification for inducing breaches of contract in the eyes of the judges.[14]

A series of decisions starting in the mid-1960s with *Stratford v Lindley*[15] has greatly expanded this liability. In that case it was alleged that an embargo placed by the Watermen's Union on the return of barges hired from Stratfords — in the context of a recognition dispute with an associated employer — amounted to an inducement both to lightermen who belonged to the union to break their contracts of employment and to the hirers of the barges to break the hiring contracts. The House of Lords unanimously found that the union officials had induced or procured breaches of the hiring contracts. Either the breaches had been indirectly procured by the unlawful means of persuading the lightermen to break their contracts of employment, or as two Law Lords thought, a letter informing an employers' association of the embargo amounted to direct persuasion of the hirers not to return the barges, a remarkably elastic view of the concept of persuasion.

All the Law Lords agreed that it was necessary to show only that the defendant union officials had a very general knowledge of the hiring contracts. Subsequent cases have established, however, that it no longer has to be shown that the defendant had any knowledge of the contract in question if he or she 'turned a blind eye' to its terms or adopted the attitude 'whether it is breach of contract or not, I care not'.[16] In these circumstances it will also be impossible for defendants to establish that they lacked the

---

12 *Camellia Tanker Ltd v ITF* [1976] ICR 274.
13 *Brimelow v Casson* [1924] 1 Ch 302. Cf. the uncertainty surrounding the existence of the defence of justification to the tort of intimidation – see Lord Devlin in *Rookes v Barnard* [1964] AC 1129, 1206 – and, if it does exist, its extent – see Lord Denning's suggestion that it could apply where unions made strike threats to secure the removal of 'troublemakers' in *Morgan v Fry* [1968] 2 QB 710, 729 and *Cory Lighterage Ltd v TGWU* [1973] ICR 339, 356–7.
14 *South Wales Miners' Association v Glamorgan Coal Co.* [1905] AC 239.
15 [1965] AC 269.
16 Lord Denning MR in *Emerald Construction Co. Ltd v Lowthian* [1966] 1 WLR 691, 700–701 and *Daily Mirror Newspapers Ltd v Gardner* [1968] 2 QB 762, 780.

necessary intention to cause breach. Indeed, it is no longer feasible to argue that the requisite knowledge and intention were absent where the defendant's acts disrupted business relations and could therefore be expected to affect the performance of commercial contracts.

The most fundamental change concerns the third requirement of the tort: breach of contract. In *Torquay Hotel Co. Ltd v Cousins*[17] the Court had to decide whether there could be liability in this tort for placing an embargo on the delivery of oil to the plaintiffs. It appeared that the contract between the plaintiffs and Esso for the supply of oil had not been broken because it contained a *force majeure* clause exempting Esso from liability for nonperformance caused by labour disputes. The majority of the Court of Appeal held that there had nevertheless been a breach of contract. This clause merely prevented Torquay Hotels from sueing Esso for damages caused by the breach; the defendant union officials could still be liable in tort for inducing breach of contract. In Lord Denning's opinion, by contrast, the time had come to extend the tort to cover 'deliberate and direct interference with the execution of a contract without causing any breach'.[18]

Contrary to popular belief, sweeping statements by Lord Denning did not of themselves suffice to change the law. But in this instance it appears that the House of Lords may have endorsed his views. In the *Merkur Island Shipping* case,[19] the issue was whether union officials were liable in tort for blacking a ship and thereby preventing the performance of a commercial contract which contained a *force majeure* clause providing that payment for hire ceased in these circumstances. All the Law Lords agreed with Lord Diplock who cited Lord Denning's views in the *Torquay Hotels* case to support his assertion that the tort covered *interference* which did not give rise to any breach of contract for which one contracting party could sue the other for damages. But Lord Diplock was extending the law beyond Lord Denning's formulation which was confined to *direct* interference. Lord Diplock applied his view of the wider liability to alleged *indirect* interference. It is now arguable, therefore, that there can be liability for either direct or indirect interference with contract even where no breach of contract occurs.

Interference with Business by Unlawful Means

There is a clear body of case law establishing the existence of a separate tort of interference with trade, business or other economic interests by unlawful means. The essential ingredients of the tort appear to be *damage* to the plaintiff deliberately and *intentionally* caused by the defendant's use of *unlawful means*. It may extend to causing damage other than economic loss but, in the context of labour disputes, the damage will almost invariably be

17 [1969] 2 Ch 106.
18 ibid. 138.
19 *Merkur Island Shipping Corporation Ltd v Laughton* [1983] 2 AC 570. See Carty (1983); Wedderburn (1983).

to the plaintiff's economic interests. These may include employment. It is therefore possible that workers who lose their jobs or are unable to work as a consequence of industrial action could have a remedy in this tort. But they would have to show that the action was deliberately and intentionally aimed at preventing them from working. In the *Lonrho* case, the Law Lords rejected the suggestion that there was a general liability for losses which are the inevitable consequence of unlawful acts. Even where economic loss is intentionally and deliberately caused, there can be no liability unless unlawful means are used. The suggestion that lawful acts could be made tortious (in the absence of a conspiracy) where they were done out of spite or malice in order to damage another was rejected by the House of Lords at the end of the nineteenth century.[20]

Considerable uncertainty exists over the ambit of unlawful means. There is no doubt that other torts can be unlawful means for the purpose of this liability. For example, in *Stratford v Lindley* two of the Law Lords gave interference with the plaintiff's business by unlawful means as a reason for granting an injunction; the unlawful means consisted of the separate tort of inducing breaches of the watermen's contracts of employment and possibly also of the hiring contracts between the plaintiffs and their customers. Similarly in *Hadmor Productions Ltd v Hamilton*,[21] Lord Diplock accepted that the decision by ACTT to black any attempt by Thames Television to show programmes made by the plaintiffs amounted to interference with the plaintiffs' business by the unlawful means of threatening to induce ACTT technicians to break their contracts of employment, which was itself actionable as the separate tort of intimidation.

In some circumstances criminal acts may amount to unlawful means. But where acts are criminal solely because they contravene statutory provisions it now seems probable that they can provide the basis for civil liability in tort only in two situations. The first is where the statutory duty which was broken was imposed for the benefit of a class which includes the plaintiff. The other is where the statute created a public right the infringement of which caused the plaintiff special damage over and above that suffered by the public generally.[22] Even more uncertainty surrounds the status of a breach of contract. In *Rookes v Barnard* the Law Lords held that it was an unlawful act for the purposes of the tort of intimidation. As a matter of logic it ought to follow that it could amount to unlawful means for the purposes of this tort as well. Otherwise it might be actionable to threaten to break a contract but not to go ahead with the actual breach.

Several attempts have been made to find unlawful means other than crimes, torts or breaches of contract as a way of outflanking the statutory immunities. In one case alleged breaches of local byelaws were held to be insufficient.[23] But operating an agreement which would be condemned

---

[20] *Allen v Flood* [1898] AC 1.
[21] [1983] 1 AC 191.
[22] *Gouriet v UPW* [1978] AC 435 (noted by Simpson, 1978); *Lonrho v Shell* [1982] AC 173, 185–6.
[23] *Camellia Tanker Ltd v ITF* [1976] ICR 274.

under restrictive trade practices legislation has been held to be unlawful means,[24] and after the *Universe Tankships* case (above) it is arguable that the use of economic duress would be sufficient as well. In *Associated Newspapers Group Ltd v Wade*,[25] Lord Denning even suggested that interference with the freedom of the press amounted to the use of unlawful means. This had occurred, he said, where union officials instructed their members not to handle advertisements from certain advertisers. He also expressed the view that the officials could be liable to public authorities which were thereby unable to publish notices in newspapers as they were required to do by statute, on the separate ground of disabling a public authority from performing its statutory duties. This opinion was based on *Meade v Haringey London Borough Council*,[26] where the defendant education authority decided to keep schools closed during a strike by ancillary workers, including caretakers who normally opened the schools. Both Lord Denning and Eveleigh LJ asserted that, in calling on an education authority to break its statutory duty to provide education, unions would be acting unlawfully and without immunity under TULRA.

This decision like that in *Universe Tankships* shows that future development of the common law could take the form of creating new liabilities, which may or may not be torts, rather than the extension of existing ones. One effect of the recent labour legislation is to increase the potential for the use of breach of statutory duties. For example, enforcing a closed shop other than a ballot-approved UMA could arguably constitute unlawful means for the purposes of the tort of interference with business by unlawful means. Alternatively, it might amount to a new form of liability. Anyone deliberately damaged by such an infringement might have a common law remedy quite apart from any rights under the 1980s legislation itself. Against this liability there would be no immunity under TULRA.

THE IMMUNITIES

Trade Unions' Immunity and its Repeal

The *Taff Vale* case,[27] in which the House of Lords held that a union itself as distinct from its officials could be liable in tort for damages, is one of the major landmarks of industrial relations history. Although trade unions had been legitimised in the eyes of the law by the Trade Union Act 1871, it had been generally thought that they lacked sufficient legal personality to be suable.[28] The decision posed a threat to the very existence of trade unions through awards of damages and legal costs — in the *Taff Vale* case they amounted to £42,000 — which would bankrupt their funds. Statutory

---

24 *Daily Mirror Newspapers Ltd v Gardner* [1968] 2 QB 762.
25 [1979] ICR 664.
26 [1979] ICR 494.
27 *Taff Vale Railway Co. v Amalgamated Society of Railway Servants* [1901] AC 426.
28 See e.g. Devonshire (1894, Pt I: para. 104).

protection against this threat was provided by s.4 of the TDA 1906, which gave trade unions a blanket immunity by prohibiting legal actions in tort against them.

Since this immunity extended to tort actions which had nothing to do with trade disputes, Kahn-Freund (1983:364) described it as 'a privilege, not a mere immunity', but he added that it would have made little difference in practice had it not existed. This was because unions would have had the benefit of the immunities provided for individuals by the rest of the 1906 Act, and that where their officials were found to have acted outside the scope of these immunities the union had usually paid the damages and legal costs. For similar reasons the Donovan Commission proposed that the complete immunity should be reduced to a qualified immunity still extending to all tort liability but confined to acts done in contemplation or furtherance of a trade dispute (paras. 902–11). This thinking overlooks the 'immense symbolic and psychological significance' of the blanket immunity (DE, 1981:para.114). Moreover, the three periods when the immunity has not been in force have all shown that its absence can contribute to creating a climate favourable to using the law in industrial disputes. The utility of this legal option turns in the first place on the extent of the liabilities that can be imposed.

From 1901 to 1906 this was the full range of economic tort liabilities, the boundaries of which had not then been clearly defined. From 1972 to 1974 the period governed by the IRA which had removed the blanket immunity through its repeal of the 1906 Act, the legal structure was more complex. While immunities against economic tort liabilities were provided for acts done 'in contemplation or furtherance of an industrial dispute' ('industrial dispute' being an amended version of the 1906 Act's definition of a trade dispute), the same acts were made subject to a series of wide-ranging statutory liabilities known as 'unfair industrial practices' before the National Industrial Relations Court (NIRC). Trade unions which registered under the IRA were immune from the basic unfair industrial practice of inducing breach of contract, but unregistered 'organisations of workers' were not. Not surprisingly the encouragement thereby provided to employers to take unregistered unions to court led to litigation concerning the central issue: when can unions be made liable, in legal terminology 'vicariously' liable, for the acts of their officials or members? As is explained below, the IRA case law may still be relevant today.[29] The immunity established by s.4 of the 1906 Act was restored on the repeal of the IRA by TULRA s.14(1),[30] but

[29] The case law on who is an 'authorised official or other person' for the purposes of the employer's duties to consult on proposed redundancies under EPA s.99 and transfers of undertakings under the Transfer of Undertakings (Protection of Employment) Regulations 1981, reg.10, could also be relevant to the vicarious liability of a union in tort.

[30] It was not in fact a total immunity because s.14(2) enabled unions to be sued for negligence, nuisance or breach of duty resulting in personal injury, or breach of duty in connection with property in respect of acts not done in contemplation or furtherance of a trade dispute. Although the ambit of this reservation, like that of its predecessor, TDA 1906 s.4(2), was uncertain, it was generally agreed that it did not concern liabilities which could arise in strikes (Wedderburn, 1974: 537–8).

was again removed when s.15(1) of EA 1982 repealed TULRA s.14. Unions as such now only have the same limited immunities as individuals from tortious liability for acts done 'in contemplation or furtherance of a trade dispute'. These immunities, now in TULRA s.13, have been greatly reduced by the 1980, 1982 and 1984 Acts.

One of the arguments in favour of this change was that it would encourage unions to exercise greater control over their members. But as the government's Green Paper pointed out (DE, 1981:paras. 127–8), it might equally have the opposite effect, since there must necessarily be some unofficial action for which unions cannot be made responsible. Moreover, by encouraging dissension within unions and weakening their internal authority, it could lead to more unofficial action. Against this it was argued that removal of the blanket immunity would enable employers to be properly compensated for losses caused by unlawful industrial action. Whether this is so depends on two factors: first, whether the union is vicariously liable for the acts of its officials or members and, second, whether the union is both liable and able to pay compensation to cover the losses incurred.

Vicarious liability. Under common law principles an employer is liable for the acts of his employees done within the course and scope of their employment and a 'principal' is liable for the acts of his 'agents' done within the scope of their authority. Between *Taff Vale* in 1901 and the time when the 1906 Act came into force, the courts treated union officials as agents of the union, but limited the circumstances in which unions were liable for their actions by applying the common law principles with 'extreme caution' (Hepple, 1972:206). The theory of vicarious liability is based on the implied power of the principal or employer to 'command'. This is difficult to apply to trade unions which generally do not have an authoritarian structure (Donovan, 1968:para.122), a point confirmed by experience under the IRA.

In the *Heatons* case[31] the House of Lords found that the TGWU was vicariously liable for the action of its shop stewards in organising the blacking of certain haulage firms in the docks, on the ground that they acted with the implied authority of the union. This authority derived less from the formal structure of the union set out in its rules than from custom and practice and its policies as evidenced, for example, by delegate conference resolutions. On this basis shop stewards could be given authority to bind the union 'from the bottom', that is, by the members, as well as from the top. But in the later *GAS* case[32] the Law Lords found that no such authority existed in respect of blacking of a company that wanted to provide baggage handling facilities at London Airport, because in this dispute union policy was apparently to achieve its goals through negotiation rather than industrial action. Overall the IRA case law made a union's vicarious liability a matter for argument in virtually all cases other than those about action which was clearly official under the rules.

---

[31] *Heatons Transport (St Helens) Ltd v TGWU* [1973] AC 15. See Davies (1973); Hepple (1972).
[32] *General Aviation Services Ltd v TGWU* [1976] IRLR 224. See Davies (1976).

The 1982 Act has tried to resolve the uncertainties surrounding vicarious liability. Section 15 sets out the conditions which must be satisfied before a union can be held liable for certain specified torts: inducing breach of or interference with contract; intimidation by threatening breach of, to induce breach of, or to interfere with a contract; and conspiring to commit one of these torts. These are the main but by no means the only economic tort liabilities which can arise in labour disputes. It is a matter for speculation which criteria on vicarious liability will be applied in other cases such as an action for interference with business by unlawful means. The courts could apply those in EA 1982 s.15, those in the *Heatons* case or some refinement of the basic common law principles, to which the case law of 1901–6 could be relevant.[33]

The basic principle of vicarious liability under EA 1982 s.15(2) is that a union is only liable for acts 'authorised or endorsed by a responsible person'. The section specifies five categories of 'responsible persons' and apparently intends unions to be liable for authorisations and endorsements by the first three of these in all circumstances. They are its principal executive committee, anyone empowered by the rules to authorise or endorse the act in question, and the president or general secretary. The other two categories are employed officials and committees to which they regularly report. For their actions a union is not liable if either they have no power to act as they did under the rules or their action has been 'repudiated' by the principal executive committee, president or general secretary. Repudiation must occur as soon as is reasonably practicable and be notified to the person whose acts are being repudiated without delay. Furthermore, if the executive committee, president or general secretary afterwards behave in a manner which is inconsistent with repudiation, it is ineffective.

Apart from the problem of what amounts to an 'authorisation' or 'endorsement', one obvious difficulty which may arise is identifying those persons or bodies who do and those who do not have the necessary authority under the rules. A union's rules for this purpose are defined to include 'any other written provisions forming part of the contract between a member and other members'. This could conceivably include, say, a shop steward's credentials or handbook. If so, shop stewards may be found to have implied authority to authorise or endorse tortious acts along the lines of the reasoning in the *Heatons* case, although it would not, under the 1982 provisions, be possible to rely on unwritten custom and practice for this purpose. The escape route of repudiation cannot be used in respect of authorisations or endorsements by most shop stewards since it applies only to acts done by officials employed by the union and committees to which they report. Does this mean that a union can never avoid liability for the acts of other 'responsible persons'? It must be arguable that a union is not liable

[33] In *Thomas v NUM (South Wales Area)* [1985] IRLR 136. Scott J held that the *Heatons* decision led to the conclusion that the union was responsible 'on ordinary principles of vicarious liability' for the acts of its branches and their officers in arranging picketing, which involved the novel tort of unreasonable interference with the right to use the public highway. See further Chapter 7.

where, for example, the rules clearly limit the powers of the president or general secretary so as to deny them the authority to 'authorise or endorse' industrial action. But it is a matter of speculation whether this or other common law principles can be applied to limit the extent of a union's vicarious liability under EA 1982 s.15.

What practical consequences might stem from this legal uncertainty? One possibility would be for unions to take steps to avoid overt authorisation of industrial action in terms of the 1982 Act. The 'spontaneous' action by NGA chapels in national newspapers, which prevented the papers from printing in November 1983 after the NGA had been fined for contempt of court in proceedings arising out of the Stockport Messenger dispute (see Chapter 19), can be seen as an example of this. Clark and Wedderburn argue that as a consequence of the 1982 Act, 'wedges will inevitably be driven between stewards and full-time officers, between both of them and the executive and the two top officers and between all of them (as "responsible persons") and the membership' (1983:204 and see generally 198–206). The Austin Rover dispute at the end of 1984, which is discussed below, provides evidence to support this view. The likelihood of such fundamental developments will be crucially influenced by the extent to which employers take or threaten legal proceedings against unions as such. In the first two years after the 1982 Act came into force, there were a significant number of tort actions brought by employers where unions were named defendants (Evans, 1985).

Limits on damages. Section 16 of the 1982 Act limits the liability of unions for damages in tort actions.[34] This provision is supposed to reduce the threat of bankrupting unions through legal actions. For a union with less than 5,000 members the maximum award of damages in any single proceedings is £10,000; for unions with between 5,000 and 25,000 members, £50,000; 25,000 to 100,000 members, £125,000; and for unions with over 100,000 members, £250,000. It must be emphasised that these limits apply as against each plaintiff. Where several employers bring separate actions which are heard together, as, for example, when several national daily newspaper owners began proceedings against the NGA over the shutdown of Fleet Street in November 1983, the maximum potential liability of the union in respect of particular industrial action (if it cannot claim immunity under TULRA s.13) becomes several times the statutory limit, and the possibility of a single strike bankrupting a union becomes a real one. But the actual amount of damages awarded in any particular case depends on what losses are proved by the plaintiff to be attributable to acts for which the union is liable. This could be well below the statutory maximum. For example, in the Stockport Messenger action against the NGA, where the union's maximum liability was £250,000, the damages (as distinct from fines for contempt of

---

[34] These limits do not apply to actions for negligence, nuisance or breach of duty which give rise to personal injury or to any action for breach of duty in connection with the ownership, occupation, possession, control or use of property (EA 1982 s.16(2)). This was also in effect the position up to 1982 under TULRA s.14(2) in respect of acts not done in contemplation or furtherance of a trade dispute.

court) awarded were £125,000, a sum which included awards of aggravated and exemplary damages which go beyond compensation for proved losses.[35]

Section 17 of the 1982 Act introduces the concept of protected property against which no award of damages or costs can be enforced. This includes a union's political fund (if it has one), any provident benefits fund (a fund used to pay sickness, accident, death, superannuation or similar benefits), and the private property of a union's trustees, officials and members. Switching money into provident benefits funds in particular may be a means of protecting a union's assets. But it must be emphasised that no property is protected against procedures to enforce payment of fines imposed for contempt of court; nor is there any limit on the amount of these fines.

In Contemplation or Furtherance of a Trade Dispute

After the repeal of the complete immunity for trade unions from tort liability, the phrase 'in contemplation or furtherance of a trade dispute' is the key to all the immunities that remain for unions and individuals who organise industrial action. Its principal function is to delimit the area in which some of the tortious liabilities will not apply. Although after the legislation of the 1980s Wedderburn's celebrated description of the phrase as the 'golden formula' (1965:222) is thus perhaps no longer entirely appropriate (see Simpson, 1983), interpretation of the definition of a trade dispute and of the limiting words 'in contemplation or furtherance' remains a vital factor in determining the extent of the immunities.

The basic definition of a trade dispute in TULRA s.29(1), as amended by s.18 of EA 1982, is as follows:

a dispute between workers and their employer which relates wholly or mainly to one or more of the following, that is to say –

(a) terms and conditions of employment or the physical conditions in which any workers are required to work;

(b) engagement or non-engagement, or termination or suspension of employment or the duties of employment, of one or more workers;

(c) allocation of work or the duties of employment as between workers or groups of workers;

(d) matters of discipline;

(e) the membership or non-membership of a trade union on the part of a worker;

(f) facilities for officials of trade unions and;

(g) machinery for negotiation or consultation, and other procedures, relating to any of the foregoing matters, including the recognition by employers or employers' associations of the right of a trade union to represent workers in any such negotiation or consultation or in the carrying out of such procedures.

---

[35] *Messenger Newspapers Group Ltd v NGA* [1984] IRLR 397. See further Chapter 19.

Subject matter of a trade dispute. The phrase 'terms and conditions' in s.29(1)(a), the most basic part of the definition, is arguably not limited to contractual terms of employment. Thus in the *Hadmor* case[36] a dispute over adherence to a consultation agreement between ACTT and Thames Television came within this part of the definition. But what determines whether the facts of particular disputes do fall within s.29(1)(a) remains uncertain. The action in *BBC v Hearn*[37] arose out of the decision of the Association of Broadcasting Staff, in conformity with its policies on racialism, to take action to prevent the BBC from transmitting television coverage of the Cup Final to South Africa. The Court of Appeal held that on the evidence there was no trade dispute but indicated that the decision would have been different had the union made a formal demand for amendment of its members' conditions of service enabling them to refuse to co-operate with broadcasts that were being transmitted to South Africa. But in the *Universe Tankships* case Lord Cross cautioned that such a demand could not create a trade dispute out of something which was not 'in reality' a trade dispute.[38]

In *Dimbleby & Sons Ltd v NUJ*,[39] journalists belonging to the NUJ who were employed by Dimbleby refused to supply copy to TBF (Printers) Ltd., a non-union company in the same group as T Bailey Forman Ltd with whom the NUJ had been in dispute for five years over the dismissal of some of its members. While it was conceded that this longstanding dispute was a trade dispute, the union argued that there was also a separate trade dispute between Dimbleby and its journalists on the basis that the journalists had asked for their terms of employment to be varied to excuse them from supplying copy to TBF. In the Court of Appeal, Lord Cross's dictum in *Universe Tankships* was cited in support of the rejection of this argument.[40] More important is Lord Diplock's astonishing statement in the House of Lords in *Dimbleby* that only current terms and conditions could be relevant, an opinion that would take a dispute over a pay claim outside the trade dispute definition!

Section 29(1)(b) appears to be wide enough to cover disputes arising out of the employment or dismissal of any person whatever the context, including victimisation after strikes and closed shop disputes. Of particular interest in recent years has been the question whether disputes motivated by a fear of future redundancies are trade disputes. While there is no doubt that they can be,[41] it may be difficult, under the post-1982 form of the definition, to establish that this is in fact the case. The point is demonstrated by the *Mercury* case.[42] The action arose out of the refusal of POEU members employed by British Telecom (BT) to interconnect Mercury with BT's telecommunications system in order to enable Mercury to run a private telecommunications service in accordance with a government licence given

---

36 [1983] 1 AC 191.
37 [1977] ICR 685.
38 [1983] 1 AC 366, 392.
39 [1984] ICR 386 (noted by Simpson, 1984a).
40 [1984] ICR 396–7, 400–401.
41 See e.g. *General Aviation Services Ltd v TGWU* [1975] ICR 276.
42 *Mercury Communications Ltd v Scott-Garner* [1984] ICR 74.

under the British Telecommunications Act 1981. The POEU opposed this 'liberalisation' of the industry and its (then) future 'privatisation' and had organised other industrial action to demonstrate its opposition to these policies. This enabled the Court of Appeal to doubt whether the refusal to interconnect Mercury 'related wholly or mainly to' fear of future job losses, as the union claimed, rather than the other wider political issues.

This decision highlights the crucial importance of the 1982 amendment which requires trade disputes to 'relate wholly or mainly to' rather than be 'connected with' any of the listed subjects. The aim of this change was to reverse one effect of the House of Lords ruling in the *NWL* case in 1979 that any genuine connection between a dispute and the subject matter listed in s.29(1) was sufficient to qualify a dispute as a trade dispute regardless of the presence of other elements, whether political, personal or of any other nature. The change has resurrected the 'predominant purpose' test wrongly applied by the Court of Appeal before the *NWL* decision (see below) and raised doubts about the status of any labour dispute where the actors may have mixed motives. The impossibility of drawing any clear line between political and industrial disputes has even been recognised by the judiciary.[43] It therefore follows that this change, like any other attempt to restrict the trade dispute definition so as to exclude disputes with a political element, must 'inevitably restrict many types of industrial action which are undoubtedly aimed at improving terms and conditions of employment' (DE, 1981: para.200). The right of workers and unions to use their industrial resources for political ends is a fundamental issue (see Kahn-Freund, 1954:127; Clark and Wedderburn, 1983:160). It is likely to become even more important as and when unions resist government cuts and privatisation policies.[44]

TULRA s.29(1)(d)–(g) identifies issues which can give rise to disputes in any industrial relations system in which the central institution is collective bargaining: union membership, union recognition, facilities for union officials and procedures in general, as well as disciplinary matters. It is of course a question of fact in each case whether a particular dispute relates wholly or mainly to one or more of these issues. In particular, recognition disputes may well be excluded if there is a significant element of ill-feeling towards the employer behind the industrial action.[45]

An important restriction on the potential subject matter of a trade dispute was made by EA 1982 in redefining the meaning of 'worker' for the purposes of the trade dispute definition. It is now confined to workers (or, in some circumstances, former workers) employed by the employer party to the dispute. Thus for example a dispute over allocation of work between groups

---

[43] Roskill LJ in *Sherard v AUEW* [1973] ICR 421, 435.

[44] The possibility of disputes between government ministers and workers being trade disputes in some circumstances is recognised by the provision that where disputes relate to matters which have been referred to joint bodies on which ministers are represented or which cannot be settled without a minister exercising a statutory power, they are treated as disputes between workers and their own employer: TULRA s.29(2). See Davies and Freedland (1984:799).

[45] Cf. *Stratford v Lindley* [1965] AC 269 and *Torquay Hotel Co. Ltd v Cousins* [1969] 2 Ch 106.

of workers can only fall within s.29(1)(c) where the workers concerned are all employed by the same employer, who must be the employer party to the dispute. Where, as in both the *Dimbleby* and *Mercury* cases, one of the issues was the allocation of work between workers of different employers — Dimbleby's own printers or TBF in the one case, BT or Mercury in the other — this could not be a trade dispute.

A final point about the subject matter of a trade dispute concerns overseas disputes. It was expressly provided that such disputes were included by TULRA s.29(3), which recognised both that business enterprise was no longer confined with national borders and the legitimacy of international trade union solidarity. This provision was amended in 1982. Overseas disputes can now only be trade disputes where those acting in contemplation or furtherance of them are 'likely to be affected in respect of one or more of the matters specified in [s.29(1)] by the outcome of the dispute'. This qualification may in fact be impossible to satisfy since it is unlikely that unions and union officers who are organising action in contemplation or furtherance of an overseas dispute — as distinct from the workers they represent — will be affected by its outcome. In particular, action organised by the ITF against ships flying flags of convenience could fail to satisfy this condition (see further below).

Parties to a trade dispute. After the 1982 amendments the parties to a trade dispute must now be 'workers and their own employer'. This change eliminates two types of dispute from the definition: disputes between different groups of workers, and disputes between employers and workers not employed by them. The exclusion of worker-worker disputes has been justified on the grounds that there should be no immunities in disputes in which employers are 'neutral' or 'innocent bystanders'. But as the majority of the Donovan Commission recognised (para.820), even in demarcation disputes employers are not necessarily neutral. Moreover, the experience of the IRA (when worker-worker disputes were excluded from that Act's industrial dispute definition) demonstrated that whether or not employers were parties to disputes over union membership was very much a question of impression. For example, in the *Cory Lighterage* case,[46] a lighterman allowed his union membership to lapse and the other lightermen then refused to work with him. His employers therefore suspended him on full pay. The Court of Appeal found that the employers were not party to this dispute, while noting minor variations of fact which would have made them a party. The law now encourages employers to do everything possible to maintain the appearance of neutrality in demarcation, union membership and inter-union recognition disputes in order to prevent them from being trade disputes.

Of profound importance is the narrowing of the range of employer-worker disputes which can be trade disputes to those between workers and their own employer. This may include a dispute between an employer and workers who have ceased to be employed by him where either their

---

[46]   *Cory Lighterage v TGWU* [1973] ICR 197, 339. See too *Langston v AUEW* [1974] ICR 180.

employment was terminated in connection with the dispute or the termination was one of the circumstances giving rise to the dispute. Thus a dispute between an employer and his former workers over their dismissal is still clearly a trade dispute. But the general exclusion of disputes between workers and an employer whose actions may affect their jobs even though he does not directly employ them reflects the narrow view that 'industrial relations and industrial action are fundamentally about what goes on at the workplace' and only about this.[47]

An employer may take a dispute out of the trade dispute definition by the creation of separate legal entities so that it may be difficult if not impossible to prove that the dispute is between workers and the entity which is legally their employer. In *Examite Ltd v Whittaker*[48] the employer, whose dismissal of certain workers had given rise to the dispute, ceased to function and a new 'front' company, the plaintiffs, was created to carry on the business. Lord Denning MR was prepared to 'pierce the veil' to discover the original employer behind the corporate facade; the dispute thus had the correct parties — even for the purposes of the post-1982 form of the definition. But the House of Lords in the *Dimbleby* case refused to consider the possibility of 'piercing the veil' of two companies run by the same individual — T Bailey Forman and TBF Printers — where to identify the two as one would have provided immunity for industrial action taken against one of them by the NUJ. Some employers may thus reorganise their businesses to take advantage of the post-1982 form of the trade dispute definition, a point which is elaborated in Chapter 5 above.

Uncertainty also surrounds action taken on an industry-wide basis where more than one employer is involved. When can it be said that there are separate disputes between each of these employers and their own workers? The question is important: action which is only in furtherance of a trade dispute between other workers and their employer will be secondary action effectively deprived of immunity by EA 1980 s.17 (see below).

The need to show a dispute between workers and their own employer could have a fateful significance for the ITF's campaign against ships flying flags of convenience. In some of the cases arising out of this campaign, the ITF has acted without the support of the crew of the ship concerned.[49] There would after 1982 be no trade dispute in these circumstances. This conclusion is reinforced by the repeal of TULRA s.29(4), which gave trade unions and employers' associations automatic standing as parties to trade disputes. The overall effect of this repeal will depend on the attitude of the courts. The 1906 definition did not expressly provide that unions could be parties to trade disputes, but the courts recognised that their representative role encompassed initiating disputes without referring back to their members.[50] This may not now be the case. In *Mercury* the Court of Appeal stressed that

---

[47]   433 HL Deb, 13 July 1982, 277 and 293 (the passage quoted), Lord Gowrie.
[48]   [1977] IRLR 312.
[49]   E.g. *Star Sea Transport Corporation v Slater* [1979] 1 Lloyds Rep 26 and *NWL Ltd v Woods* [1979] ICR 867. Cf. *Camellia Tanker Ltd v ITF* [1976] ICR 274.
[50]   See e.g. *NALGO v Bolton Corporation* [1940] AC 166, 189.

it was necessary to find out what POEU members employed by BT thought the dispute was mainly about; what the POEU itself thought the dispute was about, while relevant, could not be decisive because there could be no trade dispute between BT and the union.[51] It does seem therefore that a union may have to wait for a dispute between workers and their own employer to arise before it can take action with any prospect of retaining immunity, a state of affairs which has been judicially described as 'ludicrous'.[52]

Contemplation or furtherance. The immunities only exist where unions and individuals who organise industrial action act 'in contemplation or furtherance' of a trade dispute. The meaning of this phrase was authoritatively determined by the Law Lords in *Express Newspapers Ltd v MacShane*.[53] The NUJ was involved in a trade dispute with the proprietors of provincial newspapers over pay. It called on its members employed by the Press Association (PA), which supplies copy to both the national and provincial press, to strike in order to reduce the copy available to provincial papers. Because its PA members were divided over whether to strike, the NUJ went further and instructed its members on national newspapers to black PA copy in order to encourage its PA members to strike and to fortify the morale of those who did so. The defendant NUJ officials argued that they were protected against liability for inducing NUJ members employed by the Daily Express to break their contracts because they were acting in furtherance of the dispute between provincial newspapers and their journalists. The House of Lords upheld this claim. In the opinion of the majority a person acts in furtherance of a trade dispute if he honestly and genuinely believes that his acts will further the interests of one of the parties to the dispute. Although this is a subjective test, it envisages some limitation in the notion of contemplation or furtherance based on the actor's 'honesty of purpose'. While an objective test has been introduced for the purposes of secondary action (see below), EA 1982 s.18(7) confirms that the *MacShane* construction of contemplation or furtherance is unaffected by the amendment of the trade dispute definition.

Contemplation or furtherance also require a person's acts to be linked to a trade dispute in another way. It is only possible to act in furtherance of an existing dispute or in contemplation of a dispute that is imminent. Acts done with a view to initiating claims for improved terms and conditions which could lead to a dispute are too early in point of time to be in contemplation of a dispute.[54] It is, however, expressly provided in TULRA s.29(5) that action taken in the belief that it will achieve its objective without any dispute occurring is taken in contemplation of a dispute, if it would have given rise to a trade dispute with the person against whom it was taken had it been

---

[51] [1984] ICR 74, 106–7, 123–4.
[52] Templeman J in *Camellia Tanker Ltd SA v ITF* [1976] ICR 274, 282–3.
[53] [1980] AC 672. See Wedderburn (1980); Kerr (1980). See too *Duport Steels Ltd v Sirs* [1980] ICR 161 and *Norbrook Laboratories Ltd v King* [1984] IRLR 200.
[54] *Bents' Brewery v Hogan* [1945] 2 All ER 570.

resisted. After 1982 this is limited to action taken by workers against their own employer.

The Golden Formula Immunities

The aim of TDA 1906 was to provide qualified immunities against civil liability for individuals such as union officials who called on workers to take industrial action. They were not complete immunities since they only applied to acts done 'in contemplation or furtherance of a trade dispute'. But it was intended that their protection should extend to all the economic torts which had been developed by the courts around the turn of the century. TDA 1965 extended this protection to cover the liability imposed in *Rookes v Barnard*.

On the repeal of the IRA in 1974, TULRA sought to re-establish these immunities in a 'stronger and clearer' form. The immunity against liability for civil conspiracy in TDA 1906 s.1 was re-enacted in an amended form in TULRA s.13(4):

> An agreement or combination by two or more persons to do or procure the doing of any act in contemplation or furtherance of a trade dispute shall not be actionable in tort if the act is one which, if done without any such agreement or combination, would not be actionable in tort.

So far as liability for conspiracy to injure is concerned, this probably adds little if anything to the common law. Any action which 'relates wholly or mainly to' any of the subjects of a trade dispute set out in TULRA s.29(1) will almost certainly also have the predominant purpose of furthering workers' legitimate interests. On the authority of the *Crofter* case it will not, as explained above, be an actionable conspiracy in the first place. But TULRA s.13(4) does limit the extent of potential liability for conspiracy to commit an unlawful act. Defendants cannot be liable for this form of the tort unless the acts which they do are in themselves tortious. Conspiracies to commit torts remain actionable and are not protected by TULRA s.13(4). But since a breach of contract is not actionable in tort, the immunity would now apply, if necessary, in any action against workers for conspiracy to break their contracts of employment by taking industrial action.

The immunity against liability for inducing breach of contract in TDA 1906 s.3 and the 1965 Act's immunity against intimidation were re-enacted in a revised form in TULRA s.13(1). As amended in 1976, s.13(1)(a) covers inducing breach of, interference with, and inducing another person to interfere with any contract and s.13(1)(b) provides immunity against intimidation by threats of breach of or interference with, or to induce breach of or interference with, any contract. These extensions of immunity were intended to keep pace with the development of liability for interference with commercial contracts (see above).

In *Rookes v Barnard* in 1964 the Law Lords confirmed that the second 'limb' of s.3 of the 1906 Act provided an immunity against a form of liability which did not exist: 'interference with the trade, business or employment of another person or with the right of another person to dispose of his capital or his labour as he wills by otherwise lawful means'. It was none the less re-enacted in TULRA s.13(2) 'for the avoidance of doubt', a prudent move in the light of the House of Lords' statement in 1966 that they were now free to overrule their own previous decisions.[55] It is, therefore, open to the Law Lords to find that there is now a form of civil liability for interference with trade or business even where no unlawful means are used. If this should happen, there would now be no immunity to prevent its application to trade disputes, because TULRA s.13(2) was repealed by EA 1982 s.19(1). The justification for this step was that in the *Hadmor* case in 1982 Lord Diplock appeared to suggest that TULRA s.13(2) provided immunity against interference with trade or business *by unlawful means*.[56] Moreover the Court of Session in Scotland acted on this suggestion by finding that it was arguable that workers who were occupying their workplace were not liable for trespass if the only damage they caused was by way of interference with business.[57] Since these developments took place while the 1982 Employment Bill was before Parliament, the opportunity to head off the unlikely possibility of an extension of the immunities by judicial interpretation was seized.

It follows that there is no immunity against liability for interference with trade or business by unlawful means, a tort which it seems (as explained above) does exist. The uncertainty which surrounds this tort centres on the question of 'unlawful means'. In order to ensure that the immunities against inducing breach of or interference with contract, intimidation and (if it existed) interference with trade or business etc. could not be outflanked, TULRA s.13(3) provided:

> For the avoidance of doubt it is hereby declared that (a) an act which by reason of [s.13(1) or (2)] is itself not actionable; (b) a breach of contract in contemplation or furtherance of a trade dispute shall not be regarded as the doing of an unlawful act or the use of unlawful means for the purpose of establishing liability in tort.

Paragraph (b) was included to remove the possibility created by *Rookes v Barnard* that a breach of contract is an unlawful act for the purposes of all economic tort liabilities and not just intimidation. TULRA s.13(3) was repealed by EA 1980 s.17(8), because it was thought that it might have prevented liability being imposed for secondary action which only indirectly interfered with commercial contracts in circumstances where the intention of EA 1980 s.17 was to remove immunity (see below). But its repeal affects all

---

55 See [1966] 1 WLR 1234.
56 [1983] 1 AC 191, 229. See too his description of s.13(2) as the 'genus' immunity of which s.13(1)(a) and (b) were 'species' in *Merkur Island Shipping Corporation v Laughton* [1983] 2 AC 570, 609–10. See Wedderburn (1983:635).
57 *Plessey Co. Plc v Wilson* [1982] IRLR 198, 1983 SLT 319. See Miller, 1982. But cf. *Phestos Shipping Co. v Kurmiawan* 1983 SLT 339, where the Court of Session in effect confirmed the traditional view of TULRA s.13(2).

Trade Union Immunities 183

cases and not just those concerning secondary action. Does this enable acts which are not in themselves actionable as torts because of TULRA s.13(1) to constitute unlawful means for other torts? The Law Lords in the *Hadmor* case held that it did not; TULRA s.13(3)(a) was unnecessary because acts stated to be 'not actionable' by s.13(1) were thereby rendered not unlawful for the purposes of all tort liability. But the repeal of s.13(3)(b) restores the doubt which existed in the ten years before TULRA over whether a breach of contract is an unlawful act for the purposes of all these liabilities. If it is, then the repeal of s.13(3)(b) will have to be added to the list of restrictions on the immunities made by the 1980, 1982 and 1984 Acts.

There is another difficulty concerning the ambit of the immunities. It arises where one of the torts against which TULRA s.13 provides immunity, a 'protected' tort, is committed indirectly by the use of unlawful means for which there is no immunity. Suppose, for example, that commercial contracts are interfered with by acts which constitute an independent tort such as trespass, nuisance or defamation. Does s.13 still provide immunity against liability for the protected tort? Arguably the better view is that the s.13 immunity does still apply, although judicial opinion on the point is divided.[58]

LOSS OF IMMUNITY

The legislation of 1980, 1982 and 1984 withdraws all or a critical part of the TULRA s.13 immunities in defined circumstances. Section 16(2) of EA 1980 removes all the immunities from an act done in the course of picketing outside the narrow scope of 'attendance declared lawful' by TULRA s.15. The impact of this provision is discussed in Chapter 7. In addition, s.17 of the 1980 Act withdraws immunities from most secondary action. Section 14 of EA 1982 removes immunity from action in support of union- or recognition-only practices and s.10 of TUA 1984 takes away a key part of the immunities from acts done by unions without the support of a ballot.

Secondary Action

In popular terms, secondary action is aimed at employers who are apparently not involved in a dispute. Its objectives range from putting economic pressure on employers who are involved in the dispute, through spreading the impact of a dispute so as to influence the general climate affecting its resolution, to demonstrations of support for the workers involved, that is, sympathetic action. Before 1980 the law drew no formal distinction between

---

[58] See *Rookes v Barnard* [1964] AC 1129, 1171–3 (Lord Reid) and 1214 (Lord Devlin) cf. 1190 (Lord Evershed); *Norbrook v King* [1984] IRLR 200, 204 (Lord Lowery) cf. 208–9 (Gibson LJ). See Simpson (1984b).

primary and secondary action.[59] Certainly after the scope of TULRA s.13 was extended to cover interference with any contract, there could apparently have been immunity for a wide range of action affecting the commercial contracts of secondary employers, whether these contracts were with the employers party to the dispute or not. But this was not confirmed until the *MacShane* and *Sirs* cases in 1979–80. By then the government had already identified secondary action as a major evil which had to be eradicated because it was being used to spread the disruptive effects of disputes to industry and the community at large. Moreover, the Law Lords' opinions in these cases included several strictly unnecessary passages which appeared to invite the government to legislate to remedy this state of affairs (Wedderburn, 1980:325; Lewis and Simpson, 1981:5–6).

The response was EA 1980 s.17. The section applies where 'one of the facts relied on for the purpose of establishing liability is that there has been secondary action'. Section 17(2) provides that there is secondary action in relation to a trade dispute when a person induces breach of or interferes with a contract of employment or threatens to do so if the employer under the contract of employment is not party to the trade dispute. Unless that action can pass through one of three gateways in subss.(3)–(5), s.17(1) removes immunity for indirectly inducing breach of or interfering with commercial contracts by the unlawful means of inducing breach of or interfering with these employment contracts.

A fundamental difficulty arises because secondary action is defined 'in relation to' a trade dispute. This may turn a lot of primary action into secondary action within the definition where there are separate trade disputes involving different employers. Inducing breaches of contracts of employment by workers of the employer in the first trade dispute is clearly secondary action 'in relation to' the second trade dispute and vice versa. The facts of the *Dimbleby* case would have raised this issue had the appellate courts upheld the judge's finding that there were two relevant trade disputes in existence. It was agreed that there was a trade dispute between T Bailey Forman Ltd, the publishing company, and journalists belonging to the NUJ who had been dismissed by the company in 1978. The NUJ argued that there was also a trade dispute between Dimbleby and journalists belonging to the NUJ whom Dimbleby had suspended for refusing to supply copy to TBF (Printers) Ltd. The House of Lords rejected this argument, but Lord Diplock indicated that if this second trade dispute had existed, then s.17 of EA 1980 would not have applied.[60] The NUJ's action in inducing Dimbleby's journalists to break their contracts of employment, however, was still secondary action 'in relation to' the trade dispute between T Bailey Forman Ltd and its former journalists. There is no obvious reason why the existence of a separate dispute between Dimbleby and its journalists would have

---

[59] Except for the period when IRA s.98 was in force. See Davies and Freedland (1984:831 and 723–4) for their view that a distinction was drawn in practice before 1976 through the restriction of the immunity against liability for inducing breach of contract to contracts of employment.

[60] *Dimbleby & Sons Ltd v NUJ* [1984] ICR 386, 407.

prevented this secondary action 'in relation to' the T Bailey Forman dispute from being 'one of the facts relied upon' (s.17(1)) by Dimbleby for the purposes of establishing liability for interfering with its commercial contracts with TBF and advertisers. Lord Diplock's contrary assumption is hardly authoritative as the point was not argued.

This potential absurdity demonstrates the fallacy which underlies s.17: that industrial action can be simply categorised as either primary or secondary. Equally curious is the fact that a direct approach to a 'secondary' employer asking him to 'black' another employer who is party to a primary dispute is not secondary action within s.17. Although it might amount to inducing breach of or interfering with commercial contracts, it does not involve one of the torts in s.17(2) (inducing breach of or interfering with employment contracts) and so falls outside the definition of secondary action. This apparent lacuna could be avoided by the judges treating such direct approaches as cases of indirect inducement by threats to induce breaches of contracts of employment if the secondary employer does not black the primary employer as requested (cf. Davies and Freedland, 1984:836).

The main gateway for secondary action to pass through in order to retain the immunities of TULRA s.13(1) is in EA 1980 s.17(3). This applies where the principal purpose of the action is directly to prevent or disrupt, during the dispute, the supply (under a contract subsisting at the time of the industrial action) of goods or services between an employer party to the dispute and the employer party to the contracts of employment to which the secondary action relates. In more intelligible language this means that secondary action against the first or immediate customers and suppliers of an employer party to a trade dispute may retain the full protection of TULRA s.13(1). But the several technical conditions which have to be satisfied will be fatal to most secondary action which the gateway might seem to cover (see Wedderburn, 1981; Lewis and Simpson, 1981:204–6; Davies and Freedland, 1984:836–40).

There appear to be three main obstacles blocking the first customer/first supplier gateway. First, the purpose of the secondary action must be to prevent or disrupt supplies 'directly', which is defined to mean 'otherwise than by means of preventing or disrupting the supply of goods or services by or to any other person' (s.17(6)(b)). The problem is that most action aimed directly at commercial contracts between the employer in dispute and his first customers or suppliers necessarily affects other parties as well, for example, purchasers of goods from the first customers of the employer in dispute (see DE, 1981:para.161). Whether such action can pass through the gateway seems to depend on its 'principal purpose'.

This resurrection of the principal or predominant purpose test, which the House of Lords rejected as a limitation on the 1974 version of the trade dispute definition in *NWL*, and the need for the action to be 'likely' to achieve that purpose, which introduces an objective element into judicial assessment of secondary action which the Law Lords rejected as a qualification of the test of 'furtherance' of a trade dispute in *MacShane*, comprise the second main obstacle to negotiating s.17(3). Both these criteria give maximum scope for the judges to have the final say on whether or not the requirements of the gateway are satisfied.

The third obstacle is that it is possible to pass through this gateway only where the supply of goods or services in question is under *subsisting* contracts between the primary and secondary employers. This requirement is arguably unfair to the organisers of industrial action because in most cases they will not know whether or not there is a contract and, if there is, who are the parties to it. The precise wording of the section gave some scope for judicial construction to overcome this unfairness by finding that the gateway was satisfied where defendants could establish that their principal purpose was to disrupt contracts between the primary and secondary employer, which they believed to exist even if in fact there was no such contract or the contract was between other parties (Wedderburn, 1981). But this approach was rejected in two cases concerning the blacking of ships flying flags of convenience while they were berthed in British ports.[61] In both cases it might have appeared that the blacking was effected by interference with commercial contracts between the primary employers, the shipowners, and the secondary employers, the port authority, which employed the workers — tugboatmen, lockkeepers, etc. — whose actions, in breach of their contracts of employment, made the blacking effective. But in neither case were the contracts for port facilities for the ships made with the shipowners, the primary employers; they were made by the charterers or sub-charterers of the ships. The gateway was therefore blocked.

Moreover, the *Dimbleby* case revealed another limitation on s.17(3). It does not extend to action taken against the first customer or supplier of an associated employer of the primary employer, even where, as in that case, the association was so close that the two companies had the same shareholders, premises, telephone and controlling personality, Mr Pole-Carew, whose anti-union actions were the basic cause of the trade dispute between T Bailey Forman Ltd, the publishing company, and the journalists whom it had dismissed. The purpose of the action taken by the NUJ was to disrupt the supply of copy from Dimbleby, a secondary employer in relation to this dispute, not under a contract with the primary employer T Bailey Forman Ltd, but under a contract with its associated employer, TBF (Printers) Ltd. The Law Lords, as already indicated above, refused to 'pierce the veil' of the corporate facade of the two companies to discover the common alter ego behind them, Pole-Carew, the real party to the dispute.

In support of this refusal Lord Diplock referred to the existence of a separate gateway to legality for action against associated employers in s.17(4). This is an extension of s.17(3) in one respect. It legitimises secondary action against an associated employer of an employer party to a trade dispute and the first customers and suppliers of the associated employer, where that employer is providing goods or services in substitution for those which would otherwise be provided by the employer in dispute. The potential width of this gateway is very limited. In the first place the definition of associated employer is confined to companies subject to

---

[61] *Marina Shipping Ltd v Laughton* [1982] ICR 215; *Merkur Island Shipping Corporation v Laughton* [1983] 2 AC 570. See Wedderburn, 1983. See too the even more complex contractual relationships in *Shipping Company Uniform Inc. v ITF* [1985] ICR 245.

common control or where one controls the other (see Chapter 5). Public sector and non-corporate employers are excluded. Further, even where two companies are associated employers, it will be necessary for them to be in the same line of business so that one can substitute for the other. But where this is so, it may be difficult to prove that the commercial contracts made by the associated employer were in substitution for those of the company in dispute (DE, 1981:paras.151–3).

Section 17(5) is the licensed pickets' gateway. As is explained in Chapter 7, secondary action passes through it if it is done in the course of attendance declared lawful by TULRA s.15, either by a worker employed (or last employed) by a party to the dispute, or by a union official accompanying a member whom he represents at or near his own place of work. Even though licensed pickets are by definition attending at or near their own place of work only for the purposes of peaceful communication or persuasion, their behaviour could still amount to secondary action. A worker picketing his or her own place of work may, by holding up a placard, succeed in persuading a lorry driver to turn back and not to deliver the goods he is carrying. The picket will then have induced the lorry driver to break his contract of employment and, unless the lorry driver's employer is a party to the trade dispute in contemplation or furtherance of which the picketing was taking place, that will be secondary action as defined in s.17(2). In short, s.17(5) does no more than ensure that licensed pickets who are in dispute with their own employer do not lose the full range of the remaining immunities in TULRA s.13 by doing no more than picketing peacefully as defined in TULRA s.15.

Action in Support of Union- and Recognition-only Practices

The nature and extent of practices designed to ensure that particular work is done only by union members or by employees of firms which recognise unions and the measures designed to outlaw these practices in EA 1982 ss.12 and 13 are discussed in Chapter 2. Section 14 of the 1982 Act is the related provision which removes all the immunities in TULRA s.13 from the organisers of industrial action taken to uphold union- and recognition-only practices.

The section is in two parts. The first withdraws the immunities from acts constituting an inducement either to include a term in a contract for the supply of goods or services which is or would be void under s.12(1) or s.13(1), or to contravene the statutory duties in s.12(2) or s.13(2). Sections 12(1) and 13(1) render void clauses in commercial contracts requiring either union members (or non-members) to be used on work under the contract, or the employer to recognise, negotiate or consult with trade unions. Sections 12(2) and 13(2) create a right to sue for breach of statutory duty for a wide range of action taken effectively to impose union- or recognition-only practices. Thus unions and individuals who organise or threaten industrial action in order to uphold or secure a union- or recognition-only practice in a form which would contravene s.12 or s.13 lose the protection of the TULRA immunities.[62]

The second part of s.14 removes the immunities from acts which indirectly interfere with the supply of goods or services — whether or not under contracts — by inducing breach of or interfering with contracts of employment or threatening to do so, where at least one of the reasons for the acts is either that work done in connection with the supply has been or is likely to be done by non-unionists (or union members), or the supplier does not recognise, negotiate or consult with trade unions. This is wider than the other part of s.14 since it applies even where the organisers of industrial action do not intend to secure any infringement of s.12 or s.13.

The loss of immunities brought about by s.14 is an essential part of the policy of eroding trade union organisational strength.[63] Its potential impact may indeed go byond the areas of union- and recognition-only practices. It may have the capricious effect of removing immunity from a union which in order to bring pressures on an employer who is refusing it recognition calls on its members employed by a customer of that employer to refuse to handle supplies from him (see Lewis and Simpson, 1983). Furthermore, although organising industrial action because a supplier refuses to pay the recognised rate for the job is not formally denied immunity by s.14, it may be difficult in practice to distinguish industrial action taken for this reason from action taken because a supplier refuses to recognise unions.

Ballots before Industrial Action

In one form or another 'strike ballots' have been on the agenda of labour law reform since the late 1950s. Research indicates that union rules rarely circumscribe the freedom of negotiators by providing for obligatory ballots on support for negotiated agreements or taking industrial action. Ballots are but one form of communication. The circumstances in which they are favoured as against other forms of keeping in touch with the views of members depend on a variety of matters including the bargaining structure within which the union operates, inter-union relations, internal political pressures, distribution and structure of membership, and employer attitudes (Undy and Martin, 1984: ch.4).

Sections 10 and 11 of TUA 1984 remove some of the remaining immunities in TULRA s.13 from acts done by trade unions without the support of a ballot. The provisions only apply to 'an act done by a trade union'. This again raises the difficult question of when unions are vicariously liable for the acts of their officials and members. It is widely assumed that the 1984 Act only applies where acts have been authorised or endorsed by a union in accordance with the criteria (as described above) in EA 1982 s.15.

---

[62] It is also arguable that EA 1982 s.14(1) envisages the existence of novel tortious liabilities to which TULRA provides no immunities in any event. See Lewis and Simpson (1982:230–31).

[63] EA 1982 s.14 was one of the reasons for the absence of any immunity in *Messenger Newspapers Group Ltd v NGA* [1984] IRLR 397. But it is not clear from the judgment exactly how it applied to the facts of the case.

These criteria are indeed incorporated in TUA 1984 s.10 for the purposes of determining whether action taken by a union after a successful ballot avoids loss of immunity under the section. But they are not expressly applied for the purpose of deciding whether there has been an act done by a union which brings the section into play in the first place. While it might be logical for the courts to resolve this question by reference to s.15 of the 1982 Act, they could nevertheless decide to apply other criteria: those of the common law, those set out in the *Heatons* case in 1972, or perhaps some fresh criteria worked out by the courts especially for the purposes of these provisions.

In the first major dispute involving the 1984 Act, the Austin Rover strike in November 1984, the employers obtained injunctions against six of the unions represented on a joint negotiating committee, on the basis of their failure to hold ballots before the committee called a strike over a pay offer. Proceedings against the EETPU were dropped after it announced that a ballot would be held, while the Engineering Section of the AUEW successfully argued that it had done nothing unlawful, although even after an appeal court hearing, the legal basis for this decision remained unclear. Moreover, none of the other six unions were represented in court at this stage of the proceedings although the TGWU's subsequent support for the strike at national level appeared to leave little doubt that it was accepting responsibility.[64] The case therefore provides no clear pointers as to where the line between acts done by a union and acts not done by a union is to be drawn.

The matter is of crucial importance. In general terms, the 1984 Act does not affect unofficial action. Like the joinder provisions in cases of unfair dismissal and action short of dismissal because of non-membership of a union (see Chapter 2), and the removal of unions' blanket tort immunity, TUA 1984 makes it necessary to draw a line between what is official and what is unofficial. The strike ballot provisions in particular may encourage unions to distance themselves from their membership — as the leadership of AUEW (Engineering Section) did in the Austin Rover strike — in order to preserve the union's immunity.

Failure to get the support of a ballot does not result in the loss of all TULRA s.13 immunities. The immunities which are lost are those for inducing breach of or interference with contracts of employment and indirectly inducing breach or interfering with the performance of commercial contracts by the unlawful means of inducing breach of or interference with employment contracts (s.10(1)(2)). Of the immunities which remain, the most important in practice is that against liability for intimidation by threatening industrial action. But while such threats may remain a lawful negotiating tactic, their credibility may well be reduced by the knowledge that they cannot be carried out lawfully without the prior support of a

---

[64] See *The Guardian* and *The Times*, 15 November 1984. The TGWU was subsequently fined £200,000 for contempt of court for refusing to comply with the injunction. See *The Guardian* and *The Times*, 27 November 1984. Another union, AUEW (TASS), was also held to be in contempt for the same reason, but no penalty was imposed: *Austin Rover Group Ltd v AUEW (TASS)* [1985] IRLR 162. Austin Rover started proceedings claiming damages from all the unions concerned in January 1985.

ballot.[65] Where immunity is removed by the 1984 Act, it is not only the union which is thereby exposed to legal proceedings. The wording of s.10 makes it clear that the union officials who actually do or are responsible for the 'acts done by a union without the support of a ballot' also become open to labour injunctions and damages claims.

For unions wishing to comply with the law, the requirements for a valid ballot are both complex and controversial. The impossibility of a federal union with no or few individual members such as the ITF meeting these requirements has already been demonstrated. Although the ITF has no power to ballot the members of its affiliated unions, in *Shipping Company Uniform Inc. v ITF*[66] it was held that TUA 1984 s.10 still deprived it of immunity for failing to do so. Even where there are no such insuperable obstacles, the timing may present a difficult hurdle. Where action has already begun unofficially — in legal terms — the union's 'endorsement' of it must come within four weeks of the date when a successful ballot was held. Where it has yet to begin both the action itself and the union's 'authorisation' must come within this four-week period (s.10(3)(c)). The test of authorisation or endorsement is that in EA 1982 s.15 (see above). While it may be necessary to have some limit on the time for which ballot support can remain 'valid', four weeks was widely criticised for being too short a period. It could indeed encourage industrial action if, in order to keep legal immunity, strikes are called before the four weeks are up where otherwise industrial action might have been delayed pending the outcome of further negotiations.

The organisation of a ballot which complies with s.11 of the Act is a second hurdle. The constituency balloted must be all and only those 'who it is reasonable at the time of the ballot for the union to believe' will be called upon to take action. Any failure here — which could easily occur where for instance a union is considering tactical action by different groups at different times — will invalidate the ballot (s.11(2)). The ballot may be either postal or workplace, although voting by a show of hands is not sufficient. If workplace, the right to hold workplace ballots in EA 1980 s.2 may apply; if postal, state finance under the scheme in force under s.1 of that Act may be available (see Chapter 10). So far as is reasonably practicable, there must be secret voting, a fair count and voters must be able to vote without incurring any direct cost. Moreover, while interference (as distinct from campaigning) by the union, its members, officials or employees will invalidate a ballot, outside interference by the employer or the media does not.

The most controversial of the requirements for a valid ballot concerns what is on the ballot paper. This must include 'a question (however framed) which requires the voter to say, by answering "Yes" or "No", whether he is prepared to take part, or as the case may be to continue to take part in a strike — or industrial action falling short of a strike, where no strike is

---

[65]   It is also possible that threats by unions to call on their members to take industrial action without the support of a ballot could lead to applications for 'quia timet' injunctions to restrain them from committing threatened torts. On quia timet injunctions, see Chapter 19.

[66]   [1985] ICR 245. The judge's suggestion that the ITF could overcome this obstacle by amending its rules overlooks the practical realities surrounding the union's existence.

involved — involving him in breach of his contract of employment'. It seems clear that ballot papers may refer to other matters, but the 'breach of contract' point must be there somewhere. At this point the detail of the law suggests that the ostensible policy behind the provisions, to ensure that union leaders are responsive to their members, gives way to another objective: to bring home to workers that industrial action is almost invariably unlawful in the sense that those taking part are breaking their contracts of employment. The fact that an effective right or freedom to strike could not exist without such breaches of contract is not something which can be easily explained on a ballot paper to counterbalance the impact of a question phrased in unfamiliar legal terms. Given that the question must be drafted in this way, the final hurdle, the need to obtain a majority 'Yes' vote, may be more difficult to surmount than would otherwise be the case.

CONCLUSION

Court actions arising out of recent disputes have shown that the current state of the law on the right to organise industrial action is difficult to reconcile with the traditional notion of free collective bargaining as the central feature of British industrial relations. While this situation has resulted primarily from the limitations imposed on the immunities by the 1980s legislation, uncertainty surrounding the common law liabilities is also a cause for concern. Since the development of these liabilities is in the hands of the judges it is impossible for this aspect of the law ever to be absolutely certain, and it is at present notoriously unclear. The introduction of new forms of liability such as economic duress is one problem. Another concerns the fundamental nature of economic tort liability. It is whether, apart from conspiracy, there are a series of separate torts, as the analysis in this chapter suggests, or there is but one umbrella liability for unlawful interference with trade or business, or possibly other economic interests as well. On the latter view, inducing breach of or interference with contracts and intimidation are not necessarily the only unlawful means by which the tort can be committed.[67] While the existence of an uncertain area of residual economic tort liability is generally recognised, the better view of the current state of the law is that the separate torts have not yet been subsumed under one all-embracing liability.

If this were to happen, it would have several important implications. First, the scope of unlawful means would become even more crucial to the ambit of common law liability. Second, it would leave the criteria by which the vicarious liability of trade unions is determined totally in the hands of the judges, since it is by no means clear that those in s.15 of the 1982 Act would always be applicable. Equally important, it could make the distinction between those provisions which withdraw all the TULRA s.13 immunities, EA 1980 s.16(2) and EA 1982 s.14, and those which take away only part of

---

[67] Lord Diplock's controversial analysis of the TULRA s.13 immunities in the *Merkur Island* case arguably supports this view. See note 56 above.

these immunities, EA 1980 s.17 and TUA 1984 s.10, irrelevant. Even partial exposure to the common law might be sufficient to open the door to legal restraint. Indeed it is arguable that TULRA s.13 would no longer provide adequate immunities in the first place, especially after the repeal of s.13(3).

Apart from the selective removal of immunities, the 1980s legislation has made another fundamental alteration of the legal framework by amending the definition of a trade dispute. The phrase 'in contemplation or further-ance of a trade dispute' no longer fulfills the same function as it did up to 1982, when it was aptly described as the golden formula. It no longer attempts to draw the line between industrial conflict which is legitimate in the eyes of the law, and that which is not, at the point at which industrial relations stops and extraneous — political or other — issues alone are involved. It now denies legitimacy to many disputes which are clearly about industrial relations issues. As Clark and Wedderburn have said 'Conserva-tive government policy in the eighties has ... adapted the concept [of trade dispute] to its own political ends' (1983:164). An essential foundation of the golden formula theory has thus been undermined (see Simpson, 1983).

The tortuous complexity of a body of law based on immunities from imprecise judge-made liabilities, and the loss of those immunities in often ill-defined circumstances, has naturally led to demands for the law in this area to be recast in the form of positive rights drafted in terms intelligible to those actually affected by them. Discussion of this issue was stimulated by the 1981 Green Paper where the pros and cons were presented as a topic independent of changes in the substantive content of the law (DE, 1981:paras.339–82). This idea has attracted some support (Elias and Ewing, 1982:356–8), and must inevitably form part of the deliberations of those who favour the introduction of a Bill of Rights. But as yet no one has demonstrated clearly how they would overcome such basic difficulties as defining the boundaries of positive rights and drawing the demarcation line between them and the common law. As Wedderburn has noted, 'these matters are not technicalities ... Discussion can be meaningful only if the proponents make clear what kind of *right*, what kind of *strikes*, what extent of *legality*, they have in mind' (1985:515–16).

Debate on the merits of positive rights ought not to overlook a more fundamental issue. This is the need for a right to organise industrial action so that workers and unions have the opportunity to make collective bargaining a realistic process for joint regulation of industrial relations. Whether this can be again achieved through the traditional process of trade union immunities is a question which must now be critically examined.

Bibliography

Carty, Hazel. 1983. 'Economic Tort Liability and "Secondary Action"'. *Industrial Law Journal*, 12 (September), 166–9.

Clark, Jon, and *Lord* Wedderburn. 1983. 'Modern Labour Law: Problems, Functions and Policies'. *Labour Law and Industrial Relations: Building on Kahn-Freund*. Eds. *Lord* Wedderburn, R. Lewis and J. Clark. Oxford: Clarendon Press, 127–220.

Daniel, W.W., and N. Millward. 1983. *Workplace Industrial Relations in Britain: The DE/PSI/SSRC Survey*. London: Heinemann.

Davies, P.L. 1973. 'In Search of Jobs and Defendants'. *Modern Law Review*, 36 (January), 78–89.

——. 1976. 'Trade Union Responsibility for the Actions of Shop Stewards'. *Industrial Law Journal*, 5 (December), 251–2.

——, and Mark Freedland. 1984. *Labour Law: Text and Materials*. 2nd edn. London: Weidenfeld & Nicolson.

Department of Employment (DE). 1981. *Trade Union Immunities*. Cmnd 8128. London: HMSO.

Devonshire. 1894. Royal Commission on Labour. *Final Report*. C. 7421. London: HMSO.

Donovan. 1968. Royal Commission on Trade Unions and Employers' Associations 1965–1968. *Report*. Cmnd 3623. London: HMSO.

Elias, Patrick, and Keith Ewing. 1982. 'Economic Torts and Labour Law: Old Principles and New Liabilities'. *Cambridge Law Journal*, 41 (November), 321–58.

Evans, S. 1985. 'The Use of Injunctions in Industrial Disputes'. *British Journal of Industrial Relations*, 23 (March), 133–7.

Hepple, B.A. 1972. 'Union Responsibility for Shop Stewards'. *Industrial Law Journal*, 1 (December), 197–211.

Kahn-Freund, Otto. 1954. 'Legal Framework'. *The System of Industrial Relations in Great Britain*. Eds. A.D. Flanders and H.A. Clegg. Oxford: Blackwell, 42–127.

——. 1983. *Labour and the Law*. 3rd edn. Ed. and intr. by Paul Davies and Mark Freedland. London: Stevens.

Kerr, Tony. 1980. 'In Contemplation or Furtherance of a Trade Dispute ...'. *Dublin University Law Journal*, 1 (October), 59–91.

Lewis, Roy, and Bob Simpson. 1981. *Striking a Balance? Employment Law after the 1980 Act*. Oxford: Martin Robertson.

——, and Bob Simpson. 1982. 'Disorganising Industrial Relations: An Analysis of Sections 2–8 and 10–14 of the Employment Act 1982'. *Industrial Law Journal*, 11 (December), 227–44.

——, and Bob Simpson. 1983. Comment on M. Short, 'The Employment Act 1982: A Practitioner's Response'. *Industrial Law Journal*, 12 (June), 103.

Miller, Kenneth. 1982. 'Factory Occupations in Scotland'. *Industrial Law Journal*, 11 (June), 115–17.

Simpson, Bob. 1978. 'Gouriet: Labour Law Aspects'. *Modern Law Review*, 41 (January), 63–7.

——. 1983. 'A Not So Golden Formula: In Contemplation or Furtherance of a Trade Dispute after 1982'. *Modern Law Review*, 46 (July), 463–77.

——. 1984a. 'Trade Disputes and the Labour Injunction after the Employment Acts of 1980 and 1982'. *Modern Law Review*, 47 (September), 577–87.

——. 1984b. 'Trade Disputes and Trade Secrets'. *Dublin University Law Journal*, 6, 192–9.

Undy, Roger, and Roderick Martin. 1984. *Ballots and Trade Union Democracy*. Oxford: Blackwell.

Wedderburn, K.W. (*Lord*). 1965. *The Worker and the Law*. Harmondsworth: Penguin.

——. 1971. *The Worker and the Law*. 2nd edn. Harmondsworth: Penguin.

——. 1974. 'The Trade Union and Labour Relations Act 1974'. *Modern Law Review*, 37 (September), 525–43.

——. 1980. 'Gilt Back on the Formula'. *Modern Law Review*, 43 (May), 319–27.

——. 1981. 'Secondary Action and Gateways to Legality: A Note'. *Industrial Law Journal*, 10 (June), 113–18.

——. 1982a. 'Procuring Breach of Contract – Intimidation – Unlawful Interference – Conspiracy – Trade Disputes'. *Clerk and Lindsell on Torts*. 15th edn. Ed. R.W.M. Dias. London: Sweet & Maxwell.

——. 1982b. 'Economic Duress'. *Modern Law Review*, 45 (September), 556–64.

——. 1983. 'Lawmakers and Craftsmen'. *Modern Law Review*, 46 (September), 632–5.

——. 1985. 'The New Politics of Labour Law'. *Trade Unions*. 2nd edn. Ed. W.E.J. McCarthy. Harmondsworth: Penguin, 497–532.

7 Picketing

Roy Lewis

For over a century the law has recognised a freedom to picket peacefully. Though the definition of lawful picketing (currently embodied in TULRA s.15) was always of a narrow ambit, it has been further narrowed by the EA 1980. Pickets whose acts are unprotected by TULRA s.15 run into a range of legal liabilities both civil and criminal. The civil liabilities are an important element in the wider pattern of the legal restriction of industrial conflict. But the criminal liabilities indicate that picketing, as the physical manifestation of industrial conflict, has implications for public policy beyond the infliction of economic damage during a dispute. They point to the vital role of the police in the maintenance of public order. Indeed, in the wake of the miners' strike of 1984–5, the present government (Home and Scottish Offices, 1985) brought forward proposals to strengthen public order law and to bring picketing firmly within its framework. The policing of the miners' strike together with these proposals inevitably raise the question of police neutrality in industrial disputes. It should be apparent, therefore, that the technicalities of the law, which are this chapter's central concern, can scarcely be understood in isolation from social reality.

INDUSTRIAL AND POLITICAL CONTEXTS

Evidence from workplace surveys (Daniel and Millward, 1983:242–51, 293) suggests that in 1979–80, a period of relatively high strike incidence, 6 per cent of workplaces experienced 'primary' picketing and 8 per cent 'secondary' picketing, which was defined as picketing unconnected with any trade dispute at the picketed premises. Picketing had the effect of interfering with the movement of goods and services in about half the reported instances, and of employees in about a third. It was typically organised by shop stewards or local full-time union officers. Pickets usually operated in small numbers which varied with the number of entrances to a workplace; mass picketing was rare.

These bare facts may give a few indications as to why picketing has become so controversial. Attention has focused on violent incidents and on the spread and economic impact of secondary picketing. Public concern was first aroused by two major strikes in 1972. A national dispute in the construction industry led to confrontations between pickets and police and violent threats by 'flying' pickets against self-employed blacklegs. Mass picketing in a miners' dispute led to a number of confrontations between police and pickets (Wallington, 1972), culminating in the blockade of the Saltley coke depot. 'Saltley' was a symbolic defeat for the forces of law and order, particularly the police who were overwhelmed by sheer numbers (Kahn et al., 1983:75–6). Later, in 1976, the police employed more forceful tactics against massed pickets during the lengthy Grunwick dispute. These events caused attitudes towards picketing to harden. Secondary picketing in the public sector and road haulage strikes of 1978–9, the 'winter of discontent', was the immediate pretext for new legislation.

The government's argument for cutting back the right to picket was summarised in its Working Paper on Picketing (DE, 1979). This stated that the 1979 Conservative Party election manifesto reflected 'widespread public concern' over picketing, particularly the tendency 'in the last few years' to picket companies 'not directly involved in disputes'. Here we have the popular though not the legal essence of the distinction between primary and secondary action: the former is aimed at employers involved in the dispute and is normally action taken by their own employees; the latter is aimed at employers who are apparently not involved. (The rather different technical legal definition of 'secondary' action in EA 1980 s.17(2) is discussed in Chapter 6.) The Working Paper attributed the increase in secondary picketing to 'easier transport and communication', 'a greater degree of organisation of picketing ... sometimes the work of unofficial groups rather than official union leaders', and 'the growth and greater formalisation of the closed shop since 1974'. 'There are indications,' it added, 'of an increasing use of intimidation on picket lines, whether directly through the threat of physical violence or indirectly through the threat of loss of union membership, and, as a consequence, of jobs.' The charge of violence was again raised in connection with the bitter national steel strike during the first fourteen weeks of 1980. Despite the narrowing of the legal right to picket in 1980, violence and secondary picketing flared up during the Stockport Messenger dispute in 1983–4 and, above all, in the 1984–5 miners' strike.

Allegations of physical intimidation must be set against a tradition of peaceful picketing in Britain. This point is readily appreciated by anyone familiar with the violence which has characterised picketing in Canada (Woods, 1968:paras.425–6) and the USA (Taft and Ross, 1969). But to what extent is there substance in the view that intimidatory picketing has increased in recent years? The evidence for any connection between picketing and the closed shop is extremely tenuous (Daniel and Millward, 1983:245). The more serious charge is the alleged trend towards physical violence. A study of dispute tactics in South Yorkshire and Humberside in 1980–82 concluded that picketing was normally peaceful and that the police did not get involved in the 'vast majority' of strikes (Kahn et al., 1983:86–7). Another study of dispute tactics confirmed that most picketing was peaceful and that there was scant evidence to support the contention that secondary picketing was to be equated with intimidation (Evans, 1985a).

In the light of this research, it is clear that the level of picket-line violence can easily be exaggerated. A false impression of generalised violence may arise from the media's habit of dramatising isolated incidents. The perspective of labour history suggests that the newspapers of the Victorian era had a similar tendency (Howell, 1890:309–10). Senior policemen giving evidence to the House of Commons Select Committee on Employment in 1980 confirmed that picketing was normally peaceful, often not requiring any police presence at all, and that the problems of policing even large numbers had been exaggerated by the media.[1] Even in respect of the 1984–5 miners' dispute, with its unprecedented scenes of physical force, the NCCL (1984:8) commented that: 'contrary to the impression inevitably created by media concentration on incidents of mass picketing and violent confrontation, *most* of the picketing during the strike has been orderly and on a modest scale'.

The portrayal of secondary picketing as a novel development is also open to challenge. Leading cases at the turn of the century show that secondary picketing goes back a very long way.[2] If it increased in the late 1920s, so did the number of prolonged official disputes. The decision to engage in secondary picketing is, moreover, rooted not in political motivation, as is sometimes suggested, but rather in the logic of industrial circumstances. Empirical research has cast some light on these circumstances. Evans (1985a) found that secondary picketing arose from the perceived need to counter the substitution of the strikers' labour, the transfer of their work to other parts of the enterprise or to outside firms, and the failure of primary picketing in the face of management determination. Kahn et al. (1983) found that the choice of dispute tactics was determined by factors such as the nature of the production process, the organisation of work, the pattern of union representation, and systems of supply and distribution.

Indeed, the secondary dimension is an essential characteristic of picketing. Apart from the need to reinforce their own morale and discipline, strikers resort to picketing to achieve two objectives: to persuade other workers not to work for the employer in dispute, and to persuade third parties such as customers and suppliers not to have dealings with him. Both aspects of picketing were acknowledged by the Donovan Report (1968:para.855) in Britain and the Woods Report (1968:paras.611–12) in Canada. The TUC's Guide on the Conduct of Industrial Disputes adopted a similar perspective.[3] In reality it is impossible to separate these two functions because effective picketing of the employer in dispute must have an adverse effect on his commercial relationships with his customers and suppliers. Recognising the facts of industrial life, the Donovan Report (1968:para.875) acknowledged the frequency of persuasion of customers (it might have added suppliers) and found that 'most persons ... regard it as

---

[1]   HC Select Committee on Employment 1979–80, Minutes of Evidence, 462 (ii), 27 February 1980, p. 39.

[2]   E.g. *Temperton v Russell* [1983] 1 QB 715 (picketing and boycott of a supplier to the employer in dispute); *Quinn v Leathem* [1901] AC 495 (conspiracy to picket both the employer in dispute and his customer). On the historical context, see Clegg et al. (1964: 305–12).

[3]   This Guide (together with those on Negotiating and Disputes Procedures and Trade Union Organisation and the Closed Shop) are set out as an annex to the 'Social Concordat' document: *The Economy, the Government and Trade Union Responsibilities: Joint Statement by the TUC and the Government*, 1979, London: HMSO.

legitimate. In our opinion [the law] should be amplified so as to make such peaceful persuasion lawful.'

A basic and modern justification for secondary picketing is the need to maintain a balance of industrial power when employers operate more and more on a multi-plant, multi-company, and multi-national basis. Economic ownership and control in the private sector has become increasingly concentrated in multi-nationals, large financial institutions and groups of companies (Bullock, 1977:4–7). At the same time the overall tendency towards centralisation of power and decision-making has been intensified by the role of the modern state as employer, law-maker and manager of the economy. It is also apparent that employers at large do not necessarily regard themselves as neutral third parties in industrial conflicts. The CBI (1980), in arguing that employers in conflict with unions represent the collective interest of all employers, advocated more employer solidarity, including mutual financial support schemes and disciplinary action against workers engaged in secondary industrial action, and that employers not in dispute should refrain from taking commercial advantage of employers in dispute.

In the light of these considerations, a case may be made for a reform of picketing law in a liberal direction. In 1975 there was, in fact, an unsuccessful attempt to insert in the Employment Protection Bill a right for pickets to communicate peacefully but effectively with pedestrians and drivers.[4] Subsequently Bercusson (1977:292) suggested that the problems of picketing would diminish if employers were prohibited by law from carrying on their operations during trade disputes. While this proposal does not seem to reflect practical politics or industrial relations, its author cited some instructive examples of Canadian provisions which prevent employers from replacing striking employees or from disciplining employees who refuse to perform the duties of strikers. The British government's policy, however, is not to liberalise but – to a greater extent than in either Canada or the USA (Bellace, 1981) – to restrict the legal freedom to picket.

LEGAL FREEDOM TO PICKET

Historical Development

Until 1875 the policy of the law was generally to suppress peaceful picketing along with all other forms of industrial action (Wedderburn, 1971: 305–13). Section 7 of the Conspiracy and Protection of Property Act 1875 recognised the legal freedom to picket in a proviso to a criminal liability which is still in force. A person commits a crime if, wrongfully and without legal authority and with a view to compelling any other person to do or abstain from a lawful course of action, he does any of five specified things: uses violence to or 'intimidates' such other person, his wife or children or injures his property; persistently follows him; hides his tools or other property, or deprives him of them, or hinders their use; 'watches or besets' any house or

---

[4] HC Bill 1974–75 [119]. See HC Standing Committee F, 17 July 1975, 1485–1526.

place where he is or any approach to it; or follows him in the street with two or more others in a disorderly manner. The section sought to legalise peaceful picketing in a proviso which deemed that attending at or near a place merely in order to obtain or communicate information did not constitute the criminal offence of 'watching or besetting'.

But in *Lyons v Wilkins*[5] the Court of Appeal appeared to emasculate this proviso. Peaceful picketing which involved persuasion was held to go beyond mere attendance for the purpose of informing, and to be a common law 'nuisance' (unreasonable interference with the use of property). Since the tort of nuisance was clearly wrongful and without legal authority, peaceful picketing could after all constitute the crime of watching or besetting. In addition, the tort of nuisance provided the legal basis for civil actions for damages and injunctions against pickets who attempted by purely peaceful means to persuade other workers not to take jobs with the employer in dispute. A few years later in the *Ward Lock* case,[6] the Court of Appeal held that peaceful picketing did not necessarily or invariably give rise to nuisance or other tortious or criminal liabilities. The conflict between the two decisions remains unresolved.[7] But the immediate problem created by *Lyons v Wilkins* – that the proviso to s.7 of the 1875 Act covered only the communication of information and not persuasion – was remedied by s.2 of the Trade Disputes Act 1906.

That section declared that it was lawful, in contemplation or furtherance of a trade dispute, to attend at or near a house or place merely for the purpose of peacefully obtaining or communicating information, or of peacefully persuading a person to work or abstain from working. Section 2 of the 1906 Act was replaced by s.134 of the IRA, which was couched in similar terms, except that attendance at a place where a person resides was excluded. On the repeal of the IRA, TULRA s.15 retained the exclusion of attendance at residences but otherwise substantially restored the historic formula of the 1906 Act. Finally, EA 1980 s.16(1) (as amended by EA 1982) substituted the following as the current TULRA s.15:

(1) It shall be lawful for a person in contemplation or furtherance of a trade dispute to attend (a) at or near his own place of work, or (b) if he is an official of a trade union, at or near the place of work of a member of that union whom he is accompanying and whom he represents, for the purpose only of peacefully obtaining or communicating information, or peacefully persuading any person to work or abstain from working.

(2) If a person works or normally works (a) otherwise than at any one place, or (b) at a place the location of which is such that attendance there for a purpose

---

[5] [1896] 1 Ch 811 and [1899] 1 Ch 255, CA. See too *Charnock v Court* [1899] 2 Ch 35.
[6] *Ward Lock v Operative Printers' Assistants' Soc.* (1906) 22 TLR 327, CA.
[7] See *Hubbard v Pitt* [1975] ICR 308, CA and *Mersey Docks and Harbour Co. v Verrinder* [1982] IRLR 152. But the *Ward Lock* approach is supported by the weight of legal authority, e.g. *Fowler v Kibble* [1922] 1 Ch 487, CA; *Hubbard v Pitt* (Lord Denning MR diss.); *Galt v Philp* [1984] IRLR 156, HC of Justiciary; *Thomas v NUM (South Wales Area)* [1985] IRLR 136, 147; and of academic opinion, see Wedderburn (1971: 322–3); Bercusson (1977: 272–6); Davies and Freedland (1984: 852).

mentioned in subsection (1) above is impracticable, his place of work for the purposes of that subsection shall be any premises of his employer from which he works or from which his work is administered.

(3) In the case of a worker who is not in employment where (a) his last employment was terminated in connection with a trade dispute or (b) the termination of his employment was one of the circumstances giving rise to a trade dispute, subsection (1) above shall in relation to that dispute have effect as if any reference to his place of work were a reference to his former place of work.

(4) A person who is an official of a trade union by virtue only of having been elected or appointed to be a representative of some of the members of the union shall be regarded for the purposes of subsection (1) above as representing only those members; but otherwise an official of a trade union shall be regarded for those purposes as representing all its members.

Scope of TULRA s.15

The scope of TULRA s.15 is limited in several respects. First, the opening phrase 'it shall be lawful' gives the form rather than the substance of a positive right. Technically speaking, there is no legal 'right' to picket just as there is no legal 'right' to strike: the question is one of possible immunity from different kinds of liability.[8] Second, TULRA s.15 gives no protection for persons engaged in picketing unless their actions are in contemplation or furtherance of a trade dispute. It could not, for example, provide a defence to members of a tenants' association who were picketing an estate agent in Islington in protest against the 'gentrification' of the area.[9] But even in disputes that are clearly industrial the courts sometimes hold that the trade dispute formula is inapplicable. Thus, in advance of the EA 1980, Lord Denning was of the opinion that secondary picketing could not be in furtherance of a trade dispute: 'when strikers choose to picket, not their employer's premises, but the premises of innocent third parties not parties to the dispute – it is unlawful. "Secondary picketing" it is called. It is unlawful at common law and is so remote from the dispute that there is no immunity in regard to it.'[10] Although such reasoning is inconsistent with subsequent House of Lords decisions,[11] a variant of it was (as explained in Chapter 6) restored by EA 1980 s.17 where there is 'secondary action' within the meaning of that section. Third, even if the pickets are acting in contemplation or furtherance of a trade dispute, TULRA s.15 provides no protection where their behaviour goes beyond 'attendance' at or near a place only for the purpose of obtaining or communicating information or persuading people not to work, for example, impeding pedestrians or

8   *Kavanagh v Hiscock* [1974] ICR 282, 291, DC (Widgery CJ).
9   *Hubbard v Pitt* [1975] ICR 308, CA.
10 *Associated Newspapers Group v Wade* [1979] ICR 664, 695. For a similar line of reasoning in an undefended secondary picketing case, see *United Biscuits (UK) Ltd v Fall* [1979] IRLR 110.
11 *Express Newspapers Ltd v MacShane* [1980] AC 672, HL; *Duport Steels Ltd v Sirs* [1980] ICR 161, HL.

vehicles, a point elaborated below in the context of police control of picketing. Fourth, the permitted attendance is 'at or near' a place, not in or on it. Picketing or a workplace occupation on land against the will of the owner (or person to whom the owner has granted exclusive occupation) is not made lawful by TULRA s.15. Nor can s.15 affect the operation of any byelaws regulating the use of land.[12] In the circumstances of a 'sit in' or 'work in', therefore, the section can afford no protection against civil liability for trespass or criminal liability for watching or besetting.

The basic limitation introduced by the 1980 Act is that, subject to the qualification for trade union officials, the immunity is confined to a person who attends at or near his or her 'own place of work'. Special provision is made for the application of this concept to specific groups. If a person such as a lorry driver works at more than one place, or if it is impracticable for him to picket lawfully at his own place of work because of its location (an off-shore oil rig worker perhaps), the place of work is 'any premises of his employer from which he works or from which his work is administered'. This provision is intended to be narrowly interpreted as is made clear in the Secretary of State's Code on Picketing (1980), issued under EA 1980 s.3. In the case of lorry drivers, for example, it 'will usually mean in practice those premises of their employer from which their vehicles operate' (Picketing Code, para.13). Special provision is also made for a 'worker who is not in employment' where his last employment was terminated in connection with a trade dispute or the termination was one of the circumstances giving rise to a trade dispute. Such a person may 'in relation to that dispute' picket his former place of work. This would appear to cover a worker who was dismissed while he was on strike or locked out, providing that the picketing is in relation to that dispute. But the phrase 'not in employment' means that the worker loses the immunity for picketing the former employer if he or she finds new, even temporary, employment elsewhere.

The amended TULRA s.15 does not provide a definition of 'own place of work'. This notable omission is to some extent remedied by para. 12 of the Picketing Code:

> In general ... lawful picketing normally involves attendance at an entrance to or exit from the factory, site or office at which the picket works. It does not enable a picket to attend lawfully at an entrance to or exit from any place of work which is not his own, even if those who work there are employed by the same employer or covered by the same collective bargaining arrangements.

This formulation poses difficulties for all pickets, including those who wish to picket their own employer ('primary' pickets). For example, is an employee at one Ford plant at Dagenham entitled to regard Ford's entire Dagenham estate as his place of work? An affirmative answer to that very question was given by the National Insurance Commissioner in a decision (R(U) 1/70) on the meaning of 'place of employment' for the purposes of the

---

[12] *British Airports Authority v Ashton* [1983] IRLR 287, DC, citing as persuasive authority *Larkin v Belfast Harbour Commissioners* [1908] 2 IR 214.

trade dispute disqualification from unemployment benefit (discussed in Chapter 9). This broad interpretation had the effect of disqualifying from unemployment benefit large numbers of workers who were laid off because of a strike in one segment of the production process. In picketing the principle works in reverse: the narrower the concept of place of work the greater the likelihood of unlawful picketing. In the light of the Picketing Code, different Ford plants at Dagenham might be designated as different workplaces, and the Ford plant at Halewood certainly does not fall within the place of work of a picket from Dagenham. Many similar examples could be cited from other multi-plant employers in the private and public sectors. There is no statutory protection for the worker who ventures away from his own place of work, as narrowly understood, in order to picket at the employer's head office or at another plant belonging to his employer, even if production is being transferred from one plant to another as part of the dispute. Again, if the employer is involved in national collective bargaining through an employers' association, pickets must still remain at their own place of work if they are to retain their immunity under TULRA s.15. That is the case even if other employers are giving material support to the pickets' employer.

The restrictive impact of the 'own place of work' concept is reinforced by the trend towards operating single business enterprises through a number of different companies. If separate plants on a multi-plant site are owned by different companies, even if the companies are 'associated' employers,[13] each plant is a different place of work and a prohibited area for pickets from any other plant on the site. Any picket who confuses industrial reality with the legal fiction of separate corporate identity is legally at risk. It is noteworthy that in the Stockport Messenger dispute the unlawful secondary picketing was in response to the transfer of work between separate companies within the Messenger group (Gennard, 1984:15).

During picketing, it is good industrial relations practice for a trade union official to be present and in charge, a point in the Picketing Code (para.32) which would command general agreement. The amended TULRA s.15, however, gives an immunity to the trade union official only if he accompanies a member of his own union at the member's place of work and he personally represents that member. 'Official' in relation to a trade union means a full-time officer or a branch officer or a person elected or appointed in accordance with the rules of the union to be a representative, including a shop steward (TULRA s.30). While this definition has a wide ambit, for the purposes of TULRA s.15 the permitted official is one who personally represents the member he is accompanying: a person who is an official 'by virtue only of having been elected or appointed to be a representative of some of the members of the union shall be regarded ... as representing only those members' (TULRA s.15(4)). An official, according to para.16 of the Picketing Code, 'cannot, therefore, claim that he represents a group of

---

[13] Contrast the limited extension of lawful secondary action against an employer 'associated' with the employer in dispute: EA 1980 s.17(4). See above Chapters 5 and 6, and cf. *Dimbleby & Sons Ltd v NUJ* [1984] ICR 386.

members simply because they belong to his trade union'. Thus a shop steward may attend only with members whom he represents at a particular place of work, a branch official only with members of his branch, a district or regional official only with members of his district or region, and a national official responsible for a trade group or section only with members of that group or section.

Although multi-unionism is common throughout British industry, the member must belong to the same union as the official. This rule affects full-time officers and shop stewards, especially senior shop stewards and 'convenors'. Suppose the convenor in a factory is a member of a small craft or occupational union, but that the large majority of union members and of stewards belong to the TGWU. The office of the convenor is probably not within the statutory definition of a union 'official' because a convenor as such might not be 'a person elected or appointed in accordance with the rules of the union to be a representative of its members or of some of them' (TULRA s.30). A shop steward may come within that definition but not necessarily the convenor qua convenor, who is elected or appointed by the other shop stewards from a variety of unions to be their spokesmen for the entire plant, factory or company. The convenor who happens to be a craft worker in this example ought not to join any picket line unless it includes one of his own craft members. But the situation is only marginally different if the convenor is from the TGWU. If the pickets do not include a member from the particular small section which originally elected him as a steward, the convenor's presence with the pickets might be legally perilous both for himself and for them.

TULRA s.15 thus gives a very narrow ambit of immunity from civil and criminal liabilities. But for the section, mere attendance at the permitted place and for the permitted purposes might constitute the torts of nuisance on the *Lyons v Wilkins* principle, or possibly trespass to the highway.[14] It might also amount to the crimes of watching or besetting or wilful obstruction of the highway.

THE CIVIL LAW

Tortious Liabilities

Picketing beyond the narrow scope of TULRA s.15 involves loss of statutory protection from liability for the torts of nuisance and trespass, though, as explained above, the precise scope of these torts is a matter of conflicting judicial authority. Litigation arising from the 1984–5 miners' dispute, however, led to a novel application of the tort of nuisance. In *Thomas v NUM (South Wales Area)*,[15] a group of working miners obtained injunctions

---

[14] *Hubbard v Pitt* [1975] ICR 77, 83 (Forbes J). Contrast [1975] ICR 308, CA, esp. 316–17
     (Lord Denning MR); see too *Thomas v NUM (South Wales Area)* [1985] IRLR 136, 148 on
     the need for the plaintiff to show special damage.
[15] [1985] IRLR 136.

restraining the area union from organising mass picketing at the collieries where they had resumed work. While Scott J adopted the *Ward Lock* view that picketing is not necessarily a common law nuisance, he held that it could be tortious if it unreasonably harassed those who exercised their legal right to use the highway. Given the strong feelings against working miners in Wales, the substantial number of pickets at each of the relevant collieries, and their practice of hurling verbal abuse at the working miners, who were driven through the picket lines under police protection, the court had no doubt that the mass picketing was intimidatory. It would still have been intimidatory, in the circumstances, even if the pickets had been silent. It followed that it was an unreasonable harassment of the plaintiffs in the exercise of their right to use the highway, a species of the tort of nuisance. Such behaviour was unprotected by TULRA s.15 since it went beyond the permitted purposes. On the facts of the case, the working miners were not actually prevented from getting into work. Mass picketing which blocks the entrance to premises or prevents the entry of vehicles or people must, according to the court, constitute the tort of nuisance as well as a criminal offence under s.7 of the 1875 Act.[16]

Workers or union officials whose picketing falls outside TULRA s.15 also lose the basic immunities from liability for the so-called 'economic' torts. This is because EA 1980 s.16(2) provides that nothing in TULRA s.13, which sets out the immunities, 'should prevent an act done in the course of picketing from being actionable in tort unless it is done in the course of attendance declared lawful' by TULRA s.15. This exposes to legal liability all action in the course of picketing which is not at the right place and only for the permitted purposes. The nature of the immunities in TULRA s.13 and the corresponding tortious liabilities are fully discussed in Chapter 6. What follows is an outline to indicate their application to picketing.

TULRA s.13(1) protects against liability for inducing breach of or interfering with contract and threatening to break, induce breach of or interfere with contract. The removal of this immunity means that pickets and picket organisers who are 'unlicensed', in the sense that they fall outside TULRA s.15, including pickets at their own place of work who go beyond the permitted purposes, may be sued for inducing breach of or interfering with employment or commercial contracts or threatening to do so. The loss of immunity for inducing breach of employment contracts is fundamental: if they succeed in persuading people not to work pickets are, in legal terms, inducing them to break their contracts of employment. Hardly less sweeping is the removal of immunity for inducing breach of or interfering with commercial contracts, or threatening to do so. Furthermore, even a licensed picket within TULRA s.15 may be caught by s.17 of the 1980 Act, which removes immunity for inducing breach of commercial contract where there is secondary action as statutorily defined. But in this instance immunity may be retained provided the picketing is licensed by TULRA s.15 and the pickets are employed by a party to the dispute, or, in the case of a trade

---

[16]   At 153, in a passage on the area union's liability under its rule book.

union official, the official is accompanying a member whom he represents at or near the member's place of work.[17]

Section 16(2) of the 1980 Act entails a wider loss of immunity than other provisions restricting industrial action. Section 17 of the EA 1980 on secondary action, s.14 of the EA 1982 on action to impose union- and recognition-only practices, and s.10 of the TUA 1984 on industrial action without a valid ballot in effect remove the immunities contained in TULRA s.13(1), but leave intact the immunity in s.13(4). This subsection gives immunity from the tort of 'simple' conspiracy or conspiracy to injure. It provides that persons who combine in contemplation or furtherance of a trade dispute cannot be liable for the tort of conspiracy, unless the acts which they agree to commit are themselves tortious. The removal of this protection means that those who agree to do acts in the course of picketing outside the scope of attendance declared lawful by TULRA s.15 may be liable for conspircy, even if those acts are not themselves tortious, provided that their predominant purpose is to injure someone rather than to further their own legitimate interests.

Liability for conspiracy to commit unlawful acts, as distinct from simple conspiracy, may also feature in civil actions to restrain pickets who go beyond the bounds of TULRA s.15. They may be vulnerable to liability for conspiracy to induce breach of or interfere with contracts. It is, moreover, arguable that unlicensed pickets may conspire to break their own contracts of employment.[18] Union officials or picket organisers may also be liable for this conspiracy whether or not they actually join the picket line and even if they have no contracts of employment to break. This possibility follows from *Rookes v Barnard*[19] where one of the defendants was a full-time union officer. Even though he had no relevant contract of employment which he could threaten to break, he (together with the other two defendants who were employees of BOAC) was held liable for conspiracy to threaten a strike in breach of employment contracts. According to Lord Devlin, once the tort was proved against one defendant the plaintiff could sue 'the doer of the act and the conspirators, if any, as well'.[20] This could be particularly important since s.16(2) of the 1980 Act removes immunity from 'an act done in the course of picketing', a phrase of uncertain meaning and ambit.

Even pickets at their own place of work whose behaviour falls within the permitted purposes of TULRA s.15 may be liable for conspiracy if they act in combination with pickets who are either not at their own place of work or who go beyond the permitted purposes. It is of course possible for the licensed pickets and their organisers to dissociate themselves from the unlicensed pickets, and to adhere strictly to the Picketing Code's advice (para.34) to refuse offers of support on the picket line from outsiders. Pickets who welcome the support of fellow workers, however, run the risk of

---

[17] EA 1980 s.17(5). See further Chapter 6 above; Wedderburn (1981:117); Lewis and Simpson (1981:207–8); Davies and Freedland (1984:853–4).
[18] After the repeal of TULRA s.13(3) by EA 1980 s.17(8); see Chapter 6 above.
[19] [1964] AC 1129, HL.
[20] At 1211.

being held liable with them for conspiracy to break, induce breach of or interfere with contracts.

Further implications for civil liability arise from the Picketing Code itself. The legal effect of a Secretary of State's Code (under EA 1980 s.3(8)) is that it is admissible in evidence and, if relevant, taken into account by the industrial tribunals, the CAC, and the civil and criminal courts. As suggested in Chapter 8, failure to heed the Code's recommendations to maintain 'essential supplies' (para.37) could arguably provide the basis for a new heading of 'unlawful means', and could be relevant to the exercise of judicial discretion to grant interlocutory injunctions. The Code's impact on civil litigation was illustrated by the *Thomas* case. An injunction was granted restraining the area union, through its branches, from organising picketing or demonstrating at the relevant colliery gates by more than six persons. This number was derived from the Picketing Code, which advises (para.31) that in general the number of pickets should not exceed six at any entrance to a workplace. The court took account of this guidance in order to ensure that the weight of numbers of pickets would cease to be intimidatory to the working miners. No distinction was drawn, moreover, between the official pickets, who were stationed close to the colliery gates and normally numbered six, and the much larger number of demonstrators standing nearby.

The Picketing Code (para.36) states that a union ought not to take or threaten disciplinary action against a member because he has crossed a picket line 'which it has not authorised or which was not at the member's place of work', a point which is reiterated in the Closed Shop Code (para.62). This may be relevant not only to tortious liabilities, but also (as explained in Chapter 10) to actions against unions for unreasonable exclusion from membership contrary to EA 1980 s.4 or for breach of the rule book. The latter, contractual form of action may be used more generally to restrain unlawful picketing, a point illustrated once again by the litigation brought by working miners against the NUM and area unions. Having established that the 1984–5 strike was unlawful as a breach of the national and most area union rule books, the working miners were able to obtain injunctions restraining these organisations from calling upon their members to support the strike, not to cross picket lines, and from disciplinary action against those who did cross picket lines.[21] In addition, the *Thomas* case underlined the direct relevance of tortious and criminal liabilities for legal actions to enforce the rule book.

The working miners argued that the area union's rules implicitly restricted its authority to lawful acts, and that the court should grant an injunction against picketing at premises other than collieries (dubbed 'secondary' picketing by the judge) as it allegedly involved unlawful acts. In denying the injunction on the facts of the case, Scott J laid down a number of general principles. First, it must be ultra vires for a union deliberately to embark on

---

[21] E.g. *Taylor v NUM (Derbyshire Area) (No.1)* [1984] IRLR 440. See Ewing (1985) for an account of this litigation and Chapters 10 and 19 below for the overall development of rule book actions and enforcement procedures.

a series of criminal acts, but it would not necessarily be ultra vires if the acts merely carried the risk that criminal offences might be committed, Second, while it was not necessarily ultra vires for a union to embark on acts which carried the risk that torts might be committed, it was 'not clear' whether it was ultra vires to engage in acts which were bound to involve the commission of torts. The issue would depend upon the nature of the tort and 'in the final analysis ... considerations of public policy'.[22] Though it was 'almost certain' that the secondary picketing exposed the area union to tortious liability for interference with contract, Scott J was not prepared 'on that ground' to hold the picketing ultra vires the union.[23] Third, a crucial question for liability under the rule book was whether the picketing involved blocking the entry to premises or preventing entry through sheer weight of numbers. Mass picketing in that sense was bound to be a common law nuisance and a criminal offence under s.7 of the 1875 Act, and would, therefore, be ultra vires. But other picketing, including secondary picketing, which was peacefully and responsibly conducted at or near business premises would not automatically involve these tortious and criminal liabilities, or, by the same token, be ultra vires.

Litigation

Leaving aside the union's contractual liability to its members under the rule book and returning to the main theme of liability in tort, the *Thomas* case shows that the plaintiff who seeks to restrain unlawful picketing can be a union member, a strike breaker, who is the target of the picketing. On the facts of the case, those who brought the action were able to continue working. Damages in tort might be sought by an individual who is prevented from working if, for example, he or she is sent home without pay because there is no work, assuming that the employer has power to do this under the contract of employment. But perhaps the most obvious and more typical potential plaintiffs in actions in tort are the employer in dispute and his customers or suppliers. Whether other persons such as retail traders may sue if they can show that they have suffered loss because of the unlawful acts is perhaps arguable.

The defendants might include pickets, picket organisers and trade unions, the liability of unions depending on whether they are vicariously liable for the acts in question. The main remedies obtainable in the High Court are damages and injunctions, particularly 'interlocutory' injunctions. Failure to observe court orders may lead to penalties for contempt of court. These matters are all discussed in detail in Chapters 6 and 20. But there is one aspect of interlocutory injunction procedure which is of special relevance to picketing, namely, the identification of defendants other than trade unions.

[22] [1985] IRLR 136, 153.
[23] At 154. On the facts, the one point concerning the rule book on which the plaintiffs succeeded was in restraining the area union from making payments pursuant to a resolution that fines imposed on striking miners would be indemnified (following *Drake v Morgan* [1978] ICR 56), though the union was still free to consider each case on its merits.

In proceedings for an injunction the plaintiff must be able to identify the individuals he wishes the court to enjoin. The picket organisers are the prime target, though 'rank and file' pickets may be named as well. Who carries out the task of identification? It is not the police. As the Picketing Code (para.27) categorically states: 'the police have *no* responsibility for enforcing the *civil* law. An employer cannot require the police to help in identifying the pickets against whom he wishes to seek an order from the civil court. Nor is it the job of the police to enforce the terms of an order.' The government has acknowledged (DE, 1981:para.174) that to involve the police in this way 'might well be seen as enlisting their services on the side of the employer'. Furthermore, Home Office guidelines confiirm that employers, or at any rate 'employers' organisations' and 'commercial firms', are not normally given information by Special Branch, who keep an eye on active trade unionists during outbreaks of mass and flying picketing.[24]

The plaintiff is then responsible for identifying the pickets, though sometimes with the aid of private detective agencies. In a case brought against picketing dockers under the IRA, a firm of inquiry agents kept watch on the pickets and the agents' evidence established an overwhelming prima facie case against each of the individual dockers.[25] A plaintiff seeking to initiate contempt proceedings also has to show that there is sufficient evidence against the named defendants. In one of the famous cases under the IRA the Court of Appeal, at the request of the Official Solicitor, cancelled orders issued by the NIRC to commit defendants to prison on the ground of inadequate evidence.[26] In that instance the private detectives had failed in their task.

In the light of such apparent difficulties of enforcement, it is perhaps understandable that the Picketing Code (para.21) gives the somewhat misleading impression of a wide scope of liability of pickets not named as defendants. The true position has been succinctly summarised by Anderman and Davies (1974:33) as follows:

> an injunction against named persons restraining them from engaging in illegal picketing can be evaded if the named workers withdraw from the picket lines and from organising the illegal picketing and their place as participants and organisers is taken by other workers. It is, of course, the law that a person who aids a party enjoined to break an injunction is himself guilty of contempt, but where the enjoined pickets withdraw from participation in, or organisation of, the picket line, there would appear to be no breach by the enjoined parties for the third parties to aid and abet.

But if the named defendants under injunction fail to withdraw from the organisation of the action, then the other participants may be aiding and abetting and may consequently run into liability for contempt. Bearing that

---

24   'Home Office Guidelines on Work of a Special Branch' set out in HC Home Affairs Committee 1984–85, Fourth Report, 71, p.x.
25   *Midland Cold Storage Ltd v Turner* [1972] ICR 230, NIRC.
26   *Churchman v Joint Shop Stewards' Committee of the Workers of the Port of London* [1972] ICR 222, CA.

important qualification in mind, then, as Lord Diplock said in respect of civil actions against individual defendants, 'only those individuals are bound to observe the injunction. Everyone else involved in the industrial action can carry on with impunity doing that from which the individual defendants have been restrained.'[27]

These niceties of legal procedure have not in practice impeded employers from obtaining legal remedies. Between 1980 and 1982 several injunctions were obtained without difficulty against pickets and picket organisers. Since the repeal of the blanket trade union immunity from tort liability by EA 1982 s.15, the majority of legal actions have been against unions as such. Between September 1980 and September 1984, Evans (1985b) identified – the figures are almost certainly underestimates – seventeen instances of litigation arising from picketing. At least a dozen of these concerned picketing other than at the pickets' own place of work, though in most cases it was targeted on the premises of the employer in dispute. The examples included the Stockport Messenger litigation, which culminated in a contempt fine of £675,000, sequestration of the union's assets, and an award of damages against the NGA of £125,000. Also included was some of the litigation arising from the miners' dispute of 1984–5, notably the NCB's injunction against the NUM's Yorkshire Area, which was not enforced by way of contempt proceedings, and the action by a firm of road hauliers which led to a £50,000 contempt fine and the sequestration of the assets of the NUM's South Wales Area.[28]

For every instance of legal proceedings, there are probably several more of threats of litigation. In the study of thirty-eight mainly West Midlands disputes between September 1980 and August 1982, Evans (1983) found nine where managements sought injunctions, seven where injunctions were seriously considered and several more where management issued a warning that it might sue. The majority of plaintiffs were the employers of the defendants. Litigation or its threat offered certain advantages to management. It provided a way of exploiting divisions and fragmentation within the workforce, and a pressure on full-time union officers either to take control of a dispute or to dissociate themselves from it.[29] The conclusion of this research (Evans, 1983; 1985a; 1985b) is that, while there has been no general rush to the courts, employers are quite prepared to use and threaten to use the law against their own employees to restrain picketing.

THE CRIMINAL LAW

Picketing, whether primary or secondary, is not a criminal offence. But the police become involved because they have a duty to preserve the peace, a

---

[27] *Duport Steels Ltd v Sirs* [1980] ICR 161, 184–5.
[28] *Richard Read (Transport) Ltd v NUM (South Wales Area)* [1985] IRLR 67.
[29] Cf. *Mersey Docks and Harbour Co. v Verrinder* [1982] IRLR 152, where the full-time officer persuaded the court to strike out his name as a defendant because he was not a picket organiser.

duty which is ultimately enforced through the machinery of the criminal law. In practice, criminal prosecutions have been as important as civil litigation in establishing the ambit of the legal freedom to picket embodied in TULRA s.15 and its predecessors.

Peaceful Picketing

The following examples illustrate the narrow scope of the words 'it shall be lawful' in TULRA s.15 as far as the criminal law is concerned, the wide discretion of the police to control picketing, and the fact that peaceful pickets are prone to arrest and conviction for crimes which have the flavour of violence. A police officer decided that two pickets were enough to attend at the back gate of an employer's premises. A third picket was unwilling to accept this decision and was arrested. Although there was no obstruction of the highway and no disorder, he was held to have wilfully obstructed the officer in the course of his duty. The policeman's action was legally justified because he had reasonable grounds for believing that there might have been a breach of the peace unless he thinned out the tiny picket line.[30] Forty pickets walked in a continuous circle outside a factory in order to 'seal off the highway' and cause vehicles visiting the factory to stop so as to talk to the drivers. That, the judges found, was not made lawful by the statutory immunity since it went beyond communicating information and peacefully persuading persons to work or not to work. The conviction of the leader of the pickets for obstructing a constable in the execution of his duty by refusing to stop the circling was therefore upheld.[31]

A full-time officer of UCATT stopped a lorry by stepping out in front of it in order to urge the driver not to enter a building site. He was arrested and convicted for obstructing the highway, a criminal offence which is committed when a person, without lawful authority or excuse, wilfully obstructs the free passage along a highway.[32] This case, *Broome v DPP*, was appealed to the House of Lords.[33] The Law Lords were adamant that the statutory immunity gave no right to stop a vehicle. Lord Reid could see no ground for implying a right to require a driver to submit to any kind of constraint. 'One is familiar with persons at the side of a road signalling to a driver requesting him to stop. It is then for the driver to decide whether he will stop or not. That, in my view, a picket is entitled to do. If the driver stops, the picket can talk to him but only for so long as the driver is willing to listen.'[34] In other words, a picket's legal rights are similar to those of a hitchhiker.

If peaceful picketing by small numbers of pickets often involves criminal liability, peaceful picketing by large numbers is even more at risk. In the *Thomas* case, it was said that mass picketing involved the commission of an

---

[30] *Piddington v Bates* [1961] 1 WLR 162.
[31] *Tynan v Balmer* [1967] 1 QB 91.
[32] Highways Act 1959 s.121(1), now replaced by Highways Act 1980 s.137.
[33] [1974] ICR 84.
[34] At 89.

offence under s.7 of the 1875 Act, though the phenomenon was defined in such a way as to be inherently intimidatory: picketing so as by sheer weight of numbers to block the entrance to premises or to prevent the entry thereto of vehicles or people.[35] But it must be possible for peaceful mass picketing not to block the entrance to premises. It seems that the judges have difficulty in countenancing such a possibility. Although mass picketing was no part of the facts of *Broome v DPP*, Lord Reid took the opportunity to say that: 'it would not be difficult to infer as a matter of fact that pickets who assemble in unreasonably large numbers do have the purpose of preventing free passage. If that were the proper inference then their presence on the highway would become unlawful.'[36] On that reasoning mass picketing, however orderly and peaceful, is likely to constitute the criminal offence of wilful obstruction of the highway. That is the case even though a peaceful mass picket is akin to a peaceful demonstration, which should be viewed as a basic civil liberty.

These decisions point to the inescapable conclusion that TULRA s.15 only protects against criminal liability for very minor forms of obstruction and watching or besetting by small numbers of pickets. In practice, however, the police exercise a wide discretion and may come to some sensible arrangement with pickets. Although pickets have no legal right to stop vehicles, the police sometimes themselves stop them so that the pickets may briefly communicate without risk of a road accident. But this is purely a matter of police discretion. The police may instead choose to cordon off the pickets in such a way as to prevent them from communicating with drivers.[37]

The 1980 Act's restriction of lawful picketing to the picket's own place of work does not create any new criminal offence, but it may expand the application of existing criminal liabilities. Naturally there can be no immunity for crimes arising from any kind of force, including the physical obstruction of pedestrians and vehicles. That is not in contention. Here the concern is solely with the peaceful picket, who may have technically committed some minor degree of watching or besetting or of obstruction of the highway, but still ends up in a magistrates' court and who wishes to plead TULRA s.15 by way of a defence.

The proposition that the immunity covers such offences is supported by the legislative history. As already explained, s.7 of the Conspiracy and Protection of Property Act 1875 provided that attendance merely to communicate information was not to be deemed the criminal offence of watching or besetting, that is, it provided an immunity from criminal liability. Later s.2 of the Trade Disputes Act 1906 enacted the phrase 'it shall be lawful', words which still introduce TULRA s.15 and are wide enough to give an immunity for criminal as well as civil liability. Section 134 of the IRA was the most explicit of all: for the phrase 'it shall be lawful' it substituted the formulation that attendance for the permitted purposes would not of itself constitute a criminal offence under s.7 of the 1875 Act 'or under any other enactment or rule of law'. 'But for [s.134]', said Lord Salmon in

---

[35] [1985] IRLR 136, 153.
[36] [1974] ICR 84, 90.
[37] Cf. facts of *Kavanagh v Hiscock* [1974] ICR 282, DC, and see NCCL (1984:9).

Broome v DPP, 'the mere attendance of pickets might constitute an offence under s.7(2) and (4) of the Act of 1875 [persistent following and watching or besetting] or under the Highways Act 1959 [wilful obstruction of the highway] or constitute a tort, for example, nuisance. The section, therefore, gives a narrow but nevertheless real immunity to pickets.'[38] The 1980 amendment to TULRA s.15 reduces that immunity as it removes protection from picketing other than at the picket's own workplace. During the parliamentary debates the Attorney General confirmed that the 1980 Act had the effect of curtailing the immunity in respect of minor obstructions.[39]

The Secretary of State's Code on Picketing, which has to be taken into account by the criminal courts (under EA 1980 s.3(8)), also has implications for criminal liabilities. Confusion over the connection between the Code and criminal liabilities may be traced to the reception of the Working Paper on Picketing (DE, 1979), which baldly stated that the Code would be introduced to bring about 'a more consistent interpretation of the law by police and magistrates'. This smacked of a central government directive to the police. The chief constables, who have their own operational guidelines on handling picketing, told the House of Commons Employment Committee that they did not want the Code to apply to them as it might have the effect of limiting their discretion. In view of the need to maintain that discretion, a majority of the all-party Committee recommended that the Code ought not to specify a maximum number of pickets.[40] In response the government tried to play down the impact of the Picketing Code on the administration of criminal justice. The Code (para.1) purports to give advice only to pickets, other workers, employers and members of the public, a list which significantly omits to mention the police. Nevertheless, it is hard to imagine that the police can do anything other than take account of a Code which may be relevant to criminal proceedings.

While the Code specifically disclaims the intention of narrowing police discretion 'to limit the number of people on a particular picket line' (para.28), it requires 'pickets and their organisers' to 'ensure that in general the number of pickets does not exceed six at any entrance to a workplace; frequently a smaller number will be appropriate' (para.31). This limitation is relevant to prosecutions for a variety of criminal offences, including wilful obstruction and watching or besetting. It is again the police who have to liaise with the 'picket organiser', depicted by the Code (para.32) as an 'experienced person, preferably a trade union official'. Armed with a 'letter of authority' from his union, the picket organiser must get his 'directions' from the police on both the number and placement of pickets (para.33). According to para.34, he must ensure that the pickets understand the law and the Code and that their conduct is lawful and peaceful; the maintenance of 'essential' supplies; the clear identification of the pickets; and that any

---

38 [1974] ICR 84, 96.
39 979 HC Deb, 19 February 1980, 255, and HC Standing Committee A, 18 March 1980, 1348. Broad statements denying any relevance of EA 1980 s.16 to the criminal law (e.g. Picketing Code, paras. 3 and 22 and DE, 1981: para. 169) are misleading.
40 HC Select Committee on Employment 1979–80, Second Report, 822, para. 11.

unlicensed pickets from other places of work are kept at bay. Failure to consult with the police and to take their advice on the disposition of the pickets may be relevant to charges of obstructing the police. These provisions foreshadowed the proposals in the White Paper on public order (Home and Scottish Offices, 1985) to give the police legal powers to impose conditions on pickets and to create a criminal offence of disobedience of police directives (see below).

Physical and Verbal Force

It goes without saying that the use of force in picketing is criminal. Indeed, in the dire circumstances envisaged by the Riot Damages Act 1886, if the police fail to restrain pickets or others who behave 'riotously and tumultuously' they may themselves be liable to pay compensation to property owners. There are, however, many varieties and degrees of force. A picket may easily commit the offence of threatening words or behaviour. This arises if a person in a public place 'uses threatening, abusive or insulting words or behaviour ... with intent to provoke a breach of the peace or whereby a breach of the peace is likely to be occasioned'.[41] Other relevant criminal liabilities include wilful obstruction of the highway (Highways Act 1980 s.137), assaulting a police constable (Police Act 1964 s.51(1)), criminal damage (Criminal Damage Act 1971 s.1(3)), and the offence under s.51(3) of the Police Act 1964 of obstructing a police constable in the course of his duty. Of some 10,000 charges brought in England and Wales for offences committed in connection with the miners' dispute 1984–5, over 4,000 were for threatening words and behaviour, over 1,500 for obstructing the police, over 1,000 for criminal damage, 640 for obstructing the highway, and 360 for assaulting a police constable (Home and Scottish Offices, 1985:para.2.14).

The criminal liability under s.7 of the Conspiracy and Protection of Property Act 1875 covers a wide range of behaviour from watching or besetting through persistent or disorderly following to violence or intimidation. Prior to its use in the 1984–5 miners' dispute, there were relatively few modern examples of prosecutions under s.7.[42] An essential element is that the act complained of was done wrongfully and without legal authority and with a view to compelling a person to do or abstain from doing any act which that person has a legal right to do. Strike breakers, it should be noted, have the legal right to go to work. An act may be wrongful, moreover, even though it is immune from civil liability for the economic torts by virtue of TULRA s.13.[43] But TULRA s.15, with its distinctive history and wording (see above), arguably does provide a defence against minor forms of watching or besetting.

[41] Public Order Act 1936 s.5 as substituted by RRA s.79(6).
[42] *Galt v Philp* [1984] IRLR 156 (watching or besetting); *Elsey v Smith* [1983] IRLR 292 (following); *R v Jones* [1974] ICR 310 (intimidation); for earlier cases, see Citrine (1967:532–42).
[43] *Galt v Philp* [1984] IRLR 156 (noted by Miller, 1984).

The most serious charge under s.7 is the use of violence or intimidation. The criminal offence of intimidation is not defined in the 1875 statute, but, according to the Court of Appeal, it 'includes putting persons in fear by the exhibition of force or violence, and there is no limitation restricting the meaning to cases of violence or threats to the person'.[44] Thus displays of force and violence against buildings and equipment are sufficient for intimidation, though it is not clear what else might be included. For example, is offensive language which does not threaten violence enough? According to the *Thomas* case (see above), intimidatory mass picketing involves the commission of offences under s.7 and the picketing may be intimidatory even if the pickets are silent. Threatening a non-striker with withdrawal of his union card is almost certainly not in itself the criminal offence of intimidation.

If disorderly picketing severely disrupts public order, then a range of serious crimes may be committed, notably unlawful assembly, affray and riot. These are not defined by statute as they are judge-made common law crimes. Unlawful assembly may be committed if three or more persons have the intention of fulfilling a common purpose in such a manner as to endanger the public peace. Affray consists of unlawful fighting, or a display of force without actual violence, by one or more persons in such manner that a bystander of reasonably firm character might reasonably be expected to be terrified. The elements of the crime of riot include a display of force or violence by three or more persons with a common purpose so as to alarm a person of reasonable firmness and courage.[45] The scope of these common law crimes is uncertain and there is no maximum penalty laid down by statute.

The common law crimes together with intimidation under s.7 of the 1875 Act were among the more serious offences charged against pickets in the 1984–5 miners' dispute – where 509 of the accused were charged with unlawful assembly and 137 with riot – and also in the earlier prosecution of the 'Shrewsbury' pickets.[46] The background to the latter case was the national construction strike of 1972, which also gave rise to *Broome v DPP*. 'Flying' pickets were used in an effort to make the strike effective on the many building sites manned by self-employed 'lump' labour. Violent incidents led to the arrest, conviction and unsuccessful appeals of the Shrewsbury pickets. The notable features of this affair included the delay of five months between the alleged incidents and the charges, the massive police operation in interviewing hundreds of witnesses, the impression that the police were acting under a central government instruction, a trial which lasted for over two and a half months, and the deterrent sentences imposed on two of the accused of two years and three years of imprisonment, which were served in full. This 'show trial' effect is perhaps inevitable when serious charges are brought against groups of pickets months after the violence is

[44] *R v Jones* [1974] ICR 310, 318.
[45] The definitions of unlawful assembly and affray are drawn from Smith and Hogan (1983: 732 and 738); on riot see *Field v Receiver of Metropolitan Police* [1907] 2 KB 853.
[46] *R v Jones* [1974] ICR 310; *R v Tomlinson* [1974] IRLR 347; see Arnison (1974).

alleged to have occurred. The police may, indeed, be unable to make the evidence stick against the particular individuals who are charged, as happened in the 'Orgreave riot trial', one of the most lengthy and expensive prosecutions arising from the 1984–5 miners' dispute.[47]

A Law Commission Report (1983, noted by Morris, 1984) recommended the replacement of unlawful assembly, affray and riot by more tightly defined statutory offences carrying specified maximum penalties. This recommendation was broadly accepted by the present government in its White Paper on public order (Home and Scottish Offices, 1985). One of the likely consequences of the proposed change will be to make it easier for the prosecuting authorities to secure convictions, particularly for the comprehensive new offence of violent disorder. This is defined (1985:3.7) as the use or threat of unlawful violence to persons or property in a public or private place by three or more persons so as to cause someone of reasonable firmness, if present at the scene, to fear for his personal safety. The object of facilitating the conviction of pickets is equally clear from other proposals in the White Paper. The offence of threatening words or behaviour (Public Order Act 1936 s.5) is to contain a broader formulation of breach of the peace and – specifically in response to the picketing miners who stood on 'private' NCB property (1985:3.8) – is to be capable of being committed in private as well as public places. In the light of the experience of the miners' dispute, the government also proposed (1985:5.16) to make s.7 of the 1875 Act an arrestable offence with the maximum penalty increased from three to six months' imprisonment or a fine of £2,000.

Finally, the seriousness of a crime may be enhanced if there is a conspiracy to commit it. As mentioned in Chapter 6, the nineteenth century judges considered that combining for trade union purposes was a criminal conspiracy, a liability which received protection in trade disputes under s.3 of the Conspiracy and Protection of Property Act 1875. This section was repealed and replaced in England and Wales by the Criminal Law Act 1977. Section 1 provides that a conspiracy is a crime only when the act to be done is itself criminal, and gives an immunity for combinations, in contemplation or furtherance of a trade dispute, to commit summary offences not punishable with imprisonment. That gives no immunity, however, for conspiracy to commit other crimes which are punishable by imprisonment – for example, conspiracy to 'intimidate' – which was one of the charges against the Shrewsbury pickets. The sentences in that case were possible because the usual limits on sentence lengths for statutory offences (three months for intimidation under s.7 of the 1875 Act) were inapplicable to the common law crime of conspiracy. After the Criminal Law Act 1977 pickets may still be charged with criminal conspiracy, but s.3(3) provides that the maximum penalty for conspiracy is the maximum for the substantive offence. But some substantive offences are not tied by statute to a maximum sentence length, namely — until such times as they are replaced by statutory offences — the common law crimes of unlawful assembly, affray and riot.

---

[47] The Guardian, 18–20 July and 6 August 1985.

POLICE NEUTRALITY

Upholding the Queen's peace in an industrial dispute may involve the police in a difficult balancing act. On the one hand, an employer in dispute has the right to carry on his business and his employees, or some of them, may choose to ignore the strike and continue to work. On the other hand, the strikers may wish to exercise their freedom to picket peacefully. The police ought not to take sides. 'The police themselves attach the greatest importance to maintaining this position of neutrality. It enables them in the great majority of cases to avoid hostility and establish reasonable relations with pickets' (DE, 1981:para.174). The exercise by the police of their discretion to allow pickets to communicate with drivers and pedestrians is vital in this regard. But given the very narrow width of the pickets' legal immunity, systematic enforcement of the criminal law gives the impression that the police and the apparatus of criminal justice are being used to defeat the pickets.

One area where neutrality is sacrificed to an active police role is that of workplace occupations. Although sit-ins and work-ins are normally peaceful, they may give rise to criminal liabilities such as watching or besetting,[48] and, as already explained, TULRA s.15 can offer no defence because the permitted attendance is 'at or near' a place not in or on it. In addition, the Criminal Law Act 1977 created criminal offences ostensibly aimed at squatters but which may equally be used against occupying workers. The relevant offences are of uncertain ambit: using or threatening violence to secure entry to premises (s.6); trespassing with a 'weapon of offence' (s.8); and resisting or obstructing a court officer who is enforcing a court order for repossession of the premises (s.10). Such an order is part of a civil law procedure, but has the advantage over the injunction of enforceability against all those in possession whether or not named.[49] The police, however, may become involved in evicting the occupiers. But recognising the need to preserve police neutrality, the government (DE, 1981:paras.175–8) rejected proposals, based on the model of the repossession procedure, for injunctions against unnamed persons engaged in the act of picketing.

Leaving aside the question of workplace occupations, new tactics for dealing with mass picketing have been developed by the police since the Saltley debacle. This is evident from three disputes where the police operation allowed the employer to continue his business with the aid of working employees. The first example was the uncompromising policing of the Grunwick dispute, where there were 503 arrests between June 1977 and January 1978. Over 80 per cent of those prosecuted were convicted, mostly for the offences of obstructing a police officer in the course of his duty,

---

[48] *Galt v Philp* [1984] IRLR 156, where the court nevertheless criticised the precipitate police action in breaking up the occupation.

[49] Rules of the Supreme Court, Order 113 as amended, a procedure which is not available in Scotland; see Davies and Freedland (1984:888).

threatening behaviour, obstructing the highway, and assaulting a police officer.[50] The second example is provided by the Stockport Messenger dispute. Here, as the Chief Inspector of Constabulary (1984:53.4) reported, police tactics against mass pickets upheld public order and, at the same time, ensured continued production. According to Gennard (1984:16), the Institute of Directors 'intervened with the Home Secretary calling for sufficient police action and numbers to ensure that the Messenger Group's production was not curtailed by the mass picket ... newspaper reports suggest that the Home Secretary acted accordingly'.

The third example is the miners' dispute 1984–5, which the NCCL (1984:1) depicted as the occasion of 'the most massive and sustained deployment of the police ever experienced in Britain'. The NCCL drew attention to the numerous issues of civil liberty raised by the policing of this dispute, including allegations of over-forceful and provocative police behaviour on picket lines, the use in some instances of thousands of police to ensure the free passage of a handful of working miners, and, in contrast, the extensive use of road blocks to deny the free passage of 'presumed pickets'. As regards the administration of criminal justice, concern was expressed over the choice of charges which included not only the offences under the Police, Public Order, Highways, and Criminal Damage Acts (see above) but also the antiquated offence under s.7 of the 1875 Act, and the vague and potentially draconian common law crimes of unlawful assembly and riot. Over a quarter of those charged were eventually acquitted, though many were subject to the imposition of standard bail conditions which restricted their picketing, and their general freedom of movement, to their own pit villages. It is also noteworthy that about a fifth of those who were arrested were not charged with any offence. Another issue was the organisation of the police. In theory the police force is still organised on a local basis with roots and accountability in the community, and still operates on the basis of consent. The dispute, however, gave prominence to the National Reporting Centre at Scotland Yard, which appeared to deploy large bodies of police officers as if they were a national riot squad (see Fine and Millar, 1985).

The miners' strike raised the question of police neutrality in an acute form: were the police and the whole apparatus of criminal justice used by the government to break the strike? Apart from the massive police resources devoted to the dispute, substance to this allegation may be found in the use of road blocks and bail conditions to promote the policy of the civil law, namely, the restriction of secondary picketing. The legality of road blocks was challenged in a test case brought by miners who appealed against convictions for obstructing the police. It was held that a road block was lawful, provided the police had reasonable grounds to believe that there was 'a real risk of a breach of the peace in the sense that it is in close proximity both in place and time'.[51] Under the Police and Criminal Evidence Act

---

[50] HC Select Committee on Employment 1979–80, Minutes of Evidence, 462 (ii), 27 February 1980, pp.36–7. On the Grunwick dispute, see further Scarman (1977); Elias et al. (1980:29–59); and Chapter 3 above.

[51] *Moss v McLachlan* [1985] IRLR 76, 78, DC.

1984, which was not in force at the time of the dispute, a 'road check' is permissible only in certain circumstances, such as when a serious arrestable offence is likely to be committed in the area of the road check. Both common law and statutory principles indicate, therefore, that some of the road blocks in the miners' dispute – those imposed many miles away from mining areas – were unlawful.

Bail conditions became an issue because of the practice of magistrates' courts, particularly the court at Mansfield, of granting bail subject to the condition that the defendant should not visit any place for the purpose of picketing or demonstrating in connection with the strike, other than peacefully to picket or demonstrate at his usual place of employment. The legality of this condition was the subject of a High Court action.[52] It was held that the condition was lawful as it was not a breach of the Bail Act 1976, which in effect requires the magistrates to impose conditions necessary to prevent the defendant from committing an offence while on bail. The decision was based in part on unchallenged police evidence about the violent nature of the mass picketing in the Nottinghamshire coal field. Its consequence, according to the NCCL (1984:29), is that bail conditions can be used 'as a substitute for civil law remedies'.

There is another way in which the miners' dispute – together with other major incidents of picketing – can be said to have put paid to the policy of police neutrality: it led to the key proposals in the White Paper on public order (Home and Scottish Offices, 1985). Apart from the enlargement of some of the criminal offences applicable to pickets already discussed, the White Paper was concerned with the strengthening of police powers in respect of public order. It proposed to amend the Public Order Act 1936 to give the police wider powers to impose conditions on marches. In addition to the present test of the apprehension of serious public disorder, there would be two further tests of serious disruption to the local community and coercion of individuals (1985:paras.4.17–4.25). It also proposed to bring picketing within the framework of public order law by giving the police a power to impose conditions on 'static demonstrations' in the open-air including the highway in accordance with the same three tests (paras.5.5–5.14). The police conditions could restrict the location, size, and duration of picketing. The public disorder test might have been applied to the Grunwick or Stockport Messenger disputes in order to limit the number of demonstrators or to move them further away from the factories in question (para.5.7). Picketing was the 'obvious example' (para.5.10) for the application of the test of coercion of individuals, which predictably the White Paper illustrated with the miners' dispute. Those who organise or incite or even participate in disobedience to a police directive would, under these proposals, commit a criminal offence. Curiously, the White Paper omitted to refer to the duties of the 'picket organiser' as set out in the Picketing Code (see above). Even more curiously, and in marked contrast to the 1981 Green Paper on union immunities, no reference was made to the policy of police neutrality, which has presumably been abandoned.

[52] *R v Mansfield Justices ex parte Sharkey* [1984] IRLR 496, DC.

If it is arguable that the police and the administration of criminal justice are increasingly involved in carrying out the government's policies in respect of industrial disputes, a similar point can be made about the civil courts. Civil legal remedies may be awarded on the basis of picketing made unlawful by the 1980 Act, but the issue is more complex than that. Judicial responsiveness to a climate of 'establishment' opinion was classically illustrated by the principles set out in Scott J's judgment in the *Thomas* case: picketing which unreasonably harassed strikebreakers as users of the highway constituted the tort of nuisance; the number of pickets and demonstrators could be limited by injunction to six as advised by the Picketing Code; and intimidatory mass picketing – non-intimidatory mass picketing being apparently impossible – was both tortious and criminal and could potentially be restrained by dissenting members enforcing the union rule book. The very nature of the civil law interposes the courts between the policies of the state and the parties to a dispute. If a court order is not obeyed, the issue may be presented as one of 'law and order', in which the government is apparently not directly involved. Yet those responsible for the current legal framework ought not to be surprised if the neutrality of the law – both civil and criminal – is questioned. Perhaps there was always an element of myth in the idea that the law and the legal system could be neutral, but a much greater degree of impartiality will have to be restored to the legal framework if consent and co-operation are to replace confrontation as a durable basis for industrial relations.

Bibliography

Anderman, S., and P. Davies. 1974. 'Injunction Procedure in Labour Disputes – II'. *Industrial Law Journal*, 3 (March), 30–45.

Arnison, J. 1974. *The Shrewsbury Three*. London: Lawrence & Wishart.

Bellace, J. 1981. 'Regulating Secondary Action: The British and American Approaches'. *Comparative Labor Law*, 4 (Spring), 115–54.

Bercusson, B. 1977. 'One Hundred Years of Conspiracy and Protection of Property: Time for a Change'. *Modern Law Review*, 40 (May), 268–92.

Bullock. 1977. Committee of Inquiry on Industrial Democracy. *Report*. Cmnd 6706. London: HMSO.

Chief Inspector of Constabulary. 1984. *Report of Her Majesty's Chief Inspector of Constabulary 1983*. HC528. London: HMSO.

Citrine, N. 1967. *Trade Union Law*. 3rd edn. Ed. M. Hickling. London: Stevens.

Clegg, H.A., A. Fox and A.F. Thompson. 1964. *A History of British Trade Unions Since 1889*. Volume 1, 1889–1910. Oxford: Clarendon Press.

Confederation of British Industry (CBI). 1980. *Trade Unions in a Changing World: The Challenge for Management*. London: CBI.

Daniel, W.W., and N. Millward. 1983. *Workplace Industrial Relations in Britain: The DE/PSI/SSRC Survey*. London: Heinemann.

Davies, P., and M. Freedland. 1984. *Labour Law: Text and Materials*. 2nd edn. London: Weidenfeld & Nicolson.

Department of Employment (DE). 1979. *Working Paper for Consultations on Proposed Industrial Relations Legislation: Picketing*. London: DE.

——. 1981. *Trade Union Immunities*. Cmnd 8128. London: HMSO.

Donovan. 1968. Royal Commission on Trade Unions and Employers' Associations 1965–1968. *Report*. Cmnd 3623. London: HMSO.

Elias, P., B. Napier and P. Wallington. 1980. *Labour Law: Cases and Materials*. London: Butterworths.

Evans, S. 1983. 'The Labour Injunction Revisited: Picketing, Employers and the Employment Act 1980'. *Industrial Law Journal*, 12 (September), 129–47.

——. 1985a. 'Picketing under the Employment Acts'. *Industrial Relations and the Law in the 1980s: Issues and Future Trends*. Eds. P. Fosh and C. Littler. Aldershot: Gower.

——. 1985b. 'The Use of Injunctions in Industrial Disputes'. *British Journal of Industrial Relations*, 23 (March), 133–7.

Ewing, K. 1985. 'The Strike, the Courts and the Rule Book'. *Industrial Law Journal*, 14 (September), 160–75.

Fine, Bob, and Robert Millar (eds.). 1985. *Policing the Miners' Strike*. London: Lawrence & Wishart.

Gennard, J. 1984. 'The Implications of the Messenger Newspaper Group Dispute'. *Industrial Relations Journal*, 15 (Autumn), 7–20.

Home and Scottish Offices. 1985. *Review of Public Order Law*. Cmnd 9510. London: HMSO.

Howell, G. 1890. *Conflicts of Capital and Labour*. 2nd edn. London: Macmillan.

Kahn, P., N. Lewis, R. Livock and P. Wiles. 1983. *Picketing – Industrial Disputes, Tactics and the Law*. London: Routledge & Kegan Paul.

Law Commission. 1983. *Criminal Law: Offences Relating to Public Order*. Report 123. London: HMSO.

Lewis, R., and Bob Simpson. 1981. *Striking a Balance? Employment Law After the 1980 Act*. Oxford: Martin Robertson.

Miller, K. 1984. 'Sit-ins and s.7 of the Conspiracy and Protection of Property Act 1975 in Scotland'. *Industrial Law Journal*, 13 (June), 111–15.

Morris, G. 1984. 'The Law Commission: Criminal Law: Offences Relating to Public Order (Law Com. No. 123)'. *Modern Law Review*, 47 (May), 324–33.

National Council for Civil Liberties (NCCL). 1984. *Civil Liberties and the Miners' Dispute: First Report of the Independent Inquiry*. London: NCCL.

Scarman. 1977. *Report of a Court of Inquiry under the Rt Hon Lord Justice Scarman OBE into a Dispute between Grunwick Processing Laboratories Limited and Members of APEX*. Cmnd 6922. London: HMSO.

Smith, J.C., and B. Hogan. 1983. *Criminal Law*. 5th edn. London: Butterworths.

Taft, P., and P. Ross, 1969. 'American Labor Violence: Its Causes, Character, and Outcome'. *Violence in America: Historical and Comparative Perspectives*. Eds. H.D. Graham and E.R. Gurr. New York: Signet Books, 270–376.

Wallington, Peter. 1972. 'The Case of the Longannet Miners and the Criminal Liability of Pickets'. *Industrial Law Journal*, 1 (December), 219–28.

Wedderburn, K.W. (*Lord*). 1971. *The Worker and the Law*. 2nd edn. Harmondsworth: Penguin.

———. 1981. 'Secondary Action and Gateways to Legality: A Note'. *Industrial Law Journal*, 10 (June), 113–18.

Woods. 1968. Task Force on Labour Relations. *Canadian Industrial Relations*. Report. Ottawa: Privy Council Office.

8 Emergencies and Essential Supplies

Gillian Morris

The conception that some services are 'essential' is reflected in the law of most countries but, as Pankert (1980) demonstrates, the methods adopted for safeguarding these services vary greatly. Sometimes it is felt that the need for an uninterrupted service is so strong that workers in that service are not permitted to withdraw their labour under any circumstances. Alternatively, the legality of industrial action may be made conditional on specified workers remaining at work to ensure a minimum service, or notice of a particular length being given, or a cooling-off period observed to allow more time for a peaceful settlement to be reached. Sometimes the state is given special powers to protect the public against the full consequences of a stoppage.

What constitutes an 'essential' service differs widely between systems. In some countries the definition is confined to services necessary for public health and safety; at the other extreme, it may extend to 'all activities which the government may consider appropriate or all strikes that may be contrary to public order, the general interest or economic development' (ILO, 1983:para. 213). The developing nations, in particular, tend to include services whose disruption would damage the national economy (Pankert, 1980:728). In some systems the law specifies which services are 'essential'; in others special provisions may be invoked if a dispute is seen by a particular person or body as having defined consequences.

Limiting the freedom of groups of workers to withdraw their labour clearly reduces their bargaining power, and the Freedom of Association Committee of the ILO (1983: para. 214) has emphasised that strikes should be proscribed only where interruption of a service would endanger 'life, personal safety or health'. It has also stressed the need for any restrictions to be offset by 'adequate impartial and speedy conciliation and arbitration procedures' with binding awards which are implemented without delay. Legislation in many countries clearly goes beyond the ILO's yardstick of essentiality. Moreover, Art. 31 of the European Social Charter 1965 allows restrictions on the right to strike which are prescribed by law and 'necessary in a democratic society for the protection of the rights and freedoms of others or for the protection of the public interest, national security, public health or morals'.

The British approach to labour disputes in essential services has traditionally centred upon taking measures to secure supplies by alternative means once they have been disrupted rather than attempting to forestall disruption. The first section of this chapter looks at the powers available to the government to secure supplies in 'emergency' disputes and the use which has been made of them. In so far as it does restrict the freedom of particular groups to take industrial action, British law is a collection of piecemeal provisions rather than the product of an overall strategy. The second section analyses these provisions and also considers a number of indirect methods by which industrial action in essential services, or at least its effectiveness, may be inhibited. In the last few years pressure has grown for further restrictions. Groups which previously would not have taken industrial action, such as doctors, nurses, and higher grade civil servants, have shown themselves willing to do so, and groups which previously took only very limited forms of action are now prepared to impose more drastic sanctions. The concluding section outlines the reforms which various bodies have proposed, the union response to the challenge, and recent developments which may reduce the potential for disruption in more oblique ways.

EMERGENCY POWERS

The most far-reaching legislation in this area is the Emergency Powers Act 1920, which allows the government to take extensive powers when specific services are disrupted. In addition, the Energy Act 1976 gives broad powers of control and direction when energy supplies are threatened. The power to use troops as replacement labour, in the absence of a proclamation of emergency under the 1920 Act, is contained in the Emergency Powers Act 1964. Other sources of alternative labour, such as the police, have also been employed. The 'cooling-off' and compulsory ballot provisions of the Industrial Relations Act 1971, now repealed, present an illuminating case-study of an unsuccessful attempt to interfere in the conduct of 'emergency' disputes.

Emergency Powers Act 1920

The Emergency Powers Act 1920 enables the Crown to proclaim a state of emergency if

> at any time it appears to Her Majesty that there have occurred, or are about to occur, events of such a nature as to be calculated, by interfering with the supply and distribution of food, water, fuel, or light, or with the means of locomotion, to deprive the community, or any substantial portion of the community, of the essentials of life.[1]

The executive then has a broad power to make such regulations as the monarch deems necessary for securing essential supplies 'and for any other

---

[1] Section 1(1), as amended by the Emergency Powers Act 1964 s.1.

purposes essential to the public safety and the life of the community' (s.2(1)). The government may not, however, use this power to force strikers back to work; regulations may not impose compulsory military service or industrial conscription; nor may they make it an offence to strike or peacefully persuade others to do so. The maximum penalty the regulations may impose for their contravention, after summary trial, is three months' imprisonment, a £100 fine, or both.[2] They may not alter existing criminal procedure or allow punishment without trial (s.2(3)). The Act provides for parliamentary debate and control at an early stage. The government must communicate the occasion of a proclamation of emergency to Parliament 'forthwith', and Parliament must be specially summoned if it is not due to meet within five days of the proclamation being issued (s.1(2)). The regulations must be laid before Parliament 'as soon as may be' and require approval by both Houses within seven days of laying to continue in force (s.2(2)). A fresh proclamation and code of regulations must be issued every month and the same procedure followed (s.1(1)). It is doubtful, however, whether failure to follow these procedures would make the powers taken legally invalid (Morris, 1979:331), although it would obviously have political repercussions.

A state of emergency has been proclaimed under the 1920 Act on twelve separate occasions, all industrial disputes, including nine since 1945 and five during the Heath Government of 1970–74. The majority of these disputes involved coal miners and dockers; others involved railwaymen, electricity supply workers, seamen, and London busmen and tramwaymen. Table 8.1 outlines the course of each emergency. In 1924 and 1948 the dispute was settled before regulations were issued (although in 1948 the proclamation was not revoked). Of the remaining emergencies, six lasted for one month or less and one (1966) for six weeks. In 1921, 1926 and 1973–4, three, seven, and five successive proclamations respectively were issued during the course of the dispute. On three occasions, the government took an inordinately wide view of 'the essentials of life' in the enabling power. The 1948 and 1949 proclamations were said to be necessary to protect external trade as well as essential food supplies,[3] and in 1966 the need for powers was based on economic grounds alone.[4]

In 1921 the government introduced regulations containing 'the large majority of powers that are ever likely to be required',[5] and ever since (except in 1949 and 1955) governments have followed the practice of issuing a corpus of regulations, to which additions and changes are occasionally made, regardless of the exigencies of the immediate situation. In most emergencies only a small proportion of the powers taken have been used. The pre-war regulations reflect a greater fear of civil disturbance than the post-war, but throughout interference with property rights has been more far-reaching than restrictions on individual freedom (Morris, 1979:325–31).

---

[2] Section 2(3), as amended by the Criminal Justice Act 1982 s.41.
[3] 452 HC Deb, 28 June 1948, 1839 (Mr Attlee); 466 HC Deb, 8 July 1949, 2593 (Mr Ede).
[4] 729 HC Deb, 23 May 1966, 37 (Mr Wilson).
[5] 140 HC Deb, 5 April 1921, 341 (Mr Shortt).

TABLE 8.1
THE USE OF THE EMERGENCY POWERS ACT 1920

Year	Workers involved	Industrial action	Dispute began	State of emergency proclaimed	Dispute ended	State of emergency ended	Government in office
1921	Coal miners	Strike	31 March	31 March	1 July	26 July	Liberal-Unionist coalition
1924	Tramwaymen and busmen	Strike	22 March	27 March	1 April	1 April	Labour
1926	Coal miners (General Strike 4–12 May)	Strike	1 May	30 April	22 December	19 December	Conservative
1948	Dockers	Strike	14 June	28 June	29 June	27 July	Labour
1949	Dockers	Strike	23 June	11 July	23 July	26 July	Labour
1955	Railwaymen	Strike	29 May	31 May	14 June	21 June	Conservative
1966	Seamen	Strike	16 May	23 May	1 July	6 July	Labour
1970	Dockers	Strike	13 July	16 July	31 July	4 August	Conservative
1970	Electricity manual workers	Work to rule and overtime ban	7 December	12 December	14 December	17 December	Conservative
1972	Coal miners	Overtime ban then strike	1 November 1971 (strike 9 January 1972)	9 February	25 February	8 March	Conservative
1972	Dockers	Strike	28 July	3 August	18 August	2 September	Conservative
1973	i. Electricity power engineers; ii. Coal miners; iii. Railwaymen	i. Ban on 'out of hours' work; ii. Overtime ban then strike; iii. Ban on Sunday rest-day and overtime work	i. 1 November; ii.13 November (strike 10 February 1974); iii. 12 December	13 November	i. 28 December; ii. 8 March 1974; iii. 11 February 1974	11 March 1974	Conservative

Source: Morris, 1978: 154–7.

An overview of the regulations issued for the 1973–4 emergency[6] indicates the scope of recent regulations. They included powers to take possession of land, requisition chattels, control traffic in ports, relax restrictions relating to vehicles and driving licences, fix maximum prices for food and control its distribution, control gas, electricity, water supplies, liquid fuel and refinery products, regulate transport services and relax restrictions relating to sewerage disposal and medicines. They also included a number of specific offences: sabotage; trespassing on or near premises used for essential services; endangering, obstructing or interfering with service personnel, constables and other persons performing essential services; and inducing members of the armed or police forces to withhold their services or commit breaches of discipline. The police were given power to arrest without warrant for offences against the regulations.

It is interesting to compare the use of the regulations in the 1972 and 1973–4 miners' disputes. In 1972 the miners' action, supported by effective picketing which halted the movement of coal and prevented power stations using much of the coal they already had, proved unexpectedly damaging (Trice, 1975; Wigham, 1982:169), and by the time of the proclamation coal stocks for domestic and generating purposes stood at two weeks' supply.[7] Immediate and drastic measures were then introduced: rota power cuts were ordered; the use of electricity for advertising, display and floodlighting prohibited;[8] restrictions imposed on heating non-domestic premises;[9] and 20,000 medium-sized industrial concerns (excluding certain essential services and producers) were put onto a three-day week[10] leading to thousands of workers being laid off. The Prime Minister, Mr Edward Heath, later acknowledged that the government should have acted sooner,[11] and in 1973 he went to the other extreme, taking powers on the first day of the miners' overtime ban when power station stocks stood at twelve weeks' supply.[12] (A 25 per cent reduction in oil deliveries from Arab states was also imminent). Throughout the dispute the government 'played safe' with electricity supply, immediately restricting its use for advertising and display[13] and non-domestic heating[14] and in late December, when power station stocks were still reasonably high, introducing a three-day week for many industrial and commercial users.[15] By 7 January 1974, 885,000 workers had been laid off[16]

---

6   The Emergency Regulations SI 1973 No. 1881.
7   831 HC Deb, 14 February 1972, 155 (Mr Davies).
8   The Electricity (Advertising, Display and Floodlighting) (Restriction) Order SI 1972 No. 160.
9   The Electricity (Non-Domestic Heating) (Restriction) Order SI 1972 No. 169 (as amended by SI 1972 No. 239).
10   831 HC Deb, 14 February 1972, 193 (Sir John Eden).
11   867 HC Deb, 9 January 1974, 8.
12   863 HC Deb, 2 November 1973, 37 (written answer) (Mr Emery).
13   The Electricity (Advertising, Display etc.) (Restriction) Order SI 1973 No. 1901.
14   The Electricity (Heating) (Restriction) Order SI 1973 No. 1900 (as amended by SI 1973 No. 1913).
15   The Electricity (Industrial and Commercial Use) (Control) (No. 2) Order SI 1973 No. 2172.
16   Keesing's Contemporary Archives 1974, p. 26299.

and the cost of the three-day week was later estimated at £2,000 million.[17] These two miners' disputes — together with the 1921 and 1926 coal stoppages which, as Morris (1979:338–41) describes, involved a large-scale mobilisation of state forces and, in 1926, considerable use of public order regulations — are the only emergencies where extensive use was made of the powers taken. This is all in great contrast with the 1984–5 miners' dispute, which the government was able to defeat without invoking emergency powers.

Governments taking emergency powers have generally been anxious to emphasise that they have done so purely to protect the 'national interest' and not to influence the outcome of the dispute. In all cases except 1924, however, this rhetoric has been accompanied by a denunciation of the stoppage. All but three disputes (1948, 1949 and July 1972) concerned wages, a topic in which all governments have taken an interest, and in six of the remainder the government had a vested interest in the terms of settlement: either directly, as in 1921 and 1926 where conceding the miners' claim would have necessitated a government subsidy, or, as in 1966, December 1970, January 1972 and 1973, because of an incomes policy. Moreover, government spokesmen have sometimes deliberately fostered the atmosphere of crisis a proclamation inevitably engenders. In 1966 the Prime Minister, Mr Harold Wilson, dubbed the seamen's strike 'a strike against the state' and warned that emergency powers (which were never used) would be taken if it continued.[18] The 1949 emergency, which began when London dockers refused to unload Canadian ships blacked by a Communist-dominated union, was characterised as 'a challenge to the whole authority of the state'.[19] The 1973 miners' claim was represented as a threat to the democratic process.[20] It is disingenuous and naive to maintain that taking emergency powers is a 'neutral' act, especially where government policies are being challenged. Even where they are not being challenged, emergency powers inevitably strengthen management's hand, although they may also harden strikers' resolve.

The 1920 Act has not been invoked since 1974. The Labour Governments of 1974–9 used troops in some disputes but resisted strong opposition pressure to declare a state of emergency during a road haulage strike in 1979, arguing that co-operation with the unions was a more efficacious method of securing priority supplies. The subsequent Conservative Governments have not seen the 1920 Act as a first-line response to major disputes, and have not yet been forced into using it.

Energy Act 1976

The Energy Act 1976 ss.1 and 2 give the Secretary of State a standing power to control the use of fuel, natural gas and electricity supplies where he

---

[17] Keesing's Contemporary Archives 1974, p. 26426 (Mr Varley).
[18] Broadcast 16 May 1966: Keesing's Contemporary Archives 1965–6, p. 21547.
[19] 466 HC Deb, 8 July 1949, 2593 (Mr Ede).
[20] See, for example, 864 HC Deb, 13 November 1973, 259 (Mr Carr).

considers this desirable to conserve energy, and more extensive powers of direction over individual producers, suppliers and users when an Order in Council is in force. Such an Order may be made either because international obligations require emergency measures to be taken to deal with a threatened reduction in fuel supplies or because 'there exists or is imminent in the United Kingdom an actual or threatened emergency affecting fuel or electricity supplies which makes it necessary in Her Majesty's opinion that the Government should temporarily have at its disposal exceptional powers for controlling the sources and availability of energy' (s.3(1)). If the Order is made for the latter reason it must be laid before Parliament and approved by both Houses within twenty-eight days to remain in force. It has effect for twelve months but Parliament may renew it for a further twelve. When an Order in Council is in force the penalty for contravening a provision made by the Secretary of State can be up to two years' imprisonment and an unlimited fine (s.19). Clearly this Act could be used — though so far it appears not to have been — as an alternative to the Emergency Powers Act 1920 for disputes affecting energy supplies where the powers it gives are sufficient. However, as it provides for considerably less parliamentary supervision than the 1920 Act, it would be preferable from the viewpoint of democratic accountability for the 1920 Act to be invoked where industrial action has caused the emergency.[21]

Use of Alternative Labour

Troops. The use of troops to replace strikers goes back at least to the nineteenth century (Knowles, 1952:133). However, it was unclear whether soldiers were covered by military discipline when performing civilian tasks (Morris, 1978:86–96). The need to put this beyond challenge was an important motive for enacting the Emergency Powers Act 1920. The 1921 and 1926 regulations applied military discipline to work, declared by a Secretary of State to be 'of vital importance to the community'.[22] A similar wartime regulation of 1939 continued in force until 1964[23] when the power to use troops for non-military duties was put on a permanent basis. Section 2 of the Emergency Powers Act 1964 permits the Defence Council[24] (composed of defence ministers, service chiefs and civil servants) to authorise

---

[21] Ad hoc legislation has been introduced to deal with problems outside the scope of the Acts of 1920 and 1976. The Administration of Justice (Emergency Provisions) (Scotland) Act 1979 was passed to deal with the impact of a civil service strike on the Scottish legal system and the Imprisonment (Temporary Provisions) Act 1980 to alleviate the consequences of industrial action by prison officers. The Home Secretary has a standing emergency power to order the early release of certain categories of prisoners where necessary to make the best use of available places: Criminal Justice Act 1982 s.32.

[22] Emergency Regulations SR & O 1926 No. 556 reg. 24.

[23] The Defence (Armed Forces) Regulations SR & O 1939 No. 1304 reg. 6, continued in force by the Emergency Laws (Repeal) Act 1959 Sch. 2, Part C.

[24] The Defence (Transfer of Functions) Act 1964 substitutes references to the Defence Council for references to the Admiralty, Army Council and Air Council.

officers and men of the naval, military or air forces to be temporarily employed under military discipline in agricultural work or other work which the Council deems 'urgent work of national importance'. This would be done at the request of the appropriate civil ministry. No proclamation or parliamentary approval is required.

Since 1945 troops have performed civilian functions during disputes involving the following groups: dockers in 1945 (twice), 1947, 1948, 1949, 1950, and 1972; meat-handlers in 1946, 1947, and 1950; electricity manual workers in 1949; gas maintenance workers in 1950; petrol distribution workers in 1953; railwaymen in 1955 and 1982; seamen in 1960 and 1966; refuse workers in 1970 and 1975; firemen in 1973 and 1977; air traffic controllers in 1977; ambulance drivers in 1979, 1981, and 1982; and prison officers in 1981. On five of these occasions (1948, 1949, 1955, 1966, and 1972) a state of emergency was declared. A useful survey of the use of troops in disputes may be found in Peak (1984). Clearly troops have been involved in situations beyond the scope of the 1920 Act, such as fire, health and prison service disputes, and they have also been used where 'a substantial portion of the community' has not been affected.

The 1977–8 firemen's strike brought the most extensive use of troops to date: after 'elementary'[25] training in using old 'Green Goddess' machines preserved for civil defence, over 20,000 troops, assisted by 4,000 senior fire officers and large numbers of part-time firemen, replaced 32,000 strikers for nine weeks. But troops could not replace all workforces so effectively. First, they lack the necessary skills to perform functions which technical developments have rendered increasingly specialised. It was found in the 1960s that fewer than twenty soldiers in the entire army were able to drive railway locomotives, and since 1970 it has been public knowledge that troops could not run the power stations. They could maintain water supplies only with the help of supervisors who would probably refuse to co-operate (Jeffery and Hennessy, 1983:225, 234, 246–52). Even where the work is relatively unskilled there may be insufficient troops. Jeffery and Hennessy (1983:250) estimate that only about 15,000 troops are available without severe disruption of commitments in Northern Ireland and to NATO, and a government spokesman claimed that the services could move only 'a small fraction' of the goods moved under priority arrangements with the unions during the 1979 road haulage dispute.[26]

Nevertheless, the ability to use troops as substitute labour, albeit for a limited range of tasks, remains an important governmental power. Like declaring a state of emergency, and for the same reasons, its exercise is not a 'neutral' act. The government may be defending an incomes policy, as was the case with the firemen, and a fine line separates protecting essential services and strike breaking — a line which the Attlee Government crossed in using troops to handle all cargoes, and not just food supplies, during the 1945, 1948 and 1950 dock strikes. Bringing in troops may inflame a dispute,

---

25   940 HC Deb, 6 December 1977, 1099 (Mr Gilbert).
26   960 HC Deb, 15 January 1979, 1320 (Mr Rees). *The Guardian*, 19 January 1979 reported that troops could secure at most five per cent of normal supplies.

as happened in strikes in the docks (1949 and 1950), meat handling (1946 and 1950), and in electricity (1949). A strong case exists for subjecting such a crucial power to direct parliamentary control.

Police. During industrial action by ambulancemen in 1979, 1981 and 1982 police maintained emergency cover in areas where ambulancemen themselves withdrew cover, with troops standing by should the police and voluntary organisations be unable to cope. The employment of police as substitute labour raises substantial legal problems concerning, for example, the scope of the police discipline code (Morris, 1980). There are also political objections to such a course. Whereas the armed forces are subject to ministerial direction, the police operate as an independent and impartial law enforcement agency and using them to do the work of strikers tarnishes their impartial and independent reputation.

Civilian volunteers. No official corps of civilian volunteers exists to replace strikers. Private organisations were formed in 1911 and 1925 (Morris, 1978:535–46), in the latter case with government endorsement, and the government itself recruited nearly half a million volunteers during the General Strike.[27] Organisations established by former military commanders in the mid-1970s, 'Unison' and 'Great Britain 1975' (Morris, 1978:546–50) were denounced by government ministers as 'a near-fascist groundswell'[28] and 'at best misconceived ... and at the worst dangerous'.[29] The idea of using civilian volunteers was apparently considered, but not developed, by the present Conservative administration in 1980 (Jeffery and Hennessy, 1983:257–9). Volunteers have played a minor role in National Health Service (NHS) disputes, and although their use as alternative labour is officially encouraged,[30] it is probably a last resort for most administrators (Morris with Rydzkowski, 1984:161–3).

Industrial Relations Act 1971

The emergency procedures in the now repealed IRA ss.138–45, which were modelled on the American Taft-Hartley Act 1947, allowed the executive, with judicial sanction, to interfere directly in the conduct of disputes and were intended to make states of emergency unnecessary. The Secretary of State for Employment could apply to the National Industrial Relations Court for a 'cooling-off' order of up to sixty days if he considered there was an 'emergency situation' and delay or discontinuance of industrial action would be conducive to a settlement (s.138). Alternatively or consecutively, he could apply for a ballot order if he thought there was reason to doubt whether workers wished to participate in the action and the action would

27   197 HC Deb, 7 July 1926, 2179 (Mr Shortt).
28   *The Times*, 24 August 1974 (Mr Mason).
29   *The Times*, 4 October 1974 (Mr Jenkins).
30   DHSS Circular HC (79) 20.

either lead to an emergency situation or imperil the livelihood of a substantial number of workers in the industry (s.141). Industrial action was prohibited until the result of the ballot was known.

The definition of an 'emergency situation' was considerably broader than in the 1920 Act: it covered industrial action which caused or would cause

> an interruption in the supply of goods or in the provision of services of such a nature, or on such a scale, as to be likely (a) to be gravely injurious to the national economy, to imperil national security or to create a serious risk of public disorder, or (b) to endanger the lives of a substantial number of persons, or expose a substantial number ... to serious risk of disease or personal injury (s.138(2)).

The reference to the 'national economy' seemed to allow intervention in most major disputes. Theoretically the court had to be 'satisfied on the evidence' that there were 'sufficient grounds for believing' an emergency situation existed (ss.139(1), 142(1)), but it would have been a bold judge who overrode the Secretary of State's opinion. As Jones (1973:140) noted, 'in requiring the Industrial Relations Court to "rubber-stamp" the Minister's view ... the Act went far towards making the Court an arm of Government, not part of the independent arm of the Judiciary'.

These procedures were used only once,[31] during a rail dispute over wages in 1972 which reduced services by over 50 per cent on some lines. A fourteen-day cooling-off period failed to produce a settlement and a compulsory ballot showed a majority of five to one in favour of continuing the action. Fresh negotiations produced a settlement before it resumed. Although the procedures postponed the industrial action, they did not advance a settlement (Weekes et al., 1975:215–16). The government did not invoke them in subsequent disputes, preferring to declare a state of emergency in the case of the 1972 dock strike and 1973 campaigns by miners, electricity power engineers and railwaymen.

LIMITATIONS ON INDUSTRIAL ACTION

The law imposes direct limitations on industrial action in a variety of occupations. There are also several indirect methods by which industrial action in essential services may be inhibited.

Direct Limitations

Provisions specifically inhibiting industrial action divide into those covering particular groups of workers and restrictions on industrial action having particular consequences. Groups singled out for special treatment are the police, the armed forces, merchant seamen, and postal and telecommunica-

---

[31] *Secretary of State for Employment v ASLEF* [1972] 2 QB 443 and *Secretary of State for Employment v ASLEF (No.2)* [1972] 2 QB 455.

tions workers. Previous specific restrictions on gas, electricity and water workers under the Conspiracy and Protection of Property Act 1875 s.4 were repealed in 1971.

Police. The legislative proscription of industrial action by the police goes back to the Police Act 1919, which followed a police strike in 1918; the modern provision is s.53(1) of the Police Act 1964. This section makes it an offence to cause or attempt to cause disaffection among the members of any police force or to induce or attempt to induce any member of a police force to withhold his services or commit breaches of discipline. It is aimed at the incitement of unrest and any campaign of industrial action would involve its infringement, if not by participants, certainly by the organisers. Individual policemen taking action would commit offences under the statutory Discipline Code.[32] The statutory immunities against tortious liability for industrial action would not apply.[33] The only recorded prosecutions under s.53(1) and its predecessor arose out of activities among the unemployed between 1921 and 1932; none was against policemen (Williams, 1967:193–4).

In general, the police have acquiesced in the argument that industrial action would be incompatible with their role as a disciplined force whose members are pledged to uphold the law. But there was a break in this tradition in 1976–7 when the Police Federation (to which all ranks below superintendent automatically belong) felt obliged during a pay dispute to support a call for the right to strike. The inquiry which followed rejected this call, but accepted that restrictions on the freedom to strike must be adequately compensated for and recommended substantial pay increases, together with a formula for annual uprating linked to the monthly index of average earnings (Edmund Davies, 1978: ch. 6). The Police Federation, delighted with this solution, immediately dropped its demand for a change in the law, support for which was 'more of a gesture, an expression of frustration and discontent, than a permanent shift to the left' (Reiner, 1978:276).

Armed forces. Organising industrial action by the armed forces would infringe the Incitement to Mutiny Act 1797 s.2 which makes it illegal 'maliciously and advisedly' to seduce a serviceman from his duty and allegiance to the Crown or incite him to mutiny. It would also infringe the Incitement to Disaffection Act 1934 s.1 with its broader offence of 'maliciously and advisedly' endeavouring to seduce a serviceman from his duty or allegiance. Publications urging soldiers not to shoot strikers in 1912 and 1925, and sailors to join a strike against pay cuts in 1931 led to convictions under the 1797 Act (Young, 1976:14–18, 46–7, 53–4). Participants in industrial action would breach military law.[34]

Merchant seamen. Industrial action by merchant seamen is restricted to protect the safety of ships and interests of employers rather than the public

---

[32] The Police (Discipline) Regulations SI 1977 No. 580 Sch.2.
[33] The police (and armed forces) are excluded from the definition of 'worker' in TULRA s.30.
[34] Army Act 1955 ss.31–41; Air Force Act 1955 ss.31–41; Naval Discipline Act 1957 ss.8–18.

at large. A seaman employed in a ship registered in the UK may terminate his employment in contemplation or furtherance of a trade dispute after giving the master a minimum of forty-eight hours' notice (whatever the terms of his contract), provided that the ship is in the UK and securely moored in a safe berth when notice is given.[35] Unless these conditions are satisfied seamen taking industrial action are liable to criminal proceedings or charges under statutory disciplinary provisions.[36] But penal provisions have not been invoked for industrial action in modern times. Since 1980, the National Union of Seamen has generally advised members to sit on board ships, wherever they are, rather than terminate their employment during disputes; this tactic was used during a national dispute in 1981.

Postal workers. Restrictions on postal workers derive from provisions originally intended to deter individual acts of industrial misconduct. In *Gouriet v UPW*[37] the House of Lords held that these provisions made unlawful a proposed boycott of communications between England and South Africa. Any officer who 'contrary to his duty, wilfully detains or delays, or procures or suffers to be detained or delayed' any postal packet is liable to a maximum penalty of two years' imprisonment and an unlimited fine, and any person who solicits or endeavours to procure such action is liable to up to two years' imprisonment.[38] It seems clear that these offences make discriminatory action against particular customers illegal,[39] though beyond that their effect is uncertain. The Attorney General has said that they do not make strikes illegal because they are directed against particular acts, omissions or breaches of duty concerning one or more postal packets, which would be too remote a consequence of a strike, and they deal only with misconduct while at work. But he thought that other industrial action in breach of contract might be an offence.[40] The House of Lords judgments in *Gouriet* do not support such a distinction and, as Morris (1983:74) has argued, the Attorney General's construction of the legislation is questionable. Although recent industrial action by postal workers has not brought the threat of prosecution, it is undesirable that their legal position should remain so unclear.

Telecommunications workers. The Telecommunications Act 1984 s.45 makes it an offence, punishable by an unlimited fine, for a person engaged in the running of a public telecommunications system intentionally to intercept a message sent by means of that system otherwise than in the course of his duty. Telecommunications workers could commit this offence when taking industrial action, although if the Director General of Telecommunications

---

[35] Merchant Shipping Act 1970 s.42(2). Section 5 of the Conspiracy and Protection of Property Act 1875 does not apply to merchant seamen.
[36] See Merchant Shipping Act 1970 ss.27–32 (as amended by the Merchant Shipping Acts of 1974 and 1979); ss.34–8.
[37] [1978] AC 435.
[38] Post Office Act 1953 ss.58, 68; see also s.59.
[39] *Harold Stephen and Co. Ltd v Post Office* [1977] 1 WLR 1172.
[40] HC Standing Committee B, 3 March 1981, 581–5 (Sir Michael Havers).

issues an order of the type described below, no criminal proceedings lie against a person who commits or incites others to commit a breach of such an order (s.18(4)). More important in practice is likely to be the special civil liability, which applies to telecommunications workers, against which there is no statutory immunity.[41] Under the Telecommunications Act 1984, a telecommunications operator has a statutory duty to obey an order from the Director General to provide services in accordance with the operator's licence (ss.16,18(6)(a)). If the operator is prevented from doing so by, for example, industrial action, then any person affected, such as a customer, may sue the organiser for any act which, by inducing a breach of the operator's duty or interfering with its performance, 'causes that person to sustain loss or damage and which is done wholly or partly for the purpose of achieving that result' (s.18(5),(6)(b)). The government maintained that this would not jeopardise strikes to improve conditions which led incidentally to an order being breached; the defendant's purpose must include a desire to damage the plaintiff.[42] However, as opposition spokesmen pointed out, it will be difficult to decide when there is sufficient intent to found an action, given that a successful strike would necessarily interfere with an order.[43]

Restrictions in terms of the consequences of industrial action. The Conspiracy and Protection of Property Act 1875 s.5 makes it an offence 'wilfully and maliciously' to break 'a contract of service or of hiring, knowing or having reasonable cause to believe that the probable consequences of ... so doing, either alone or in combination with others, will be to endanger human life, or cause serious bodily injury, or to expose valuable property ... to destruction or serious injury'. The penalty is a maximum of three months' imprisonment or a £50 fine. Clearly industrial action by a number of workers — for example, firemen, and workers in the health service and the public utilities — could come within this provision. Moreover, as any industrial action, except a strike preceded by notice of termination or a ban on non-contractual duties, will amount to a breach of contract,[44] there have been many disputes where it could have been invoked. But there is no record of any prosecutions under it.

Another provision which may be relevant is HSWA s.7(b), which makes it the duty of every employee while at work 'as regards any duty or requirement imposed on his employer or any other person by or under [health and safety legislation] to co-operate with him so far as is necessary to enable that duty or requirement to be performed or complied with'. Breach of this duty is an offence punishable by up to two years' imprisonment and an unlimited fine. Any employees who blacked essential safety

---

41   See 448 HL Deb, 20 February 1984, 597–8 (Lord Mackay).
42   58 HC Deb, 9 April 1981, 140 (Mr Baker); 448 HL Deb, 20 February 1984, 559; 449 HL Deb, 19 March 1984, 1010 and 450 HL Deb, 29 March 1984, 378 (Lord Mackay).
43   448 HL Deb, 20 February 1984, 599 (Lord Donaldson); 450 HL Deb, 29 March 1984, 378 (Lord Wedderburn).
44   *Simmons v Hoover Ltd* [1977] ICR 61. See Chapter 9 below.

work could arguably be guilty of the offence. To date there have been no prosecutions for industrial action.

Between 1927 and 1946 strikes and lockouts having any object other than or in addition to the furtherance of a trade dispute within the strikers' trade or industry and 'designed or calculated to coerce the Government either directly or by inflicting hardship upon the community' were declared illegal by s.1 of the Trade Disputes and Trade Unions Act 1927. Anyone organising or acting in furtherance of such a strike or lockout, otherwise than by merely ceasing to work or refusing to accept employment, was liable to up to two years' imprisonment. There was no detailed consideration by the courts of the range of strikes and lockouts declared illegal under this provision before the Act was repealed.[45]

Indirect Limitations

In addition to direct restrictions, there are a number of means by which industrial action in essential services may be inhibited indirectly: these concern restrictions on union membership, interlocutory injunctions, union immunities, protection from union discipline and the effect of the Code of Practice on Picketing.

Restrictions on trade union membership. Limiting freedom of association prevents workers organising effective collective action. Since 1919 the police, as well as being unable to take industrial action, have been prohibited from joining or affiliating to trade unions and the Police Federation may not associate with outside bodies.[46] Workers in most state security and intelligence agencies have traditionally been unable to join trade unions,[47] and in January 1984 the government announced that workers at Government Communications Headquarters (GCHQ), who had previously been encouraged to join civil service unions, would henceforth be allowed to belong only to a departmental staff association approved by their director. The association is not permitted TUC affiliation and industrial action is prohibited.[48] The government claimed that only banning union membership could ensure the necessary continuous operation of GCHQ, threatened seven times by industrial action between February 1979 and April 1981, and prevent future conflicts of loyalty for staff encouraged to participate in national campaigns. The announcement was made without consultation with staff and unions at GCHQ, a course condemned by the House of Commons Employment Committee,[49] which urged the govern-

---

45 In *R v Trease* [1944] 2 All ER 403, the issue on appeal was whether the defendants could be acting in 'furtherance' of a strike which had not yet begun. There was no appeal against the decision of the Assize Court that the strike, whose purpose was to secure the exemption of apprentices from liability to direction to work in the mines, was illegal.
46 Police Act 1964 ss.47(1), 44(2).
47 53 HC Deb, 31 January 1984, 120 (written answer) (Mrs Thatcher).
48 53 HC Deb, 1 February 1984, 227 (written answer) (Sir Geoffrey Howe).
49 HC Select Committee on Employment 1983–84, First Report, 238.

ment to try to reach an agreement with the unions to maintain continuity of operations. But the government rejected union proposals, which included a condition of service for GCHQ staff not to take action which might interfere with the uninterrupted operation of essential security and intelligence services.[50] The legal challenge to the government's action, which focused ultimately on the lack of consultation, is discussed in Chapters 2 and 20.

Interlocutory injunctions. Interlocutory injunctions, which are discussed in detail in Chapter 19, prevent the defendant carrying out an allegedly unlawful activity pending the full trial of an action. In deciding whether or not to grant an interlocutory injunction a court is required by virtue of TULRA s.17(2) to 'have regard to the likelihood' that the defendent will establish a defence of statutory immunity at the full trial. In *NWL Ltd v Woods*[51] the House of Lords stated that normally an interlocutory injunction would be refused where the defendant had shown that such a defence was likely to succeed, but the court still retains a discretion to grant it regardless. 'Cases may exist', said Lord Diplock, 'where the consequences to the employer or to third parties or the public and perhaps the nation itself, may be so disastrous that the injunction ought not to be refused, unless there is a high degree of probability that the defence will succeed'.[52] In a later decision Lord Fraser affirmed that even where the defence seemed highly likely to succeed 'if the probable result of the threatened act would be to cause immediate serious danger to the public safety or health and if no other means seemed to be available for averting the danger in time', it would not be wrong to grant the injunction.[53]

Scope of immunities. The statutory immunities from specified kinds of liability depend on industrial action being taken 'in contemplation or furtherance of a trade dispute'. Before 1982 a dispute had only to be 'connected with' one of the objects of 'collective bargaining', as legislatively defined, to constitute a 'trade dispute'; it now must relate 'wholly or mainly' to one of these matters.[54] The government intended this amendment to direct inquiry into the predominant object of a dispute and to make unlawful those which are judged primarily political.[55] Clearly the line between a 'trade' and a 'political' dispute may be particularly difficult to draw in the public sector where a dispute over wages or job cuts, for example, may involve challenging broader government policies. In addition, dispute organisers may be held liable for wrongs not protected by the immunities. In the late 1970s the Court of Appeal opened up the possibility of liability for inducing the breach of a statutory duty or interfering with its performance.[56]

---

[50] 55 HC Deb, 27 February 1984, 30–31 (Sir Geoffrey Howe).
[51] [1979] ICR 867.
[52] At 881–2. (The correction of the phrase cited was approved by Lord Diplock: see note [1980] ICR 167.)
[53] *Duport Steels Ltd v Sirs* [1980] ICR 161, at 187.
[54] TULRA s.29(1), as amended by EA 1982 s.18(1)(c), discussed in detail in Chapter 6 above.
[55] See *Mercury Communications Ltd v Scott-Garner and the POEU* [1983] IRLR 494.
[56] *Meade v Haringey London Borough Council* [1979] ICR 494; *Associated Newspapers Group Ltd v Wade* [1979] ICR 664. See further Morris (1983:77–8) and Chapter 6 above.

If accepted as a cause of action this could jeopardise lawful industrial action in all public services having statutory duties to perform.

Protection from union discipline. A number of provisions aim to protect employees instructed by their union to take industrial action from disciplinary action by the union. Clearly such provisions may weaken union bargaining power. The Code of Practice issued under the IRA, which has remained in force, states (para. 22) that a professional employee should not be called upon by his union to take action which would conflict with the standards of work laid down for the profession if that action would endanger: the public health or safety; the health of an individual needing medical or other treatment; the well-being of an individual needing care through the personal social services. The Secretary of State's Closed Shop Code goes further in providing (para. 61) that unions should not threaten disciplinary action against members who refuse to take part in industrial action where, among other things, there were reasonable grounds for believing the action was unlawful, involved a breach of statutory duty or the criminal law or constituted a serious risk to public safety, health or property, or where the member believed that it contravened his professional or other code of ethics. This is relevant (as explained in Chapter 10) to the rights of members against unions. It could be invoked by non-participants threatened with disciplinary action in most essential service disputes. In addition, the Closed Shop Code (para. 24) and EPCA s.58(8) provide legal protection for employees whose professional ethics inhibit union membership or participation in industrial action (see Chapter 2). The disciplinary body for nurses[57] has warned that industrial action could amount to professional misconduct if it put patients at risk (Morris, 1983:79–80).

Code of Practice on Picketing. The Secretary of State's Picketing Code (paras. 37–8) states that pickets should ensure the movement of essential goods and supplies, the carrying out of essential maintenance of plant and equipment and the provision of services essential to the life of the community, and urges prior agreement on arrangements to guarantee this between unions and employers. Examples of supplies to be protected include heating fuel for schools, residential institutions and private residences; goods and services necessary for the maintenance of plant and machinery; supplies for the production, packaging, marketing and distribution of food, animal feeding stuffs and pharmaceutical products; and supplies to health and welfare institutions and those needed in the interests of public health and safety. Failure to comply with the Code may be taken into account in any proceedings, but these particular provisions do 'not seem to impinge very closely on the legal obligations of pickets' (Davies and Freedland, 1984:885). The courts may, however, consider non-compliance

---

[57] Until July 1983, the General Nursing Council for England and Wales, now the United Kingdom Central Council for Nursing, Midwifery and Health Visiting.

relevant to the exercise of their discretion to grant interlocutory injunctions (Lewis and Simpson, 1981:174).

ALTERNATIVE STRATEGIES AND PROPOSALS FOR REFORM

The issues raised by industrial action in essential services were not widely discussed in Britain before the 1970s. Trade unions usually took pains to safeguard public health and safety during disputes and the practice of maintaining essential supplies by alternative means worked sufficiently well. However, the technological complexity of areas such as electricity and water supply and the increased willingness of highly-trained professional groups to take industrial action mean that the state cannot now rely on sending in troops as a last resort. In the last few years pressure has grown for a change in policy.

The majority of the House of Commons Employment Committee, reporting in mid-1981, concluded that 'industrial action which puts public health or public safety at risk poses a very serious problem, which must be tackled without delay', and recommended the introduction of legislation 'at an early date'.[58] The Institute of Directors (1984) advocates compulsory binding arbitration, possibly on a 'final offer' basis, as the last stage of disputes procedures in essential services, with no immunity for industrial action in breach of procedure. It also favours (1983) decentralising collective bargaining in public sector monopolies and establishing separate employer units, together with substantial elements of privatisation. The Centre for Policy Studies (1983), another influential organisation, has proposed that strikes in the fire, health, nuclear power[59] and sewerage services and the public utilities should be prohibited altogether, with particularly severe punishment where withdrawal of the service leads to death or serious injury. It suggests linking the pay of workers in these services to the retail price index and compulsory arbitration for disputes over other matters. The Social Democratic Party advocates compulsory arbitration where industrial action threatens life and limb (SDP, 1982:26–8). The Engineering Employers' Federation wants employers to be relieved of the obligation to pay employees laid off because of essential services being disrupted.[60]

The 1979 Conservative election manifesto, which followed the 'winter of discontent' disputes in the road haulage industry, NHS, and national and local government, promised that industrial action in essential services would be restricted, but the Green Paper on Trade Union Immunities (DE, 1981) was much less enthusiastic. It emphasised that existing legal provisions had been little used and that workers in key industries generally exercised restraint, and pointed out the difficulties of identifying the groups to be restricted, the disruption to industrial relations introducing restrictions would cause, and the difficulties of enforcing sanctions. It concluded that

---

[58] HC Select Committee on Employment 1980–81, Second Report, p.ix, paras. 24 and 29.
[59] On industrial action in the nuclear power industry, see Lewis (1978).
[60] HC Select Committee on Employment 1980–81, Second Report, pp.244–6.

voluntary 'no strike' agreements, where these could be negotiated, seemed the best avenue to pursue. Unions considering 'no strike' agreements, however, would clearly require guarantees that earnings and other conditions of employment would be adequately protected. The present government opposes the extension of index-linking, applied to the police and firemen, to other services, and is unlikely to accept unrestricted binding arbitration in the public sector. A number of bodies which recently examined proposals for restricting industrial action by particular groups in return for specific pay determination procedures (Merrison, 1979; May, 1979; Megaw, 1982) rejected such schemes as unworkable. In the words of the Megaw Inquiry (para. 261) 'neither side would be likely to be able to pledge itself to honour the bargain, nor would it be easy to reach a deal at a price acceptable to all parties, including the taxpayer'.

The 1983 water strike reawakened the Conservative Party's enthusiasm for restrictions, and its 1983 election manifesto stressed the need for 'adequate procedure agreements' in essential services and promised consultations on removing immunity for industrial action in breach of procedure. It did not mention any quid pro quo arrangement to protect wages. This proposal would leave it to employers to bring private proceedings against the organisers of industrial action. Official spokesmen have since reiterated their intention to conduct consultations and this area seems a likely future target for the 'step by step' approach to labour law reform. Meanwhile the government is attempting to discourage industrial action by nurses and professions allied to medicine by reserving the right to exclude from the recommendations of their recently-established Review Body any groups which do resort to industrial action.

The trade unions also recognise the desirability of avoiding disruption to essential services. They are firmly opposed to legal restrictions, however, and they advocate voluntary joint regulation by workers and employers. The TUC Guide on the Conduct of Industrial Disputes[61] advises unions to ensure that their members maintain supplies and services essential to the health or safety of the country or otherwise required to avoid causing serious hardship or exceptional pollution. This should be done in consultation, and preferably by agreement, with the relevant employer. This formula was applied to the NHS in 1981 when TUC-affiliated unions published a more detailed Code (TUC, 1981:para. 10.11). It states that any action which restricts services to patients should be consistent with respect for 'human life, safety and dignity' and urges unions involved in any dispute to arrange in advance with management to maintain supplies and services essential for emergency services and high dependency patients. Emergency services are defined as those which 'directly involve the life, limb or ultimate safety of a patient'.

The 'joint regulation/self-restraint' approach carries the quid pro quo that management should not draw on its full range of sanctions or resources to counter the impact of the action. The NHS unions warned that observ-

---

[61] See annex to the 'Social Concordat': *The Economy, the Government and Trade Union Responsibilities: Joint Statement by the TUC and Government* (London: HMSO, 1979).

ance of their Code was dependent on a 'sensible local management response' (TUC, 1981:para.10.9), and that measures such as suspending participants in industrial action or refusing to negotiate on, or pay for, emergency cover, could turn limited industrial action into a full stoppage.[62] During the 1983 water strike unions justified departures from their code of conduct on the ground that white-collar staff had been doing strikers' jobs. Such an approach may also involve employer representatives in agreeing to curtail services. In a survey undertaken by Morris and Rydzkowski (1984) of senior administrators in thirty-one health districts in South-East England, administrators in nine districts said they had restricted services during a national dispute in 1982 in return for the unions providing agreed levels of cover, and those in twenty districts could envisage entering such agreements, although many would do so only if the alternative were more drastic disruption.

Making such arrangements has advantages for both sides: for the unions, it demonstrates the effectiveness of the action while avoiding accusations of irresponsibility; for management, it limits and defines its impact. It may also prolong disputes, however, and employers may take advantage of workers who observe a code of conduct. In 1982 the NHS unions 'committed themselves to a lengthy and ultimately unsuccessful dispute with a government which saw itself as fighting for an essential element in its economic policy and which was unmoved by the hardship caused to the community by the withdrawal of non-essential medical services' (Davies and Freedland, 1984:886). The general secretary of one large union later said that the unions had fought 'with one hand tied behind our back'.[63] But where the employer genuinely wants to negotiate a settlement rather than sit out a dispute, and both sides adhere to their agreements, the 'joint regulation' approach can offer the cheapest and most efficacious method of securing the continuation of basic services.

No discussion of industrial action in essential services can ignore recent developments which may undermine union power in more oblique ways. The present government is strongly in favour of contracting out certain health and local government services to private enterprise, one factor being their reduced vulnerability to disruption. Relaxing public sector monopolies in posts, telecommunications, and electricity will weaken unions by making available alternative sources of supply. The decentralisation of collective bargaining urged by the Institute of Directors has begun on a small scale in the water industry, where regional water authorities are no longer bound to observe nationally-agreed conditions. A more specialised tactic, employed by the Ministry of Defence after work was disrupted at the Polaris submarine bases during the 1981 civil service dispute, is to replace civilians in key jobs with military personnel. These strategies may prove much more significant in reducing the impact of industrial action in essential services than the more direct methods upon which the literature has generally concentrated.

[62] DHSS Circular HC 79 (20) had encouraged a tougher management response to industrial action.
[63] *NUPE Journal*, no. 1 (1983) (Rodney Bickerstaffe).

Bibliography

Centre for Policy Studies (CPS). 1983. *The Right to Strike in a Free Society*. London: CPS.

Davies, Paul, and Mark Freedland. 1984. *Labour Law: Text and Materials*. 2nd edn. London: Weidenfeld & Nicolson.

Department of Employment (DE). 1981. *Trade Union Immunities*. Cmnd 8128. London: HMSO.

Edmund Davies. 1978. Committee of Inquiry on the Police. *Reports on Negotiating Machinery and Pay*. Cmnd 7283. London: HMSO.

Institute of Directors (IOD). 1983. *Democracy and Competitiveness: Further Steps Towards Trade Union Reform*. London: IOD.

——. 1984. *Settling Disputes Peacefully*. London: IOD.

International Labour Office (ILO). 1983. *Freedom of Association and Collective Bargaining*. Geneva: ILO.

Jeffery, Keith, and Peter Hennessy. 1983. *States of Emergency*. London: Routledge & Kegan Paul.

Jones, Aubrey. 1973. *The New Inflation*. Harmondsworth: Penguin.

Knowles, K.G.J.C. 1952. *Strikes – A Study in Industrial Conflict*. Oxford: Blackwell.

Lewis, Roy. 1978. 'Nuclear Power and Employment Rights'. *Industrial Law Journal*, 7 (March), 1–15.

——, and Bob Simpson. 1981. *Striking a Balance? Employment Law after the 1980 Act*. Oxford: Martin Robertson.

May. 1979. Committee of Inquiry into the United Kingdom Prison Service. *Report*. London: HMSO.

Megaw. 1982. *Report of an Inquiry into the Principles and the System by which the Remuneration of the Non-Industrial Civil Service should be Determined*. Cmnd 8590. London: HMSO.

Merrison. 1979. Royal Commission on the National Health Service. *Report*. Cmnd 7615. London: HMSO.

Morris, Gillian S. 1978. 'A Study of the Protection of Public and Essential Services in Labour Disputes 1920–1976'. PhD thesis, University of Cambridge.

——. 1979. 'The Emergency Powers Act 1920'. *Public Law* (Winter), 317–52.

——. 1980. 'The Police and Industrial Emergencies'. *Industrial Law Journal*, 9 (March), 1–12.

——. 1983. 'The Regulation of Industrial Action in Essential Services'. *Industrial Law Journal*, 12 (June), 69–83.

——, with Stephen Rydzkowski. 1984. 'Approaches to Industrial Action in the National Health Service'. *Industrial Law Journal*, 13 (September), 153–64.

Pankert, A. 1980. 'Settlement of Labour Disputes in Essential Services'. *International Labour Review*, 119 (November–December), 723–37.

Peak, Steve. 1984. *Troops in Strikes: Military Intervention in Industrial Disputes*. London: Cobden Trust.

Reiner, Robert. 1978. *The Blue-Coated Worker*. Cambridge: Cambridge University Press.

Social Democratic Party (SDP). 1982. *Reforming the Trade Unions*. London: SDP.

Trades Union Congress (TUC). 1981. *Improving Industrial Relations in the National Health Service: A Report by the TUC Health Services Committee*. London: TUC.

Trice, J.E. 1975. 'Methods of and Attitudes to Picketing'. *Criminal Law Review* (May), 271–82.

Weekes, B., M. Mellish, L. Dickens and J. Lloyd. 1975. *Industrial Relations and the Limits of Law: The Industrial Effects of the Industrial Relations Act, 1971*. Oxford: Blackwell.

Wigham, Eric. 1982. *Strikes and the Government 1893–1981*. London: Macmillan.

Williams, David. 1967. *Keeping the Peace*. London: Hutchinson.

Young, T. 1976. *Incitement to Disaffection*. London: Cobden Trust.

9 Industrial Action and the Individual

John Mesher and Frank Sutcliffe

While the law of industrial conflict usually focuses on the legal liabilities of strike leaders and trade unions, industrial action has profound legal implications for individual employees. The common law tends to treat industrial action as a violation of the individual contract of employment. The development of social security, and then of statutory employment protection rights, has raised many issues concerning the legal position of individual employees engaging in industrial action. What is the effect of such action on, for example, the right not to be unfairly dismissed, or to claim statutory redundancy pay, or entitlement to social security benefits? To what extent is the answer to these questions influenced by the contract of employment? There is one further introductory point about the overall direction of legal policy: since 1979 the state has cut back the rights of individual employees engaging in industrial action. This is intended to deter individual employees from taking industrial action and thus complements the reduction of trade union immunities.

THE CONTRACT OF EMPLOYMENT

The common law is strangely equivocal about the employment relationship. On the one hand, the employer and employee are seen as two individuals of equal bargaining power who freely enter a contract. On the other hand, the common law, through the device of implied terms, loads the employee with obligations derived in part from the traditional master and servant relationship (see further Chapter 12 above, and Fox, 1974:184). This reinforces the inequality which the law pretends does not exist. Efforts by employees to establish a 'countervailing power' (Kahn-Freund, 1983:20) to that of the employer by combining together have been traditionally viewed with suspicion by the judges, who tend to see industrial action as a challenge to the legitimate authority of the employer as embodied in the contract of employment. The employer's capacity to coerce through his economic power is recognised not as problematic but as a legitimate property right. Moreover, the common law's approach to industrial action is undiscriminating. All forms of action are treated in essentially the same way, that is, as a breach of contract by the employee. This breach is important in two respects. First, it may provide one of the ingredients of the economic torts for which trade unions may be liable (see Chapter 6). Second, and more importantly for the purposes of this chapter, it may entitle the employer to take disciplinary action against the individual employee.

Strikes and Other Industrial Action

The effect of a strike on the contract of employment is that it is a breach by the employee of the central obligation under the contract to work. In *Simmons v Hoover*[1] Phillips J said that 'a real strike' would always be a repudiatory breach of contract. A repudiatory breach is one which entitles the employer to dismiss the employee without notice if he so wishes. In saying this the judge was aware that in most strikes both sides desire to continue the employment after the strike is over, so that in practice permanent dismissals are rare. But English law has not developed a more realistic alternative analysis to that of breach.

Industrial action other than striking will usually, if not invariably,[2] involve a breach of contract of some kind. The contract of employment may be seen as a continuing open-ended commitment 'in which the manager's discretion defines the nature of the job to be done' (Forrest, 1980:364). This discretion is backed in law by the standard implied term that employees must obey all reasonable commands of the employer. As any reasonable order from an employer has contractual force, industrial action involving the withdrawal of co-operation is likely to be in breach of contract. This was established by *Secretary of State for Employment v ASLEF (No.2)*.[3] The question in that case was whether a work to rule by employees could be a breach of contract. On the face of it, the employees were strictly observing all the rules of the British Railways Board. How could that be a breach? According to Lord Denning MR:

> The instruction was intended to mean, and it was understood to mean, 'keep the rules of your employment to the very letter, but, whilst doing so, do your very utmost to disrupt the undertaking'. Is that a breach of contract? Now I quite agree that a man is not bound positively to do more for his employer than his contract requires. He can withdraw his goodwill if he pleases. But what he must not do is wilfully to obstruct the employer as he goes about his business.[4]

Such wilful obstruction was a breach of contract. For Buckley LJ the railwaymen were in breach even if they did not break any express term of the contract because there was an implied term that 'the employee must serve the employer faithfully with a view to promoting those commercial interests for which he is employed'.[5] The combined effect of the judgments in

---

1   [1977] ICR 61, 76.
2   'Other industrial action' within the meaning of EPCA s.62 (see below) does not necessarily involve a breach of contract: *Power Packing Casemakers v Faust* [1983] ICR 292, CA.
3   [1972] ICR 19, CA. Cf. *Metropolitan Borough of Solihull v NUT* [1985] IRLR 211 (arguable contractual obligation on the part of teachers to perform lunchtime duties).
4   At 55.
5   At 62.

this case is to establish a negative duty on the employee not wilfully to disrupt the employer's undertaking, and a positive duty to promote the commercial interests for which he is employed. Industrial action designed to put pressure on the employer is likely to fall foul of this rule.

In *Power Packing Casemakers v Faust* the industrial action was a ban on non-contractual overtime, that is, a refusal to do something that the contract did not require the employee to do. Stephenson LJ acknowledged, obiter, that the effect of the *ASLEF* case could be to make such action a breach of contract.[6] This approach takes the duty of co-operation to its outer limits. Rideout with Dyson (1983:461) has commented that the contract of employment can be extended by the use of implied terms to turn what the courts regard as unreasonable conduct into a breach of contract for which the employee may be dismissed.

Procedure Agreements and Suspension of Contract

Statute law affects the common law analysis in respect of the potential effect of collective agreements. As explained above in Chapter 4, TULRA s.18 reaffirms the presumption that collective agreements are not intended to create legal relations as between the collective parties. It was thought, however, that suitably worded collectively agreed peace obligations might be incorporated into the individual contract of employment.[7] This would have amounted to a form of 'back door' legal enforceability of collective agreements, contrary to the policy of the Social Contract labour legislation. TULRA s.18(4) therefore provides that collectively agreed limitations on industrial action shall not form part of the contract of employment, unless five conditions are satisfied. These are that the collective agreement is in writing, contains a clause expressly permitting the incorporation of the peace obligation, is reasonably accessible to workers, is agreed to by independent trade unions, and that the contract of employment actually incorporates the peace obligation. These requirements usually preclude the incorporation of such clauses. But this is of little practical significance. As already explained, industrial action is usually in breach of employment contracts for reasons other than the effects of collectively agreed peace obligations.

One way of modifying the common law analysis would be to introduce a rule that industrial action suspends rather than breaks the contract of employment. Most European countries have accepted the principle of suspension of contracts in industrial disputes as part of the provision of a positive right to strike. The difficulty is that 'suspension is only accepted in case of a lawful strike, and it is therefore necessary to draw a borderline between those strikes and the unlawful strikes for which a system of termination of the contract is still applicable' (Blanc-Jouvan, 1972:185).

---

6 Though he declined to express a firm opinion on the matter: [1983] ICR 292, 296.
7 In *Rookes v Barnard* [1964] AC 1129, HL the peace obligation was worded to apply to employees, and it was conceded that it was incorporated into their contracts of employment.

The difficulties of suspension were considered by the Donovan Commission (1968:paras. 941–52), which recommended that further detailed work was required before changes could be made. At about the same time Lord Denning attempted to introduce suspension of contracts during industrial disputes into the common law,[8] but his approach was not adopted in any subsequent case. In a detailed consideration of the matter in *Simmons v Hoover*,[9] Phillips J correctly concluded that the principle of suspension could not be incorporated into the law without legislation.

Rideout with Dyson (1983:241) has commented that English law is 'remarkably unsophisticated' in its approach to industrial action. All action is treated in a similar fashion – as a breach of contract. Yet a more discerning approach which protected certain kinds of industrial action might affect the overall pattern: 'the law could be used to further a variety of policies. Protection of official as compared to unofficial strikes would tend to lend support to the central organisation of trade unions. Distinction between constitutional and unconstitutional strikes would emphasise the effectiveness of collectively agreed procedures.'

Employers' Responses to Industrial Action

Since the late nineteenth century the courts have refused to grant orders of specific performance to compel employees to work (Freedland, 1976:272–8). TULRA s.16 now expressly prohibits the courts from making orders to compel individual employees to work, or to attend at a place of work. Thus it is not open to the employer to curtail industrial action by using the courts to order individuals to return to work, although a return to work may be achieved by obtaining injunctions to require union leaders to call off industrial action. In any event, other legal options are available against individuals under the contract of employment. These options are theoretical in many situations, as employers will not wish to exercise them, though they may still use the threat of them as a deterrent to industrial action.

Dismissal. Dismissals during the course of a dispute are rarely intended to be permanent in practice, and the dismissal letter often contains an offer of re-engagement provided that the worker returns by a given date.[10] In an era of economic decline and high unemployment, however, dismissals may more often be intended to sever relations permanently. At common law most forms of industrial action are sufficiently serious breaches of contract to justify dismissal, and repudiatory acts justify summary dismissal without notice. In reality employers are rarely required to defend such dismissals, as the common law remedy for wrongful dismissal is so puny: damages amounting to wages that would have been earned if proper notice had been given. Over the last decade and a half the dismissal option has been affected by the unfair dismissal legislation. In particular, EPCA s.62 limits to some

---

[8] *Morgan v Fry* [1968] 2 QB 710, CA.
[9] [1977] ICR 61.
[10] E.g. facts of *Marsden v Fairey Stainless Ltd* [1979] IRLR 103, EAT.

extent the employer's ability to be selective in dismissals for industrial action (see below).

Self-dismissal. It is common for employers to claim that a course of industrial action has resulted in the employees' self-dismissal, or will do so if persisted in. The reasoning is that any conduct which amounts to a repudiatory breach by the employee 'automatically' terminates the contract without the need for the employer to dismiss the employee. In one case[11] a number of employees walked out when a colleague was dismissed. They gave no warning of the walk out, and left a high pressure steam system switched on. This was a dangerous act. They were later informed that they had lost their jobs. The EAT held that there had been a repudiatory act by the employees which was accepted by the employer as an indication that their contracts were at an end. There had been no dismissal by the employer.

While this approach seems to represent a degree of rough justice, its effect is to undermine the scheme of employment protection legislation. If self-dismissal is not a dismissal by the employer, then there can be no right to claim unfair dismissal or redundancy pay. Other cases have, however, firmly rejected the notion of self-dismissal. In *Simmons v Hoover* Phillips J said that 'refusal to work during a strike did not involve "self-dismissal" by the strikers, but left the parties to the contract hoping that the strike would one day be settled, and the contract be alive, unless and until the employer exercised his right to dismiss the employee'.[12] This approach was adopted by Waterhouse J,[13] who took the view that the policy of the unfair dismissal legislation required dismissal by the employer in the face of a repudiatory breach if the contract was to be terminated. But it would still be true to say that, notwithstanding these unfair dismissal cases, the effect of repudiatory breach has not been finally determined at common law.

Damages. Industrial action involves breaches of contract. It is therefore possible to sue individual employees for damages, though this is rare, primarily because of the industrial relations implications. In addition, the scale of damages may be very small. In *NCB v Galley*[14] a pit deputy took part in a ban on Saturday shift working. The shift could not be worked because of his absence and the NCB claimed damages for loss of profit caused by him. It was held that damages were limited to loss caused by the individual breach, that is, the cost of hiring a replacement.

Stopping pay. While a complete stoppage of work entitles the employer to stop pay, problems may arise if there is a partial stoppage, as in a work to rule, blacking of machinery or refusal to perform certain duties. The

---

[11] *Gannon v Firth Ltd* [1976] IRLR 415.
[12] [1977] ICR 61, 73, EAT.
[13] *Rasool v Hepworth Pipe Co. Ltd* [1980] ICR 494, EAT.
[14] [1958] 1 WLR 16, CA. Contrast *Strathclyde Regional Council v Neil* [1984] IRLR 12 and 14, a case where there was an express agreement as to what should be paid in the event of premature termination of contract by the employee.

employer may wish to stop pay or threaten to do so, but is he entitled to take this action? In *Bond and Neads v CAV Ltd*[15] Bond refused to work one of his four machines because of a dispute over bonus money. The employers warned him that he would not be paid unless he worked normally, but nevertheless facilitated his work. He worked for five days in this way and the employers refused to pay him on the grounds that he was not ready and willing to work normally. The court held that the appropriate question was whether Bond was ready and willing to work in accordance with the terms of his contract rather than 'normally'. It was held that, although Bond was in breach of his contract by refusing to work the machine, the employers had waived the breach by facilitating his work, and thus could not withhold payment. Napier (1984:337) criticised this case by arguing that the correct rule is that if work has been done, then entitlement to wages is established without any need to inquire into the matter of being ready and willing to work. The employee is entitled to payment in full for work done provided that any defective performance does not deprive the employer of a substantial benefit under the contract. In *Bond*'s case no substantial benefit was lost and he should have been entitled to his pay without further question.

In two other cases employers attempted to stop pay for partial performance of the contract and the courts at first instance allowed a deduction from pay to represent the extent of the defective performance. In *Royle v Trafford Borough Council*[16] the court allowed a deduction of five thirty-sixths of a teacher's pay when he refused to teach an extra five pupils as part of a union campaign against increasing class sizes. The deduction was supposed to represent that part of his duties unfulfilled. In *Miles v Wakefield Metropolitan District Council*,[17] the plaintiff, a superintendent registrar, was a Crown servant and not an employee of the council, though the council was responsible for his pay. He usually conducted weddings on Saturdays but, as part of a campaign of industrial action, rearranged his work so as to do other duties instead. The court at first instance held that Miles was in breach of his obligations in respect of Saturday working and that it was appropriate to withhold three thirty-sevenths of his salary for the period of the industrial action, as representing the extent of defective performance. No attention was paid to the fact that Miles had worked his full contractual hours albeit at other duties. But the Court of Appeal held by a majority that the council was obliged to pay him in full. There was no entitlement to stop the pay of an 'office holder' (see Chapter 12). Parker LJ also thought that there would be no right to withhold the pay of an employee in the absence of accepted repudiatory conduct or a specific right to suspend. This case supports Napier's view of entitlement to pay being established by work done, calls into question the validity of the *Royle* decision, and casts doubts on the legality of threats by education authorities to make deductions from pay during teachers' industrial action in 1985. The employer is entitled to claim

15   [1983] IRLR 360.
16   [1984] IRLR 184.
17   [1984] ICR 332, ChD; [1985] IRLR 108, CA.

damages for breach of contract, but that is quite different from withholding pay for work done.

The question whether an employee is ready and willing to work is a relevant one when the claim is not pay for work actually done but for damages representing wages lost because of some action by the employer. In *Bond and Neads v CAV Ltd*, part of the claim concerned two days in which Bond had turned up for work but had been prevented from working because the employers had cut off power to his machines. He was held to be entitled to his pay (as, strictly speaking, damages) because he was ready and willing to work. If the employee is clearly not ready and willing to work in accordance with his contract, then the employer may refuse to pay him. In *Cresswell v Board of Inland Revenue*[18] tax officers refused to work a new computerised system and insisted on working the old manual system. The employer refused to allow them to work the old method and refused to pay them until they began to work the computerised system. The court held that there had been a proper refusal to pay until such time as the employees were prepared to work as required.

Lock-outs. Davies and Freedland (1984:889) divide lock-outs into offensive and defensive categories. Offensive lock-outs are undertaken by employers to compel employees to accept certain terms and conditions of employment. More common is the defensive lock-out in which the employer suspends employees who are taking strike or other industrial action, or closes an establishment in response to action taken by some of the workers there or, at a further remove, because of a dispute at some other establishment. In all of these cases the employer is intent on saving money and putting pressure on employees.

What is the legal status of the lock-out? There is no general right to suspend or lay off employees without pay at common law,[19] but it is possible and quite usual to provide such a right in contracts of employment. It is also possible in theory to establish a 'custom of the trade', though successful cases are rare. Guaranteed week agreements also limit the discretion of the employer to lay off, though they usually expressly provide for such a right in industrial disputes. If the contract provides a power of suspension, it may require an elaborate procedure to be gone through first, or stipulate that suspension must be on full pay. It was for this reason that the employers in *Royle* and *Cresswell* were anxious to avoid suspending the employees.

As Davies and Freedland (1984:892) observe, the offensive lock-out is a repudiatory breach of contract by the employer, which gives the employee a claim for notice-period damages rather than an effective remedy. If the employer locks out employees already engaged in industrial action, however, he is simply accepting their prior breach of contract, which does not entitle them to a legal remedy. An exception was the *Bond v CAV* case, in which Bond was locked out one week after he had begun industrial action. The court held that by the time the lock-out took place he was no longer in

[18] [1984] IRLR 190.
[19] *Devonald v Rosser* [1906] 2 KB 728, CA.

breach of contract, as he had given notice to terminate the 'supplemental' agreement covering the disputed fourth machine. He was therefore entitled to damages for the employer's breach in locking him out.

A lock-out is sometimes a response to the selective withdrawal of key workers. This happened in *Chappell v Times Newspapers Ltd.*[20] The Court of Appeal held that a defensive lock-out by employers of employees not at that moment engaged in industrial action, but who refused to give an undertaking that they would not join the selective action if called on by their union, was not a breach of contract by the employers. The men had shown themselves prepared to break their contracts, and this entitled the employers to take the action. A lock-out further removed than this, for example, of employees not taking action or even directly interested in it, would be a breach of contract.[21]

STATUTORY EMPLOYMENT PROTECTION RIGHTS

Continuity of employment is not broken by the employee being on strike or locked out, but any such period does not count towards continuous service for the purposes of the statutory rights.[22] If an employee is dismissed during a strike or lock-out, continuity is still preserved provided the employee is re-engaged. It is not possible to contract out of the continuity provisions; any such attempt will be void by virtue of EPCA s.140.

Unfair Dismissal

Two conflicting policies of the EPCA come into play in this area. First, trade union activity at an appropriate time is given enhanced protection under EPCA ss.23 and 58 (discussed in detail in Chapter 2 above). Second, following the analysis of the Donovan Commission (1968:para.576) the unfair dismissals law is withdrawn from cases in which industrial action has taken place. This latter policy, described as 'a kind of legal laissez-faire or neutrality',[23] finds its current expression in EPCA s.62, which provides immunity for employers against complaints of unfair dismissal where the dismissed employees are engaged in industrial action.

To resolve the conflict between the two policies would require a clear demarcation line between protected trade union activity and unprotected industrial action. There is no clear demarcation line; the same behaviour may be trade union activity at one point and industrial action at another. Carrying out health and safety duties[24] and attending mass meetings[25] are

20 [1975] ICR 145, CA.
21 On the EEF's proposal for a power to suspend employees whose work is affected by industrial action elsewhere, see Davies and Freedland (1984: 930–31).
22 EPCA Sch.13, para.15. See further Chapter 12 below.
23 Phillips J in *Gallagher v Wragg* [1977] ICR 174, 178, EAT. See generally on EPCA s.62 Davies and Freedland (1984: 909–29).
24 *Drew v St Edmundsbury Borough Council* [1980] ICR 513, EAT.
25 *Rasool v Hepworth Pipe Co. Ltd* [1980] ICR 494, EAT.

trade union activities, which may be classed as industrial action if done with the intention of bringing industrial pressure to bear on the employer. Thus the courts are required to engage in the difficult exercise of exploring the motives of the employees and the nature and effects of their actions.

Section 62 prohibits an industrial tribunal from considering a claim for unfair dismissal if at the time of the dismissal the employer was conducting a lock-out, or the complainant was taking part in a strike or other industrial action. The protection for the employer is lost only if he has engaged in victimisation,[26] which is shown if he has failed to dismiss one or more relevant employees but has dismissed the complainant, or he has re-engaged a dismissed employee within three months of dismissal but has not re-engaged the complainant. If there has been victimisation, then the complaint of unfair dismissal can be heard in the normal way, and it is open to the employer to defend the dismissal or the failure to re-engage on the grounds that he has acted reasonably. If the claimant can show that the dismissal was for union membership or activity, then it is automatically unfair.

Lock-out, strike, or other industrial action. Section 62 applies where the employee is locked out, or engaged in strike or other industrial action. These phenomena are not statutorily defined for the purposes of s.62. This has led the courts to examine statutory definitions which are provided for other purposes. In *Fisher v York Trailers*,[27] Slynn J adopted the statutory definition (now in EPCA Sch.13 para.24 (1)) of lock-outs provided for the purpose of establishing continuity of employment: 'the closing of a place of employment, or the suspension of work, or the refusal by an employer to continue to employ any number of persons employed by him in consequence of a dispute, done with a view to compelling those persons, or to aid another employer in compelling persons employed by him, to accept terms or conditions of or affecting employment'. If there is simply a dismissal without some prior suspension it might not be a dismissal during a lock-out within this definition, with the consequence that the employee might not be denied by s.62. A 'refusal to continue to employ' is a lock-out, which means that there would have to be a subsequent dismissal if the protection of s.62 is to be claimed for the employer. But if the dismissal is in response to a go-slow (as in *Fisher*), it could be argued that the go-slow constitutes 'other industrial action' and the complications of the lock-out ought not to arise.

Strike is defined in EPCA Sch.13 para.24 as

the cessation of work by a body of persons employed acting in combination, or a concerted refusal or a refusal under a common understanding of any number of persons employed to continue to work for an employer in consequence of a dispute, done as a means of compelling their employer or any person or body of

---

[26] There was a short-lived attempt in *Thompson v Eaton* [1976] IRLR 308 to allow consideration of unfair dismissal claims where the strike had been provoked or engineered by the employer. This development was curtailed by the EAT in *Marsden v Fairey Stainless Ltd* [1979] IRLR 103. See Napier (1980).

[27] [1979] ICR 834, EAT, noted by Townshend-Smith (1980).

persons employed, or to aid other employees, in compelling their employer or any person or body of persons employed, to accept or not to accept terms or conditions of or affecting employment.

The definition is provided for the purpose of establishing continuous employment and judges have warned against the transplantation of statutory definitions provided for different purposes.[28] In practice, the definition of a strike has not been a critical issue. Any action that approaches being a strike is likely to come within s.62's notion of 'other industrial action', for which there is no current statutory definition.[29]

'Other industrial action' was intended to be a catch-all category covering all the well-known forms of industrial action. After the *ASLEF* case, it was clear that any industrial action would almost inevitably involve a breach of the contract of employment. It seemed to be assumed that a breach of contract was required to establish 'other industrial action' for the purpose of s.62, perhaps on the basis that some blameworthy conduct was thought to be necessary in order to lose the right to bring a claim for unfair dismissal. This assumption was demolished by *Power Packing Casemakers v Faust*.[30] It was held that three employees who had refused to work overtime in order to impose pressure on the employer during a pay dispute had taken part in other industrial action and were debarred from claiming unfair dismissal. This was so even though there was no contractual obligation to work overtime, and the employees were as individuals guilty of no misconduct in refusing.

Relevant employees. Section 62 was designed to ensure equal treatment of those caught up in industrial disputes. If a complainant can show that a relevant employee has been treated more favourably by not being dismissed or by being re-engaged then an unfair dismissal claim might be heard.

'Relevant employees' in relation to a lock-out (as opposed to a strike or other industrial action) are defined as 'employees who were directly interested in the dispute in contemplation or furtherance of which the lock-out occurred' (s.62(4)(b)). Before the EA 1982 the wording was 'trade dispute' rather than 'dispute'. Section 18 of the 1982 Act narrowed the definition of 'trade dispute' in TULRA s.29 in order to restrict immunity from liability in tort. As this would also have narrowed the scope of operation of s.62, the word 'trade' was removed from that section.

The problem for employers contemplating lock-outs is that the category of relevant employees is so wide that there is a danger of overlooking and not dismissing one of the relevant employees and thus losing the protection of s.62. This danger is increased by the wording (taken from social security law) 'directly interested in', which includes not only those actually locked out, but also any other employees affected by the outcome of the dispute. In *Fisher v York Trailers* the relevant employees were the seven actually locked out and dismissed, plus the twenty-seven others who had agreed to work at

---

[28] See Waterhouse J in *Rasool v Hepworth Pipe Co. Ltd* [1980] ICR 494.
[29] See *Thompson v Eaton* [1976] ICR 336, 341 (per Phillips J).
[30] [1983] ICR 292, CA.

the normal incentive pace and returned to work. It seems that employers have to dismiss all employees with a direct interest in order to claim s.62 protection. This can be contrasted with the narrower scope of required dismissals in relation to strikes or other industrial action. Relevant employees in relation to a strike or other industrial action means 'those employees at the establishment who were taking part in the action at the complainant's date of dismissal' (s.62(4)(b)(ii)).

What is meant by 'taking part'? In *McCormick v Horsepower Ltd*[31] the Court of Appeal held that an engineer, who temporarily and individually refused to cross a picket line of boilermakers, was not taking part in their strike, as he was not acting in concert with them or anyone else. Even if he had been taking part in the strike, he was found to have been dismissed for redundancy prior to the tribunal hearing, which meant that the complainant was unable to show the essential element of unfair treatment and that the tribunal was therefore unable to hear the complaint. A different result, one that allowed the dismissed strikers to have their unfair dismissal claims heard, was achieved in *Coates v Modern Methods and Materials Ltd.*[32] Unrest among the workforce led to a factory gate meeting. Mrs Leith had turned up to go to work, but decided not to go in as she was frightened of possible abuse from fellow workers. She stayed at the factory gates for about an hour and then went to a prearranged appointment with her doctor, who gave her a sick note. She attended union meetings during the strike, but did not draw strike pay, and explained to the union official that she was sick and not on strike. This was accepted by the industrial tribunal as being the position after her visit to the doctor. The question was whether she had taken part in a strike for the hour she spent at the factory gates. For the Court of Appeal this was a question of fact and not one of law as the EAT had claimed. The majority of the Court laid down an objective test 'participation in a strike must be judged by what the employee does, and not by what he thinks or why he does it. If he stops work when his workmates come out on strike and does not say or do anything to make plain his disagreement, or what could amount to a refusal to join them, he takes part in their strike.'[33]

Selective dismissal and re-engagement. Section 62 was intended to prevent victimisation through discriminatory treatment, though the EA 1982 amendments have reduced the protection available in a number of ways (Ewing, 1982; Wallington, 1983; Mailly, 1983). The definition of relevant employees is limited to those taking part in the industrial action at the time of the complainant's dismissal, which allows employers to retain those who had begun industrial action but ceased it and resumed work before the complainant was dismissed. This paves the way for employers to use the threat of dismissal to force a substantial return to work.[34]

[31]   [1981] ICR 535, CA.
[32]   [1982] ICR 763, CA.
[33]   At 777 (per Stephenson LJ).
[34]   EPCA s.62(2)(b) as amended puts paid to *Stock v Frank Jones (Tipton) Ltd* [1978] ICR 347, HL.

A further restriction on the meaning of 'relevant employee' is that such an employee must work at the same 'establishment' as the complainant. Despite its importance for the scope of s.62, no definition of establishment is given. It could relate either to the physical premises of work or to the staffing structure.[35] Clearly, the notion of establishment was introduced to enable employers to dismiss those taking industrial action at one plant and not at another, without fear of unfair dismissal liability. It enables employers to be selective about the plants to be retained or closed down at a time of continued industrial contraction.

Another 1982 amendment was the introduction of a time limit. This allows employers to offer re-engagement on a selective basis three months after the date of dismissal of the person offered re-engagement (s.62(2)(b)). The time limit may be criticised in that employers can simply sit out a dispute, perhaps having engineered the strike in the first place, and selectively re-engage with impunity three months after dismissing everyone. Against a background of high unemployment, this possibility does not seem far-fetched.

Even before the 1982 amendments there was a certain flexibility for employers in re-engagement. In *Marsden v Fairey Stainless Ltd*[36] all the employees had a letter dismissing them but offering re-engagement provided the offer was accepted by a deadline. Marsden's letter was wrongly addressed and he did not receive it. He did not go back to work by the deadline and was dismissed. The tribunal found that as a shop steward he must have had knowledge of the letter and that it applied to him. He could not therefore complain of selective discrimination.

The re-engagement can, moreover, be in the job[37] the complainant held before the dismissal 'or in a different job which would be reasonably suitable in his case' (s.62(4)(c)) with the same employer, his successor or an associated employer. In *Williams v National Theatre Board Ltd*[38] about thirty men went on strike. One woman struck in sympathy for a couple of days and then returned to work. All were dismissed. The men were offered re-engagement, though they were to be treated as on second warning in a three-warning disciplinary procedure, and the woman was offered re-engagement without disciplinary action. The Court of Appeal said that it was for management to decide the terms of re-engagement and the men could not complain of the different treatment for the woman. The offer made to the men was held to come within the statutory definition. The disciplinary point did not affect the capacity in which the men were offered re-engagement. The decision is important for two reasons. First, Lord Denning MR clearly saw it as permissible for employers to offer changed terms and conditions to those previously worked. In a dispute over working

---

35 See Lord Denning MR in *Noble v David Gold & Son (Holdings) Ltd* [1980] IRLR 253, CA for consideration of possible interpretations of establishment.
36 [1979] IRLR 103.
37 'Job' defined in EPCA s.153(1) as 'the nature of the work which the employee is employed to do in accordance with his contract, and the capacity and place in which he is so employed'.
38 [1982] IRLR 377, CA.

arrangements as this was, the power to vary contracts unilaterally and still to claim the protection of s.62 is of great advantage to the employer. Second, it is clear that an employer can offer re-engagement to different strikers with different disciplinary conditions, and not fall foul of the anti-victimisation principle. This is another powerful advantage for the employer, who can single out the ringleaders for special disciplinary attention. It remains to be seen how far this can be taken in practice. There would arguably need to be some reason other than mere participation in the strike itself to justify greater penalties for some rather than for others.[39]

The final point on victimisation is not directly relevant to EPCA s.62, but concerns the employee who has worked normally through industrial action, and has been victimised by fellow employees who have themselves taken industrial action. The employer may have to take active steps to protect the employee if unfair dismissal liability is to be avoided. In one case[40] the applicant succeeded in a constructive dismissal claim against the employer who failed to protect her against abuse.

Redundancy Payments

Entitlement to a statutory redundancy payment arises if the reason for dismissal is redundancy. The broad principle is that dismissals during a strike will be for redundancy only if the strike occurs after notice of dismissal for redundancy has been given. Any strike action taken prior to a redundancy notice is likely to be a repudiatory breach of contract giving the employer the right to dismiss without making a redundancy payment.[41] This is the case even if a redundancy situation is known to be imminent and the strike is in response to that knowledge.

Even when redundancy notice has been given the employee may forfeit the right to redundancy payment if he is guilty of misconduct which would entitle the employer to dismiss without notice (EPCA s.82(2)). Strike or other industrial action would usually be such misconduct, though the right to redundancy pay may be preserved by EPCA s.92: if the industrial action occurs during the individual employee's obligatory period of notice, that is, his individual notice period based on length of service under EPCA s.49. Any time lost by strike action may have to be made up (EPCA s.110), and the tribunal may make a deduction from the redundancy pay if it thinks fit.

The redundancy provisions of EPCA s.82(2) and s.92 are complex and uncertain. There is a limited recognition of accrued rights preserved during industrial action taken in response to redundancy notice, but the preservation of rights is capricious, in that it depends on how the employer chooses to react to the industrial action and whether EPCA s.82(2) operates.

---

[39] See *Bernard Matthews Turkeys Plc v Rowland* (1983) IDS Brief supplement 37 (March), EAT; *Laffin v Fashion Industries (Hartlepool) Ltd* [1978] IRLR 448, EAT.

[40] *Adams v Southampton and SW Hants Health Authority* (1984) IDS Brief 284 (September).

[41] *Simmons v Hoover* [1977] ICR 61.

Guarantee Payments

The EPCA ss.12–18 provides a limited right to guarantee payments during a period of lay off. The right is based on the employer's failure to provide work and entitles the employee to be paid by the employer a maximum of five days' guarantee pay in any period of three months. EPCA s.13(3) provides that the employee will not be entitled to a guarantee payment 'if the failure to provide him with work occurs in consequence of a strike, lock-out or other industrial action involving any employee of his employer or of an associated employer'.

The dispute does not have to be the only cause of the lay off. If it is the final straw which causes a closure, that will be sufficient.[42] If there is some causal connection between the dispute and the lay off entitlement is lost, provided that some employees of the employer or an associated employer are involved in the dispute. 'Involving' means something more than affecting. In *Newman v Edward Hanson Ltd*[43] employees of a firm which normally supplied contract labour to British Steel were laid off because of a national steel strike. The employees had not participated in the dispute in any way, but were merely affected by it. They were held to be entitled to guarantee pay. But refusal to cross a picket line may be sufficient to establish involvement.[44]

SOCIAL SECURITY

The availability of social security benefits may have a considerable impact on the individual circumstances of strikers and their families. The extent to which the rules about benefits are actually known to workers or unions and influence decisions to strike or to settle on particular terms is highly contentious (see Gennard, 1977). None the less, recent reforms in this area have been based on the assumption that the availability of benefits affects the activities of unions and workers. The major benefits concerned are unemployment benefit and supplementary benefit, but it is necessary to look at their interaction with a wide range of other benefits, for example, housing benefit and family income supplement as well as with the tax system.

Unemployment Benefit

The 'trade dispute disqualification' has been part of the unemployment benefit scheme since its introduction in 1911. It is now imposed by s.19(1) of

---

[42] *Thompson v Priest (Lindley) Ltd* [1978] IRLR 99.
[43] (1984) IDS Brief 268 (January).
[44] *Garvey v J & J Maybank Ltd* [1979] IRLR 408, IT.

the Social Security Act 1975 (the 1975 Act), as amended by the EPA. This provides that

> A person who has lost employment as an employed earner by reason of a stoppage of work which was due to a trade dispute at his place of employment shall be disqualified for receiving unemployment benefit so long as the stoppage continues, except in a case where, during the stoppage, he has become bona fide employed elsewhere in the occupation which he usually follows or has become regularly engaged in some other occupation; but this subsection does not apply in the case of a person who proves ... that he is not participating in or directly interested in the trade dispute which caused the stoppage of work.

It is often said that the aim of this disqualification is 'neutrality'. The quid pro quo for the disqualification of those involved in a trade dispute is said to be that vacancies caused by a trade dispute are deemed not to be suitable employment, so that no claimant can be disqualified for refusing to strike break (1975 Act s.20(4)(a)). The overall aim of 'state neutrality' is considered later, but the word neutrality is often used in the unemployment benefit context in a peculiar way. This is seen in the Tribunal of Commissioners' decision R(U) 17/52,[45] which describes the 'manifest object' of the disqualification as to 'prevent the insurance fund from being used for financing employees during strikes or lock-outs'. The merits of the dispute are irrelevant. In this sense the adjudicating authorities are neutral. It does not matter if the strike or lock-out is good or bad, justified or unjustified, legal or illegal.

The immediate effect of the disqualification is of course that the claimant receives no unemployment benefit for himself or his family. Since no wages will be received for the period without employment, no social security contributions will be made by or for the claimant. Nor can any contributions be credited while the disqualification lasts.[46]

Trade dispute. The first issue to be proved by the adjudication officer is that there is a trade dispute at the claimant's place of employment. 'Trade dispute' is defined in s.19(2)(b) of the 1975 Act as

> any dispute between employers and employees, or between employees and employees, which is connected with the employment or non-employment or the terms of employment or the conditions of employment of any persons, whether employees in the employment of the employer with whom the dispute arises, or not.

[45] Reported decisions of the Social Security Commissioners, whose decisions bind tribunals and adjudication officers, are printed and published by HMSO. 'R' stands for reported, and 'U' stands for unemployment benefit. Then decisions are numbered within each year. Unreported decisions have the prefix 'C', for Commissioner, and do not have brackets round the letter marking the type of benefit. 'S' is added for Scottish decisions. Reported decisions can be inspected at local DHSS offices, as well as in some libraries.

[46] The Social Security (Credits) Regulations SI 1975 No. 556 reg. 9. The circumstances in which such credited contributions count are exceptionally complicated (see, e.g. CPAG, 1984c:118–21).

This definition is essentially the same as that originally provided in the Trade Disputes Act 1906 in relation to immunities from liability for industrial action. The definition for that purpose has been considerably narrowed (see Chapter 6), but here, where the wider the definition the more claimants will be disqualified, nothing has changed.

A broad approach has always been taken to what was connected to terms or conditions of employment. For instance, in R(U) 12/62 the refusal of the captain of a fishing boat to allow the crew to take their meals at the same table as him since they were not members of the Close Brethren was held to affect conditions of employment. It follows from the neutrality principle, as stated in R(U) 17/52, that it makes no difference if the employer has locked out the claimants or is in breach of a collective agreement or even of the criminal law. In *R v National Insurance Commissioner ex parte Thompson*,[47] the dispute was about who should pay for protective overalls needed in dusty working conditions. Even if the employer's action was in breach of the HSWA, this would still be a trade dispute and the disqualification would apply. From 1924 to 1927 there was an exception to the disqualification if the employer had acted in breach of certain collective agreements (Ewing, 1981). The TUC's continuing representations to restore the exception seem to have faded away, and it was not seriously considered by the Donovan Commission (1968:paras.993–4).

Place of employment. It is only if claimants lose their employment because of a trade dispute at their own place of employment that the disqualification applies. Those laid off at other places are not subject to the disqualification. The basic rule has been given a wide meaning, covering, for example, the whole port of Port Talbot (R(U) 8/71) or the whole of Ford's Dagenham plants (R(U) 1/70). Thus, as in R(U) 8/71, the operations of a number of different employers in the same 'place' may be covered. Although the test is related to the claimant's actual place of work (questions do not seem to be raised about where the claimant could contractually be required to work), it could catch excessive numbers if it were not for the exception in s.19(2)(a), which allows a separate department to count as a separate place of employment if the work carried on in it is commonly carried on as a separate business. This can sometimes involve complicated evidence of commercial practice which is beyond anything which an individual claimant could produce. In evidence to the Donovan Commission, the CBI and the TUC argued for a widening and narrowing respectively of the definition, based on contradictory arguments about tendencies towards the integration of production processes. The Commission (1968:paras.970–72) stuck with the present definition, being concerned not to allow evasion of the disqualification by selective strike action.

By reason of a stoppage of work due to a trade dispute. The claimant must have lost employment by reason of a stoppage of work. The disqualification applies if the stoppage precipitates the loss of employment at a

[47] Appendix to R(U) 5/77; (1979) *Current Law Yearbook*, para.2559.

particular date. It is this initial loss of employment which is crucial. It does not matter that the claimant's employment would have ended later for some other reason if, for instance, he was under notice of dismissal (R(U) 12/72, R(U) 13/72). There is usually no difficulty in showing that the stoppage was due to a trade dispute. But if the stoppage is due to 'a decision to cease to be employed or to give employment' (R(U) 17/52), it is not due to a trade dispute even if that is the background to the dismissal. This rule only applies, however, when the decision to sever relations initiates the stoppage (R(U) 1/65). If the decision comes in the course of the stoppage, the principles set out in the next section apply.

So long as the stoppage of work continues. The disqualification lasts as long as the stoppage, not the trade dispute, subject to the rules (described below) on participation and direct interest in a trade dispute. Stoppage here refers not to the claimant's individual loss of employment but to the general stoppage. The principle is that this general stoppage ends when the employer has sufficient workers that his work is no longer hindered by the refusal of workers to work on his terms, or by his refusal to employ workers on theirs (R(U) 25/57). Thus the employer has to be back more or less at pre-strike production levels. This can take a long time (see CSU 2/81 (below)). It has been shown above that it does not matter that employment would not have been available for some other reason. In R(U) 12/80 the claimant was a casual worker who only worked for two or three days a week. Even if a regular pattern of non-employment on certain days could have been shown, he would still have been disqualified for every day covered by the stoppage.

The stoppage may therefore last long after the dispute is settled, or dies a natural death. It may indeed last indefinitely if the employer never gets back to pre-strike production levels. There are two ways out of this: one is the proviso discussed in the next two sections, the other is if the stoppage ceases to be due to a trade dispute. For the latter to happen some independent cause must intervene. It is not enough for the employer to dismiss or not to re-engage strikers (R(U) 1/65), or even to close down his business completely, if the cause is the trade dispute. But if the general closure is due to bad trade or some other independent cause, the stoppage ceases to be due to the trade dispute (R(U) 15/80).

A common situation is where work cannot be resumed immediately because repairs or safety work have to be carried out. In *R v National Insurance Commissioner ex parte Dawber*[48] a furnace could be kept going during a strike by two alternative methods. The employers chose the cheaper but more hazardous alternative. It went wrong and the roof of the furnace fell in. It took four weeks to repair after the dispute was settled. The Commissioner decided that the continuance of the stoppage was still connected with the trade dispute; it was not necessary that the events should be the inevitable result of the dispute. The Divisional Court would not interfere with this decision, saying that there is a connection if the event is a

[48] Appendix to R(U) 9/80.

natural and probable result of the trade dispute and reasonably foreseeable by the parties to that dispute.

A particularly stark illustration of how such a connection can survive commercial decisions by the employer is provided by CSU 2/81. A strike by direct production workers collapsed and the strikers wanted their old jobs back. However, the employer decided to abandon direct production and to sub-contract that work. This decision was held to be a result of the trade dispute, so that the disqualification continued for several more months until the sub-contracted production had built up to pre-existing levels.

Bona fide employed elsewhere or regularly engaged. A claimant may escape disqualification by getting within either limb of the exception. Then if the new occupation ends while the original stoppage of work is continuing, unemployment benefit is available in the ordinary way. The first limb applies where the claimant has become employed elsewhere under a contract of service in his usual occupation. There may be difficult problems in defining the claimant's place of employment. But the main issue is whether the employment was 'bona fide'. Here the leading case is R(U) 6/74, where it was held that the phrase means that the employment is genuine, that is, not created simply to avoid the disqualification and is taken up for an honest motive, for example, to earn some money. It does not require an intention permanently to sever relations with the employer. The fact that the employment turns out to be temporary, or even was known in advance to be temporary, does not in itself make it not bona fide, but is simply one of the circumstances to be considerd.

The second limb of the exception applies when the claimant has become regularly engaged in some other occupation. This covers self-employment as well as employment under a contract of service. There seems to be no modern British authority on the meaning of 'regularly', although in R(U) 6/74 it was said to embody similar notions of genuineness. The Supreme Court of Canada has held that in this context regularity refers to a pattern of work rather than to any fixed period of employment.[49] Thus the work must have continued for long enough for it to be said that the claimant 'has become' regularly engaged, but the work need not be long term and it does not matter that the claimant intends to go back to the old employer. This general approach is likely to be followed in Britain.

Not participating or directly interested. The final escape route is for the claimant to show that he is neither participating nor directly interested in the trade dispute which caused the stoppage of work. The task originally was much harder, requiring proof that he was also not financing the dispute and was not a member of a grade or class of workers any of whom was outside the terms of the proviso. Following the recommendations of the Donovan Commission (1968:paras.973–81, 983–91), these provisions were repealed by EPA s.111.

The claimant must show both that he is neither participating nor directly interested in the dispute. The Commissioners have in general refused to

[49] In *Re Abrahams and Attorney-General of Canada* (1983) 142 DLR (3d) 1.

provide a positive definition of participation. R(U) 5/66 decides that the claimant does not have to show an 'active disassociation' from the dispute. So failing to attend a union meeting at which a vote was taken about a strike by another class of workers was not participation. A worker faced with a picket line is put into an impossible situation. Acquiescence in the arguments of the pickets and a failure to go into work means that the claimant has participated in the pickets' dispute (R(U) 3/69). This is so even if the pickets have imported their dispute from elsewhere: the dispute is still at the claimant's place of employment (R(U) 1/74). On the facts in R(U) 3/69 the Commissioner held that the claimant was prevented from working by force or intimidation and that this could not amount to participation.[50] The problem, however, is that there then arises a dispute between the pickets and the claimant about whether the claimant should work or not, which clearly falls within the definition of trade dispute (see R(U) 3/69 and R(U) 1/74). It seems impossible then to say that the claimant is not participating in this dispute, although that is what was held in R(U) 3/69 (distinguishing R(U) 2/53) and in CU 39/1985. If the strict view is correct, the claimant has the choice of crossing the picket line or being disqualified for unemployment benefit.

On 'direct interest' there is, by contrast, an excess of authority culminating in the decision of the House of Lords in *Presho v DHSS*.[51] The first issue is the meaning of 'interest'. It is clear that it does not require an active association with the dispute. It is enough that the claimant might be affected in a real sense although only to a small extent. The interest can be imposed on him by the actions of others (R(U) 3/69). It is also clear that the interest must be in the subject matter of the dispute, not just in the fact that a dispute exists and is preventing the claimant from working.[52] The different phrases used in various decisions led to uncertainty about whether the interest has to be in the dispute, or in the outcome of the dispute. In *Presho*'s case the House of Lords cut through the confusion in the Court of Appeal by holding that the interest must be in the *possible* outcome of the dispute – as that defines its subject matter – but not in the outcome of the dispute in the sense of the ending of the dispute regardless of what it is about.

The crucial issue is when an interest is 'direct'. There was a line of Commissioners' decisions holding that the test was whether the claimant would be affected by the possible outcome of the dispute virtually automatically, without intervening contingencies. This test was applied by the Commissioner in R(U) 1/84 to disqualify Mrs Presho. She was a member of USDAW. The pay dispute which led to her being laid off was with the AUEW. Although the employers, Brooke Bond Oxo, had separate procedure agreements with USDAW and the AUEW, it was their practice to apply any increase conceded to one part of their workforce across the board. The House of Lords upheld the Commissioner's decision, but narrowed the test of directness. According to Lord Brandon (who gave the single judgment), it is necessary that the outcome of the dispute will be automatically

---

[50] Cf. the discussion of cases such as *Coates v Modern Methods* in text to notes 31–3 above.
[51] [1984] AC 310; appendix to R(U) 1/84.
[52] *Watt v Lord Advocate* 1979 SC 120; appendix to R(U) 6/78.

applied to the claimant as a result of a collective agreement (legally binding or not) or 'established industrial custom and practice' at the place of work. He considered that the tighter test proposed by the Court of Appeal, which excluded custom and practice, would have left the way 'wide open for deliberate and calculated evasions of the basic provision'.[53]

A highly significant development arose in one of the many appeals concerning the 1984–5 coal dispute (on which see Mesher (1985)). The previously accepted rule, established in R(U) 4/79, was that if a claimant had participated or had a direct interest in the dispute at any time during the stoppage then this proviso could not be used. However in CU 39/1985 a Tribunal of Commissioners overruled the earlier decisions and held that if a claimant ceased during the stoppage to participate or have a direct interest then the disqualification should be lifted. But this did not help the individual claimant, whose notice of dismissal for redundancy expired after the strike had begun. The Commissioners held that the dispute which caused the stoppage was a general one covering wages as well as pit closures, so that he still had a direct interest in the possibility of receiving arrears of a wage increase even though he had left the industry. None the less, the decision raises the possibility of escape from disqualification for many claimants caught by the rigour of the rule that disqualification lasts as long as the stoppage, not the dispute.

Statutory Sick Pay and Sickness Benefit

There is no trade dispute disqualification for sickness benefit. If the claimant becomes incapable of work during the stoppage, there may be entitlement to sickness benefit. The DHSS will examine extremely strictly any such claim made during a dispute. The interaction with employer's statutory sick pay is more complex.[54] If at the date on which the stoppage begins the claimant is already entitled to statutory sick pay, that entitlement continues as long as the incapacity continues up to the maximum period. If the claimant falls ill after that date, then if the trade dispute rule applies, statutory sick pay is not payable by the employer. In this case, the claimant can immediately claim sickness benefit under the ordinary rules. The employer may also be bound to pay contractually agreed sick pay.

Supplementary Benefit

If the unemployment benefit disqualification goes back to 1911, the policy of the Poor Law goes back much further. The famous judgment in *Attorney-General v Merthyr Tydfil Union*[55] upheld the common practice that, while a striker could not be granted poor relief so long as he remained in health, his family could be supported. This principle was taken over in the

---

53 [1984] AC 310, 319.
54 Social Security and Housing Benefits Act 1982 Sch.1 paras.2(g) and 7. On statutory sick pay, including the maximum periods, see further Chapter 13 below.
55 [1900] 1 Ch 516.

supplementary benefits scheme, but not put into statutory form until 1966. The current provision starts with s.8 of the Supplementary Benefits Act 1976 (the 1976 Act), which requires that if a person is caught by the trade dispute rule his or her personal requirements must be disregarded in the calculation of supplementary benefit. This basic provision was not altered in the major reform of supplementary benefit legislation in 1980, which removed large elements of discretion that had previously been exercised by the Supplementary Benefits Commission and replaced them almost entirely by maximum entitlements rigorously defined in regulations.[56] But many of the consequences of the basic rule have been altered.

The form of s.8 of the 1976 Act is almost entirely the same as that of s.19 of the 1975 Act. Although theoretically the supplementary benefit authorities should make their own decision on the evidence available, it is not surprising that they follow the decisions of the unemployment benefit authorities. However, there is one crucial difference in the wording of the two sections. While s.19 of the 1975 Act applies to a person who has 'lost employment' by reason of a stoppage of work, s.8 of the 1976 Act refers to a person being 'without employment for any period' by reason of a stoppage. It is arguable that s.8 does not impose a continuous disqualification, as s.19 does, but requires a day by day (or at least week by week) assessment of whether the stoppage is currently the reason for the absence of employment. It was suggested, but not decided, in R(U) 12/80 that a claimant who normally only worked on some days of the week might be without employment on the other days by reason of that pattern of work rather than the stoppage. The argument would be the same if the claimant resigned or was dismissed for some reason independent of the trade dispute. It has recently been applied to award supplementary benefit to a miner made redundant during the 1984–5 dispute (*CSB 214/1985*).

Claimants with families. Entitlement to supplementary benefit depends on the defined requirements of the 'assessment unit' (the claimant plus any other people he can claim for) being more than its resources. Benefit then makes up the difference. If a claimant caught by s.8 has a partner (married or unmarried) or dependants, then their normal requirements will be allowed. Housing requirements such as mortgage interest will be met. Rent and general rates fall within the housing benefit scheme, administered by local authorities. If there is an entitlement to supplementary benefit, then all of the rent and rates will be paid. Even if there is no such automatic entitlement, a family may qualify on the general low income test. Only a very limited range of additional requirements – for extra heating or a special diet, for example – are allowed and no single payments or normal urgent need payments can be made if any member of the assessment unit is disqualified.[57] The only recourse is to the restrictive conditions of the Supplementary Benefit (Trade Disputes and Recovery from Earnings)

---

56 For discussion of the 1980 reforms generally, see Mesher (1981).
57 Supplementary Benefit (Requirements) Regulations SI 1983 No.1399 regs. 12(2), 13(3) (4), Sch.3 para.12; Supplementary Benefit (Single Payments) Regulations SI 1981 No.1528 reg. 6(1)(b); Supplementary Benefit (Urgent Cases) Regulations SI 1981 No. 1529 reg.6(1)(b).

Regulations.[58] These apply only to a few closely defined needs and require all other sources of credit or assistance to be exhausted. The only relatively open-ended provision under these regulations requires a member of the assessment unit to be affected by a 'disaster'. But in R(SB) 24/85 a Tribunal of Commissioners stressed the difficulty of applying the provision to a striking miner's family. The 1984–5 coal dispute brought into prominence many restrictive provisions in the legislation, the full effect of which had been masked by their being scattered around several regulations. For instance, the discovery that a payment could not be made even for the cost of a child's funeral led to the Minister intervening to order ex gratia payments to be made and to an amendment to the Trade Disputes Regulations.

All the ordinary rules on resources apply. The income of all members of the assessment unit must be looked at. For example, most other social security benefits, like child benefit or unemployment benefit paid to a spouse, count in full. Final earnings are taken into account for the length of the period to which they relate from the date on which they are payable. If the earnings are the claimant's, there is no entitlement to supplementary benefit for the period covered. A person paid a week in hand will thus be excluded for the first two weeks of the stoppage. There is a special rule allowing final earnings to be spread forward for an extra week if the last week's are more than two and a half times the assessment unit's normal (non-trade dispute) requirements.[59] Any strike pay received up to £17 per week is disregarded altogether, except under the Trade Disputes Regulations.[60] This is the compensation for the deduction mentioned in the next paragraph. If, exceptionally, any income tax rebate is received, it counts as income.[61] There are many other forms of income whose treatment under the regulations, which are especially complex here, is unclear. During the 1984–5 miners' strike controversial guidance, mainly adverse to claimants, was issued to his offices by the Chief Adjudication Officer (CPAG, 1984a; 1984b; Luba, 1984 and see also R(SB) 29/85).

Once the calculation of resources against requirements has been made, s.6(1) of the Social Security (No.2) Act 1980 requires that the sum of £17 (which is index-linked) is deducted from any entitlement to benefit, except under the Trade Disputes Regulations. Entitlement may thus be wiped out completely. The rule applies regardless of whether the claimant is receiving strike pay or not, or indeed of whether he is a union member or not. It is a straightforward penalty, although this part of the 1980 legislation was avowedly aimed at forcing trade unions rather than the state to provide financial support for strikers and their families. The deduction rule was the subject of a legal challenge. An ingenious argument contesting the application of the rule to claimants with partners was not considered by the Divisional Court on the ground that the issue should have been taken

[58]   SI 1980 No.1641.
[59]   Supplementary Benefit (Resources) Regulations SI 1981 No.1527 reg.10(2)(e).
[60]   SI 1980 No.1641 reg. 12.
[61]   SI 1981 No.1527 reg. 3(2) (d).

through the ordinary appeal process.[62] But after an expedited appeal procedure, the claimant's argument anyway failed before a Tribunal of Commissioners (R(SB) 25/85).

Single claimants. A single claimant with no dependants is an entire assessment unit, which thus has nil requirements and no entitlement to ordinary benefit. The only possibility is through the Trade Dispute Regulations described above, but there are further difficulties. For instance, it is even more difficult to establish a 'disaster' if the only person affected in the assessment unit is the claimant. Housing benefit will be available to meet rent and rates though. The overall position marks a sharp contrast to that before 1980 when payments for essential living expenses were made by the Supplementary Benefits Commission to single claimants once their resources were exhausted. Although only small amounts were paid on a national scale (Gennard, 1977:28), even this protection against destitution has gone. Now single claimants have to become incapable of work before ordinary benefit can be received. They may therefore be attracted to picketing by expenses payments from unions (Hartley et al., 1983:57).

Return to work. On return to work at the end of the stoppage, a claimant is entitled to benefit for the first fifteen days (counting any income tax refund received as a resource with a £4 disregard), but the amount paid is recoverable from future earnings (1976 Act s.9). It appears that a claimant returning to work before the end of the stoppage is entitled to benefit for the first fifteen days under the ordinary regulations,[63] where there is no power of recovery.

Claims by a spouse. Until recently, if a man and a woman were living together, only the man could claim supplementary benefit or family income supplement (FIS). Since the Supplementary Benefit (Equal Treatment) Regulations 1983[64] and corresponding amendments to the FIS legislation, it has been possible, subject to conditions, for a couple to choose which of them should be the claimant. If a spouse claims supplementary benefit, this can avoid the special final earnings rule at the beginning of a dispute, and some problems on return to work afterwards. More fruitful could be a claim for FIS if the spouse is in full-time work and providing the family is not already receiving FIS. Here the main controversy is whether the striker's normal earnings when not on strike should count as part of the family's normal income in the FIS calculation. A Tribunal of Commissioners in R(FIS) 2/85, upheld in the Court of Appeal,[65] decided that they should, without dealing with the precise calculation. If the spouse is independently entitled to, say unemployment benefit, there is entitlement to a dependant's increase for the striker.

---

[62] *R v Chief Adjudication Officer ex parte Bland* (1985) The Times, 6 February.
[63] The Supplementary Benefit (Conditions of Entitlement) Regulations SI 1981 No.1526 reg.9(2)(a).
[64] SI 1983 No.1004.
[65] *Lowe v Adjudication Officer* [1985] 2 All ER 897.

Other Benefits

The availability of housing benefit and child benefit has already been mentioned. Any other benefits not based on unemployment (such as an existing FIS award) are also available. An award of supplementary benefit or FIS provides an automatic passport to benefits like free school meals, school clothing grant, free prescriptions, free dental treatment, vitamins and milk tokens. Even if there is no such automatic passport, there may be entitlement on general low income grounds, for which purposes the family's requirements should be calculated in the ordinary way, without the £17 deduction. A local authority social services department may make payment under s.1 of the Child Care Act 1980 to prevent children from being taken into care.

Income Tax

Unemployment benefit is subject to PAYE income tax,[66] as is supplementary benefit paid to the unemployed or to those who fall within the trade dispute disqualification.[67] The effect of this is that no repayment of income tax is made while the benefit is being paid, but a calculation is made when entitlement ceases or at the end of the tax year.[68] Even if a person is not receiving unemployment or supplementary benefit, however, neither the tax authorities nor the employer are to make any repayments of PAYE tax if the person is or would be disqualified under s.19 of the 1975 Act.[69] The one exception is that if wages are paid during the disqualification period – for example, wages due for work before the strike – the employer can take into account repayments due in calculating the deduction of PAYE tax from those wages. Thus availability of tax refunds, which in the past has been the subject of much controversy as an alleged encouragement to striking (Donovan, 1968:para.996 and App.8; Durcan and McCarthy, 1974), is no longer an issue.

CONCLUSION

That the common law allows virtually no scope for legitimate industrial action is not surprising. That legislation has omitted to do so is perhaps

---

[66] Income and Corporation Taxes Act 1970 s.219(1)(a), as amended.
[67] Finance Act 1981 s.27. An exception is that payments under s.4 of the 1976 Act, i.e. urgent needs payments under the Trades Disputes Regulations, are free of tax.
[68] Income Tax (Employments) Regulations SI 1973 No.334 regs.53–69, inserted by the Income Tax (Employments)(No.13) Regulations SI 1982 No.66 reg. 14.
[69] Finance Act 1981 s.29, implemented by reg.7 of the Income Tax (Employments) (No.13) Regulations SI 1982 No.66, amending reg.24 of the Income Tax (Employments) Regulations SI 1973 No.334.

surprising. The loss of accrued employment protection rights in conditions of high unemployment is a matter which may be reversed by a future government. In particular, thc taboo on the tribunals examining the 'merits' of industrial disputes might be removed. Collective issues and the merits of industrial action are already reviewable by tribunals over a range of matters including the rights to associate and dissociate. There is therefore less reason today than in the past to exclude other industrial dispute cases from scrutiny. But would such changes assist employees? It has been suggested that the decisions of the courts in the employment protection sphere entrench and institutionalise managerial powers (Collins, 1982). This is arguably inevitable as the judges who interpret the legislation are steeped in the individualist traditions of the common law (Forrest, 1980). It is possible that even if tribunals had jurisdiction the merits would normally be decided in favour of the employer.

Given the consequences of engaging in industrial action in terms of loss of statutory rights, the question arises whether they are to any degree in the contemplation of employees before they take industrial action. It is thought not, primarily because the action is not viewed by employees as something likely to sever the relationship, so that the consequences of dismissal are not considered. Section 11 of the Trade Union Act 1984 (discussed in detail in Chapter 6), which requires the ballot paper to specify that industrial action is in breach of the individual's contract, is unlikely to make much difference to this perception. It may not in itself have much meaning without an explanation of the consequences of breach of contract. Also there will be no ballots in those strikes which are spontaneous and unofficial. Moreover, trade unions are unlikely to highlight this negative side when faced with the prospect of taking industrial action. As Hartley et al. (1983:19) point out:

> Organisations do not just passively or reactively confront problems and issues 'delivered' to them by their circumstancs, but play a significant role in their construction, by selective perception, definition and action. In decision-making rationalisation more often characterises organisational enactment than rationality. Rather than conforming to the prescribed ideals of problem-solving, problems are defined to fit the range of available or acceptable solutions.

So far as the social security system goes, there is an exceptionally complex disqualification applying not just to strikers, but also to those who are locked out and to certain non-strikers at the same workplace. The disqualification hits not just at the claimant but also at his family and has been tightened severely in 1980. On what principles can the present scope of the disqualification be justified? The Donovan Commission (1968:para.956) referred to the original purpose of the insurance scheme as being to protect those who lost employment through 'the ordinary fluctuations of trade or business', rather than through trade disputes. This is sometimes translated into the distinction between involuntary and voluntary unemployment, which is reflected in the limited disqualifications for misconduct, leaving voluntarily, and refusing suitable work (see Chapter 13). However, the principle of not compensating for voluntary unemployment cannot justify the scope of the trade dispute disqualification. The dispute and a direct interest in it may be imposed on the claimant, yet he is still disqualified. The disqualification may continue when a claimant wants to return to work, but is prevented by circumstances quite beyond his control.

Another general principle that could justify the scope of the disqualification is that of state neutrality in trade disputes. In its strongest form this asserts that it is wrong for the state to provide support for strikers and their families at all.[70] Few would go so far as to withdraw all social security benefits, however, and most proponents of this approach accept some kind of middle position centring on the withdrawal of unemployment and supplementary benefits. Then the argument shades into the proposition that in the past the provision of benefits has in fact encouraged workers to strike or, once in a dispute, to stay out for longer or to demand higher settlements. The empirical evidence to support this argument is lacking. Durcan and McCarthy (1974) have shown that the overall level of strike activity is not affected by changes in benefit levels, though this does not exclude specific effects on individuals (Hunter, 1974; Gennard, 1977:ch.7). It seems intuitively unlikely that the availability of supplementary benefit will affect an initial decision to strike, if only because of the immense complexity of the legal rules. Furthermore, financial support is likely to come only after the dispute has lasted two weeks or more (because of the final earnings rule) and planning this far ahead is rare. It does appear to be the case that strikers generally try to get by on savings, not paying bills and by borrowing, regarding supplementary benefit as a last resort (Gennard, 1977:ch.5). Again intuitively, the fact that benefit is being paid for a striker's family might make him or her less ready to return to work on terms seen as unsatisfactory. But such an effect is almost impossible to test.[71]

It is some variant of this principle which has nevertheless informed the changes to the legislation carried out since 1979 on the basis that state provision for strikers had been too generous and that more of the financial burden ought to be shifted to the trade unions. In so far as the argument rested on the proposition that Britain was much more generous than other countries in providing for strikers' families, it is clear that it is unfounded (Lasko, 1975:35; Gennard, 1977:30–34). The common foreign pattern is of disqualification for unemployment insurance (although sometimes this is more limited than in Britain), but with provision for families and sometimes strikers through a social assistance system.

It seems impossible to define any point at which the state can be strictly neutral. Withdrawing support from one side inevitably aids the other. The question is whether there is the appropriate balance between subsidising

---

[70] For an example see Society of Conservative Lawyers (1974), comprehensively demolished by Lasko (1975).

[71] A Gallup poll carried out for the Radio 4 programme 'What about the Workers?' apparently found that over half of workers thought that strikers could claim social security benefits (as reported in *The Guardian*, 4 October 1984). Such a misconception might reinforce an individual's decision to strike, but perhaps suggests that publicity for the previous stringent rules might have had more effect on such decisions than increasing the stringency.

industrial action and the prevention of destitution. But two final points can
be made. First, the more serious the consequences of disqualification, the
stronger become the arguments for distinguishing between claimants on the
basis of the merits of the dispute. Second, what is the reality of the right to
strike for a non-unionist or a member of a union which cannot or will not pay
strike pay, if the result of striking is the necessity of living a long way below a
subsistence level of income?

Bibliography

Blanc-Jouvan, X. 1972. 'The Effect of Industrial Action on the Status of the Individual Employee'. *Industrial Conflict: A Comparative Legal Survey*. Eds. B. Aaron and K.W. Wedderburn. London: Longman, 175–253.

Child Poverty Action Group (CPAG). 1984a. 'Welfare Rights and the Miners' Strike'. *Welfare Rights Bulletin*, 60 (July), 1–3.

——. 1984b. 'Miners' Strike Update'. *Welfare Rights Bulletin*, 61 (August), 9–10.

——. 1984c. *Rights Guide to Non-Means Tested Benefits*. London: CPAG.

Collins, H. 1982. 'Capitalist Discipline and Corporatist Law'. *Industrial Law Journal*, 11 (June and September), 78–93, 170–77.

Davies, P.L., and M.R. Freedland. 1984. *Labour Law: Text and Materials*. 2nd edn. London: Weidenfeld & Nicolson.

Donovan. 1968. Royal Commission on Trade Unions and Employers' Associations 1965–1968. *Report*. Cmnd 3623. London: HMSO.

Durcan, J.W., and W.E.J. McCarthy. 1974. 'The State Subsidy Theory of Strikes'. *British Journal of Industrial Relations*, 12 (March), 26–47.

Ewing, K.D. 1981. 'Collective Agreements, Trade Disputes and Unemployment Benefit – The Employer's Breach Exemption'. *Northern Ireland Legal Quarterly*, 32 (Winter), 305–27.

——. 1982. 'Industrial Action: Another Step in the "Right" Direction'. *Industrial Law Journal*, 11 (December), 209–26.

Forrest, H.G. 1980. 'Political Values in Individual Employment Law'. *Modern Law Review*, 42 (July), 361–80.

Fox, A. 1974. *Beyond Contract: Work, Power and Trust Relations*. London: Faber.

Freedland, M.R. 1976. *The Contract of Employment*. Oxford: Clarendon Press.

Gennard, J. 1977. *Financing Strikers*. London: Macmillan.

Hartley, J., J. Kelly and N. Nicholson. 1983. *Steel Strike: A Case-Study in Industrial Relations*. London: Batsford.

Hunter, L.C. 1974. 'The State Subsidy Theory of Strikes: A Reconsideration'. *British Journal of Industrial Relations*, 12 (November), 438–44.

Kahn-Freund, O. 1983. *Labour and the Law*. 3rd edn. Ed. and intr. by Paul Davies and Mark Freedland. London: Stevens.

Lasko, R. 1975. 'The Payment of Supplementary Benefit for Strikers' Dependants – Misconception and Misrepresentation'. *Modern Law Review*, 38 (January), 31–8.

Luba, J. 1984. 'Strikers and Social Security Benefits'. *Legal Action* (July), 77–80.

Mailly, R. 1983. 'Dismissal for Taking Part in Industrial Action: A Right to Strike?'. *Trade Union Law Bulletin*, 4 (January–March), 50–59.

Mesher, J. 1981. 'The 1980 Social Security Legislation'. *British Journal of Law and Society*, 8 (Summer), 119–27.

——. 1985. 'Social Security in the Coal Dispute'. *Industrial Law Journal*, 14 (September), 191–202.

Napier, B.W. 1980. 'Strikes and the Law of Unfair Dismissal'. *Cambridge Law Journal*, 39 (April), 52–4.
——. 1984. 'Aspects of the Wage-Work Bargain'. *Cambridge Law Journal*, 43 (November), 337–48.
Rideout, R.W., with J.C. Dyson. 1983. *Rideout's Principles of Labour Law*. 4th edn. London: Sweet & Maxwell.
Society of Conservative Lawyers. 1974. *Financing Strikes*. London: Conservative Political Centre.
Townshend-Smith, R. 1980. 'Note on *Fisher v York Trailers*'. *Industrial Law Journal*, 9 (March), 48–52.
Wallington, P. 1983. 'The Employment Act 1982: Section 9 – A Recipe for Victimisation'. *Modern Law Review*, 46 (May) 310–17.

PART IV
Trade Unions

10 Trade Union Government and Democracy

Kenneth Miller

In their formative years during the nineteenth century trade unions had to operate in a hostile legal climate. The Trade Union Act 1871 was the first major piece of legislation concerned with trade union government. It negated certain judicial decisions which had held that the purposes of trade unions were unlawful as being in restraint of trade.[1] Until recently the aim of subsequent legislation was to provide a legal environment in which trade unions could operate effectively and independently without external interference. Kahn-Freund (1983:274) observed that 'in this country, it has, on the whole, been common ground that in th[e] dilemma between imposing standards of democracy and protecting union autonomy the law must come down on the side of autonomy'. This policy broke down, of course, during the period of the Industrial Relations Act 1971 (IRA). The Trade Union Act 1984 (TUA) represents an even more radical change in the state's policy towards the internal affairs of trade unions. Its aim is to lay down minimum standards of behaviour which must be adhered to by all trade unions.

Prior to the Act of 1984 the main source of authority for trade unions were the provisions of their own rule book. These rule books, many of them first drawn up in the late nineteenth and early twentieth centuries, lack the level of clarity and precision of other forms of rules regulating the conduct of legal entities such as limited companies or partnerships.[2] One reason for this has been the 'non-interventionist' tradition established by the late nineteenth and early twentieth century legislation. Rideout (1965:153) has indeed argued that the principal reason why union rules are sometimes meaningless or ambiguous is because they were compiled in the belief that the courts would interfere as little as possible in the internal workings of what were regarded as voluntary associations.

Parliament may have historically avoided any general involvement in internal union affairs, but the same cannot be said for the courts. Yet arguably the common law also recognises the importance of union autonomy. This is because the legal model used to regulate the relationship of the

---

[1] See, for example, *Hornby v Close* (1867) LR 2 QB 153; *Farrer v Close* (1869) LR 4 QB 602.
[2] A point accepted by the House of Lords in *Heatons Transport (St Helens) Ltd v TGWU* where Lord Wilberforce counselled judges not to construe rule books as if they were drafted by 'parliamentary draftsmen': [1972] ICR 308, 393.

union to the individual member is based on contract. The application of contractual principles might in theory allow the trade union a very wide discretion to set out the conditions of membership and to provide rules for the regulation of the relationship with members. The practice, however, has been different. As Elias et al. (1980:309) have argued, the very contractual principles which might have kept the courts out have allowed them to interfere in union affairs by 'implying terms and striking out rules contrary to public policy [so as] to effect a significant amount of control over union constitutions'. Judicial intervention has gone even further. Although a trade union may be a voluntary association in the eyes of the law, it exercises important public functions through the practice of the closed shop and through its involvement in collective bargaining. Thus principles of public law have also been applied to trade unions. This has been accomplished mainly through the application of the rules of natural justice to trade union disciplinary activities. The interaction between judicial and legislative policies is thus the underlying theme of this chapter which considers in turn the legal framework of union administration, the TUC's important role in inter-union relations, the legal rights of individual members and applicants for membership, and the question of democracy within trade unions.

LEGAL FRAMEWORK OF UNION ADMINISTRATION

Statutory Definition and Legal Status

At common law a trade union was regarded as an unincorporated voluntary association with no legal persona separate from its members. The Trade Union Act 1871 did not alter this state of affairs. It did provide for the first time, however, a definition of what was to be regarded in law as a trade union, and it established voluntary machinery for registration with the Chief Registrar of Friendly Societies. The 1871 definition, apart from requiring that a trade union had to be a temporary or permanent combination, concentrated exclusively upon its principal objects. Thus to be regarded as a trade union an association had to pursue one or more of the following objects: 'the regulation of the relations between workmen and masters, or between workmen and workmen, or between masters and masters, or the imposing of restrictive conditions on the conduct of any trade or business, and also the provision of benefits to members'. Employers' associations and even trade associations unconnected with industrial relations could fall within this statutory definition (Grunfeld, 1966:7–8). It applied for a hundred years until repealed by the IRA. This statute instituted a dichotomy between 'organisations of workers' and 'trade unions'. The status of trade union (to which were attached important rights and immunities) was reserved for those organisations of workers which registered with the Chief Registrar of Trade Unions and Employers' Associations. The 1971 Act also introduced a separate definition applicable to employers' associations.

The present definition contained in s.28 of TULRA concentrates upon both the nature of the organisation and upon its objects. Thus to be regarded as a trade union the organisation (whether permanent or temporary) must consist 'wholly or mainly of workers' and must have principal purposes which include 'the regulation of relations between workers ... and employers or employers' associations'. The definition of trade union also covers organisations which are made up wholly or mainly of constituent associations or affiliates. It was unclear whether this included the TUC. According to the Certification Officer (1978:16), the TUC falls within the definition.

The requirements of s.28 are not a major obstacle for most workers' organisations. The definition hinges upon two elements: the organisation should consist wholly or mainly of workers, and should include the regulation of worker–employer relations among its principal purposes. Section 30(1) of TULRA defines the meaning of 'worker'. It covers not only a person employed under a contract of employment, but also anyone employed under any sort of contract so long as that person is required to perform personally any work for another party to the contract who is not a professional client. The definition of worker also includes civil servants but not members of the armed services or police force. The scope of an organisation's principal purposes was tested in two cases under the IRA. In both it was held that a joint shop stewards' committee in the docks could not be an 'organisation of workers' because it did not seek to bargain with employers – it existed merely as an influential pressure group.[3]

The legal status of a trade union is regulated by TULRA s.2. This provision regularises the status of trade unions and brings certainty to the law after the series of confusing legislative developments and judicial decisions.[4] The Donovan Commission (1968:para.784) had recommended the grant of corporate status to all trade unions, based on registration. This recommendation was enacted in the IRA, although that Act placed greater significance on registration than Donovan envisaged. In the event the majority of TUC-affiliated trade unions deregistered. To that extent most unions were merely unincorporated organisations of workers under the IRA. But unregistered organisations, although they were not corporate bodies, could still be sued in their own name (IRA s.154).

In considering the provisions of TULRA s.2, two points arise concerning the pre-1971 position. The first concerns the scope of legal remedies available against unions. The decision of the House of Lords in *Bonsor v Musicians' Union* firmly established that damages as well as a declaration and an injunction could be awarded against a union. TULRA s.2(1)(c) accepts this point and provides ways of enforcing a judgment for damages. An important circumstance where damages may be awarded against the union is in a closed shop where loss of employment follows from an expulsion. The second point concerns the judicial interpretation of s.3 of the

---

[3] *Midland Cold Storage Ltd v Turner* [1972] ICR 230; *Midland Cold Storage Ltd v Steer* [1972] ICR 435.

[4] *Bonsor v Musicians' Union* [1956] AC 104, HL. See also *Taff Vale Railway Co. v Amalgamated Society of Railway Servants* [1901] AC 426, HL; *ASRS v Osborne* [1910] AC 87, HL.

1871 Act, which provided that the purposes of trade unions were no longer to be regarded as unlawful by being in restraint of trade. The fact that the section did not expressly exempt the rules of the union was eventually used by the judges as a pretext for striking down specific rules.[5] Consequently, TULRA s.2(5) protects both the purposes and the rules of a trade union from the doctrine of restraint of trade.

Section 2 of TULRA could be regarded as enacting a 'halfway house' between corporate and unincorporated status. Although the Act states that a trade union shall not be, or be treated as if it were, a body corporate,[6] trade unions are accorded certain quasi-corporate characteristics. Thus s.2 declares that trade unions are capable of making contracts, suing or being sued in their own name, and of being the subjects of criminal prosecution. (Trade union liability for economic torts is dealt with in Chapter 6 as part of the discussion of union immunities.) Further TULRA s.2(1)(e) ensures that any judgment, order or award made against a union by a court can be enforced against the union to the same extent and in the same manner as if the union were a body corporate. Nevertheless, it would appear that the purpose of the enactment of such characteristics is to overcome procedural difficulties and not to create a near corporate entity. This point was accepted in a case where the EETPU sued for libel,[7] O'Connor J held that such an action had to be based on the possession of a legal personality which could be libelled. The opening words of TULRA s.2(1) indicated that trade unions did not have that personality. Consequently, the union could not maintain an action in its own name in relation to its reputation.

Like the 1871 Act, TULRA vests all the property belonging to the trade union in trustees in trust for the union. The beneficiaries under this arrangement are all the members of the union together and separately. The vesting of property in this way is a mandatory requirement under s.2(1)(b). It was held under the equivalent provisions of the 1871 Act that a trade union could not create a company to own its property even where the company's directors were the union's trustees.[8] TULRA does simplify, however, some of the procedural requirements of trust law as it applies to trade unions. Thus under s.4 a trustee of a listed trade union can be appointed or discharged by a written instrument of the union rather than by means of a deed which is the normal requirement for trusts. Finally, there are circumstances where the trustees can be removed from office for a failure to carry out their duties and a receiver appointed by the court to administer the union's assets.[9]

---

[5] See *Edwards v SOGAT* [1971] Ch 354, CA. But cf. *Faramus v Film Artistes' Association* [1964] AC 925, HL.
[6] An exception is made for 'special register bodies' who retain their corporate status under s.2. These are bodies who became incorporated either by Royal Charter or under the Companies Acts. The two most important are the British Medical Association and the Royal College of Nursing. No new special register bodies can be created.
[7] *EETPU v Times Newspapers Ltd* [1980] QB 585. For an earlier decision which took a different view based on the 1871 Act, see *National Union of General and Municipal Workers v Gillian* [1946] KB 81, CA.
[8] *Re National Union of Railwaymen's Rules* [1968] 1 All ER 5.
[9] *Clarke v Heathfield* [1985] ICR 203. See further Chapter 19.

TULRA also deals with the status of employers' associations. They can be either bodies corporate or unincorporated associations. If the association is of the latter type, TULRA s.3(2) bestows upon it the same attributes as those provided to trade unions by s.2(1). In the EETPU case, however, O'Connor J was of the opinion that an employers' association, as distinct from a trade union, was a quasi-corporation and so could sue to protect its reputation as TULRA s.3 lacked the opening restrictive words of s.2.

Role of Certification Officer

The Certification Officer (CO) exercises an independent statutory authority over a number of trade union matters.[10] When the office of CO was first created by the EPA it was given new functions and also had transferred to it duties formerly exercised by the Chief Registrar of Friendly Societies. The CO is required to maintain a list of trade unions and employers' associations and to determine any question concerning the independence of trade unions. He also has the authority to ensure that unions maintain proper accounts and submit annual returns, as well as supervising union superannuation schemes. He is responsible for ensuring that unions comply with the balloting requirements of the Trade Union (Amalgamations) Act 1964 concerning transfers of engagement and amalgamations and that they comply with the requirements of TUA 1913 (as amended) concerning ballots for the creation of a political fund. The CO also hears complaints alleging malpractices under both Acts.

These functions are in keeping with the traditional legislative philosophy towards trade unions. Despite his legal powers, the CO cannot generally dictate to trade unions over the contents of their rule books or tell them how they should conduct their internal affairs. He has, for example, none of the extensive powers of his predecessor under the IRA Sch.4 to ensure that a union's rules satisfy certain statutory criteria before the organisation can be registered. Since 1980, however, the authority of the CO to interfere in the internal affairs of trade unions has expanded in two ways. First, the EA 1980 charges the CO with the power to supervise the scheme under s.1 of that Act for refunding certain costs incurred by trade unions in the holding of secret ballots. Second, the TUA 1984 gives the CO a jurisdiction (which is shared with the courts) to hear complaints that a ballot for the election of the principal executive committee of a trade union is not in conformity with the terms of that Act. Both of these provisions are analysed below as aspects of 'trade union democracy'.

Listing. The CO maintains a list of organisations which satisfy the statutory definition of trade union[11] and also a list of employers' associa-

---

10 EPA ss.7–9 and Sch. 1 require ACAS to provide the CO with staff, finance and accommodation. Nevertheless, he is independent of both ACAS and the Secretary of State.
11 Organisations of workers were automatically entered in the list by the CO when TULRA took effect if they were either affiliated to the TUC or registered under previous legislation, unless it appeared that they did not satisfy the definition of a trade union in TULRA s.28 (see above).

tions. The principal benefit of listing is that it is a condition precedent for the application to the CO for a certificate of independence. The only other advantage is that it guarantees the organisation tax relief for expenditure on provident benefits.

There are certain obligations, however, which are imposed upon trade unions irrespective of listing. Both listed and unlisted unions are required to maintain proper accounting records, to have those accounts audited, and to submit annual returns to the CO. These are requirements which are backed up by the threat of criminal sanctions against both the union and its responsible officials (TULRA s.12), though who is supposed to instigate these criminal proceedings is unclear.

Certificates of independence. It is a cardinal rule in most market economy countries that effective collective bargaining depends on the independence of trade unions from employers. In the United States, for example, s.8(a)(2) of the National Labor Relations Act makes it an unfair labour practice for an employer 'to dominate or interfere with the formation or administration of any labor organisation or contribute financial or other support to it'. In Britain this problem has been tackled by conferring authority on the CO over the award of certificates of independence. In contrast to listing, a trade union which has obtained a certificate of independence enjoys a number of legal advantages which are designed in the main to facilitate collective bargaining. These rights, which may accrue to a trade union or its members, are listed in Chapter 3 in the context of legal support for collective bargaining.

The CO is guided by the definition of independence provided in s.30(1) of TULRA. This defines an independent trade union as one which is not under the domination or control of an employer or a group of employers or of an employers' association, and is not liable to interference by an employer (arising out of the provision of financial or material support or by any other means) tending towards such control. Most unions which have not been awarded certificates have failed because they were liable to interference tending towards employer's control. Other factors such as the effect which the issue of a certificate might have on good industrial relations or collective bargaining structures, or whether it is desirable to allow a new trade union to operate in a particular area, cannot be considered. The task of the CO is simply to assess the independence of the applicant union. To that extent proof of the effectiveness of the organisation in collective bargaining is irrelevant except so far as it impinges on independence.

In exercising his functions over the award of certificates the CO has drawn up a list of criteria which have been approved in principle by the EAT and the Court of Appeal.[12] First, history: if there is evidence in the recent past that the union has received employer support and encouragement, it is a powerful argument against the award of a certificate. Second, membership base: a union which recruits from the employees of a single employer only is

---

[12] See *Blue Circle Staff Association v CO* [1977] ICR 224, EAT and *Squibb UK Staff Association v CO* [1979] ICR 235, CA.

more vulnerable to employer interference than a broadly based union. Third, organisation and structure: this is assessed not only on the basis of the formal rules but upon practices as well. The union should be organised in such a way as to enable the members to play a full part in the decision-making process free from employer interference or involvement. Fourth, finance: a union with weak finances and inadequate reserves is more likely to be susceptible to employer interference than one with a strong financial base. Fifth, the degree of reliance on employer-provided facilities: 'a strong record and the display of a robust attitude in negotiation are items on the credit side which may outweigh other factors unfavourable to the union's case' (CO, 1976:11). It is not necessary for a union to satisfy each of these criteria separately. The award of a certificate is based on 'a careful assessment of the whole nature and circumstances' of the case (CO, 1977:7).

The major area of controversy has concerned the CO's handling of applications for certificates from staff associations. In many of these cases TUC-affiliated trade unions unsuccessfully objected to the applications. The CO has suggested in his annual reports that it is difficult to generalise about the character of staff associations. They range from organisations whose very existence relies upon the benign approval of the employer to others which maintain quite separate administrative procedures and who display a 'robustness' in collective bargaining. As the CO has also argued, it is pointless to criticise him if staff associations with the potential to de-stabilise collective bargaining arrangements obtain certificates. Any blame for this lies with the statutory definition of independence. Nevertheless, the CO has introduced two mechanisms in order to allay fears about his certification function. First, he amended his procedures in 1977 so as to provide greater information to objecting unions and to enable discussions with objectors to take place as a matter of course.[13] Second, the CO took the further step in 1978 of instigating a system whereby around a hundred unions who had shown some reliance on employer-provided facilities in the past had their affairs monitored in order to assess their continued independence. Ultimately, the CO can withdraw a certificate from a trade union if he considers that it is no longer independent (EPA s.8(7)).

Mergers. The Trade Union (Amalgamations) Act 1964 provides for two forms of merger: a transfer of engagements and an amalgamation. In the case of a transfer of engagements, the membership of the transferor organisation joins the transferee union and the transferor union ceases to exist. Only the members of the transferor union are required to be balloted. In an amalgamation two or more unions come together to form a new union with new rules after a favourable vote of the membership of each of the organisations concerned.

[13] An objecting union cannot appeal to the EAT against the award of a certificate to another union: *General and Municipal Workers' Union v CO* [1977] ICR 183. But the CO's decision to refuse or withdraw a certificate can be appealed by the applicant union to the EAT and thence to the ordinary civil courts (EPA s.8(9)). Appeals to the EAT are competent on both law and fact (EPCA s.136(3)).

Before any transfer or amalgamation can be implemented, however, there are a number of steps laid down in the Act and the accompanying Regulations.[14] It is the function of the CO to ensure that all these requirements are complied with before authorisation for a merger is forthcoming. As a first step, the CO must be given the opportunity to approve the instrument setting out the terms of the transfer of engagements or the amalgamation. The next step is to provide a notice which explains the merger proposals to the members, who will have the opportunity to vote on it. Like the instrument, the notice must also be approved by the CO. The ballot takes the form of a resolution which is voted on by the members.

Section 1(2) of the 1964 Act lays down three fundamental requirements for the conduct of the ballot. First, every member of the union must be entitled to vote. The CO has held that the reference to 'every member' in the Act means that the union cannot restrict the vote to certain classes of member even if the union rule book so restricts voting rights.[15] Thus members who are in arrears with their subscriptions can vote in merger ballots. Second, every member of the union must be allowed to vote without interference or constraint and must, so far as is reasonably possible, be given a fair opportunity of voting. Third, the method of voting must involve the marking of a voting paper by the person voting. The Act does not demand that voting should be carried out in secret, or that postal ballots should be used. If postal ballots are used, however, application can be made to the CO for refund of the costs involved in organising them under the scheme authorised by s.1 of the 1980 Act. Subject to these requirements, the Act allows a union's governing body to arrange for the vote of its members 'to be taken in any manner which the body thinks fit' (s.2(2)). The major change introduced by the 1964 Act is that for the resolution to be carried all that is required is a simple majority of those voting (s.2(3)). It is not possible for a union to require a higher level of support unless it specifically excludes this provision by declaring expressly in its rules that s.2(3) should not apply.[16] In such a case the union can demand either a larger majority for the resolution to be carried or a certain proportion of the members to vote in the ballot.

If the resolution is approved in the ballot, the next step is to request the CO to register the instrument. The CO can refuse registration if the instrument is inconsistent with the rules of a participating union. In the *AUEW* case,[17] where an application was made for judicial review of the procedures by which the Construction Workers and Foundry Workers Sections proposed to transfer their engagements to the Engineering Section, the Court of Appeal held that the rules of the AUEW were part of and incorporated into the rules of each of the four sections making up the federal union. Since the AUEW's rules demanded that the number of sections must

[14] Trade Unions and Employers' Associations (Amalgamations, etc.) Regulations SI 1975 No. 536 (as amended by SI 1978 No. 1344 and SI 1981 No. 1631). For a detailed analysis, see Grunfeld (1966); Elias (1973).

[15] *McLaren and Ognall and Association of Cinematograph Television and Allied Technicians*, CO (1979:18); *Young and National Union of Agricultural and Allied Workers*, CO (1982:21).

[16] *Gormley and Amalgamated Society of Boilermakers*, CO (1982:22).

[17] *R v CO ex parte AUEW(E)* [1983] ICR 125.

be maintained at four, and since the effect of the instrument was to reduce this number, the CO was entitled to refuse registration. The merger cannot become effective until the instrument is registered. Before it can be registered, however, the CO must wait for six weeks to enable complaints about the conduct of the merger process to be received. The receipt of any complaint during this time prevents the instrument from being registered until the complaint is determined.

The right to complain is restricted to members of the transferor union in the case of a transfer, or a member of any of the unions involved in the case of an amalgamation. The nature of the complaint must relate to one of the three fundamental requirements in s.1(2) of the Act, or to the conduct of the ballot itself. The CO has the power to dismiss the complaint with or without a hearing or, after hearing both sides, he can uphold the complaint as justified. If he takes this latter course he can either make a declaration that the complaint is justified without any order, or else make an order which specifies the steps which must be taken before an application to register the instrument will be entertained. The CO has has the power to award costs to either side after a hearing. Appeals on points of law lie to the EAT.

THE TUC: A LEGAL PERSPECTIVE

The TUC plays a crucial role in inter- and intra-union relations. It has produced model rules and recommendations for the content of union rule books on such matters as the admission and discipline of members (TUC, 1970:141–4), it exercises authority over union organisational disputes by means of its 'Bridlington Principles', and it can deal with complaints about arbitrary exclusion or expulsion through its Independent Review Committee. These two latter matters will be dealt with in more detail. Before discussing them, however, mention should be made of the penalties for an affiliated union which fails to comply with a decision of the TUC or one of its committees. Rule 13 of the TUC's constitution entitles the TUC to discipline affiliated organisations. The ultimate sanction provided by this rule is the general council's power to suspend a union from membership until the next annual congress. The union is entitled to an appeal at the congress where the powers available to the delegates are re-admission, further suspension or expulsion. Rule 13 may be invoked against a union which refuses to accept TUC decisions made under the Bridlington procedure. It can also be used against a union which rejects the assistance of the general secretary or general council in an industrial dispute which affects other TUC affiliates, and against a union which the general council believes is involved in activities 'detrimental to the interests of the trade union movement or contrary to the declared principles or declared policies of Congress'.

Inter-union Disputes

The TUC's 'Principles Governing Relations between Unions' (the Bridlington Principles) apply to all affiliated unions. They are not intended to be legally binding on TUC unions but they are regarded as constituting 'a code of conduct accepted as morally binding by affiliated organisations' (TUC, 1979a:7).[18] Their aims are to minimise disputes over organisational rights between unions and to provide a forum to resolve them in the shape of a TUC disputes committee.

The principles have a long pedigree. They were extended and formalised at the congress held at Bridlington in 1939. They were expanded in 1969 by recommendations adopted by a special congress held at Croydon. The effect of the 'Croydon Principles' was to give the TUC considerably greater powers over both official and unofficial industrial action taken in furtherance of inter-union disputes. No affiliated union should authorise industrial action in pursuance of an inter-union dispute until the TUC has had the opportunity to consider the matter. Further, in the case of an unauthorised stoppage of work, the relevant union should take immediate steps to get its members back to work and to inform the TUC of the problem.

The principles create rules for transfers of members between unions and also set out the circumstances in which a union can commence organising activities where another union is already involved. A union should not accept new members without inquiry of their present or former union. It is up to the latter union to explain whether the members in question have tendered their resignations, or are in arrears with contributions, or are under discipline or penalty, or whether there are other reasons why an applicant should not be accepted by the inquiring union. This exchange should take place on forms prescribed by the TUC. If the inquiry does show that there are members who are under discipline, engaged in a trade dispute or in arrears with contributions, the requesting union is proscribed from accepting them into membership. If the relevant unions cannot agree about a person's entitlement to membership, the matter should be referred to the TUC and can ultimately form the basis of a decision by a disputes committee.

The issue of organisation rights is tackled by principle 5, which declares that 'no union shall commence organising activities at any establishment or undertaking in respect of any grade or grades of workers in which another union has the majority of workers employed and negotiates wages and conditions, unless by arrangement with that union.' In construing principle 5 it is important to consider the notes which are attached to it and which have equal status and validity. These notes stress the need for consultation between unions competing for members in the same area, and emphasise factors such as a union's previous recruitment efforts, the period of those efforts, and the extent of any difficulties it encountered. The notes also declare that a disputes committee will have regard to 'any existing collective bargaining or other representation arrangements in the establishment, company or industry.' Principle 5 acknowledges, therefore, the desirability of orderly and stable representation. Indeed, disputes committees have been keen to protect unions which enjoy an established position in bargaining. To

---

[18]   But on the possible legal enforceability of the Bridlington principles, see note 19 below and Lewis and Simpson, 1981:242, note 13.

that extent, principle 5 has been 'an important barrier to any extension of multi-unionism' (Ball, 1980:13; cf. Kalis, 1977).

If a disputes committee finds that a union has breached any of the principles, it may order the expulsion of persons accepted into membership. It is at this stage that there is likely to be friction between the TUC and the courts because a legal challenge based on the contract contained in the union rule book may come from the expelled member.[19] As Davies and Freedland (1984:617) argue, 'the whole [Bridlington] procedure is one in which the interests of the individual are disposed of by reference to collective interests; and this will always arouse the sensibilities of the courts'. Many of the recent alterations to the principles can best be seen as attempts by the TUC to shield their procedures from judicial review (Ball, 1980), a point which is underlined by an examination of the case law.

In one case,[20] it was held that an expulsion in conformity with an award of a disputes committee was unlawful. The fact that the union had no specific or express rule to cover this type of expulsion meant that it had acted beyond its powers. The court refused to accept the argument that a term providing the union with such authority could be implied into its rules. The response of the TUC was to advise all unions to incorporate into their rules a 'model rule' giving them the power of expulsion in compliance with a disputes committee award.

A decision of considerable importance for the TUC was that of Foster J in *Rothwell*.[21] This case arose out of the decision by APEX to agree to accept a transfer of engagements of the Staff Association General Accident (SAGA). ASTMS, which was already organising in General Accident, claimed that this amounted to organisation activities and was in breach of principle 5. A disputes committee agreed with ASTMS, recognised it as the appropriate union and ordered APEX to expel the members which it had recently acquired as a result of the merger. When APEX sought to comply with the award, Rothwell, a former general secretary of SAGA, sued APEX and the TUC to prevent the expulsions taking place. Although APEX had incorporated the TUC's model expulsion rule into its constitution, Foster J held that the purported expulsions were invalid because both the award of the disputes committee and the decision of the TUC to implement it were based on a mistaken interpretation of the Bridlington principles. The committee had acted unlawfully in three ways. First, the decision in favour of ASTMS went beyond the scope of its remit since it had only been asked to order a termination of the merger between APEX and SAGA. Second,

---

[19] The only instance of a union, as opposed to an aggrieved individual, seeking to challenge an award of a disputes committee was the abortive attempt by the Engineers' and Managers' Association to apply to the courts for a declaration that the TUC had acted unlawfully in supporting TASS's application for organisation rights at General Electric (see facts of *EMA v ACAS* [1980] ICR 215, HL and Ball, 1980:21–2).

[20] *Spring v National Amalgamated Stevedores and Dockers Society* [1956] 2 All ER 221. See too *Andrew v NUPE* (1955) The Times, 9 July.

[21] *Rothwell v APEX* [1976] ICR 211. See too *Walsh v AUEW* (1977) The Times, 15 July and *Phillips v NALGO* [1973] IRLR 19.

since ASTMS had recruited only 25 per cent of General Accident employees, an application of principle 5 was inappropriate in the circumstances. Third, SAGA's transfer of engagements to APEX did not amount to the commencing of organisation activities under principle 5. Foster J held further that the TUC had acted ultra vires by trying to force APEX to break its legal obligations concerning the merger.

The most fundamental aspect of *Rothwell* was the holding that discussions about the possibility of merging do not amount to organisation activities. As Ball (1980:17) has explained, this has caused disputes committees to make an uneasy distinction between traditional recruitment activities which are covered by principle 5 and talks about mergers which are legitimate. Moreover, the TUC has recognised that a dispute committee's inability to rule on mergers with non-affiliated unions is a significant omission. It advises that unions considering mergers with non-affiliates should consult with other unions and, in the event of disagreement, any union concerned should refer the matter to the TUC, but for conciliation only.

Undoubtedly the most fundamental challenge to the legality of Bridlington was mounted by Lord Denning in the Court of Appeal in *Cheall v APEX*.[22] APEX had decided to expel Cheall in order to comply with the decision of a disputes committee. When Cheall was given notice of the termination of his membership under the authority of the union's model rule, he raised an action in the High Court challenging the validity of that notice. Although Cheall was not employed under a closed shop, Lord Denning held that his purported expulsion was unlawful. He argued that everyone had the right to join the union of their choice. In support of this assertion he referred to Art. 11(1) of the European Convention on Human Rights, which enshrines a right to form and join trade unions. In his view, this right was an integral part of British law. Further, it was also a basic right not to be expelled from a union except for reasonable cause and in accordance with the rules of natural justice. Both the provisions of APEX's model rule and the decision of a disputes committee were, according to Lord Denning, unreasonable and contrary to public policy. This decision was reversed on appeal by the House of Lords, which held that there was nothing in law to prevent unions making arrangements between themselves which they considered to be in the best interests of their members in improving industrial relations and enhancing bargaining strength. Nor did the rules of natural justice apply to invalidate the award of the disputes committee or, in the circumstances, APEX's decision to expel in conformity with the TUC's ruling. But the door was left slightly ajar by Lord Diplock: if the effect of such an expulsion was that someone lost their job because of the existence of a closed shop, then different considerations might apply.

[22] [1982] ICR 543, CA; [1983] ICR 398, HL. See further Simpson (1983) and Chapter 2 (above) where the case is discussed from the point of view of freedom of association.

Independent Review Committee

The Donovan Commission (1968: paras. 658–69) suggested that a review body should be created to hear complaints concerning arbitrary exclusions or expulsions from unions. No such body was ever created by statute, although the IRA did contain provisions in s.65 prohibiting arbitrary or unreasonable discrimination against applicants or members. A similar provision contained in s.5 of TULRA was repealed by TULR(A)A in 1976. In response to this repeal, the TUC established its Independent Review Committee (IRC) in April 1976 to provide a voluntary forum for hearing cases alleging unreasonable exclusion or expulsion (see Ewing and Rees, 1981). Under its terms of reference, the IRC can only hear complaints from people who have been dismissed or who have been given notice of dismissal as a result of their exclusion or expulsion from a union where union membership is a condition of employment.

The IRC's awards are not legally binding but all TUC affiliated unions have agreed to abide by them. Its remedy is to recommend that a union admits or re-admits the complainant into membership; it has no authority to award compensation. The IRC can only hear a case if the complainant has exhausted all union appeals procedures. If a case goes to a hearing, the parties before it are the complainant and the union(s) involved. The employer who is a party to the closed shop, and whose decision to dismiss is a prerequisite for IRC involvement, has no right of appearance; nor is an award of the IRC effective against any employer. It has been claimed that this is a major weakness: if the IRC makes a recommendation that a complainant should be re-admitted into the union and the union complies, there is nothing that can be done to force the employer to offer reinstatement (IRRR, 1978).

There has been some recognition of this problem by the IRC itself, since it has introduced the novel concept of post-hearing conciliation to explore the possibility of finding an agreed solution in order to help the complainant find a way back into gainful employment. Moreover, Lord Wedderburn, the chairman of the IRC, has stated that 'once satisfied on the preliminary question that the rules have been observed, the Committee always goes on to inquire into the merits and reasonableness of the case presented both by the union and the complainant' (TUC, 1979b:391).

RIGHTS OF MEMBERS

The last two decades have witnessed an increasing tendency to subject internal union affairs to legal regulation. Although the Donovan Commission (1968: para. 622) found that 'it is unlikely that abuse of power by trade unions is widespread', it still recommended that the Chief Registrar of Friendly Societies be given a supervisory function over the content of union rules and that an independent review body should be created to deal with arbitrary exclusion and expulsions.[23] Section 65 of the IRA laid down a number of 'guiding principles' for trade union rules which forbade, among other things, arbitrary or unreasonable exclusion from membership and unfair or unreasonable disciplinary action. The original provisions of TULRA also proscribed arbitrary or unreasonable exclusion or expulsion from a trade union (s.5). Fresh provisions outlawing unreasonable exclusions or expulsions where a closed shop operates were enacted in EA 1980 ss.4 and 5. Moreover, the judge-made common law has played a major role in the trend towards intervention in internal union affairs.

The starting point for judicial involvement has traditionally been the contract of membership. It has been held repeatedly that the union rule book constitutes a contract between the individual member and the union or, perhaps, between the union members themselves.[24] There is no doubt that the fundamental assumption underpinning the court decisions is the freedom of the individual. Indeed, the contractual techniques which the courts have devised have been built around this precept. But it is not just the rules of private law which are relevant to internal union affairs. The courts have also relied upon concepts derived from public law, notably, the rules of natural justice.

Some judges have been prepared, however, to dig deeper into the public law chest to find ways of controlling union behaviour. Thus Lord Denning has perceived union rules which regulate membership as analogous to bye-laws. Although this view has been criticised in both the Court of Appeal and House of Lords,[25] Lord Denning returned to it in his judgment in *Cheall*. The most significant feature of the bye-law approach is that it gives the courts the ability to strike down union rules as being unreasonable. In other words, even if a union complies with the terms of its rule book, there can be no guarantee that it is acting lawfully since the rule which authorises the action might itself be unlawful. Clearly, such an approach would give the courts a wide power over all facets of union behaviour. But other judges have not been prepared to support Lord Denning in his bye-law theory, though it can be seen as the theoretical underpinning of ss.4 and 5 of EA 1980.

The courts, however, have not always been consistent with their application of public law notions to trade unions. It is a well known principle of public law that litigants should exhaust all their internal remedies before a court will entertain an application for review. This point was once accepted for trade union cases,[26] but, subsequently, the need to exhaust internal

---

[23] This was consistent with Kahn-Freund's argument (1970) that the protection of the individual from arbitrary exclusion by a union was complementary to protection from arbitrary dismissal by an employer.

[24] See Lord Macdermott's decision in *Bonsor v Musicians' Union* [1956] AC 104 for the idea that the contract is between a member and the other members.

[25] Per Diplock LJ in *Faramus v Film Artistes' Association* [1963] 2 QB 527, at 554, CA; per Lord Evershed [1964] AC 925, at 943, HL.

[26] *White v Kuzych* [1951] AC 585, PC.

procedures has not been regarded as a bar to any court proceedings.[27] Even where there is an express provision in the rule book requiring members to exhaust their domestic rights first, this will not bind the courts since their jurisdiction cannot be ousted.

Admission to a Union at Common Law

The lack of a contractual relationship between the union and the applicant for membership has made it difficult for the courts to find a theoretical basis for review in exclusion cases. Indeed, in two decisions the House of Lords construed the fact that the plaintiffs had been admitted wrongly into membership as meaning that they had never been members of the relevant unions.[28] In neither case was the House of Lords willing to disturb the discretion given to the unions to decide their own rules over membership. The *Faramus* case even recognised that it was legitimate for a union to control the supply of labour in a particular industry by specifying restrictive conditions for membership as part of its closed shop policy.

The concept of the 'right to work', however, provided the judges with a doctrinal rationalisation for their review of decisions on admission. This development has been carried out almost single-handedly by Lord Denning. Its essence is that powerful trade unions should not be permitted to prevent persons exercising their skills in their chosen area of employment. Although first articulated in 1952,[29] the right to work theory was used for the first time in 1966 in *Nagle v Feilden*[30] to invalidate the Jockey Club's refusal to grant a trainer's licence to a woman on the ground of her sex. Lord Denning declared that the primacy of a person's right to work gave the courts the authority to intervene where any organisation which exercised 'a predominant power over the exercise of a trade or profession' sought to reject an application 'arbitrarily or capriciously'.[31]

Edwards v SOGAT[32] constituted the most radical application of the doctrine. The starting point here was the recognition that the union's decision not to re-admit Edwards into membership meant loss of employment. In such circumstances, Lord Denning opined, 'the courts of this country will not allow so great a power to be exercised arbitrarily or capriciously or with unfair discrimination neither in the making of the rules nor in the enforcement of them'.[33] Wedderburn (1971:432) characterised this decision as 'a subversion of the democratic process of trade unions'.

How have other judges reacted to this theory? In the *Nagle* case both Salmon and Dankwerts LJJ referred to its existence, and in *Edwards* Sachs

---

[27] *Lawlor v UPW* [1965] Ch 712; *Leigh v NUR* [1970] Ch 326; *Radford v NATSOPA* [1972] ICR 484.
[28] See *Martin v Scottish TGWU* 1952 SC (HL) 91; *Faramus v FAA* [1964] AC 925, HL.
[29] *Lee v Showmen's Guild* [1952] 2 QB 329, CA.
[30] [1966] 2 QB 633, CA.
[31] ibid., at 646.
[32] [1971] Ch 354, CA.
[33] ibid., at 376.

LJ considered it to be a right of equal opportunity to obtain work. More recently in *McInnes v Onslow Fane*[34] Megarry V-C accepted that there exists a 'liberty to work'. Hepple (1981:80) suggested that the right to work is merely 'a reformulation in positive terms of the old doctrine of restraint of trade' applied from an individual standpoint. Certainly TULRA s.2(5) ensures that restraint of trade does not apply either to the purposes or the rules of a trade union. Slade J, however, acknowledged that the right to work was a category of public policy wider than restraint of trade allowing judicial intervention against job controls applied by unions and professional bodies.[35]

Elias (1979) has demonstrated the importance of *McInnes*. In that case Megarry V-C recognised that unions had to act fairly when exercising their authority to exclude or expel. This duty varied with the type of function exercised. In a forfeiture of membership case the rules of natural justice should be applied to their full extent. In other admission cases a union should ensure that its decision was reached honestly and without bias or caprice. But in a third category of case – the legitimate expectation case where someone would expect to have their membership confirmed or to be re-admitted – higher standards of fairness were required. The nature and extent of this duty, however, was never spelled out. The *McInnes* case went further than *Nagle* because it would apply procedural fairness to union admissions even where there is no closed shop.

Discipline and Expulsion at Common Law

There are two principal methods applied by the courts to control trade union disciplinary action. The first is the requirement that a union should comply strictly with its rules as a contract.[36] The second is the need for a union's procedures to conform with the rules of natural justice. Furthermore, courts should also take into account, if relevant, the Secretary of State's Closed Shop Code. This states (para.57) that unions should adopt clear and fair rules covering the offences for which disciplinary action can be taken, the appropriate penalties, the disciplinary procedure, the right to appeal and the appeals procedure.

Strict compliance with rules. Union rule books tend to provide for two types of disciplinary offence – the specific and the blanket offence. The latter entitles the union to take disciplinary action against a member for activity detrimental to the interests of the union. In both cases the courts have construed the provisions strictly. Even where there is no ambiguity in the terms of the specific offence, a union must ensure that it acts on the basis

---

[34] [1978] 3 All ER 211.
[35] *Greig v Insole* [1978] 3 All ER 449.
[36] For surveys of union rule books see Gennard et al. (1980) and IRRR (1982).

of those terms to the letter.[37] Moreover, where the rule itself is, in the opinion of the court, either ambiguous or capable of two meanings, then it will be interpreted in favour of the disciplined member.[38]

Where a member is alleged to have committed a 'blanket' offence, the traditional approach of the courts is to assess whether the facts proved are reasonably capable of establishing the offence or, alternatively, whether a reasonable tribunal would have come to the conclusion which the union's disciplinary committee came to on those facts. In *Kelly v NAT SOPA*,[39] for example, it was held that Kelly had not indulged in 'conduct detrimental to the interests of the Society' by taking daytime work when he was already employed by the Daily Mail at night. The essence of the union's case was that by taking daytime work he had made himself a danger to the colleagues he worked with at night. The court refused to accept that Kelly's extra work did make him a danger. There was no evidence to show that he was too tired to carry out his night work properly. But, in *Wolstenholme v Amalgamated Musicians' Union*[40] it was held that Wolstenholme had brought the union into 'discredit' by making unsupported allegations about irregularities at his branch and serious misconduct by local officials, which he later refused to withdraw. In neither of these cases was there any real attempt to consider whether the protection of the individual should override the collective interests of the union.

The need for such assessment took on considerable significance as a result of the Court of Appeal's decision in *Lee v Showmen's Guild*,[41] a case which continues to provide the basis for the courts' intervention in expulsion cases. Lee had been fined and subsequently expelled from the Guild for participating in 'unfair competition' by taking a site at a fair which the union had allocated to another member. Two important points were raised. First, the Court recognised that a decision to expel deprived a person of his livelihood. Second, although there was a reiteration of the traditional view that the task for the courts was to consider whether the facts were reasonably capable of supporting the decision reached, Lord Denning, in particular, spelled out the circumstances in which such a decision could be reviewed. He considered that union disciplinary committees exercised two functions: they construed the rules, which was a question of law, and they applied the rules to the facts. The fact that the second function could not in practice be separated from the first enlarged the scope for judicial intervention. Indeed, in the *Lee* case the Court of Appeal finally decided that the Guild had not applied the correct meaning to the phrase 'unfair competition' so that the facts did not establish the offence. It had come to a conclusion which no reasonable tribunal would have reached. Hence any purported expulsion

---

[37] The classic examples are *Bonsor* (note 4 above) and *Edwards* (note 32). A further example is *Blackall v National Union of Foundryworkers* (1923) 39 TLR 431 where Blackall's expulsion was considered invalid because he had been expelled two days earlier than the union's rules allowed. See also *MacLelland v NUJ* [1975] ICR 116.

[38] E.g. *Amalgamated Soc. of Carpenters v Braithwaite* [1922] 2 AC 440.

[39] (1915) 31 TLR 632.

[40] [1920] 2 Ch 388.

[41] [1952] 2 QB 329.

was invalid. The effect of this decision, therefore, was to allow the courts to substitute their own view of the meaning of a blanket offence for that of the union.

Industrial action. The manner in which the courts have extended contractual principles to deal with blanket offence cases is illustrated most vividly by the case law on unions' powers to discipline members who have failed to participate in industrial action (cf. Davies and Freedland, 1984:606–11). It is clear that this is an area where the tension between individual rights and collective interests is most sharply defined. This tension is also highlighted by the Closed Shop Code of Practice which specifies (paras. 61–2) circumstances where disciplinary action should not be taken against a member who has failed to participate in industrial action. A member should not be disciplined if he has crossed a picket line which the union has not authorised or which was not at his own place of work; or there are reasonable grounds for believing that the industrial action was unlawful; or the action would contravene a member's professional or other code of ethics; or it is in breach of a procedure agreement; or the action has not been affirmed in a secret ballot. The courts, of course, are entitled to take this advice into account in any case before them.

In *Esterman v NALGO*[42] the union had instructed members not to assist in administering local elections. Esterman defied this instruction and, in consequence, was to be disciplined by the union on the basis that she was guilty of conduct rendering her unfit for membership. Before a disciplinary meeting could be held, however, she sought an injunction in the High Court to prevent the meeting taking place. Not only did Templeman J entertain her application despite the fact that the domestic tribunal had not yet convened, he also held that any purported disciplinary proceedings were unlawful. Despite his assertion that his decision was based on the traditional analysis that no reasonable tribunal could have found Esterman guilty of any unfitness for membership, the real basis appeared to be the belief that union members, if asked to participate in industrial action have the right to question the authority and wisdom of the union in giving such instructions. This undermines the union's ability to maintain its collective authority and strength. As Davies (1975:114) has argued, it is a recipe for trade union weakness because 'it encourages union members to express themselves at the point of conflict with the employer, where the need for organisational solidarity is the greatest'. Equally the case was based on an interpretation of union rules which *assumed* the superiority of individual over collective interests (Kidner, 1976:94).

This approach has been followed in two subsequent cases where the courts again entertained actions prior to the disciplinary proceedings being exhausted. The apparent effect of these decisions is that industrial action has not only to comply strictly with the terms of the rule book, but also must not involve a member in breaching an agreement between the union and the

[42] [1974] ICR 625.

employer. Thus in *Partington v NALGO*[43] the expulsion of Partington, who had returned to work during an industrial dispute to provide emergency cover for Scottish Gas, was held invalid because the industrial action was in breach of an agreement between the union and the Gas Board. In *Porter v NUJ*[44] the ground on which the Court of Appeal found for Porter was that, since the industrial action was unconstitutional as there had been no ballot as required by the rules, any expulsion for refusal to participate in it must also be unlawful. The Law Lords in this case agreed with the principle of the Court of Appeal's decision but were not prepared to rule on the validity of the strike on interlocutory proceedings. Finally, in cases arising from the miners' strike 1984–5, injunctions were awarded to prevent disciplinary action being taken against members who refused to cross picket lines, which the courts categorised as unofficial.[45]

Natural justice. In relation to trade union disciplinary functions, the discipline tribunal is taken to operate as a quasi-judicial body. This means that the rules of natural justice require two things. First, a disciplined member must have a right to proper notice of the complaint and an opportunity to be heard by the appropriate committee. Second, the tribunal must act in an unbiased manner and reach an honest decision. These two requirements must be strictly observed.

The courts' approach to the first requirement is illustrated by the *Lawlor* case.[46] Lawlor had been expelled from the union on a resolution passed by the executive committee. He had been given no notice of the charge against him, nor any real opportunity of attending a hearing. In the circumstances of this case, the minimum requirements of natural justice were a notice of the charge or complaint and an opportunity to be heard in answer to it. Since Lawlor had been denied both, his expulsion was invalid. It is also clear that changing the nature of the charges during any disciplinary proceedings without giving the member fresh notice is a breach of the rules of natural justice.[47]

The other requirement is for an unbiased tribunal to adjudicate upon the merits of the case. Clearly, the disciplinary proceedings of trade unions are controlled by lay people and the law cannot demand the same level of impartiality that would be required of a judge or an arbitrator. Instead, their task is to have 'a will to reach an honest conclusion after hearing what was argued on either side and a resolve not to make their minds up beforehand'.[48]

An example of a case of alleged bias was *Roebuck v NUM (Yorkshire*

---

43 [1981] IRLR 537, Ct Sess. In the earlier case of *Silvester v National Union of Printing, Bookbinding and Paper Workers* (1966) 1 KIR 679 Goff J also considered the relevance of a trade agreement in construing the terms of the union rule book.
44 [1979] IRLR 404, CA; [1980] IRLR 404, HL.
45 *Clarke v Chadburn* [1984] IRLR 350; *Taylor v NUM (Derbyshire Area) (No.1)* [1984] IRLR 440.
46 *Lawlor v UPW* [1965] Ch 712.
47 *Annamunthodo v Oilfield Workers' Trade Union* [1961] AC 945, PC.
48 *White v Kuzych* [1951] AC 585, PC.

Area) (No.2),[49] where Roebuck had given evidence on behalf of a newspaper in a libel action brought by Arthur Scargill, then President of NUM's Yorkshire Area. Scargill believed that the giving of evidence against him amounted to 'conduct detrimental to the interests of the union'. The union's area council referred the matter to the area executive. The executive resolved to bring charges alleging conduct detrimental to the interests of the union. A further meeting of the executive held that these charges had been made out. All these meetings were chaired by Scargill, who participated in the hearing but did not vote on any resolution. Templeman J found that it was irrelevant to consider whether Scargill's presence and conduct had an influence on the result. The real issue concerned the fact that his presence at all stages of the discipline procedure gave the impression that the dice were loaded against Roebuck. The decision to discipline Roebuck, therefore, could not stand since justice had to be seen to be done.

Statutory Control of Admissions and Expulsions

In addition to their common law rights, individuals are protected from unreasonable exclusion or expulsion from a trade union under EA 1980 ss.4 and 5. This is a right to apply initially to an industrial tribunal for a declaration. There is also a right to receive compensation. The amount of compensation awarded depends upon whether the union has admitted or re-admitted the applicant into membership in accordance with the declaration. If the declaration has been complied with, the applicant may apply to a tribunal for compensation. The amount awarded cannot exceed the maximum of thirty times the maximum week's pay for a basic award for unfair dismissal plus the maximum compensatory award available in such cases. But if the applicant has not been admitted or re-admitted into membership the application for compensation will go to the EAT. In addition to the two heads of compensation already mentioned, that tribunal can make an additional award of fifty-two times a week's pay. The award of compensation can be reduced if the applicant fails to mitigate his loss or if he has caused or contributed to the rejection by the union.[50]

A major reason given for this measure was that it was part of a legislative package the aim of which was to control the abuses of the closed shop.[51] It is for this reason that the statutory protection against unreasonable exclusion or expulsion from a trade union applies only where the person is in or is seeking employment in respect of which a UMA operates (s.4(1)). The concept of reasonableness is at the nub of these provisions. Section 4(5) states that 'whether a trade union has acted reasonably or unreasonably shall be determined in accordance with equity and the substantial merits of the case'. It is made plain, however, that compliance or non-compliance with the union rule book will not be conclusive in assessing the reasonableness or

---

[49] [1978] ICR 676.
[50] *Howard v NGA* [1984] IRLR 489, EAT.
[51] Accepted by the EAT in *Goodfellow v NATSOPA* [1985] IRLR 3.

otherwise of the union's conduct (s.4(5)). This creates, as Lewis and Simpson (1981:111) argue, 'a whole range of uncertainties for trade unions', particularly in respect of their recruitment and disciplinary functions.

Three important points have emerged from the case law. First, s.4 does not prevent a union from creating its own categories of membership,[52] and, further, the provision is not effective where a person was refused transfer to another category.[53] Second, the state of unemployment among union members in a particular industry can be taken into account as a factor in deciding whether a union's refusal to admit was reasonable. This point was established by the EAT in the *Howard* case, which followed the advice in the Closed Shop Code (para.56) that the number of applicants may be important for admission policies where unemployment might undermine negotiated terms and conditions of employment. Third, the concept of unreasonable expulsion in s.4(2) is not broad enough to cover cases of 'constructive' expulsion, that is, where the union's conduct is such as to give the member no alternative but to resign.[54]

The value of the statutory protections is open to question as far as individual applicants are concerned. Use of the legislation has been at best patchy, and the cases have not uncovered clear and obvious examples of union malpractice. It is arguable, in fact, whether disaffected members might fare better under the IRC's procedures (Ewing and Rees, 1983). Further, the provisions may cause friction with the TUC's operation of its Bridlington procedure and, as already suggested, may have dangers for the principle of union autonomy. It is arguable that the real purpose behind ss.4 and 5 is to weaken union negotiating power. This is particularly true as far as expulsion for non-participation in industrial action is concerned. When assessing reasonableness, the tribunal has to take cognisance of the Closed Shop Code's advice about disciplinary action against those refusing to participate in industrial action (see above).

TRADE UNION DEMOCRACY

Although most unions possess certain common features of government like the branch, the delegate conference and the national executive, they vary markedly both in terms of their internal structure and in the methods by which their officers are appointed or elected (Undy et al., 1981). Forms of government, moreover, vary from the federal structure of the NUM, to the trade group structure of the TGWU, the regional system of the GMBATU, and the centralised decision-making system of the EETPU. Equally, there is no uniform system of election for union officers or officials (see Undy and Martin, 1984:ch. 2).

---

[52] *NATSOPA v Kirkham* [1983] IRLR 70.
[53] Discussed by the EAT in both *Kirkham* and *Goodfellow*.
[54] *McGhee v TGWU* [1985] IRLR 198.

Rule Book as Contract and Constitution

The courts treat the rule book as both the contract of membership and the constitution of the union. Members' rights to participate in the union's affairs, in the eyes of the law, depend just as much upon a strict construction of the rule book as their rights concerning discipline or expulsion. In certain circumstances these two elements – the right to participate in union affairs and the right not to be disciplined save in conformity with the rules – can operate in tandem. Thus in *Clarke v Chadburn*[55] the court was at pains to ensure that a purported rule change was not implemented in breach of the union's procedure for mandating area councils. This rule change would have allowed the union to discipline miners who had crossed picket lines. Further, in *Taylor v NUM (Derbyshire Area) (No.1)*[56] a declaration was made that the suspension of a number of working miners was void and an injunction was awarded to prevent the union disciplining them for continuing to cross picket lines, since the strike had been called in breach of the area rules.

The importance of using balloting procedures was repeatedly stressed in the cases raised by working miners against various areas of the NUM during the miners' strike of 1984–5. In most of these cases, however, the judges relied on a strict construction of the rule book to establish the requirement for conducting ballots. In *Taylor v NUM (Derbyshire Area) (No.1)* Nicholls J held that the local area was required by its rules to obtain 55 per cent support in a ballot for strike action before such action could be official, and in *Taylor v NUM (Yorkshire Area)*[57] it was held that a ballot held three years previously was too remote to be acceptable under the rules. In both cases the judges accepted that to all intents and purposes the strike constituted national action, which was also unlawful in the absence of a national ballot. In a subsequent case[58] Vinelott J held that it was ultra vires for the union to authorise expenditure on strike action which had been called in breach of the area's rules. Further, the officials who had misapplied union moneys in this way were in breach of the fiduciary duty which they owed to the members, and could be personally liable for such unauthorised expenditure. There is also a parallel between the miners' cases and other litigation involving disciplinary action for failure to participate in industrial action: the miners' cases demonstrated the readiness of the judges to issue interlocutory injunctions to restrain the repetition or continuance of alleged unlawful behaviour. Indeed, in the *Yorkshire* case Nicholls J went further by awarding a mandatory order on interlocutary proceedings to ensure that branches held committee meetings and elections.

In some cases arising out of strikes, however, the union has successfully defended the constitutionality of its action. In *Sherard v AUEW*[59] members

---

55 [1984] IRLR 350. Exceptionally a declaration was awarded on interlocutory proceedings.
56 [1984] IRLR 440.
57 [1984] IRLR 445.
58 *Taylor v NUM (Derbyshire Area) (No.3)* [1985] IRLR 99.
59 [1973] ICR 421.

of the union sought an injunction to prevent a one-day strike called by the national executive to protest against the government's counter-inflation legislation. They argued that the strike was political in nature and contrary to the union's rules. But the Court of Appeal held that the union's rules were wide enough to cover strikes which had a political object, and that the rules also gave the executive power to call such action.

It is clear that a union must comply not only with the terms of its own rule book but also with that of any organisation to which it is affiliated. Thus in *AUEW (TASS) v AUEW(E)*[60] it was held that the Engineering Section's rule change which enabled it to increase the size of its national committee was unlawful. It was held that the Engineering Section had to comply not only with the requirements of its own rule book but also with that of the federal organisation. Since the effect of the purported rule change meant that the Engineering Section had created a larger national committee than it was permitted to send to the national conference of the federal AUEW, such a change was in breach of the rules of the AUEW.

Notwithstanding the general requirement for strict compliance with the rule book, the circumstances in which an individual member can complain to the courts about irregularities in union procedures may sometimes be uncertain. In *Cotter v NUS*[61] the Court of Appeal adopted the company law principle of 'the rule in *Foss v Harbottle*' to prevent members challenging a resolution of the union passed at a special general meeting which authorised a loan to the 'Miners Non-Political Movement'. The thrust of this rule is that the majority of members should govern the administration of the association and not the courts. Where it is claimed that a wrongful act has been committed against the union, the proper plaintiff may be the organisation itself rather than the individual member. One exception where the rule does not apply is where the union engages in ultra vires activity. A recent example of the application of this exception is *Taylor v NUM (Derbyshire Area) (No.3)*,[62] where Vinelott J held that members of the area union could seek an injunction against the union restraining use of its funds in support of strike action in breach of the rule book. Other exceptions have also been allowed. In *Edwards v Halliwell*[63] it was accepted that an individual member had standing to raise an action where the effect of the procedural irregularity was to invade the personal and individual rights of the members. Further, in *Hodgson v NALGO*[64] Goulding J recognised the practical difficulties of an over-zealous application of the rule in *Foss v Harbottle*. He held that where it was impossible to go through the appropriate procedure to correct the alleged irregularity before the decision was implemented, the individual should have title to sue.

Another area of concern for the judiciary is the union's treatment of its officers. In most cases the court's task involves interpreting the rule book as

[60] [1983] IRLR 108.
[61] [1929] 2 Ch 58.
[62] [1985] IRLR 99.
[63] [1950] 2 All ER 1064.
[64] [1972] 1 All ER 15.

a contract. Thus in *Leigh v NUR*[65] it was held that the union was not entitled to insist that any candidate for the office of president had to belong to the Labour Party. Even though the president was required by the rules of the union to attend TUC and Labour Party conferences, this did not mean that a person had to be a member of the Labour Party at the time of nomination.

It is also clear that the rules of natural justice may apply in relation to a union's dismissal of an employed official. As in the case of a member who is being expelled, union officers are entitled to notice of the charge against them and the right to a hearing since the courts have accepted that the decision to dismiss an official is a judicial one.[66]

The rules of natural justice may apply to dismissals, but what of the circumstances where a duly elected shop steward's credentials are not renewed by the union? This problem arose in *Breen v AEU*[67] where an experienced shop steward found that his election to that office was disallowed. Lord Denning MR argued that since Breen had been a shop steward for a number of years he had a legitimate expectation that the district committee would approve his election. If there were reason why approval was not to be forthcoming, he was entitled to be heard in his defence. But the majority held that, in the absence of a special reason, there was no requirement that Breen should be present and entitled to speak when the committee deliberated on the renewal of his credentials. All that was required of the committee in the circumstances was that it should reach its decision in good faith. The majority would have been prepared to follow Lord Denning's decision, however, had they been able to upset the finding of fact of the judge at first instance that an unsubstantiated allegation of fraud against Breen was not taken into account by the district committee. There is no doubt, therefore, that in certain circumstances the full principles of natural justice could be applied to a candidate who has been refused office.

Ballots by Statute

A ballot for whatever purpose may be required under union rules, a point which is amply demonstrated by the saga of litigation arising from the 1984–5 miners' strike. Such a requirement is of course consistent with the principle of union autonomy from the state. But the legislation enacted since 1979 has marked the most radical and significant statutory intrusion into internal union government through the policy of promoting the use of ballots. There are two main aspects of this policy. First, s.1 of EA 1980 and ensuing regulations provide for a scheme which is administered by the CO for the refund of expenses incurred by independent trade unions in the

---

[65] [1971] 2 QB 175. See now TUA 1984 s.2(1) which proscribes requiring that a candidate in an executive election, whether directly or indirectly, be a member of a political party. Cf. *Birch v NUR* [1950] Ch 602. See further Chapter 11 below.

[66] *Stevenson v United Road Transport Union* [1977] ICR 893.

[67] [1971] 2 QB 175.

conduct of postal ballots. In addition, EA 1980 s.2 provides a procedure whereby an independent trade union can request an employer to permit a ballot to be held on his premises. The other and more important intervention is brought about by the provisions of TUA 1984. This requires unions to hold secret ballots for the election of members to their executive committees (see below), for the calling of industrial action (see Chapter 6) and for the maintenance of their political funds (see Chapter 11).

State subsidy. The EA 1980 s.1 was enacted to encourage unions to hold secret ballots in the hope that 'responsible' union leaders would be elected (DE, 1983:para.7; cf. Undy and Martin, 1984:ch.5). Thus it enables the Secretary of State to create a scheme for the refund of certain expenses incurred in conducting secret ballots. The scheme which was actually introduced is narrower, however, since it applies only to postal ballots and not to non-postal or workplace ballots. It is an essential requirement of the regulations[68] that those voting should return their ballot papers by post either to the union or to another person responsible for counting the votes. The scheme restricts the purposes for which funds for ballots are available. Thus it covers ballots to amend the union's rules and amalgamation ballots required by the 1964 Act. It also applies to ballots for elections to the union's executive either as required by the union's own rules or by the Act of 1984, or elections for the positions of president, chairman, secretary or treasurer or any other position which the person elected holds as an employee of the union. Further, the scheme covers ballots to obtain members' views on the calling or ending of industrial action or to ascertain members' views on the acceptance or rejection of a proposal made by the employer regarding remuneration, hours of work, level of performance, holidays or pensions. Ballots under the 1913 Act are also covered. But the scheme still does not apply to ballots for the election of employee representatives.

The scheme also lays down conditions about the conduct of the ballot which have to be satisfied before payment can be made. The first condition is that the method of voting must be by the marking of a voting paper. Any person voting should be allowed to vote without interference or constraint from the trade union. Also, so far as reasonably practicable, any voter should have a voting paper sent to his or her home address, and be given a convenient opportunity to vote by post. Finally, the voting papers must be fairly counted, and the outcome of the ballots determined solely on the votes cast.

Executive elections. Part I of the TUA requires a ballot to ensure that voting members (including ex officio members with a vote) of a union's principal executive committee are elected to it and are re-elected at least every five years (see Kidner, 1984). This requirement applies despite anything to the contrary in the union's rule book. Forms of indirect election like voting through a delegate or the block branch vote are excluded. The

Act demands that all members of the union should have an equal opportunity to vote and that those voting can exercise their rights without any interference or constraint on the part of the union. So far as reasonably practicable, the voting must be in secret and the person voting must be entitled to return the ballot paper without incurring any direct cost. It is clear that the preferred system of voting under the Act is by postal ballot. But s.3 does allow a union to hold a workplace ballot where it is satisfied that such a ballot can meet the necessary requirements of secrecy and freedom from interference or constraint. It is for the union to make such a decision and it must be prepared to show that it was held on reasonable grounds. If a workplace ballot is chosen it must take place immediately before, after or during working hours at the member's place of work (or a more convenient place) without direct cost to that member. In order to assess who is entitled to vote, the Act places a novel and onerous obligation on trade unions to compile and thereafter maintain, by means of a computer or otherwise, a register of the names and addresses of their members. It is permissible under the Act for a union to maintain separate constituencies for executive elections where there is authority in the rules. Thus seats can be restricted to members in particular occupations or trades, geographical areas, or sections of the union. As far as being a candidate is concerned, s.2(9) creates a general right not to be unreasonably excluded from standing for office. It is arguable that this right is infringed where a union prohibits members of a particular political party from so standing. There is also an obligation on the union not to require, whether directly or indirectly, that a candidate be a member of a particular political party. This provision reinforces the decision in the *Leigh* case, discussed above.

Part I is enforced through rights provided to every member of the union. Complaints that there has been a breach of the Act can be made by a member either to the High Court (Court of Session in Scotland) or the CO. The CO, however, has power to make a declaration only. The declaration specifies the breaches of the Act which the union has committed. The more potent remedy – the enforcement order – is available only before the courts. The courts can make a declaration where the CO has refused one and, of course, they have the power to make an enforcement order which can be issued along with the declaration or after it, since an enforcement order can also be made where the CO has awarded a declaration but it has not been complied with. The order may require the union to secure the holding of an election, to take specified steps to remedy its breach of the Act, and to abstain from specified acts so that a repetition of the breach does not take place. If the enforcement order is not observed, any member (and not just the one who made the initial application) can apply to the courts to enforce obedience. The final sanction under the Act, therefore, is through contempt of court proceedings.

Part I of the Act came into force on 1 October 1985. Its impact depends to a large extent on the willingness of members to complain about breaches of the Act by their unions. A union, however, ignores these provisions at its peril, for it cannot guarantee down to the last member that no action will be raised.

CONCLUSION

At the beginning of this chapter it was suggested that the legislation enacted since 1979 constitutes the state's most extensive intrusion into the internal affairs of trade unions. It is clear that state policy has moved away from merely providing a framework in which unions can operate effectively free from unnecessary legal restraint to one in which a great deal of their activity is subject to legislative standards. Thus their admission and expulsion procedures are subject to scrutiny by a tribunal where there is a UMA; they must follow the recommendations in the Closed Shop Code on the treatment of members and applicants; and, perhaps most fundamental of all, they must adhere to detailed statutory requirements in their executive elections, in the methods used for consulting members before industrial action and as regards their maintenance of a political fund.

Yet it is arguable that these statutory innovations were anticipated to some extent by the judiciary in their development of the common law rules applicable to cases involving trade unions. Thus the concepts of the right to work and of 'fair treatment' in union admission procedures provide the courts with a similar jurisdiction to that exercised by the tribunals and the EAT under EA 1980 ss.4–5. In the sphere of union democracy, while the courts have been on the whole content to rely on a strict construction of the rule book, there appears to be an underlying theme that union decisions should be implemented only after the widest possible consultation with the membership. Again this foreshadowed the legislative intervention in the form of the TUA. But perhaps the clearest example of the way in which the judges have anticipated statutory developments is their willingness to intervene in cases where disciplinary action is taken against a member because of a failure to participate in industrial action. This complex interplay reinforces the combined effect of judicial and legislative policies on trade union government and democracy.

Bibliography

Ball, Chris. 1980. 'The Resolution of Inter-Union Conflict: The TUC's Reaction to Legal Intervention'. *Industrial Law Journal*, 9 (March), 13–27.

Certification Officer (CO). 1976–1983. *Annual Reports of the Certification Officer 1975–1982*. London: Certification Office for Trade Unions and Employers' Associations.

Davies, Paul. 1975. 'Refusal by Individual Member to Follow Union Instructions'. *Industrial Law Journal*, 4 (June), 112–14.

——, and Mark Freedland. 1984. *Labour Law: Text and Materials*. 2nd edn. London: Weidenfeld & Nicolson.

Department of Employment (DE). 1983. *Democracy in Trade Unions*. Cmnd 8778. London: HMSO.

Department of Employment and Productivity (DEP). 1969. *In Place of Strife: A Policy for Industrial Relations*. Cmnd 3888. London: HMSO.

Donovan. 1968. Royal Commission on Trade Unions and Employers' Associations 1965–1968. *Report*. Cmnd 3623. London: HMSO.

Elias, Patrick. 1973. 'Trade Union Amalgamations: Patterns and Procedures'. *Industrial Law Journal*, 2 (September), 125–36.

——. 1979. 'Admission to Trade Unions'. *Industrial Law Journal*, 8 (June), 111–13.

——, Brian Napier and Peter Wallington. 1980. *Labour Law: Cases and Materials*. London: Butterworths.

Ewing, K.D., and W.M. Rees. 1981. 'The TUC Independent Review Committee and the Closed Shop'. *Industrial Law Journal*, 10 (June), 84–100.

——, and W.M. Rees. 1983. 'Exclusion from Trade Union Membership'. *Industrial Law Journal*, 12 (June), 106–9.

Gennard, John, Mark Gregory and Stephen Dunn. 1980. 'Throwing the Book: Trade Union Rules on Admission, Discipline and Expulsion'. *Employment Gazette*, 88 (June), 591–601.

Grunfeld, C. 1964. 'Trade Union (Amalgamations, etc.) Act, 1964'. *Modern Law Review*, 27 (November), 693–704.

——. 1966. *Modern Trade Union Law*. London: Sweet & Maxwell.

Hepple, Bob. 1981. 'A Right to Work?'. *Industrial Law Journal*, 10 (June), 65–83.

Industrial Relations Review and Report (IRRR). 1978. 'Independent Review Committee Describes its Methods'. *Industrial Relations Review and Report*, no. 184 (September), 4–5.

——. 1982. 'Union Procedures on the Admission and Expulsion of Members – A Survey of Current Practice'. *Industrial Relations Review and Report*, no. 272 (May), 2–7.

Kahn Freund, Otto. 1970. 'Trade Unions, the Law and Society'. *Modern Law Review*, 33 (May), 241–67.

——. 1983. *Labour and the Law*. 3rd edn. Ed. and intr. by Paul Davies and Mark Freedland. London: Stevens.

Kalis, P.J. 1977. 'The Adjudication of Inter-Union Membership Disputes: The TUC Disputes Committee Revisited'. *Industrial Law Journal*, 6 (March), 19–34.

Kidner, Richard. 1976. 'The Individual and the Collective Interest in Trade Union Law'. *Industrial Law Journal*, 5 (June), 90–106.

——. 1984. 'Trade Union Democracy: Election of Trade Union Officers'. *Industrial Law Journal*, 13 (December), 193–211.

Lewis, Roy, and Bob Simpson. 1981. *Striking a Balance? Employment Law after the 1980 Act*. Oxford: Martin Robertson.

Rideout, R.W. 1965. 'The Content of Trade Union Disciplinary Rules'. *British Journal of Industrial Relations*, 3 (July), 153–63.

Simpson, Bob. 1983. 'The TUC's Bridlington Principles and the Law'. *Modern Law Review*, 46 (September), 635–43.

Trades Union Congress (TUC). 1970. *TUC Report 1969*. London: TUC.

——. 1979a. *TUC Disputes Principles and Procedures*. London: TUC.

——. 1979b. *TUC Report 1978*. London: TUC.

Undy, R., V. Ellis, W.E.J. McCarthy and A.M. Halmos. 1981. *Change in Trade Unions: The Development of UK Unions since 1960*. London: Hutchinson.

——, and R. Martin. 1984. *Ballots and Trade Union Democracy*. Oxford: Blackwell.

Wedderburn, K.W. (*Lord*). 1971. *The Worker and the Law*. 2nd edn. Harmondsworth: Penguin.

11   Trade Unions and Politics

Keith Ewing

Collective bargaining is only one of the ways trade unions seek to promote their members' interests. Also important is the development of political action 'to establish and maintain the legal and economic conditions in which unions can flourish' (Flanders, 1970:30). Political activity takes several forms, but perhaps the most important, yet the most controversial, is the close links which the unions have with the Labour Party. In 1983, 47 unions affiliated 6.1 million members to the Party, this accounting for 79 per cent of the income to Labour's general fund. In addition, the unions donated the bulk of the funds used by the Party to fight the general election in that year and they are the source of much of the money made available to constituency parties. But by no means all British trade unions are affiliated to Labour, as is evident from the fact that also in 1983 there were 10 million members in 97 organisations affiliated to the TUC. Yet while the non-affiliated unions are significant — they include NALGO and the civil service unions — their non-affiliation does not seriously suggest that organised labour can function effectively without a foothold in the political arena, nor does it undermine the important role of the Labour Party in securing that foothold. For not only does the Party continue directly to represent a substantial number of trade unionists, but even the so-called non-political unions have some influence in its affairs through bodies such as the TUC–Labour Party Liaison Committee, which has played an important part in shaping Labour's economic strategy (Elliott, 1978:31).

The flow of money from the unions for political purposes has always been closely controlled by law. In 1908 WV Osborne, the secretary of the Walthamstow branch of the railwaymen's union, sought a declaration that the compulsory political levy of his union was unlawful and an injunction to restrain the union from raising and distributing money for political purposes. The case turned mainly on the Trade Union Acts 1871–6 — organised labour's charter of freedom — which for the first time conferred a legal status upon the unions and brought them within the law. For the purposes of this legislation trade unions were defined as meaning any combination for the regulation of relations between masters and men or for the imposition of restrictive conditions on any trade or employment.[1] Both the Court of Appeal and the House of Lords held that because the definition did not

---

[1]   Trade Union (Amendment) Act 1876 s.16. (For the current definition of a trade union, see Chapter 10 above).

make any reference to political action, this was not contemplated by Parliament as being a lawful object of trade unionism, and therefore was beyond the powers of a union registered under the Acts.[2] This was clearly a great threat to the future of the Labour Party, with injunctions being imposed subsequently on a considerable number of other unions (Ewing, 1982:38). If this process had continued the Party would have been slowly starved to death. The Liberal Government of the day responded in two different ways. First, in 1911 public money was made available to provide salaries for the hitherto unpaid MPs. This at least provided Labour MPs with a guaranteed source of income and relieved the Party of what had been a substantial burden. Second, the government introduced a Bill to remove the legal restraints on trade union political spending, it being readily accepted that trade unions had a right to seek the realisation of their goals by representation in Parliament and that they should not be disabled from so doing by economic and legal barriers (Ewing, 1982:41).

The Liberal Government was unwilling to reverse *Osborne* completely, however, largely because the closed shop allowed unions in effect to require workers to make a political contribution as a condition of obtaining or retaining a particular employment (Ewing, 1982:43). The TUA 1913 therefore imposed a number of preconditions with which unions had to comply before they could lawfully incur political expenditure as defined by the Act which (as amended) is still in force.

Unions are required to ballot their members on a resolution for the adoption of political objects (s.3(1)). If a majority of the members voting in the ballot approve, the union may adopt rules to establish a separate political fund which alone can be used for the purpose of financing the political objects. The rules must provide that every member has a right to be exempt from the obligation to contribute to the fund (s.3(1)(a)), a measure which is reinforced by the additional requirement that individuals exercising this right must not be denied any of the benefits of the union, or exposed to any disability or disadvantage (except in relation to the control and management of the political fund) for so doing (s.3(1)(b)). Breach of any of the political fund rules may be enforced by an aggrieved member making a complaint to the government appointed Certification Officer (CO) who inherited this jurisdiction from the Chief Registrar of Friendly Societies (EPA s.7). If, after a hearing, the CO concludes that a breach of the political fund rules has been committed, he may make such an order for remedying the breach as he thinks just under the circumstances (s.3(2)). An appeal lies on a point of law from a decision of the CO to the EAT (s.5A), from there to the Court of Appeal, and ultimately to the House of Lords.

The balance struck by the 1913 Act between the collective and individual interest was generally much more favourable to the individual than that struck by the law of many other western democracies on this issue. In Sweden and in the federal laws of Australia and Canada, trade unionists have no legally enforceable right to claim exemption from the obligation to

---

[2] *Amalgamated Society of Railway Servants v Osborne* [1909] Ch 163, CA; [1910] AC 87, HL, cf. *Steele v South Wales Miners' Federation* [1907] 1 KB 361.

finance the political activities of their unions (Ewing, 1982:ch.8). Yet the 1913 Act has never been fully accepted as striking a fair balance and its terms have since been revised on two occasions. The first revision was made by the Trade Disputes and Trade Unions Act 1927, passed in the wake of the general strike, which altered the arrangements for paying the levy from a system of contracting-out to one of contracting-in, whereby union members were presumed unwilling to pay unless they had positively agreed to do so. The 1913 settlement was restored by the post-war Labour Government in 1946,[3] and a subsequent attempt to re-introduce the 1927 arrangement was considered but rejected by the Donovan Commission (1968:para.924). The second major revision of the 1913 Act was by the TUA 1984, Part III of which implemented proposals raised in the Green Paper *Democracy in Trade Unions* (DE, 1983), in which trade union political activity was subjected to a wide-ranging examination. The major change introduced by the 1984 Act is the requirement that unions periodically ballot their members for approval to continue to pursue political objects. But although this is the principal change, it is not the only one. The Act extends the definition of political objects; it limits the potential sources of financing of trade union political funds; and it prohibits the practice where, because of the operation of the check-off, a political levy is deducted from the wages of contracted-out members against their wishes.[4]

POLITICAL OBJECTS

The key to the 1913 and 1984 Acts is the definition of political objects. Where the action in question is outside the terms of the definition, unions are free to spend money from general funds and members have no right to contract out of that expenditure. Also, unions which do not have a political fund may lawfully engage in this expenditure without the need for such a fund. As originally enacted, s.3(3) of the 1913 Act defined political objects to mean expenditure in relation to representation in Parliament and local government, and also expenditure on the holding of political meetings and the distribution of political literature. In the Green Paper (DE, 1983:paras.103–4) the government argued that s.3(3) was out of date and too narrowly drawn. First, the 1913 definition did not apply to expenditure on elections for the European Assembly, and as a result unions could meet any expenditure in relation to these elections from their general funds. Second, the definition pre-dated the use of radio, television, film and video for political purposes and it was unclear to what extent the existing definition applied to such publicity. Third, the administration of the 1913 Act had revealed a number of anomalies, one example being that while the definition applied to expenses incurred in distributing political literature, it did not

---

³ Trade Disputes and Trade Unions Act 1946.
⁴ This chapter's analysis of the 1984 Act draws heavily on Ewing (1984b). The author is grateful to the editor of the *Industrial Law Journal* for permission to use the material.

apply to expenses incurred in the printing or preparation of the literature. These alleged defects have been cleared up by the amended definition of political objects which was introduced by s.17 of the 1984 Act.

The amended s.3(3) of the 1913 Act is written in wide and expansive terms, though it is perhaps not significantly wider than the old definition as is sometimes claimed. Section 3(3)(a) and (b) expressly apply to contributions to the funds of a political party; the payment of expenses incurred directly or indirectly by a political party; and the provision of any service or property for use by or on behalf of a political party. A contribution is defined to include affiliation fees and loans (s.3(3C)), and would also cover payments to Labour's election fund. Expenses incurred by a party would catch matters such as salaries, rents and administration. And in addition to buildings, 'property in this context could include equipment such as computers and printing presses. Services that unions might provide could include the provision of staff as, say, research assistants or facilities such as transport ... mailing services and data processing'.[5] Although in contrast the original definition of political objects did not expressly refer to donations to political parties, it was readily assumed that these were covered, on the ground that they were made 'in furtherance' of the defined objects.[6] In fact it was also held that the original definition was wide enough to require the unions to use their political funds to finance the provision of new headquarters for the Labour Party.[7] In the view of the EAT, 'whatever else is comprehended in the word "furtherance", the expenditure of money in providing premises for the benefit of a political party which, to the knowledge of the union, will in the ordinary course of performing its functions as a political party use those premises for the purposes specified in [the definition of political objects] is undoubtedly expenditure in furtherance of those objects'.[8]

Section 3(3)(c) relates to electoral matters and covers expenditure in connection with the registration of electors, the selection of any candidate for political office, and the candidature itself. In addition, s.3(3)(d) applies to expenditure incurred in the maintenance of any holder of a public office.[9] A candidate is defined as meaning a candidate for selection to a political office and includes a prospective candidate (s.3(3C)). This is broadly similar to the provisions contained in the original s.3(3), though there are some important differences. These arise from the definition of political office, which now means not only the office of MP or membership of a local authority, but also membership of the European Assembly, and any position within a political party (s.3(3C)). This last provision would cover expenditure incurred in the election of a Labour Party leader or deputy leader, an inclusion which is ensured by the fact that s.3(3)(c) applies also to the holding of a ballot by the union in connection with any election to political

---

5 HC Standing Committee F, 28 February 1984, 1316.
6 *Parkin v ASTMS* [1980] IRLR 188.
7 *ASTMS v Parkin* [1983] IRLR 448.
8 ibid. at 453.
9 On the meaning of maintenance in this context, see *ASTMS v Parkin* [1983] IRLR 448.

office. There was some doubt as to whether this expenditure was covered before the 1984 Act. It is true that the original definition of political objects included the expenditure of money on the holding of political meetings or on the distribution of political literature. In *Coleman v POEU*,[10] however, the CO held that it was aimed at expenditure on literature or meetings held by a party which has or seeks to have MPs, or directly and expressly in support of such a party. This could have been interpreted to exclude meetings held not by a party but by factions, and also by organisations other than political parties.

Section 3(3)(e) applies to expenditure on the holding of any conference or meeting by or on behalf of a political party, or of any other meeting the main purpose of which is the transaction of business in connection with a political party. It is expressly provided that expenditure incurred by delegates or participants (but apparently not observers) in connection with their attendance shall be treated as expenditure incurred on the holding of the conference or meeting (s.3(3A)). Again, much of this expenditure would have been caught by the original definition of political objects, which applied to the holding of political meetings. It is true that this was qualified in the sense that it did not cover expenditure on the holding of meetings where the main purpose was the furtherance of statutory objects, a term which was defined to relate directly to industrial relations issues.[11] In *Richards v NUM*,[12] however, the qualification was restrictively interpreted: if a union made a payment towards the holding of a meeting by a political party, this would be a political meeting — and so within the scope of the political objects — unless the main purpose of the party holding the meeting was to promote the statutory objects. In practice that was not likely to arise very often, with the result that a contribution to a meeting organised by a political party would normally have had to be met by political funds. It appears then that this aspect of the 1984 amendment may not significantly extend the definition of political objects, though as initially drafted it was written in much wider terms and applied to any meetings at which the business of a political party was transacted.[13]

The most controversial part of the amended definition is contained in s.3(3)(f). This concerns expenditure on the production, publication or distribution of any literature, document, film, sound recording or advertisement, the main purpose of which is to persuade any person to vote or not to vote for a political party or candidate. This modernises the original definition, though in enacting s.3(3)(f) it is clear that the government also

---

10 [1981] IRLR 247, at 430.
11 Statutory objects were defined by TUA 1913 s.1(2) to mean 'the regulation of relations between workmen and masters, or between workmen and workmen, or between masters and masters, or the imposing of restrictive conditions on the conduct of any trade or business, and also the provision of benefits to members'. This was repealed by the TUA 1984 s.17(3).
12 [1981] IRLR 247.
13 This would have meant, for example, that trade union annual conferences would have had to have been financed exclusively from the political fund if any political fund business was transacted in any of the sessions. A conference is a single meeting rather than a series of meetings. See *Parkin*'s case (CO, 1984:57.)

had other targets in its sights, namely, the electoral expenditure of public sector unions concerned to protect their members' interests in the face of privatisation and cuts. The £1 million campaign against the cuts conducted by NALGO before and during the 1983 general election campaign was singled out as a clear example of tendentious political advertising which would now be unlawful unless financed from a political fund. The view of the opposition was that this amounts to political censorship by the government of its critics,[14] while the government claimed that such advertising was already caught by the 1913 Act.[15] There may be substance to each of these views, albeit that the opposition claim is not strengthened by the fact that the membership of NALGO, and other unions, is free to vote in a ballot for the establishment of a political fund if it wishes the union to engage in activity of this kind. In fact, in 1983 the Society of Telecom Executives successfully balloted its members to set up a fund, which is to be used only to finance campaigns designed to protect the public sector.

The assertion that NALGO's expenditure fell within the original definition of political objects may be doubted in the light of *Coleman*'s case[16] where, as already explained, the CO held that the original definition applied only to expenditure directly and expressly in support of a party. In any event, it is also arguable that the expenditure was undertaken in furtherance of statutory objects. On the other hand, there is the CO's admission that his narrow interpretation of the provision 'may invite scepticism in the world of today'[17] and the fact that any challenge to expenditure such as that by NALGO would be in the High Court where the union could expect a much less sympathetic audience than before the CO. In addition, it may be that the statutory objects' proviso in the original definition was much less significant in this context than was assumed. As was held by the CO in *McCarthy v APEX*, 'although the words "the main purpose ... of the distribution" imply a test which is primarily subjective, it is to my mind straining the rule to suggest that the main purpose was to further the statutory objects where that purpose could only be indirect and the direct and obviously apparent purpose was to bring about the election of a Labour Government'.[18] Although NALGO did not openly encourage electors to vote for a particular party, it is widely thought that it sought to influence the result of the election. The CO's dictum would have been just as applicable in such a case and a similar approach may well have been adopted by the High Court.

BALLOTS

As stated in the introduction, a union is required to ballot its members on a resolution to adopt political objects, should it wish to spend money in the

---

[14]   HC Standing Committee F, 28 February 1984, 1312 (Mr John Smith).
[15]   ibid. 1308 (Mr Alan Clark).
[16]   [1981] IRLR 427.
[17]   ibid. at 430.
[18]   [1980] IRLR 335, at 338.

furtherance of these objects. A simple majority of those voting is sufficient (s.3(1)). Under the 1913 Act, once a resolution was passed, there was no duty on a union to test the opinion of the membership as to whether the union in question should continue to promote political objects. In the Green Paper, the government objected to this once-for-all requirement of the 1913 Act and pointed out that it was not self-evident that 'a majority of the present members of a trade union in which a ballot was held many years ago would wish their union still to pursue political objects or to continue previous affiliations' (DE, 1983:para. 85).

Section 12 of the 1984 Act gives effect to the government's objections by providing that a political fund resolution will automatically cease to have effect (if it has not been previously rescinded) ten years from the date of the ballot on which it was passed. So if a union is to retain an unbroken authority to devote funds for political objects, it must ballot its members before the ten-year period lapses. Although unions are thus required to ballot their members every decade for authority to continue to operate their political funds, this did not give them ten years from the commencement date of the legislation in which to hold the first ballots. If a political fund resolution was approved more than nine years before the commencement date, it was deemed to have been passed nine years before that date (s.12(3)). This means that resolutions passed more than nine years before 31 March 1985[19] expired one year thereafter. Most unions with political funds were in fact in this position.

Both the initial and the review ballots must be conducted in accordance with rules to be approved by the CO, who under s.4(1) of the 1913 Act was required simply to ensure that every member had an equal right and, if reasonably possible, a fair opportunity of voting, and that the secrecy of the ballot was properly secured. This provision was amended, however, so that political fund ballots are to be conducted in accordance with procedures not unlike those prescribed by Part I of the 1984 Act for elections to trade union executive committees.[20] Part I is considered in Chapter 10. There are, however, a number of differences. First, although entitlement to vote in political fund ballots must be extended to all union members, there is no exception — in contrast to s.2 of the 1984 Act — for members who are unemployed, apprenticed or in arrears. The only exception to the wide franchise lies in s.13(7)(a), which provides that where ballot rules are drawn up before a resolution expires, overseas members may lawfully be excluded. So the right to vote in political fund ballots extends to members who are exempt from paying the levy, and to those who may be ineligible to pay it because of the rules of the union. Second, there is no statutory preference for postal ballots as there is in s.2(7). The provisions for distribution of ballot papers and voting are similar in fact to the alternative arrangements in s.3, which provides for distribution of ballot papers at the workplace or at a

---

[19] The commencement date for Part III (TUA 1984 s.22(5)).
[20] TUA 1984 s.13 amended s.4(1) of the 1913 Act by substituting new requirements as to ballot rules. These provisions now constitute s.4(1A)–(1F) of the TUA 1913.

place more convenient to the member, and for voting at the workplace or by post.

Although the workplace thus plays an important part in the distribution of ballot papers and in voting, the 1984 Act fails to impose any duty on an employer to co-operate in the conduct of the ballots. There is not even an obligation on employers to allow union officials access to the workplace to deliver ballot papers. Yet a ballot may be annulled for breach of the rules even though the breach was caused largely by the employer's conduct. This point is qualified, however, in two respects. In the first place, on hearing a complaint by a member alleging a breach of the ballot rules, the CO is empowered to make such order as he thinks just to remedy the breach. Where employer resistance has led to some members being disenfranchised or to some other breach of the rules, the CO is not required to invalidate the ballot, and it may be improper for him to do so if the breach of the rules did not affect the result.[21] In the second place, unions and their members may assert legal rights under the EPCA and EA 1980. So it would be possible for a union official to distribute ballot papers on the employer's premises without the consent of the employer, provided that this is done outside working hours.[22] In some cases, moreover, an employer could be required under s.2 of the 1980 Act to provide facilities for the ballot to be conducted, though this applies only where the union in question is recognised and only where the employer employs more than twenty people.

THE POLITICAL FUND

Where a resolution is approved by a majority of the members voting, the union must then adopt rules — also to be approved by the CO — providing that any payments in furtherance of the political objects 'are to be made out of a separate political fund' (TUA 1913 s.3(1)(a)). Two issues arise here: first, how is the fund to be financed; and second, what happens to the fund if the members should subsequently decide in the course of periodic review not to vote in favour of the continued operation of political objects?

As originally enacted, the 1913 Act required unions to use only their political funds for political purposes, but apart from the members' right of exemption it did not restrict the sources for financing the fund. Section 4(2) of the 1927 Act supplemented the contracting-in provision by preventing unions from adding any assets to their political funds other than the money raised by the political levy. But this was repealed in 1946. Section 14 of the 1984 Act now provides that at any time when there is a resolution in force no property shall be added to a union's political fund other than contributions to the fund by members of the union or any other person, and property which accrues to the fund in the course of administering the assets of the

---

21 See *Brown v AUEW* [1976] ICR 147.
22 EPCA s.23 as construed by *Zucker v Astrid Jewels* [1978] IRLR 385, applying dicta of Lord Reid in *Post Office v UPW* [1974] ICR 378 (see Chapter 2 above).

fund. This means that unions may not add to their political funds income which is yielded by the investment of other funds. It also means that unions are prevented from borrowing money or running an overdraft, a restriction which may not be insignificant. At the end of 1982 four unions had a political fund deficit, at least one of which was financed by an unsecured overdraft (CO, 1984:50–52), a practice which was held by the EAT not to involve a breach of the political rules before the enactment of the 1984 Act.[23]

Section 14 also provides that no liability of a political fund shall be discharged out of any other fund of the union, regardless of whether an asset of that other fund has been charged in connection with the liability. Quite simply this means that a creditor will not be able to secure payment of a political fund debt out of the general fund of the union, or out of the assets of that fund. It is not altogether clear whether this measure introduces any change to the law since the matter was expressly left open when the position under the pre-1984 law was considered by the EAT in *ASTMS v Parkin*.[24] But although the issue has been clarified, the solution adopted could have inequitable consequences. The position could easily arise whereby a union with a low balance holds a ballot to renew political objects, the resolution is lost, and the union has a number of debts which exceed the balance in its funds, with no income to meet these debts.

When a political fund resolution ceases to have effect, members can no longer be required to contribute to that fund (TUA 1984 s.14(2)(b)), and the union is required to take such steps as are necessary to ensure that the collection of political fund contributions is discontinued as soon as reasonably practicable (s.15(3)(a)). This will involve giving notice to employers to modify check-off arrangements. But because check-off agreements require varying periods of notice before any change can be made, the decision of the members of the union in question may not be implemented immediately. The duty to discontinue collecting the levy is reinforced by s.16 of the 1984 Act which provides that a union member may apply to the High Court, or to the Court of Session in Scotland. Where the members' claim is upheld, the court is empowered to grant a declaration and, if it considers it appropriate, to make an order requiring the union to take steps necessary to secure that the collection of contributions is discontinued. Any member of a union may apply under these provisions, including those who may not be directly affected in the sense that the union is not collecting contributions from them. Section 16 also provides that where an order is made, it may be enforced by any of the members, as if they had made the original application. This is qualified only by the requirement that the applicant in such a case must have been a member of the union at the time when the order was made.

The 1984 Act also provides that no property shall be added to the political fund after a resolution has ceased to have effect (s.14(2)(a)). So in principle money from any source may not be added to the fund following the expiry of a resolution. But what happens to the money left in the fund at that date?

---

[23] *ASTMS v Parkin* [1983] IRLR 448.
[24] ibid.

Here, a union may have three options. First, it may freeze the fund in the hope that the members will approve a new resolution some time in the future. Second, it may transfer the money to other funds, notwithstanding any rules of the union in question or any trusts on which the political fund is held (s.14(2)(c)). Third, in certain circumstances the union may spend from the fund for political purposes. Section 15(1) of the 1984 Act provides that where a ballot is held before the expiry of a resolution, and the adoption of a fresh resolution is not approved, the union may continue to use its funds for political purposes for up to six months beginning with the date of the ballot. But otherwise political funds cannot be spent for political purposes after the expiry of a resolution. This is the effect of s.3(1) of the 1913 Act which prohibits the use of any union funds for political purposes unless there is a resolution for the time being in force.

THE RIGHT OF EXEMPTION

Section 14 of the 1984 Act now makes clear that trade union political funds may be financed only by the contributions of members or other persons; or by money which accrues from the administration of the assets of the fund. By s.3(1)(a) of the 1913 Act a union's political fund rules must permit the exemption of a member of the union from any obligation to contribute to the fund. A union is required under s.5 of the 1913 Act to notify its members of their right of exemption following the passing of a political fund resolution. The notice, which is to be given in accordance with rules to be approved by the CO, should also advise members that an exemption form may be obtained from the head office or branch office of the union, or from the CO. But it is not necessary to use the form provided by the union and it is sufficient to use a form similar to that prescribed by the statute.[25] It has been held that the members may write out their own forms and hand them to the appropriate union officials,[26] and it has been suggested that there may be circumstances where an oral notification will suffice.[27] The effect of a notice of exemption depends on when it was delivered to the union. If it is given within 28 days of receiving a notification of the right of exemption following the passing for the first time of a political objects resolution, it has immediate effect. In all other cases, however, it does not become effective until 1 January immediately following the date of delivery. After a periodic review ballot a union is required to notify its members of their right of exemption.[28] But any exemption delivered thereafter becomes effective only from the following January (TUA 1984 s.13(a)).

A question which has given rise to considerable difficulty is the use of the

---

[25] *Hewett and ETU* Report of Selected Disputes referred to the Chief Registrar of Friendly Societies 1938–1949.
[26] *Valentine and ETU* Registrar's Report 1957. See also Donovan (1968:para. 926).
[27] *Templeman and AUEFW* Registrar's Report 1969.
[28] This is the effect of TUA s.5(1) which requires notification to be made after the passing of the political fund resolution.

check-off as a method of collecting the political levy. In practice some employers have been willing to grant check-off facilities only if the dues paid by union members are fixed and regular. This has meant that these employers have been reluctant to deduct a smaller trade union subscription from employees who are exempt from paying the political levy. Consequently, many unions benefiting from check-off facilities required exempt members to pay the political levy and then claim a rebate from the union periodically. This proved to be a controversial practice which gave rise to two quite different legal problems. The first point is whether this practice amounts to a breach of the Truck Acts 1831–1940. These Acts — which generally apply only to manual workers — require that wages due must be paid to the worker concerned in the current coin of the realm. In *Hewlett v Allen*,[29] however, the House of Lords held that there was no violation if money was withheld from the wage packet by the employer and transferred to a third party at the request of the employee. The third party might be a trade union, which means that in principle the operation of the check-off does not run foul of the Truck Acts.[30] It has never been decided, however, whether it is lawful for an employer to check-off a full trade union contribution where the employee has assented to only a portion being deducted. The matter was raised before the EAT in *Reeves v TGWU*[31] but not decided for lack of jurisdiction.

The litigation which has taken place has related directly to the second issue, namely, whether the operation of the practice of rebates constituted a breach by the unions of their political fund rules. By s.6 of the 1913 Act a union may adopt one of two methods for the collection of the political levy. First, it may impose a separate levy of the members. In that case it was held by the CO in *Elliott v SOGAT 1975*[32] that 'if the same deduction is made from the pay of both exempt and non-exempt members a separate levy of non-exempt members is not being made',[33] even though contracted-out members were reimbursed and their money never reached the political fund. Alternatively, unions may adopt a system which relieves exempt members of the whole or any part of any periodical contribution payable to the union, in which case relief is to be given 'as far as possible to all members who are exempt on the occasion of the same periodical payment'. In *Reeves v TGWU*[34] the EAT construed these words to mean that if it is not possible, because of the operation of the check-off, to relieve exempt members when dues are actually paid, there is no breach of the rules if the union adopts a system of rebating the political contribution to exempt members. The EAT added, however, that the rebates should be paid in advance where possible, yet accepted that there would be sufficient compliance if in the circumstances rebates in advance were not possible, and the union paid the rebate in

---

29 [1894] AC 383. See also *Penman v Fife Coal Co. Ltd* [1936] AC 45.
30 See *Williams v Butlers Ltd* [1975] ICR 208.
31 [1980] IRLR 307. See Ewing (1981); Newell (1980).
32 [1983] IRLR 3.
33 ibid. at 6.
34 [1980] IRLR 307.

arrears as soon as reasonably possible after the date when collection was made by the employer. But the EAT concluded by making clear that, for the purposes of its decision, it presumed that the rebates would be made automatically without the need for the exempt member to make a claim. If the complainant in a future case was required to claim a rebate, 'that might wholly change the position'.[35]

In practice most unions adopted the second method for exempting their members and so were governed by *Reeves*. Although the decision seemed to strike a reasonable balance between the interests of the unions in the effective operation of the check-off and the interests of exempt members, it did not satisfy the government. Section 18 of the 1984 Act now makes it unlawful for an employer to deduct a political levy after written notification by an employee that he or she is exempt from the obligation to contribute to the political fund or that written objection to contributing to the fund has been lodged with the union. The employer must comply as soon as reasonably practicable, and may do so by refusing to operate the check-off in respect of contracted-out members. Clearly, this will put an end to the system of rebates in the case of employees who exercise this right, for an amount in respect of the levy is not to be deducted at source regardless of whether a refund has been paid. If employers refuse to deal with differential contributions, they will either have to suspend the operation of the check-off or simply deduct a flat rate general contribution from all members and leave the unions to collect the political levy by separate procedures. Because the obligations under these new provisions are owed by the employer, enforcement is not by way of complaint to the CO but to the county court, or to the sheriff if in Scotland (s.18(6)). If the court finds the employer in breach of the section it may make a declaration and may also make an order requiring the employer to take whatever steps the court may specify to ensure that the breach is not repeated (s.18(4) and (5)).

PROTECTION FROM DISCRIMINATION

The right to claim exemption from the obligation to pay a political levy is reinforced by s.3(1)(b) of the 1913 Act, which requires political fund rules to provide that exempted members 'shall not be excluded from any benefits of the union, or placed in any respect either directly or indirectly under any disability or at any disadvantage as compared with other members of the union (except in relation to the control or management of the political fund)'. It is also provided that 'contributions to the political fund of the union shall not be made a condition for admission to the union', though there are doubts as to whether this measure could be effectively enforced in the event of breach by a union. Protection from discrimination is limited to non-contribution to the political fund and does not include other forms of political discrimination by unions against their members. Thus the Chief

---

[35] At 313.

Registrar held that he had no jurisdiction to make an order where the complainant had been denied the right to be a delegate to the London Trades Council, not because he did not pay the political levy, but because of his association with a rank and file movement which was regarded by the union as a disruptive organisation.[36]

The exclusion of a member from the benefits of the union would cover the withholding of unemployment benefit or strike pay from the member concerned. A disability or disadvantage as compared with other members is a more difficult concept. Although it has been held that a union may not impose a higher general contribution on exempt members in lieu of the political levy,[37] it has also been held that the rule is not wide enough to protect members who have been discriminated against in their jobs because of their exemption. In a rather doubtful decision, the Chief Registrar held that the rule applies only to cases where exempt members have been deprived of their rights or put under some disability or at some disadvantage within the union itself, as compared with other members.[38] The scope of the protection has also been cut down in a number of recent decisions, including *Richards v NUM*,[39] where the CO rejected a complaint that Richards had been discriminated against as an exempt member because he had been denied the opportunity of inspecting the union's political fund account: 'someone who does not contribute to the political fund and has no say in how it is spent has no interest in the books of that fund; and consequently ... he suffers no disability or disadvantage by being denied the opportunity to inspect them'.[40]

The statutory proviso permitting discriminatory treatment in relation to the control and management of the political fund is an important qualification of the duty not to discriminate. Discrimination on this ground, however, is permissive rather than mandatory and unions may properly include exempt members in decisions relating to the political fund. Indeed, it was held in *Hobbs and Clerical and Administrative Workers' Union*[41] that if a union is to take advantage of its power of exclusion it must do so by passing a rule to that effect. Where this is done, recent cases suggest that the power of exclusion will be construed in favour of the union. In *Parkin v ASTMS*[42] one of the questions which arose was whether an exempt member could be lawfully excluded from voting on a motion for the union's annual conference which concerned the reselection of Labour MPs. In answering this question in the affirmative, the CO rejected the narrow construction argued by the complainant, namely, that the phrase was restricted to matters affecting the amount of expenditure from the fund, changes in the persons managing the fund, and changes in auditing arrangements for the investments of the fund.

---

[36] *Cleger and Amalgamated Union of Operative Bakers, Confectioners and Allied Workers* Registrar's Report 1935.
[37] *Griffiths and NUGMW* Registrar's Report 1928.
[38] *Bond and TGWU* Registrar's Report 1933.
[39] [1981] IRLR 247.
[40] ibid. at 254.
[41] Registrar's Report 1956.
[42] CO's Report 1979. Also *Double v EETPU* CO's Report 1982.

The CO's view was that where a union spends money from its political fund which could not lawfully be spent from any other fund of the union, matters of policy on which the union has a decision to take only because of that expenditure, for example, decisions which solely relate to the internal affairs of a political party, are matters within the expression 'control or management of the political fund'.

Although a narrow interpretation of 'control or management' was thus resisted in *Parkin* and in subsequent cases, the phrase is not open-ended. In *Birch v NUR*[43] the rules of the union prohibited exempt members from holding any office which involved control or management of the political fund. Mr Birch, who had been removed from his post as branch secretary when it was discovered that he did not pay the levy, sought a declaration in the High Court that the rule was inconsistent with the plain language of the statute, which simply enables unions to discriminate against members in relation to the control or management of the fund. For the union, it was argued, however, that the proviso to the rule was not confined to functions concerned with control or management of the political fund, and that exempt members must suffer disabilities of the kind to which Birch was subjected for, as a matter of practical branch administration, it was necessary to combine the control and management of the general fund and the political fund in the hands of the same branch officials. But this argument was firmly rejected by Danckwerts J, who, in granting the declaration, concluded that 'it is entirely reasonable that a non-contributor should be excluded from control or management of the political fund; it is quite another matter that he should be excluded from any office in his union or branch'.[44]

The approach adopted by the High Court in *Birch*'s case was strongly criticised by Grunfeld (1966:305), who contended:

> A necessary distinction must be drawn between union office at local, and district or other intermediate level where these exist, and union office at the highest or national level. To take away from the executive committee or executive council, including the general secretary of a union, their supervisory control and management of the political fund and of all the union's major political activities, would be profoundly damaging to the efficient organisation of the union's political work and to the effectiveness of the union's participation in the political affairs of the labour movement.

Grunfeld (1966:306) continues by arguing that *Birch* should be confined to local positions in a union and that, although the Act provides that exempt members shall not be placed at any disability or disadvantage, this should be construed to mean any disability or disadvantage in any *reasonable* respect. But contrary to what is implied by Grunfeld, trade unions are not compelled to exclude exempt members from the control and management of the political fund. There is no reason in principle why the leading officials should

---

[43] [1950] Ch 602.
[44] ibid. at 613.

not be responsible for the management of the fund even though they do not contribute to it. In practice, however, a union may well feel it expedient that those officials do pay the levy and that they take an active involvement in the affairs of the wider labour movement.

Before the enactment of TUA 1984 Part I, however, this need could have been met without seeking to invoke Grunfeld's argument. It is a common practice for trade unions to insist that leading officials be members of the Labour Party. Under the rules of the Party, members must pay the political levy of their respective trade unions. Such a requirement clearly has the effect indirectly of excluding non-contributors from union office: in order to hold office candidates must be members of the Labour Party; and in order to be a member of the Labour Party there is an obligation to pay the political levy of any union to which the individual belongs. Yet conditions of this kind appear to have been accepted by the Chief Registrar as not constituting a breach of the political fund rules.[45] So in effect unions could require senior officials to pay the levy, despite the decision in *Birch*. This practice is now unlawful with regard to the positions to which s.2 of the 1984 Act requires elections on a five-yearly basis, that is, elections to union executive committees. Section 2(10) provides that no candidate for election to any such office shall be required whether directly or indirectly to be a member of a political party. As a result if a union wishes its senior officials to pay the levy, it can do so by making Labour Party membership a condition of office for only the officials with regard to whom there is no statutory duty to elect on a periodic basis. It is true that in some cases this will include the president and general secretary where they are not members of the executive committee or where they are non-voting members of that committee. But if a union wishes to insist on a political levy contribution from those to whom s.2 does apply, it will have to convince the courts that *Birch* should be qualified along the lines suggested by Grunfeld.

ADMINISTRATION AND ADJUDICATION

As has already been pointed out, the CO has an important role to play in the administration of trade union political funds and in the adjudication of disputes. These are (as explained in Chapter 10) in addition to the other duties which have been conferred upon the CO since the creation of the post in 1976. Although the CO clearly has judicial as well as administrative functions, neither he nor his predecessor are lawyers. This contrasts with the Chief Registrar of Friendly Societies who was required on appointment to be a barrister of twelve years' standing.[46]

The CO's jurisdiction in political fund disputes is confined under s.3(2) of the 1913 Act to complaints made by members who are aggrieved by the breach of a rule made pursuant to the requirements of the Act. This means

---

[45] *Vaughan and National Association of Operative Plasterers* Registrar's Report 1932.
[46] Friendly Societies Act 1974 s.2(1), repealed by Friendly Societies Act 1981 s.1.

that non-members have no right to complain, a not insignificant point in view of the fact that the political fund rules must provide that contribution to the political fund shall not be made a condition of admission to the union.[47] In principle it is not clear what remedy would be available to the individuals faced with such a precondition of membership. In practice, however, the answer may be that they should accept the condition in order to obtain membership and then complain to the CO once they have standing to do so. Another requirement is that the member is aggrieved by the breach. The complainant himself must have been wronged: there is no vicarious right of complaint. So in *Parkin v ASTMS*[48] the CO had no jurisdiction to deal with a complaint from a non-exempt member to the effect that exempt members had been excluded from voting on a political matter which did not relate to the control and management of the political fund.

The number of complaints received by the CO varies annually, though in practice only a handful are made each year, the details being provided in Table 11.1.

TABLE 11.1
POLITICAL FUND COMPLAINTS

Year	Number of Complaints	Number of Formal Hearings
1976	3	0
1977	18	0
1978	12	0
1979	105	4
1980	20	1
1981	12	2
1982	24	3
1983	21	0

Source: *Annual Reports of the Certification Officer 1977–1983.*

On receiving a complaint the CO notifies the union concerned and explains the nature of the complaint. In practice the union will then normally propose a course of action satisfactory to the complainant and the complaint will be withdrawn. This helps to explain the very low number of formal hearings relative to the number of complaints.

Where a hearing is held and the complaint is well-founded, the CO is empowered to make such order to remedy the breach as he thinks just in the circumstances (TUA 1913 s.3(2)). Unions have been ordered to transfer

---

[47] See Citrine (1967:431) and Rideout with Dyson (1983:399). Citrine suggests, however, that the applicant may apply to the High Court for a declaration.
[48] CO's Report 1979.

money from the general to the political fund;[49] to stop discriminating against an exempt member,[50] and to return money wrongly obtained from an exempt member.[51] Any such order may be recorded in the county court and may be enforced as if it had been an order of that court. An appeal lies from a decision of the CO to the EAT and from there to the Court of Appeal, but the courts have no original jurisdiction to hear political fund complaints. Although the possibility of the High Court and the CO having a concurrent jurisdiction was left open by Eve J in *Forster*'s case,[52] it would be contrary to the principle that if 'Parliament has created new rights and duties and by the same enactment has appointed a specific ... body for their enforcement, recourse must be had to that body alone' (De Smith, 1980:358–9).

The courts do, however, have an original jurisdiction on some issues of trade union political funding. First, as in *Birch v NUR*,[53] the courts may be called upon to determine whether a political fund rule complies with the requirements of the 1913 Act. Second, where the political fund rules of the union include matters which are not required by the statute, the CO has no jurisdiction and any breach of these rules may be enforced only in the High Court.[54] Third, as has already been stated, the 1984 Act has given the High Court jurisdiction to deal with complaints that a union has not taken appropriate action to discontinue the collection of the political levy in cases where a resolution has ceased to have effect. Finally, s.16 of the 1984 Act extends the discrimination rule to make it unlawful for a union to place at a disability or disadvantage any member who did not pay the levy before the expiry of the resolution. But, unlike the rule itself, this measure is enforced by the High Court and not by the CO.

CONCLUSION

A curious feature about the present law on trade union political expenditure is that the 1984 amendments, which increase the protection for individuals, have been introduced at a time when the closed shop, the principal justification for any legal regulation in this area, is in retreat. In his classic work, Kahn-Freund (1983:247–8) wrote:

> The 'political fund' and the ceremony of 'contracting out' have become part of the pattern of British social life. They are taken for granted. But if something like a closed shop had not been also taken for granted in 1913 and ever since, this would

49   *Richards v NUM* [1981] IRLR 247; *ASTMS v Parkin* [1983] IRLR 448.
50   *Griffiths and NUGMW* Registrar's Report 1928.
51   *Robinson and NACODS* Registrar's Report 1966.
52   *Forster v National Amalgamated Union of Shop Assistants, Warehousemen and Clerks* [1927] 1 Ch 539.
53   [1950] Ch 602. The CO has power only to hear complaints alleging the breach of political fund rules. He may not entertain any challenge to the legality of the rules. See *Birch and NUR* Report of Selected Disputes referred to the Chief Registrar of Friendly Societies 1938–1949.
54   *Coleman and POEU* Registrar's Report 1974.

be incomprehensible. The history of the political fund demonstrates how deeply the principle of the closed shop is rooted in this country. In a sense the political fund is an institution complementary to the closed shop.

Yet as a result of the Acts of 1980 and 1982 it is now unfair for an employer to dismiss an employee on grounds of non-union membership, unless there is a UMA in force which has been approved within the preceding five years in a secret ballot, by either 80 per cent of those eligible to vote, or 85 per cent of those voting. Even where such an agreement has been made and approved, it may still be unfair to dismiss an employee for non-membership if the employee genuinely objects on grounds of conscience or other deeply-held personal conviction to being a member of any trade union whatsoever or of a particular trade union (see further Chapter 2). The importance of these measures is that, particularly in view of the small number of successful ballots which have been conducted, for most trade unionists they reinforce the right of exemption with an effective right of resignation. In such circumstances a case could be argued to loosen rather than to tighten the legal controls on trade union political expenditure.

The new restrictions on the closed shop do not, however, remove the need for all legal protection of members' rights in the area of political expenditure. Frequently there will be only one recognised union in a particular workplace, and only one union which will be able effectively to represent the interests of the employees. There is substance in the view that in such circumstances people should not be discouraged from joining the union simply because they would be compelled to contribute to its political fund. But although the 1913 Act could be justified even in the absence of legal support for the closed shop, the extension of these controls by the 1984 Act is more difficult to defend. Trade unions were already subject to quite exceptional legal regulation in this area. While it is true that trade unions and companies perform different functions and are regulated in different ways, comparison on the question of political expenditure seems irresistible. as *The Times* pointed out, 'although political contributions by companies are not directly comparable, the parallel is so close that it would be widely seen as unfair to legislate on the levy without reference to shareholders' rights'.[55] Yet the only specific statutory protection for shareholders is to be found in the Companies Act 1985 Sch.7, which provides that company directors must disclose in their annual report to shareholders any political donation in excess of £200. A company is treated as giving money for political purposes if, directly or indirectly,

(a) it gives a donation or subscription to a political party of the United Kingdom or of any part thereof; or (b) it gives a donation or subscription to a person who, to its knowledge, is carrying on, or proposing to carry on, any activities which can, at the time at which the donation or subscription was given, reasonably be regarded as likely to affect public support for such a political party as aforesaid.

---

[55]   25 May 1983. On company political donations see Ewing (1984a).

In contrast to a trade union, a company is not required to ballot its members or to introduce a procedure for the exemption of objectors. So unlike the shareholder who is compelled to contract-out of membership altogether, the trade union member already had the right to contract-out of an incident of membership.

Moreover, the 1984 amendments were introduced without it ever being clearly established that the procedures of the 1913 Act gave rise to any serious difficulty in practice. In view of the effective removal of legal protection for the post-entry closed shop, there was a heavy onus on the government to establish the inadequacy of the existing law. The most significant change introduced by the amendments has been the requirement for periodic review, which, as has already been shown, was justified by the government on the ground that 'it is not self-evident that a majority of the present members of a trade union in which a ballot was held many years ago would wish their union still to pursue political objects' (DE, 1983:para. 85). Yet trade unions were not bound irrevocably to maintain their political funds, with s.3(4) of the 1913 Act providing that political fund rules may be rescinded in the same manner as any other rule of the union. So it is possible for a union to revoke its political fund at any time where there is a call of this kind from the members. The fact that in 1983 a political levy was paid by 81 per cent of the members of unions with political funds suggests that there is little demand among trade unionists for such a step to be taken and, contrary to the government's claims, that there is in fact a broad measure of support for the continued operation of political funds. It is true, of course, that it is not 81 per cent of the members of all trade unions who pay the political levy and that in some cases fewer than 50 per cent of the members contribute. But at best all this suggests is that there may be a case for introducing mandatory ballots when the number of levy payers falls below a certain level. It is certainly no justification for imposing compulsory ballots on all unions.

This is not to deny that the government might have had a strong case for periodic review had it been able to show that the high level of contributions to political funds was due to a failure of the 1913 Act to ensure that people had an effective right to contract out. But the government did not produce any evidence to demonstrate that, despite the formal right of exemption, trade unionists were systematically compelled to pay the levy against their will. In fact all the credible and reliable evidence points in the other direction. The Donovan Commission (1968:para. 924) found no evidence (despite having sought it) that the procedures of the 1913 Act 'are ineffective, and that the protection conferred by the Act ... is illusory'. More recently, the EEF alleged that the Labour Party was 'significantly dependent upon the unwilling or unconscious contributions of a probably large number of union members'.[56] Yet in the course of examination by the Commons Select Committee on Employment, the EEF was unable to produce evidence to support its allegation.[57] It would in fact be highly

[56]   HC Select Committee on Employment 1982–3, 243 (i).
[57]   ibid.

surprising if anything other than isolated examples of abuse were to be found. There are now some 1.3 million trade unionists who do not pay the levy in those unions with a political fund (CO, 1984:52). As Grunfeld (1966:296) has written, 'it is most ingenuous to allege that other individuals are not perfectly free to do the same when so large a company stands as an example before them'.

Bibliography

Certification Officer (CO). 1984. *Annual Report of the Certification Officer 1983*. London: Certification Office for Trade Unions and Employers' Associations.

Citrine, N. 1967. *Trade Union Law*. 3rd edn. Ed. M. Hickling. London: Stevens.

De Smith, S. 1980. *De Smith's Judicial Review of Administrative Action*. 4th edn. Ed. J.M. Evans. London: Stevens.

Department of Employment (DE). 1983. *Democracy in Trade Unions*. Cmnd 8778. London: HMSO.

Donovan. 1968. Royal Commission on Trade Unions and Employers' Associations 1965–1968. *Report*. Cmnd 3623. London: HMSO.

Elliott, J. 1978. *Conflict or Co-operation? The Growth of Industrial Democracy*. London: Kogan Page.

Ewing, K.D. 1981. 'The Check-off and the Problem of the Political Levy'. *Modern Law Review*, 44 (March), 219–22.

——. 1982. *Trade Unions, the Labour Party and the Law: A Study of the Trade Union Act 1913*. Edinburgh: Edinburgh University Press.

——. 1984a. 'Company Political Donations and the Ultra Vires Rule'. *Modern Law Review*, 47 (January), 57–75.

——. 1984b. 'Trade Union Political Funds: The 1913 Act Revised'. *Industrial Law Journal*, 13 (December), 227–42.

Flanders, A.D. 1970. 'Trade Unions and Politics'. *Management and Unions: The Theory and Reform of Industrial Relations*. London: Faber, 24–37.

Grunfeld, C. 1966. *Modern Trade Union Law*. London: Sweet & Maxwell.

Kahn-Freund, O. 1983. *Labour and the Law*. 3rd edn. Ed. and intr. by P. Davies and M. Freedland. London: Stevens.

Newell, D. 1980. 'Trade Union Political Funds and the Check Off System'. *Industrial Law Journal*, 9 (June), 122–4.

Rideout, R.W., with J.C. Dyson. 1983. *Rideout's Principles of Labour Law*. 4th edn. London: Sweet & Maxwell.

PART V
Modern Employment Law

12 The Contract of Employment
Brian Napier

The content of individual employment law has altered dramatically in the last twenty years, mainly as a result of changes which occurred in the 1970s, the decade in which legislation brought a new framework of rights for employees, and created specialised labour courts — the industrial tribunals — before which these rights can be claimed. Important though these rights are, however, it remains true — and this is perhaps one of the leading paradoxes of the contemporary employment law — that they complement rather than oust the common law of the contract. Today the common law fulfils a dual function. It operates as a backcloth, providing a set of rules important in the many situations left unregulated by specific statutory measures, or where the legislative remedies that do exist are either inadequate or restricted in their application. It also has a crucial role to play in the operation of the statutory rights themselves, however, for Parliament has typically incorporated contractual terms and concepts in defining these. Thus, for example, there can be no proper understanding of what amounts to a 'dismissal' for the purposes of unfair dismissal without a knowledge of the common law rules regarding repudiation of contract, and no real grasp or redundancy law without an appreciation of the limits placed on job mobility by the implied terms of the contract of employment.

It follows that the history of the common law of the contract deserves attention too. For, through the system of binding precedent, the response of the courts to problems arising today is conditioned by what their predecessors had to say about similar problems in the past. This account of the modern contract thus begins with an examination of the historical antecedents of the present law.

DEVELOPMENT OF THE CONTRACT OF EMPLOYMENT

Status and Contract

Although there has been systematic legal regulation of the employment relationship since the fourteenth century, it has only been in the last hundred and fifty years or so that this regulation has taken contract as its primary model. Before then the relationship was shaped in part by the criminal law, operating through a line of statutes which imposed compulsory labour and gave magistrates the power to fix wages, in part by the civil law regulating the status of different categories of persons. The great jurist Blackstone, writing in 1765, analysed the relationship of master and servant in ways which, to modern eyes, are both revealing and deficient. For Blackstone, employment was akin to the relationships of husband and wife, parent and child and guardian and ward, and was classed by him alongside these as one of the 'great relations in private life'. Moreover, his world of servants was peopled almost exclusively by workers in domestic service and engaged in agricultural labour. As Kahn-Freund (1977:508–13) has shown, Blackstone's concept of employment was seriously out of date even against the social conditions of late eighteenth century England. His treatment of the topic tells us not only that the understanding of employment as the product of a free bargain between individuals had not yet been achieved, but also that the leading jurist of the age was little concerned with explaining and classifying the diverse forms of engagement of labour which, from other sources, we know existed in English society of the time. Why did Blackstone ignore the position of the factory labourer, the office clerk, indeed the urban worker in general? Probably for two reasons: the conditions of employment of the new working classes took them outside the terms of the disused but still-venerated Elizabethan and Jacobean criminal statutes, and there was no incentive for lawyers of his time to concern themselves with the details of such employment. The workers did not have the resources to go to law to ascertain the dimensions of their employment obligations, and, if their employers did, they lacked the inclination to do so.

The nineteenth century saw fundamental changes in the legal attitude towards the employment relationship, changes which still underpin many of the assumptions found in the law. To begin with there was, in the first half of the century, a transformation in the basic legal model. Instead of being part of the law dealing with personal status, employment was brought within the fold of the expanding law of contract. Most famously expressed in Maine's dictum that the movement of civilised society was from status to contract and that the status of the slave was superseded by the contractual relations of the servant to his master (cf. Kahn-Freund, 1977:512), the view that the key to understanding the history of employment in the nineteenth century lies in an appreciation of how contract replaced status has recently been attacked by writers who rightly warn against over-simple explanations of complex phenomena (Merritt, 1982; Foster, 1983). None the less, it would be a mistake to underestimate the impact of the shift towards contract at both theoretical and practical levels. On a theoretical level, the embracing of contractual notions was seen as an important part of the general liberal trend in labour law which, in the second half of the century, led in 1875 to the repeal of the Master and Servant Acts and gave a measure of protection to those engaged in certain trade union activities (Ruegg, 1901:277–9). To explain the employment relationship as a bargain, the terms of which lay entirely within the control of two independent parties, was to stress the even-handedness of the law, and was a view which accorded well with Benthamite thinking on individualism which, as Dicey (1962:63–4) noted, exercised such a potent intellectual force in the middle years of the century. But the influence of contract was also felt in the content of specific legal rules with practical consequences.

In the shape of the doctrine of common employment, for example, it was used as a means of developing a particular legal doctrine which had dramatic and disastrous effects for many thousands of working people and their families (Bartrip and Burman, 1983:103–25). The legal rule that an employee, injured at work by the negligence of a fellow employee, could not hold the common employer liable for the tort originated in the case of *Priestley v Fowler* in 1837.[1] At first the rule was expressed as turning on what, in modern terminology, would be seen as the employer's 'duty of care' to his employees. But, as it was refined and enthusiastically developed by the English courts (in Scotland the courts were far more cautious), it was explained in contractual terms. The employee (or his successors) could not sue because he had bargained away his right to do so as a term (albeit implied) of the contract he had entered into with his employer: 'the negligence of a fellow servant is taken to be one of the risks, which a servant as between himself and his master undertakes, when he enters into the service.'[2] The convenience and plausibility of the contractual analysis was a potent factor in the spread of a doctrine which became one of the most controversial aspects of the law of tort, and which was eventually to provide the impetus for the introduction of workmen's compensation legislation in 1897.

As the example of common employment illustrates, the transition from status to contract was far from being the unqualified improvement it seemed to many Victorian and Edwardian jurists. As the form of the relationship of master and servant changed, so too did its content. The transition from what Fox (1974:181–90) has called a 'high-trust' to a 'low-trust' relationship brought with it the abandonment of some of the rules which had existed in the earlier law for the protection of the weaker party. In the case of *Limland v Stephen*[3] at the beginning of the century, Lord Kenyon could say there were 'reciprocal duties between masters and servants. From the servant is due obedience and respect; from the master protection and good treatment.' While the principle of employer's control remained largely unaffected under the changing law, except in so far as the duty to obey was now explained as an implied term of the contract and not as an essential part of the relationship of master and servant (Selznick, 1969:136), the master's obligations in respect of welfare were watered-down in several important respects. For example, the obligation to pay wages and to provide medical assistance to sick servants was cut back by a judiciary increasingly aware of the phenomenon of industrial employment and the appropriateness of linking payment of wages directly with productive effort.[4]

Judges had the opportunity of developing the law in this and other ways because, to an unprecedented extent, cases on the master and servant relationship were coming before them. This was not just due to a change in attitudes as to the desirability of recourse to law as a means of settling disputes, although no doubt the rise of a commercial middle-class did have

---

[1] (1837) 3 M & W 1.
[2] *Swainson v North-Eastern Railway Co.* (1878) 3 ExLR 341, at 343 (per Pollock B).
[3] (1801) 3 Esp 269, at 270.
[4] See, e.g. *Sellen v Norman* (1829) 4 C & P 80.

some influence here, but also to the workings of the poor law. Parish fought parish in the courts over who had the burden of looking after the poor, and often the answer was given by where the unfortunate pauper had previously acquired a 'settlement' of a year's duration. This in turn was largely dependent on the terms of the employment over the period, and thus the courts were brought to consider the terms of service of even the most menial workers.

A range of other developments in the detail of the master and servant relationship are also associated with judicial activity in the nineteenth century (Haines, 1980:271–84). As tort liability became more important, so too it was increasingly important to distinguish between the acts of servants (for whom the employer was vicariously liable) and those of independent contractors (for whom he was not). So detailed case law also emerged to decide what acts were carried out 'in the scope of employment', and which were not.[5] Gradually, the courts recognised that employment relationships were not governed by rules appropriate to an agricultural economy; periods of hiring, it was accepted, might be terminated by the giving of notice, although the presumption that, unless the contrary was indicated, a hiring was to last for the rotation of the year was not abandoned by English law until 1969.[6] More generally, the nineteenth century saw the development and, in some instances, creation of many of the basic principles within the contract of employment relating to the payment of wages and dismissal which still apply today.

But no account of the many changes in individual employment law in this period should neglect the tension which arose between the standards tolerated by the common law and those laid down by statute. For although the judges, by and large, embraced contractualism and laissez-faire ideas of economic behaviour with energy and enthusiasm — except, it should be noted, in developing the notion of contractual terms unenforceable because they were incompatible with the fundamental principles of freedom of trade — the nineteenth century also saw legislative intervention to maintain minimum standards of civilised conditions of labour. One commentator (Friedmann, 1959:99) has concluded from this and other evidence that the judges are incapable of effecting major social adjustment by using the common law device of contract as a social equaliser. The most notable example of statutory intervention is to be found in the history of factory legislation. But mention can also be made of the Truck Acts, which sought to protect the worker's right to payment of wages, and lesser measures such as the Merchant Shipping Acts of 1844 and 1854 which gave close regulation of the terms of employment of sailors (Atiyah, 1979:543–4). Thus the significance of the nineteenth century from the point of view of the history of employment law is not simply the displacement of status by contract; it is also that during this period English law accepted the propriety of imposing, by legislation, certain protections for workers outside the realm of contract (Hepple, 1982:399). In so doing, some of the worst effects of unbridled

[5] *Mitchell v Crassweller* (1853) 13 CB 237.
[6] *Richardson v Koefod* [1969] 1 WLR 1812.

individualism were mitigated, and a pattern for legal intervention was set which was to have profound consequences for the subsequent development of the law.

Characteristics of the Modern Law

The story of the contract of employment during the present century can be more briefly told, notwithstanding the many fundamental changes in society and industrial relations which have taken place in this period. There has been no truly radical alteration in the conception of the individual employment relationship similar to that which occurred in Victorian England. By 1914 most of the great legislative and judicial battles in this field had been fought, and the foundations of social and industrial legislation had been well and truly laid. Thus, in particular, the doctrine of freedom of contract has remained central to the common law's understanding of employment throughout this century, although this understanding has had to be modified in various ways in order to accommodate new phenomena such as the growth in collective bargaining, and different forms of statutory intervention in the employment relationship. During World Wars I and II it is true that commitment to the basic ideal of freedom to contract — the principle that the right to choose his master was the main difference between a servant and a serf[7] — was temporarily suspended (Pritt, 1970:64–5, 83–9), but the limited forms of compulsory labour in these times of emergency were removed in peace-time. Also, of course, a powerful reason for the relative stability of the law of the contract of employment has been the tradition of 'absentionism' (Kahn-Freund, 1954) which, in keeping with the wishes of the parties, kept industrial disputes in both the collective and individual areas of labour law largely outside the courts. As Lewis has explained (1976:7), the pressure for protective legislation which in the nineteenth century had brought such measures as the Truck Act 1831 and the Factory Act 1833 became, under the direction of the trade union movement, narrowly focused in the areas of safety, health and welfare; with few exceptions (of which the guaranteeing of minimum wages in certain industries was probably the most important), the regulation of basic terms and conditions of employment was, until the 1960s, seen as appropriately covered by collective bargaining, and not by legislation interfering with the content of the employment relationship.

Notwithstanding this essentially static background, however, the history of labour law over this century does show three interesting developments which are significant for an understanding of the current contract of employment. The first is that that the contract, as a legal concept, acquired early on an importance which took it beyond the sphere of the regulation of the direct relations between employer and employed. Indeed, this tendency was already becoming apparent in the previous century, when the application of the law of workmen's compensation turned, among other things, on

---

[7] *Nokes v Doncaster Amalgamated Collieries Ltd* [1940] AC 1014.

the question whether the claimant was engaged under a contract of employment or not. But the early years of the twentieth century saw the concept used in connection with the first statutes dealing with unemployment and sickness insurance, the measures which were the forerunners of the present welfare state. The contract of employment was there deployed as a means of determining the applicability of the new rules, and as a result it became established as a useful concept denoting the archetypal employment relationship. Similarly, in revenue law, the contract of employment (or service) became centrally important in deciding whether taxation on earnings was paid under Schedule D or Schedule E of the tax legislation (Tiley, 1981:109). One consequence of these developments was that there came to exist several distinctive groupings of case law on the interpretation and content of the contract, each relative to its own particular context. Unfortunately, little or no attempt has been made to integrate these collections into a single coherent body of law, and even today labour lawyers or judges will not necessarily follow, or even be properly acquainted with, the interpretations of the contract of employment in areas outside their own.

The second feature to note concerns what might be termed the 'classlessness' of the contract of employment. In contrast with the relationship of master and servant, where classification as a servant entailed acceptance of a low social position, the new relationship of employer and employee was seen as socially neutral. This was so despite the attachment of the judiciary to the old terminology and to the continued description of the parties to the relationship as 'master' and 'servant'. This change did not take place overnight, however, and in some areas the old thinking remained evident. In 1905, for example, in a case dealing with a claim for compensation made by a mine manager under the Workmen's Compensation Act 1897,[8] the Court of Appeal refused to extend the Act to cover such a claim, notwithstanding the argument that the mine manager was employed under a contract of service. Collins MR insisted upon the need to 'interpret the Act as applying to persons whom *ex hypothesi* the legislature regards as not being in a position to protect themselves', and that meant excluding claims from relatively well-off middle-class employees such as the plaintiff. Elsewhere, however, the ubiquity of the contract of employment was a strong force in promoting its classlessness. When doctors, teachers and other professionals were seen as employed under a contract of employment (as they were for tax and national insurance purposes), it became unrealistic to maintain otherwise. This change is perhaps most clearly reflected in the detailed legal rules, discussed below, which show a movement away from the idea that it is the employer's right to control the work done by the employee which distinguishes the contract of employment from other relationships for the doing of work in exchange for money.

The third feature to mention here is the broadening of the concept of service under a contract of employment to include employment relationships within the public sector. The tremendous growth in the number of public

---

[8]   *Simpson v Ebbw Vale Steel Iron and Coal Co.* [1905] 1 KB 453.

sector employees in the last hundred years required some rethinking of original concepts — the contract of employment, and the relationship of master and servant before it, having evolved to deal exclusively with employment in the private sector. By and large, public sector workers have been assimilated to those in the private sector, and the device of the contract of employment has been extended to them. This contrasts with the position found in continental Europe, where typically the employment relation of the public servant is governed by a quite separate regime, based upon the principles of public rather than private law.

The uniformity of British law extends even to civil servants, a class of workers historically denied a contractual relationship with the Crown,[9] although in their case the contract of employment that now probably governs them allows for immediate dismissal at the discretion of the Crown. The justification for this severe rule (which does not reflect what generally happens in practice) is a matter of public law — the argument that the freedom of the executive to act in the best interests of the state must not be restricted by contract. In the *GCHQ* case,[10] the Court of Appeal considered and rejected the argument that this power, which is derived from the royal prerogative, had been lost as a result of the passing of the Trade Disputes and Trade Union Act 1927. This point was not argued when the case went on appeal to the House of Lords, though Lord Diplock did observe that the rule allowing for the instant dismissal of civil servants was 'beyond doubt'.

Although this is just one of many important differences between public and private employment (Hepple, 1982), the extension of the contract of employment to this group has not proved unduly problematical. But the fact remains that a public body acting as employer is likely to be exercising powers granted by statute, and operates under special responsibilities. Its activities are subject to the rules of public law, and sometimes this can have important repercussions on its behaviour as an employer. In 1925, for example, the courts intervened to strike down a wage award by a local authority which was seen as ultra vires because it exceeded the standard set by market forces.[11] In recent times, however, the peculiarity of public employment has more often been a factor which has operated to the benefit of the employee, especially in the area of dismissal: the doctrine of ultra vires has been applied to restrain the improper use of delegated powers through the remedy of judicial review.[12] One writer (Ganz, 1967:288) has commented that 'occasionally it is possible in case of public employment to catch a glimpse of a totally different approach to the employment contract as something more permanent than a contract determinable at pleasure by giving notice'.[13]

---

[9] *IRC v Hambrook* [1956] 2 QB 641; *Riordan v War Office* [1959] 1 WLR 1046.
[10] *Council of Civil Service Unions v Minister for the Civil Service* [1984] IRLR 3, EAT; [1985] ICR 14, HL. See Wade (1985).
[11] *Roberts v Hopwood* [1925] AC 578.
[12] *R v Birmingham City Council ex parte NUPE* (1984) The Times, 24 April (noted by Fredman, 1984).
[13] A good illustration is to be found in *R v Secretary of State for the Home Department ex parte Benwell* [1985] IRLR 6. See the discussion of 'wrongful dismissal' below.

IDENTIFICATION OF THE CONTRACT OF EMPLOYMENT

Limitations of the Contractual Model

Reliance on the contract of employment as the main vehicle for ensuring the availability of statutory rights gives rise to an unsatisfactory state of affairs for a growing number of persons. The problems of the 'marginal' workers are detailed in Chapter 18, but it can be mentioned here that there are two principal ways in which persons whose employment relationship is atypical may find themselves excluded from statutory benefits. It may be, as is the case with part-time workers, that they do not work for the required minimum number of hours per week (usually sixteen) to qualify for protection, or that, as with seasonal workers or those on fixed term contracts, they do not work with one employer for long enough to build up the continuity of employment which is also necessary for the making of most claims. The other possibility, even more worrying from the point of view of eligibility for employment protection rights, is that the legal nature of the relationship under which work is done is seen as being something other than that of a contract of employment. Should this be so, most of the statutory employment protection rights will not apply to them, irrespective of hours worked or length of service.

More recently the mantle of the contract of employment has been withheld from other groups of working people who have much to lose but little to gain from being excluded from it. A leading example is provided by the many young people who work on the Youth Training Scheme (YTS), and who, most probably, are in law classed as trainees not possessing contracts of employment.[14] As Freedland has observed (1983:231), the YTS shows up a lacuna in our employment protection legislation, but as such it does not stand alone. Persons who give their services through the intermediacy of an employment agency are also excluded from many statutory rights,[15] as are many casual and home workers. As different forms of working relationships emerge and develop, labour law ought to show flexibility in meeting new needs. Continued reliance on the institution of the contract of employment may be one factor which contributes to the phenomenon of a relatively underprivileged sector of employment existing alongside those fortunate enough to be in conventional employment (Craig et al., 1982:77–9).

Elements of the Contract

In order for there to be a contract in English law, certain basic requirements must be met. There must be behaviour which can be construed as the making and acceptance of an offer by the parties, and the resulting bargain

---

14 *Daley v Allied Suppliers Ltd* [1983] ICR 90.
15 *Wickens v Champion Employment* [1984] ICR 365.

struck must be supported by a 'consideration', which is the term lawyers use for a price. In the context of employment, offer and acceptance generally occur at the stage when the employee is first engaged by the employer, and the 'price' for their bargain is found in the reciprocal promises of the employer to pay wages and the employee to perform services. These elements are rarely lacking, although it is sometimes a matter of some difficulty to know precisely when the bargain was made and how the basic rules are to be applied to it. Is the contract made, for example, when the offer of employment is made (typically, at the end of a job interview), or is it concluded only later when the employee receives a formal letter of appointment (which may contain conditions additional to or even inconsistent with what was said at the time of the interview)? No simple general answer can be given to this important question, for it will depend on the facts and how the courts interpret the intention of the parties. Some light can be shed, however, by examining the finding of the Court of Appeal in *Robertson v British Gas Corporation*[16] where it was necessary to pronounce upon a conflict between a letter of appointment and the issuing by the employer of statutory written particulars. The view which prevailed was that the letter and not the statutory particulars constituted the written contract, and one of the judges (Ackner LJ) went so far as to say that not only was the written statement devoid of contractual effect, it might not even be used for the purposes of interpreting the meaning of the earlier document. Another problem concerns not the classification of particular elements of the contract, but the larger question of differentiating the type of agreement known in law as a contract of employment from the various other possible arrangements concerned with the performance of services in exchange for remuneration. The answer to this question leads to a consideration of the features which make the contract of employment unique.

Distinguishing Features of the Contract

It is conventional to begin any account of the criteria for identifying a contract of employment or service with the series of tests which the courts have evolved over time for this purpose. As already mentioned, the original concept was that of control. The employer controlled the employee in the doing of the work, or at least had the power to do so if he wished, which could not be said of the relationship between employer and independent contractor working under a contract for services.[17] With the growing democratisation of the concept of contractual service, however, this simple notion, which harked back to the time when service was associated with inferior social status (Kahn-Freund, 1951), became increasingly unsuitable. In its place there arose the 'integration' test, by which a contract of service was seen as existing where a worker was taken on as part of the employer's

16 [1983] ICR 351.
17 *Yewens v Noakes* (1880) 6 QBD 530; *Performing Rights Society Ltd v Mitchell and Booker Ltd* [1924] 1 KB 762.

undertaking or organisation.[18] But this too was found defective, largely because, by asking whether the worker was integrated in the organisation, the application of the test begged the question in issue. To the extent that this test ever worked it did so only by relying on unstated assumptions about persons in employment possessing a particular recognisable social role.

In the place of the 'organisational' test there emerged, after the decision in *Ready Mixed Concrete (South East) Ltd v Minister of Pensions and National Insurance*,[19] the so-called 'multiple' test. According to this test the finding of a contract of service depended on the balancing of a number of factors, none of which was classed as sufficient in itself, but some of which — the existence of control, for example, or payment of a wage or other consideration — were seen as essential. The core of the 'multiple' test was the idea that the other, non-essential provisions of the contract should not be inconsistent with the existence of a contract of service, and, under this heading, the judge was empowered to take note of factors such as ownership of plant and materials, and where the chance of profit and risk of loss lay. Perhaps because of the high degree of flexibility and discretion this test allows, the 'multiple' test has stood up well, and still, in a somewhat modified form, represents the law.

Nowadays it would appear that the law pays particular attention to what has become known as the 'economic reality' of the situation between the parties, but this is really only an application of the idea behind the 'multiple' test and not a new concept. The underlying principle is whether the individual whose status is in question could be described as being in business on his or her own account. Most recently, however, there are indications that a variation of this, expressed in terms of 'mutuality of obligation', has been gaining ground.

The leading case is *O'Kelly v Trusthouse Forte Plc*[20] where the Court of Appeal had to decide whether certain waiters, employed as 'regular casuals' in the catering trade, were qualified to claim in respect of allegedly unfair dismissals by reason of having worked under a contract of employment. The industrial tribunal which first heard the claim applied the 'multiple' test and concluded that the ingredient of mutuality of obligation was missing from the relationship between the waiters and Trusthouse Forte. This seems to have meant that neither side was obliged to carry forward the relationship: the 'employers' were not obliged to offer work, and the 'workers' were under no obligation to accept work when offered. The Court of Appeal held that the industrial tribunal had been acting within its proper jurisdiction in so concluding, and upheld that body's decision that there was no contract of employment. Although the case is primarily important as marking out the classification of the contract as a matter of fact and not law, it also stands as the first acceptance by the Court of Appeal of a test which has subsequently been specifically approved.[21] It would now appear that for there to be a

[18] *Stevenson Jordan and Harrison Ltd v MacDonald and Evans* [1952] TLR 101.
[19] [1968] 2 QB 497.
[20] [1983] IRLR 369; discussed in Chapter 18 below as part of the analysis of the legal problems of temporary work.
[21] *Nethermere (St Neots) Ltd v Taverna and Gardiner* [1984] IRLR 240.

contract of employment, there must be some continuing obligation on the employer to supply work, and a corresponding obligation on the worker to do it. The question whether this is so in any particular case, however, is classed as a matter of fact. In consequence of EPCA s.136(1), which allows an appeal only on matters of law, the decision of an industrial tribunal either in favour of or against the existence of such a contract can accordingly only be challenged if there was no evidence to support it.

Although the substance of the tests for identifying a contract of employment have been generally agreed by the judges, the necessarily broad statements of principle these produce must be supplemented with more detailed observations. There will be occasions when a superior court will take a more 'interventionist' approach and show itself willing to set aside an inferior tribunal's determination for or against the existence of a contract of employment. This can be seen, most notably, in *Ferguson v John Dawson & Partners*,[22] a case in which a finding in favour of the presence of a contract of employment was a necessary prerequisite to a successful claim by the plaintiff, injured in an industrial accident, for damages for breach of statutory duty. In the event the majority of the Court of Appeal did not depart from the finding made by the judge at first instance, but the judgments show clearly that this was a decision reached on the substance of the facts themselves, and not on any narrow jurisdictional ground. In that situation, of course, appeal lay to the Court of Appeal on issues of fact as well as law, a point which draws attention to the need always to consider the legal context in which the question of the identification of a contract arises. Context is important also in the sense that the receptiveness of courts or tribunals to arguments about the presence of a contract of employment will be influenced by the merits of the case. The well-informed and calculating litigant, who seeks to set aside a self-employed status earlier claimed for financial advantage, in order to pursue a claim for unfair dismissal or redundancy, is unlikely to meet with much success.[23] But there are signs that the courts will to some extent use their discretion to find a contract of employment exists where this is a way of assisting an under-privileged group of workers, such as those who work at home,[24] to achieve basic statutory rights.

THE CONTRACT AS AN AUTHORITATIVE SOURCE OF RULES

Although the parties are free (within the limits imposed by the general law and particular statutory rules) to contract on their own terms, the great majority of contracts of employment share certain common features. The employee undertakes, in exchange for the payment of remuneration, to

---

[22] [1976] 3 All ER 817.
[23] *Massey v Crown Life Insurance Co.* [1978] ICR 590; cf. *Young & Woods Ltd v West* [1980] IRLR 201.
[24] *Airfix Footwear Ltd v Cope* [1978] IRLR 396; *Nethermere (St Neots) Ltd v Taverna and Gardiner* (above); cf. *Mailway (Southern) Ltd v Willsher* [1978] ICR 511.

obey the lawful and reasonable orders of the employer, and to take reasonable care in the carrying out of his employment duties. There is also a duty of fidelity towards the employer, which is translated into particular obligations not to enter into competition with him during working time, not to divulge or improperly use confidential information acquired in the course of his employment, and, within certain limits, to disclose to the employer information harmful to the employer's interests. The employee is, however, under no general duty to disclose personal misconduct, although he may be required to inform the employer of the misbehaviour of fellow employees.[25]

The employer is bound by a duty to take reasonable care for the safety of the employee, to pay wages, and to exercise due respect and consideration in dealings with the employee. This duty of respect may be seen as the counterpart of the employee's duty of fidelity. It is not of recent creation, but it is a duty which, through the operation of the law of unfair dismissal and, in particular, that part of it concerned with 'constructive' dismissal (see below), has acquired a much-increased significance in recent years.

Express and Implied Terms

Although the parties are free to make the bargain of their choice, in practice many of the key features of their relationship are left undefined, and are settled by the courts through the device of the implied term. Implied terms are, in legal theory, of secondary significance in defining the contract, in the sense that they will not override express terms which state the contrary, nor can they be used as a basis for an interpretation having this effect. In reality, however, it would be hard to overemphasise either the contribution made by such terms in building up the content of the contract, or the flexibility and power this operation gives to the judges whose job it is to construe the contract. The importance is only enhanced by the closer link (explained below) between implied contractual terms and the legal effect of collective bargaining.

Implied terms are often divided by lawyers into those implied in fact, and those implied in law.[26] The difference betwen the two is not as clear in practice as it appears on paper, but its basis is that, in relation to the former category, the courts will seek to justify their findings by reference to the presumed but unexpressed wishes of the parties. As an aid in so doing they will, among other things, have regard to what is established practice in the trade or industry in question, and to what they are sure must have been in the parties' contemplation. In the past, the standards to be met before such a power of implication was exercised were high, and imposed, in theory at least, a limit on judicial creativity. Judges were supposed to imply terms only where it was necessary to do so to give business efficacy to the contract,[27] or

---

[25] *Bell v Lever Brothers Ltd* [1932] AC 161; *Sybron Corporation v Rochem Ltd* [1983] 2 All ER 707.
[26] *Howman & Son v Blyth* [1983] IRLR 139.
[27] *The Moorcock* (1889) 14 PD 64.

where the term was one which would immediately have been accepted by both parties when their attention was drawn to it.[28] Today, although it is going too far to say openly that the judges have power to imply all terms which they think reasonable,[29] the case law has developed in that direction. It has recently been said judicially that 'we can treat as an agreed term a term which would not have been at once assented to by both parties at the time when they made the contract, for example where one party would at once have assented to it and the other would have done so after it had been made clear to him that unless he did so there would be no contract',[30] and it has also been held that the conduct of the parties under the contract is highly relevant to deciding the content of any implied terms which may be contained in it.[31]

In relation to terms implied in law, as opposed to fact, the basis for judicial intervention is a legal requirement that the employment relationship contains a term dealing with a particular matter. Sometimes this will be as a result of statute, but, more often, the legal requirement will arise as a result of judicial interpretation of the rules of the common law. There the judges obviously enjoy a great measure of discretion. The term implied by law is seen as a necessary incident of the constitution of the employment relationship.[32]

One of the best illustrations is to be found in the *ASLEF* case,[33] where the Court of Appeal in an important judgment (Napier, 1972) held that a 'work to rule' on the railways amounted to breach of an implied duty of co-operation, which was a part of the contract of employment. Such a finding could in no sense be justified by reference to the common intentions of the parties, since it was so contrary to the interests of the workers concerned. Nevertheless, the term in question was held, as a matter of law, to form part of the contract. The case provides the clearest evidence of what the judges think are the proper dimensions of the employment bargain, and an object lesson in the discovery and application of one of the most significant implied terms to be found in the contract.

Statutory Provisions

While statute, through the creation of such individual rights as unfair dismissal and redundancy protection, plays a major part in regulating the individual employment relationship, its effect on the contract of employment itself is more limited. Basically, it operates in one of three ways: by compulsorily introducing terms into the contract of employment, by rendering ineffective particular terms which otherwise would stand part of that

---

28   *Shirlaw v Southern Foundries Ltd* [1939] 2 KB 206.
29   *Liverpool City Council v Irwin* [1977] AC 239.
30   *Mears v Safecar Security Ltd* [1982] ICR 626, at 651 (per Stephenson LJ).
31   *Wilson v Maynard Shipbuilding Consultants AB* [1978] ICR 376.
32   *Lister v Romford Ice and Cold Storage Co. Ltd* [1957] AC 555.
33   *Secretary of State for Employment v ASLEF (No.2)* [1972] ICR 19.

contract, and by limiting the operation of contractual rights in situations where there is a statute giving comparable protection. In addition, the statutory provisions concerning written particulars of employment have given rise to difficulties, and are of sufficient importance in practice to require explanation. The statutory concept of continuity of employment is dealt with as a separate heading towards the end of this chapter.

Statutory incorporation. Taking first the introduction by statute of terms into the contract, examples include the equality clause which by s.1 of the EqPA is inserted in all contracts under which men and women are employed in Great Britain, and which renders illegal sexual discrimination within the contract (see Chapter 17 below). Here the introduction of the term proceeds directly from the parent statute: more commonly, statute authorises the introduction of a term through the intermediacy of the decision of the CAC. Where, for instance, an employer has failed to disclose information to a recognised trade union for the purposes of collective bargaining as required under EPA s.17 (see Chapter 3 above) then it is possible that, at the end of a lengthy process of compulsory arbitration, the CAC will make an award of terms and conditions of employment which the employer is required to observe in respect of the workers affected, and which takes effect as part of the contracts of employment of these workers (EPA s.21(6)). Further provisions for statutory incorporation are contained in the Wages Councils Act 1979 s.14.

It is of course one thing to introduce a term into the contract, and another to make it stay there. The contract of employment is distinguished by the changing content of its substance, and, in principle, whatever the source of a term of the contract, there is no reason why it should not be abandoned or varied by the subsequent agreement of the parties. The mandatory approach of the EqPA precludes such an occurrence in relation to the equality clause — 'if the terms of a contract ... do not include ... an equality clause they shall be deemed to include one' — but a different solution is provided by the EPA. Terms and conditions compulsorily introduced by virtue of an award of the CAC under EPA s.21 may be superseded or varied only in one of three ways: by a subsequent award of the CAC, by a collective agreement between the employer and the union representing the employee, or by agreement between the parties in so far as that agreement effects an improvement in these terms and conditions.

Contracting-out. Another way in which legislation may directly affect the substance of the contract is by rendering invalid attempts to contract-out of rights conferred by statute by means of a private bargain between employer and employee. Although there is limited acceptance of the possibility of allowing contracting-out under the auspices of collective bargaining — see EPCA ss.18 (guarantee pay), 65(2) (unfair dismissal), and 96 (redundancy pay) — the principle set out in EPCA s.140 is clear: any attempt, whether contained in a contract or not, to exclude or limit the operation of any provision of the EPCA is deemed void. Unfortunately, this sweeping statement does not do away with all difficulties. In the absence of any general principle of construction giving entrenched effect to terms of employment derived from a statutory source, separate provision must be made in every case against contractual derogation. Thus equivalent but not identical measures to s.140 are to be found in relation to the operation of the law of truck (Truck Act 1831 s.1) and the law of patents (Patents Act 1977 s.40(4)), to name but two instances out of many. Moreover, in practice, if not in strict law, there can be effective contracting-out where the parties successfully elect for an employment relationship based on something other than a contract of employment, as occurred, for example, on the facts of the *Ready Mixed Concrete* case.[34] The difference between fashioning a contract to meet a particular classification so that a statutory obligation does not apply and excluding by way of express term that same statutory obligation is a fine one, but it represents a barrier which so far the courts have been unable to cross.[35]

Overlapping rights. Statute may impinge on contractual rights by providing that the substance of closely overlapping rights drawn from both sources is to be taken into account when claims are made under either. A good example is to be found in relation to sick pay. Whether or not sick pay is due to an employee is a matter of contract. But, since April 1983, there has also existed a scheme of statutory sick pay, under which employers have a general obligation to pay fixed amounts to certain employees who cannot work because of sickness (see Chapter 13 below). Where there is a contractual right to sick pay this is taken into account in assessing a claim to statutory sick pay, and vice versa.[36]

Written particulars. Lastly, there is the obligation imposed by EPCA s.1 on an employer to issue written particulars of employment to his employees. The employer must within the period of thirteen weeks from the start of the employee's employment, give to him a written statement covering: the scale or rate of remuneration, and when this is paid; hours of work; any terms relating to holiday entitlements, holiday pay, incapacity for work due to sickness or injury, sick pay or pensions; length of notice the employee must give or is entitled to receive in order for the contract to be lawfully terminated; and job title.

The obligation does not compel the parties to introduce terms to cover all these points, but if there is no term then the employer must state that this is so. But there is also an obligation to include in the written statement certain information relating to disciplinary procedure, and the employer must also state whether a contracting-out certificate (under the Social Security Pensions Act 1975) is in force. Arguably (Hepple and O'Higgins, 1981:120), this second obligation imposes a duty on the employer to have disciplinary rules, so that he does not fulfil his statutory responsibilities if he merely says in the

[34] [1968] 2QB 497.
[35] See, however, the remarks of the EAT in *Secretary of State for Employment v Deary* [1984] IRLR 180 on the scope of EPCA s.140.
[36] Social Security and Housing Benefits Act 1982 s.10, Sch.2.

written statement that no such rules exist. In relation to all the matters covered by the obligation to provide written particulars, the statement may refer to another document (typically, a collective agreement) which the employee has a reasonable opportunity of reading in the course of his employment. Use of this option facilitates the incorporation of terms from such documents into the individual contract of employment, but, since the written particulars themselves do not have contractual status, it does not automatically ensure that such incorporation will take place. Conversely, the absence of such a reference does not preclude incorporation.

The operation of this duty has given rise to problems bearing upon the construction of the contract of employment. The difficulties relate to the status of the document provided by the employer, and to the erroneous but plausible belief that the contents of the document fix the terms of the contract. This is clearly not so as a matter of law, and was never the intention of Parliament — the original legislation dealing with the issuing of written particulars being only to promote the right of workers to know the most important terms of their employment (Leighton and Dumville, 1977:137). It has taken the courts some considerable time to accept in principle the limited function of the written particulars, and even now, in relation to the incorporation of terms and conditions of employment from collective agreements, no clear distinction is made between the prescriptive and informative roles of the written statement.

The decision of the Court of Appeal in *Gascol Conversions Ltd v Mercer*[37] was for long a source of controversy, as it appeared to overrule previous authority and to assume that the act of an employee in signing for the receipt of the written statement given to him by his employer was to be taken as constituting his acceptance of a written contract of employment. The written statement, in other words, was seen not as a record of the contract, but was identified with the contract itself. More recently, however, the EAT has reaffirmed the orthodoxy which *Gascol v Mercer* put in doubt. The *Gascol* case was distinguished as concerned with the special situation where the parties had chosen to express their contract in writing, 'but in the case of an ordinary statutory statement served pursuant to the statutory obligation, the document is a unilateral one merely stating the employer's view of what those terms are'.[38] It followed that the act of signing for the receipt of this document did not in itself commit the employee to a contractual acceptance of its content, and the document provided no more than persuasive evidence of the actual terms of the contract of employment.

The same presiding judge, in another decision two days later,[39] pursued this line of reasoning further. Not only did the written statement and the employee's written acknowledgment of receipt not give authoritative guidance as to the actual terms of the contract, the act of the employee in not objecting to a unilateral variation of the original written statement was not

---

[37] [1974] ICR 420.
[38] *Systems Floor Ltd v Daniel* [1982] ICR 54, at 58 (per Browne-Wilkinson J). Approved by the Court of Appeal in *Robertson v British Gas Corporation* [1983] ICR 351.
[39] *Jones v Associated Tunnelling Co. Ltd* [1981] IRLR 477.

to be taken as committing him to these varied terms. In that case the employers successfully argued that a variation in terms had taken place, but the EAT was extremely wary about the general principle at stake. It would be unrealistic, it was said, to expect employees to read and react to erroneous changes in their written particulars, so that their effective consent could be inferred from their silence. This most important observation not only counters the argument that by failing to object the employee may be taken to have varied the terms of his contract; it also gives an answer to the technically separate point that silence may be relied on as working against an employee,[40] so that the employee's silence will not, as a matter of law, preclude him from later raising objections to the terms of the written particulars he has received.

Incorporation from Collective Agreements

The contract of employment may incorporate or borrow from many sources, such as works rules or arbitration awards, but in practice it is incorporation from collective agreements which gives rise to the most interesting as well as the most important legal issues. The problems found here are of both a general and technical nature, and thus some comment about the general framework within which the discussion takes place is appropriate before consideration of the details of the law itself.

It is commonplace to affirm that the lawyer's model of the employment relationship is far removed from that of the reality of industrial relations, but perhaps in no context is this gap more evident than in relation to the legal explanation of the status of collectively agreed terms and conditions of employment. Collective agreements are only exceptionally legal binding agreements (see Chapter 4 above), and, to quote Kilner Brown J, they 'are not of themselves of any legal significance unless and until they are translated into a contractual relationship between employer and employee'.[41] Thus, in law, something which is the product of collective action *par excellence* is seen as having meaning only within the individual employment relationship. Not only does this give rise to considerable difficulty when it comes to adapting the content of the collective agreement into a suitable form for inclusion in the contract of employment, it may also distort the significance and sometimes the function of the norms involved. The cart of the individual contract of employment is put before the horse of the collective agreement. This means, for example, that, in principle, the standards set by collective agreements and translated to individual contracts via the process of incorporation enjoy no special status. They exist as terms of the contract of employment, and may as such be abandoned or varied by the simple agreement of the parties. This contrasts sharply with the position found in many other countries, where the collective agreement is recognised

---

[40] Cf. *Smith v Blandford Gee Cementation Co. Ltd* [1970] 3 All ER 154; *Evenden v Guildford City Association Football Club Ltd* [1975] QB 917.
[41] *Land v West Yorkshire Metropolitan County Council* [1979] ICR 452, at 458.

as akin to legislation guaranteeing minimum rights to the workers affected, and as such, productive of standards which may be raised to the workers' benefit, but from which there can be no derogation by private bargain.[42]

In order to explain the translation from collective agreement to individual contract, two main legal models have been advanced. Sometimes it is said that incorporation occurs as a result of the union acting as agent for the workers, so that in concluding an agreement it can be said to be acting on their behalf. But this explanation, while viable in principle and occasionally followed in practice, is widely accepted as being only of marginal importance. Not the least of the difficulties it faces is that, in Britain, the binding effect of a collective agreement is not generally considered as restricted to those workers who happen to be members of the union which negotiated it. The fact of union membership alone will not suffice to create a relationship of agency; something more is required before the courts will accept this analysis in a particular case.[43] Much more important than agency is the explanation which sees incorporation as proceeding from a term, express or implied, within the individual employment contract. Strictly speaking, there can be no doubt that a reference to a collective agreement in the statutory written statement of particulars does not of itself constitute a separate basis for incorporation, although in practice it is likely to be treated as conclusive evidence of such an occurrence.

In relation to the problems associated with the incorporation of contractual terms from collective agreements, the legal difficulties can be grouped around two main issues — identifying the substance of the terms incorporated, and relating the mechanics of incorporation to the changing nature of collective bargaining. As far as substance is concerned, there is only one formal limitation, which relates to those provisions known as 'no-strike' or 'peace' obligations. If a union agrees collectively not to strike, or, more probably, not to strike until certain dispute-settlement procedures have been tried, is that obligation reproduced in the contract of employment? As explained in Chapter 9, TULRA s.18(4) makes it difficult, though not impossible, for such an argument to succeed, by requiring certain fairly stringent conditions to be met in the form and content of the collective agreement. But even without the 'protection' offered by s.18(4) — which in many cases will be more apparent than real, given that at common law the taking of industrial action is almost always a breach of the contract of employment, irrespective of any incorporation — there is another argument against the incorporation of such clauses. Strikes, it can be argued, are essentially collective activities, and thus clauses in collective agreements limiting or restricting them can have no counterpart in individual contracts of employment. In a word, such clauses are not appropriate for being incorporated. This notion of appropriateness, while probably not persuasive in relation to 'no-strike' clauses,[44] has had more success in limiting other borrowings from collective agreements.

---

[42] See, e.g., the French Code du Travail, art.L.132–10 (Aliprantis, 1980:261–81). For the position in the USA, see *JI Case Co. v NLRB* (1964) 321 US 332, and Gould (1982:66–94).
[43] *Burton Group Ltd v Smith* [1977] IRLR 351.
[44] See, e.g., *Rookes v Barnard* [1964] AC 1129 and *Partington v NALGO* [1981] IRLR 537.

In *British Leyland (UK) Ltd v McQuilken*,[45] for example, it was used successfully to counter the contention that an employee acquired a contractual right to be consulted by his employer, notwithstanding that the latter had agreed to do this as part of a collective agreement made with his trade union. While the notion of appropriateness will serve to exclude many matters found in the collective agreement, it will not necessarily have this effect with regard to procedural provisions which set out how individual grievances between employer and employee are to be handled,[46] and, bearing in mind the massive growth in formal disciplinary procedures in British industry in the 1970s (Daniel and Millward, 1983:163), the incorporation of such matters may now be said to be fairly widespread.

As regards the second source of difficulty, that of making incorporation work against a 'dynamic' background of collective bargaining arrangements, the cases show that the judges have made some effort to make legal theory accord with practice. They have, for example, rejected an argument that the process of incorporation should be undertaken in a literal way, so that there should be a precise copying of the wording of the collective agreement in the terms of the individual contract, when this would conflict with the interpretation required by common sense.[47] So too they have acknowledged that rights acquired by incorporation are not easily lost as a consequence of changes in the power relationship between union and employer. The collective agreement and the contract are seen, correctly, as separate entities, and it follows that the termination of a collective agreement, which might proceed from the unilateral act of either employer or union, will not oust from individual contracts terms which the doctrine of incorporation had previously placed there.[48]

But the variation of the content of the contract to take account of collectively agreed changes at the collective level is something which falls to be explained by the device of the implied term. It is not difficult, once the contract has been construed so as allow for incorporation, to go further and to imply a term to the effect that the relevant terms of the contract will change in accordance with what is the outcome of negotiation. At its simplest, once the principle of the incorporation of wage rates has been established, it is manifestly reasonable to accept also that alterations in the established rates will, as they are settled collectively, take effect within the contract of employment. It does not follow, however, that a union has complete discretion to bind the workers to whatever it should agree. While an implied term allowing for movement in wage rates within certain parameters might be easily read into the contract of employment, this does not mean that such a term would cover, say, a substantial drop in wage levels or other significant deterioration in conditions of employment following collective bargaining.

[45] [1978] IRLR 245.
[46] *Barber v Manchester Regional Hospital Board* [1958] 1 WLR 181; *Jones v Lee* [1980] ICR 310.
[47] *Burroughs Machines Ltd v Timmoney* [1977] IRLR 404.
[48] *Morris v CH Bailey Ltd* [1969] 2 Lloyd's Rep 215; *Robertson v British Gas Corporation* [1983] ICR 351; *Gibbons v Associated British Ports* [1985] IRLR 376.

The courts have been rather less successful in coming to terms with another feature of British collective bargaining: the fact that there is not one single system of negotiation between employers and unions, but a number of overlapping and sometimes inconsistent layers, which exist at different organisational levels and different geographical locations. Even if it is accepted that incorporation does operate to fill the contract of employment, which particular collectively agreed bargain takes priority? The question becomes crucial when, as not infrequently happened in the past, local level bargains provided for improvements on standards laid down in agreements negotiated at national level. No simple solution to this problem of selection between competing levels of collective bargaining exists. All that one can say is that a particular line of approach, associated with the decision of the Court of Appeal in *Gascol Conversions Ltd v Mercer*[49] which tended to discount for the purposes of incorporation informal types of collective bargaining, is open to serious challenge. The approach found in the *Gascol* case has probably been superseded by one which shows the courts more circumspect and flexible, and more prepared to take account of the content of local level collective agreements.[50]

Collateral Agreements

It is customary to consider the employer–employee relationship as governed by one contract, which itself contains a range of terms, express and implied. An alternative model, however, allows for the existence of additional contractual agreements which are as a matter of law separate from the obligations contained in the main contract of employment. The purpose of such collateral agreements may be to regulate special situations which do not fall within either the express terms of the contract, or the range of matters covered by an implied term. There are some signs that the idea of seeing the obligations of the basic contract of employment as supplemented in this way is growing more acceptable, and this trend deserves attention because it can have important practical consequences. Thus, in *Land and Wilson v West Yorkshire Metropolitan District Council*,[51] the Court of Appeal accepted that firemen who were employed by a local authority to do extra duties (additional to their full-time work as ordinary firemen) were employed for these extra duties under a separate part of their contract of employment. The significance was that when the employers gave notice to end that separate and particular part of the contract, this did not amount to a dismissal in law of the employees under the main part of their contract.

Another example arose in the litigation which took place during the teachers' pay dispute in 1985. In the context of considering the legality of the refusal by teachers to participate in the supervision of pupils during lunch hours, it was argued that, even though such duties were not required under

---

[49] [1974] ICR 420.
[50] *Barrett v NCB* [1978] ICR 1101.
[51] [1981] IRLR 87.

the contract of employment itself, by undertaking such duties in return for certain benefits the teachers had become obliged to carry on with them under a separate collateral agreement.[52] Such an agreement could, of course, itself be terminated by the giving of notice — but the point of the argument was that by terminating it as had been done without the giving of reasonable notice of termination, the teachers had committed a breach of contract. Unfortunately, the point was not decided in the course of the legal proceedings, but on the authority of *Land* (and another later decision)[53] there would seem to be no objection in principle to augmenting the totality of the obligations arising within the employment relationship in this way.

SUBSTANCE OF THE CONTRACT

The following discussion, which is in no sense exhaustive, is intended to illustrate the duties arising in three important areas: the employee's duty of obedience, payment of wages, and termination of the contract.

Duty of Obedience

As noted above the employee's duty to obey the reasonable orders of his employer constitutes one of the traditional distinguishing features of the contract of employment. In the modern law, the legal basis for this feature is a term implied into the contract as a matter of law. In the past, breach of this duty left the employee open to the sanction of summary dismissal, and this remains true today, although the standards of behaviour expected of employees have been somewhat relaxed in line with changing social attitudes.[54] Some of the most interesting developments, however, have taken place elsewhere. In the past, the ambit of the duty of obedience was explored by the courts only in the context of allegedly wrongful dismissals; not so today, when the existence of the range of statutory employment protection rights directs attention on to what may legitimately or reasonably be required by an employer of his employee. Examples may be drawn from the law of unfair dismissal and redundancy, topics which are discussed in detail in Chapter 15.

In unfair dismissal law the question whether an order falls within the scope of the powers of command given by the contract to the employer may be relevant at the stage of deciding either the reasonableness of a dismissal, or whether or not a dismissal took place. With regard to the former, while the issue whether the employee was contractually bound to obey is not decisive one way or the other as to fairness,[55] this test allows the courts to

---

52 *Metropolitan Borough of Solihull v NUT* [1985] IRLR 211.
53 *Bond and Neads v CAV Ltd* [1983] IRLR 360. But cf. *Gibbons v Associated British Ports* [1985] IRLR 376.
54 *Wilson v Racher* [1974] ICR 428; *Laws v London Chronicle (Indicator Newspapers) Ltd* [1959] 2 All ER 285.
55 *Ladbroke Racing Ltd v Arnott* [1979] IRLR 192; *Brandon and Goold v Murphy Bros* [1983] IRLR 54.

evaluate and criticise the exercise of managerial prerogative. The cases show, for example, the courts' readiness to express views on such diverse matters as the scope of the employer's right to specify the details of his employee's dress, and to implement badly thought-out systems for assessing work performance.[56] By contrast, in proving a constructive dismissal — where the employer's improper conduct has allegedly justified the employee in leaving — the test is based on contract.[57] A tribunal will often have to decide whether the giving of orders which the employee has found unacceptable amounts to a serious breach of the employer's implied duty of good and reasonable conduct, and as such warranted the employee's departure.[58]

Another example may be taken from the law of redundancy, where the concept of job mobility has become of fundamental importance. An employee who is dismissed because of refusal to comply with a lawful order to take up another job with the same employer in another part of the country is dismissed for misconduct, not redundancy, and accordingly it is often vital to know the extent to which such a right on the part of the employer to direct movement forms part of the contract.[59]

As these particular examples demonstrate, under the influence of the framework of individual statutory rights, the courts have, to a much greater extent than in the past, been given opportunities of passing judgment on the orders given by an employer to his employees. Under the influence of these rights, the prevailing view which has emerged favours a much more restrictive interpretation of the right to command than was previously found acceptable. The right to command is seen as more limited in scope and is itself subject to the employer's contractual duty to maintain the employee's trust and confidence. Some (for example, Napier, 1977; Elias, 1981) have seen in these changes a movement among the judiciary towards a more pluralistic analysis of the employment relationship, although this argument has not gone unchallenged (Collins, 1982; Glasbeek, 1984).

Payment for Work Done

While the law recognises that the payment of remuneration in exchange for services is fundamental to the constitution of the contract of employment, there is a somewhat surprising lack of certainty about the precise implementation of this aspect of the relationship. To begin with, a conventional distinction exists between payment provided for by the ordinary terms of the contract and that which comes from overtime. A practical reason for making this distinction is of course that overtime usually attracts a higher rate of pay, but the distinction also has a less obvious significance in relation to the

---

[56] *Boychuk v Symons Holdings Ltd* [1977] IRLR 395; *Payne v Spook Erection Ltd* [1984] IRLR 219.
[57] *Western Excavating (ECC) Ltd v Sharp* [1978] ICR 221.
[58] *Woods v WM Car Services (Peterborough) Ltd* [1982] IRLR 413.
[59] *O'Brien v Associated Fire Alarms* [1969] 1 All ER 93; *Jones v Associated Tunnelling Co. Ltd* [1981] IRLR 477.

many statutory rights which require the calculation of weekly hours of work, either for the purposes of eligibility or calculation of benefits due. In most cases overtime working, even if sanctioned by long practice, will be classified as extra-contractual,[60] and so will not count for the relevant statutory purposes.

There are, moreover, distinctions to be made between different payment systems. Probably the most well-known is between the worker who is paid for what he produces (piece-work) or for a set number of hours worked each week, and the worker who is paid a fixed salary for the doing of a job, without reference to his productivity or number of hours. Both the first two types of remuneration are usually associated with wage-earners, while the fixed salary appointment is customary in higher-status white-collar employment. The legal significance of this distinction is that it is easier to argue that the consideration or price for the wages paid is the actual doing of work in the first two situations, as opposed to the readiness of the employee to perform work in the case of a salaried job. But another approach (Napier, 1984), arguably more in keeping with the views expressed in the cases, is to accept that in a contract of employment 'it is the service that earns the remuneration',[61] and that the question of what constitutes service is something which has to be decided according to the terms of the contract. It is a mistake to think of service merely in terms of direct working effort. The employee who is on stand-by, waiting to do work as and when required by his employer, is offering performance (and earning wages) no less than the operative who is actually engaged in production at his machine.

The law makes various provisions for protecting security of earnings. The main statutory measures are contained in the Truck Acts 1831–1940, supplemented recently by the rights to receive an itemised statement of pay (EPCA s.8), guarantee payments (EPCA s.12), payment for suspension on medical grounds (EPCA s.19), and maternity pay (EPCA s.33). Of these measures, the provisions of the Truck Acts alone impinge directly on the terms of the contract of employment, by making it, among other things, illegal to contract for the payment of wages 'otherwise than in the current coin of the realm', and by prohibiting (subject to closely regulated exceptions) deductions from wages. Potentially, these provisions are of very wide application, notwithstanding that they govern only those engaged in manual labour. But empirical evidence (Goriely, 1983) shows that they are widely ignored in practice and very imperfectly enforced by the responsible state body, the wages inspectorate. Deductions from the wages of staff to take account of shortages found on stock-taking are fairly common in certain trades and yet, despite being contrary to the legislation, go largely unchallenged. The government has published a consultation paper (DE, 1984), in which the abolition of this protective legislation is mooted.

When wages have been earned by performance, the employee's claim to payment arises strictly not as part of the law of contract, but in debt. That is to say, it is money which is owing to the employee because of services he has

---

[60] *Tarmac Roadstone Holdings v Peacock* [1973] ICR 273.
[61] *Automatic Fire Sprinklers v Watson* [1944] CLR 435, at 465 (per Dixon CJ).

rendered. It follows that the legal rules appropriate to contractual claims have no bearing at this stage. Thus, for example, an employee has no duty to mitigate his loss in respect of wages earned but unpaid. This important point has sometimes been overlooked by the courts when actions are brought to recover wages following industrial action short of strikes. This issue is discussed in Chapter 9 in terms of the employer's right to stop pay, but certain aspects must be considered here as they illustrate the nature of the contract of employment.

While it is probable that working to rule is the kind of repudiatory breach that justifies summary dismissal,[62] it would appear that if the employer does not exercise this option to terminate the contract he is bound to pay wages for the, albeit imperfect, performance offered. In one case dealing (though only indirectly) with this point, the Court of Appeal indicated otherwise, suggesting that someone working to rule could not prove that he was ready and willing to perform his contract.[63] But that requirement is properly applied to a claim for damages for breach of contract; not (as in the case of unpaid wages) to a claim for payment of money due. That point aside, however, judicial observations in the *ASLEF* decision stand as authority for the view that the employer is entitled to refuse to pay wages for partial performance of the contract of employment by the employee, at least where that partial performance occurs in connection with industrial action and where it has a seriously disruptive effect on his business.

Other jurisdictions see the situation differently. In Australia, for example, it has been held in the High Court that wages could be claimed in circumstances of partial performance where the employer had allowed the contract to continue and had taken the benefit of that portion of the work that was done by the employee.[64] A related point concerns the legitimacy of deductions being made from salaries by employers to take account of the impact made by lesser forms of industrial action.[65] Such deductions may properly reflect only the actual economic loss attributable to the breach of contract suffered by the employer.[66] Where, however, the industrial action takes the form of a direct refusal to work in accordance with the lawful directions of the employer, then no remuneration at all is due.[67]

Wrongful Dismissal

The contract of employment, which is usually of indefinite duration, may be terminated in a variety of ways. The law of wrongful dismissal is mainly

---

[62] *Secretary of State for Employment v ASLEF (No.2)* [1972] 2 QB 455, at 492 (per Lord Denning MR).
[63] *Henthorn and Taylor v Central Electricity Generating Board* [1980] IRLR 361.
[64] *Welbourn v Australian Postal Commission* [1984] 52 ALR 669. Cf. *Australian National Airlines Commission v Robinson* [1977] VR 87.
[65] *Royle v Trafford Borough Council* [1984] IRLR 184; *Miles v Wakefield Metropolitan District Council* [1985] IRLR 108.
[66] *National Coal Board v Galley* [1958] 1 WLR 16.
[67] *Cresswell v Board of Inland Revenue* [1984] IRLR 190.

concerned with termination brought about by the employer, and is either preceded by no notice, or by shorter notice than is required either under the contract or the relevant statutory rules. Under EPCA s.49 an employee who has worked for two years is entitled to two weeks' notice of termination (or wages in lieu) and for each additional completed year of service, he gains an entitlement to an extra week's notice or pay in lieu, up to a maximum of twelve weeks. An employee who has worked for a month or more but less than two years is entitled to one week's notice. This protection cannot be lost by private agreement between employer and employee, although the parties may by contract extend the period of notice.

Only where the employee has been guilty of serious misconduct amounting to a repudiation of his contract of employment is the sanction of summary dismissal warranted, and the point has been made that the concept of serious misconduct is one which has changed to become narrower than it was previously. Whereas, for example, in earlier days there was no requirement that the employer's orders be 'reasonable' (McCarry, 1984), this is arguably different today. It is, of course, no part of an employee's duty to obey instructions which would lead him to commit a crime, or to expose himself to the serious risk of death or injury.[68] The most interesting recent developments in the law of wrongful dismissal raise, in general, the question whether the contract of employment is properly seen as subject to the ordinary rules of contract, or has an independence from them. In particular, they involve consideration of the remedies available where dismissal constitutes a breach of contract by the employer, and of the operation of the principles of natural justice within the employment relationship.

Traditionally, the only course of action open to an employee dismissed in breach of contract was a claim for damages against his ex-employer, based on the loss suffered by him when the contract was terminated by the unlawful act. The contract, in other words, was seen as coming to an end without need for any action on the part of the employer, an analysis which has been dignified with the name of the 'automatic theory' of termination (Elias, 1978:17–18; McMullen, 1982:111–23). On this analysis, the contract of employment stood on its own in this respect, because there was no possibility of the injured party electing not to accept the repudiatory dismissal as ending the contract. This reasoning was endorsed by Sir John Donaldson when President of the National Industrial Relations Court.[69] It was, however, overturned by two decisions which appeared to bring the mechanics of termination back into line with mainstream contract doctrine by requiring acceptance of the repudiation by the innocent party.[70] But the practical significance of this development was lessened by the readiness with which the judges indicated they would find evidence of such acceptance. None the less, to quote the words of Buckley LJ in *Gunton's* case, it was not

---

[68] *Bouzuru v Ottoman Bank* [1930] AC 271. Cf. *Turner v Mason* (1845) 14 M & W 112.
[69] *Sanders v Earnest A Neale Ltd* [1974] ICR 565.
[70] *Thomas Marshall (Exports) Ltd v Guinle* [1979] Ch 227; *Gunton v Richmond-upon-Thames London Borough Council* [1980] ICR 755.

'impossible that in some cases incidental or collateral terms might cause the injured party to want to keep the contract on foot.'[71] Such special cases might arise where, for example, keeping the contract alive might open up entitlement to a particular statutory right by virtue of the employee's length of service. Similarly, prolonging the existence of the contract could be significant for pension entitlement calculated by reference to length of service.

The most recent indication, however, voiced by the Court of Appeal in *R v East Berkshire Health Authority ex parte Walsh*,[72] is that the choice between an 'automatic' or 'elective' theory of termination has not yet been authoritatively settled in favour of the latter. In that case two members of the Court of Appeal (including Donaldson MR) expressed reserve over the precise effect of the *Gunton* decision. May LJ openly preferred the dissenting view of Shaw LJ in that case, in support of the 'automatic' theory of termination.

A related but separate point to the above is whether an employee is at common law entitled to the protections of natural justice before being dismissed for alleged misconduct or other good reason. This may of course be specifically covered by an express term within the contract, but will it be implied by operation of law irrespective of what the parties themselves have provided for? In certain exceptional situations this has always been so; for example, where the employee (usually high-ranking) has been fortunate enough to enjoy, in addition to any contractual rights, the exceptional status of office-holder. Because the holding of office was originally linked with the owning of a right of property, the common law has been careful to protect the person whose rights were potentially infringed by removal or dismissal, and this concern was translated into a requirement that certain minimum procedural standards be observed prior to an effective removal. But the class of persons protected in this way was very restricted — the leading modern example of such a person being someone holding the position of chief constable.[73]

Recently, however, there have been indications that the courts were prepared to widen this category. Dicta at the level of the House of Lords[74] and Court of Appeal[75] suggested not only that many ordinary employees might benefit from the extended scope of such protection, but that in an appropriate case the courts would use the discretionary remedies of declaration and injunction to prevent dismissals in breach of natural justice going ahead. This movement in favour of the spread of natural justice entitlements in employment cases was further endorsed by the decision of Woolf J in *R v British Broadcasting Corporation ex parte Lavelle*[76] to the effect that, in all cases where the contract of employment incorporated

---

[71] At 772.
[72] [1984] IRLR 278.
[73] *Ridge v Baldwin* [1964] AC 40.
[74] *Malloch v Aberdeen Corporation* [1971] 2 All ER 1578, at 1595 (per Lord Wilberforce).
[75] *Stevenson v United Road Transport Union* [1977] ICR 893, at 902 (per Buckley LJ).
[76] [1983] ICR 99.

procedural safeguards, the employee could claim the kind of protection previously thought only to be available to office-holders.

While none of these decisions has so far been overruled or even specifically disapproved, the decision of the Court of Appeal in *R v East Berkshire Health Authority ex parte Walsh*[77] is an example of a different approach. That case dealt with an attempt by a senior nursing officer employed within the National Health Service to obtain judicial review to stop his dismissal, which he alleged to be in breach of natural justice. Expressed narrowly, the decision was that the remedy of judicial review for failure to comply with alleged breach of natural justice was not available to workers such as Mr Walsh. Judicial review was held by the Court of Appeal not to be available in respect of public employment which was underpinned by statute, but where there was no direct statutory control of the grounds of dismissal. More broadly, however, the decision casts doubt on the willingness of the Court of Appeal to support any generalised extension of procedural limitations on dismissals by operation of the doctrines of the common law, and that approach may well extend to proceedings brought under the heading of an ordinary contractual claim as well as to those where the somewhat specialised remedy of judicial review is sought. Nevertheless, judicial review remains important for certain public sector workers whose terms of employment are not based on contract, and where the nature of their employment imparts the necessary public law character to the relationship.[78]

CONTINUITY OF EMPLOYMENT

The final topic dealt with is a statutory concept, but makes extensive use of the contract of employment. The requirement of continuous employment is fundamental to the working of the system of statutory employment rights, for, in general, these are extended only to persons who have been employed for a certain length of time with one employer, or a series of linked employers. Even when eligibility for a particular right is not dependent on length of service, the calculation of compensation for infringement usually is. Many 'marginal' workers find themselves excluded from statutory rights because they were unable to fulfil the conditions required for continuous employment (see Chapter 18), and this is so notwithstanding the statutory presumption that employment during any period is continuous, so that the burden of proof lies with the employer (or Secretary of State) who is contesting this.

The concept of continuity, as expresssed in EPCA Sch.13 (as amended), seeks to classify the various vicissitudes and interruptions which, to some extent, are likely to be found in normal working life. Generally, the effect of the law is that such incidents do not work to the disadvantage of employees

77 [1984] IRLR 278.
78 *R v Secretary of State for the Home Department ex parte Benwell* [1985] IRLR 6.

seeking to claim statutory rights, but there are several important exceptions to this rule.

Weeks that Count

In order for a week to count towards a period of continuous employment, it must normally either be one in which the employee is employed for sixteen hours or more, or be one in which, although less than sixteen hours are actually worked, the employee is governed by a contract of employment which normally involves employment for sixteen hours or more (Sch.13, paras.3,4). Thus, for example, a week during which the employee is on holiday counts for continuity purposes by virtue of the operation of the second principle. If the week does not qualify under these tests then in principle it does not count in building up continuity and, furthermore, it breaks any period of continuity already accrued. To this basic rule, however, there are several exceptions.

Reduction in contractual hours. If, having worked under a contract for sixteen hours or more, an employee is then employed under a contract normally involving between eight and sixteen hours, he will continue to build up continuity for a period of up to twenty-six weeks (Sch.13, para.5). If he has been employed for five years or more, then continuity is for all purposes assessed on the basis of a minimum of eight hours weekly contractual or actual working, so that a person in this position is not subject to this twenty-six week limitation, and, indeed, need never have worked for more than eight hours weekly since his employment began. In addition, once qualified for a particular statutory right by virtue of a period of continuity, an employee will only lose that qualification by reason of a reduction in his working hours if his relations are governed by a contract which normally involves employment for less than eight hours weekly, and he is employed in any week for less than sixteen hours (Sch.13, para.7). These two conditions are cumulative, so that it is not enough for actual hours worked to drop below sixteen if the contractual obligation remains above this limit.[79]

No contract of employment. Certain periods when there is no contract of employment in existence none the less will count towards continuity. This rule (Sch.13, para.9) applies to weeks where the employee is for the whole or part of it: incapable of work in consequence of sickness or injury; or absent from work on account of a temporary cessation of work; or absent from work in circumstances such that, by arrangement or custom, he is regarded as continuing in the employment of his employer for all or any purposes; or absent from work wholly or partly because of pregnancy or confinement. In the case of incapability in consequence of sickness or injury

---

[79] See, e.g., *Booth v Times Furnishing Co. Ltd* (1984) IDS Brief 281 (July) 8. See too the discussion of *Secretary of State for Employment v Deary* [1984] IRLR 180 in Chapter 18.

or absence because of pregnancy, the maximum period covered is twenty-six weeks, although this time-limit has no application to a woman exercising her right to return to work after pregnancy under EPCA s.45. In such a situation every week of her absence counts for the purposes of continuity, whether or not her contract of employment continued during her absence (Sch.13, para.10).

The interpretation of all these provisions has been a rich source of case law, the details of which cannot be explored here. An important point is that Sch.13, para. 9 only applies where there is no contract of employment in existence. It follows therefore that it is unnecessary and wrong to invoke the provision when the absence is already provided for by the terms of the contract. Commonly this will be the case in the event of absence through sickness. But it is this paragraph which may maintain continuity in situations where there is a practice of dismissing workers during slack periods and re-engaging them when demand picks up, or the granting of exceptional leave of absence to an employee. The question whether in terms of para.9 the cessation of work was 'temporary' must be answered with hindsight, that is, after the resumption of the employment.[80] But the cessation must be transient, in the sense of lasting only for a relatively short time by contrast to the periods of continuous employment before and after it.[81] Many part-time and seasonal workers will find that breaks in their employment will not be covered by the provisions of para.9, although the decision of the House of Lords in the *Ford* case has improved their position by holding that teachers and others employed over a series of academic years (excluding the summer vacations) may be able to show continuous employment spanning this annual break. Where workers are employed on a series of fixed term contracts regularly renewed, then again continuity should be assured, either because the new contract will begin in the same week as the old one ends (and so there will be no interruption), or because any gap will be held to be covered by the provision on temporary cessation.

Industrial action. An employee who takes part in a strike (defined as a concerted cessation of work or a concerted refusal to continue to work, done as a means of compelling an employer to accept or not to accept terms and conditions of employment (Sch.13, para.24(1)) is in a special position. Any week during any part of which there is such participation will not count in building up a period of continuous employment but, unusually, neither that week nor a week during which the employee is absent from work because he has been locked out by his employer breaks continuity already accrued (Sch.13, para.15). Since 1982, the outcome is that a employee who has gone on strike for any number of days will find that the beginning of his period of continuous employment is postponed by that number of days (EPCA s.151, as amended), and so he must work longer in order to qualify for the various rights conditional on periods of continuous employment.

---

[80] *Fitzgerald v Hall, Russell & Co. Ltd* [1970] AC 984.
[81] *Ford v Warwickshire County Council* [1983] IRLR 126.

These provisions emphasise the importance of distinguishing participation in a strike from the act of an employee who, perhaps because he is intimidated, does not go to work at the time of an industrial dispute. The meaning of 'intimidation' in this context is open to debate. What will be seen by one person as the removal of effective freedom of choice by threats, will be seen by another as no more than vigorous persuasion. It should also be noted in this context that there is no requirement that the industrial action involves a breach of the contract of employment. So here, as elsewhere,[82] the imposition of an overtime ban may satisfy the definition.

Change of Employers

Business take-overs. Schedule 13 also contains provisions designed to preserve continuity in certain circumstances where an employee moves from one job to another with a different employer, or continues doing the same job with another employer. In the situation where the trade, business or undertaking is transferred as a going concern, then the continuity of the employee who goes to work for the new employer will be maintained (para.17(2)). But the cases show that it is not always easy to distinguish such a situation from one where assets alone are transferred, and continuity is broken.[83]

If the employee does not go along with working for the new employer, and there is thus no transfer of continuity in this way, then the employee may be entitled to receive a redundancy payment. This will only be so, however, if he has not unreasonably refused an offer of employment made by the new owner (EPCA ss.94(3), 82(3)(5)). In situations where the Transfer of Undertakings (Protection of Employment) Regulations[84] apply (typically where there is a take-over of a business otherwise than by share purchase), then there is no room for the application of Sch.13, para.17, and no threat to continuity, as the contracts of employment, together with any accrued periods of continuous employment of the relevant workers, are automatically transferred to the new employer.

Other changes. Some of the most important situations provided for by Sch.13 are that the transfer of an employee to an associated employer does not break continuity (para.18), nor does the transfer which occurs on the death of an employer, or a change in the constitution of a partnership which acts as an employer (para.17(4)(5)). And an employee who is reinstated or re-engaged by an employer (or a successor or associated employer) following the making of a claim of unfair dismissal does not suffer any break in continuity.[85]

---

82   *Faust v Power Packing Casemakers Ltd* [1983] IRLR 117. See Chapter 9 above.
83   *Woodhouse v Peter Brotherhood Ltd* [1972] ICR 186; *Melon v Hector Powe Ltd* [1981] ICR 43.
84   SI 1981 No. 1794.
85   Labour Relations (Continuity of Employment) Regulations SI 1976 No.660.

FUTURE PROSPECTS

No signs exist at the moment that the contract of employment will develop in any startlingly novel directions over the next few years. The innate conservatism of the lawyers concerned with the preparation of legislation means that, should any new statutory employment rights (such as, for example, a right to paternity leave) be introduced it is more than likely that their scope would be set by using the contract of employment as a limiting device. No doubt the courts will also continue to tussle with the task of defining the identifying characteristics of a contract of employment, and perhaps if, as Clark and Wedderburn (1983:155) have suggested, the growth of artificial forms of self-employment is seen as constituting a real threat to employment protection and trade union organisation, the judicial answers to this perennial problem may show a greater, more explicit, awareness of the policy implications.

It may also happen that, as the impact of statutory employment rights becomes less under a government disinclined to do anything which might be seen as increasing the cost of employing labour, the rules of the common law become more valued as a means of developing employment protection. The most fruitful area for the development of the common law is that concerned with remedies for dismissal. For the obtaining of declarations and injunctions (which have the effect of stopping dismissals taking place or being implemented), may be seen as increasingly desirable against a background of high unemployment and a scheme of statutory compensation which places a value of no more than a few hundred (or even thousand) pounds on the loss of a job. But significant change in the law here would require the active participation of the judges. As noted above, few indications exist that the senior judiciary will respond positively to any such innovatory developments of the common law.

Bibliography

Aliprantis, N. 1980. *La Place de la Convention Collective dans la Hierarchie des Normes*. Paris: Librairie Générale de Droit et de Jurisprudence.

Atiyah, P.S. 1979. *The Rise and Fall of Freedom of Contract*. Oxford: Clarendon Press.

Bartrip, P.W.J., and S.B. Burman. 1983. *The Wounded Soldiers of Industry*. Oxford: Clarendon Press.

Clark, J., and *Lord* Wedderburn. 1983. 'Modern Labour Law: Problems, Functions, and Policies'. *Labour Law and Industrial Relations: Building on Kahn-Freund*. Eds. *Lord* Wedderburn, R. Lewis and J. Clark. Oxford: Clarendon Press, 127–242.

Collins, H. 1982. 'Capitalist Discipline and Corporatist Law'. *Industrial Law Journal*, 11 (June and September), 78–93, 170–77.

Craig, C., J. Rubery, R. Tarling and F. Wilkinson. 1982. *Labour Market Structure, Industrial Organisation and Low Pay*. Cambridge: Cambridge University Press.

Daniel, W.W., and N. Millward. 1983. *Workplace Industrial Relations in Britain: The DE/PSI/SSRC Survey*. London: Heinemann.

Department of Employment (DE). 1984. *Protection of Wages: Legislative Proposals*. London: DE.

Dicey, A.V. 1914. *Lectures on the Relation between Law and Public Opinion in England during the Nineteenth Century*. 2nd edn. London: Macmillan. Reissued 1962. London: Macmillan.

Elias, P. 1978. 'Unravelling the Concept of Dismissal'. *Industrial Law Journal*, 7 (March), 16–29.

——. 1981. 'Fairness in Unfair Dismissal: Trends and Tensions'. *Industrial Law Journal*, 10 (December), 201–17.

Foster, K. 1983. 'The Legal Form of Work in the 19th Century: The Myth of Contract?'. Paper presented to conference on 'The History of Law, Labour and Crime', University of Warwick, September. (Unpublished).

Fox, A. 1974. *Beyond Contract: Work, Power and Trust Relations*. London: Faber.

Fredman, S. 1984. 'Contractual and Public Law Remedies in Respect of Unilateral Alterations'. *Industrial Law Journal*, 13 (September), 177–81.

Freedland, M.R. 1983. 'Labour Law and Leaflet Law: The Youth Training Scheme of 1983'. *Industrial Law Journal*, 12 (December), 220–35.

Friedmann, W. 1959. *Law in a Changing Society*. London: Stevens.

Ganz, G. 1967. 'Public Law Principles Applicable to Dismissal from Employment'. *Modern Law Review*, 30 (May), 288–302.

Glasbeek, H.J. 1984. 'The Utility of Model Building — Collins' Capitalist Discipline and Corporatist Law'. *Industrial Law Journal*, 13 (September), 133–52.

Goriely, T. 1983. 'Arbitrary Deductions from Pay and the Proposed Repeal of the Truck Acts'. *Industrial Law Journal*, 12 (December), 236–50.

Gould, W.B. 1982. *A Primer on American Labor Law*. Cambridge, Mass.: MIT Press.

Haines, B.W. 1980. 'English Labour Law and the Separation from Contract'. *Journal of Legal History*, 1 (December), 262–96.

Hepple, B.A. 1982. 'Labour Law and Public Employees in Great Britain'. *Labour Law and the Community: Perspectives for the 1980s*. Eds. *Lord* Wedderburn and W.T. Murphy. London: Institute of Advanced Legal Studies, 67–83.

——. 1983. 'Individual Labour Law'. *Industrial Relations in Britain*. Ed. G.S. Bain. Oxford: Blackwell, 393–417.

——, and P. O'Higgins. 1981. *Employment Law*. 4th edn. B. A. Hepple. London: Sweet & Maxwell.

Kahn-Freund, O. 1951. 'Servants and Independent Contractors'. *Modern Law Review*, 14 (October), 504–9.

——. 1954. 'Legal Framework'. *The System of Industrial Relations in Great Britain*. Eds. A.D. Flanders and H.A. Clegg. Oxford: Blackwell, 42–127.

——. 1959. 'Labour Law'. *Law and Opinion in England in the 20th Century*. Ed. M. Ginsberg. London: Stevens, 215–63.

——. 1967. 'A Note on Status and Contract in British Labour Law'. *Modern Law Review*, 30 (November), 635–44.

——. 1977. 'Blackstone's Neglected Child: The Contract of Employment'. *Law Quarterly Review*, 93 (October), 508–28.

Leighton, P.E., and S.L. Dumville. 1977. 'From Statement to Contract – Some Effects of the Contracts of Employment Act 1972'. *Industrial Law Journal*, 6 (September), 133–48.

Lewis, R. 1976. 'The Historical Development of Labour Law'. *British Journal of Industrial Relations*, 19 (March), 1–17.

McCarry, G.J. 1984. 'The Employee's Duty to Obey Unreasonable Orders'. *Australian Law Journal*, 58 (June), 327–32.

McMullen, J. 1982. 'A Synthesis of the Mode of Termination of Contracts of Employment'. *Cambridge Law Journal*, 41 (April), 110–41.

Merritt, A. 1982. 'The Historical Role of Law in the Regulation of Employment – Abstentionist or Interventionist'. *Australian Journal of Law and Society*, 1 (1), 56–82.

Napier, B.W. 1972. 'Working to Rule – A Breach of the Contract of Employment?'. *Industrial Law Journal*, 1 (September), 125–34.

——. 1977. 'Judicial Attitudes towards the Employment Relationship – Some Recent Developments'. *Industrial Law Journal*, 6 (March), 1–18.

——. 1980. 'Office and Office-Holder in British Labour Law'. *International Collection of Essays in Memoriam Sir Otto Kahn-Freund*. Eds. F. Gamillscheg et al. Munich: C.H. Beck, 593–607.

——. 1984. 'Aspects of the Wage-Work Bargain'. *Cambridge Law Journal*, 43 (November), 337–48.

Pritt, D.N. 1970. *Employers, Workers and Trade Unions*. London: Lawrence & Wishart.

Rideout, R. 1966. 'The Contract of Employment'. *Current Legal Problems*, vol. 19, 111–27.

Ruegg, A.H. 1901. 'Changes in the Law of England Affecting Labour'. *A Century of Law Reform. Twelve Lectures on the Changes in the Law of England During the Nineteenth Century*. London: Macmillan, 241–79.

Selznick, P. 1969. *Law, Society and Industrial Justice*. New York: Russell Sage Foundation.

Tiley, J. 1981. *Revenue Law*. 2nd edn. London: Butterworths.

Wade, H. W. R. 1985. 'Procedure and Prerogative in Public Law'. *Law Quarterly Review*, 101 (April), 180–99.

13 Employment Protection and Social Security

Erika Szyszczak

The relationship between employment protection and social security occupies a twilight world rarely entered by academic lawyers. The two areas are popularly and traditionally polarised: a person is either in work and looks to contractual and statutory guarantees to protect rights at work or is out work and looks to the benefits offered by the social security system. But this view is too simple; the relationship between employment protection and social security provision is complex in many respects. The interrelationship of the two areas has implications for the operation of the labour market as a whole: it may affect the size of the labour market, determining how and when a person enters or leaves the labour market and how employers adjust to fluctuations in supply and demand, not only of labour, but also of the quantity of products or services produced. It may also determine how and when the state intervenes in the labour market in order to offset market failure.

Before an attempt is made to shed light on this complex interrelationship, it is necessary to describe the main elements of employment protection and social security. Once the broad scope of these areas has been identified, the relationship between the two can be illuminated by focusing in greater detail on four aspects: the decision to participate in the labour market, short-time working, maternity benefits and sickness benefit. In all four areas the state has actively intervened to regulate the labour market both through employment protection legislation and social security.

EMPLOYMENT PROTECTION

Successive post-war governments have established a degree of legal protection for employees through legislative intervention in the labour market. This development has been variously interpreted as part of an intended transition towards a more equal and democratic society, as a strategy to modernise British industrial relations in conformity with both international standards and the reformist prescription of the Donovan Commission, and as an indication of an overall trend towards corporatist control (cf. Clark and Wedderburn, 1983:184–98; Lewis, 1983:368–81; Collins, 1982). Whatever the purpose, by 1979 the Conservative Government perceived that the balance had swung too far in favour of workers' rights and set about dismantling some of them.

This chapter concentrates upon individual employment protection rights. By so doing, the role of collective rights and their importance and influence on individual rights should not be underestimated. In tracing the historical development of employment protection, Kahn-Freund (1983:37–51) categorises three layers. The first layer comprises the development of health and safety at work standards and the protection of wages through the Truck Acts. The second layer has its starting point in the Trade Boards Act 1909 when the state broadened its interest away from merely looking at methods of payment of wages to take an interest in the quantum of wages. The introduction of a statutory form of minimum wages was eventually extended to include rights to holidays and holiday pay and other conditions of employment (Wages Councils Act 1959 s.11). The third layer, to which attention will be paid, is the development of modern employment protection.

A striking feature of modern employment protection legislation is its ad hoc arrival on the industrial relations scene. The earliest of measures, the Contracts of Employment Act 1963, introduced the statutory right to written details of the particulars of employment and gave minimum periods of notice for termination of employment with guarantees of income during the notice period. This was followed by the Redundancy Payments Act 1965, which provided compensation for enforced job loss due to economic circumstances. Protection against arbitrary dismissal was introduced by the IRA of 1971. These measures established what has been termed a 'floor of rights' (Wedderburn, 1971:8, 16). This was built upon in the EPA 1975 which introduced, among other things, the right to guarantee payments, the right to maternity pay and leave, the right to time off work, trade union rights, and guarantees by the state in the event of the employer's insolvency. Davies and Freedland (1984:347) point to the significance of this Act in extending the concept of employment security from the termination of employment to the content of the employment relationship. An attempt was made to consolidate this new era of rights in the EPCA 1978. While this remains the major piece of employment protection legislation, several important areas of employment protection remain outside the scope of this Act which has itself been subject to several ad hoc amendments.

A major area of rights outside the EPCA is the legislation relating to race and sex discrimination (see Chapter 17). New forms of employment protection, such as the rights to protection of confidential information contained in the Data Protection Act 1984, have also developed outside the scope of the EPCA. A further complication is that the European Community has been actively involved in legislating in the area of labour law (see Chapter 20; Hepple, 1983a). Most of this legislation has been enacted in the form of Directives and has been incorporated into British law. European Community law, however, remains a separate and underlying source of employment protection law, which may in certain circumstances be relied upon by individuals in the national courts (Wyatt, 1983).

A second distinctive feature of employment protection is its relationship with collective bargaining. As Hepple (1983b:385) observes, 'the design of the legislation is an expressed preference for collective bargaining, and the content of statutory rights is generally below that of the best results of collective bargaining from the workers' viewpoint'. The idea behind the 'floor of rights' approach was that the weaker, poorly unionised workers would be guaranteed minimum rights which could be extended but not restricted by individual or collective agreement. But the individual nature of the rights, 'means that, even where collective bargaining is well-established, individual workers are free to assert and enforce their rights without the assistance of a trade union or, what is more, even against its wishes' (Hepple, 1983b:394).

There is scope for collective bargaining to replace the statutory rights in the areas of unfair dismissal (EPCA s.65), guarantee payments (EPCA s.18), redundancy payments (EPCA s.96) and the handling of redundancy situations (EPA s.107). Application must be made to the Secretary of State who must be satisfied that the collectively agreed arrangements are at least of the same standard as the statutory rights. They need not be more favourable. But these exemption provisions have been under-utilised (Bourn, 1979).

A third characteristic of the legislation is that the rights are not universal. Certain categories of employment are excluded from part or all of the legislation, for example, 'mariners' (EPCA s.144), the police (EPCA s.146) and those working ordinarily outside Great Britain (EPCA s.141(2); SDA s.10). Small firms are also exempted from certain employment protection legislation; for example, firms employing less than five employees are exempt from the employment provisions of the SDA (s.6(3)), although the European Court of Justice[1] has ruled that this provision is contrary to the Equal Treatment Directive.[2] Another exemption was that the continuous service qualification for unfair dismissal was increased for employees working in small firms (EPCA s.64A). Now, however, all employees must have at least two years' continuous service to gain the protection of the unfair dismissal provisions.[3]

Certain categories of employees may voluntarily or involuntarily exclude themselves from the rights guaranteed in the legislation. This may be achieved by agreeing to waive their rights to employment protection, but this is permitted only in limited circumstances.[4] Alternatively the rights may not be enforced through fear of victimisation, lack of awareness of legal rights, or failure to act within the prescribed time limitation (usually three

---

[1] Case 165/82 *EC Commission v United Kingdom* [1984] IRLR 29.
[2] Council Directive 76/207, OJ L39/40 (14 February 1976). See Chapter 1, note 62.
[3] The new rules only apply where the period of continuous employment begins after 1 June 1985: Unfair Dismissal (Variation of Qualifying Period) Order SI 1985 No. 782.
[4] EPCA s.142 allows an employee to waive rights to unfair dismissal and/or a statutory redundancy payment on the expiration of a fixed term contract. This must be carried out in writing during the currency of the contract, which must be for a minimum of two years in the case of a redundancy payment and one year for an unfair dismissal waiver.

months). Financial constraints may also be a barrier since legal aid is not available to commence industrial tribunal proceedings (see generally Chapter 19).

An important feature and limitation is that the rights are contingent upon the employee satisfying minimum periods of continuous employment. This varies according to the type of right, the number of hours worked under the contract of employment, and, in some cases, according to the size of the firm. These rules are summarised in Table 13.1.

The emphasis on minimum periods of continuous service has repercussions which are significant for the relationship between employment protection legislation and social security. Briefly, problems arise if the employee is absent from work for any period of time. Therefore special technical rules have been built into the EPCA to preserve continuity where the employee is absent from work due to 'acceptable' reasons such as sickness, maternity leave and lay-offs (EPCA s.151, Sch.13). The operation of these continuous service rules results in crucial distinctions being drawn between permanent and temporary (or casual) employees, between full-time and part-time employees, and between the status of employees in large firms and small firms. There is evidence to suggest that the operation of the rules in this way is not neutral; in particular, divisions are created along gender lines. More women than men tend to occupy part-time work as a result of domestic and child-care responsibilities or interrupt their career patterns for similar reasons (Elias and Main, 1982; Dex, 1984). Although the SDA may provide an additional or alternative form of protection for employees lacking the necessary continuous service qualification, the results are not as effective as the 'floor of rights' approach to employment protection (Disney and Szyszczak, 1984; O'Donovan and Szyszczak, 1985). To use Leighton's terminology (Chapter 18), certain groups of employees are 'marginalised' in the labour market by falling through the rather flimsy safety net of employment protection.

A final characteristic of employment protection legislation is the effect it has had on employers' attitudes. There has been a hostile response on the part of some employers since the legislation is viewed as adding to costs and thus as a disincentive to recruitment. This argument has been utilised by the Conservative Government to justify loosening the legislation for small firms, and to oppose any extension of employment protection proposed by the European Community. The empirical evidence, however, by no means supports the proposition of disincentive effects. Survey evidence suggests that many firms do not feel their costs to be significantly affected by employment protection legislation; indeed some welcomed the legislation as offering a degree of formalisation of existing informal rules (Daniel and Stilgoe, 1978). Furthermore, even if the legislation acts as a disincentive to recruitment, it also raises the cost of dismissals. Therefore the net effect on employment of a rise in hiring and firing costs is unclear. One clear implication, however, given some empirical support in Disney and Szyszczak (1984), is that employers facing such costs will tend to adjust labour input by varying the quantity of labour obtained from a given workforce (for

TABLE 13.1
MINIMUM QUALIFYING PERIODS FOR EMPLOYMENT PROTECTION

Employment Protection Rights	*Qualifying Period of Continuous Service*[a] *Number of Hours worked per week*		
	Under 8 hours	*Between 8 and 16 hours*	*16 or more hours*
1. Written statement of employment terms	No right	5 years	13 weeks
2. Redundancy payment	No right	5 years[b]	2 years[b]
3. Guarantee payment	No right	5 years	1 month but the contract must be for at least 3 months
4. Medical suspension pay	No right	5 years	1 month
5. Maternity pay	No right	5 years at the beginning of the 11th week before confinement	2 years at the beginning of the 11th week before confinement
6. Right to return after confinement			
7. Itemised pay statement	No right	5 years	No qualifying period
8. Time off for trade union official's duties	No right	5 years	No qualifying period
9. Time off for trade union activities	No right	5 years	No qualifying period
10. Time off for public duties	No right	5 years	No qualifying period
11. Time off for redundant employee to seek work	No right	5 years	2 years
12. Time off for safety representatives	2 years	2 years[c]	2 years
13. Time off for ante-natal appointment	No qualifying period		
14. Written statement of reasons for dismissal	No right	5 years	6 months
15. Dismissal or action short of dismissal for trade union membership or activities (or non-membership)	No qualifying period		
16. Exclusion or expulsion from trade union in closed shop	No qualifying period		
17. Unfair dismissal	No right	5 years	1 year or 2 years in firms employing less than 20 employees[d]
18. Sex and race discrimination	No qualifying period		

Sources: EPCA; EA 1980 and 1982; SDA; RRA; EqPA; Safety Representatives and Safety Committees Regulations SI 1977 No. 500; and *Voluntary Part-Time Work*, Evidence to the House of Lords Select Committee on the European Communities, 19th Report, HL 216, 22–31 (Prof. BA Hepple).

example, by varying overtime hours) rather than the size of the workforce itself. Nevertheless, the disincentive argument has been used in order to justify a reduction in employment protection rights in the Employment Acts of 1980 and 1982 (Lewis and Simpson, 1981: ch.2; Newell, 1983) and further reductions on this ground are anticipated (DE, 1985a; 1985b; DTI, 1985a; 1985b).

SOCIAL SECURITY

Ogus and Barendt (1982:11) provide a useful working definition of social security as 'a system of cash benefits conferred on individuals satisfying conditions of entitlement'. Such a definition has the attraction of simplicity but perhaps presents an overly narrow view of the operation of the modern welfare state in providing a measure of public 'social security'. Some might argue that benefits in kind such as public housing, public health or the social services should be included. While this chapter will consider some new forms of state intervention such as special employment measures which interact with social security and employment protection legislation, it will concentrate upon the 'narrow' financial aspect of social security benefits since these are the most pertinent to the issue under consideration.

The core of the British social security scheme is financed from national insurance (NI) contributions made by employers and insured persons who are (or have been) at work as employees or self-employed. The revenue raised through social security contributions is also used to finance the NHS and the 'refundable' employment protection rights paid through the Redundancy and Maternity Pay Funds.

A first point to note is the sheer cost of the social security scheme. NI contributions do not cover all social security payments, which form the largest single component of public expenditure, totalling over 30 per cent of planned public expenditure for 1985–6 (Treasury, 1985). Unlike other areas of public expenditure, the social security budget is not constrained by cash limits. Recent governments have attempted to reduce this area of expenditure arguing for a greater role for 'individual responsibility' and a policy of 'rolling back the frontiers of the welfare state'. Such retrenchment has involved transferring some elements of social security provision into the sphere of employment protection: for example, guarantee payments for short spells of unemployment. A related strategy involves transferring some of the administrative burden on to employers – for example, maternity pay and statutory sick pay – or on to other agencies, such as the administration of housing benefit by local authorities. A further strategy has been to reduce eligibility for social security. This is seen in the limiting of allowances for board and lodging,[5] or restricting the right of young people to receive social security as an alternative to accepting places on a Youth Training Scheme.

An important characteristic of the social security scheme is the provision of different kinds of benefits. Some benefits are universal and are not contingent upon contributions to the NI scheme. Child benefit is one example. Others such a supplementary benefit are means-tested. These benefits are classified as non-contributory on the grounds that they are not contingent upon the beneficiary having sufficient NI contributions. Initially they were envisaged by Beveridge (1942) as providing a 'safety-net' for persons not covered by the contributory NI scheme. It was anticipated that their role would diminish with the development of a comprehensive NI system. Changing circumstances have resulted in a plethora of new schemes tacked on to the basic social security provisions and financed out of general taxation. In contrast, a third category of benefits is classified as contributory and reveal the close relationship between the social security scheme and participation in the labour market. Such benefits are contingent upon the claimant having paid a certain requisite value of NI contributions. Table 13.2 shows the broad distinctions between these three kinds of benefit.

TABLE 13.2
DIFFERENT KINDS OF BENEFITS AVAILABLE UNDER
THE SOCIAL SECURITY SCHEME

Contributory	*Non-Contributory Means-Tested*	*Non-Contributory Universal*
Retirement pension;	Non-contributory pension;	Maternity grant;
Unemployment benefit;	Disability benefits;	Child benefit;
Sickness benefit;	Supplementary benefit;	Death grant;
Industrial disablement benefit;	Supplementary allowance;	Attendance allowances
Invalidity benefit	Supplementary pension;	
Widow's benefit	One parent benefit;	
	Family income supplement;	
	Rent rebate;	
	Rent allowance	

Source: Treasury (1985).

[5] This policy was challenged in *R v Secretary of State ex parte Cotton* (1985) The Times, 14 December.

The NI contribution system varies according to the status of the contributor. In particular, distinctions are drawn between employed and self-employed persons. Such distinctions may have important consequences for employment law, particularly in relation to the employment protection legislation which is normally contingent upon a contract of service. Under the social security system, however, these matters are dealt with by the Secretary of State rather than by industrial tribunals (Social Security Act 1975 (SSA) s.93).

Work incentive strategies are a further link between the labour market and the social security scheme. Until abolished by the Social Security (No.2) Act 1980, an earnings-related supplement was available to 'top up' many contributory benefits including unemployment benefit. The earnings-related supplement was introduced in the mid-1960s along with the Redundancy Payments Act in order to encourage 're-structuring' of British industry. Such a scheme has, however, also been regarded as acting as an employment disincentive and this argument encouraged the government to abolish the earnings-related supplement.

Another work incentive is the refusal of social security benefits to the so-called 'work shy'. Until recently, when administrative cost-saving changes were introduced, entitlement to unemployment and supplementary benefits was conditional on registering as available for employment. It is now difficult to enforce this eligibility requirement as claimants no longer have to register for employment. The unemployed are now counted by eligibility for benefits not by attachment to the labour market.

Despite these changes some vestiges of the attachment to work requirement remain in the rules relating to eligibility for social security. Thus unemployment benefit is unavailable if claimants have made themselves 'voluntarily unemployed' through misconduct or by voluntarily leaving their work without just cause or refusing an offer of suitable employment (SSA s.20(1)(a)(b); see Chapter 9 for the 'trade disputes' disqualification). Similarly, although there is now no requirement of registration, the claimant must be 'available for work' (SSA s.17(1)(a)). These requirements are carried through into the conditions for supplementary benefit eligibility. With increasing unemployment, the government is caught between its commitment to 'individual responsibility' to reduce reliance on the social security system and the economic reality that it is unrealistic 'to insist on the notional availability of social security claimants being available for work when there is an increasingly chronic shortage of work for them to do' (Davies and Freedland, 1984:25).

As with employment protection legislation, the operation of the social security scheme is not neutral in terms of how men and women are treated. Unlike the employment protection legislation, however, the assumptions underlying the social security scheme are sometimes explicit. The Beveridge ideal family unit was composed of a male breadwinner and a dependent wife. Although the National Insurance Act 1946 recognised that some married women worked, it was perceived that their needs were not as great as those of male workers. Married women were given the choice of opting for lower NI contributions, thereby receiving lower social security benefits.

This was phased out under the SSA. But many married women work part-time, and the NI contribution system provides a financial inducement to restrict earnings below the lower contribution threshold. This excludes some part-time women workers from the contributory benefits of the social security scheme and may amount to a form of indirect discrimination (see below).

The assumption that married or cohabiting women were not primary participants in the labour market is also seen in the fact that until recently they could not claim non-contributory benefits in their own right. These rules have now been altered (Luckhaus, 1983; Partington, 1983), but some commentators have suggested that they are phrased in such a way so as to continue discrimination against married or cohabiting women (Rights of Women Europe, 1983:84).

Although the SDA s.51 excluded the social security system from the statute's ambit, the European Community equality legislation has eroded certain discriminatory aspects (O'Donovan, 1983). The anomalies of the disparity between men and women in issues relating to retirement and widowers' pensions, and the government's refusal to change the discriminatory rules relating to the non-contributory invalidity pension and the housewives' non-contributory invalidity pension, were partially off-set by the March 1985 Budget, which introduced a new severe disablement allowance and changes in the earnings rules for invalidity and widowers' pensions (Treasury, 1985:174). Previously the government had refused to alter the housewives' non-contributory invalidity pension or the invalid care allowance on the ground that 'housewives' did not form part of the 'working population', as defined in Art.2 of the EC Council Directive on the implementation of equal treatment for men and women in matters of social security.[6]

A further point to note is the interrelationship between NI and the financing of some of the employment protection rights. The state has played an important role in facilitating the cross-subsidisation of the employment protection rights through the use of the NI Fund. Some of the costs of employment protection are recoverable from funds established by the state and financed from employers' contributions and the Treasury. Furthermore, these rebates are not 'experience-related', that is, the employer is not penalised for drawing on the funds. The rebates vary according to the type of claim: full compensation is available from the Maternity Pay Fund for maternity pay,[7] while the employer receives only 35 per cent of a statutory redundancy payment from the Redundancy Fund.[8]

A new form of 'social security' is the state's guarantee of the employment protection rights, either through facilitating the enforcement of rights

---

6 Council Directive No. 79/7, OJ 1979, L6/24 (10 January 1979). On the invalid care allowance see *The Times*, 2 March 1985, 'Ruling Paves Way For Married Women's Right to Care Allowance'; *The Guardian*, 30 March 1985, 'Benefits Test Case Sent to Europe'.
7 EPCA ss.37–43; Maternity Pay (Rebate) Regulations SI 1977 No. 322.
8 EPCA ss.103–9. The rebate was decreased from 41 per cent to 35 per cent by the Redundancy Payments (Variation of Rebates) Order SI 1985 No. 250.

through the industrial tribunal system or guaranteeing payments in the event of the employer's insolvency (EPCA s.121). The latter has assumed increased significance in the present economic recession and, in fact, has been strengthened by EA 1982 (Sch.3, Part 1, paras. 3,4). While such a policy might seem inconsistent with 'rolling back the welfare state', Davies and Freedland (1984:569) point out that it is not inconsistent with the aim of reducing the impact of employment protection on individual employers.

Having outlined the scope of employment protection legislation and social security, the relationship between the two schemes can now be examined looking first at the labour market and the decision to participate and then at three specific areas: short-time working, maternity provision and sickness provision.

THE LABOUR MARKET AND THE PARTICIPATION DECISION

The NI system plays an influential role in determining the optimal extent of labour market participation. Under the present contribution conditions, if an employee earns above the lower earnings limit (£35.50 per week, April 1985), the employer and employee become liable to pay NI contributions on the whole amount of earnings. There is of course an incentive for the employer and employee to avoid this payment by opting for the status of 'homeworker' or 'self-employment' or by agreeing to limit either hours of work or earnings. Obviously this will result in an immediate gain to the weekly pay packet and decrease employers' costs, although limiting hours may result in employees falling outside the scope of the minimum hours requirement of the employment protection legislation as well as denying them access to contributory social security benefits such as unemployment benefit, maternity allowance and sickness benefit. This problem is exacerbated where these low paid and 'marginal' employees are unable to provide themselves with adequate compensatory coverage through private social insurance plans.[9]

Related to this decision of whether to enter the labour market and on what terms are the issues of the 'unemployment trap' and the 'poverty trap'. In the case of the 'unemployment trap', Minford et al. (1983), for example, argue that a combination of trade union power and generous unemployment benefits have led to the situation where a large number of workers in the non-unionised sector are equally well off out of work as in work (net of taxes and NI contributions). Other commentators such as Dilnot et al. (1984) argue that there is very little hard empirical evidence in support of this proposition. In contrast, the 'poverty trap' concerns people who have entered employment: as their earnings rise the reduction in eligibility for means-tested benefits combined with tax and NI deductions result in an overall financial loss, thus creating a disincentive to accept wage increases or work harder. In the March 1985 Budget the government introduced new rate

---

[9] *Voluntary Part-Time Work*, Evidence to House of Lords Select Committee on the European Communities, Session 1981–82, 19th Report, HL 216, 118–27 (Low Pay Unit).

bands on the NI contributions to encourage employers to take on lower paid workers.[10] But the thresholds of the initial and then the higher rates still have a disincentive effect and are unlikely to eliminate the problem. Atkinson and King (1985) have argued that they create new tiers of the poverty trap.

The relationship between social security and employment protection may also be relevant to the question of whether to stay in or leave the labour market. For example, the availability and level of social security may determine whether an employee is persuaded to accept a voluntary redundancy situation. Fryer (1973) has exposed some of the inadequacies and limitations of the statutory redundancy scheme and, while private redundancy schemes have improved upon the statutory scheme (IDS, 1984b), individuals who exhaust their unemployment benefit after fifty-two weeks will also be ineligible for supplementary benefit if their capital resources exceed £3,000. This rule therefore reduces the level of long-term financial provision and may act as a disincentive to leave the job, especially for those workers whose prospects of alternative employment look bleak.

Similarly the relationship between unfair dismissal compensation and social security is complicated by the fact that individuals may be denied social security benefit if they are regarded as being unemployed by their own voluntary act. An employee may therefore be compelled to pursue an unfair dismissal claim in order to make out a case for social security benefit. Prior to 1977 the industrial tribunal deducted any social security benefits that the applicant had received (or was expected to receive) from the unfair dismissal award. This was to the advantage of the employer in that the award was reduced by the level of the social security benefits. Now the employer is issued with a recoupment notice which notifies the amount of social security benefits which should be deducted from the award and paid to the DHSS.[11] The employee meanwhile is disentitled to unemployment benefit and may therefore suffer a 'cash-flow' problem until the unfair dismissal award is paid[12] (Hepple et al., 1977).

Another issue which may affect the decision as to whether or not an individual leaves the labour market is the eligibility rules surrounding the state pension. At present there is a disparity in the age of eligibility for pension benefit. Women are eligible at the age of sixty and men at the age of sixty-five (SSA ss.27–9). These provisions are exempt from the legislation dealing with discrimination (EqPA s.6(1A); SDA s.6(4)) and also from

---

[10] From November 1985 these will be 5 per cent on all earnings between £35.50 and £55.00 per week; 7 per cent on all earnings between £55 and £90; 9 per cent on all earnings between £90 and £265 for employees and between £90 and £130 for employers; 10.45 per cent for employers between £130 and £265. (Note that different, lower rates apply for contracted-out employees.)

[11] Employment Protection (Recoupment of Unemployment Benefit and Supplementary Benefit) Regulations SI 1977 No. 674; Employment Protection (Recoupment of Unemployment Benefit) (Amendment) Regulations SI 1980 No. 1608.

[12] Social Security, Unemployment, Sickness, Invalidity Benefit Amendment Regulations SI 1984 No. 1608; on the duty to mitigate loss cf. *Westwood v Secretary of State* [1984] IRLR 209.

European Community law.[13] Similarly, employees lose the benefit of the unfair dismissal and redundancy provisions once they reach retirement age (EPCA ss.64(1)(b), 82(1)(a)(b)).

Thus, in the same way that 'part-time' and 'casual' employees become marginalised, the interaction of social security and employment protection may also disadvantage these older workers who wish to continue working beyond the retirement age, perhaps because they do not regard their pension provisions as an adequate source of income maintenance.

Finally, new forms of 'social security' such as the special employment measures which have developed in the last decade may also be relevant to the decision whether or not to participate in the labour market. Many of these schemes are designed to reduce the unemployment statistics but their impact upon the employment relationship is significant; for example, the withdrawal of supplementary benefit eligibility from young people who refuse to participate in the Youth Training Scheme combined with the denial of employment protection if they are employed under the scheme result in a new form of employment relationship for young people (Freedland, 1983). In similar fashion, workers covered by the Temporary Short-Time Working Compensation Scheme were denied unemployment benefit (see below). In contrast, the Job Release Scheme and the Part-Time Job Release Scheme allow for the payment of allowances to those workers who retire early in order to create employment for a person who would otherwise be unemployed.

SHORT-TIME WORKING[14]

History reveals that short-time working as a means of responding to fluctuations in labour demand is not a new concept. This century has, however, witnessed three developments which have radically changed perceptions of its definition and the issue of who should bear the risk of shortages of work. The first development stems from the growing belief in the early part of this century that there should be some form of state compensation for unemployment. From 1912 onwards limited public unemployment benefit was available to compensate for short spells of unemployment. Prior to this the solution to a shortage of work was fairly simple. An employment relationship based on the 'work-wage' bargain and thus the concomitant 'no work – no wage' provided a framework in which employers could hire and fire at will leaving employees to chance their luck in the

---

[13] Art.7, Council Directive 79/7 (see note 6 above); Case 43/75 *Defrenne v Sabena SA* [1976] 2 CMLR 98; Case 149/77 *Defrenne v Sabena SA* [1978] 3 CMLR 312; Case 69/80 *Worringham and Humphreys v Lloyds Bank Ltd* [1981] 2 CMLR 1; Case 12/81 *Garland v BREL* [1982] 2 CMLR 174; Case 19/81 *Burton v BRB* [1982] 2 CMLR 136; cf. *Southampton and South West Hampshire Health Authority (Teaching) v Marshall* [1983] IRLR 237, EAT, now referred to the ECJ, Case 152/84, OJ C187/7 (14 July 1984). See further Chapters 14 and 17.

[14] The author's research in this area was financed by an ESRC Monitoring of Labour Law Research Award (No. EO 3250002).

market place. This was by no means an optimal solution, for while it provided flexibility, technological change demanded increased skills and training. Thus both employer and employee had a vested interest in retaining the specialist skills acquired for particular jobs. Historical evidence suggests that employers and employees often colluded in sharing out the available work in times of shortages (Turner, 1962).

The second development has been the attitude of the judiciary and their willingness to curtail the wide powers of lay-off without pay previously attributed to the employer. The turning point was the decision in *Devonald v Rosser and Sons Ltd*[15] where the Court of Appeal found an implied obligation on the part of the employer to provide a piece-rate worker with sufficient work to enable him to earn remuneration bearing a reasonable relation to earnings when work was fully available.

The other development which has changed perceptions of short-time working is the growth of modern employment protection rights. Procedures were introduced in the Redundancy Payments Act (now contained in EPCA ss.87-9) to prevent employers avoiding a redundancy payment by putting employees on short-time working (see Chapter 15). But the complexity of the procedures coupled with the existence of unemployment benefit and the introduction of a claim for unfair dismissal have rendered these provisions largely inoperative.

As explained above, the employment protection rights are contingent upon the employee satisfying minimum periods of continuous employment. Greater emphasis is therefore placed upon maintaining the employment relationship at a formal level. Since the consequences of short-time working are closely related to many of the principal employment rights (such as guarantee and redundancy payments and unfair dismissal), special provisions have been built into the statutory framework to preserve continuity of employment during short-time working (EPCA ss.12, 87 and Sch.13, para.9). Thus short-time working has assumed a special and technical meaning as a result of employment protection legislation, and this, along with the economic recession, may have increased employees' resistance to termination of employment.

The availability of unemployment benefit to compensate short-time working led to its widespread use in the inter-war period. Employers and employees openly colluded in the use of the 'OXO' system; so called because employees alternated days of employment, 'O', with days of unemployment 'X', in order to maximise unemployment benefit (see Bakke, 1935). There has been much dissatisfaction with the use of the social security system to finance short-time working in this way. Some critics have argued that the availability of benefits actually increased the number of unemployed (Benjamin and Kochin, 1979; cf. Metcalf et al., 1982). Unlike other countries which have created special schemes for 'partial unemployment', Britain has relied upon the general unemployment benefit scheme to compensate short-time working (EIRR, 1983; Grais, 1983). This policy has been

---

[15] [1906] 2 KB 728.

subjected to many criticisms. Conceptually problems arise when unemployment benefit is payable despite the existence of an employment contract. To deal with this a series of complicated administrative rules have developed (see Ogus and Barendt, 1982:90). Additionally, the administrative costs of paying unemployment benefit for short and irregular spells of unemployment are high and the employment services are not suited for dealing with such situations.

Apart from these administrative problems, the existence of unemployment benefit arguably leads to absenteeism and may encourage employers and employees to adapt patterns of short-time working to attract the maximum amount of unemployment benefit (Ogus, 1975; DE, 1978). A further criticism relates to the fact that because unemployment benefit is financed by employers, employees and the state, it is inequitable to allow firms who regularly resort to short-time working to be subsidised in this way (Ogus and Barendt, 1982:91). Given this dissatisfaction, the post-war period has seen a range of rather cumbersome and ineffective methods of shifting the burden of short-time working away from the social security system and on to individual employers.

In the immediate post-war period, the state placed emphasis on encouraging the development of collective guaranteed week agreements. These were not widespread, however, and with the social security system providing a convenient fall-back, they were riddled with exclusion, limitation and suspension clauses. The state actively intervened in order to shift the burden of short-time working away from the social security system by discounting the first six days of lay-off in the computation for the earnings-related supplement (National Insurance Act 1966 s.2) and indicating that unemployment benefit would not be payable for the first six days of unemployment.[16] These are known as 'waiting days'. A three-year transitional period was envisaged to facilitate the negotiation of guaranteed week agreements. The agreements did not materialise on a widespread scale and the 'six waiting days' rule was postponed.[17] Although the Conservative Government announced that it would resurrect the rule, to come into operation on 1 January 1972, this course of action was also postponed after strong representations from both sides of industry.[18] Instead, the Labour Government put forward proposals for a compulsory guaranteed wage (DE, 1974, paras.1–9), which became the basis of the statutory guarantee payment provisions of the EPCA ss.12–18.

Statutory Guarantee Pay and Unemployment Benefit

Employees with four weeks' continuous service, working under a contract of employment involving at least sixteen hours per week and lasting for at least three months, are entitled to a maximum statutory guarantee payment of

[16] 724 HC Deb, 7 February 1966, 43–4.
[17] 1579 HC Deb, 19 December 1968, 1579.
[18] 814 HC Deb, 31 March 1971, 401–2; 828 HC Deb, 15 December 1971, 143–4 (Written Answers).

£10.50 per day[19] for up to five workless days in any three-month 'rolling' period.[20] There is provision to off-set any contractual guarantee payment against the statutory scheme (EPCA s.16), and it is also possible to obtain an exemption from the statutory scheme where alternative collective arrangements have been made (EPCA s.18). To date, twenty-two exemption orders have been granted. The statutory scheme is limited, however, and social security remains an important source of compensation for those workers who suffer prolonged spells of short-time working and are not covered by a collective agreement. In spite of this, the rules governing the interaction of statutory guarantee payments and unemployment benefit have been extensively criticised. Phrases such as 'awkward and ill-fitting' (Bourn, 1983:241), 'unwieldy and complex' (Ogus and Barendt, 1982:92), 'poorly thought through' (Hepple et al., 1977:56) prevail in the texts.

Employees are ineligible for unemployment benefit on days they are eligible for a statutory guarantee payment. Prior to 1977 (when the statutory provisions came into force), employees laid off were eligible for unemployment benefit after the first three days of lay-off, and until 1982 the earnings-related supplement was payable after six consecutive days of lay-off. Thus employees laid off for three days in any three-month rolling period are now better off as they receive compensation for the initial spell of unemployment, but employees laid off between five and eight days suffer financially as unemployment benefit is no longer payable during this period. Although the statutory scheme may have helped underpin the contract of employment through the creation of a 'floor' of payments for the low paid and least unionised employees, the existence of the low 'ceiling' for the payments and the fact that the rates have failed to keep pace with inflation has left statutory guarantee payments an inadequate source of income for short spells of unemployment.

Employees may also find themselves in financial difficulties if the employer disputes the claim for a statutory guarantee payment. If an employee claims unemployment benefit, the insurance officer will check the situation with the employer. If it is decided that the employer should make a statutory guarantee payment, unemployment benefit will be refused until eight days have elapsed (calculated as five 'guarantee pay' days and the three 'waiting' days). The employee must either appeal against the insurance officer's decision within twenty-eight days, or bring a claim to an industrial tribunal against the employer for a guarantee payment within three months of the day for which guarantee pay is claimed, or both. The procedures are complex and confusing and the situation is exacerbated by the interaction of the statutory guarantee pay provisions with any collective agreements on the guaranteed week or any special employment measures such as the Temporary Short-Time Working Compensation Scheme (TSTWCS). Little litigation has arisen, however, perhaps because the sums involved are too small for an employee to risk the legal costs.

---

[19] Employment Protection (Variation of Limits) Order SI 1984 No. 2019.
[20] Originally this was a fixed quarter but was altered to a rolling period by EA 1980 s.14.

Two cases show that if the employee does choose to litigate the process is lengthy, thus supporting the view put forward by Drake and Bercusson (1981) that the legal provisions seem better designed for the protection of the NI Fund than for the protection of employees. The circumstances of *Robinson v Claxton and Garland Teeside Ltd*[21] were rather unusual in that the case was concerned with the hiatus caused when an exemption order, granted under what is now EPCA s.18, came into effect one day after the statutory guarantee pay provisions came into force. The applicant had been laid off since 17 January 1977 and had received one week's guarantee pay under a collective agreement. He was then advised to claim unemployment benefit as the lay-off was expected to last for some time. Unemployment benefit was paid until 31 January 1977 but then ceased when the guarantee pay provisions came into effect on 1 February 1977. It took over seven weeks before the industrial tribunal confirmed that the employer was liable to make a guarantee payment on 1 February 1977. But in another case, *Clemens v Peter Richards*[22] the DHSS was held to be wrong. Three and a half months after the worker had been denied unemployment benefit, the industrial tribunal decided she was not entitled to a guarantee payment.

Such practical problems and the underlying rationale of transferring the financial burden of initial short-term working away from the NI Fund to individual employers has been subject to critical comment (Hepple et al., 1977:58). The distribution of the costs of these measures is unclear, especially since there are no statistics on the level and amounts of guarantee payments.[23] While evidence suggests that employers as a whole can pass on most of the NI contributions in the form of lower wages or higher prices (Beach and Balfour, 1983), whether individual employers facing an unequal incidence of claims for guarantee payments can do so is less clear.

Employment Subsidies and Guarantee Pay

As the economic recession deepened neither side of industry was appeased by the statutory initiative. The DE (1978) canvassed the idea of re-structuring the financing of short-time working by establishing a Short-Time Working Fund comprising two tiers: one permanent, the other temporary. The permanent tier would have required employers to provide employees on short-time working with compensation amounting to 75 per cent of gross normal pay for each day lost, with a maximum limit of one week's continuous lay-off. The payments would have been taxable and recipients ineligible for unemployment benefit. An upper limit of payment was envisaged in line with the weekly pay limits set for the calculation of redundancy and unfair dismissal awards. A minimum figure was also envisaged to ensure that no full-time worker got less than the statutory guarantee pay provisions (or full normal pay if this figure was lower).

[21] [1977] IRLR 159.
[22] [1977] IRLR 332.
[23] 995 HC Deb, 10 December 1980, 452–3.

Compensation would not have been payable if employees were put on indefinite lay-off or were laid off because of an industrial dispute. The Short-Time Working Fund was to be financed equally by employers and the state. Employers were to receive a 50 per cent rebate of any compensation paid under the permanent tier. The temporary tier was to exist at times of high unemployment. Then the state would refund all the costs of short-time working provided employers could satisfy the DE that short-time working was adopted as an alternative to redundancy, that the firm would remain solvent and that there were good prospects of returning to normal working. Partington (1978) pointed to the vague criteria for triggering the temporary tier and the likely ineffectiveness of a temporary measure to deal with large and permanent increases in the level of unemployment. In a slightly modified form, however, these DE proposals were the basis of the Short-Time Working Bill presented to Parliament in March 1979.[24] This Bill was lost in the dissolution of Parliament for the General Election of June 1979.

In the event, no re-structuring of short-time compensation was implemented. Instead industry saw the arrival and departure of a series of ad hoc interventions in the labour market. Some such as the Temporary Employment Subsidy (TES) and the TSTWCS were designed to off-set redundancies; others such as the Job Release and Youth Training Schemes were designed to create flexibility in the labour market and alleviate unemployment through the creation of new jobs. Section 1 of the Employment Subsidies Act 1978 facilitated the introduction of these discretionary schemes, implemented through brief pamphlets and unpublished administrative rules. The era of 'leaflet law' was fully established (Freedland, 1980; 1983).

Turning to the subsidies affecting short-time working, the first measure, the TES, came into operation on 18 August 1975. Provided employers were prepared to defer impending redundancies affecting ten or more workers, they were eligible for a subsidy of £20 per week for each full-time job maintained. The TES closed for applications on 31 March 1979 after complaints by the EC Commission that it infringed the state aid provisions of Art.92 of the Treaty of Rome 1957 (see Deakin and Pratten, 1982).

The TSTWCS came into operation on 1 April 1979 and closed for applications on 31 March 1984. It resembled the temporary tier proposals of the DE (1978). While the TES subsidised jobs to continue producing output, TSTWCS subsidised short-time working. Compensation was payable at the discretion of the Secretary of State to employers who agreed to withdraw a redundancy notice issued under the redundancy consultation provisions of the EPA s.100. The short-time working could be rotated throughout the whole workforce. Originally employees on short-time working had to be paid at least 75 per cent of their normal pay for each day without work, provided they had carried out a normal day's work after a maximum of seven consecutive days without work. The employer was reimbursed the short-time payments, related NI contributions and holiday pay credits.

[24] 964 HC Deb, 21 March 1979, 1499–1500; HC Bill 1978–9 [116].

Compensation could be paid for a maximum of twelve months.[25] These rules were changed over time; for example, the reimbursement of holiday pay credits was abolished and the levels and length of TSTWCS support was varied as shown in Table 13.3.

The interaction of TSTWCS and statutory guarantee pay was complex and unclear. After a complaint to the Parliamentary Commissioner for Administration,[26] the rules were clarified: in any week in which employees covered by TSTWCS were entitled to a statutory guarantee payment, employers had to pay at least the TSTWCS rate of normal daily pay if that amounted to more than the maximum guarantee payment, or the maximum guarantee payment if that amounted to more than the maximum TSTWCS rate, or full normal pay if that amounted to less than the maximum guarantee payment. Employers were reimbursed for these payments (up to a maximum of £120 per employee per week) and also for their share of NI contributions. In effect the financial burden of guarantee payments shifted to the state. Furthermore, when the TSTWCS funding came to an end the employer's liability to make statutory guarantee payments was discharged for up to a further three months.[27] The employee, therefore, had to fall back upon the social security system and, after a period of short-time working, was unlikely to be in a financial position to cushion the consequences of the lack of fit between the various statutory schemes supposedly designed to deal efficiently with short-time working.

TSTWCS was a massive scheme. An estimated 1,025,700 jobs threatened with redundancy were covered by TSTWCS and 3,101,097 people were placed on short-time to avoid redundancies. Gross public spending on supporting these jobs cost over £1 billion (1983–4 prices). At the peak of its coverage in March 1981, firms were receiving compensation for 984,000 employees working short-time. In contrast, just under 20,000 people were claiming unemployment benefit for short-time in that month (Richards and Szyszczak, 1985). With the closing of TSTWCS in March 1984 the legal

TABLE 13.3
LEVELS AND LENGTH OF TSTWCS SUPPORT

Date Application Received	*Percentage of Normal Wages Paid to Employees Working Short-time*	*Duration of Support (in Months)*
April–June 1979	75	12
July 1979–October 1980	75	6
November 1980–June 1982	50	9
July 1982–March 1984	50	6

[25] For details see DE Leaflet PL 692; DE (1980); Freedland (1980).
[26] Case C591/81 – Mishandling of application for assistance under the TSTWCS. Parliamentary Commissioner for Administration, First Report, Session 1982–83 (1982) Vol. 4, 21.
[27] *Cartwright v Clancy* [1983] IRLR 355.

framework has reverted back to the position pre–1979. But at a practical level the situation has changed in that the recession has deepened, leading to a rise in short-time working and also a greater use of suspension and limitation clauses in collectively agreed guarantee week agreements (IDS, 1981). The meagre statutory guarantee pay provisions are unlikely to provide sufficient compensation and therefore the state may be compelled to assume greater financial responsibility for short-time working through the social security system.

MATERNITY PROVISION

Maternity rights are a feature of social security law, factory legislation and employment protection. Under the social security system a woman may obtain a lump sum maternity grant for each child born and surviving for at least twelve hours.[28] The grant is still set at the 1969 figure of £25, but as from 4 July 1982 it is a non-contributory benefit financed out of general taxation.[29] A maternity allowance is also available based upon the mother satisfying certain contribution conditions (SSA s.22). It is a flat-rate benefit, the earnings-related supplement having been abolished from 1982. It is revised annually, currently (1984–5) stands at £27.25 per week, and is payable for eighteen weeks, beginning eleven weeks before the birth, provided the woman has stopped working.

The desire to protect the function of motherhood was an important contributory factor in the development of factory legislation in the nineteenth century. The Factory and Workshop (Amendment) Act 1891 made it a criminal offence for an employer knowingly to employ any woman in a factory or workshop within four weeks of her giving birth.[30] Apart from such isolated measures, and despite two major ILO initiatives,[31] it was only in the mid-1970s, in response to the increased participation of women in the labour market, that the UK introduced maternity rights enforceable by women against their employers. In theory these rights improve upon the social security scheme by increasing the financial benefits relating to maternity and by granting working women a measure of job security.

The employment protection legislation provides that all pregnant women, regardless of their length of service, are entitled not to be unreasonably refused paid time off work during working hours in order to receive antenatal care (EA 1980 s.13). This right is conditional on the woman producing for the employers' inspection (and on request) a medical certificate from a midwife or health visitor showing that she is pregnant, plus an

---

[28] Social Security (Maternity Benefit) Regulations SI 1975 No.553.
[29] Social Security (No.2) Act 1980 s.5; Social Security (Maternity Grant) Regulations SI 1981 No. 1157.
[30] The Factory and Workshop (Amendment) Act 1891 s.17. This rule was carried over in the Factory and Workshops Act 1901 s.61.
[31] Maternity Protection Convention 1919; in 1952 it was revised to become the Maternity Protection Convention (Revised) 1952 No.103 and accompanying Recommendation No.95.

appointment card or other document showing that an appointment has been made. These conditions do not apply to the first appointment. Once an employer has allowed a woman time-off over several weeks payment may not be refused: by allowing the woman time off it will be taken that the employer has accepted it was reasonable.[32] If the employer refuses the request for time off work, an employee has the right to complain to an industrial tribunal which may award compensation (EPCA s.31A(6)(8)). This right was introduced as a 'social policy' measure designed to reduce ill-health and infant mortality, but the costs of the right are borne by individual employers.

The EPCA s.60 provides protection against unfair dismissal on the grounds of pregnancy. The right is circumscribed in that it is not applicable, if, at the date of the woman's termination of employment, she has become incapable of doing her work because of pregnancy or if her continued employment would be in breach of a statutory duty or restriction. To qualify for this protection the woman must have been continuously employed for at least two years. These restrictions are a bar to many women, especially those working part-time. The SDA may provide an alternative remedy for such women since it does not require a minimum qualifying period. But an industrial tribunal and the EAT refused to accept that discrimination on the grounds of pregnancy constituted direct discrimination.[33]

A woman also has a right to return to the job originally specified in the contract of employment and on terms and conditions which are not less favourable than would have been applicable to her had she not been absent on maternity leave (EPCA s.45). The entitlement is to a maximum of forty weeks' maternity leave (eleven weeks before and twenty-nine weeks after the birth). This right has been curtailed, however, by EA 1980 in that it no longer applies to employers who employ five or fewer employees and who can show that it is not reasonably practicable to permit the woman to return to the original job or offer her 'not less favourable' or 'alternative' employment (EPCA s.56A).

Irrespective of the size of the firm, employers will have a defence to an unfair dismissal claim if they can show that it is not reasonably practicable to reinstate the woman in the original job (for a reason other than redundancy) and suitable alternative employment is offered, which is either accepted or unreasonably refused (EPCA s.56A(2)–(4)). If it is not reasonably practicable for the employer to permit the woman to return to work by reason of redundancy, EPCA s.45 provides that the woman may be offered alternative employment by the employer. This also must be 'suitable', 'appropriate' and 'not less favourable' than the original job. If no such vacancy exists, then the woman is treated as dismissed for the purposes of a redundancy claim (EPCA s.86). An employee who has a right both under the EPCA and under her contract of employment, or otherwise, to return to work may not

---

[32] *Gregory v Tudsbury Ltd* [1982] IRLR 267.
[33] *Reaney v Kanda Jean Products* [1977] IRLR 159, IT; *Turley v Allders Department Stores Ltd* [1980] IRLR 4, EAT; cf. *Hayes v Malleable Working Men's Club* [1985] IRLR 367, EAT and *Maugham v NE Magistrates' Court Committee* [1985] IRLR 367.

exercise the two rights separately, but may in returning to work take advantage of whichever right is the more favourable (EPCA s.48).

The right to return to work has been extended by recent decisions under the SDA. In *Home Office v Holmes*,[34] a woman successfully claimed that a condition requiring her to return to full-time work amounted to indirect discrimination on the grounds that a smaller proportion of women than men could comply with the condition because of women's domestic and childcare responsibilities. The EAT was careful to explain that the decision turned upon the particular facts of the case and that it was open for an employer to show that the condition of full-time work was justifiable. Despite this caveat, the principles of *Holmes* have been applied in subsequent decisions.[35]

The right to return to work has, however, been complicated by extra and more stringent notice requirements imposed by EA 1980. A woman must give written notice that she intends to return to work at least three weeks before she commences maternity leave and three weeks before she intends to return to work. The employer may ask for additional written notice of the intention to return to work not earlier than forty-nine days from the expected date of confinement. A failure to comply with this request within fourteen days (or as soon as is reasonably practicable) will result in the loss of the right to return to work (EPCA s.33(3A)(3B)).

Maternity pay is also included within the scope of employment protection. A woman is entitled to six weeks' maternity pay from the employer at a rate of nine-tenths of her gross weekly pay, provided she remains at work until the eleventh week before the expected date of confinement and she has two years' continuous service with the employer (EPCA ss.34–5). The flat-rate maternity allowance payable under SSA s.22 is deducted from the statutory payment regardless of whether or not the employee is entitled to it. Employers do not bear the financial burden of maternity payments since they are entitled to a full rebate from the Maternity Pay Fund, which is financed by contributions from employers' NI contributions. The rebate does not cover any additional payments which may have been made as a result of more favourable individual or collective agreements. As with other statutory rights to pay, any contractual payments are off-set against the statutory right.

The state acts as a guarantor of the financial provisions relating to maternity pay by allowing a woman to complain to an industrial tribunal if the employer fails to make maternity payments (EPCA s.36). The Maternity Pay Fund may be used to make payments directly to the woman where the employer is insolvent, or fails to make payments, and the employee has taken all reasonable steps (other than proceedings to enforce a tribunal award) to recover payment from the employer (EPCA s.40).

From the woman's point of view, maternity pay is taxable and the payment will result in her receiving less than her normal earnings since she only receives nine-tenths of her gross pay. This figure was chosen because it

---

[34] [1984] IRLR 299 (noted by O'Donovan and Szyszczak, 1985).
[35] *Wright v Rugby Borough Council* (1984) COIT No. 235 28/84; *Fulton v Strathclyde Regional Council* (1985) EAT 949/83, 15 January.

was calculated that the earnings-related supplement (since abolished) of the maternity allowance would make up approximately one-tenth of a week's earnings. A further problem arises if a woman has two employers. In *Cullen v Creasey Hotels (Limbury) Ltd*,[36] the EAT held that each employer should deduct the maternity allowance from each statutory maternity payment. The woman's earnings from her two part-time jobs were so low that she received no maternity pay from either employer. This situation could be remedied if one employer was prepared to make an ex gratia payment equivalent to the maternity allowance. This sum might be recoverable, at the discretion of the Secretary of State, from the Maternity Pay Fund (EPCA s.39(2)).

These complex maternity provisions involve employers, employees, the DHSS and the DE in an intricate relationship. The DHSS (1980a) reviewed this relationship and suggested reforms, not only to simplify and reduce the administrative costs of maternity provision but also to attempt a more equitable redistribution of the resources available. The political climate did not seem to facilitate this and the proposals were dropped.

Ogus and Barendt (1982:249) argue that 'the statutory right to maternity pay from the employer has to a large extent superseded in importance the social security allowance as an instrument of income maintenance'. This assertion is not borne out by research undertaken by the DHSS (1980a) which discovered that less than 16 per cent of women having a child qualified for maternity pay. The major impediment to this right is the continuous service qualification, which debars women who work part-time or who have limited labour market experience as a result of previous childbirth or other domestic responsibilities. Similar factors limit the right to the maternity allowance. Conversely, the level of employer's maternity pay ignores the abolition in 1982 of the earnings-related supplement to the maternity allowance. The failure to increase the level of statutory maternity pay has thus eroded income maintenance for some women.

Although the introduction of employment protection legislation has increased awareness in the private sector of the need to provide maternity provision, the state, in its wider role of the provider of adequate 'social security', has not encouraged a comprehensive strategy for maternity provision. An obvious omission is the lack of any statutory paternity leave. Several firms have agreed a limited form of such leave[37] and the European Commission has recently proposed a Directive on parental leave.[38] Furthermore, the present statutory length of maternity leave is inadequate. It does not protect parents who wish to share childcare responsibilities, or women who wish to continue breast-feeding their children for a longer period, or children who are in need of constant care and attention as a result of illness or disability.

---

[36] [1980] IRLR 59.
[37] See IDS (1980) and Bell et al. (1983) for surveys of paternity leave.
[38] Amended proposal for a Council Directive on Parental Leave and Leave for Family Reasons, Com(84) 631 final. Cf. Case 163/82 *Re Italian Sex Equality Laws: EC Commission v Italy* [1984] 3 CMLR 169; Case 184/83, *Hoffmann v Barmen Ersatzkasse* (1984) The Times, 24 July.

Similarly, the financial provisions are limited, forcing women to return to work or assume the status of being 'dependent' upon the state or the family. While recent decisions under the SDA have provided a few women with some flexibility as to when and how they return to work, the state has not made 'flexi-time' or temporary or part-time work attractive by making employment protection rights available. Social security benefits which are available as a result of childbirth, such as child benefit, may help cushion the financial loss, but they cannot replace the status presently accorded to a full-time and permanent worker under the employment protection legislation. Finally, the right to return to work is rendered even more illusory by the lack of any positive right to childcare facilities accorded to parents. Indeed, the state has been instrumental in reducing such facilities through public expenditure cuts and the taxing of childcare facilities in the private sector.

SICKNESS PROVISION

Income maintenance during sickness has traditionally been regarded as a matter to be dealt with under the contract of employment or by the social security system rather than through employment protection legislation. The EPCA ss.19–22 covers only suspension from work on medical grounds due to the operation of specified health and safety provisions (set out in Sch.1), which apply only to a small minority of employees. An employee is entitled to a week's pay (as defined in Sch.14) for each week of suspension up to a maximum of twenty-six weeks. Employees who are incapable of work through ill-health, or refuse suitable alternative work, or who fail to comply with reasonable attendance requirements render themselves ineligible for payment under these provisions.

The omission of sickness provision from the employment protection legislation can be explained by various factors. Frequently, provision for payment of wages during short spells of sickness was dealt with under the contract of employment, though the courts have not always taken a generous view of a presumption in favour of sick pay when the contract has been silent on the issue.[39] At the time of the passing of the EPA, moreover, occupational sick pay schemes were becoming widespread. By 1974 80 per cent of male full-time workers and 78 per cent of full-time female workers were covered by occupational sick pay schemes (DHSS, 1977). There was, therefore, a tendency in industry to favour voluntary provision as opposed to state regulation of sick pay. As with the collective guaranteed week agreements, however, the occupational sick pay schemes varied across industries and excluded many part-time workers. Finally, the availability of comprehensive sickness benefit under the social security scheme was crucial.

Under the SSA, sickness benefit was available for persons satisfying the same contribution conditions as for unemployment benefit. The self-

---

[39] Cf. *Marrison v Bell* [1939] 2 KB 183; *Mears v Safecar Security Ltd* [1981] ICR 409; *Howman and Son v Blyth* [1983] ICR 416. See Chapter 12 above.

employed were also eligible on the basis of their NI contributions. The level of sickness benefit was the same as unemployment benefit and provision was made for dependants' allowances. Similarly, three 'waiting' days had to be served before sickness benefit was payable. It was possible to link periods of sickness; any two days within a period of six consecutive days could count as a period of interruption of employment and any two such 'continuous' periods within thirteen weeks of each other could be linked to form a single period. The claimant had to prove that sickness benefit was payable in respect of 'a day of incapacity for work', which was defined in s.17(1)(a)(ii) as a day when the claimant is, or is deemed ... to be, incapable of work by reason of some specific disease or bodily, or mental disablement'. The claimant could be disqualified from sickness benefit through misconduct or by refusing to submit to a medical examination or treatment.

The late 1970s, however, saw several changes to the social security scheme to provide more generous treatment of long-term incapacity. In the 1980s this was followed by a reduction in state provision for short-term sickness benefit, mainly as a financial and administrative cost-cutting measure. The earnings-related supplement was abolished by the Social Security (No.2) Act 1980 and the 'linked spells' rule was reduced from thirteen weeks to eight. The Social Security and Housing Benefits Act 1982 (SSHBA) introduced a new policy for the short-term sick. This Act transferred the administration of claims for sick pay lasting less than eight weeks to employers, who were then under an obligation to pay statutory sick pay (SSP) at three rates according to earnings.[40] In addition, SSP was brought into taxable income and was also liable to social security contributions. The scheme contained other radical departures from the social security sickness benefit, including the abolition of the contributions requirement for short-term claimants and dependants' allowances. The short-term industrial injury benefit was also abolished and replaced by the SSP scheme. In addition, changes were made to the system of notifying sickness. It is now no longer necessary to produce a medical certificate for the first eight days of illness or injury; self-certification will suffice.[41]

As with maternity pay the financial burden of SSP does not fall on employers since they are able to deduct payments of SSP out of their NI contributions. In the original Green Paper (DHSS, 1980b), the government had hoped to reduce its own administrative costs by refunding SSP claims through an across-the-board cut to all employers. This proposal to end the cross-subsidisation inherent in sickness benefit provision met general opposition, which led to the current system of full refunds. There were fears that SSP might be abused by employers during trade depressions to compensate short-time working. Therefore, the full refund system requires

---

[40] As from 6 April 1985 these rates are £44.35 where the employee's normal weekly earnings are not less than £71; £37.20 where the employee's normal weekly earnings are less than £71, but not less than £53; £30 where the employee's normal weekly earnings are less than £53: Statutory Sick Pay Up-rating Order SI 1984 No. 2037.

[41] Social Security (Medical Evidence, Claims and Payments) Amendment Regulations SI 1982 No. 699.

monitoring of sick pay records by the state to confirm that they do not show an excessive rise. Although IDS (1984a) report that SSP has been introduced with few hitches, SSP refunds have in fact shown a steady rise (Disney, 1985). There is also evidence to suggest that occupational sick pay schemes have continued to improve (IDS, 1984a). One of the justifications for SSP was that the social security sickness benefit duplicated existing occupational sick pay schemes. Although there is a high average level of coverage, certain groups such as part-time and women employees are still under-represented in these schemes. Furthermore, there is no evidence that groups with above average risks of industrial illness have a greater incidence of occupational sick pay coverage (Creedy and Disney, 1985).

SSP is of significance since it represents clear signs of dismantling the system of 'social insurance' developed under the National Insurance Act 1946. Some commentators have gone as far as characterising this as 'privatisation' of the sickness scheme (Lewis, 1982), although this would seem to be over-stating the case. But the government intends to extend SSP to cover the first twenty-eight weeks of sickness from April 1986, thereby leaving social security benefit only a residual role for short-term sickness for the self-employed. Being solely dependent upon employment status rather than on contributory requirements, the scheme introduces a new element of income maintenance into the employment relationship.

While SSP falls into the ambit of the employment relationship, it still bears the hallmarks of the social security system (Davies and Freedland, 1984:351). This is particularly so in relation to the adjudication of the scheme, which is entrusted to the Secretary of State for determining issues on the scope of SSP (with an appeal to the High Court or Court of Session in Scotland on issues of law) and to the social security authorities for determining questions of entitlement (SSHBA ss.11–12). This is in contrast to the use of industrial tribunals for other aspects of employment protection. In determining eligibility for SSP, the terminology used in SSHBA s.1 follows the social security definitions of 'day of incapacity for work' and 'specific disease or bodily or mental disablement'. Similarly, the three 'waiting days' rule applies (s.2), but the 'linking' period is reduced to five weeks (as opposed to eight weeks in the social security scheme). The day for which SSP is claimed must be a 'qualifying day', that is, a day on which the employee is required by the employer to be available for work (s.4). The employer may not terminate the contract of employment to avoid making SSP payments (s.3 (7)). Once entitlement to SSP is exhausted, the employee transfers to the social security invalidity benefit. The relationship with the social security scheme is also maintained if the employee is entitled to the maternity allowance which, once payable, supersedes SSP.

CONCLUSION

This chapter has sketched out some aspects of the intricate interrelationship between employment protection and social security. Although this interrelationship reveals only one facet of the complexity of the modern employment relationship, it does provide an explanation for that complexity. Highlighted by, for example, the provisions governing compensation for short-time working, it reveals that state intervention in the labour market has been conditioned by short-term responses to immediate problems, such as economic recession. Provision has, therefore, often taken the form of an ad hoc combination of existing institutionalised practices (such as the use of the 'OXO' scheme in the 1930s), state provision through social security schemes, attempts to induce alterations to institutional practices (seen in the introduction of statutory guarantee pay), and special measures, such as TSTWCS, which exist uneasily with the other arrangements.

The relationship between employment protection and social security may also lead to both inequity and an inefficient use of resources. In the case of maternity provision, for example, the employment protection legislation provides a right to maternity pay but, in the interrelation with the social security system, does not guarantee equity of treatment: for example, women working part-time or with interrupted work histories may be entitled to neither maternity pay nor maternity allowance. In the case of SSP, a similar pattern emerges except that, with the extension of the employer's liability to twenty-eight weeks in 1986, recipients are eligible for supplementary benefit in addition to SSP if their incomes fall below the minimum standard. This guarantees equity of treatment with other groups of sick and disabled people but at a cost in economic efficiency. Having passed the administrative cost of the short-term sick on to employers, the DHSS will find itself assessing SSP claimants after all, in order to assess entitlement to other, means-tested, benefits.

In the introduction to this chapter it was suggested that, for those people who are in work, in good health, not pregnant and with no risk as to loss of job, the relationship between employment protection and social security might seem to be of little importance. Because of rising unemployment and the enlargement of the 'marginal' labour market, however, the interrelationship between social security and employment protection is likely to be of growing importance, not only for the young and female sections of the labour force, but for every actual or potential participant. Indeed, the decision to participate, particularly for part-time workers, is very much affected by the overlap and the growth in part-time, primarily female, employment has been one of the major characteristics of the changing labour market since 1945.

Bibliography

Atkinson, A.B., and M.A. King. 1985. 'Working ... But Trapped in Poverty'. *The Guardian*, 22 March.

Bakke, E.W. 1935. *Insurance or Dole? The Adjustment of Unemployment Insurance to Economic and Social Facts in Great Britain*. New Haven, Conn.: Yale University Press.

Beach, C.M., and F.S. Balfour. 1983. 'Estimated Payroll Tax Incidence and Aggregate Demand for Labour in the United Kingdom'. *Economica*, 50 (February), 35–48.

Bell, C., K. McKee and K. Priestley. 1983. *Fathers, Childbirth and Work*. Manchester: Equal Opportunities Commission.

Benjamin, D.K., and L.A. Kochin. 1979. 'Searching for an Explanation of Unemployment in Interwar Britain'. *Journal of Political Economy*, 87 (June), 441–78.

Beveridge. 1942. Inter-Departmental Committee on Social Insurance and Allied Services. *Social Insurance and Allied Services: Report by Sir William Beveridge*. Cmd 6404. London: HMSO.

Bourn, C. 1979. 'Statutory Exemptions for Collective Agreements'. *Industrial Law Journal*, 8 (June), 85–99.

——. 1983. *Redundancy Law and Practice*. London: Butterworths.

Clark, J., and *Lord* Wedderburn. 1983. 'Modern Labour Law: Problems, Functions and Policies'. *Labour Law and Industrial Relations: Building on Kahn-Freund*. Eds. *Lord* Wedderburn, R. Lewis and J. Clark. Oxford: Clarendon Press, 127–242.

Collins, H. 1982. 'Capitalist Discipline and Corporatist Law'. *Industrial Law Journal*, 11 (June and September), 78–93 and 170–77.

Creedy, J., and R. Disney. 1985. *Social Insurance in Transition: An Economic Analysis*. Oxford: Oxford University Press.

Daniel, W.W., and E. Stilgoe. 1978. *The Impact of Employment Protection Laws*. London: Policy Studies Institute.

Davies, P., and M. Freedland. 1984. *Labour Law: Text and Materials*. 2nd edn. London: Weidenfeld & Nicolson.

Deakin, B.M., and C.F. Pratten. 1982. *Effects of the Temporary Employment Subsidy*. Cambridge: Cambridge University Press.

Department of Employment (DE). 1974. *Employment Protection Bill: Consultative Document*. London: DE.

——. 1978. *Compensation for Short-Time Working: Consultative Document*. London: DE.

——. 1980. 'Temporary Short-Time Working Compensation Scheme'. *Employment Gazette*, 88 (May), 478–81.

——. 1985a. *Employment: The Challenge for the Nation*. Cmnd 9474. London: HMSO.

——. 1985b. *Consultative Paper on Wages Councils*. London: DE.

Department of Health and Social Security (DHSS). 1977. *A Survey of Occupational Sick Pay Schemes*. London: DHSS.

——. 1980a. *A Fresh Look at Maternity Benefit*. London: DHSS.

——. 1980b. *Income During Initial Sickness: A New Strategy*. Cmnd 7864. London: HMSO.

Department of Trade and Industry (DTI). 1985a. *Burdens on Business: Report of a Scrutiny of Administrative and Legislative Requirements*. London: HMSO.

——. 1985b. *Lifting the Burden*. Cmnd 9571. London: HMSO.

Dex, S. 1984. *Women's Work Histories: An Analysis of the Women and Employment Survey*. Research Paper no. 46. London: Department of Employment.

Dilnot, A.W., J.A. Kay and C.N. Morris. 1984. *The Reform of Social Security*. Oxford: Clarendon Press for the Institute of Fiscal Studies.

Disney, R. 1985. 'Social Security'. *Public Expenditure Policy 1985–86*. Ed. P. Cockle. London: Macmillan.

——, and E.M. Szyszczak. 1984. 'Protective Legislation and Part-Time Employment in Britain'. *British Journal of Industrial Relations*, 22 (March), 78–100.

Drake, C.D., and B. Bercusson. 1981. *The Employment Acts 1974–1980: With Commentary*. London: Sweet & Maxwell.

Elias, P., and B. Main. 1982. *Women's Working Lives: Evidence from the National Training Survey*. Coventry: Institute for Employment Research, University of Warwick.

European Industrial Relations Review (EIRR). 1983. 'Short-Time and Lay-Offs'. *European Industrial Relations Review*, no. 111 (April), 15–19.

Freedland, M.R. 1980. 'Leaflet Law: The Temporary Short Time Working Compensation Scheme'. *Industrial Law Journal*, 9 (December), 254–8.

——. 1983. 'Labour Law and Leaflet Law: The Youth Training Scheme of 1983'. *Industrial Law Journal*, 12 (December), 220–35.

Fryer, R.H. 1973. 'The Myths of the Redundancy Payment Acts'. *Industrial Law Journal*, 2 (March), 1–16.

Grais, B. 1983. *Lay-Offs and Short-Time in Selected OECD Countries*. Paris: OECD.

Hepple, B.A. 1983a. 'Harmonisation of Labour Law in the European Communities'. *Essays for Clive Schmitthoff*. Ed. J. Adams. Abingdon: Professional Books, 14–28.

——. 1983b. 'Individual Labour Law'. *Industrial Relations in Britain*. Ed. G.S. Bain. Oxford: Blackwell, 393–417.

——, T.M. Partington and R.C. Simpson. 1977. 'The Employment Protection Act and Unemployment Benefit: Protection for Whom?'. *Industrial Law Journal*, 6 (March), 54–8.

Incomes Data Services (IDS). 1980. 'Maternity Provisions'. *IDS Study*, 230 (November).

——. 1981. 'The Guaranteed Week'. *IDS Study*, 235 (February).

——. 1984a. 'Sick Pay and SSP'. *IDS Study*, 316 (June).

——. 1984b. 'Redundancy Terms'. *IDS Study*, 327 (December).

Kahn-Freund, O. 1983. *Labour and the Law*. 3rd edn. Ed. and intr. by P. Davies and M. Freedland. London: Stevens.

Lewis, Richard. 1982. 'The Privatisation of Sickness Benefit'. *Industrial Law Journal*, 11 (December), 245–54.

Lewis, Roy. 1983. 'Collective Labour Law'. *Industrial Relations in Britain*. Ed. G.S. Bain. Oxford: Blackwell, 361–92.

——, and B. Simpson. 1981. *Striking a Balance? Employment Law After the 1980 Act*. Oxford: Martin Robertson.

Luckhaus, L. 1983. 'Social Security: The Equal Treatment Reforms'. *Journal of Social Welfare Law* (November), 325–34.

Metcalf, D., S. Nickell and N. Floros. 1982. 'Still Searching for an Explanation of Unemployment in Interwar Britain'. *Journal of Political Economy*, 90 (April), 386–99.

Minford, P., D. Davies, M. Peel and A. Sprague. 1983. *Unemployment: Cause and Cure.* Oxford: Martin Robertson.

Newell, D. 1983. *The New Employment Law Legislation: A Guide to the Employment Acts 1980 and 1982.* London: Kogan Page.

O'Donovan, K. 1983. 'The Impact of Entry into the European Community on Sex Discrimination in British Social Security Law'. *Essays for Clive Schmitthoff.* Ed. J. Adams. Abingdon: Professional Books, 87–98.

——, and E. Szyszczak. 1985. 'Indirect Discrimination – Taking a Concept to Market'. *New Law Journal*, 135 (January) 15–18 and 42–4.

Ogus, A.I. 1975. 'Unemployment Benefit for Workers on Short-Time'. *Industrial Law Journal*, 4 (March), 12–23.

——, and E.M. Barendt. 1982. *The Law of Social Security.* 2nd edn. London: Butterworths.

Partington, T.M. 1978. 'Compensation for Short-Time Working: New Government Proposals'. *Industrial Law Journal*, 7 (September), 187–90.

——. 1983. 'Equality of Treatment'. *Industrial Law Journal*, 12 (December), 264–5.

Richards, J., and E. Szyszczak. 1985. 'Short-Time Working in Great Britain: Historical Developments and the Decline of Unemployment Benefit for Short-Time Compensation'. Short-Time Working Project, Working Paper no. 15. Canterbury: University of Kent.

Rights of Women Europe. 1983. *Women's Rights and the EEC: A Guide for Women in the UK.* London: Rights of Women Europe.

Treasury. 1985. *The Government's Expenditure Plans 1985–86 to 1987–88.* Vol. 2. Cmnd 9428–II. London: HMSO.

Turner, H.A. 1962. *Trade Union Growth, Structure and Policy.* London: Allen & Unwin.

Wedderburn, K.W. 1971. *The Worker and the Law.* 2nd edn. Harmondsworth: Penguin.

Wyatt, D. 1983. 'The Direct Effect of Community Social Law – Not Forgetting Directives'. *European Law Review*, 8 (August), 241–8.

14 Occupational Pensions

Graham Moffat and Sue Ward

The provision and regulation of occupational pension schemes have not traditionally been identified as topics appropriate for inclusion in a text on labour law. For the lawyer the raw material of conventional analysis was sparse, there being a dearth of legal cases. For the industrial relations specialist there was no incentive to devote space to a subject seemingly concerned with post-retirement income rather than existing employment relationships. This stance was reinforced both by the apathy of unions and employees and by a broadly accepted paternalist view of a pension as a reward for long-service. It has been aptly noted that 'at one time the few employers outside the public sector who provided occupational pensions specifically preserved them for long-serving employees' and 'the older schemes were frequently initiated by employers without pressure from employees' (OPB, 1981:paras. 1.11, 1.12). Indeed, many trade unions were either hostile or indifferent to occupational pensions; they preferred to concentrate on campaigning for better state pensions.

The perception of occupational pension provision as essentially a voluntary act was reflected in a legal framework which imposed few obligations or restrictions on employers. There was no legal duty to provide a pension scheme or to make it available to all employees, and until recently the law did not require minimum levels of scheme benefits or regulate the circumstances in which scheme members could be deprived of their pension rights. The only restrictions on level of benefits were maxima imposed by the Inland Revenue under the Finance Acts principally to prevent the use of pension schemes for tax avoidance. Most schemes were established and administered under trusts law, which in theory protected the interests of scheme members by imposing obligations on the trustees responsible for the scheme's funds.

This system has in the last two decades come under increasing pressure from four sources. First, the expansion of state pensions has indirectly resulted in compulsory minimum standards for vesting and preservation of occupational pension benefits. Second, the expansion and increased value of benefits of occupational pension schemes made pension entitlement of great financial significance to many employees, for whom it may represent their most substantial investment exceeding even their interest in their own homes.[1] Recognition of this led to criticism of the existing legal framework.

---

[1] Treating pension entitlement as a capital asset of the individual significantly alters wealth distribution estimates. IR, 1983a:Table 4.9 and accompanying text.

The Wilson Committee (1980:para.1224) recommended the introduction of a pension schemes statute analogous to a Companies Act: 'to produce a clear and systematic statement of the legal duties and obligations of employing companies, scheme trusts and their professional advisers and to make it easier for members of a scheme and their representatives to monitor its management and solvency'. Third, the perception of pensions was transformed. Under the stimulus of the exemption of pension scheme benefits from incomes policies between 1972 and 1974 and 1975 and 1978, unions came to regard pension provision as a matter for collective bargaining. Although not without criticism (Morgan, 1984:65; OPB, 1981:paras. 1.12–1.14), the view of pension entitlement as deferred pay rather than employer gratuity has been widely accepted. One consequence of the deferred pay analogy is support for the claim that scheme members should acquire a greater collective say in the management and control of schemes. The final source of pressure sprang from the belief that the traditional system hindered mobility in the labour market. The present government has responded to this view by bringing forward new legislation.

This chapter explains the present regulatory framework and assesses whether the pressures referred to above are likely to undermine the model of a thinly regulated voluntary system of occupational pensions. It describes in broad outline the system of occupational pension provision and then concentrates on three areas of legal regulation: the provision and content of pension schemes, the protection of employee rights and expectations, and scheme administration including employee involvement.

STRUCTURE AND SIGNIFICANCE OF OCCUPATIONAL PENSION SCHEMES

State Provision and Occupational Pensions

Occupational schemes are part of a complex set of arrangements, closely linked with the state's two-tier system. The first tier is the basic pension, currently (1985–6) £38.30 a week per single person, payable in practice to everyone who has paid national insurance contributions for nine-tenths of their working lives. The second tier is a state additional pension: an earnings-related pension introduced by the Social Security Pensions Act 1975 (SSPA), which came into force in 1978. This scheme was not retrospective, so that those who were already pensioners, or who became pensioners in the first few years after the Act, have little or no earnings-related pension. When fully implemented this pension will provide an earnings-related element based on the highest twenty years' annual earnings of the employee within statutory lower and upper limits. Each year's earnings will be revalued to reflect estimated annual average increases in earnings (SSPA s.21). The additional pension cannot exceed 25 per cent of those earnings, a figure below that promised by many occupational schemes.

Each proposal for a state earnings-related scheme since 1959 has included provision for the peculiarly British system of contracting-out. At present an employer who is prepared to set up a scheme which provides a guaranteed minimum pension (GMP) equivalent to the earnings-related component of the state scheme is allowed to contract-out employees from that component; in return both employer and employee pay a reduced rate of national insurance contribution.

There is no compulsion on schemes to contract-out. It is possible to receive three types of pension: state basic, state additional, and occupational. In fact, almost all public-sector employees and approximately 80 per cent of those in private sector schemes are contracted-out (Government Actuary, 1981:table 5.1).

Types of Occupational Scheme

Occupational pensions can be classified into statutory and non-statutory schemes. A number of schemes in the public sector with 3.7 million members in 1979 (Government Actuary, 1981:table 2.7) are statutory. Their rules are embodied in Acts of Parliament, extensively amplified in regulations contained in statutory instruments. Unlike other occupational schemes, they do not have trustees and are therefore not regulated by trusts law.

Certain statutory schemes — for example, those covering the civil service, police, fire services and armed forces — are 'pay-as-you-go'. There is no separate fund built up in advance to pay for pensions. Other schemes, such as those for teachers and the NHS, have a notional fund. Here the contributions, calculated as for a funded scheme, are remitted to the Treasury and accounted for as a fund with interest being added at the rate earned on certain government stocks. No actual stock is held, however, and the benefits when due are paid out of current government revenues. Other statutory schemes, notably the local government scheme, are funded on the same actuarial basis as private schemes.

The remaining schemes with 8.1 million members in 1979 (Government Actuary, 1981:tables 2.2 and 2.6) are funded by contributions made by the employer and employee, together with investment income. These schemes are usually established under irrevocable trusts in accordance with Inland Revenue guidance. They range from very large schemes in both the nationalised industries and the private sector to small self-administered schemes for twelve people or fewer, including many single-member schemes. It is with these schemes that the remainder of this chapter is principally concerned.

Social and Economic Significance

According to the Government Actuary (1981:tables 2.8 and 5.1), in 1979 approximately 100,000 employers operated pension schemes and the total membership in the UK was 11.8 million employees out of a workforce of 23.15 million. Of those not in pension schemes, 7.15 million were employed by employers with schemes but were either ineligible or unwilling to join. The same survey showed (table 3.2) that 3.7 million pensions were being paid to former employees or their dependants. Thus around 15 per cent of employers operate a pension scheme, half the workforce is involved and half the retired are in receipt of an occupational pension. While there exists wide variation in the level of pensions paid, for most occupational pensioners the pension is at least sufficient to lift them well above supplementary benefit thresholds although scarcely into affluence (Government Actuary, 1981:table 3.3). In addition, some schemes offer a proportion of pension entitlement as a tax-free lump sum on retirement, an attractive benefit, particularly for middle- and upper-income earners.

The significance of this extensive provision stretches beyond the social objective of alleviating insecurity in old age. On average, employees pay 4.5 per cent of their earnings into occupational schemes with the average contribution from employers being 10.9 per cent. (NAPF, 1985). The effect of this very high level of contractual (and therefore compulsory) savings on the British economy is a matter of debate. The Wilson Committee (1980:para. 332) concluded that 'funded pension schemes provide at least the opportunity for higher savings and real investment'. What is beyond debate is that the assets of pension funds have increased substantially, particularly in the last decade. By the end of 1982 total assets of self-administered pension funds were £83.5 billion compared with £12 billion in 1972. This does not include the long-term investment funds of life assurance companies valued at £79 billion, a substantial proportion of which represents pension business. At a conservative estimate total pension fund assets are at least £100 billion.[2] This channelling of personal savings into financial institutions has increasingly concentrated ownership of company ordinary shares in their hands. A recent Stock Exchange survey (1983:table 2.16) shows that 47.2 per cent of ordinary shares are beneficially owned by insurance companies and pension funds (20.5 per cent and 26.7 per cent respectively), compared with 21 per cent just over a decade earlier.[3]

PROVISION AND CONTENT OF PENSION SCHEMES

Framework of Law

The legal framework for the administration and regulation of occupational pension schemes is a curious melange of labour law, social security law, and tax law amplified by Inland Revenue procedures and practice notes, all superimposed on the fundamental basis supplied by the law of trusts.

The minimum requirements imposed by the SSPA in respect of contracting-out have already been referred to. In addition, the OPB, which was

---

[2] See *Financial Statistics*, June 1984, cols. 7.11 and 7.12.
[3] For comment on the political and economic implications of the potentially dominant role of institutional investments see: Bolton (1971); NEDO (1975); Drucker (1976); Minns (1980); Wilson (1980); Plender (1982).

established under the Social Security Act 1973, has limited supervisory powers over contracted-out schemes, and also over the requirements on equal access and preservation of benefits in all schemes. Not surprisingly, given the net value of the tax reliefs currently assessed at £3.25 billion,[4] tax law figures pre-eminently in the regulation of pension schemes. The 1970 Finance Act (FA) ss.19–26 as amended, gives the Inland Revenue the power to approve pension schemes for tax relief. The legislation sets out basic conditions which entitle a scheme to approval, supplementing these with a discretionary power for the Inland Revenue to approve schemes which do not comply fully with these conditions. It issues Notes on Approval, commonly called Practice Notes (IR, 1979), which give guidance as to the manner in which the discretion is exercised. Tax law directly influences the structure of schemes in two ways. It imposes upper limits on scheme benefits if the tax reliefs on members' contributions and investment income are to be retained. Equally significantly, in order to obtain the exempt approved status which is a prerequisite for the favoured tax treatment, it is necessary for a scheme to be established by means of 'an irrevocable trust' (FA s.21(1)). The consequence is that the regulation and administration of all exempt approved schemes is provided by the law of trusts.

Under this system pension contributions, whether from employer or employee, are paid into the trust fund separate from the employer's business assets. The administration and management of the fund are the responsibility of trustees whose powers are laid down in a trust deed and supplemented by what can be loosely termed the common law of trusts.

This adoption of trusts law as a basic legal framework introduces three potential protections for scheme members. One, already mentioned, is the separation of the fund from the employer's business assets. This provides an element of security against employer insolvency since the trust fund is not available to the employer's creditors. The second protection is that trustees are liable for losses caused through their negligent, incompetent or fraudulent conduct. This protection is largely fictional since an individual trustee's personal assets are most unlikely to be adequate to compensate the fund in the event of substantial losses. Finally, and more significantly, the flexibility of the trust device and the basic legal duties imposed on trustees, for example, to act solely in the best interests of the scheme members, make trusts law in principle a suitable device for the disinterested management of pension schemes.

A more sceptical opinion on the appropriateness of trusts law is discernible in a report of the OPB (1982), which argued for a new statutory basis for pension schemes, broadly supporting the recommendation of the Wilson Committee. This chapter attempts to assess the validity of criticisms of the existing legal framework. There are three separate strands of criticism. The law is too fragmented and uncertain, the procedures for enforcement of members' rights are too cumbersome, and the standard of legal protection of

---

[4] The gross tax relief of £5.10 billion is reduced by the estimated tax yield of £1.85 billion from pensions in payment: IR (1983b).

members' interests is unsatisfactory partly because trusts law is inadequate to control potential conflicts of interest between employer and scheme member.

Access to Pension Schemes

Employers have substantial legal autonomy over access to pension schemes. A scheme may be open to all employees or it may be restricted at the employer's discretion. Those employees defined as 'marginal' (see Chapter 18) are frequently excluded, particularly in the private sector. In 1979, two million employees were excluded because they were too young or their service was too short, and a further four million part-timers were either not eligible or had opted not to join (Government Actuary, 1981:tables 2.8, 2.9). But for most employees eligible to join a pension scheme, membership is a condition of service. In fact trade unions have accepted and at times pressed for compulsory pension scheme membership, if only to prevent the equivalent of wage undercutting by non-members for whom the employer would have no contribution to make.

The employer's discretion over access and benefit levels is marginally limited by the statutory constraints on discrimination on grounds of race (RRA s.4(2)) and, arguably, of trade union membership and non-membership (EPCA s.23(1)(a) and (c)). In sharp contrast the SDA does not apply to 'any provision made in relation to death or retirement' (s.6(4)). A similar exclusion is contained in the EqPA s.6. The abandonment of protection against sex discrimination is modified as regards access by the SSPA s.54(1), which requires trustees to ensure that scheme rules comply with the Act's equal access requirements for men and women. The OPB has power to override or modify scheme rules to ensure compliance, but effectiveness of the provision is weakened by its not covering indirect discrimination. An OPB recommendation (1976a:para.15(a)(3)) that indirect discrimination in relation to scheme entry should be governed by provisions analogous to those in the SDA has not been implemented.

For a scheme to obtain Inland Revenue approval all employees eligible to join must be notified of their rights (FA s.19(2)(b)), an obligation supplemented by the requirements under EPCA s.2(3) to notify a new employee in writing of the existence of 'any terms and conditions of employment relating to pensions and pension schemes'.

Contract of Employment

The EPCA's written notice requirement can be satisfied by referring the employee to a document describing the pensions arrangements. This will commonly contain a pension promise which specifies the pension an employee can anticipate receiving on retirement. But the legislation does not require the employer to make clear whether the pension promise is enforceable as a term of the contract of employment (DHSS, 1984a:para. 52).

In the absence of clear legal authority it is conventionally accepted (for example, Ellison, 1979:29) that the employer is under no contractual obligation to employees, whatever the moral or industrial relations pressures, to see that the scheme is able to honour its promises; nor is there any enforceable obligation on the employer directly to pay benefits to the scheme member. The government has proposed that the EPCA be amended to require employers to clarify whether the pension promise forms part of the contract of employment (DHSS, 1984a); but any clarification is likely merely to confirm that the present negative understanding is correct. It is of course quite possible for an employer to contract with employees to pay pensions direct to them. The Inland Revenue (1979:para.2.6) specifically recognises this but will not grant 'exempt approved status', with the result that the tax reliefs are normally lost if this method of pension provision is adopted (Langham and Sparks, 1976).

However ambiguous the employer's contractual liability as to scheme benefits may be, recent case law confirms that the employee does have a contractual claim against the employer for the payment of the latter's agreed pension contribution. In an action arising out of the collapse of Court Line Ltd in 1974, a merchant navy officer established that a failure to pay the employer's pension contribution was a breach of contract and he recovered in damages the value of the unpaid contribution.[5] In deciding that employer contributions could properly be regarded as part of an employee's total wage, Brandon J categorically accepted the view of pensions as deferred pay.[6]

There is a significant limitation on this contractual liability. Most pension scheme trust deeds contain a discontinuance clause enabling the employer on giving the requisite notice, commonly three months, to cease contributions and possibly wind up the scheme. Any new statutory requirement to clarify the employer's contractual pension obligations is likely to result in the unambiguous insertion of a discontinuance clause in the statement of terms of the contract of employment. This will further reduce the already remote likelihood of an employee resigning and successfully claiming 'constructive' dismissal when a scheme is discontinued. Although a major fringe benefit of the employment can be said to have been lost, a decision to discontinue contributions to the pension scheme in accordance with a term of the contract of employment can scarcely be said to satisfy the requirements of contractually repudiatory conduct necessary to show a 'constructive' dismissal (see Chapter 15).

EEC Law and Scheme Benefits

An additional legal influence is to be found in EEC law concerning equal pay, which provides wider rights than those contained in domestic legisla-

---

5   *The Halcyon Skies* [1976] 1 All ER 856.
6   At 863, citing Lord Reid: 'the products of the sums paid into the pension fund are in fact delayed remuneration for his current work. That is why pensions are regarded as earned income' (*Parry v Cleaver* [1969] 1 All ER 559, 560).

tion, although the extent of the additional protection is uncertain. Article 119 of the Treaty of Rome enshrines the principle of equal pay for equal work for men and women (see generally Chapter 17). The application of this principle to occupational pension schemes has recently been established, albeit in limited form, through two decisions of the ECJ. Both decisions are difficult to reconcile with the intention and wording of the UK statutes.

Two female employees of Lloyds Bank complained that the Bank's pension scheme for women infringed their right to equal pay under Art. 119. The Court of Appeal referred two questions to the ECJ: whether the employer's contribution and the employee's rights or benefits came within the definition of pay. The ECJ decided that the particular contributions did constitute pay but did not examine the broader issue of the status of scheme benefits.[7] This issue resurfaced in *Garland v British Rail Engineering Ltd* over the provision by British Rail of concessionary rail travel facilities in retirement. The ECJ ruled that the provision of more generous special travel facilities to retired male employees constituted discrimination contrary to Art. 119.[8] Subsequently the House of Lords was able to hold that this view was not inconsistent with SDA s.6(4) if the words of that section — 'provision in relation to retirement' — were construed narrowly so as to exclude a privilege that had existed during employment and merely carried over into retirement.[9]

Left unanswered was the question of whether those benefits payable only after retirement are within the definition of pay in Art. 119. Acceptance of pension benefits as deferred pay suggests a positive answer. Support for this view can be gleaned from the language of the ECJ, which endorsed a broad interpretation of Art. 119: 'the concept of pay ... comprises any other consideration whether in cash or in kind, whether immediate or future, provided that the worker receives it, albeit indirectly in respect of his employment from his employer'.[10] The gloss on the language of Art. 119 provided by the addition of the words 'whether immediate or future' is potentially of some significance as regards the treatment of pension benefits. The sweeping nature of the statement, however, must be viewed in the context that European law permits discrimination in state pension schemes.[11] Consequently it is possible to argue, as did the Advocate General to the ECJ in the bank employees' case, that an occupational scheme designed not as a supplement to a state scheme but as a substitute for it or part of it should be regarded as outside the scope of Art. 119. If this were not so a contracted-out scheme would be obliged to afford equal rights to men and women, yet the state scheme it replaces would not. The ECJ's determination to decide each case on the narrowest basis possible reflects a reluctance to be drawn into an area where, as Ellis and Morrell (1982) have

---

[7] *Worringham and Humphreys v Lloyds Bank Ltd* [1981] IRLR 178, ECJ, [1982] IRLR 74, CA.
[8] [1982] IRLR 111, ECJ.
[9] [1982] IRLR 257, HL.
[10] *Garland v British Rail Engineering Ltd* [1982] IRLR 111, at 115.
[11] Equal Treatment for Men and Women in Matters of Social Security. Directive 79/7/EEC OJ 1979, L6/24, Art. 7(a).

argued, any attempt to impose equal treatment where unequal retirement ages are permitted to exist is fraught with interlocking legal and practical difficulties.[12]

PROTECTION OF EMPLOYEE EXPECTATIONS

Hepple (1983:417) suggests that 'the extension of individual rights cannot be expected to transcend the economic and social structure of the labour market'. Economic insecurity is an established facet of the employment relationship and much employment law can be seen as an attempt to moderate it. One attraction of membership of an occupational pension scheme is that it appears to provide some guarantee of security of income in retirement. This expectation is fuelled by and reflected in the promises of occupational pension scheme rules. Yet are the promises in the nature of aspirations creating only an illusion of security? Whether employee expectations of security are fulfilled is dependent on provision for the unpredictable factors of a working life. Any system of occupational pensions which ignored the existence of job-changers or job-losers, which imposed no financial controls in relation to a scheme's solvency, and which relied on the employer both continuing in business and being willing to maintain a pension scheme could be said to be contributing to the illusion. But expectations are not limited to the pension payment in the first week of retirement. A system which allowed the real value of pensions in payment to decline could be similarly criticised. The absence of a comprehensive legal framework will not inevitably result in pensions expectations being frustrated, and the present system relies on a combination of voluntary practice and legal protection to counter these possible deficiencies.

Voluntary Early Leaver

In a White Paper (DHSS, 1971:para. 67) a previous government commented that 'reliance on occupational provision as a central and expanding sector of the total provision for retirement could not be justified if job mobility, whether voluntary or enforced, continued to undermine it to the extent it does now'. There was a sound basis for this welfare-oriented concern for early leavers, defined by the Inland Revenue and OPB simply as those scheme members who withdrew from pensionable service before the normal retirement age without an immediate pension (OPB, 1981:para. 1.7). Before 1973 the minimum legal entitlement of early-leavers in private sector schemes depended solely on scheme rules subject to an Inland Revenue defined maximum entitlement.[13] The common practice was that they were entitled to a refund of their own contributions only. There existed no

---

[12] See OPB (1976a) and McGoldrick (1985) for a comprehensive review of equal status.
[13] The current limits are detailed in IR (1979: paras. 13.1–13.28).

statutory entitlement to benefit from the employer's contribution, nor was there any statutory obligation to maintain the real value of a preserved pension, if provided, or to make a transfer payment to another scheme. Statutory protection has since tentatively emerged in three stages, culminating in the Social Security Act 1985 which substantially amends the SSPA.

The Social Security Act 1973 Sch.16 made the first inroads into the autonomy of scheme rules on minimum entitlement to what are termed short service benefits. As amended by s.1 of the 1985 Act it imposes a limited prohibition against discriminatory treatment of early leavers and requires the provision of preserved benefits for those who have completed at least five years' pensionable service. Further protection came with the SSPA ss.33–7, which require contracted-out schemes to preserve an individual's GMP, and revalue it in line with statutory formulae for each succeeding year up to the state scheme's pensionable age, for all members with five or more years' service irrespective of age. Alternatively s.38 permits the transfer of the GMP by mutual agreement of all parties to another contracted-out scheme. Those with less than five years' service can be bought back into the state scheme.

The absence of any statutory obligation to revalue any other element of a preserved pension prompted substantial criticism. The problem was encapsulated in the pension entitlement of the occupationally mobile employee who might acquire several preserved pensions, the total of which, assuming no revaluation, would inadequately reflect final salary. The absence of a legal obligation to revalue did not mean that increases were not made. But available statistical and anecdotal evidence suggests that such voluntary increases as existed were in the large majority of cases inadequate to compensate for either prices or earnings increases (Government Actuary, 1981:para.10.6; OPB, 1981:ch. 3).[14] In the OPB report (1981) on this subject, a majority of Board members recommended a mandatory revaluation of preserved benefits broadly in line with national average earnings increases but with a ceiling of 5 per cent per annum over the period of deferment as a whole.

The reliance on voluntary initiative to provide the desired improvements eventually gave way to legislation. The Social Security Act 1985 broadly implements the OPB majority revaluation recommendation, except that movement in prices rather than earnings has been chosen as the benchmark, while retaining the 5 per cent ceiling. The protection is not retrospective, applying only to those leaving pensionable employment after 1 January 1986 and then only to their pension entitlement accruing after 1 January 1985. The legislation is of a type familiar to labour lawyers. It imposes a minimum standard of protection, overriding any conflicting scheme rules. A more generous uprating provision can be granted where scheme resources and Inland Revenue rules permit. Whether employers and employee representatives will see that as a priority use of scarce resources is doubtful. According to a government consultation document (DHSS, 1983:para. 2), 'much of the

---

[14] A loophole permitting extensive erosion of the non-GMP element of a preserved pension has been closed by the Health and Social Security Act 1984 s.20 and Sch.6.

difficulty relating to the early leaver springs from his lack of adequate representation'. Nothing in the new legislation alters that position.

The 1985 Act also breaks with the non-interventionist approach to the availability of transfers and the calculation of transfer values. The OPB (1981:para. 9.32) accepted that the choice between a preserved pension and a transfer should in principle be financially neutral, but rejected legislation as a means of achieving this. As an alternative to a preserved pension, the Act provides the early leaver with the right to a 'cash equivalent' of accrued benefits. This notional entitlement can be used at present only to acquire transfer credits in a new employer's scheme or to purchase a deferred annuity from an insurance company. But nothing in the legislation requires a scheme to accept transfers and in this respect it merely reflects current practice as transfers are already widely available. The NAPF survey (1985) showed that nearly all occupational pension schemes provided in their rules for the payment and acceptance of transfers. Nevertheless, the absence of an accepted basis for calculating transfer values has been an inhibiting factor. The government is more tentative on this vexed issue, placing its faith in the actuarial profession to provide an agreed set of principles while reserving to itself the possibility of imposing standards by regulation if necessary.[15] Unless a satisfactory agreed basis can be attained, it seems unlikely that transfer of pension rights will in practice become as widespread in the private sector as it is in the public.

Involuntary Early-Leavers

The protection of the rights and expectations of the involuntary early leaver are broadly as explained in the previous section. An employee who is dismissed prior to retirement retains entitlement to a preserved pension (Social Security Act 1973 Sch.16). Loss of pension rights accrued to that point is thus not available to the employer as a disciplinary measure. Additional protection applicable in some circumstances is outlined below.

Ill-health and early retirement. Entitlement for those who retire early because of ill-health depends on scheme rules, subject only to Inland Revenue maxima. A pension can be awarded based on pensionable earnings at actual retirement date but taking account of all actual and potential service (IR, 1979:para. 10.6). Similar provisions apply to voluntary early retirement except that stricter Inland Revenue criteria prevent the inclusion of potential service and prohibit payment of pension before the age of fifty.

Redundancy. A distinction must be drawn between those redundant pension scheme members who receive an early pension and those whose entitlement is preserved. To reiterate, statutory protection of the preserved pension is the same as that of any early leaver. Improved protection of expectations in scheme rules is a matter for negotiation and no statutory

---

[15] See 68 HC Deb, 26 November 1984, 674 (Secretary of State).

change is likely. Scheme rules may provide for an early pension and Inland Revenue practice is to apply the ill-health and early-retirement limits. In practice, scheme rules covering 30 per cent of private sector and 50 per cent of public sector members provide special benefits to those made redundant (Government Actuary, 1981:para. 12.9). The value of this is reduced as the employer can exclude or reduce the statutory redundancy payment where a pension is payable immediately.[16]

Unfair dismissal. Loss of pension rights is a permissible head of claim for compensation where an employee is unfairly dismissed,[17] and for many successful claimants it represents a substantial proportion of total compensation. Compensation can be awarded for both loss of pension position already earned at the date of dismissal and loss of future opportunity to improve that position. Numerous judgments have indicated that assessment of compensation is 'a rough and ready matter',[18] but a wide divergence of approach has been avoided by general acceptance of guidelines published in 1980 and prepared by a group of tribunal chairmen and members of the Government Actuary's Department.[19] Although the guidelines have no statutory status tribunals adhere to them. It is possible for parties to present their own actuarial evidence, although the EAT inclines to the view that 'elaborate or other statistical evidence is to be discouraged in the industrial tribunal'.[20] Any compensation awarded is supplementary to the preserved pension entitlement required by scheme rules or statute for early leavers. Where a wrongful dismissal action is preferred to an unfair dismissal claim, the damages for lost pension rights will depend on the terms of the contract. Usually the compensation will be limited merely to the payment of the employer's contributions for the notice period.

Security of Pension Benefits and Expectations

An obvious feature and potentially an obvious failure of pension provision tied to individual employers is that security of pension expectation depends on the security of the specific employment relationship. The disadvantages this has presented for early leavers have been commented on. Similarly for the worker who remains with the same employer the economic security of pension entitlement and expectation depends both on the ability and willingness of the employer to continue funding the scheme and on the solvency of the scheme's fund. Although the issues of scheme continuation and fund solvency in practice present overlapping problems, they raise sufficiently diverse problems of legal regulation to merit separate treatment

---

[16] EPCA s.98 and Redundancy Payments Pensions Regulations SI 1965 No. 1932.
[17] Confirmed in *Copson v Eversure Accessories Ltd* [1974] IRLR 247.
[18] Cf. *Manpower Ltd v Hearne* [1981] IRLR 281, 284.
[19] The full guidelines are reproduced in Hepple and O'Higgins (1981: app.1).
[20] *Manpower Ltd v Hearne* loc cit. See also *Tradewind Airways Ltd v Fletcher* [1981] IRLR 272. The more favourable view expressed in *Copson v Eversure Accessories* predates the guidelines.

here. This section also considers the maintenance of the real value of pensions in payment.

Security of the pension fund. The security offered by external funding depends crucially on fund solvency, which in turn depends on an assessment of the timing and quantum of contributions necessary to fulfil defined expectations. The member's expectation may be that the scheme will continue in existence and that the contribution rate will be sufficient to ensure a fund adequate to provide the promised pension at retirement. The member may also expect that if the scheme is discontinued the fund will be sufficient to meet the accrued entitlement. These two expectations have different implications for the meaning of solvency and suggest a plurality of approaches to the valuation of fund solvency (OPB, 1982:ch. 6; Young and Buchanan, 1981:ch. 3).

The present statutory system of control over fund solvency is limited. The SSPA s.41 requires the OPB to supervise contracted-out schemes primarily to ensure that GMPs are safeguarded, and empowers it to cancel contracting-out certificates where appropriate. This does not provide any check on total scheme solvency since GMPs constitute a small proportion of its liabilities. Section 32(4) enables the Board also to cancel a certificate, however, where 'there are circumstances relating to the scheme or its management which make it inexpedient that the employment should continue to be contracted-out employment'. This discretion, applicable only to contracted-out schemes, can be used to require a level of funding above the minimum necessary for GMPs. The OPB asserts (1982:para. 5.37) that 'the legislation has provided an adequate framework for the supervision of the financial resources of contracted-out schemes' and, in the absence of major scheme failures, does not recommend additional statutory controls other than the imposition of a greater obligation of disclosure. The government (DHSS, 1984a) has endorsed this approach.

Voluntary scheme discontinuance. For most members of funded pension schemes the rules provide a formal guarantee of entitlement, ultimately enforceable not against the employer but against the trustees or administrators. Paradoxically where those same rules contain a discontinuance clause this can undermine employee expectations. Assuming adequate funding, accrued benefits will be met but the build-up of further entitlement for the member will be frustrated if the scheme is discontinued. There is nothing inherently contrary to the tenets of trusts law in reserving the discretion to discontinue to the employer. It is, however, less easy to reconcile with the FA s.21(1) whereby an exempt approved scheme must be established under an irrevocable trust. The Inland Revenue's view that the existence of this discretion does not infringe the section seems a narrow reading of its language.

Where a discontinuance clause is activated and the scheme wound up, the order of priority in meeting claims is of crucial importance. Scheme rules usually detail the order to be followed in allocating the fund on winding-up where inadequate funding exists. An OPB survey (1982:app.5) indicates that, after administrative costs, pensions in payment are overwhelmingly the foremost consideration. The rules may also indicate how a surplus should be allocated, subject to the Inland Revenue requirement that any residue must be returned to the employer. The same regulations (IR, 1979) also permit the augmentation of benefits for the members up to the maximum permitted levels. Potentially a tension exists here between the interest of the members and the interest of the employer. Unless the scheme rule on winding up specifies which interest should take priority, and the OPB survey is inconclusive on this, the obligation of the trustees to act solely in the best interests of the scheme members indicates that priority should be given to augmenting benefits.

Voluntary discontinuance of a scheme is rare but the existence of the discretion emphasises the essentially voluntary nature of the employer's obligation and the uncertainty of the pension expectation. In addition, the Inland Revenue requirement that the residual surplus be returned to the employer fits uncomfortably with an analysis of pension provision as deferred pay.

Company transfer. There are two types of transfer — one where the complete business changes hands and the other where a part only of the business is sold — and the consequences for the scheme member can be different. In addition, control of a company may be transferred by a purchase of shares but this would not directly affect the pension status of an employee.

The pension fund will usually not be part of the business assets that the new owner obtains when the complete business changes hands. Where the scheme is adequately funded the member's accrued pension entitlement is protected, though the expectation of increasing entitlement may be affected by a discontinuance provision. Although the new owner may undertake to continue the existing scheme or indeed to offer entry to an improved scheme, there is no legal obligation to do this, and the scheme can be discontinued with the previously mentioned consequence for the member. The significance which the absence of a discontinuance clause makes to a member's entitlement was apparent in British Airways' attempt to reduce its pensions commitment prior to privatisation. The trust deed contained a clause prohibiting amendments that could diminish or prejudicially affect the rights of members. The employer was compelled to offer substantial cash inducements to attempt to persuade existing members to surrender their entrenched rights[21]

Where a partial transfer occurs the original pension scheme remains intact but the status of the scheme member whose employment is transferred to the new proprietor is merely that of an early leaver. There is no obligation to offer entry to the new employer's scheme, assuming one exists.

The relative lack of protection where the whole or part of a business is transferred is compounded by the express exclusion of contractual pension

---

[21] *Financial Times* 26, 27 January 1984.

obligations from the scope of the Transfer of Undertakings Regulations,[22] although there remains the theoretical possibility of claiming constructive dismissal from the original employer where the pension arrangements are terminated or substantially altered to the detriment of the employee. The only positive statutory intervention is the limited procedural requirement that an employer must consult with the recognised trade unions before a contracting-out certificate can be varied or surrendered to the OPB as would be necessary in a corporate transfer.[23] The weakness of the formal protection of expectations would matter less if the pensions arrangements ultimately agreed resulted from negotiations between old and new employers and recognised trade unions within a financial framework substantially dictated by actuarial valuations of accrued and prospective liabilities. In practice, pensions considerations are frequently treated as a low priority.

Employer insolvency. The most likely reason for a discontinuance rule to be activated will be when an employer ceases business altogether by voluntary liquidation or compulsory bankruptcy. Then the separation of the fund from the employer's business assets and from the grasp of creditors provides the main protection. Assuming that full contributions have been paid the scheme would be discontinued in accordance with the rules with the consequences for employee pension rights and expectations mentioned previously. Limited additional protection is provided in SSPA s.58 in respect of certain unpaid employer contributions and members' contributions deducted from pay but not passed over to the scheme. These are granted priority over claims on the insolvent employer's assets. In addition EPCA s.123 provides for the Redundancy Fund to meet claims of the pension scheme against the insolvent employer, not exceeding the equivalent of the employee's pension contributions in the twelve months preceding insolvency, where the employer's assets are inadequate.

Pensions in payment. The expectation of a stable standard of living in retirement related to the standard achieved in the last years of working life will not be protected by a guarantee that only the nominal value of pension entitlement is secure. Recent historically high rates of inflation linked to the emergence of final-salary schemes have highlighted the failure to adjust pensions to changing money values. It is here that the divergence between public and private sector schemes is most visible. The great majority of public sector schemes in practice award pension increases in line with the retail price index. For most there exists a legal obligation either in statute or in the scheme rules.[24] In the private sector only 20 per cent of members have any entitlement in scheme rules to a regular pension increase and this is

---

[22] SI 1981 No. 1794 reg. 7.
[23] Occupational Pension Schemes (Certification of Employments) Regulations SI 1975 No. 1927 reg. 10(4). Contracted-Out and Preservation (Further Provisions) Regulations SI 1978 No. 1089 reg. 4.
[24] Pensions (Increases) Act 1971, and for a comprehensive review see Scott (1981:app. 3).

usually stated in specific percentage terms. Here again there exists a divergence between scheme rules and practice as 60 per cent of scheme members receive pension increases, although only exceptionally do these match the rate of increase in the retail price index (Government Actuary, 1981:table 10.2).

Reliance on practice rather than scheme rules to evaluate the protection of expectations is unsatisfactory. Although some schemes, by using conservative assumptions about investment returns, have compiled surpluses from which pension increases can be paid, many increases have been unfunded and paid directly by the employer. There is no guarantee that the practice would be continued, which leaves existing pensioners particularly vulnerable to employer insolvency. In contrast to its proposals on preserved pensions, the OPB (1982:paras. 9.20–9.27) did not recommend any statutory mandatory increase of pensions in payment and the government has endorsed this approach (DHSS, 1984a).

SCHEME ADMINISTRATION: EMPLOYEE INVOLVEMENT AND CONTROL

In rejecting proposals to prescribe statutory minimum levels of funding, the OPB (1982:para. 6.27) placed its faith in 'freedom with disclosure'. The Board favoured a large measure of freedom to choose the appropriate method and level of funding but that all parties concerned should have access to sufficient information to enable informed choices to be made. The less sanguine approach evident in the Board's evaluation of the legal structure of pension schemes, referred to previously, has not appealed to the government. It has expressed itself satisfied that 'trust law provides a suitable framework for regulating the conduct of pension schemes' (DHSS, 1984a:para. 60). The potential protection afforded by trusts law to scheme members lies in the fundamental duties imposed on trustees. These require trustees to administer the trust fund honestly for the benefit only of all the members, to invest the funds in a proper manner, and to be impartial in their treatment of members. When a power of delegation — most commonly used to appoint specialists to manage investments—is added, the picture emerges of trustees as selfless managers of capital, the ultimate owners of which are the beneficiaries, in this context the scheme members, separated from this management function.

Closer investigation raises questions about the appropriateness of this subtle division of ownership, management and control. This section focuses on four central issues: membership participation, conflicts of interest, disclosure of information, and the effectiveness of remedies.

Membership Participation

The adoption of freedom with disclosure as a guiding principle involves no necessary commitment to employee participation in the administration of a scheme. Trusts law views the members as passive policemen rather than active administrators, and implementation of more extensive disclosure requirements merely creates better informed policemen. Despite this fundamental division of functions, there is equally nothing in trusts law which prevents a scheme member being appointed a trustee.

In fact a considerable increase in membership participation in the management of schemes has developed during the last decade (Schuller and Hyman, 1983a; Government Actuary, 1981:ch. 13). The trend, which mirrors consistent OPB recommendations (see OPB, 1982), is not a direct result of legal duties. The only existing statutory obligation is the contracting-out consultation requirement previously mentioned. No extension of participation through legislation is envisaged at present, though a White Paper (OPB, 1976b) did propose to grant recognised trade unions a right of appointment to 50 per cent of the membership of any controlling body of an occupational pension scheme. The White Paper proposals were never enacted, running into a deadlock similar to that afflicting proposals for worker directors (Bullock, 1977).

The Government Actuary's survey (1981:table 13.3) disclosed that employee participation at trustee level in the private sector occurred in 50 per cent of schemes covering 70 per cent of scheme members. A more limited survey by Schuller and Hyman (1983a), confirming employee participation in just over 50 per cent of schemes with trustees, indicated a major shift towards participation in the 1976–80 period. It is tempting to attribute the growth to the threat of legislation but the survey findings are more tentative; pension managers, for example, strongly rejected such a claim. An increased recognition of pension entitlement as deferred wages, with the corollary that members should be able to exercise some control over their property, may have contributed to a climate favouring participation, as may the view that it gives members 'a better appreciation of the extent of claims on resources constituted by a pension scheme' (OPB, 1976b:para.29). The clear acceptance by the OPB, and less enthusiastically the NAPF (1982), of the value of participation probably helped establish a favourable ethos.

The concentration of employee involvement is uncertain. The Government Actuary's survey (1981:75) suggested that in about 40 per cent of those schemes in the public and private sectors where employee representation existed, whether by election or nomination, the representatives formed 50 per cent or more of the trustees. Employee involvement, however, does not imply union involvement, the object of the 1976 White Paper. According to the most recent NAPF Survey (1985), two-thirds of schemes have trustees nominated by the employer while only 2 per cent have union nominees. Schuller and Hyman's survey (1983a) suggested a higher proportion of union nominees (16 per cent) and elected members, but showed that senior management constituted 50 per cent of employee trustees.

In principle the identity and method of appointment of trustees is irrelevant to the regulation of pension schemes. The duties are common to all trustees. Moreover, the 1976 White Paper drew a careful distinction between the fixing of levels of benefit and contributions, matters for collective bargaining, and scheme administration, a matter for participative management. This differentiation of functions so readily drawn in principle may prove less easy to sustain in practice and conceals several potential conflicts of interests (see Nobles, 1985).

Conflicts of Interest

Self-investment. To the employer a disadvantage of external funding of pension schemes is that it requires alienation of capital from the business. This disadvantage is alleviated if the fund can subsequently be invested with the employer. One consequence of self-investment is to undermine the degree of security provided by the initial separation of assets. The close relationship that often exists between trustees and employer, particularly where trustees are the employer's nominees, opens up the possibility of a conflict of interest between the trustees' duty to act solely in the best interests of the members and a wish not to act to the detriment of the employer's interest. The temptation for the employer to draw on a source of accessible capital, possibly on preferential terms, is self-evident but formal constraints do exist.

In its statutory regulation of contracted-out schemes, the OPB requires the submission of an annual statement advising whether self-investment exceeds 10 per cent of a scheme's total resources. According to the OPB, 'there is often a measure of self-investment ... although this is less common in the larger funds' (OPB, 1982:para.3.19). While the Board cannot prohibit self-investment, they have the residual powers referred to previously to cancel a contracting-out certificate when the security of the GMP is at risk. An additional limitation is imposed by the Inland Revenue on small self-administered schemes involving less than twelve members where self-investment may not exceed 50 per cent. Trusts law imposes potential constraints on self-investment, although the terms of a trust deed may limit their effectiveness by specifically permitting it. In particular, if the employer is also a sole trustee, the equitable obligation that a trustee should not allow a position to arise where personal interest could possibly conflict with his duties to the trust, in this case the obligation to the members, suggests that self-investment could be successfully challenged by a scheme member. Otherwise it is not prohibited provided trustees act solely for the benefit of members and not to improve the employer's financial position, even though this could result.

Self-investment may not always cause a conflict of interest between employer and all scheme members. On the contrary the employer and some scheme members can have an identity of interest in applying fund resources to help protect employees' jobs, a use that will not necessarily financially benefit existing pensioners. This raises the question of how far the notion of benefit can be stretched and whether trusts law assumes an identity of interest among scheme members. In the context of a specific trust deed, Brightman J commented: 'it would in my view be wrong to suppose that the trustees are forbidden to give the parent concern financial accommodation on preferential terms if the trustees consider that the security of the employment of their members may otherwise be imperilled'.[25]

The implication that benefit can include the interests of members as employees rather than as future pensioners is difficult to sustain after the mineworkers' case. The pension scheme for all industrial employees of the National Coal Board had ten trustees, five each appointed by the Board and the NUM. The union appointees were held to be in breach of their duty as trustees when they refused to approve a new investment policy for the fund unless it complied with certain guidelines established by the union conference, which were claimed to be in the union members' interests. The judgment confirmed that, except in rare cases, 'the paramount duty of the trustees is to provide the greatest financial benefits for the present and future beneficiaries'.[26]

This seems to require an investment policy directed towards achieving the best possible financial return consistent with security of capital and *for no other purpose* unless directly relevant to the employees as members of the pension scheme. Paradoxically, in those schemes where pension entitlement accrues with length of service, the overwhelming majority, security of employment is directly relevant to the employee not just as employee but also as pension scheme member. As explained previously, a scheme member may suffer financial detriment if forced through redundancy to join the ranks of early leavers with only a preserved pension.

Over-funding. A problem analogous to self-investment is that of over-funding. Recent substantial reductions in workforce levels and improved investment returns have drastically affected assumptions concerning future pension commitments, resulting in notional surpluses in some pension schemes. Regulation of over-funding is the province of the Inland Revenue, which, conscious of the fiscal attractions of pension funds as a haven for capital, has required any significant surplus to be disposed of. This has usually been by increasing benefits or, less commonly, reducing contributions and only exceptionally by refund to the employer. A change of practice in 1983 altered the order of priorities. In confirming the change the Financial Secretary to the Treasury commented that:

> it is of course the duty of the trustees to administer the scheme in the best interests of the members, but they may well consider — and the members may agree — that these interests would best be served by a refund to the employer if the alternative is, for example, the failure of the company and the loss of the members' jobs.[27]

This statement attempts to take account of the potential conflict of interest between employer and members, but assumes a community of interest among all members which may not exist. If trustees approve a refund for the benefit of existing employees without considering increasing

[25] *Evans v London Co-operative Society Ltd* (1976) The Times, 6 July.
[26] *Cowan v Scargill* [1984] IRLR 260, 266.
[27] 53 HC Deb, 2 February 1984, 304.

preserved pensions or pensions in payment, it is questionable whether the trustees could be said to be acting in the interests of all the members. But fear of imminent insolvency is not a prerequisite for disposal of an actuarial surplus and methods not necessarily involving trustee discretion exist. Employer and employees may agree not to increase benefits but to reduce their respective contributions for a limited period, indirectly providing a refund for both parties. The Inland Revenue now see this as the most acceptable option.[28] This leaves the interests of the early leavers and present pensioners formally unprotected and reliant on employer and employee goodwill.

Investment policy. Although both pension managers and employee trustees consider investment policy and the monitoring of fund performance as their most important activities (Schuller and Hyman, 1983b:89), the view of professional advisers and fund managers is a significant, at times dominant, influence. This had led Minns (1980) to suggest that a concentration of control of investment exists within certain financial institutions. This concentration exercises a decisive influence in shaping conventional investment criteria, critised by the TUC as being 'too often over-cautious, passive and short-term' (TUC, 1982:21).

Trusts law requires the trustee in exercising the power of investment 'to take such care as an ordinary prudent man would take if he were minded to make an investment for the benefit of other people for whom he felt morally bound to provide'.[29] The standard is nebulous but the prudent man would certainly take skilled advice, which is likely to reflect conventional investment criteria. This does not prevent employee trustees from arguing for different criteria to be applied, but they must show these are reasonable and chosen solely with the best interests of scheme members in mind. In this context 'the best interests of the beneficiaries are normally their best financial interests', according to the judgment in the mineworkers' case.[30] The case demonstrates the difficulty of establishing that an investment policy is in the members' best interests where it is influenced by trade union conference decisions, whether reflecting the collective views of the members or not, and whether of purported indirect benefit to the members as employees or not. Similarly, individual investment decisions taking account of union recognition policies or non-compliance with safety standards would seem in breach of the duty to act in the best interests of the members, unless these factors could be shown directly to relate to the profitability or security of the investment.

Surveys suggest (Schuller and Hyman, 1983b; Minns, 1980:ch. 5) that disagreement between trustees over investment policy and practice is in fact infrequent. This does not mean that the potential for conflicts of interests between trustees and among scheme members does not exist. In the private

---

[28] See the letter from the Superannuation Funds Office in *Pensions World* (July 1984), 409, clarifying Inland Revenue practice, and 83 HC Deb, 26 July 1985, 874.
[29] *Re Whiteley* (1886) 33 Ch D 347, at 355 (per Lindley LJ).
[30] *Cowan v Scargill* loc. cit.

family trust the conflict is defined out of existence by assuming a consensus on the objective of financial benefit, disagreements on investment policy being resolved by resort to objective professional advice. Scant room is left for the beneficiary's opinion since he is the mere recipient of the trust founder's bounty. In the mineworkers' case the court was unconvinced that pension funds were materially different.

But striking factual differences do exist. Employees partly fund the scheme by their own contributions and, if the view of pension entitlement as deferred wages is accepted, by the employer's contribution. They may wish to exercise some direct collective control over policy guiding the investment of their property. For the employer the contribution level is fixed in relation to assumptions about investment return and scale of benefits. Again the direct interest in investment policy is evident and the distinction between collective bargaining issues, such as benefit and contribution levels, and participative management issues, such as investment, begin to look artificial.

This raises in acute form the appropriateness of the standards of trusts law as regulator of the conflicts of interest that may arise. In fact, trusts law recognises their existence and attempts formally to resolve them by prohibiting trustees from furthering their own interests or those of the trust founder, the employer,[31] and by imposing the duty of impartial treatment of beneficiaries. It accepts the conflicts and obliges the trustee to resolve them impartially, while reserving ultimate control in the hands of the beneficiaries. Its effectiveness depends both on whether the conflicts in the context of pension funds are susceptible to impartial objective resolution and the members are equipped with adequate information to carry out their policing role.

Disclosure of Information

Prior to the Social Security Act 1985, the law regulating disclosure of information to the members of occupational pension schemes was extremely fragmented and uncertain. The general obligations on the employer to provide written particulars on pensions (EPCA s.1(3)(d)(iii)) and to disclose information to recognised unions (EPA s.17) were of limited value. They did not extend to the provision of information about the administration of the scheme by trustees. This the scheme member had to seek from the trustees direct. Trusts law provides rights of access to information to members based on their equitable ownership of scheme funds. 'The beneficiary is entitled to see all the trust documents because they are trust documents and because he is a beneficiary. They are in a sense his own'.[32] While this principle would not permit disclosure of confidential information concerning the exercise of a trustee's discretion in individual cases,[33] it

---

[31] *Turner v Turner* [1983] 2 All ER 745.
[32] *O'Rourke v Darbishire* [1920] AC 581, at 626 (per Lord Wrenbury).
[33] Cf. *Re Londonderry's Settlement* [1965] Ch 918.

would give the member a right of access to, for example, an actuary's reports and details of investment holdings. In fact the right seems to be little known or used (OPB, 1982:para. 4.12), and a weakness is that the obligation arises only where the member requests access to the information.

Despite these legal limitations and uncertainties, the practice of voluntary disclosure developed albeit inconsistently (Schuller and Hyman, 1983b; 1983c). But the OPB, having eschewed statutory regulation of funding and placed its faith in membership control, recommended (1982:ch. 7) a statutory obligation of disclosure. The government has introduced this in the Social Security Act 1985. Schedule 2 empowers the Secretary of State to make regulations for the disclosure of information about a scheme's constitution, its administration and finances, and the rights and obligations that may arise under it. The details to be disclosed are at present uncertain but the government's view (DHSS, 1984a:app. B) is that they should be 'sufficient to enable an expert pension adviser to form a complete picture of the scheme and its financial soundness'. The implication is that reliance on voluntary regulation of pension schemes by scheme members depends substantially on those members and their advisers acquiring the necessary expertise. In this respect it is significant that the SSPA is amended by the 1985 Act so as to require disclosure to recognised trade unions as well as scheme members. An additional disclosure duty requires pension schemes to submit information, including copies of scheme rules and annual reports, to a registrar for inclusion on a register open to public inspection. The shift away from reliance on voluntarism is also apparent in the enforcement provisions. The new enforcement provisions enable an 'aggrieved person' to obtain a county court order requiring disclosure, and empower the registrar to prosecute trustees who are in default of the registration obligations.

The position is less satisfactory where the information disclosed reveals possible breaches of trust. The effectiveness of the system of voluntary control then depends on the legal remedies available to the scheme member. The government, having decided to rely on the substantive standards of trusts law for regulation, seems willing also to rely for enforcement on its remedies. Although the threat of court action may generally be sufficient (DHSS, 1984a:para. 27), a costly journey through the High Court is the only enforcement mechanism. Robert Evans, a retired London milkman, did bring a successful action against the trustees of the London Co-operative pension scheme, but this should not engender complacency. The time involved and the financial cost he incurred for little personal reward are more likely to discourage than encourage potential litigants.[34]

CONCLUSION

Four sources of pressure were initially identified as pushing pensions into greater prominence in labour relations and labour law at both collective and

---

[34] See note 25 above. In 1977 the case was settled when London Co-operative Society paid £1.4m into its pension fund. The direct benefit for Mr Evans was an increase of £1.81 in his weekly pension: *The Guardian*, 17 November 1977.

individual levels. The fourth and now most compelling of these, state intervention into the voluntary provision and regulation of schemes, is at an embryonic stage but the government's strategy is becoming clearer and the implications for occupational pension schemes can be assessed.

The provisions of the 1985 Act to ease the transfer of pension entitlement for job-changers and to provide some inflation protection for preserved pensions can certainly be portrayed as increasing the choices and protecting the expectations of early leavers. Contemporaneously the legislation is perceived as a necessary adjunct to improving the efficiency of the labour market. 'The government must ... have regard to the need for national economic purposes, to remove artificial and unnecessary obstacles to job mobility' (DHSS, 1983:para. 2).[35] The legislation is now to be supplemented with a more fundamental reform. The government appears committed to enabling employees to opt out of their occupational pension schemes, and out of the state earnings-related scheme, subject to their arranging a personal pension, one that can be taken with the employee when changing jobs (DHSS, 1984c). While the avowed intention is to increase peoples' 'freedom to choose the pension arrangements that suit them best' (DHSS, 1984c:1), equally influential is the view that personal pensions, unaffected by job changes, will encourage occupational labour mobility.

In addition, the Centre for Policy Studies (CPS, 1983), from where the proposal originates, envisages personal pensions as reversing the trend towards stock market domination by institutional investors. Yet the attractiveness of this option for many employees will be considerably diluted if there is no statutory obligation on employers to contribute more than rebated national insurance contributions, a much lower percentage figure than most employers currently contribute to occupational pension schemes. This limitation is a consequence of the policy constraints of not wishing to be seen to undermine existing occupational pension schemes, or to impose unnecessary compulsory financial burdens on employers. Indeed, it looks more as if a fundamental objective is to encourage those at present in the state scheme to opt for personal pensions, reducing the potential public expenditure burden of the pay-as-you-go state scheme (DHSS, 1984d).[36]

Despite this, the full range of government proposals may yet affect the structure of occupational pension schemes. While no statutory regulation of funding or obligation to increase pensions in payment is proposed, the move towards inflation-proofed preserved pensions will itself increase costs. The government estimates that the total annual average increase in costs will be equivalent of between 1 and 2 per cent of payroll, although this will vary between schemes.[37] Faced with this, employers may use the opportunity presented by the government's initiative to seek to reduce costs and restructure pension schemes by offering to contribute voluntarily to personal pension plans for certain groups of employees, while retaining a more

---

[35] See McCormick and Hughes (1981), for a view that job mobility has been hindered.
[36] A Green Paper – *Reform of Social Security* (Cmnd 9517, HMSO, 1985) – proposed the phasing out of SERPS and its replacement by compulsory personal pension provision or membership of an occupational scheme.
[37] 68 HC Deb, 26 November 1984, 672 (Secretary of State).

generous contribution level and final salary scheme for other employees. Personal pension provision may benefit some highly mobile employees, assuming an adequate level of employer contribution, but it could result in a deterioration in terms and conditions for others. Such a development would reflect the growing division of the workforce into core and marginal groups. From this perspective a consequence of pension reform will be the reinforcement of a segmented labour market.

The same unwillingness to impose undue financial or administrative burdens on either employers or the state, which limits the protection given to early leavers and influences the government's proposals on personal pensions, underpins the approach to the issue of security of members' rights and expectations. The OPB (1982:para. 3.28) has stated that the existing system, to be satisfactory, requires an adequate level of funding, an adequate legal structure, and security for the value of benefits. The government has rejected extensive statutory controls to achieve these objectives; it has reaffirmed support for the voluntary system of regulation, buttressed by a statutory duty of disclosure, and, more contentiously, has declared itself broadly satisfied with the existing legal structure. It is evading the issue to rely on trusts law to resolve conflicts arising out of attempts to increase employer accountability and responsibility while encouraging the genuine separation of trustees from the employer. The same criticism applies to conflicts between members that reflect the competing demands of security of employment and security of pensions expectations. The trust is an adaptable medium but a belief that its present standards can provide universally acceptable, objective solutions to what are in essence conflicts of policy is unwise. Equally, appeals to more extensive legislation as a panacea are futile if these same conflicts are not confronted.

Reliance on the voluntary system to resolve policy conflicts and protect employee expectations may push collective bargaining on pensions more towards centre-stage, but now with a different emphasis. Instead of negotiating to increase pension benefits, unions may be faced, as suggested above, with proposals to individualise pension provision and to limit scheme access or reduce scheme benefits. Indeed, recognition of the full cost of protecting expectations engendered by present pension promises may mean that security of benefits, rather than constituting a fundamental requirement, will itself now become a negotiable scheme benefit, a possibility clearly envisaged by the OPB (1982:para. 11.30).

The government's approach is moderately reformist but the result may yet be to fracture the consensus on pensions that has existed since the mid-1970s and re-open debate on the reliance on occupational pensions to provide security in retirement in an uncertain economic climate, particularly when their attractiveness as a savings medium is partly dependent on privileged tax treatment. As Fogarty (1982:205) has commented: 'if we could write on a clean sheet a formula for organising income support in non-working periods ... would we choose one based on occupation, or at least based on occupational units?'

Bibliography

Bolton. 1971. Committee of Inquiry on Small Firms. *Report*. Cmnd 4811. London: HMSO.

Bullock. 1977. Committee of Inquiry on Industrial Democracy. *Report*. Cmnd 6706. London: HMSO.

Centre for Policy Studies (CPS). 1983. *Personal and Portable Pensions – for All*. Memorandum by the Personal Capital Formation Study Group. London: Centre for Policy Studies.

Department of Health and Social Security (DHSS). 1971. *Strategy for Pensions: The Future Development of State and Occupational Provision*. Cmnd 4755. London: HMSO.

——. 1983. *Improved Protection for the Occupational Pension Rights and Expectations of Early Leavers from Occupational Pension Schemes*. London: DHSS.

——. 1984a. *Greater Security for the Rights and Expectations of Members of Occupational Pension Schemes*. London: DHSS.

——. 1984b. *Improved Transferability for Early Leavers from Occupational Pension Schemes*. London: DHSS.

——. 1984c. *Personal Pensions: A Consultative Document*. London: DHSS.

——. 1984d. *Population, Pension Costs and Pensioners' Incomes: A Background Paper for the Inquiry into Provision for Retirement*. London: HMSO.

Drucker, P.F. 1976. *The Unseen Revolution: How Pension Fund Socialism Came to America*. London: Heinemann.

Ellis, E., and P. Morrell. 1982. 'Sex Discrimination in Pension Schemes: Has Community Law Changed the Rules?'. *Industrial Law Journal*, 11 (March), 16–28.

Ellison, R. 1979. *Private Occupational Pension Schemes*. London: Oyez Press.

Fogarty, M. (ed.). 1982. *Retirement Policy: The Next Fifty Years*. London: Heinemann.

Government Actuary. 1981. *Occupational Pension Schemes 1979: Sixth Survey*. London: HMSO.

Hepple, B. 1983. 'Individual Labour Law'. *Industrial Relations in Britain*. Ed. G.S. Bain. Oxford: Blackwell, 393–417.

——, and P. O'Higgins. 1981. *Employment Law*. 4th edn. B. A. Hepple. London: Sweet & Maxwell.

Inland Revenue (IR). 1979. *Occupational Pension Schemes: Notes on Approval under the Finance Act*. Thames Ditton: Inland Revenue Superannuation Funds Office.

——. 1983a. *Inland Revenue Statistics 1983*. London: HMSO.

——. 1983b. *Cost of Tax Reliefs for Pension Schemes – Appropriate Statistical Approach*. London: Board of Inland Revenue.

Langham, F.R., and J.D. Sparks. 1976. 'Tax Treatment of Pension Provision'. *Journal of Institute of Actuaries*, vol. 103, 323–30.

McCormick, B., and G. Hughes. 1981. 'The Influence of Pensions on Job Mobility'. Discussion Paper 8118. Southampton: University of Southampton, Department of Economics.

McGoldrick, A. 1985. *Equal Treatment in Occupational Pension Schemes: A Research Report*. Manchester: Equal Opportunities Commission.

Minns, R. 1980. *Pension Funds and British Capitalism*. London: Heinemann.

Morgan, E. Victor. 1984. *Choice in Pensions*. Hobart Paper 100. London: Institute of Economic Affairs.

National Association of Pension Funds (NAPF). 1982. *A Guide to Good Practice: Member Participation in Pension Schemes*. Croydon: NAPF.

——. 1985. *Tenth Annual Survey of Occupational Pension Schemes 1984*. Croydon: NAPF.

National Economic Development Office (NEDO). 1975. *Finance for Industry*. London: HMSO.

Nobles, R. 1985. 'Conflicts of Interest in Trustees' Management of Pension Funds'. *Industrial Law Journal*, 13 (March), 1–17.

Occupational Pensions Board (OPB). 1976a. *Equal Status for Men and Women in Occupational Pension Schemes*. Cmnd 6599. London: HMSO.

——. 1976b. *The Role of Members in the Running of Schemes*. Cmnd 6514. London: HMSO.

——. 1981. *Improved Protection for the Occupational Pension Rights and Expectations of Early Leavers*. Cmnd 8271. London: HMSO.

——. 1982. *Greater Security for the Rights and Expectations of Members of Occupational Pension Schemes*. Cmnd 8649. London: HMSO.

Plender, J. 1982. *That's the Way the Money Goes: The Financial Institutions and the Nation's Savings*. London: André Deutsch.

Schuller, T., and J. Hyman. 1983a. 'Pensions: The Voluntary Growth of Participation'. *Industrial Relations Journal*, 14 (Spring), 70–79.

——, and J. Hyman. 1983b. 'Trust Law and Trustees: Employee Representation in Pension Schemes'. *Industrial Law Journal*, 12 (June), 84–98.

——, and J. Hyman. 1983c. 'Information, Participation and Pensions: Strategy and Employee-Related Issues'. *Personnel Review*, 12 (3), 263.

Scott. 1981. Committee of Inquiry into the Value of Pensions. *Report*. Cmnd 8147. London: HMSO.

Stock Exchange. 1983. *The Stock Exchange Survey of Share Ownership*. London: Stock Exchange.

Trades Union Congress (TUC). 1982. *Report on Fund Investment and Trusteeship*. London: TUC.

Wilson. 1980. Committee to Review the Functioning of Financial Institutions. *Report*. Cmnd 7937. London: HMSO.

Young, M., and N. Buchanan. 1981. *Accounting for Pensions*. Cambridge: Woodhead-Faulkner.

15   Unfair Dismissals and Redundancy

Steven Anderman

The statutory provisions on unfair dismissal and redundancy are the core of employment protection legislation. This is so in part because the overwhelming majority of cases that are brought to industrial tribunals concern unfair dismissal and redundancy. Even more important, however, these provisions purport to give protection against the loss of the job itself as opposed to the protection of rights during the course of employment and, in this sense, are the 'cutting edge' of employment legislation. They offer a perspective with which to assess the extent to which the interests of employees in job security are actually protected against what managers consider to be an essential prerogative, their right to terminate the employment relationship.

At first glance, the unfair dismissal and redundancy enactments appear to provide extensive legal protection from managerial decisions to dismiss employees by giving workers a legal means to question those decisions. Thus the legislation gives individual employees a right to complain about the unfairness of most types of dismissal (EPCA ss.54–80). Moreover, once recognised by an employer, a trade union has a statutory right to be informed and consulted before that employer makes redundancies within the grade of employees whom the trade union represents, and employers have an obligation to notify the DE about impending redundancies (EPA ss.99–107). Furthermore, the EPCA provides a cluster of employment rights which give employees some protection against the effects of management decisions to make workers redundant (see Gennard, 1982). These include a right to a minimum payment of compensation for redundancy (ss.81–120); a right to a minimum period of notice of dismissal or pay in lieu of notice (ss.49–52); a right to reasonable time off from work with pay during the notice period to look for another job or make arrangements for training for future employment (s.31); a right to a guaranteed weekly payment in case of lay off or short time (ss.12–18); and protection for employees in cases where the employer has become insolvent (ss.121–7). In addition, there is protection for employees in certain cases of transfers of undertakings (Transfer of Undertakings (Protection of Employment) Regulations 1981).

The legislation establishing these rights has been viewed as a barrier against redundancy and loss of job security (Bourn, 1983:24), or as 'property rights in the job against the employer' (Davies and Freedland, 1984:429).

Yet it is somewhat misleading to characterise employment protection legislation solely as employee rights constraining the exercise of managerial discretion. For this ignores the point that the policy underlying the legislation has also been to reform managerial practice in order to enable management to achieve its economic objectives more effectively in the sphere of redundancy and discipline.

A related misconception of 'individual employment legislation' has been the tendency to regard it as purely a floor 'on which we can all stand ... a ground floor for an edifice of collective bargaining' (Kahn-Freund, 1977:73), or to discern in its structure the primacy of collective bargaining (Wedderburn, 1980:84), as if the effects of individual employment legislation upon the machinery of collective bargaining are relatively insignificant. For this too tends to underestimate the dual purpose of such individual labour legislation – managerial efficiency and employment protection – as well as the actual impact upon labour relations of the legislatively stimulated reforms of managerial policies and procedures. The theme of this chapter is that the legislation concerning redundancy and disciplinary dismissals can most usefully be viewed as part of an overall public policy of attempting to promote efficient management as well as to secure individual rights in employment.

UNFAIR DISMISSAL

A law on unfair dismissal was planned by the Labour Government in the 1960s following the recommendation of the Donovan Report (1968:para.545), but was first enacted by the Conservative Government in the IRA. It was later retained by successive governments, appearing to provide, rather unusually, a relatively stable feature in the framework of labour law. In appearance the statutory right not to be unfairly dismissed, now embodied in Part V of the EPCA, takes the form of a fundamental workers' right based on the ILO Termination of Employment Recommendation No.119 (1963), which asserted the principle that an employer should not dismiss an employee without valid reason and sufficient cause and without the dismissed employee having a right to have recourse to an independent tribunal to determine the issue and decide an appropriate remedy. The legal position of employees at common law was that, as long as proper contractual notice of termination was given, an employer was legally entitled to dismiss an employee for whatever reason he wished. There was no obligation on the employer to reveal his reason for dismissal to the employee much less to justify it. And even if the employer dismissed an employee without notice or with inadequate notice, the only remedy open to the employee was that of claiming wrongful dismissal in the ordinary courts – a course of action for which the only remedy was damages generally limited to pay for the notice period (Anderman, 1985:4; and see further Chapter 12 above). In a radical departure from common law principles, the Act proclaims that every employee who is qualified has the right not to be dismissed unfairly by his or her employer (EPCA s.54). Consequently it provides that a dismissed employee has the right to complain to an industrial tribunal that the dismissal is unfair (s.67), and to have that tribunal determine the 'reasonableness' of the employer's decision (s.57(3)) in the light of the employer's reason for dismissal. If the tribunal finds that the employee's complaint is well founded, then it has the discretion to order a remedy of reinstatement, or re-engagement or compensation. In addition, the statute provides a separate right for the employee to receive upon request a written statement of the reason for dismissal (s.53).

The introduction of the statutory procedure, however, was, as already suggested, not solely motivated by the desire to give protection to employees in their contractual relationship with employers; it had a second aim of improving personnel management. The predominant method of achieving this aim was to convince managers to adopt formal disciplinary and dismissal procedures. The Donovan Commission (1968:para.533) had indicated that a statute would provide managers with a clear incentive to devise such procedures as a means of avoiding recourse to the statutory procedure and yet of defending a case should one arise. Once established, formal disciplinary and dismissal procedures, it was thought, would enable employers to manage their workforce more efficiently by ensuring that they refrained from the more arbitrary forms of dismissal and that dismissal decisions were not taken until they could be shown to the workforce to be fair and justified. Moreover, the formal procedures would help management to plan disciplinary decisions and to present them to the workforce in ways that would avoid precipitating strikes to reverse disciplinary dismissals. Hence the 1971 Act was accompanied by a Code of Practice (1972) which had a special section on Disciplinary and Dismissal Procedures providing for a system of warnings, a hearing, and a right of appeal. These recommendations on discipline were later updated and replaced by a separate Code on Disciplinary Practice and Procedures in Employment (1977) prepared by ACAS.

There was also some suggestion that the provision of a statutory procedure to resolve dismissal disputes might have a direct impact upon the incidence of industrial action over dismissals by providing an acceptable alternative channel whereby contested decisions could be challenged without the need for industrial action (Donovan Commission, 1968:para.528; DE, 1970; Dickens et al., 1985:224). At all events, it was clear that the statute was not only intended to have a protective function; it was also intended to promote managerial efficiency and thereby reduce industrial conflict.

Limitations on the Right not to be Unfairly Dismissed

The statutory right to complain of unfair dismissal is far from being a universal right as only qualified employees may complain to a tribunal. To be qualified an employee must have two years' service or more if hired after 1 June 1985; if hired before that date, an employee must have at least one year's service or, if working in a firm of twenty or fewer employees, two years' service or more (EPCA s.64).[1] If part-time, an employee must work for sixteen hours per week or more or eight hours per week or more after five years' service (Sch.13, paras.4 and 5). Moreover, employees must not have reached the normal retiring age for their position or, if there is no normal retiring age for employees in their position, then they must not be over sixty if a woman or sixty-five if a man (s.64(1)(b)). They must not be normally working outside Great Britain (s.141), and, if working on a fixed term contract of at least one year's duration, not have agreed in writing to exclude any claim to a right of unfair dismissal (s.142).

In addition, workers who do not meet the statute's technical definition of 'employee', that is, an individual who works under or who has worked under a contract of employment (s.153) are excluded from its protection. The line between employees and non-employees established by this definition is not always clear. In order to establish whether an individual is an employee tribunals may resort to a test of whether he is 'in business on his own account', [1a] or of the degree to which the employer has 'control' over the work,[2] or of whether it can be shown that the employer is contractually obligated to provide work and the individual to perform work.[3] Industrial tribunals have a wide discretion to decide which of these tests to apply and how to weigh the factors involved in each test because the question is viewed essentially as one of fact, subject only to a limited appeal on questions of law.[4]

The cumulative effect of these statutory exclusions has been to deny large groups of workers the protection of what was thought to be a basic employee right. Equally important, they provide opportunities for employers to avoid the effect of the legislation by adopting forms of contract such as part-time or short-term employment or sub-contracting that take the employment out of the scope of the legislation (Leighton, 1983:23 and Chapter 18 below). In this respect, business efficiency has been accorded a greater priority than employment protection.

Has the Employee been Dismissed?

Assuming that an employee is qualified to bring a claim for unfair dismissal, the first step in presenting a case is to prove that he or she has been 'dismissed', a concept which includes failure to permit a woman to return to work after confinement (s.56). The EPCA (which applies an identical requirement for claims for redundancy payments) provides that three and only three types of dismissal will entitle an employee to complain of unfair dismissal (s.55); first, where the employer terminates the employee's

---

[1] As amended by the Unfair Dismissal (Variation of Qualifying Period) Order SI 1985 No. 782.

[1a] *Market Investigations Ltd v Minister of Social Security* [1969] 2 QB 173. For a more detailed analysis of the tests of an employment contract, see Chapter 12.

[2] *Young & Woods Ltd v West* [1980] IRLR 201, EAT.

[3] *Nethermere (St Neots) Ltd v Gardiner and Taverna* [1983] IRLR 103, EAT; [1984] IRLR 240, CA; *O'Kelly v Trusthouse Forte Plc* [1983] ICR 728, CA.

[4] ibid.

contract of employment with or without notice; second, where the employer decides not to renew a fixed term contract; and third, constructive dismissal, where the employee resigns, with or without giving notice, in circumstances such as he is entitled to do so without notice because of the conduct of the employer.

In theory, this third category of dismissal extends the statutory protection in order to prevent employers from forcing employees to resign as a method of avoiding claims for unfair dismissal or redundancy. But the statute has been interpreted to provide such protection in practice only to employees who can show that the conduct of the employer that forced them to leave amounted to a contractual repudiation. A contractual repudiation is defined technically as either a breach of a particular fundamental term of a contract or a renunciation of the terms of a contract as a whole. Under the case law there have been three main categories of repudiation: a failure by the employer to meet a positive contractual obligation such as the duty to pay agreed remuneration[5] or to provide a safe system of work;[6] an insistence by the employer upon a fundamental change in the nature of the employee's contractual performance such as the kind of work he could be required to perform, or his hours or place of work;[7] and conduct by the employer which amounts to a breach of a particular implied obligation such as the duty not to destroy the mutual confidence and trust of the employment relationship.[8] In principle any of these actions by the employer will entitle the employee to resign and claim unfair dismissal. While the statutory test of constructive dismissal was held to be a 'contractual' as opposed to a pure reasonableness test because of the language of the statutory provision,[9] a wide range of unreasonable conduct by the employer may constitute constructive dismissal provided that it can fit into one of the recognised categories of contractually repudiatory behaviour. For example, the duty not to destroy the mutual confidence and trust of the relationship has been extended to a wide range of employer mistreatment of employees including false accusation of dishonesty and theft,[10] harsh language,[11] and harassment.[12] Moreover, the EAT has on occasion held that it was possible for tribunals to imply a term that employers will not treat their employees arbitrarily, capriciously or inequitably in matters of remuneration.[13]

Some commentators have been influenced by these decisions to argue that the judicial development of implied terms has achieved results comparable to those which would have resulted from a statutory reasonableness test for constructive dismissal (Elias, 1978:105–6; Hepple and O'Higgins, 1981:263).

---

5 *Hill Ltd v Moroney* [1981] IRLR 259, EAT.
6 *British Aircraft Corporation Ltd v Austin* [1978] IRLR 332, EAT.
7 *McNeill v Charles Crimin (Electrical Contractors) Ltd* [1984] IRLR 179, EAT.
8 *Woods v WM Car Services (Peterborough) Ltd* [1982] ICR 693, CA.
9 *Western Excavating (ECC) Ltd v Sharp* [1978] IRLR 27, CA; see also *Post Office v Roberts* [1980] IRLR 347, EAT.
10 *Robinson v Crompton Parkinson Ltd* [1978] IRLR 61, EAT.
11 *Palmanor Ltd v Cedron* [1978] IRLR 303, EAT.
12 See *Garner v Grange Furnishing Ltd* [1977] IRLR 206, EAT.
13 *Gardner Ltd v Beresford* [1978] IRLR 63, EAT.

Yet the contractual test falls short of comparability in important respects. It continues to place certain limits upon the extent to which unreasonable behaviour can be shown to be a contractual repudiation. For example, where the employer has *express* contractual authority to a transfer of an employee and he exercises this power by transferring the employee to less attractive work or surroundings unreasonably,[14] it will be more difficult for an employee to argue that the employer repudiated the contract as a whole by breaking an *implied* term, since generally an express term is superior to an implied term.[15] Moreover, the fact that constructive dismissal has been contractually defined has brought unnecessary legal technicalities into the determination of whether or not an employee has been dismissed. Thus, on the one hand, employees must be careful not to leave their employment prematurely in response to a warning,[16] or to any announcement that creates uncertainty about the future of their jobs.[17] They must wait until the point when the employer actually commits a repudiation[18] or run the risk of being held to have resigned voluntarily rather than to have been constructively dismissed. On the other hand, employees must not remain on the job too long after a repudiation because this might have the effect of waiving it and affirming the contract.[19]

Statutory Test of Fairness

Once, however, an employee succeeds in proving that he or she has been dismissed under the statute, the next step is for the industrial tribunal to determine whether or not that dismissal was fair. The EPCA s.57 asks the tribunal to test the fairness of a dismissal in two stages. The first stage requires the employer to show his reason for dismissal and that it fits into one of the reasons in s.57(2) or 57(1)(b), that is, the capability or qualifications of the employee for performing work of the kind which he was employed by the employer to do, the conduct of the employee, redundancy, the inability of the employee to work in the position which he held without contravention (either on his part or on that of his employer) of a statutory duty or restriction, or was some other substantial reason of a kind such as to justify the dismissal of an employee holding the position which that employee held. Normally this stage requires the employer only to provide sufficient evidence to prove what in fact his motive was and not to justify it. Nevertheless, a dismissal can be found to be unfair at the first stage if an employer fails to show that his reason for dismissal was one which was presumptively valid under the statute. Moreover, the employee may be able

---

14   *Milbrook Furnishing Ltd v McIntosh* [1978] IRLR 309, EAT. But see *BBC v Beckett* [1983] IRLR 43, EAT.
15   E.g. *Express Lifts Ltd v Bowles* [1977] IRLR 99, EAT.
16   *Morton Sundour Fabrics Ltd v Shaw* (1967) 2 ITR 84.
17   *British Leyland (UK) Ltd v McQuilken* [1978] IRLR 245, EAT.
18   E.g. *Maher v Fram Gerrard Ltd* [1974] ICR 31, NIRC.
19   E.g. *Cox Toner Ltd v Crook* [1978] ICR 823, EAT; *Western Excavating (ECC) Ltd v Sharp* [1978] IRLR 27, CA.

to show that the employer's reason for dismissal was one which is automatically unfair under the statute. These reasons relate to trade union membership or activity or non-membership (s.58), redundancy in breach of an agreed procedure (s.59), pregnancy (s.60) and (as explained in Chapter 17) sex or race.

The second stage requires industrial tribunals to be satisfied that the employer's decision was reasonable in the circumstances (including the size and administrative resources of the organisation) and in accordance with equity and the substantial merits of the case (s.57(3)). Taken at face value, this test of reasonableness would appear to be both comprehensive and searching. It applies to dismissals for a wide range of reasons a general test of reasonableness, which involves an examination of the factual and procedural circumstances as well as the substantial merits of the case. It also appears to include the application of standards of equity to the determination of the reasonableness of the employer's decision, which implies that tribunals could apply objective standards of reasonableness to management decisions. And, indeed, industrial tribunals have been described as 'industrial juries' having a wide power to apply the test of reasonableness as a question of fact,[20] and subject only to a limited appeal where they make mistakes of law.

Yet in the process of interpreting the statute, appellate courts have often sought to circumscribe tribunal discretion in the application of the reasonableness test. For example, the EAT and the Court of Appeal have decided that in testing whether the employer had a reasonable factual basis for his decision to dismiss for misconduct, an industrial tribunal cannot require an employer to prove that the employee actually committed the act of misconduct complained of. The employer may only be required to show that he had reasonable grounds for his belief that this was the case.[21] In *British Home Stores Ltd v Burchell* the EAT indicated that this test could be broken down into three separate elements: 'first of all, there must be established by the employer the fact of that belief; that the employer did believe it. Secondly, that the employer had in his mind reasonable grounds upon which to sustain that belief. And thirdly, we think that the employer, at the stage at which he formed that belief on those grounds, at any rate at the final stage at which he formed that belief on those grounds, had carried out as much investigation into the matter as was reasonable in all the circumstances of the case.'[22]

Since *Burchell's* case, s.57(3) has been amended by EA 1980 to remove from the employer the formal burden of proving the reasonableness of the dismissal. Nevertheless the rules in *Burchell's* case continue to apply in a wide range of misconduct cases. Industrial tribunals are guided that they must not make their own determination of the fact whether or not employees had committed an act or acts for which they have been dismissed;

[20] E.g. *Grundy (Teddington) Ltd v Willis* [1976] IRLR 118, EAT.
[21] See *British Home Stores Ltd v Burchell* [1978] IRLR 379, EAT; *Monie v Coral Racing* [1978] IRLR 379, EAT; [1980] IRLR 464, CA.
[22] [1978] IRLR 379, 380.

their function has been limited to that of determining whether the belief of the employer at the time the employer took the decision to dismiss was justified in the light of the evidence available to him and the extent of the investigation he had undertaken.[23] In so far as tribunals are thus circumscribed in deciding the 'facts' of the case, the description of tribunals as 'industrial juries' may be somewhat misleading.

In cases of dismissals for misconduct, industrial tribunals apply a test of procedural reasonableness influenced by the guidelines laid down by the ACAS Code of Practice on Disciplinary Practice and Procedures. The Code states that employers should have formal disciplinary procedures which provide that before dismissal an employee is given adequate warnings in case of misconduct short of gross misconduct, as well as a fair hearing and a right of appeal. The recommendations of the Code do not have the force of law, but they must be taken into account by tribunals when relevant (EPA s.6(11)). Moreover, the EAT has urged that not only the Code but also the tenets of good industrial practice must be taken into account by tribunals when applying the test of reasonableness.[24] Yet while industrial tribunals have the discretion to decide that an important procedural omission by itself makes a dismissal unfair,[25] a procedural omission does not necessarily make a dismissal unfair under the statutory test of reasonableness.[26]

The cases where an employer can omit an important procedural step and nevertheless be found to have fairly dismissed an employee can be divided into two categories. One category consists of the cases which are so obvious on the merits that formal defects in the employer's investigative procedure are not significant. For example, where the employer already has strong evidence of misconduct[27] or the employee has already indicated his views in another context, the omission of a formal hearing has not been conclusively unfair conduct.[28] In such cases the procedural failure is considered to be either superfluous or unimportant by comparison with the substantive merits of the case and hence the employer could not be said to have acted unreasonably in the circumstances.

There is a second category of cases, however, where procedural omissions by the employer are treated rather more cavalierly in the guidelines given to industrial tribunals by appellate courts. Thus in *British Labour Pump Co. Ltd v Byrne*[29] it was suggested that in cases of procedural failures by the employer there should be a second stage test as a matter of course to determine whether the procedural omission was likely in the circumstances to have had any effect upon the ultimate result. As a result of this

---

23 *W Weddel Ltd v Tepper* [1980] IRLR 96, CA; *Monie v Coral Racing Ltd* [1980] IRLR 464, CA.
24 *Williams v Compair Maxam Ltd* [1982] IRLR 83, EAT.
25 *W Devis & Sons Ltd v Atkins* [1977] IRLR 314, HL.
26 *W & J Wass Ltd v Binns* [1982] IRLR 283, CA.
27 See *Bailey v BP Oil (Kent Refinery) Ltd* [1980] IRLR 287, CA; *Harris and Shepherd v Courage (Eastern) Ltd* [1982] IRLR 509, CA.
28 E.g. *James v Waltham Holy Cross UDC* [1973] IRLR 202, NIRC; *Retarded Children's Aid Society Ltd v Day* [1978] IRLR 128, CA.
29 [1979] IRLR 94, EAT.

downgrading of the importance of procedural omissions under the statutory test, dismissals have been held to be fair even where the employer had failed, as agreed in the procedure, to include an employee's trade union official at a hearing,[30] or to give an employee an opportunity to be heard in a case of serious misconduct,[31] or to give a warning.[32] In these cases the industrial tribunals found that the procedural defect was not likely to have affected the outcome of the decision.

The *British Labour Pump* doctrine has been severely criticised on several counts by courts and commentators. Thus in *Sillifant v Powell Duffryn Timber Ltd*,[33] the then president of the EAT objected to the fact that the second stage test required industrial tribunals to apply the reasonableness test on the basis of hypothetical conclusions and guesswork. It has also been pointed out that the test fails to give sufficient weight to the factor of equity in the statute[34] and should not be applied when the failure was part of the procedure of investigating the facts.[35] Moreover, academic commentators have pointed out that the test of the potential outcome of a procedural failure is not the most appropriate method of determining the reasonableness of a decision in a context where procedural justice must not only be done but also be seen to be done (Anderman, 1985:133–4; Schofield, 1983:171).

Although the *British Labour Pump* doctrine has been endorsed by the Court of Appeal, it establishes only a guideline to industrial tribunals rather than a binding precedent.[36] Industrial tribunals can in their discretion decide either that a dismissal is unfair because of a procedural defect or that a procedural defect is insufficiently serious in the circumstances to make a dismissal unfair. But in so far as the *British Labour Pump* guidelines are applied by tribunals, there is a considerable weakening of the procedural test of fairness under the statute as it was originally conceived.

Finally, the courts have urged that industrial tribunals may not apply their own standard of 'reasonableness'.[37] Instead, they must ask whether or not the employer acted within the 'range of reasonable employers' in taking the decision that he did.[38] As applied to disciplinary dismissals, for example, this standard places limits on a tribunal's discretion to decide that an employee's decision to dismiss rather than impose a lesser penalty was reasonable in view of the nature of the disciplinary offence, the employee's record, and the extent to which the employer met his own responsibility to give adequate warnings and to act consistently (Anderman, 1985:149–72). 'The function of the tribunal, as an industrial jury, is to determine whether in the particular circumstances of each case the decision to dismiss the

---

30 *Bailey v BP Oil (Kent Refinery) Ltd* [1980] IRLR 287, CA.
31 *W & J Wass Ltd v Binns* [1982] IRLR 283, CA.
32 *Retarded Children's Aid Society Ltd v Day* [1978] IRLR 128, CA.
33 [1983] IRLR 191, EAT.
34 E.g. *Murray McKinnon v Forno* [1983] IRLR 7, EAT.
35 *Henderson v Granville Tours Ltd* [1982] IRLR 494, EAT.
36 E.g. *Siggs & Chapman Contractors Co. Ltd v Knight* [1984] IRLR 83, EAT.
37 *UCATT v Brain* [1981] IRLR 224, CA.
38 *British Leyland (BL) Ltd v Swift* [1981] IRLR 91, CA.

employee fell within the band of reasonable responses which a reasonable employer might have adopted. If the dismissal falls within the band it is fair; if it falls outside it is unfair'.[39]

The net effect of this approach is to require industrial tribunals to adopt a standard of fairness which reflects the lower reaches of acceptable managerial practice rather than to allow tribunals to establish standards which reflect their view of a more objective standard of fair industrial practice (Elias, 1981; Anderman, 1985). Although the Court of Appeal has been generally concerned over the last few years to ensure that industrial tribunals retain a wide jurisdiction over questions of fact, a failure by a tribunal to apply the test of a range of reasonable responses provides a basis of appeal.[40] While appellate decisions have thus acted generally to inhibit industrial tribunals in their applications of standards of fairness directly to managerial decisions in the areas of discipline and discharge, ill health, employee job performance and work reorganisation (see Anderman, 1985), they have sought to impose particularly strong inhibitions on tribunal scrutiny of management prerogative in two types of dismissals: dismissals in the context of reorganisation and dismissals for unfair redundancy.

Unfair Redundancy

In redundancy situations where an employee alleges that he was dismissed unfairly, the statute prescribes three grounds upon which he can base a complaint. The first is where the real reason for the selection for redundancy was trade union membership and activity or non-membership (s.59(a)) (see Chapter 2). The second is where the employee is selected in unjustified contravention of a customary arrangement or agreed procedure relating to redundancy (s.59(b)). To fit within this provision the employee must show that the employer contravened the criteria for selection contained in the procedure; other types of contraventions, such as a failure to meet a procedural requirement for consultation, will not satisfy this subsection.[41] Where the employer fails to act in compliance with an agreed procedure or collective agreement in respect of selection, then, unless the employer can show that he had special reason justifying his failure, the dismissal is automatically unfair.

The third ground for complaint is where a dismissal for redundancy is not thought to be reasonable in all the circumstances, whether or not a redundancy procedure has been followed. In principle, this appears to require the tribunal to determine whether the employer's decision in terms of the factual and procedural circumstances as well as the merits of the case was a fair one. Thus it has become accepted practice for industrial tribunals to consider whether the employer had a genuine factual basis for his application of criteria for selection for redundancy,[42] and whether he had

39   *Iceland Frozen Foods v Jones* [1982] IRLR 439, 442.
40   E.g. *Richmond Precision Engineering Ltd v Pearce* [1985] IRLR 179, EAT.
41   E.g. *McDowell v Eastern British Road Services Ltd* [1981] IRLR 482, EAT.
42   E.g. *Williams v Compair Maxam Ltd* [1982] IRLR 83, EAT.

followed a reasonable procedure of warnings, consultations and investigation of the possibilities of alternative employment before taking a decision to lay off the employee.[43] Moreover, the test includes an examination of the reasonableness of the timing of the redundancy as well as the basis for selection of the particular employee for redundancy.[44]

Owing to appellate decisions, however, considerable limitations have been placed upon the exercise of tribunal discretion to decide whether or not a dismissal for redundancy is unreasonable. Thus, under the reasonableness test of s.57(3), industrial tribunals have been urged not to require too high a standard of proof from the employer to show that his criteria for selection have been met.[45] Moreover, certain guidelines given by appellate courts and the EAT have reduced the impact of the norms of fair industrial practice in respect of the status and security of employees recommended by paras.44–6 of the Industrial Relations Code of Practice.[46] The Code's recommendations for warnings, consultation and investigation of the possibilities of alternative employment should be taken into account by tribunals, and the EAT has held that a tribunal that fails to give sufficient weight to these factors can be found to have made a legally perverse decision.[47] Nevertheless, a tribunal finding that an employer had omitted an important procedural step is not necessarily a sufficient basis for a finding of unfairness. The tribunal must go on to find whether that procedural error or omission was likely to have had an effect on the eventual result.[48] Where the tribunal finds that the effect of a procedural error or omission would have been minimal it has an option to find either that the dismissal was fair despite the procedural error, or to find that the dismissal was unfair but then reduce compensation accordingly.

Whether or not a formal procedure exists, the case law suggests that there is a further aspect of reasonableness in the nature of a procedural duty on management. Where an employer is planning to make workers redundant, he ought on their behalf to seek alternative positions among relevant job categories within the firm or associated firms. In exceptional circumstances,[49] this may require the retention of a particular employee through the practice of 'bumping',[50] that is, the transfer of an employee into the job of another employee with shorter service, who is in turn dismissed.[51]

Another aspect of the law of unfair redundancy is the way in which the procedural duty of the employer to engage in collective consultations with recognised trade union representatives before making redundancies has

---

[43] E.g. *Grundy (Teddington) Ltd v Plummer* [1983] IRLR 98, EAT; *Freud v Bentalls Ltd* [1982] IRLR 443, EAT.

[44] E.g. *Hammond Scott v Elizabeth Arden Ltd* [1976] IRLR 166, IT.

[45] E.g. *Buchanan v Tilcon Ltd* [1983] IRLR 417, Ct Sess.

[46] The Code was issued in 1972 under the IRA and was kept in force by TULRA Sch.1, which requires tribunals to take its recommendations into account where relevant. Disciplinary decisions are the subject of a separate ACAS Code (see above).

[47] *Williams v Compair Maxam Ltd* [1982] IRLR 83, EAT, but see now *Rolls Royce Ltd v Dewhurst* [1985] IRLR 184, EAT.

[48] *British United Shoe Machinery Co. Ltd v Clarke* [1978] IRLR 297, EAT.

[49] *Huddersfield Parcels Ltd v Sykes* [1981] IRLR 115.

[50] *Thomas and Betts Manufacturing v Harding Ltd* [1980] IRLR 255, CA; but see *Barratt Construction Ltd v Dalrymple* [1984] IRLR 455, EAT.

[51] On the legal complications of 'bumping', see Davies and Freedland (1984:561–2).

been undervalued. Despite the recommendations of the Code and the requirements of the EPA for collective consultation,[52] a failure to consult a union representative over a redundancy is treated on a par with any other procedural omission. An industrial tribunal does not have to decide that such a procedural defect makes the dismissal unfair; it can go on to ask the further question whether or not it would have produced a different result in the case of that particular employee.[53] It is only where the failure to consult is so extreme that a finding of fair dismissal would be a perverse decision by an industrial tribunal.[54]

These inhibitions upon tribunals attempting to treat procedural omissions as an important basis for a finding of unfair redundancy are mild compared to the limits that have been placed by appellate decisions on the test of the substantive merits of redundancy decisions. In this respect the courts have shown great zeal to ensure that the unfair dismissals law is not used to restrict the managerial view of the logic of the market place and of the most efficient use of labour. Some indication of this may be given by the language of *Moon v Homeworthy Furniture Ltd*,[55] a case where an employer decided to shut down a factory in part as a response to an organising drive by a trade union. The employees argued that the economic basis for the decision was questionable because the business remained viable. It therefore asked the industrial tribunal to examine whether the decision to close the factory and dismiss employees was a reasonable one on the merits. Despite the fact that the statutory language provided a strong basis for such a claim, the EAT reacted rather testily to this attempt to extend the unfair dismissal test to questions beyond those of selection for redundancy or procedure. As the EAT put it:

> The employees ... were and are seeking to use the industrial tribunal and the Employment Appeal Tribunal as a platform for the ventilation of an industrial dispute. The Appeal Tribunal is unanimously of the opinion that if that is what this matter is all about it must be stifled at birth ... the decision of the industrial tribunal was right and there could not and cannot be any investigation into the rights and wrongs of the declared redundancy.[56]

Even in cases of selection for redundancy, however, there have been considerable limits placed on the discretion of industrial tribunals. Where the employer selects employees in accordance with an agreed procedure, there is a strong presumption that the selection is reasonable unless the criteria in the agreement themselves are unreasonable.[57] Yet where there is no pre-arranged procedure, industrial tribunals are adjured not to interfere

---

[52] It is true that EPA s.99(8) states that there is no other remedy for a failure to consult than those provided in Part IV of the Act, but this itself would not operate to limit the scope of EPCA s.57(3).

[53] E.g. *Freud v Bentalls Ltd* [1982] IRLR 443, EAT, but see *Grundy (Teddington) Ltd v Plummer* [1983] IRLR 98, EAT.

[54] *Williams v Compair Maxam Ltd* [1982] IRLR 83, EAT.

[55] [1976] IRLR 298, EAT.

[56] At 299.

[57] E.g. *Evans v AB Electronic Components Ltd* [1981] IRLR 111, EAT.

too strongly in the selection question. Thus tribunals have been urged not to substitute their own views for those of the employer, but confine themselves to asking whether the selection process fell within the band of reasonable selection processes in industry.[58] In particular, industrial tribunals cannot impose upon employers a requirement to observe the principle of 'last in first out'. Not surprisingly, despite the extensive case law, it has been relatively rare for an employee to win a case of unfair redundancy.

Reorganisation and Unfair Dismissal

The tribunal review of managerial discretion has also been quite strictly constrained by the courts in cases of dismissals arising from reorganisations. Where employees refuse to accept a change in their contractual terms and conditions of employment caused by a reorganisation of the business, employers have tended to dismiss them outright by serving them with notices of termination of existing contracts combined with an offer of new contracts on changed terms, or to place them in a position to resign and claim 'constructive dismissal' (see above). In either case the dismissed employees might attempt to persuade an industrial tribunal that the dismissal was for redundancy or was otherwise unfair because of the absence of a valid reason. The defence mounted by employers has been usually to claim that the dismissal was for 'some other substantial reason'.

The EAT first gave its unreserved support to the notion that such dismissals could qualify as 'some other substantial reason' in *Ellis v Brighton Co-operative Society Ltd.*[59] In that case a reorganisation of the business which had been agreed with the trade union involved a longer working week for Mr Ellis, a foreman. Instead of a basic work week of forty-eight hours, he was required to work an average of fifty-eight hours as well as to assume more onerous duties. Contractually he had no obligation to go along with the new duties because, as a non-member of the union, he was not bound by the change. Nevertheless, the EAT considered that his refusal amounted to grounds for dismissal for 'some other substantial reason' and that the employers had acted reasonably in the circumstances.

In *Ellis* the EAT appeared to suggest that before an employer could reasonably impose a change in contractual terms as a result of a reorganisation there would have to be a finding that the reorganisation was prompted by business necessity and that there had been prior consultation with employees. In *Hollister v National Farmers' Union*,[60] however, the Court of Appeal decided that the EAT's insistence upon consultation 'nearly always before a person was dismissed' went too far in putting a gloss on the statute. Whereas in *Hollister* an industrial tribunal could satisfy itself that consultation was not essential to the employer's decision, it was not open to an appellate tribunal to reverse the tribunal. Moreover, the Court of Appeal

---

[58]   *BL Cars v Lewis* [1983] IRLR 58, EAT.
[59]   [1976] IRLR 419, EAT.
[60]   [1979] IRLR 238, CA.

made it clear that the standard implied by *Ellis* that the reorganisation if not done would 'bring the business to a standstill' was not a fixed and immutable requirement. It was enough for the tribunal to find that there was a 'sound, good business reason' for the reorganisation. This and subsequent cases established that the Court of Appeal and the EAT were attempting to restrict the role of industrial tribunals in examining the employer's motivation for the reorganisation.[61]

In *Richmond Precision Engineering*,[62] moreover, the EAT made it clear that a tribunal's discretion to decide that a dismissal in the course of a reorganisation was unreasonable was restricted to cases where it could find that the decision was outside the range of reasonable employer decisions. Nevertheless, as part of the test of reasonableness, an industrial tribunal may insist on evidence of the factual basis of the employer's reasons for reorganisation and can go on to ask the further question of whether the change in contractual terms imposed upon the employee was reasonable in the sense of being reasonably related to the reasons for the reorganisation.[63] For example, in *Evans v Elemeta Holdings Ltd*[64] an employer had sought to change the provisions of his employee's contracts from voluntary overtime paid after the first five hours to a position where all overtime was to be unpaid and unlimited in extent except on Saturdays, and the additional payment for overtime was to be withdrawn. Mr Evans refused to accept the new terms because the obligation to work compulsory unpaid overtime was so open-ended. The EAT overturned the industrial tribunal's finding of fair dismissal, indicating that the tribunal had to address itself more carefully to the question of the reasonableness of the change in terms, in the light of the employer's evidence of the need for the particular type of change in the contractual provisions. Yet an industrial tribunal may find such a dismissal unfair only where the employer's decision falls outside the band of reasonable employers' decisions. They do not have the authority to decide for themselves whether the employer's decision was reasonable by balancing the disadvantage to the employee against the advantages to the employer.[65]

These cases also show that where an employer in the course of a reorganisation chooses to abrogate existing employment contracts and collective agreements, the courts have allowed the reasonableness test as applied to 'some other substantial reason' to be used to undermine the expectations created by such agreements. It is true that technically reasonableness as a statutory test can override contractual obligations. But since the statute was arguably enacted to enhance employee rights, it would have been perfectly proper to treat the contract and collective agreement as establishing minimum rights for employees to be improved upon by the statute. The interpretation of s.57(1)(b) (some other substantial reason) in respect of the

---

[61] E.g. *Bowater Containers v McCormack* [1980] IRLR 50, EAT.
[62] *Richmond Precision Engineering Ltd v Pearce* [1985] IRLR 179, EAT.
[63] E.g. *Ladbrooke Courage Holidays Ltd v Asten* [1981] IRLR 63, EAT; *Orr v Vaughan* [1981] IRLR 63, EAT.
[64] [1982] IRLR 143, EAT.
[65] *Richmond Precision Engineering Ltd v Pearce* [1985] IRLR 179, EAT; but see *Chubb Fire Security Ltd v Harper* [1983] IRLR 311, EAT.

rights of employees in the course of reorganisation operates to undermine the protective purpose of the legislation and creates insecurity for employees in respect of their job rights generally.

The effects of this interpretation also reach into and undermine the provisions of the Transfer of Undertakings (Protection of Employment) Regulations.[66] Under reg.8, where there is a relevant transfer of the business resulting in the dismissal of an employee, the dismissal is treated as automatically unfair, unless the employer can establish that it arose from an economic, technical or organisational reason entailing changes in the workforce. In such a case the dismissal is no longer automatically unfair but is treated as dismissal for a substantial reason and made subject to the normal test of the reasonableness of the employer's decision under EPCA s.57(3). To take the dismissal out of the automatic unfairness provisions of reg.8(1), the employer must show that the reorganisation actually caused the dismissal and that there was in fact a change in the workforce. Thus in *Berriman v Delabole Slate Ltd*,[67] where an employer sought to reduce wages after acquiring a company, the resultant constructive dismissal was not a dismissal within the meaning of the regulations because a change in pay was not a 'change in the workforce' within the meaning of reg.8(2). Once an employer can show that the dismissal falls within this provision, it may qualify as a dismissal for either redundancy[68] or some other substantial reason.[69] In the latter case, owing to the limitations on the tribunal's application of the reasonableness test, there is a possibility that an employee can be dismissed in the course of the sale of the business without compensation (Collins, 1985:62–4).

Remedies for Unfair Dismissal

Once an industrial tribunal finds that an employee has been unfairly dismissed, it must choose between three remedies: reinstatement, re-engagement or compensation. The statute gives formal priority to reinstatement and re-engagement. Industrial tribunals must first determine whether the employee wishes to obtain re-employment in either form and then whether it is practicable to order such a remedy (EPCA ss.68–9). When looking at the practicality of reinstatement, tribunals ought to consider the industrial relations consequences of making such an order,[70] the likelihood of friction with supervisors or fellow employees,[71] as well as the size and scale of the organisation,[72] the capabilities of the individual and the availability of the job itself, though the absence of a vacancy cannot be decisive.[73] Moreover, where the tribunal finds that an employee has caused

---

66 SI 1981 No. 1794.
67 [1984] ICR 636, [1984] IRLR 394, EAT; [1985] IRLR 305, CA.
68 *Gorictree v Jenkinson* [1984] IRLR 391, EAT.
69 *McGrath v Rank Leisure* [1985] IRLR 323.
70 *Pirelli Cable Works Ltd v Murray* [1979] IRLR 190, EAT.
71 *Coleman v Magnet Joinery* [1975] IRLR 46, CA.
72 *Nothman v London Borough of Barnet (No.2)* [1980] IRLR 65, CA.
73 *Enessy Co. SA v Minoprio* [1978] IRLR 489, EAT.

or contributed to some extent to the dismissal it must determine whether it would be 'just' to make such an order (s.69(5)(c)).

Where re-employment is ordered, the penalty for non-compliance with the order is purely financial. The statute in s.71 states that an employer who without good cause refuses to comply will be required to pay compensation to the employee in the form of an 'additional' award, amounting in most cases to thirteen to twenty-six weeks' pay, on top of the compensatory and basic awards. In cases of dismissal because of racial or sex discrimination, the scale of the additional award is raised from twenty-six to fifty-two weeks' pay. In cases of dismissal for trade union membership and activity or non-membership, a 'special' award is made (see Chapter 2). But before an industrial tribunal can make an additional award, it is open to an employer to show that it was not practicable for him to comply with the order.[74]

If an industrial tribunal finds that a dismissal is unfair and makes no order of reinstatement or re-engagement, it must make an award of compensation under two headings: a 'basic award' and 'a compensatory award' (ss.72–5). The basic award is designed to provide compensation for the loss of accrued rights owing to past service and in particular to compensate for the decrease in the value of a redundancy payment should the employee ever be made redundant in the future. It is therefore calculated as the equivalent of a redundancy payment (see below). The basic award can be reduced even to a nil award by four types of deduction: a proportionate reduction representing the tribunal's judgment of the extent to which the employee contributed to his own dismissal; a reduction by the amount of any redundancy payment either awarded by a tribunal or made by the employer; a failure by the employee to mitigate his loss by accepting a reasonable offer of reinstatement; or a reduction for any conduct which was not taken into account in calculating the basic award because it was discovered after the dismissal but would make it just and equitable to reduce the basic award.

The compensatory award in principle is designed to compensate an employee for all other financial loss to the employee caused by the employer's decision to dismiss the employer. The statute (s.74) states that such loss should include any benefit which the dismissed employee might reasonably be expected to have had but for the dismissal and any expense incurred as a result of the dismissal. In practice this award includes mainly loss of earnings and other benefits before the hearing and for a period into the future owing to unemployment or obtaining a lower paid job. It also includes loss of pension entitlement and expenses where relevant. Yet the compensation which an employee receives under this head will not necessarily provide full financial compensation. For higher paid employees there is currently a maximum limit to the compensatory award of £8,000. For all employees there are a number of deductions from the figure representing the calculation of actual financial loss. Thus an employee has a duty to mitigate his loss by making reasonable efforts to find new employment. Also where an employee to some extent causes or contributes to the dismissal, the compensatory award may be proportionately reduced including in extreme

---

[74]   See *Timex Corp. v Thomson* [1981] IRLR 522, EAT; *Freemans Plc v Flynn* [1984] ICR 874.

cases a reduction to nil. Finally where an employer paid an employee a redundancy payment greater than the employee's entitlement to a basic award, the difference is deducted from the compensatory award.

The tribunals and the judges have tended to apply the remedies for unfair dismissal conservatively. Although the statutory provisions were amended specifically to make reinstatement the primary remedy, the tribunals have been reluctant to order this remedy in practice (Williams and Lewis, 1981:41; Dickens et al., 1985:111–13). Reinstatement and re-engagement have been ordered in less than 5 per cent of successful cases, and the proportion of re-employments secured at the conciliation stage has been about 8 per cent (Dickens et al., 1985:158 and see further Chapter 19 below). In those cases where tribunal orders have been made, about one half have been effective in the sense that the employees continued in employment for six months or more (Williams and Lewis, 1981:24).

While the rarity of re-employment is largely due to the reluctance of tribunals to make appropriate orders, it is also true that employees do not always take advantage of the option when it is offered to them (Dickens et al., 1985:114–19). One factor that undoubtedly influences the majority of non-unionised complainants of unfair dismissal is that they may be isolated and vulnerable where there is no organisation at workplace level that could help them face up to the day to day pressures of being back at work after a reinstatement or re-engagement order. At all events, the statistics puncture the myth that the statute offers a form of job security by providing an effective remedy of reinstatement. At most it provides a form of compensation for loss of employment, though at levels which are barely adequate. The median award of compensation was £1,345 in 1983, the equivalent of about two months' average wages. Moreover, some employers may be wary about hiring an employee who has taken an unfair dismissal complaint to an industrial tribunal.

Effects of the Legislation

Another important measure of the effectiveness of the unfair dismissal law is the 'success rate'. From 1976 to 1981 there was a decline in the rate of successful complaints of unfair dismissal as a proportion of all such complaints from 37.6 per cent to 23.3 per cent. This decline has been explained by the fact that employers screened out the more obvious unfair decisions and then made greater use of legal counsel at tribunal hearings (Williams, 1983:160). Also, redundancy dismissal complaints, with their greater propensity for failure, have increased as a proportion of all unfair dismissal complaints (Davies and Freedland, 1984:507). But it is also possible that the restrictive judicial interpretation of the reasonableness test has made a significant contribution to the decrease in cases won by complainants (Anderman, 1985:323). The success rate did improve somewhat in 1982 and 1983 (though it was still less than a third), perhaps because of the greater freedom of tribunals to determine issues of fact.

The impact of the legislation upon collective labour relations has been equally complex. The legislative aim to prompt a procedural reform in management has clearly been realised. Daniel and Stilgoe (1978:49) found that 84 per cent of the firms they studied had adopted formal procedures for discipline and dismissals. A Warwick University survey found that between 94 and 99 per cent of firms with a hundred or more employees had adopted written disciplinary and dismissals procedures (Dickens et al., 1985:236). The effects of this increase in formal procedures upon management have been partly to restrict the discretion of supervisors and lower line management to dismiss and partly to give greater importance to the personnel function in companies (Brown, 1981:32; Daniel and Stilgoe, 1978:41; Dickens et al., 1985:264). This in turn has operated as a control over arbitrary decisions by first line management and has resulted in the introduction of greater due process and natural justice in industry (Dickens et al., 1985:252, and Chapter 19 below). Yet voluntary procedures do not solely operate as an employee protection. They also provide a basis for processing dismissals more effectively by management. Formal procedures can provide a virtual 'conveyor belt for dismissals' (Dickens et al., 1985:257). They also tend to centralise control in higher management and help to legitimise management decisions to the workforce (Dickens et al., 1985:266).

It has been argued, however, that the direct impact of the statutory procedure upon the trade union sector and collective action has been relatively insignificant: although the intention of the unfair dismissals legislation was to individualise potential collective disputes, the law has not been put into effect in practice for organised workers (Mellish and Collis-Squires, 1976:164; Clark and Wedderburn, 1983:189). It is true that those employees making the most use of the tribunal procedures have tended to be non-unionised employees, with the highly unionised sectors being under-represented in the complaints of unfair dismissals to industrial tribunals (Davies and Freedland, 1984:510). It is also true that there is little hard evidence that the legislation has reduced the incidence of industrial conflict over disciplinary dismissals. Strikes over non-redundancy dismissals which on average constituted about 10 per cent of stoppages in the 1964–6 period still accounted for about 9 per cent of stoppages in 1982 (Dickens et al., 1985:224–7). This in turn may be related to the low rate of success and the paucity of reinstatement orders. As the statute has been interpreted, it fails to offer employees, collectively dissatisfied with a managerial decision, a credible alternative (Anderman, 1985:326–7). Nevertheless, it is not correct to conclude from this evidence that the overall impact of dismissals legislation upon collective labour relations has been minimal. For the procedural reforms concerning discipline and dismissal introduced by management in response to the legislation have occurred more in the unionised than in the non-unionised sectors. These reforms, while providing formal trade union representation in disputes procedures, make a significant contribution to managerial control over discipline and dismissal in the organised sectors (Dickens et al., 1985:250–52).

STATUTORY REDUNDANCY PAYMENTS

The Redundancy Payments Act 1965 marked the first use of statute to create an entitlement to a minimum lump sum payment for employees who were dismissed for redundancy, thus recognising the principle that an employee who lost his job through no fault of his own was entitled to compensation. The decision to enact such a statutory right to a redundancy payment was in part prompted by a concern that employees who suffered unemployment as a result of redundancy should not be left without compensation for the loss. Yet the legislation was also impelled by a concern to improve managerial efficiency by helping managers to convince employees to accept redundancy as a necessary concomitant of industrial change and greater efficiencies in the use of manpower (Fryer, 1973:221). Against a background of full employment, it was thought that the redeployed workers would move into the expanding sectors of the economy. Consequently, rather than simply enhancing unemployment benefit, the government drafted a statute in 1965 providing for a lump sum payment to be made to those employees whom management had decided must be redundant, whether or not such employees were able to obtain other employment immediately after losing their existing job through redundancy (Daniel, 1985:70–71).

Under the RPA (now EPCA Part VI) an employee with a minimum of two years' service over the age of eighteen who is dismissed, or laid off or put on short time,[75] owing to redundancy, is entitled to a lump sum payment which varies with his age, length of continuous service,[76] and weekly pay (currently a maximum of £152) for each of twenty years' service. Thus employees who are made redundant between the ages of eighteen and twenty-one are entitled to half a week's pay for each year of service, between twenty-one and forty one week's pay for each year of service, and between forty-one and sixty-four one and a half week's pay for each year of service. Female employees upon reaching the age of sixty and male employees upon reaching the age of sixty-five are excluded from a right to a redundancy payment and they lose one-twelfth of their entitlement for every month they have worked after their preceding birthday. The employer is required to pay the sum to the employee but can recover 35 per cent from the Redundancy Fund which is managed by the DE but is financed by a surcharge on employers' national insurance contributions.[77] The remaining 65 per cent may be set off as an expense against corporation tax. Any questions about the employee's entitlement whether raised by employee, employer or the Secretary of State for Employment may be referred to an industrial tribunal for decision (see generally Grunfeld, 1980).

---

[75] An employee is laid off (not provided with work or pay) or put on short time (where the work provided by the employer results in less than half a week's pay) over a period of four weeks, or six weeks out of thirteen: EPCA ss.87, 88.

[76] On the statutory definition of 'continuous service' (EPCA s.151, Sch.13) and the extensive case law, see Chapter 12 above.

[77] Redundancy Payments (Variation of Rebates) Order SI 1985 No. 250.

If these provisions open the door to an entitlement to a sum of compensation for the loss of a job under certain circumstances, they carefully limit the scope of these circumstances. Thus, entitlement to a redundancy payment has been confined to situations where employees can prove that they have been 'dismissed', which is strictly defined in the same way as for unfair dismissal (s.83). A dismissal is taken to be by reason of redundancy under s.81(2) only if it is attributable wholly or mainly to:

> (a) the fact that [the] employer has ceased, or intends to cease, to carry on the business for the purposes of which the employee was employed by him, or has ceased, or intends to cease, to carry on that business in the place where the employee was so employed, or (b) the fact that the requirements of that business for employees to carry out work of a particular kind, or for employees to carry out work of a particular kind in the place where they were so employed, have ceased or diminished or are expected to cease or diminish.

In other words, redundancy as defined in the Act can consist of a decision of the employer to close a business or a part of a business, or to move an employee's or group of employees' place of employment or to declare an employee or group of employees surplus to the requirements of his business.

Partly because the reason for the dismissal is so clearly within the employer's discretion, once an employee proves that he or she was dismissed and alleges that the dismissal was for redundancy, the statute in effect shifts to the employer the burden of proving that the dismissal was not wholly or mainly due to redundancy (s.91(2)). The onus is therefore on the employer to show that the main cause of the dismissal was a reason other than redundancy such as misconduct, illness, bad attendance, incompetence or a reorganisation of terms and conditions. Where the employer justifiably dismisses the employee for misconduct or some other contractual violation, the employee is not entitled to a redundancy payment by reason of the dismissal (s.82(2)), unless the dismissal occurred within the actual period of notice of dismissal for redundancy. In that case a tribunal may decide that the employee can receive that part (up to 100 per cent) of the redundancy payment he would otherwise have received which the tribunal finds is just and equitable depending on the circumstances of the case (s.92(3)). These provisions also apply to a dismissal of an employee for participation in a strike which is technically a dismissal for misconduct entitling the employer to dismiss without notice (see Chapter 9).

Even where employees succeed in showing that they have been dismissed owing to redundancy, they can be disqualified from a payment if they unreasonably refuse suitable alternative employment to take effect immediately or within four weeks, which is offered to them by their employer (s.82(3)–(5)), or an associated employer (s.82(7)), or a new employer to whom the business had been transferred (s.94). To constitute an offer of suitable employment a job must be substantially similar but it can be offered with less attractive terms and conditions (see Grunfeld, 1980:256–305). The statute provides for a trial period of four weeks during which the employee may try out the new job without prejudice to his chances of refusing it (s.84(3)). Yet at the end of the trial period the employee must still make a decision whether or not to accept the offer knowing that a refusal could constitute an unreasonable refusal and hence disqualify him or her from a redundancy payment.

There are two features of the statutory definition of redundancy which are of particular importance. First, the test of cessation or diminution of work of a particular kind consists simply of whether, in the employer's opinion, fewer employees are required to perform the kind of work the employee is doing at the place where the employee has been employed. The statute thus puts no limitation upon the employer's decision to make workers redundant, other than levying the cost of the employer's proportionate contribution to the redundancy payment. Second, the case law suggests that the decisions on whether or not an employee qualifies for a payment are strongly influenced by a concern that employee rights under their contracts should be construed to provide a measure of flexibility and adaptability to the needs of the business.

Work of a Particular Kind

Both features can be illustrated by the way the courts have interpreted the statutory term 'work of a particular kind'. At an early stage of the case law it was made plain that the phrase should be defined by reference to the contract of employment, rather than to the job that the employee was actually performing. Hence where employees worked under a contract with a flexibility clause providing that they could be transferred to other types of work, the work they were doing or even their job description had little legal consequence; what counted in defining the phrase 'work of a particular kind' was the width of the contractual flexibility clause, that is, the work the employee could be contractually required to perform. For example, in *Nelson v BBC*[78] a BBC Caribbean Service producer who worked under a contract of employment with a flexibility clause requiring him to serve when, how and where the BBC demanded was dismissed when the Caribbean Service was discontinued. Owing to the flexibility clause, the Court of Appeal decided that his job was that of general producer rather than that of producer in the Caribbean Service. Consequently, when the Caribbean Service job disappeared and he refused another production job with the BBC, he could not be regarded as dismissed for redundancy as defined by the statute.

Similarly, where the contract provides an express term for geographic mobility, the place of work is not confined to the place where the employee is currently working. For example, in *Sutcliffe v Hawker Siddeley Aviation Ltd*[79] an employee worked under a contract that contained a term that the employee should be prepared and willing to work at the request of the company as an aircraft electrician at any station within the UK. When he refused to transfer to another station following the cessation of work for him at his existing station, he was unable to claim that he was dismissed for

[78] [1977] ICR 649, CA.
[79] [1973] IRLR 314, CA.

redundancy. He had simply refused to obey a lawful contractual order by the employer and hence had been dismissed for that reason.

Where an express flexibility clause is drawn extremely widely, it may be limited by judicial interpretation. For example, in *Cowen v Haden Ltd*[80] the employee was a regional surveyor with a flexibility clause in his contract that said: 'the employee's job title will be regional surveyor – southern region. He will be required to undertake, at the direction of the company, any and all duties which reasonably fall within the scope of his capabilities.' The Court of Appeal decided that when his job as regional surveyor ended, his dismissal was for redundancy despite the flexibility clause. This was because the effect of that clause was not to entitle the employer to transfer the employee to any job as quantity surveyor within the organisation but only to require him to perform any duties reasonably within the scope of his capabilities as a regional surveyor.

In the absence of an express term on mobility or flexibility, there may be disagreement over the existence or scope of an implied term. In *O'Brien v Associated Fire Alarms*[81] the employer argued that the contract gave him implied authority to require the employee, after working seven years in Liverpool, to transfer to work in Barrow 120 miles away. The Court of Appeal held that the tribunal could not on the facts imply a term that the employee could be sent anywhere in the north-western area. The only term to be implied in their contracts was that they should be employed within daily travelling distance of their homes, or, within a reasonable distance of their homes. Later cases confirm that geographical mobility is a matter on which a contractual term should normally be implied, though its content will vary.[82]

In each of these cases the statutory phrases 'work of a particular kind' or 'place of work' were viewed as being defined by reference to the contract of employment. The work was a package of contractual terms and conditions, some express and some implied. It is clear from the above cases that the contractual view of 'work of a particular kind' and 'place of work' does not prevent flexibility being read into employment contracts by judicial interpretation. This may sometimes take the form of a very explicit support for managerial efficiency. Thus in *North Riding Garages v Butterwick*,[83] an employee worked as a workshop manager, the job consisting mainly of supervision of maintenance work. After another firm took over his employer, his job was drastically reorganised and he was asked to take on the administrative as well as maintenance work. When he proved unable to match up to the new type of job, he was dismissed. It was held that he could not qualify for a redundancy payment. His job had not disappeared. His employer still had a continued need for workshop managers, albeit of a different type. The court rather sanctimoniously asserted that for the purpose of the Act an employee who remained in the same kind of work was

---

80 [1982] IRLR 314, CA.
81 [1968] 1 WLR 1916.
82 *Jones v Associated Tunnelling Co. Ltd* [1981] IRLR 477, EAT, but see too *Murphy v Epsom College* [1985] IRLR 80, CA.
83 [1967] 2 QB 56, DC.

expected to adapt himself to new methods and techniques, and could not complain if his employer insisted on higher standards of efficiency than those previously required.

The kind of work employees do consists not only of the tasks performed but also other important contractual elements of the job, including hours of work, pay etc. When an employer reorganises work so as to retain the need for the specific tasks performed by employees but drastically changes their hours of work or terms of compensation, despite the blow to the employee's contractual expectations, the courts have not been prepared to recognise that this constitutes a change in 'work of a particular kind'. Instead they have viewed the statutory phrase quite narrowly in terms of the tasks performed in the job. In *Johnson v Nottinghamshire Combined Police Authority*,[84] for example, a decision to reorganise the working hours of two women from a five-day week to a shift system and a six-day week was held not to be a change in the kind of work. It was only a change in hours, which was not mentioned specifically in the statute. It did not matter that the contractual expectations of the women who took the job on the original terms were that the job was one for parents taking care of children of school age. For the purposes of the statute, it was held that a change in hours of work did not cause a change in the particular kind of work unless it was so fundamental as to change the nature of the work. Furthermore, in *Chapman v Goonvean and Rostowrack China Clay Co. Ltd*,[85] an employer's withdrawal of free transport was held not to be a reduction in the requirement for an employee to carry out 'work of particular kind', even though it was an important element of the job to the employee and a part of his package of rights under his contract of employment.

The net effect of these decisions is to allow managerial reorganisations of terms and conditions of jobs without satisfying the technical definition of redundancy. An employer is thus entitled to reorganise his business so as to improve its efficiency and in so doing to propose to his staff a change in terms and conditions, and to dismiss them if they do not agree, without necessarily triggering the right to a statutory redundancy payment. One consequence of these decisions is that employees resigning because of the denial of their contractual expectations may be regarded as constructively dismissed, but may still be denied redundancy pay because the reason for dismissal is not redundancy as narrowly interpreted by the judges. While such interpretations ensure that the payment fund is carefully protected, they do not further the legislative aim that employees dismissed through no fault of their own should receive a measure of compensation.

Impact on Collective Bargaining

Nevertheless, away from the margins of interpretation in case law, the individual right to a redundancy payment has had a strong impact upon

---

[84] [1974] ICR 170, CA; see also *Lesney Products Ltd v Nolan* [1977] ICR 235, CA.
[85] [1973] ICR 310, CA.

collective bargaining. This has not taken place through the exclusion of tribunal complaints by virtue of the Secretary of State exempting collective redundancy agreements under EPCA s.96, a provision which has been virtually ignored. Instead collective agreements have been made which have incorporated improvements upon the level of redundancy payments provided by statute. Equally important, the statute has had the effect of helping to win wider acceptance among employees of the practice of voluntary redundancy. While the 1965 Act itself did not prescribe any specific procedures for consultation or selection, 'procedures for redundancy' were usually agreed to in a collective agreement providing for an enhanced redundancy payment. These procedures usually provided for some form of collective notice and consultation as well as agreed criteria for selection such as 'last in, first out'. They also suggested that redundancies would be acceptable in certain situations. As the provision of a lump sum severance payment made redundancy somewhat less unattractive to employees, especially long service employees, it contributed to the growth of the practice of voluntary redundancy (Gennard, 1982:121,134).

This practice consisted of giving workers in certain grades the opportunity to volunteer to be made redundant and receive a payment. Technically, such workers have to be dismissed in order to qualify for a redundancy payment.[86] If sufficient numbers step forward, compulsory redundancies which could otherwise give rise to an industrial dispute may be avoided. It was insufficiently appreciated at the time, however, that eventually collective resistance to compulsory redundancies would also be undermined by the practice of the lump sum redundancy payment (Gennard, 1982:134). As Daniel (1985:74) describes it, the trade union after a while was 'caught in a pincer movement between managerial strategy and individualist opportunism on the part of its members' and 'had no alternative but to adopt two stances in relation to redundancy. The first was to insist upon "no redundancy other than voluntary redundancy". The second was to bargain over the inducements to volunteer, and in particular, to try to bid up the size of the employer's supplement to the statutory minimum payments.'

The law became a significant factor in managing redundancies in other ways as well. Managers increasingly publicised that those who engaged in industrial action to resist compulsory redundancies could, if dismissed during such action, lost their redundancy pay entitlement. This is the so-called redundancy payments 'trap' under EPCA s.82, in which a dismissal because of industrial action prior to formal notice of dismissal for redundancy results in a complete loss of redundancy pay. Furthermore, under EPCA s.92, dismissal for industrial action during the notice period may result in a complete or partial loss of payment (see Levie et al., 1984:202). Finally, as part of the general legal pressure to deter individuals from striking (see Chapter 9), employees who are dismissed when taking industrial action are often prevented from complaining of unfair dismissal (EPCA s.62).

---

[86]   *Morton Sundour Fabrics Ltd v Shaw* (1967) 2 ITR 84, DC; *Devon County Council v Cook* (1977) 12 ITR 347, EAT; *British Leyland (UK) Ltd v McQuilken* [1978] IRLR 245, EAT.

COLLECTIVE CONSULTATION OVER REDUNDANCIES

The redundancy payments and unfair dismissal legislation were complemented by a third statute, which required employers to consult with recognised trade unions as well as to notify the government in advance of redundancies. Enacted as part of the Social Contract programme of legislation, ss.99–107 of the EPA were essentially an implementation of the EC's Directive on Collective Redundancies. They have since been supplemented by the Transfer of Undertakings (Protection of Employment) Regulations 1981 which also implement an EC Directive.[87]

Under EPA s.99 an employer who proposes to make a person redundant has an obligation to inform and consult about such a decision with a trade union which has been recognised for that grade of employee. It is vital that the union is recognised for collective bargaining within the statutory definition of EPA s.126(1), which is discussed above in Chapter 3. The consultation must begin at the earliest opportunity regardless of the number of employees proposed to be redundant. But if a hundred or more employees at an establishment are to be dismissed in a ninety-day period, then consultation must begin ninety days before the first dismissal takes effect. If between ten and ninety-nine employees are to be dismissed in a ninety-day period, then the statutory minimum period for consultation is thirty days. At first sight, the statutory rights appear to be quite formidable. The information that is required to be disclosed in writing for the purpose of consultation by the employer is wide-ranging. It includes the reasons for his proposal, the numbers and descriptions of employees whom it is proposed to dismiss as redundant, the total number of employees of any such description employed by the employer at the establishment in question, the proposed method of selecting the employees who may be dismissed, and the proposed method of carrying out the dismissals, with due regard to any agreed procedure, including the period over which the dismissals are to take effect. As the EAT put it in *Spillers-French (Holdings) Ltd v USDAW*,[88] the object of this legislation was

> to give an opportunity for consultation between employer, trade unions and [the DE]. The consultation may result in new ideas being ventilated which avoid the redundancy situation altogether. Equally it may lead to a lesser number of persons being made redundant than was originally thought necessary. Or it may be that alternative work can be found during the period of consultation.

At the same time, however, the requirement that the employer must consult with trade union representatives is defined rather weakly as little more than a right to discussion. Thus, according to EPA s.99(7), the

---

[87] On the EC Directives on the Approximation of the Laws of the Member States Relating to Collective Redundancies (OJ 1975, L48/29) and to Safeguarding Employees' Rights in the Event of Transfers of Undertakings (OJ 1977, L61/26), see further Chapter 20 below.
[88] [1980] ICR 31, 37.

employer need only consider any representations made by the trade union representatives, reply to them, and state his reasons if he rejects any of those representatives. Moreover, the statute contains an escape clause where there are 'special circumstances which render it not reasonably practicable' (s.99(8)) for the employer to comply with any of the statutory require- ments. In such a case, an employer need only take all such steps towards compliance with the requirements as are reasonably practicable in those circumstances. The courts have given a broad interpretation to this escape clause. Although gradual insolvency has not been sufficient,[89] sudden financial disasters – such as insolvency due to a withdrawal of a prospective purchaser and a bank calling in a receiver,[90] or a failure to procure a government loan[91] – have been held to be special circumstances justifying no consultation by the employer.

Where an employer fails to meet his obligation to inform and consult at the earliest opportunity, the statute gives the initiative to the trade union to enforce its rights by making a complaint to an industrial tribunal. The penalty provided for a failure to consult falls short of a court order compelling the employer to comply with his statutory duties towards the union. Although the union initiates the complaint and the complaint is concerned with the employer's failure to meet his responsibilities towards the union, the remedy consists solely of financial compensation which the employer must pay to individual employees who have lost the opportunity of being represented by their union in the requisite consultation process. The amount of compensation is provided in the form of a protective award (s.102(1)), consisting of a week's pay for every week in a 'protected period', that is, a period determined by the tribunal to be just and equitable in all the circumstances having regard to the employer's default. Hence while it is up to the union to initiate a complaint, it is left to the individual employee to enforce the penalty for the employer's failure to comply by presenting a complaint to an industrial tribunal (s.103).

The maximum amount of the award varies with the required consultation period, which in turn is related to the number of workers involved. Thus in the case of a collective dismissal of over a hundred employees in a ninety-day period, the maximum protective award consists of ninety days' pay. In the case of redundancies of ten to ninety-nine employees, the maximum amount is thirty days. In all other cases the maximum award is twenty-eight days' pay. Subject to the maxima, the courts have tended to assess the protective period in terms of the loss to employees of the wages which they would have obtained during a period of proper consultation rather than the severity of the employer's failure to consult. As the EAT put it in *Talke Fashions Ltd v Amalgamated Society of Textile and Kindred Trades*,[92] 'the seriousness of the default ought to be considered in its relationship to the employees and not in its relationship to the trade union

[89] *Clarks of Hove Ltd v Bakers' Union* [1978] IRLR 366, CA.
[90] *USDAW v Leancut Bacon Ltd* [1981] IRLR 295, EAT.
[91] *Hamish Armour (Receiver of Barry Staines Ltd) v ASTMS* [1979] IRLR 24, EAT.
[92] [1977] ICR 833, 836, EAT.

representative who has not been consulted'. Moreover, in *Spillers-French (Holdings) Ltd v USDAW*,[93] after the EAT concluded from the authorities that the purpose of the statute was to compensate the individual employee in the event of the default of the employer, it defined the key element in the assessment of compensation as 'not the loss or potential loss of actual remuneration during the relevant period by the particular employee [but rather] the loss of days of consultation which have occurred'. Thus the individualistic form of remedy has influenced the method of assessing the penalty on the employer for failure to carry out his collective procedural obligations.

Finally, the statute (s.102) does not treat the protective award as the equivalent of a requirement that the employer actually retains the employee in employment for a protected period, on the analogy of interim relief in cases of dismissal for trade union membership and activity or non-membership. Instead of providing for actual earnings to be paid during the period, the award is measured by the employee's pay for normal working hours, a formula which excludes non-compulsory overtime. Furthermore, where the employee actually works during the protected period, any contractual payment made by the employer can be set off against his liability to the employee under the protective award (s.102(3)).

One consequence of the form of the statutory remedy has been that employers can buy out employees' legal rights to consultation by paying them the full protective award in cash and avoiding the actual consultation process.[94] A complication that faces an employer who is planning a redundancy on such a basis is the relationship between his obligation to consult under EPA s.99 and his obligation to provide notice of termination to employees under EPCA s.49. In principle an employer who issues notices of termination during the process of consultation is not consulting over proposed redundancies but presenting the trade union and employees with a fait accompli.[95] In practice, however, as long as the notices of dismissal have not actually expired during the minimum period for the consultation process, it is possible for employers to encompass some of the period of notice of dismissal within the period of consultation (see Bourn, 1983:57).

In addition to the obligation to consult recognised trade unions, employers are required to notify the DE when they propose to dismiss ten or more employees for redundancy (s.100). Periods of advance notification correspond to the same periods as those set out for consultation with trade unions. A failure to meet this statutory duty is punishable by a fine of £400 or loss of 10 per cent of the redundancy rebate (s.104). The idea behind these provisions is to put the DE in a position to help to place redundant employees in new jobs or in government retraining courses. Yet this recognition of a public interest in redundancies is relatively modest. Employers are required only to notify, not to obtain the consent of public

93 [1980] ICR 31, 40.
94 E.g. *ASTMS v Hawker Siddeley Aviation Ltd* [1977] IRLR 418, IT.
95 *GMWU (MATSA) v British Uralite Ltd (No.2)* [1979] IRLR 413, IT.

authorities, before making large scale redundancies (Davies and Freedland, 1984:249).

It would be a mistake to suppose that the redundancy consultation provisions effectively enhance job security, or even the influence of trade unions or governments over managerial decisions concerning redundancies. The formal requirements of the statute have not proved in practice to be onerous for managers and, despite the extensive formal obligations, there has been relatively little litigation intitiated by trade unions (Bourn, 1983:56). One reason for this is the fact that the statute requires employers only to consult with trade unions and is therefore purely procedural in nature. As a consequence, little is offered to protect weak trade unions with minimal bargaining power. At a time of high unemployment, moreover, the provisions have been less than effective even when used by the stronger unions as the legally required consultations have often produced very little in the way of substantive modifications of employer decisions (Levie et al., 1984:202–3).

The sustained depression and the high level of unemployment since 1979 have undermined the unions' bargaining strength and so exposed the weakness of the purely procedural legal duty to consult. Nevertheless, had the collective redundancy provisions operated in a more favourable economic climate in the last few years, voluntary redundancy (as encouraged by the statutory redundancy payments scheme) and the increased tendency of managers to plan the implementation of redundancy decisions would have undermined trade union attempts at resistance. Acting on their own initiative, employers had – in order to minimise industrial conflict – already begun to incorporate consultation with unions into their system of managing redundancy before the 1975 Act (Gennard, 1982:136). As Daniel (1985:79) has persuasively argued, the practice of collective consultation and voluntary redundancy ensured 'very little organised resistance, disputes or disruption' and thus helped to facilitate the enormous increase in redundancies in the 1970s and 1980s, which reduced employment in manufacturing industry by one quarter.

CONCLUSION

The public policy ramifications of the law of redundancy and dismissals have only occasionally been understood. There has been a tendency for commentators to regard the law as contributing to a new 'floor of employment protection', a form of job security, and even a property right in the job, as if the law operated exclusively to provide employees with rights against employers. There has also been a tendency to regard the legislation as having a minor impact on voluntary collective bargaining. The experience of the legislation suggests, however, that these approaches are inadequate.

In the realm of individual rights, it is clear that the legislation has failed to provide a floor of employment protection in the sense of a safety net for employees: too many groups have been excluded from the statutory protection while many of those who are covered have the additional protection of collective bargaining. Hepple (1981:82) has drawn attention to the importance of universal individual legal rights which are not dependent upon membership of trade unions in a labour market divided between a 'primary' sector with relatively high pay and job security and a 'secondary' sector where pay and job security are relatively low. The exclusions and qualifications in unfair dismissals law tend to belie the description of such laws as 'purely' protective and suggest that the policy is more concerned to give weight to the needs of industry for flexibility.

Similarly, the conceptualisation of individual employment protection legislation as a means of conferring a form of job security or property rights in the job is problematical. For legislation to be viewed in this way it must be capable of reversing managerial decisions to dismiss employees, which in turn presupposes that the legislation provides effective remedies. Yet there has been a palpable failure of the remedies provided by the unfair dismissals legislation to reverse managerial decisions. It is true that the statute has indirectly improved job security by stimulating the growth of dismissals and disciplinary procedures, which have tended to be associated with a reduction in the incidence of disciplinary dismissals (Daniel and Stilgoe, 1978:62; Daniel and Millward, 1983:171; Dickens et al., 1985:256). Moreover, the legislation may have had some deterrent effect upon managerial decisions because of the costs of processing a dismissal through the tribunal system. Yet a view that it has operated directly upon management decision-making to enhance job security by the provision of a legal remedy is unconvincing. Equally it is odd to portray the redundancy payments legislation as a measure to improve job security when it is clearly designed to facilitate redundancy decisions (Fryer, 1973). The operation of the collective consultation provisions in conjunction with the redundancy payments legislation has not reversed managerial decisions but rather has raised the price to management of making these decisions. In this sense, therefore, it is misleading to describe the legislation as providing a form of job security; at most it has produced a basis for compensation for the loss of such security. Nor does the legislation provide an effective 'property right' in the much more limited sense of a right to compensation which increases in value with age and length of service, as exemplified by the calculation of redundancy pay and the basic award (cf. Davies and Freedland, 1984:430). For the development of the case law relating to employers' efforts to reorganise terms and conditions of employment often effectively removes the right of employees to receive compensation for unfair dismissal or redundancy even where their contractual rights have been broken.

This is one aspect of a wider problem of judicial interpretation. That the judges have proved reluctant to interpret the legislation so as to effectuate its protective purposes is difficult to deny. They have been concerned to construe the statutory protections so as not to interfere unduly with managerial prerogative. Of the numerous examples given in this chapter, perhaps the most important is the judicial insistence that tribunals cannot decide the reasonableness of managerial decisions to dismiss according to their own standards of fairness but must apply the test of whether the decision fell within a band of reasonable managerial responses. This is itself an interpretation of the legislation that falls at one extreme end of the range of reasonable judicial responses to the statutory language. The test also means that the tribunals must restrict themselves to an administrative law standard of review, a standard applicable to public bodies such as government departments or local authorities making decisions which affect the public. To apply a public law standard to the private law decisions of management reflects a view that the exercise of discretion by managers in pursuit of profitability is somehow in the general interest. Yet how realistic is this view? Managerial decisions are not always and automatically efficient. The purpose of legislation is to socialise managerial behaviour in the interests of efficiency as well as justice. It is arguable that the judges' own ideology has taken them further than the parliamentary intention and any future reform of the legislation should take this into account.

Finally, the full range of the effects of unfair dismissal and redundancy legislation upon collective bargaining have not always been appreciated. From the beginning the draftsman of the legislation intended that it should have a profound impact upon managerial policy and practice and stimulate procedural reform in industry (see Lewis, 1979:218–21; Davies and Freedland, 1979:199). But the view persisted, nevertheless, that the impact of the legislation upon collective bargaining would be minimal, not seriously intervening in its machinery and institutions. Initially this view may have been held because the legislation provided that parties to collectively agreed procedures could preserve their voluntarist position by being formally excluded from the tribunal jurisdiction in respect of unfair dismissals (EPCA s.65), redundancy payments (EPCA s.96), or redundancy consultation (EPA s.107). While these procedures have rarely been used (see Bourn, 1979), the empirical evidence cited earlier in this chapter points to the impact of the employment protection laws on the substance and procedures of collective bargaining.

While acknowledging a degree of 'juridification', some commentators (Wedderburn, 1980:84; Clark and Wedderburn, 1983:188–9) argue that industrial relations in sectors with strong union organisation are relatively less affected by the employment protection laws. It is of course true that strikes over disciplinary issues persist and a typical tribunal applicant is likely to be a non-member. But it should be noted that the so-called 'voluntary' procedures in industry have been powerfully influenced by legal norms. According to Dickens et al. (1985:252), the way in which unfair dismissal provisions stimulated the development, formulation and modification of procedures for handling discipline/dismissal issues, incorporating notions of due process and natural justice and encouraging the quasi-judicial managerial review of decisions, may be identified as a further aspect of 'juridification'. Similarly, Daniel and Millward (1983:126) point out that the form and operation of voluntarily agreed norms and procedures have been effectively modified and guided by an awareness of the legal provisions and their operation. Increased specialisation and importance of the personnel function contribute to this awareness.

That collective labour relations have been 'juridified' in this way, however, is perhaps less important than that the process has proved to be a means to enhance managerial prerogatives. Though the number of disciplinary dismissals in those sectors with formal procedures has decreased as lower line managers have been subjected to controls, there has been a noticeable tendency for control to be centralised and new techniques employed to make use of union involvement to legitimise managerial disciplinary policies and decisions (Dickens et al., 1985:241, 265–6). Moreover, it is difficult to conceive of redundancy legislation as acknowledging in its structure the primacy of voluntary collective bargaining. The legislation has always been aimed directly at influencing the development of managerial policies, including prior consultation and even negotiation over redundancy. As Daniel (1985) and Levie et al. (1984) have shown, the legislation has increased management planning of redundancies both in terms of orchestrating redundancy decisions and negotiating redundancy agreements, and it has thereby increased the control of managers over mass dismissals and closures. As Gennard (1982:137) points out, moreover, collective resistance to redundancy has been relatively small partly because of a shift from a unilateral to bilateral procedures.

This perspective of individual employment legislation as both rights legislation and as a catalyst to managerial efficiency helps to explain why these laws have been accepted by all political parties, despite their fundamental differences over legislation which is directed more explicitly at collective labour relations. It also calls into question the rationality of political decisions to break this consensus by the erosion of employment protection in general and unfair dismissal in particular.

Bibliography

Advisory, Conciliation and Arbitration Service (ACAS). 1977. *Disciplinary Practice and Procedures in Employment*. Code of Practice 1. London: HMSO.

Anderman, S.D. 1985. *The Law of Unfair Dismissal*. 2nd edn. London: Butterworths.

Bourn, C. 1979. 'Statutory Exemptions for Collective Agreements'. *Industrial Law Journal*, 8 (June), 85–99.

——. 1983. *Redundancy Law and Practice*. London: Butterworths.

Brown, William (ed.). 1981. *The Changing Contours of British Industrial Relations: A Survey of Manufacturing Industry*. Oxford: Blackwell.

Clark, Jon, and *Lord* Wedderburn. 1983. 'Modern Labour Law: Problems, Functions and Policies'. *Labour Law and Industrial Relations: Building on Kahn-Freund*. Eds. *Lord* Wedderburn, Roy Lewis and Jon Clark. Oxford: Clarendon Press, 127–242.

Collins, Hugh. 1982. 'Capitalist Discipline and Corporatist Law – Part II'. *Industrial Law Journal*, 11 (September), 170–77.

——. 1985. 'Dismissal for Economic Reasons'. *Industrial Law Journal*, 14 (March), 61–4.

Daniel, W.W. 1985. 'The United Kingdom'. *Managing Workforce Reduction: An International Survey*. Ed. M. Cross. London: Croom Helm, 67–90.

——, and N. Millward. 1983. *Workforce Industrial Relations in Britain: The DE/PSI/SSRC Survey*. London: Heinemann.

——, and E. Stilgoe. 1978. *The Impact of Employment Protection Laws*. London: PSI.

Davies, P.L., and M. Freedland. 1979. *Labour Law: Text and Materials*. London: Weidenfeld & Nicolson.

——, and M. Freedland. 1984. *Labour Law: Text and Materials*. 2nd edn. London: Weidenfeld & Nicolson.

Department of Employment (DE). 1970. *Industrial Relations Bill: Consultative Document*. London: DE.

Dickens, L., M. Jones, B. Weekes and M. Hart. 1985. *Dismissed: A Study of Unfair Dismissal and the Industrial Tribunal System*. Oxford: Blackwell.

Donovan. 1968. Royal Commission on Trade Unions and Employers' Associations 1965–1968. *Report*. Cmnd 3623. London: HMSO.

Elias, P. 1978. 'Unravelling the Concept of Dismissal – II'. *Industrial Law Journal*, 7 (June), 100–12.

——. 1981. 'Fairness in Unfair Dismissal: Trends and Tensions'. *Industrial Law Journal*, 10 (December), 201–17.

Fryer, R.H. 1973. 'Redundancy and Public Policy'. *Redundancy and Paternalist Capitalism*. R. Martin and R.H. Fryer. London: Allen & Unwin, 216–60.

Gennard, J. 1982. 'Great Britain'. *Workforce Reductions in Undertakings*. Ed. E. Yemin. Geneva: ILO, 107–39.

Grunfeld, C. 1980. *The Law of Redundancy*. London: Sweet & Maxwell.

Hepple, B.A. 1981. 'A Right to Work?' *Industrial Law Journal*, 10 (June), 65–83.

——. 1982. 'The Transfer of Undertakings (Protection of Employment) Regulations'. *Industrial Law Journal*, 11 (March), 29–40.

——, and P. O'Higgins. 1981. *Employment Law*. 4th edn. B. A. Hepple. London: Sweet & Maxwell.

Kahn-Freund, O. 1977. *Labour and the Law*. 2nd edn. London: Stevens.

Leighton, Patricia E. 1983. *Contractual Arrangements in Selected Industries*. Research Paper no. 39. London: Department of Employment.

Levie, H., D. Gregory and N. Lorentzen (eds.). 1984. *Fighting Closures*. Nottingham: Spokesman.

Lewis, Roy. 1979. 'Kahn-Freund and Labour Law: An Outline Critique'. *Industrial Law Journal*, 8 (December), 202–21.

Mellish, M., and N. Collis-Squires. 1976. 'Legal and Social Norms in Discipline and Dismissal'. *Industrial Law Journal*, 5 (September), 164–77.

Schofield, P. 1983. 'The British Labour Pump Principle'. *Industrial Law Journal*, 12 (September), 171–5.

Wedderburn, K.W. (*Lord*). 1980. 'Industrial Relations and the Courts'. *Industrial Law Journal*, 9 (June), 65–94.

Williams, Kevin. 1983. 'Unfair Dismissal: Myths and Statistics'. *Industrial Law Journal*, 12 (September), 157–65.

——, and D. Lewis. 1981. *The Aftermath of Tribunal Reinstatement and Reengagement*. Research Paper no. 23. London: Department of Employment.

16 Health and Safety at Work

Philip James and David Lewis

Injuries and diseases resulting from workplace activity constitute a moral, political, social and economic problem. Although the cost of accidents and disease to the country as a whole is extremely difficult to calculate, especially when a substantial proportion of accidents are of a minor nature and are not reported, Morgan and Davies (1981:485) estimate that the total cost of occupational accidents and diseases during 1978–9 ranged between 0.8 per cent and 1.2 per cent of gross national product. Indeed, the number of working days lost owing to industrial accidents and illness is normally far greater than those lost through strikes (Beaumont, 1983:1–2).

This chapter outlines the scope of HSWA and assesses its significance. Having indicated some of the interrelationships between health and safety and other aspects of labour law, it goes on to describe the sources of compensation available to injured persons. Finally, it considers the role the law can play in reducing accidents and illness at the workplace, and discusses the implications of the economic recession for industrial health and safety. The first task, however, is to note the Report of the Robens Committee (1972), which exercised a decisive influence over the current legal framework.

THE ROBENS REPORT

The history of protective occupational health and safety legislation[1] can be traced back to the passing of the first factory statute in 1802, enacted as a result of concern about the appalling working conditions of pauper children in cotton mills. The next 170 years saw the piecemeal extension of protective legislation to cover other types of worker, workplaces and hazards. Initially these legislative developments were restricted to the textile industry, though non-textile activities were gradually affected by them. The ad hoc fashion in which the statutory framework for occupational health and safety evolved meant that a highly complex body of law had developed by the early 1970s. The Robens Report noted that there were then in force no less than nine main groups of statutes relevant to occupational health and safety, these being supported by nearly five hundred supplementary statutory instruments. This body of legislation included the Factories Act 1961, the Mines

---

[1] See generally Hutchins and Harrison (1966).

and Quarries Act 1954, the Offices, Shops and Railway Premises Act 1963, and the Explosives Acts 1875 and 1923.

Not surprisingly, therefore, the Robens Report (1972:para.28) concluded that 'the first and perhaps most fundamental defect of the statutory system is simply that there is too much law'. The Report accepted the argument that the sheer mass of law was counter-productive: 'people are heavily conditioned to think of safety and health at work as in the first and most important instance a matter of detailed rules imposed by external agencies'. The Report assumed that apathy, which it identified as the most significant reason for accidents at work, could not be cured so long as people were encouraged to think that health and safety could be ensured by an 'ever expanding body of legal regulations enforced by an ever increasing army of inspectors. The primary responsibility for doing something about the present levels of occupational accidents and disease lies with those who create the risks and those who work with them' (Robens, 1972:para.28).

Another criticism raised by the Report was that too much of the existing law was 'intrinsically unsatisfactory'. Apart from being 'written in a language and style that renders it largely unintelligible to those whose actions it is intended to influence' (1972:para.29), the existing legislation laid down no general standard of care but dealt with problems in an ad hoc fashion. Attention had been focused on statutorily defined places and physical processes, and duties had historically been owed by specified persons such as 'occupiers' to other specified persons. No statute was applicable to all workers. The Robens Report was also concerned by the 'fragmentation of administrative jurisdictions' (1972:para.32). At the time the Committee was conducting its inquiry, responsibilities for administration and enforcement were divided between five government departments and seven separate inspectorates, which diffused and compartmentalised the expertise and facilities that were available to deal with occupational hazards.

The Report identified two main objectives of reform: a unified and more integrated system to improve the state's contribution to health and safety, and the creation of conditions which would lead to a more effective self-regulatory system. It recommended, first, that the existing statutory measures should be replaced by a comprehensive and orderly set of revised provisions under a new enabling Act. This Act would include a clear statement of the basic principles of safety responsibility and be supported by regulations and non-statutory codes of practice. Second, the scope of the new legislation would extend to all employers and employees (except for specific exclusions), and to the self-employed where their acts and omissions could endanger other workers or the general public. Third, the existing inspectorates would be amalgamated to form a unified service. Finally, where sanctions were needed to ensure the rectification of unsatisfactory conditions, a range of alternatives should be available to the inspectorate, including improvement or prohibition notices.

The assumptions and analysis of the Robens Report were the subject of some criticism. Thus Phillips (1976) suggested that the main reason for accidents at work was not apathy but the economic cost of eliminating risks. Woolf (1973) saw rigorous enforcement of the criminal law as potentially more effective than self-regulation. Nevertheless, the Report commanded widespread support and was the basis of the legal framework introduced by the enactment in 1974 of the HSWA.

THE HEALTH AND SAFETY AT WORK ACT

The HSWA is an enabling statute providing the framework within which earlier provisions can be revised and replaced. Its implementation, therefore, did not herald the large-scale repeal of existing statutes and statutory instruments. This earlier legislation has, for the most part, continued in force pending its gradual replacement by new requirements developed under the 1974 framework, a vast task that is proceeding slowly and will certainly not be completed by the turn of the century.

The HSWA applies to England, Wales and, with certain exceptions, to Scotland.[2] Its broad objectives are outlined in s.1(1). These are to secure the health, safety and welfare of persons at work; to protect persons other than those at work against risks to health and safety arising out of or in connection with the activities of persons at work; to control the keeping and use of explosives or highly flammable or otherwise dangerous substances; and to control the emission into the atmosphere of noxious or offensive substances. These objectives refer to the health and safety of persons at work. Unlike most of the earlier legislation, the Act's application is not limited to those working under a contract of employment at particular types of premises, or engaged in particular types of activities, though domestic servants are excluded (HSWA s.51). Moreover, the Act covers not only those at work, but also other persons who may be affected by their activities. The importance of protecting the public from risks associated with work-related activities is therefore acknowledged. Two bodies have responsibility for implementing these objectives: the Health and Safety Commission (HSC) and the Health and Safety Executive (HSE).

Health and Safety Commission and Executive

The HSC is a body corporate whose members are appointed by the Secretary of State for Employment. In accordance with HWSA s.10, it consists of a chairman and between six and nine other members. Three of the latter must be appointed after consultations with organisations representing employees, and three following consultations with those representing employers. With regard to the appointment of any other members, the Secretary of State is required to consult with local authorities and other appropriate organisations. In fact since its formation the Commission has consists of a chairman and between six and nine other members. Three of local authority representatives.

---

[2] Regulations largely modelled on the Act have been introduced into Northern Ireland: Health and Safety at Work (Northern Ireland) Order SI 1978 No.1039.

The HSC has the duty to promote the general purposes of the Act (s.11). It also has a number of more specific duties, perhaps the most important of which is its duty to prepare regulations.[3] In drafting these the HSC is required to consult with government departments and other appropriate bodies (s.50(3)(a)). To that end the Commission has adopted a policy of issuing consultative documents outlining its regulatory proposals, and has also formed eighteen advisory committees dealing with particular hazards and industries (HSC, 1984a).

Initiatives developed by the European Commission (EC) have exerted an important influence over how the HSC has carried out this regulatory function in recent years. EC Directives have, for instance, significantly influenced the development and content of regulations dealing with such matters as the classification, packaging and labelling of dangerous substances, the notification of hazardous installations, and the use of tachographs in goods vehicles. ILO conventions and recommendations have also influenced the development of domestic regulations (see Drake and Wright, 1983:249–55).

The HSC's powers are outlined in HSWA ss.13–16. One of these merits particular mention. The Commission may, for the purpose of providing practical guidance on the requirements imposed by statutory provisions, approve and issue codes of practice (s.16(1)). Where such a code is issued, s.17(1) provides that a failure on the part of a person to observe any of its provisions does not of itself render that person liable to civil or criminal proceedings. Where, however, it is alleged that persons have contravened a requirement of any relevant statutory provision and it is shown that they have failed to observe a relevant code, then this will be taken as conclusive evidence of their guilt, unless the court is satisfied that the defendants complied with their obligations in some other way.

The HSE is in effect the operational arm of the Commission (see ILO, 1982), and its members are appointed by the Commission with the approval of the Secretary of State. It was created on 1 January 1975 and at that time became the employer of most of the inspectors who had been appointed under earlier statutes. Inspection functions are also carried out by local authority inspectors. Prior to the HSWA these inspectors had been responsible for enforcing the Offices, Shops and Railway Premises Act 1963. Their enforcement activities still cover largely the same types of premises, but they are now able to enforce certain other relevant statutory provisions.[4] Currently, the HSC (1985) is considering whether to expand the role of local authority inspectors.

[3] The scope and purposes of regulations are outlined in HSWA s.15 and Sch.3. Section 1 (2) provides that regulations and codes of practice should be designed to maintain or improve the standards of health, safety and welfare established by or under the enactments specified in Sch.1.

[4] See Health and Safety (Enforcing Authority) Regulations SI 1977 No.746. 'Relevant statutory provisions' are the provisions of the statutes listed in HSWA Sch.1 together with those contained in Part I of the Act and any regulations made under these statutes.

General Duties

To aid the achievement of its objectives the HSWA ss.2–9 specifies a number of general duties. These impose obligations on employers and employees as well as the self-employed, the controllers of premises, and the designers, suppliers, manufacturers and importers of articles and substances for use at work. Most of these duties are qualified by the words 'so far as is reasonably practicable', a phrase which is not defined in the Act. Judicial decisions in various civil cases do, however, provide guidance on its meaning and indicate that the duty involves a balancing of the risk to health and safety against the cost and trouble associated with its control and removal.[5] The test of reasonable practicability can therefore be seen to involve a form of cost-benefit analysis. Also the test is subjective in so far as it involves a consideration of the particular circumstances of a case rather than the imposition of an overall objective standard.[6] There is, however, some uncertainty as to whether courts can take account of an employer's financial position.[7]

The inclusion of the qualifying phrase 'so far as is reasonably practicable' was the subject of controversy when the Health and Safety at Work Bill was going through Parliament, with some MPs seeking unsuccessfully to substitute the more onerous obligation to take precautions and measures 'so far as is practicable'.[8] The latter phrase is used in the Mines and Quarries Act 1954 and certain sections of the Factories Act 1961, and requires measures to be taken that are possible in the light of current knowledge and invention.[9]

Duties of employers. Section 2(1) of the Act imposes a duty on all employers to ensure, so far as is reasonably practicable, the health, safety and welfare at work of their employees. The effect of this section was therefore formally to close the gaps in coverage which had existed under the earlier framework of occupational health and safety legislation. As a result, up to eight million workers received protection for the first time. These 'new entrants' included those employed in hospitals, schools, universities and road haulage depots. Section 2(2) details a number of matters to which – so far as is reasonably practicable – this overall duty of the employer extends: the provision and maintenance of plant and systems of work that are safe and without risks to health; arrangements for ensuring safety and absence of risks to health in connection with the use, handling, storage and transport of articles and substances; the provision of information, instruction, training

---

5 See e.g. *Edwards v National Coal Board* [1949] 1 KB 704. For more recent discussions of the duty, see *West Bromwich Building Society v Townsend* [1983] IRLR 147 and *Associated Dairies v Hartley* [1979] IRLR 171.
6 In *Martin v Boulton and Paul (Steel Construction) Ltd* [1982] ICR 366 it was held that the test can require an employer to adopt methods safer than those universally practised in a particular industry.
7 See *TO Harrison (Newcastle-under-Lyme) Ltd v K Ramsey* [1976] IRLR 135.
8 HC Standing Committee A, 2 May 1974, 71 & 78. The duty to use the best practicable means in HSWA s.5 (see below) imposes a higher standard of care.
9 *Marshall v Gotham Co. Ltd* [1954] All ER 937, at 942 (per Lord Reid).

and supervision to ensure the health and safety at work of his own employees; the maintenance of a workplace under his control in a condition which is safe and without risks to health, and the provision and maintenance of means of access to and egress from it that are safe and without such risks; and the provision of a working environment for his employees that is safe, without risks to health, and adequate as regards facilities and arrangements for their welfare at work.

These duties are owed by employers to their own employees, defined as individuals who work under contracts of employment or apprenticeship (HSWA s.53(1)). But against a background of concern about the health and safety of trainees on the MSC's Youth Training Scheme (YTS), and uncertainty about their employment status (see IRS, 1983; Freedland, 1983 and Chapter 18 below), regulations now provide that YTS trainees not employed under a contract of employment shall be treated as employees of the person whose undertaking is the provider of training.[10]

Prior to this amendment YTS trainees not falling within the definition of employee were covered by the duty of employers under s.3(1) to conduct their undertaking in such a way to ensure, so far as is reasonably practicable, that non-employees are not exposed to risks to their health and safety. Section 3(2) imposes a similar duty on the self-employed with regard to themselves and others. In the *Swan Hunter* case,[11] the Court of Appeal confirmed that the duty of employers under s.3(1) could extend to the provision of appropriate instruction and information to non-employees. It further held that the provision of such instruction and information may be necessary if employers are to comply with the duty to provide a safe system of work for their own employees. Current trends involving the greater use of contract labour suggest that s.3(1) and (2) could become of increasing importance (Atkinson, 1984).

The *Swan Hunter* decision additionally serves to highlight an important point about the duties imposed on employers under the HSWA. This is that they represent a shift in the emphasis of occupational health and safety legislation away from a pre-occupation with the provision of physical safeguards – although this is still essential – towards a greater concern with management systems and arrangements.[12] The duty of employers under s.2(3) to prepare a written statement of their safety policy further illustrates this point. Employers are required to prepare and, as often as may be appropriate, revise a written statement of their general policy with respect to the health and safety of their employees and the organisation and arrangements for the time being in force for carrying out that policy. They are further obliged to bring this statement and any revision of it to the notice of

---

[10] Health and Safety (Youth Training Scheme) Regulations SI 1983 No.1919. These regulations also state that while undergoing YTS training, such trainees will be considered to be at work, except where this training consists of a course at a university, polytechnic, college, school or similar educational or technical institute.

[11] *R v Swan Hunter Ltd* [1981] IRLR 403.

[12] Barrett et al. (1983). For information on management safety specialists at the workplace level, see HSE (1976); HSC (1983); EMAS (1976).

their employees.[13] Research indicates that the content, communication and implementation of many policies could be substantially improved (see HSE, 1980; Dawson et al., 1984; Barrett and James, 1981). Moreover, regulations exempt employers who carry on undertakings in which they employ less than five employees from the requirements relating to safety policies.[14] Nevertheless, the duty to prepare and circulate safety policies reflects the importance the legislature attaches to involving employees in the maintenance and improvement of health and safety, a point best illustrated by the consultative duties discussed later in the chapter.

Duties of employees. Employees are required to take reasonable care for the health and safety of themselves and others who may be affected by their acts or omissions (HSWA s.7). They are also required to co-operate with employers and any other persons so far as is necessary to enable such persons to perform any duties imposed on them by relevant statutory provisions. It is an offence for *any person*, including an employee, to 'intentionally or recklessly interfere with or misuse anything provided in the interests of health, safety or welfare in pursuance of any relevant statutory provisions' (HSWA s.8). With regard to the services and equipment made available by employers, s.9 forbids employers to levy or permit to be levied on employees any charge in respect of 'anything done or provided in pursuance of any specific requirement of any of the relevant statutory provisions'.[15]

Controllers of premises and manufacturers. The remaining general duties of the 1974 Act impose obligations on categories of persons other than employers and employees, although the former may also fall within these categories. HSWA s.4 applies to those who have, to any extent, control of non-domestic premises which are made available to persons not in their employment either as a place of work, or a place where they may use plant or substances, for example, a coin-operated laundrette. The duty imposed on controllers is to take such measures as it is reasonable for persons in their position to take to ensure, so far as is reasonably practicable, that the premises and any plant or substances on the premises are safe and without risk to health. In addition, controllers of premises of prescribed classes are required to use the best practicable means for preventing emission into the atmosphere of noxious or offensive substances and for rendering harmless and inoffensive such substances as may be so emitted (HSWA s.5). To date no such classes of premises have been prescribed.

---

13   CA 1985 Sch. 7 empowers the Secretary of State to make regulations requiring prescribed classes of companies to include in directors' reports information about their arrangements for securing the health, safety and welfare of employees and other persons. No regulations have so far been made under this section. The government plans to raise this threshold to 20 employees: OMWP (1985).

14   Employers' Health and Safety Policy (Exception) Regulations SI 1975 No.1584 reg.2; see *Osborne v Bill Taylor of Huyton Ltd* [1982] IRLR 17.

15   But HSWA s.2 duties are general rather than specific: *Associated Dairies Ltd v Hartley* [1979] IRLR 171.

A person who designs, manufactures, imports or supplies any article for use at work has the duty under HSWA s.6 to ensure, so far as is reasonably practicable, that the article is so designed and constructed as to be safe and without risks to health when properly used. Similar duties are imposed on the importers, manufacturers and suppliers of substances for use at work, who are additionally required to carry out or arrange for the carrying out of any necessary research in order to discover and, so far as is reasonably practicable, to eliminate or minimise risks to health and safety. Finally, a person who erects or installs any article for use at work is required to ensure, so far as is reasonably practicable, that nothing about the way in which it is erected or installed makes it unsafe or a risk to health when properly used.[16]

The duties contained in s.6 were regarded as being of considerable importance when the Act came into force. Their primary purpose was to lay duties on all those involved in the chain of supplying articles and substances for use at work to ensure that they were safe when put to their intended use. Restrictive judicial interpretations have, however, made it difficult for the HSE to enforce the section and meant that it has been less effective than originally hoped. Problems have particularly emerged with regard to the interpretation of the phrases 'when properly used' and for 'use at work'.[17]

Enforcement of Act

Local authority and HSE inspectors are given wide-ranging powers under HSWA s.20(2) and s.25. These relate to such matters as the right of entry to premises; the making of examinations and investigations; the taking of measurements, photographs and samples; the production and inspection of books and documents; the provision of facilities and assistance; the questioning of people; and the seizing and rendering harmless of articles and substances. In addition, following the Robens Report's recommendation concerning the use of administrative sanctions, inspectors are also given the power to issue improvement and prohibition notices.[18] In 1982 factory and local authority inspectors issued 11,038 improvement and 2,594 prohibition notices (HSE, 1984).

An improvement notice can be served on a person where an inspector is of the opinion that the person is contravening one or more relevant statutory provisions, or has done so in circumstances that make it likely that the contravention will continue or be repeated.[19] Such a notice requires the

---

[16] See also Health and Safety (Leasing Arrangements) Regulations SI 1980 No.907.
[17] See e.g. the discussion of *McConnachie v Dancheats Woodworking Machinery Ltd* (unreported) in *HSIB*, 42 (1979), 5–7. Also see HSC (1984b).
[18] Section 48(1) exempts the Crown from the enforcement provisions of HSWA, although they still apply to Crown employees. The HSE, however, follows a policy of issuing non-statutory notices where an improvement or prohibition notice would usually have been appropriate.
[19] The High Court has suggested, however, that an improvement notice which only asserts that an employer is in contravention of HSWA s.2(1) is insufficiently specific: *West Bromwich Building Society v Townsend* [1983] IRLR 147.

person to remedy the contravention or the matters occasioning it within a specified period (s.21). This period must not be less than the time allowed for bringing appeals against notices (see below).

Prohibition notices can be served by inspectors where they believe that activities are being or are about to be carried on, which involve a risk of serious personal injury.[20] The actual contravention of a relevant statutory provision is therefore not always necessary before a notice is served. A prohibition notice directs that the activities to which the notice relates should not be carried on by or under the person on whom the notice is served, unless the matters specified in the notice have been remedied (s.22(3)). It may be issued with immediate effect where the inspector is of the opinion that there is an imminent risk of serious personal injury.

A person on whom a notice has been served has a right of appeal to an industrial tribunal within twenty-one days of the serving of a notice.[21] In the case of an improvement notice, the effect of an appeal is to suspend its operation until the appeal is withdrawn or disposed of by the tribunal (s.24(3)(a)). A prohibition notice continues to operate, however, unless the tribunal chooses to order its suspension at the appeal or at a specially convened hearing to deal with the issue as a preliminary point. A tribunal hearing an appeal is empowered to cancel or affirm a notice either in its original form or with such modifications as it thinks fit.[22]

It is an offence for any person or body corporate to contravene any of the relevant statutory provisions. In addition, s.37(1) provides that where an offence committed by a body corporate is proved to have been committed with the consent or connivance of or to have been attributable to any neglect on the part of any director, manager, secretary or other similar officer, that person is also guilty of the offence.[23] Thus the Director of Roads for Strathclyde Regional Council was successfully prosecuted on the grounds that the Council's failure to prepare a safety policy was attributable to his neglect.[24]

Section 33 of the Act details fifteen different types of offences. These fall into two categories: those triable summarily, and those triable either summarily or on indictment. The latter more serious category covers such offences as a failure to comply with an improvement or prohibition notice, and a failure to discharge any duties imposed under ss.2–9 and any health and safety regulations made under the Act. The maximum penalty applic-

---

[20] Such notices can only be served in respect of activities which are the subject of relevant statutory provisions (s.22(1)). See note 4 above.

[21] Industrial Tribunals (Improvement and Prohibition Notices Appeals) Regulations SI 1974 No.1925. An appellant may apply for an extension of time on the grounds that it was not reasonably practicable for an appeal to be brought within 21 days.

[22] Section 82(1)(c) defines 'modifications' to include additions, omissions and amendments. A tribunal cannot, however, modify a notice so as to introduce a duty not raised in the notice: *British Airways Board v Henderson* [1979] ICR 77. For a review of the appeals procedure see Drake and Wright (1983: 144–57).

[23] Section 36(1) provides that where the commission of an offence is due to the act or default of some other person, proceedings may be brought against that person even where no action is taken against the person initially committing the offence.

[24] *Armour v Skeen* [1977] IRLR 310.

able to a person found guilty of an offence on summary conviction is a fine of £2,000. Where proceedings are brought on indictment, however, a Crown Court may impose an unlimited fine and, in the case of certain offences, up to two years' imprisonment. To date nobody has been sentenced to imprisonment.

Where a person is convicted of an offence under any of the relevant statutory provisions in respect of matters which appear to the court to be within its powers to remedy, the court may, in addition to or instead of imposing any punishment, order specified steps to be taken within a fixed time (s.42(1)). A failure to comply with an order is an offence and may lead to a fine of up to £100 for each day on which the order is contravened. Such a fine can also be imposed where persons are found guilty of contravening an improvement or prohibition notice and continue to do so after their conviction (s.33(5)).

Proceedings in respect of any of the relevant statutory provisions can only be instituted in England and Wales by an inspector or by or with the consent of the Director of Public Prosecutions (the Procurator-Fiscal in Scotland). In practice HSE and local authority inspectors are largely responsible for determining the extent to which such proceedings are brought. The enforcement policy of the HSE, and the factory inspectorate in particular, has been the subject of some criticism. Traditionally, the factory inspectorate has tried to secure compliance through persuasion, prosecutions tending to be considered only in cases of gross non-compliance, or where persuasion has failed or is considered unlikely to succeed (Carson, 1970). This approach has been defended on the grounds that it is the most cost-effective policy in terms of time and resources. Critics such as Woolf (1973) have argued, however, that a more vigorous enforcement policy, together with the imposition of higher fines where an offender is successfully prosecuted,[25] would make a significant contribution to improved standards of health and safety. This argument recently received some support from an ILO mission on the effectiveness of labour inspection in the UK, one of whose conclusions was that improvement and prohibition notices should be served more often by inspectors (ILO, 1982:71).

EMPLOYEE PARTICIPATION UNDER HSWA

Prior to the HSWA employee participation in health and safety had largely depended on voluntary developments at the workplace, usually involving the setting up of consultative committees and the use of normal collective bargaining machinery (Williams, 1960; Howells, 1974). The 1974 Act introduced a statutory framework for employee representation. Section 2(4) provides that regulations may require, in prescribed cases, the appointment by recognised trade unions of safety representatives from among employees to represent those employees in consultations with their employer. Originally

[25] The average fine was £265 in 1983: HSE (1984).

s.2(5) also provided for regulations to enable employees to elect safety representatives, but this sub-section was subsequently repealed as a result of trade union opposition.[26] Thus non-unionised workplaces and work groups are excluded from the statutory framework, a point that has been the subject of some criticism (Barrett, 1977: 175–6).

Where safety representatives are appointed, s.2(6) obliges employers to consult them with a view to co-operating effectively in promoting and developing measures to ensure the health and safety of the employees. An employer is additionally required, in such cases as may be prescribed, to establish, in accordance with regulations made by the Secretary of State, a safety committee if requested to do so by the safety representatives (s.2(7)). This committee is to have the function of keeping under review the measures taken to ensure the health and safety of employees and such other functions as may be prescribed.

An employer's duty to consult with safety representatives is not defined in the Act. Traditionally, joint consultation has been distinguished from negotiation on the grounds that the former involves an exchange of information but no infringement of managerial prerogatives, whereas the latter entails an element of joint decision-making.[27] The inclusion of a duty to consult rather than bargain very much echoed the Robens Report's argument (1972:21) that 'there is no legitimate scope for "bargaining" on safety and health issues, but much scope for constructive discussion, joint inspections and participation in working out solutions'. This reflected in turn the committee's views that there was a 'greater natural identity of interest between the "two sides" in relation to safety and health problems than in most other matters'. The Report's reliance on consultation arguably under-estimated the conflicts of interest that can occur over health and safety matters (Lewis, 1974:98).

Proposals for regulations to activate HSWA s.2(4) and (7) were issued by the HSC in the form of a consultative document, along with an accompanying draft Code of Practice and Guidance Notes at the end of 1975. Proposals agreed by the Commission were not, however, laid before Parliament until March 1977 and came into effect in October 1978.[28]

Safety Representatives and Safety Committees Regulations

The regulations enable an independent trade union to appoint safety representatives from among the employees of an employer by whom it is recognised (reg.3(1)). A recognised union is defined as one which is

---

[26] EPA s.116 and Sch.15, para.2. See the discussion on 'single channel' representation in Chapter 3.

[27] Clegg (1960:36). Research findings suggest that in practice the process of joint consultation frequently involves an element of bargaining: Derber (1955); Cressey et al. (1981:20).

[28] Safety Representatives and Safety Committees Regulations SI 1977 No.500. The regulations and the HSC's Code of Practice (Safety Representatives and Safety Committees) and Guidance Notes are reproduced in HSC (1977).

recognised by the employer for the purposes of negotiations over one or more of the matters specified in TULRA s.29(1).[29] As far as reasonably practicable, safety representatives should either have been employed by their employer throughout the preceding two years or have had at least two years' experience in similar employment.[30]

In addition to representing employees in consultation with the employer under s.2(6) of the 1974 Act, reg.4(1) accords safety representatives the following functions: to investigate potential hazards and dangerous occurrences and to examine the causes of accidents; to investigate complaints relating to an employee's health, safety or welfare at work; to make representations to the employer on these and on general matters affecting the health, safety or welfare of employees; to carry out inspections in accordance with the regulations; to represent employees in consultations at the workplace with inspectors; to receive information from inspectors in accordance with HSWA s.28(8); and to attend meetings of safety committees.

Safety representatives are entitled to inspect the whole or part of the workplace at least every three months, although they are required to give employers reasonable notice in writing of their intention to conduct an inspection (reg.5). More frequent inspections can, however, be carried out by agreement with the employer. Additional inspections can be made if there has been a substantial change in the conditions of work or new information has been published by the HSE relevant to the hazards of the workplace. Inspections may also be conducted to determine the cause of notifiable accidents, dangerous occurrences or notifiable diseases (reg.6). An employer is required to provide such facilities and assistance as safety representatives may reasonably require, including facilities for independent investigation by them and private discussion with the employees.

Safety representatives who have given the employer reasonable notice are entitled to inspect and take copies of relevant documents. An employer is also required to make available to safety representatives information which is necessary to enable them to fulfil their functions (reg.7(2)). Paragraph 6 of the HSC's Code of Practice amplifies this provision by listing various types of information which should be disclosed. Regulation 7(2) details a number of exemptions to this duty of disclosure. These for the most part mirror those relating to the disclosure of information for collective bargaining purposes in EPA s.18 (see Chapter 3). One important difference, however, is that the regulations do not specifically exempt information that has been provided to an employer in confidence. Also the procedures applicable where a failure to disclose is alleged differ, and a failure to comply with the regulations constitutes a criminal offence. Health and safety inspectors, moreover, have a duty to disclose information in circumstances where it is necessary to assist

---

[29] *Cleveland County Council v Springett* [1985] IRLR 131. On 'recognition' see further Chapter 3.

[30] Safety representatives do not need to be employees of the employer concerned where they are appointed to represent members of the British Actors' Equity Association or the Musicians' Union (reg.8(2)).

in keeping employees or their representatives adequately informed about matters affecting their health and safety (HSWA s.28). This duty of disclosure relates to factual information obtained by them concerning the employer's premises and information regarding action they have taken or propose to take in connection with those premises.

Under reg.4(2) an employer must permit safety representatives to take such time off with pay for performing their functions and to undergo training as may be reasonable in all the circumstances having regard to the provisions of an approved Code of Practice.[31] The amount of pay to which a representative is entitled during time off is similar to that for union officials under EPCA s.27 (see Chapter 2). Indeed, payment made in respect of time off under EPCA s.27 discharges an employer's liability under the safety regulations. The clear implication of this is that a safety representatives may also be a trade union official for the purposes of the latter section. A representative may complain to an industrial tribunal that the employer has either failed to permit him time off or to pay him in accordance with the regulations (reg.11(1)).[32] If the complaint is well-founded the tribunal must make a declaration and may award compensation.

Finally, two safety representatives may in writing ask an employer to form a safety committee (reg.9). On receiving such a request, the employer is initially required to consult with the safety representatives and the representatives of recognised trade unions. He is then obliged to form the committee not later than three months after the making of the request and to post a notice stating its composition at the workplace (or workplaces) to be covered by it in a place where it may easily be read by employees. There is no statutory guidance on the operation of these committees, but the Guidance Notes indicate that their functions might include assistance in the development of safety rules and the analysis of accident statistics and trends.

Enforcement and Impact of the Law

The regulations represented a departure from the voluntary manner in which collective relations at the workplace have historically evolved in Britain. But, as Davies and Freedland (1984:232) note, the legislature seems to have drawn back from the consequences of this departure in that many items of detail are left to trade unions and employers at the workplace. These include the number of safety representatives and their method of appointment, the precise arrangements for notifying and carrying out inspections, and the provision of facilities for safety representatives. Indeed, it should not be overlooked that trade unions are under no obligation to activate the system of participation laid down in the regulations.

This attempt to maintain a balance between legal intervention and traditional voluntarism is also seen in the approach adopted towards the

---

[31] HSC Code of Practice: Time Off for the Training of Safety Representatives, 1978.
[32] The leading case is *White v Pressed Steel Fisher* [1980] IRLR 176. See also *IRLIB*, 268 (6 November 1984).

enforcement of the regulations. Paragraph 3 of the HSC's Code states that employers and unions should make full use of the existing industrial relations machinery to reach agreement in order to achieve the purposes of the regulations and to resolve any differences. The significance of this advice was subsequently underlined by guidance on the enforcement of the regulations issued to local authorities and HSE inspectorates by the HSC.[33] This suggests that inspectors should not consider enforcement action until they are satisfied that all voluntary means of resolving a disagreement have been tried. Where enforcement action is considered necessary, it is suggested that the issuing of an improvement notice will normally be the most appropriate first step. To date no prosecutions have been brought for breaches of these regulations.

There is still only limited research available on how the legislative provisions have been implemented at the workplace.[34] In 1985 the TUC estimated that around 130,000 safety representatives had been appointed. According to a survey of 6,630 workplaces carried out by HSE inspectors in October 1979, statutory safety representatives had been appointed in only 17 per cent of workplaces (DE, 1981). But a very different picture emerged when safety representative coverage was measured in terms of the proportion of employees as opposed to workplaces covered, the relevant figure rising to 79 per cent.

Research suggests that the statutory provisions have served to increase considerably the number of workplaces possessing safety committees, as well as stimulating the restructuring of those that had previously existed. In a survey of some 2,000 establishments, Daniel and Millward (1983:142) found that 37 per cent of establishments possessed joint health and safety committees and another 12 per cent had consultative committees dealing with health and safety as well as other matters. Of particular significance was the finding that two-thirds of the former committees had been established since mid-1975, with nearly half of them having been set up after mid-1977 when the regulations had already been laid before Parliament (cf. Brown, 1981:75).

HEALTH AND SAFETY AND EMPLOYMENT PROTECTION

Health and safety issues impinge on several legal provisions for the protection of individual employees, notably in respect of sex discrimination, statutory payments for suspension on medical grounds, and unfair dismissal. It is not unlawful to discriminate on the grounds of sex if it is necessary to do so in order to comply with a requirement imposed by a statute or regulation.[35] This is designed to preserve the special protection afforded by

[33] Reproduced in *HSIB*, 36 (December 1978).
[34] For a review of relevant research, see Glendon and Booth (1982). Also see Holgate (1982); Beaumont (1983); and LRD (1984).
[35] SDA s.51. See *Page v Freight Hire Ltd* [1981] IRLR 13, where it was held that in order to satisfy SDA s.51 an employer does not have to show that debarring a woman from taking up the job was the only method of meeting the requirements of HSWA s.2.

the Factories Act 1961 to women in relation to their hours of work. Section 55 of the SDA, however, obliges the EOC to review the question of discriminatory health and safety provisions in consultation with the HSC. In 1979 it was recommended that the discrimination should be removed and protection provided on equal terms (EOC, 1979). The government has announced its intention of lifting restrictions on women's hours (OMWP, 1985).

Employees who are suspended from work in consequence of a requirement imposed by specified health and safety provisions or a recommendation contained in a code issued under HSWA s.16 are entitled to a week's pay for each week of suspension up to a maximum of 26 weeks.[36] This right can only be invoked where the specified safety legislation has affected the employer's undertaking. Employees are not entitled to remuneration under this provision for any period during which they are incapable of work by reason of injury or illness, although they are likely to be entitled to statutory sick pay (see Chapter 13).

The impact of health and safety on the law relating to discipline and dismissal is of considerable practical significance. At common law employees are required to exercise reasonable care in the performance of their duties and to obey orders, unless doing so would lead to injury or disease. The reciprocal duty of care which is placed on employers includes the provision of safe systems of work. Moreover, there are statutory obligations which compel employers, either explicitly or implicitly, to control their employees' behaviour, for example, employers' duties under HSWA s.2. It follows that on occasions employers will be forced to take disciplinary action in order to perform their legal obligations and that employees will seek redress if they feel that they have been unfairly treated.

The law on unfair dismissal is discussed in Chapter 15. Some mention, however, must be made of its specific application to the field of health and safety. While not every breach of a statutory or common law duty by an employer will amount to a constructive dismissal,[37] employers have an obligation to act reasonably in dealing with safety matters.[38] Several of the potentially fair reasons for dismissal could be invoked in cases where health and safety feature, but perhaps the most frequently relied on are those related to the capability or conduct of the employee (Anderman, 1985:chs.4–6). As regards EPCA s.58(1)(b) – which makes unlawful dismissal for taking part in the activities of an independent trade union at an appropriate time – the EAT has decided that a distinction should be drawn between a trade union's activities to promote health and safety and those of an individual trade unionist.[39]

---

[36] EPCA s.19 (as amended). The relevant health and safety provisions are listed in EPCA Sch.1.

[37] *Graham Oxley Tool v Firth* [1980] IRLR 135.

[38] *British Aircraft Corporation v Austin* [1978] IRLR 332.

[39] *Chant v Aquaboats Ltd* [1978] ICR 643; cf. *Drew v St Edmundsbury Borough Council* [1980] IRLR 459. See further Chapter 2.

In applying the test of reasonableness under EPCA s.57(3), which is the crux of many unfair dismissal claims, tribunals can take into account a wide variety of factors. They include the content of the employer's rules and the way in which they were applied, the manner of investigating breaches and the possible alternatives to dismissal. Thus, even where detailed rules have been formulated and drawn to the attention of employees, a dismissal could still be unfair if a tribunal considers that it was based on the contravention of an unreasonable rule, for example, a requirement to use unsuitable safety equipment. Not only must the content of the rules be reasonable, but they must also be applied in a fair and consistent manner.[40] Finally, dismissal is usually regarded as the last resort among the options available to employers, and in handling disciplinary matters (including those arising from safety issues) they must ensure that the penalties imposed are reasonable in relation to the offences committed and the circumstances surrounding them.[41]

COMPENSATION

Injured employees may get compensation for occupational accidents and diseases through state benefits and civil actions in tort. So far as state benefits are concerned no question of blame arises, but in actions for damages the plaintiff must prove some degree of fault.

State Benefits

An employee who is incapable of work can claim statutory sick pay, and subsequently invalidity and disablement benefits. Traditionally, a distinction was maintained between industrial injury and sickness benefits, those suffering from industrial accidents or diseases receiving more favourable treatment than those afflicted by other causes. However, industrial injury benefit was abolished by the Social Security and Housing Benefits Act 1982. Since April 1983 the statutory sick pay scheme (as explained in more detail in Chapter 13) has provided benefits paid by employers for periods of incapacity for work. A person who is, or is deemed to be, incapable of work by reason of some specific disease or bodily or mental disablement can claim sickness benefit only if he or she has no entitlement to statutory sick pay or it has been exhausted.

Disablement benefit is regulated by the Social Security Act 1975. It is payable to an 'employed earner' who 'suffers personal injury caused by accident arising out of and in the course of employment' or where such a person suffers from a prescribed disease (ss.50, 76–8). Owing to the complex

[40] See *Taylor v Parsons Peebles Ltd* [1981] IRLR 119.
[41] On referring employees to the HSE as an alternative to dismissal, see *HSIB* 95, November 1983 (agreements in the West Yorkshire wool textile industry dealing with persistent failure to wear hearing protectors).

development of the law entitlement to benefit is by no means easy to establish, although there is a presumption that an injury in the course of employment arises out of that employment. Benefit is available where the claimant 'suffers as a result of the relevant accident from loss of physical or mental faculty' assessed at more than one per cent. Payments are calculated in accordance with a table of deemed percentage loss, for example, 30 per cent for loss of a foot.[42]

If the degree of disablement is assessed at less than 20 per cent benefit is paid in the form of a lump sum; if it is 20 per cent or greater it takes the form of a weekly pension. Since this benefit is not linked to income loss there could well be hardship where the claimant's earning capacity has been affected. Where the claimant is 'incapable of work and likely to remain so permanently', he or she may get unemployability supplement.[43] If the claimant is fit to do some work but 'incapable of following his regular occupation' or employment of an 'equivalent standard which is suitable in his case', he or she may be eligible for special hardship allowance to compensate for any continuing loss of earnings.[44] Finally, a flat rate benefit is available for those who have suffered 100 per cent disablement and require constant attendance, and if the need for attendance 'is likely to be permanent' an exceptionally severe disablement allowance may be paid.[45]

It has been observed that disablement benefit can be claimed only if it is shown that the personal injury was caused by an accident. In some occupations, however, workers risk the onset of certain diseases, and if a disease is contracted it may be ascribed to a 'process' rather than an 'accident'. As a result, the industrial injuries scheme deals separately with a number of specified diseases which are known to be caused by certain types of employment. Under the Social Security Act 1975 s.76(2), the Secretary of State may prescribe a disease if satisfied that it ought to be treated as a risk inherent in an occupation, and that in any particular case there will be reasonable certainty that the disease can be attributed to the nature of the employment. A disease may be prescribed for an occupation or for a type of work which is performed in a range of occupations. To obtain benefit people who suffer from a disease must demonstrate that it is prescribed for their particular occupation or for a general activity in which they engage as part of their job. It must also be shown that the disease was in fact caused by the performance of this particular occupation.[46] Major changes to the schedule

---

[42] See also the Social Security (Industrial Injury) (Benefit) Regulations 1975, Sch.1. In November 1985 a 100 per cent assessment for disablement benefit was worth £62.50 per week. Assessment of the degree of disability is by a medical board or medical appeal tribunal.

[43] This is at a flat rate £38.30 for a single person at November 1985, with increases which vary with the claimant's age and number of dependants.

[44] The maximum weekly figure was £25 in November 1985.

[45] The value of each allowance was £25 at November 1985. If an industrial accident turns out to be fatal, relatives may claim industrial death benefit.

[46] If the disease is prescribed for an occupation it is presumed to have been caused by it unless the adjudication officer proves the contrary: Social Security (Industrial Injuries) Prescribed Diseases Regulations SI 1980 No.377 reg.4(1).

of occupational diseases were implemented in 1983.[47] These fell short, however, of the proposal of the Industrial Injuries Advisory Council (1981) that the scheme should be extended to allow claims to be brought on a case by case basis where a disease was not listed in the schedule if it could be shown that, on the balance of probabilities, the disease was caused through the claimant's work.

The receipt of state benefits does not prevent a claimant from suing for damages, but if a successful action is brought the question arises as to how far the court should take into account the value of any benefits received. One view is that the benefits should be regarded as emanating from an insurance scheme and therefore should not be deducted.[48] The counter-argument stems from the fact that employers pay national insurance contributions and, if state benefits are not deducted, injured parties would receive double compensation. The current position is that in calculating damages, a court must take into account half of the sums that have accrued or may accrue to the injured plaintiff in respect of state benefits for a maximum of five years.[49]

Common Law Actions for Damages

Negligence. Employers have a duty of reasonable care towards their employees while they are in the course of employment. Although such a duty constitutes an implied term in all contracts of employment, for procedural reasons and because the basis of assessing damages is more favourable, it is normally advantageous to bring an action in tort rather than in contract. In essence liability for the tort of negligence depends on the absence of reasonable care to prevent reasonably foreseeable dangers. Foresight is judged in the light of the knowledge and experience possessed or reasonably expected at the time of the alleged negligence, the standard of care required changing with advances in scientific knowledge.[50] The duty of care involves balancing the risks against the precautions necessary to eliminate them. In assessing risks all the circumstances of the case are to be considered, including their seriousness and frequency as well as the vulnerabilities of the employee[51] and his or her particular knowledge, skill and experience.[52] In theory the employer's duty is simply one of reasonable care for the safety of his or her employees, although over the years this duty has been subdivided into: safe place of work,[53] safe system of work, safe tools

---

[47] Social Security (Industrial Injuries) (Prescribed Diseases) Amendment (No.2) Regulations SI 1983 No.1094.
[48] *Parry v Cleaver* [1970] AC 1.
[49] Law Reform (Personal Injuries) Act 1948 s.2 (as amended).
[50] See *Thompson v Smiths Shiprepairers Ltd* [1984] IRLR 93 on noise and damage to hearing.
[51] *Paris v Stepney Borough Council* [1951] AC 367.
[52] *Qualcast Ltd v Haynes* [1959] AC 743.
[53] This duty of care applies even where the employee is engaged in activities outside the employer's premises: *General Cleaning Contractors v Christmas* [1953] AC 180.

and equipment,[54] and safe fellow-workers.[55] While the common law duty appears similar to that imposed by HSWA s.2, different standards of care may be required in the different contexts.

In tort actions it is for the plaintiff to prove that the defendant's acts or omissions amounted to negligence and that this negligence was the cause of the injury. Where the injury results from the negligence of more than one person (joint tortfeasors), the Civil Liability (Contribution) Act 1978 enables the plaintiff to bring an action against any of the tortfeasors, leaving the defendant to seek a contribution from the others. Often it will be very difficult for the injured employee to ascertain how an accident occurred, and in certain exceptional cases, the courts will be prepared to infer from the circumstances of the injury a chain of facts leading to the conclusion that the defendant had been negligent. In two respects injured employees may be better placed than some other plaintiffs on the question of proof. First, HSWA s.28(9) provides that information obtained by a health and safety inspector may be released to an injured employee for the purpose of bringing a civil action. Second, the plaintiff may be able to demonstrate that the employer has failed to comply with the recommendations of an approved code of practice issued under the HSWA. Such codes are admissible in evidence in criminal proceedings (HSWA s.17), but there is no reason why a breach of a code should not also be admissible in civil proceedings.

Breach of statutory duty. An action for breach of statutory duty allows a person to sue for damages where the defendant's conduct which caused the injury contravened a duty imposed by statute. Since the statutory duty may be stricter and more precise than the common law duty of care, this independent tort is now of greater practical importance in the context of industrial injuries than an action for negligence. The statute upon which the action is based must, however, be one which supports civil liability.[56] Clearly it is desirable for Parliament to indicate whether statutes can be used as a basis for civil liability. HSWA s.47(2) states that a breach of duty imposed by regulations issued under the Act 'shall, so far as it causes damage, be actionable except in so far as the regulations provide otherwise'. HSWA s.47(1) provides that a contravention of ss.2–8 does not confer a right of action in any civil proceedings. Nevertheless, breaches of duty imposed by any previous legislation remain actionable.

Before damages can be recovered the plaintiff will have to prove a number of matters. First, that there was a breach of a statutory duty which had been imposed on the defendant.[57] Second, that the injury was caused by the defendant's breach of duty, a principle which may conflict with the promotion of positive safety provision. Liability may thus be avoided if an

---

[54] On liability for defective equipment supplied by third parties see the Employers' Liability (Defective Equipment) Act 1969 s.1.
[55] *Hudson v Ridge Manufacturing Ltd* [1957] 2 QB 348.
[56] The safety provisions of the Factories Act 1961 give rise to civil actions. On health and welfare provisions, see Fife and Machin (1982:3).
[57] For the duties of occupiers of premises see the Occupiers' Liability Acts 1957 and 1984.

employer who has failed to supply safety equipment demonstrates on the balance of probabilities that the employee would not have used it had it been provided.[58] Third, that the damage suffered was of a kind which the statutory provision was intended to prevent.[59]

Vicarious liability. The essence of this doctrine is that employers are held liable for the civil wrongs committed by their employees in the course of employment. As well as providing redress for third parties, this doctrine also enables a person to sue the employer if he or she is injured as a result of the tortious act of a fellow employee. Until it was abolished by the Law Reform (Personal Injuries) Act 1948, the concept of common employment deemed workers to have consented to the risk of negligence by other employees. Vicarious liability can be justified on the basis that the employer will normally have created the situation from which the injury arises, although liability is imposed without any necessary personal fault on the employer's part. A practical consequence of this doctrine is that while both employer and employee are liable in tort, it is the former who is likely to be sued. In theory, however, an employee may be required to reimburse the employer for any damages paid out as a result of his or her failure to take care.[60]

Determining what is 'in the course of employment' in this context has caused immense difficulties over the years but the present position may be summarised as follows. Employees act in the course of employment if they carry out an act which is authorised by the employer. In addition, employees are also deemed to be acting 'in the course of employment' where they carry out work which they have been appointed to do but they perform it in an unauthorised way. This is so despite the fact that they would not have been so authorised if the employer had known about it. An employer may be liable even though an employee performs an act which is expressly prohibited, so long as the act was a mode of doing what he or she was employed to do.[61]

Defences. The two main defences are *volenti non fit injuria* and contributory negligence. *Volenti* (the voluntary assumption of risk) is based on the principle that a plaintiff should not recover damages if a risk that he or she has agreed to take materialises. There must be both knowledge and acceptance of the likelihood of a tortious act (not merely of danger), however, and it would be unreal to hold that someone has accepted a risk simply because they have not left their job. Although still theoretically available, this defence will rarely succeed and, as a matter of principle, it cannot be applied in actions for breach of statutory duty by the employer, since its effect would be to permit an employee to contract out of protection provided by Parliament.[62]

---

[58] *McWilliams v Sir William Arrol Ltd* [1962] 1 WLR 295.
[59] *Close v Steel Co. of Wales* [1962] AC 367.
[60] *Lister v Romford Ice Co.* [1957] AC 555.
[61] *Rose v Plenty* [1976] All ER 97; *Harrison v Michelin Tyre Co. Ltd* [1985] 1 All ER 918.
[62] *Wheeler v New Merton Board Mills* [1933] 2 KB 669.

Prior to the Law Reform (Contributory Negligence) Act 1945 any degree of contributory negligence could totally defeat a plaintiff's claim. The Act states that where the plaintiff's fault and that of another contribute to the injury, damages must be reduced to 'such extent as the court thinks just and equitable having regard to the claimant's share in the responsibility for the damage'. For there to have been contributory negligence, the plaintiff must have shown a lack of reasonable care for his or her own safety. Nevertheless, owing to the stress of the work environment, the courts have been prepared to excuse a certain amount of inattention.[63] Clearly a breach of statutory duty by the employee can amount to contributory negligence, and HSWA ss.7–8 (see above) may be useful to employers in this respect. Finally, it has been held to be within the principle of contributory negligence that the plaintiff, while not helping to bring about the accident by his or her negligence, has contributed to the severity of the injury.[64] This is important because of the number of industrial injuries which are exacerbated by the failure to use safety equipment.

CONCLUSION

The law on health and safety could serve two basic functions. It could act positively by aiming to reduce the risk of accidents and illness, or negatively by merely compensating the victims. It is clear that the main function of the common law is not to prevent accidents but to provide reparation where losses have been incurred. Of course, one effect of the availability of damages may be that preventative measures are introduced, but generally the concentration on compensation has distracted attention from prevention.

Normally the compensation payable to employees is covered by insurance. Under the Employers' Liability (Compulsory Insurance) Act 1969, every employer carrying on a business must maintain an approved policy with authorised insurers covering bodily injury or disease of employees arising out of and in the course of their employment.[65] Theoretically the cost of insurance premiums could have a deterrent effect if the performance of individual employers was evaluated. But in practice these premiums, which are usually determined by the average experience in the relevant class of business, have come to be regarded as just another cost of production which may be passed on to the consumer (Atiyah, 1980:574).

Although much of the legislation prior to the HSWA was undoubtedly designed to advance safety, lawyers tended to approach it as if its primary purpose was to determine fault after an injury had been sustained. Over the years the concept of fault liability has been criticised on a number of

---

[63] *Caswell v Powell Duffryn Ltd* [1940] AC 142.
[64] *Froom v Butcher* [1975] 3 All ER 520.
[65] For exceptions, see s.3 and the Employers' Liability (Compulsory Insurance) Exemption Regulations SI 1971 No.1933.

grounds. Most fundamentally, the tort system is based on the cause of accidents rather than their consequences. Tort proceedings are also slow and expensive, and plaintiffs – many of whom will be ineligible for legal aid and will not have the support of a trade union – may have great difficulty proving fault. Moreover, the present system still fails to provide a remedy for the majority of those injured at work as only one in five work accident victims obtains damages (Harris et al., 1984:317).

No-fault liability systems have been introduced in other countries. In New Zealand the Accidents Compensation Act 1972 introduced state insurance for all injuries and prohibited actions in tort for personal injury caused by accident. But the Pearson Report (1978), which examined the issue of civil liability in this country, did not recommend the abolition of tort actions for personal injury or the imposition of strict liability.

Finally, there are the questions of how the post-1974 system of occupational health and safety has operated, and the extent to which it has been affected by the recession. For much of the period since the passing of the HSWA the trend in reported accidents has generally been downward, and it would seem that the Act may have served to increase the attention paid to health and safety in many workplaces (Daniel and Stilgoe, 1978). The HSE notes, however, that it has recently had to cope with a combination of staff cuts and the recession at a time when considerable extra responsibilities have been assumed. This has meant that minor hazards have been given less attention than they should during a period when the recession has affected employers' own health and safety priorities.[66] The Chief Inspector of Factories has similarly observed that many companies under financial pressure have cut their maintenance activities to the bone or dispensed with the services of safety specialists (HSE, 1984). He has also pointed to the lessening influence of trade unions and safety representatives, especially at the workplace level.

While it is accepted that accident statistics are not the only measure of safety performance, the provisional number of major injuries reported to the Factory Inspectorate in 1984 was 10,288 (HSE, 1985), confirming an increasing trend also discernible in 1982 and 1983. Furthermore, it would seem that the incidence of major and fatal injuries per 100,000 employees also increased during this period. Although it would be unfair to conclude on the basis of three years' statistics that there has been a change in the underlying pattern of safety, the latest figures suggest that it would be unwise to assume that the beneficial impact of the HSWA will be maintained in the immediate future.

[66] Press Notice, *HSE,* 2 October 1984.

Bibliography

Anderman, S.D. 1985. *The Law of Unfair Dismissal*. 2nd edn. London: Butterworths.

Atiyah, P.S. 1980. *Accidents, Compensation and the Law*. 3rd edn. London: Weidenfeld & Nicolson.

Atkinson, John. 1984. 'Manpower Strategies for Flexible Organisations'. *Personnel Management* (August), 28–31.

Barrett, Brenda. 1977. 'Safety Representatives, Industrial Relations and Hard Times'. *Industrial Law Journal*, 6 (September), 165–78.

——, Hilda Brown and Philip James. 1983. 'Achieving Health and Safety at Work: The Problem of Evaluating Management Effectiveness'. *Personnel Review*, 12 (2), 16–20.

——, and Philip James. 1981. 'How Real is Worker Involvement in Health and Safety?'. *Employee Relations*, 3 (4), 4–7.

Beaumont, P. 1983. *Safety at Work and the Unions*. London: Croom Helm.

Brown, W.A. (ed.) 1981. *The Changing Contours of British Industrial Relations: A Survey of Manufacturing Industry*. Oxford: Blackwell.

Carson, W.C. 1970. 'White-Collar Crime and the Enforcement of Factory Legislation'. *British Journal of Criminology*, 10 (October), 383–98.

Clegg, H.A. 1960. *A New Approach to Industrial Democracy*. Oxford: Blackwell.

Cressey, P., John Eldridge, John MacInnes and Geoffrey Norris. 1981. *Industrial Democracy and Participation: A Scottish Survey*. Research Paper no. 28. London: Department of Employment.

Daniel, W.W., and Elizabeth Stilgoe. 1978. *The Impact of Employment Protection Laws*. London: Policy Studies Institute.

——, and Neil Millward. 1983. *Workplace Industrial Relations in Britain: The DE/PSI/SSRC Survey*. London: Heinemann.

Davies, P., and Mark Freedland. 1984. *Labour Law: Text and Materials*. 2nd edn. London: Weidenfeld & Nicolson.

Dawson, Sandra, Philip Poynter and David Stevens. 1984. 'Is Your Safety Policy Adequate?'. *Health and Safety at Work* (August), 51–4.

Department of Employment (DE). 1981. 'Safety Appointed'. *Employment Gazette*, 89 (February), 55–8.

Derber, M. 1955. *Labor-Management Relations at the Plant Level under Industry-Wide Bargaining*. Chicago: University of Illinois, Institute of Labor and Industrial Relations.

Drake, Charles, and Frank Wright. 1983. *Law of Health and Safety at Work: The New Approach*. London: Sweet & Maxwell.

Employment Medical Advisory Service (EMAS). 1977. *Occupational Health Services: The Way Ahead*. London: HMSO.

Equal Opportunities Commission (EOC). 1979. *Health and Safety: Should we Distinguish between Men and Women?* Manchester: EOC.

Fife, Judge Ian, and E. Arthur Machin (eds.). 1982. *Redgrave's Health and Safety in Factories*. 24th edn. London: Butterworths.

Freedland, M. 1983. 'Leaflet Law: The Youth Training Scheme of 1983'. *Industrial Law Journal*, 12 (December), 220–35.

Glendon, A., and Richard Booth. 1982. 'Worker Participation in Occupational Health and Safety in Britain'. *International Labour Review*, 121 (July–August), 399–416.

Harris, Donald, Mavis Maclean, Hazel Genn, Sally Lloyd-Bostock, Paul Fenn, Peter Corfield and Yvonne Brittan. 1984. *Compensation and Support for Illness and Injury*. Oxford: Clarendon Press.

Health and Safety Commission (HSC). 1977. *Safety Representatives and Safety Committees*. London: HMSO.

——. 1983. *Professional Training and Qualifications in Occupational Health and Safety*. London: HSC.

——. 1984a. *Annual Report 1983–4*. London: HMSO.

——. 1984b. *Proposed Changes to Section 6 of the Health and Safety at Work etc. Act 1974*. London: HSC.

——. 1985. *Draft Proposals for Revising the Health and Safety (Enforcing Authority) Regulations 1977*. London: HMSO.

Health and Safety Executive (HSE). 1976. *Safety Officers: Sample Survey of Role and Functions*. London: HMSO.

——. 1979. *Health and Safety Statistics 1976*. London: HMSO.

——. 1980. *Effective Policies for Health and Safety*. London: HMSO.

——. 1984. *Manufacturing and Service Industries: 1983 Report*. London: HMSO.

——. 1985. *Manufacturing and Service Industries: 1984 Report*. London: HMSO.

Holgate, G. 1982. 'Union Policy in Appointing Safety Representatives'. *Employee Relations*, 4 (2), 28–32.

Howells, R. 1974. 'Worker Participation in Safety (1): The Development of Legal Rights'. *Industrial Law Journal*, 3 (June), 87–95.

Hutchins, B.L., and A. Harrison. 1966. *A History of Factory Legislation*. 3rd edn. London: Cass & Co.

Industrial Injuries Advisory Council. 1981. *Industrial Diseases: A Review of the Schedule and the Question of Individual Proof*. Cmnd 8393. London: HMSO.

Industrial Relations Services (IRS). 1983. *Guide to the Youth Training Scheme*. London: Eclipse Publications.

International Labour Organisation (ILO). 1982. *Report of the Tripartite Mission on the Effectiveness of Labour Inspection in the United Kingdom*. Geneva: ILO.

Labour Research Department (LRD). 1984. *Safety Reps in Action*. London: LRD.

Lewis, David B. 1974. 'Worker Participation in Safety (2): An Industrial Relations Approach'. *Industrial Law Journal*, 3 (June), 96–104.

Morgan, P., and N. Davies. 1981. 'Costs of Occupational Accidents and Diseases in Great Britain'. *Employment Gazette*, 89 (November), 477–85.

Office of the Minister without Portfolio (OMWP). 1985. *Lifting the Burden*. Cmnd 9571. London: HMSO.

Pearson. 1978. Royal Commission on Civil Liability and Compensation for Personal Injury. *Report*. Cmnd 7054. 3 vols. London: HMSO.

Phillips, J. 1976. 'Economic Deterrence and the Prevention of Industrial Accidents'. *Industrial Law Journal*, 5 (September), 148–63.

Robens. 1972. Department of Employment. Committee on Safety and Health at Work. *Report of the Committee 1970–72*. Cmnd 5034. 3 vols. London: HMSO.

Williams, J.L. 1960. *Accidents and Ill-Health at Work*. London: Staple Press.

Woolf, A. 1973. 'Robens Report: The Wrong Approach?'. *Industrial Law Journal*, 2 (June), 88–95.

17 Women and Minorities

Mary Redmond

This chapter is concerned with the law affecting discrimination in employment. Although many forms of discrimination are encountered – for example, discrimination on the basis of trade union membership and activities, disablement or chronic ill-health – this chapter is confined to discrimination in employment on two grounds: sex and race. Because of their structural similarity the Race Relations Act 1976 (RRA) and the Sex Discrimination Act 1975 (SDA) are considered together. The SDA applies to discrimination on the basis not only of sex but also marital status.[1] Equal pay forms another major part of the subject-matter; discussion ranges over the Equal Pay Act 1970 (EqPA) and the Equal Pay (Amendment) Regulations 1983 (EqPAR). The chapter then takes as a separate theme the strategic enforcement of anti-discrimination laws. It examines the Commission for Racial Equality (CRE) and the Equal Opportunities Commission (EOC), concentrating on their investigative powers. Throughout the chapter the importance of European law will be apparent. The influence of EC law on sex discrimination in employment and equal pay is increasing, affording rights more extensive than national law. Article 119 of the Treaty of Rome is binding on the UK. It lays down the principle of 'equal pay for equal work'. Article 1 of the EC Directive on Equal Pay[2] has amplified this to mean, 'for the same work or for work to which equal value is attributed, the elimination of all discrimination on grounds of sex with regard to all aspects and conditions of remuneration'. A second important EC Directive on Equal Treatment[3] concerns achieving equality generally in employment, training, promotion and working conditions.[4]

DISCRIMINATION IN THE LABOUR MARKET

It is useful to be aware of the context in which anti-discrimination laws operate. The *Labour Force Survey* (DE, 1981) provides information about

[1] Section 3. Discrimination against a single person on grounds of his or her status is not covered. Protection from victimisation is afforded under both Acts for persons who proceed under the SDA, EqPA or RRA (SDA s.4; RRA s.2).
[2] 75/117 OJ February 10, 1975, L45/19.
[3] 76/207 OJ February 9, 1976, L39/40.
[4] Chapter 20 deals with the enforcement of EC law in the United Kingdom. Maternity rights are dealt with in Chapter 13.

the composition of the labour force broken down by sex, economic status and ethnic origin. Immigrant and female labour in Britain is heavily concentrated in less desirable, non-skilled manual jobs. This effective stratification in the labour market points to the need for a far-reaching legal framework. The *Survey* (Table 4.24) examined the industrial distribution of the labour force by ethnic group. It found that different ethnic groups were clustered in certain divisions. West Indian men, for instance, were concentrated in 'metal goods, engineering and vehicles' and in 'transport and communication'. A high percentage of Indian, Bangladeshi and Pakistani men worked in 'distribution, hotels and catering, repairs' and 'other manufacturing'. The majority of West Indian or Guyanese women worked in 'other services', while nearly half of all Indian, Pakistani or Bangladeshi women worked in 'other services' or in 'other manufacturing'.

The *Labour Force Survey* (Table 4.25) also analysed the socio-economic groups of those in employment. Similar proportions of white and non-white persons were classified as skilled manual, but a higher proportion of white persons were in non-manual occupations. Among the non-white ethnic groups, far more Indian (35 per cent) were in non-manual occupations compared with West Indian or Guyanese men (13 per cent). A smaller proportion of non-white than white women were non-manual, though differences in distribution by ethnic group were found to be less pronounced for women.

Women workers are heavily concentrated in relatively few occupations and industries, often those where part-time labour is in high demand (Martin and Roberts, 1984; see further Chapter 18 below). Figures from the DE's *New Earnings Survey* show that this concentration in manual employment has been on the increase over the last decade. In 1983, for example, 60 per cent of female manual workers were employed in catering, cleaning, hairdressing or other personal service occupations. In 1975 the corresponding figure was 47 per cent. But in non-manual employment, the degree of concentration has lessened. Differences in occupational class can have far-reaching effects. There is a major difference in character, security, conditions and fringe benefits of work as between manual and non-manual grades. Most indices of work deprivation also correlate with low earnings (Townsend, 1979).

DISCRIMINATION IN EMPLOYMENT DUE TO RACE OR SEX

Equality before the law is traditionally regarded as a characteristic of the rule of law. But real equality must be sensitive to economic factors. Great substantive inequalities in legal protection are compatible with formal conditions of equality. This is not to diminish the importance of the principle of equality before the law, but to indicate its narrow limits. This principle must be distinguished from the right to be treated as an equal (Dworkin, 1977:227), a right which lies at the heart of anti-discrimination measures.

Judge-made common law has not generally been able to address the right to be treated as an equal. Freedom of contract was the prevailing legal

TABLE 17.1
SEGREGATED NATURE OF THE LABOUR FORCE

ETHNIC ORIGIN	MEN				WOMEN			
	Numbers of Economically Active (000s)	Numbers in Employment (000s)	Numbers Unemployed (000s)	Unemployment Rate/100 Economically Active	Numbers of Economically Active (000s)	Numbers in Employment (000s)	Numbers Unemployed (000s)	Unemployment Rate/100 Economically Active
White	14,758	13,325	1,434	9.7	9,799	8,945	854	8.7
Non-white	575	476	99	17.2	334	281	53	15.8
West Indian or Guyanese	150	120	31	20.6	126	107	18	14.5
African	14	13	2	11.0	10	9	1	10.3
Indian	205	174	32	15.4	113	93	20	17.7
Pakistani or Bangladeshi	87	69	18	20.4	13	10	2	19.0
Other	117	101	17	14.2	72	61	11	15.3
No reply	167	161	6	3.6	104	102	2	1.9
All ethnic origins	15,500	13,962	1,538	9.9	10,237	9,328	909	8.9

Source: Labour Force Survey, Table 4.22.

notion, a freedom which developed when discrimination had not yet been formulated as a legal problem. Judges never affirmed that acts of sexual or racial discrimination offended against public policy, notwithstanding the passage of legislation such as the Representation of the People Act 1918, which enfranchised all women over thirty who were householders, wives of householders, or university graduates, and the Sex Discrimination (Removal) Act 1919, still in force, under which, among other things, women were given a right of access to occupations previously closed to them.[5] Only in 'monopoly' and 'closed shop' situations did British judges step in to protect against discrimination.[6] Statutory intervention was necessary: nothing except legislative action could have dealt with the human right to be treated as an equal.

Direct Discrimination

The Acts outlaw direct and indirect discrimination. Direct discrimination is loosely defined in each (SDA, s.1(1)(a); RRA, s.1(1)(a)). It arises where an employee is treated 'less favourably' than a person of the opposite sex or of another racial group is or would be treated.[7] It took some time before judges grew accustomed to discrimination which was not structured on the traditional notion of overt prejudice.[8] An employee may complain against discriminatory conduct or, more significantly, against discriminatory assumptions where there has been no intention to discriminate. The legislation is concerned only with the factual and objective nature of an act, and with the effect of that act. Thus it is unlawful for an employer to treat a married woman worker on the assumption that her husband is the breadwinner,[9] or that she wishes to live with her husband.[10] Even if a group statistically possesses a particular characteristic, individuals will be regarded as discriminated against if assessed on the basis of that statistical prediction and not on their actual possession of that characteristic.

Discrimination involving separateness is also envisaged; there is provision for a notional comparator ('would be treated') in the definitional section of each Act. Under the SDA this could be invoked in favour of persons in

---

5   Although the Act was rarely invoked. It was directly in issue only in two cases over a span of 60 years: *Price v Rhondda UDC* [1928] 2 Ch 472 and *Nagle v Feilden* [1966] 2 QB 633.
6   *Nagle v Feilden* above; *Edwards v SOGAT* [1971] Ch 354. See further Chapter 2.
7   Contrast cl.1 of the Sex Equality Bill 1983 (HC Bill 1983–84 [18]) introduced by Jo Richardson MP which, although not comprising a statement as to rights, is a clear improvement on the existing text: 'the purpose of this Act is to redress and eliminate disadvantage based on sex, marital status and sexuality by improving the condition of those suffering such disadvantage; and the provisions which follow shall be construed accordingly.'
8   See *Peake v Automotive Products Ltd* [1978] QB 233; distinguished in *Greig v Community Industry* [1979] ICR 356. *Peake* was recanted from in *Ministry of Defence v Jeremiah* [1980] QB 87. See, too, *Din v Carrington Viyella Ltd* [1982] ICR 256.
9   *Coleman v Skyrail Oceanic Ltd* [1981] ICR 864.
10 *Horsey v Dyfed County Council* [1982] IRLR 385. See, analogously, *Phillips v Martin Marietta Corp.* (1971) 400 US 542, 3 FEP 40.

segregated employment, although difficult questions of proof would arise. Here, and throughout the SDA, discrimination is also proscribed if it is to a man's detriment.[11]

Indirect Discrimination

The proscription of indirect discrimination represents a landmark in British anti-discrimination legislation. The continuing absence of women and of minority groups from important areas of employment is due, in large measure, to indirect discrimination. This has become a major issue of social policy. Although it has also become an issue of legal policy, the translation from social concern to legal problem has not been entirely satisfactory.

The SDA and RRA employ a similar formula in relation to indirect discrimination. Section 1(1)(b) of the SDA proscribes discrimination against a woman where a person applies to her a requirement or condition which he applies or would apply equally to a man but

> (i) which is such that the proportion of women who can comply with it is considerably smaller than the proportion of men who can comply with it, and (ii) which he cannot show to be justifiable irrespective of the sex of the person to whom it is applied, and (iii) which is to her detriment because she cannot comply with it.

The RRA s.1(1)(b) refers to 'racial groups' rather than 'women' and an employer has to show the requirement or condition is 'justifiable irrespective of the colour, race, nationality or ethnic or national origins of the person to whom it is applied'.

The inspirational source for British legislation on indirect discrimination was American law. After the Civil Rights Act was passed in 1964 discrimination in the USA received new and more subtle meanings.[12] There were two particularly difficult categories of discrimination: the perpetuation in the present of the effects of past discrimination, and 'adverse impact', that is, acts which disproportionately affect minorities adversely. The new approach asked questions relating women and minority groups to the economic and political systems of the wider society.[13] Structural and institutional factors were taken into account such as personnel management policies, trade union rules, collective agreements, social conventions, and custom and practice.[14] The use of, for example, aptitude testing and language proficiency tests, or reliance on seniority or continuity in employment for determining redundancy and promotion was found to have a disproportionately adverse impact on women and minority workers. Different institutions and practices can serve as barriers to the economic advancement of either category. For instance, a

---

[11] SDA s.3(2). See *Peake* in note 8 above. References hereafter in the text to the treatment of women apply equally to the treatment of men.
[12] Rustin (1976); Rainwater and Yancey (1967). The process of change is well documented by McCrudden (1982).
[13] Zubaida (1972: 125); Pole (1978).
[14] This is the approach adopted, e.g. by Hepple (1971, 157–8).

'part-timers first' rule in redundancy is damaging to women workers, almost a third of whom work part-time.

In 1969 in an important American case a court declined to accept as a defence under the Civil Rights Act an employment standard which had the effect of locking victims of racial prejudice in an inferior position.[15] After this decision, discriminatory policies had to to give way unless there was a legitimate, business purpose which was non-racial or non-sexual. Judicial recognition of 'adverse impact' discrimination is generally traced to the Supreme Court case of *Griggs v Duke Power Co.*[16] The Court adopted the 'business necessity' test in order to determine whether criteria were lawful or unlawful. 'The touchstone is business necessity. If an employment practice which operates to exclude Negroes cannot be shown to be related to job performance the practice is prohibited.' Good intent did not 'redeem employment procedures or testing mechanisms that operate as "built-in head-winds" for minority groups and are unrelated to measuring job capability'.[17] Although the Court used 'job relatedness' and 'business necessity' as though they were synonymous, the two concepts are not interchangeable. Generally if the purpose of an employment policy or practice is successful job performance, 'job relatedness' is the only means of establishing 'business necessity'. Otherwise an employer's defence is likely to turn on the burden or benefit to the business. Because Britain turned to *Griggs* for its definition of indirect discrimination,[18] these uncertainties regarding an employer's defence are also found in British law.

The road to be travelled by a person alleging indirect discrimination is strewn with complexities.[19] Broadly, however, under the statutory definition of indirect discrimination three questions have to be faced by a complainant. First, does the employer have a requirement or condition[20] – for example, in respect of promotion – which he applies to, say, Pakistani and English workers? Second, if he has, is this requirement (it may be a language proficiency test) such that the proportion of Pakistanis who can comply with it is considerably smaller than the proportion of English workers who can comply? Third, is the person who is alleging detriment himself not able to pass the test? If the person complaining of discrimination has been able to establish these three things, a prima facie case exists. Then the employer (or whoever discrimination is alleged against) must show the requirement to be justifiable. If he does not, the claim will have been proven.

[15] *Local 189, Papermakers v US* (1968) F Supp 505 (DC Va 1968) and *Teamsters v US* (1977) 431 US 324, 346 n. 28, 14 FEP 1514, 1523.
[16] (1971) 401 US 424, 3 FEP 175.
[17] *Griggs*, note 16 at 431 and 432.
[18] There are, however, several differences: McCrudden (1982: 338, 345).
[19] See *Francis v BA Engineering Overhaul Ltd* [1982] IRLR 10; see too the rather misleading *Watches of Switzerland v Savell* [1983] IRLR 141.
[20] *Perera v Civil Service Commission* [1982] IRLR 147: condition or requirement cannot simply be a 'plus factor', it has to be a 'must factor', non-compliance with which means complete failure for an applicant/employee. See, too, *Home Office v Holmes* [1984] IRLR 299: requirement that women work full-time held to be unlawful discrimination in the circumstances.

The phrase 'can comply' occurs twice in the definition of indirect discrimination. It means 'can in practice' comply, not that a person can theoretically do so.[21] An employer may try to argue that an employee is not suitable because of the exercise of free choice, that is, the employee is disabled by reason of having chosen one course of action rather than another. The employer's defence of free choice is rebutted if there has been a lack of awareness on the complainant's part as to the implications of his or her individual choice.[22] The relevant point of time to establish an applicant's ability or inability to comply with a requirement or condition is the date on which the allegation as to detriment is made. It is unlawful to select part-timers first for redundancy and the EAT has held that past opportunities to comply in the sense of past opportunities to become a full-time worker are irrelevant.[23]

A claimant alleging indirect discrimination must establish that he has been adversely affected personally by the practice or rule he is challenging. Most often this requirement presents no difficulty: detriment is self-evident.[24] The racially or sexually discriminatory conduct must be the activating cause of the detriment. An employer cannot disclaim liability for the unlawful discriminatory behaviour of an employee just because the detriment flowing from that unlawful conduct involved a step taken by another, innocent employee.[25] But he will be absolved from liability if the behaviour forming the subject matter of a complaint is too remote from the allegedly unlawful act.[26]

Case law on the employer's defence of 'justifiability' is, as yet, unsatisfactory. In part it reflects *Griggs*. In part it suggests industrial tribunals are taking a very broad approach, not limiting themselves to, still less defining or distinguishing between, factors such as 'business necessity' and 'job relatedness'. In the mid-1970s Parliament deliberately eschewed a defence involving 'necessity', in the main so as not to upset seniority systems long established in British industrial relations. But Phillips J, following the reasoning in *Griggs*, espoused this criterion in the most important EAT analysis of an employer's defence under the SDA, *Steel v UPW*:[27]

---

[21] *Price v Civil Service Commission* [1978] ICR 27: requirement that job applicants be under 28 years likely to be indirectly discriminatory because of usual child-bearing pattern of women of that age; *Home Office v Holmes* (note 20 above). See too Chapter 13, text to notes 34–5.

[22] *Bohon-Mitchell v Council of Legal Education* [1978] IRLR 525.

[23] *Clarke v Eley (IMI) Kynock Ltd* [1983] ICR 165. The EAT made it clear however that whereas redundancy criteria for selecting part-timers first will be regarded as unjustifiable, a standard of 'last in, first out' should be viewed as justifiable, even if indirectly discriminatory. But see *Kidd v DRG* [1985] IRLR 190.

[24] *Bayoomi v British Railways Board* [1981] IRLR 431; *BL Cars Ltd v Brown* [1983] IRLR 193. *Watches of Switzerland* note 19 above may be regarded as a bad decision in relation to 'detriment'.

[25] *Seide v Gillette Industries Ltd* [1980] IRLR 427; *Din v Carrington Viyella Ltd* [1982] IRLR 281.

[26] *Kingston v British Railways Board* [1982] IRLR 274.

[27] [1978] ICR 181, 187–8.

First, the onus of proof lies upon the party asserting [justifiability]. Secondly it is a heavy onus[28] in the sense that at the end of the day the industrial tribunal must be satisfied that the case is a genuine one where it can be said that the requirement or condition is necessary. Thirdly, in deciding whether the employer has discharged the onus the industrial tribunal should take into account all the circumstances, including the discriminatory effect of the requirement or condition if it is permitted to continue. Fourthly, it is necessary to weigh the need for the requirement or condition against that effect. Fifthly, it is right to distinguish between a requirement or condition which is necessary and one which is merely convenient, and for this purpose it is relevant to consider whether the employer can find some other and non-discriminatory method of achieving his object.

Later decisions suggest that the standards set out in *Steel* have been relaxed.[29] Considerably more weight has been given to managerial prerogative, and the EAT has shown itself willing to consider matters other than those relating to the broad needs of the business enterprise. Yet it is always proper to ask whether a particular condition or requirement can be validated. The complainants in *Ojutiku and Oburoni v Manpower Services Commission*[30] challenged the defendant's selection process for training sponsorship. Among the criteria applied by the Commission was the requirement that applicants should already have had experience in a post of commercial, administrative, professional or industrial responsibility. Because the complainants lacked such experience they were unable to secure sponsorship for the course they wished to pursue. They failed in their claim. The Court of Appeal declared the standard applicable to the test of justifiability to be 'lower than business necessity'.[31]

Although at first sight this is sweeping, the scope of the decision can be restricted. The material facts in *Ojutiku* concerned selection processes for sponsorship by a non-employer body for training, not selection processes for training or employment by an actual employer. None the less, as an indication of the judicial attitude to anti-discrimination legislation, the case is significant. According to Eveleigh LJ, if a person produces reasons for doing something which would be 'acceptable to right-thinking people as sound and tolerable reasons for so doing', he has justified his conduct.[32] Although a purely subjective approach is rejected, the standard of objectivity is far from clear. Does it mean that where, for example, an employer requires educational qualifications which have a disparate impact on women or minority workers, it is sufficient for the employer to argue in his defence

28 This must be read in the light of *Vulcan Ltd v Wade* [1978] ICR 800: onus is on balance of probabilities, as in other civil cases.
29 E.g. *Singh v Rowntree Mackintosh Ltd* [1979] ICR 554; *Panesar v Nestlé Co.* [1980] IRLR 60. Contrast *Hurley v Mustoe* [1981] ICR 490 and *Chiu v British Aerospace Plc* [1982] IRLR 56 which adhered to *Steel*.
30 [1982] IRLR 418.
31 ibid., at 422 (per Kerr LJ). In a later case, *Clarke v Eley* (note 23 above, at 174) the President of the EAT acknowledged that the view expressed in *Ojutiku* must be taken to have overturned Phillip J's definition of 'justifiability' in terms of necessity, and expressed some apprehension as to the direction in which the decisions of the courts were going on this issue.
32 Note 30 above, at 421.

that common sense and the views of most people are in favour of the most education a person can have? Stephenson LJ, rejecting a test of employer's convenience as a possible basis for justifiability, employed a standard requiring the party applying the discriminatory condition to prove it to be justifiable 'in all the circumstances' by balancing its discriminatory effect against the discriminator's reasonable need for it.

In another case which concerned discrimination in education rather than employment, the House of Lords declared that the condition which the alleged discriminator seeks to apply must be 'in all circumstances justifiable'.[33] Lord Fraser indicated that 'justifiable', in his view, meant less than 'necessary'.[34] As Davies and Freedland (1984:57) aptly put it, 'the courts have ... travelled quite a long way from the notion of justification as consisting in independently validated job relatedness, which may be regarded as describing the pure milk of the doctrine as it originally developed in United States case law'.

Difficulties of proof beset both parties in cases of alleged indirect discrimination (Lustgarten, 1980:213). The Acts envisage group rather than individual disputes. In all but the most straightforward cases, statistics on group patterns are of vital relevance, whether or not British courts and tribunals actually welcome such evidence.[35] In the USA, since *Griggs*, statistics have played a crucial role (see Schlei and Grossman, 1983). The principal statistical comparisons used to establish a prima facie case of employment discrimination are generally concerned with 'pass/fail' and 'population/workforce' comparisons. The former compare the percentage of the protected group (based on sex or race) who pass a given test, or satisfy a requirement or condition laid down by the employer, with the success rate for the majority group (for example, whites, males or white males). Population/workforce statistics compare the availability of the protected group in the general population or labour force in a relevant geographic area with the percentage of that protected group in an employer's workforce or section thereof.

A practical difficulty in Britain is the unavailability of precise and accurate data. British employers, unlike their American counterparts, are not required to collect statistics regarding the racial composition of their workforce. In 1983 the CRE (1983:7, 14) recommended mandatory record keeping for employers. Some information about women in employment may be gained from the Census of Population, but the classifications are in the main too broad to provide the sort of finely tuned statistics required for litigation. Unless the availability of more precise statistical information becomes a priority, claimants seeking redress for alleged indirect discrimination may face an almost insurmountable hurdle, above all where the discrimination being challenged concerns sub-groups within a group.

---

[33] *Mandla v Dowell-Lee* [1983] ICR 385, at 394.
[34] ibid.
[35] In general statistical evidence has not been welcome, see e.g. *Fletcher v Clay Cross (Quarry Services) Ltd* [1979] ICR 1, at 8; *Perera*, note 20 above, at 148. For the common sense approach which is more prevalent, see *Holmes*, note 20 above.

Eligibility to Claim

SDA. 'Sex' is not defined in the SDA although 'women' are defined in terms of 'females of any age' and 'men' as 'males of any age'.[36] Unlike the EqPA there are several exceptions to the operation of the SDA relating either to the nature of the job, its requirements or the character of the employment relationship. 'Special cases' in ss.17–21 exclude liability for discrimination in respect of the police force, prison officers, organised religions and mine workers. Midwives used to be excluded but restrictions on the training and employment of men as midwives were lifted with effect from September 1983.[37] In November 1983 the European Court of Justice (ECJ) ruled that the exception for private households and small employers (five or fewer employees) in the SDA s.6(3) was contrary to the EC Directive on Equal Treatment,[38] although the Court accepted that there may be some kind of employment in a private household which could come within the general exemption in the Directive.[39] The Court also held that the Directive covers all collective agreements, internal rules and rules governing independent professions, whether these are legally binding or not, because of the far reaching de facto consequences for employees. The Court directed that UK legislation should therefore provide for the removal of unlawful discrimination in such collective agreements and rules. Draft legislation is awaited. Other exclusions are found in s.43 (charities) and in s.51 (acts done under statutory authority)[40] and s.52 (acts safeguarding national security). The exclusion in s.51 is designed to avoid a clash between the Act and such provisions as are found in, for example, the Factories Act 1961 (restriction on night working for women) and associated legislation concerning hours of work, health and safety, and so on (cf. EOC, 1979).[40a]

Section 6(4) declares that some of the main protections for employees 'do not apply to provision in relation to death or retirement'. A similar exclusion is found in the EqPA (see below). In both Acts the exclusion is loosely phrased. This has enabled courts and tribunals to cast the net very widely.[41] In supporting individual complaints at law the EOC has sought to limit the application of the exemption for provisions relating to death or retirement. Where cases have proceeded to the ECJ, concern has additionally been focused on the extent to which the European Directives are deemed to be

---

[36] SDA s.82(1). See *White v British Sugar Corporation* [1977] IRLR 121.
[37] Sex Discrimination (Amendment of s.20) Order SI 1983 No. 1202.
[38] *Commission of the EC v United Kingdom* [1984] IRLR 29.
[39] At 33.
[40] See *Page v Freight Hire (Tank Haulage) Ltd* [1981] IRLR 13; and *Hugh-Jones v St John's College* [1979] ICR 848.
[40a] The government has recently proposed to remove restrictions on women's bonus (OMWP, 1985), and to repeal the small firms' exemption in the SDA as well as making discriminatory terms in collective agreements void (DE, 1985).
[41] *Roberts v Cleveland Area Health Authority* [1979] ICR 558; *Garland v British Rail Engineering*, note 42 below; *MacGregor Wallcoverings v Turton* [1979] ICR 558; *Southampton and SW Hamps Health Authority v Marshall* [1983] IRLR 237.

directly applicable in Member States.[42] The subject of women's entitlement under state and occupational pensions is more fully discussed in Chapter 14.

RRA. The RRA s.1 proscribes discrimination on 'racial grounds', that is, 'colour, race, nationality or ethnic or national origins'. The unlawful grounds have deliberately been expressed in imprecise words, intended to refer to unfair and sometimes prejudiced behaviour rather than to divide people into racial groups. It is impossible to classify people on the basis of 'colour'; similarly, contrary to popular belief, 'race' is not an objective scientific term, and 'national origins' does not provide a precise definition of a person's legal status in terms of his nationality and citizenship.[43] 'Ethnic origins' is not the same as 'ethnicity'.

In *Mandla v Dowell-Lee*[44] the House of Lords considered the meaning of 'ethnic'. In holding that Sikhs were protected by the RRA the Lords laid down a check-list to determine whether a particular group is a 'racial group'. The essential factors are a long shared history and a cultural tradition. In addition some of the following are likely to be present: a common geographical origin or descent from a small number of common ancestors; a common language; a common literature; a common religion; and being either a minority or a majority within a larger community. The Lords further held that a person is a member of such a group if he considers himself a member of it and is accepted by others as a member.[45] Although unfavourable treatment of a socially distinct minority, whose distinctiveness includes religion, constitutes unlawful discrimination on grounds of ethnic origin (Lester and Bindman, 1972:157), it cannot be affirmed that the Act applies where the victim's religion is the direct cause of the discrimination or where the exclusion follows from the sectarian character of a particular institution. It is still an open question whether in such cases the Act protects members of, for example, the Jewish faith (Williams, 1981).

Unlike the position under its forerunner, the Race Relations Act 1968, there are few exceptions to the Act of 1976. The Act does not apply to employment for the purposes of a private household (s.4(3)), nor to charities (s.34). If an employer acts in pursuance of an enactment, order or instrument, he has a defence (s.41(1)). Discrimination on grounds of nationality, or ordinary residence, or the length of time for which a person has been resident in the UK is not proscribed if the act is done under arrangements made by or with the approval of a Minister or in order to comply with a condition imposed by a Minister (s.41(2)). Discrimination under civil service rules which restrict Crown employment on grounds of birth, nationality, descent or residence are not outlawed (s.75(5)), nor are acts done to safeguard national security (s.42).

---

[42]   *Garland v British Rail Engineering* [1982] IRLR 111; *Burton v British Railways Board* [1982] IRLR 116. In general, see Ellis and Morrell (1982).

[43]   Discrimination against nationals of the EC is unlawful by virtue of Art. 48 of the Treaty of Rome and the implementing Reg. 1612/68, OJ 1968 L257/2.

[44]   [1983] ICR 385.

[45]   *ibid.*, at 390 (per Lord Fraser).

Scope of the Acts

Acts of racial or sexual discrimination usually do not spring up in isolation. They are typically one knot in a tangle of bad employment practices. The SDA (s.6) and the RRA (s.4) make it unlawful for a person, in relation to employment by him at an establishment in Great Britain, to discriminate, on the grounds of sex or race, against applicants in selection arrangements and job offers, and against those employed in access to promotion, transfer or training or as regards any other benefits, facilities or services, and by dismissal or subjection to any other detriment. 'Dismissal' here covers termination of employment whether voluntary or involuntary. In practice, involuntary dismissals or redundancies are more likely to be challenged as being unlawfully discriminatory as well as unfair.

The Acts place primary liability on the employer, although 'anything done by a person in the course of his employment' is to be treated as done by his employer as well as by him, whether or not it was done with the employer's knowledge or approval.[46] The Acts apply to employees in the strict sense and to those who work under contracts for services.[47] Also covered are 'contract workers', that is, employees who work for persons (principals) who are not in law their employers.[48] The Acts also apply to partnerships of six or more partners,[49] to organisations of workers or of employers and to professional and trade associations,[50] as well as to bodies which can confer an authorisation or qualification needed for or facilitating engagement in a particular trade or profession.[51] They outlaw discrimination by vocational training bodies,[52] employment agencies,[53] and the Manpower Services Commision.[54] The SDA and the RRA apply to the Crown in the same way as to any other employer.

The law against discrimination in selection for employment is indirectly strengthened by sections in the legislation which make it unlawful to publish a discriminatory job advertisement,[55] for example, seeking a 'craftsman', 'handyman' or 'manageress'. Only the EOC or the CRE may bring proceedings against the publisher or advertiser. An individual may, however, have a remedy in respect of discriminatory advertising even though he cannot initiate proceedings himself.[56]

Workplace sexism may be said to constitute a recognisable 'detriment', capable of destroying trust and confidence in the employment relationship

[46] SDA s.41; RRA s.32. *CRE v Imperial Society of Teachers of Dancing* [1983] IRLR 315. The employer may safeguard himself by taking such steps as are reasonably practicable to prevent the employee from doing an unlawful act.
[47] SDA s.82(1); RRA s.78.
[48] SDA s.9; RRA s.7. *Rice v Fon-a-Car* [1980] ICR 133.
[49] SDA s.11; RRA s.10.
[50] SDA s.12; RRA s.11.
[51] SDA s.13; RRA s.12. *British Judo Association v Petty* [1981] IRLR 484.
[52] SDA s.14; RRA s.13.
[53] SDA s.15; RRA s.14.
[54] SDA s.16; RRA s.15.
[55] SDA s.38; RRA s.29.
[56] *Brindley v Tayside Health Board* [1976] IRLR 364.

and so amounting to a repudiatory breach of the contract of employment.[57] Proof of employees' detriment will generally reside in the persons concerned either being treated adversely or being given to believe they will if they do not yield to some form of sexual relationship (Rideout, 1983:337).

A comparison of the cases of persons of different sex or racial group must be such 'that the relevant circumstances in the one case are the same, or not materially different, in the other' (SDA s.5(3); RRA s.3(4)). The comparable man in a case of alleged unlawful sex discrimination may have to be taken to be married if the complainant is also married, thus coming within a sub-class of the protected group. But under the SDA s.2(2) no account may be taken of special treatment afforded to women in connection with pregnancy or childbirth. A majority of the EAT has held that a woman with child has no masculine equivalent and hence that it is not unlawful under the SDA to dismiss her because she is pregnant.[58]

Affirmative Action

Even if employment discrimination were to stop overnight this would not be sufficient to enable women and ethnic minorities to compete for jobs from a basis of genuine equality. They would still suffer from the effects of past discrimination and disadvantage. Affirmative action is only a means to an end, a means which recognises temporary and limited exceptions in favour of members of disadvantaged groups. There is perhaps no other aspect of employment law that so brings tensions into focus as affirmative action or, as it is often inaptly styled, 'reverse discrimination'. The best known American cases in recent years have been in this specific area.[59]

Nothing in the British legislation requires 'reverse discrimination' in favour of women or of minorities. But provision is made for exceptional situations in which special treatment may be given to members of a particular racial group or sex. The SDA allows discriminatory training for members of one sex by certain training bodies (s.47), by employers, and by trade unions and similar organisations (s.48) where, during the preceding twelve months, no persons of that sex were doing the job in question or their number was comparatively small. Trade unions and similar organisations may reserve seats on elective bodies for members of one sex (s.49). Discriminatory training may be offered by training bodies to those who have been discharging domestic or family responsibilities in order to equip them for employment (s.47(3)). The RRA permits affirmative action in providing for the special needs of particular racial groups in regard to education, training and welfare (ss.35, 37–8). Discriminatory education and training is also allowed for persons not ordinarily resident in Great Britain who intend

57 *Western Excavating (ECC) Ltd v Sharp* [1978] ICR 221, at 229 (per Lawton LJ), see Rubenstein (1983). A potentially important case is *Porcelli v Strathclyde Regional Council* [1984] IRLR 467.

58 *Turley v Allders Department Stores Ltd* [1980] ICR 66. But see now *Hayes v Malleable Working Men's Club* [1985] IRLR 367.

59 *Regents of the University of California v Bakke* (1978) 438 US 265; *United Steelworkers of America v Weber* (1979) 443 US 193; *Fullilove v Klutznick* (1980) 448 US 448. See Dworkin (1977: 223–39); McKean (1983: 243).

to leave at the end of the period of education or training (s.36). Trade unions or similar organisations may give discriminatory training for posts in the organisation or do any act to encourage persons of a particular racial group to join the organisation. The Acts retain the prohibition on giving preference at the stage of selection for employment or promotion, that is, permitted discrimination is confined to the stages leading up to selection. But the consequences of affirmative action at this juncture should not be underestimated: the practical effect of recruiting additional female or minority trainees may be to give them preference also in recruitment, assuming there are sufficient vacancies upon completion of their training.

In December 1984 the EC Council adopted a Recommendation on the promotion of positive action for women.[60] Member states are recommended, among other things, to adopt a positive action policy designed to eliminate existing inequalities affecting women in working life and to promote a better balance between the sexes in employment.

Genuine Occupational Qualification

Both the SDA s.7 and the RRA s.5 list circumstances where being a member of one sex or belonging to a particular racial group is a 'genuine occupational qualification' (GOQ). Along with the provisions concerning affirmative action these form an important part of the Acts' remedial structure. The list of circumstances constituting a GOQ is considerably longer in the SDA than in the RRA. Examples in the former are where the essential nature of the job calls for a person of one sex for reasons of authenticity in dramatic performance or other entertainment, or to preserve decency or privacy, or where the job is to be performed outside the UK in a country whose laws and customs preclude a member of that sex from performing those duties. Certain hospital and prison staff are also covered. Examples in the RRA include personal welfare counsellors and jobs involving 'working in a place where food or drink is (for payment or not) provided to and consumed by members of the public or a section of the public in a special ambience for which, in that job, a person of that racial group is required for reasons of authenticity'. There is evidence that the EAT is prepared to stretch the language of the Act in favour of protected groups.[61]

The statutory GOQ defence and the defence of justifiability to an allegation of indirect discrimination must be distinguished. Illustrating this by reference to the SDA, the former arises only where an employer takes adverse action against or excludes a person because of sex, for example, a rule that no females may work in a prison for men. An employer must be able to show that it is a GOQ. In contrast the defence of 'business necessity' comes into play where an employer has a criterion for work that is on the face of it neutral but excludes members of one sex at a higher rate than members of the other, thus creating an adverse impact. The focus of an employer's defence would not be upon the legitimacy of an assigned

---

[60] OJ L331, 19 December 1984.
[61] *Timex Corporation v Hodgson* [1981] IRLR 530. See too *Jeremiah*, note 8; *White*, note 36.

stereotype but upon the validity of the stated job 'qualification' and its relationship to the work performed. Where a GOQ is established an employer may refuse to consider all persons of the protected group. Where a 'business necessity' defence is established an employer may exclude all persons who cannot meet the criterion regardless of whether the criterion has an adverse impact on a particular protected group.

Burden of Proof

Under the RRA and SDA the burden of proof lies on the claimant as in civil proceedings at common law, that is, on the balance of probabilities. He who alleges must prove. This is in contrast to unfair dismissal and to redundancy law (see Chapter 15 above) and can operate to the severe disadvantage of complainants. Both Acts attempt to offset this imbalance by enabling the complainant to obtain information in order to decide whether to institute proceedings and, if he decides to do so, to formulate and present the case most effectively (SDA s.74; RRA s.65). The procedure is a novel one. The complainant may submit questions to the respondent on a prescribed form.[62] Although the latter is not obliged to reply, the tribunal is entitled to draw an inference that unlawful discrimination has occurred if the respondent fails to reply or is evasive or equivocal.[63] In other words, an employer may find himself obliged to answer questions which may affect him adversely from a legal point of view before proceedings have begun. In practice this special form procedure has been ineffectual.

Industrial tribunals are not unsympathetic to the plight of complainants. Only in exceptional or frivolous cases, according to the EAT, would it be right for an industrial tribunal to find at the end of an applicant's presentation that there was no case to answer.[64] Once it is shown that there is a prima facie case of discrimination, it is generally sufficient to shift the evidential burden and it is then for the employer to produce evidence that discrimination is not unlawful.[65] Furthermore, the tribunal should look at the evidence as a whole and decide whether the case has been established, taking into account the fact that direct evidence of discrimination is seldom available and that affirmative evidence normally consists of inferences to be drawn from the primary facts.[66] Where the primary facts indicate discrimination, in the absence of a satisfactory explanation, discrimination should be found. Where relevant, evidence may be admitted of events subsequent to the alleged act of discrimination, whether the act was overtly discriminatory or

---

62　Sex Discrimination (Questions and Replies) Order SI 1975 No. 2048 as amended by SI 1977 No. 884; Race Relations (Questions and Replies) Order SI 1977 No. 842. *Oxford v Department of Health and Social Security* [1977] IRLR 225.

63　*Virdee v ECC Quarries Ltd* [1978] IRLR 295.

64　*Humphreys v Board of Managers of St George's C of E Primary School* [1978] ICR 546. See Bindman (1980).

65　*Wallace v SE Education and Library Board* [1980] IRLR 193, NI Court of Appeal; *Conway v Queen's University of Belfast* [1981] IRLR 137 (same). This approach is directly parallel to the standards developed by the US Supreme Court in cases stemming from *McDonnell Douglas Corp. v Green* (1973) 411 US 792.

66　*Khanna v Ministry of Defence* [1981] IRLR 331.

not.[67] Likewise discrimination which took place before the Acts came into force or before the relevant time within which a complaint must be filed, although not actionable, may be taken into account in determining whether there has been discriminatory conduct within the relevant period.[68] Once proceedings have commenced a power arises to obtain information by an application for discovery and inspection of documents.[69] The EAT took a fairly liberal view of the power to order disclosure in early cases, a trend confirmed by the House of Lords in *Science Research Council v Nassé*.[70] The House confirmed the wide discretion of industrial tribunals to order disclosure, subject to suitable safeguards where this is necessary for disposing fairly of the case and for saving costs. The fact that documents are confidential is irrelevant. In a complaint of unlawful discrimination the EAT may, on an appeal concerning discovery and inspection of documents, review the industrial tribunal's exercise of discretion and substitute its own view.[71]

Remedies for Individual Complainants

Both the SDA and the RRA accept that the victim of unlawful discrimination should be entitled to obtain a remedy in his or her own right before an industrial tribunal. The EOC or CRE may assist a complainant, for example, by giving advice or arranging representation. When exercising discretion in the matter, the relevant Commission must consider whether the case raises a question of principle, or is complex, and must have regard to the claimant's position and any other special considerations.[72] In employment discrimination cases, a copy of every complaint is sent to ACAS. An officer of ACAS may attempt to 'conciliate'. There is provision for a conciliation officer to attempt conciliation before a complaint is made to a tribunal in the same way as when a complaint has been made.[73]

The Acts require that a complaint be presented to an industrial tribunal within three months of the act complained of, subject to a discretion, vested in the industrial tribunal, to hear an out-of-time complaint where 'in all the circumstances of the case it considers that it is just and equitable to do so'.[74] The practice in sex discrimination cases is to ensure that the tribunal consists of men and women members. In race discrimination cases, wherever possible, at least one of the lay members will have been appointed because of his special knowledge or experience of race relations though there is no statutory requirement to that effect. Basing itself on natural justice principles, the EAT has declared that if the facts relied on for believing that a

---

[67] *Chattopadhay v Headmaster of Holloway School* [1981] IRLR 487.
[68] *Eke v Commissioners of Customs and Excise* [1981] IRLR 334.
[69] Industrial Tribunals (Rules of Procedure) Regulations SI 1985 No. 16.
[70] [1979] ICR 921.
[71] *British Library v Palyza* [1984] IRLR 306.
[72] SDA s.75; RRA s.66.
[73] SDA s.64(2); RRA s.55(2).
[74] SDA s.76; RRA s.68. *Hutchison v Westward TV Ltd* [1977] IRLR 69.

tribunal member has special knowledge are capable of being shown to be wholly inaccurate, the Divisional Court or the EAT might interfere.[75]

The SDA and the RRA aim to provide compensation for the victim and future change. The first unsophisticated attempts to provide a remedy for unlawful discrimination appeared in the Race Relations Act 1968. The model of the Race Relations Board, which alone had the power to investigate complaints and, where conciliation failed, to bring civil proceedings, was unsatisfactory. Now an industrial tribunal, upon upholding a complaint by an individual of unlawful discrimination, is empowered 'as it considers just and equitable' to do one or more of the following: make an order declaring the rights of the parties, award compensation, or recommend that the respondent take within a specified period action appearing to the tribunal to be practicable for the purpose of obviating or reducing the adverse effect on the complainant of the act of discrimination.[76]

The amount of compensation awarded may not exceed the maximum compensatory award for the time being prescribed for unfair dismissal under the EPCA. The tribunal must award damages on the principles of tortious liability,[77] though, for the avoidance of doubt, both Acts stipulate that damages may include compensation for injury to feelings.[78] The EAT has held that compensation under this head should be moderate, calculated in accordance with the guidance given in defamation cases.[79] An indication of the low level of tribunal awards for unlawful discrimination is given in Chapter 19.

Recommendations are not specifically enforceable. If a recommendation is not complied with and if non-compliance is 'without reasonable justification', an industrial tribunal may make an order of compensation or increase an existing order of compensation subject to the maximum compensatory award.[80] An upper limit on compensation could originally be justified on the basis that it was desirable to standardise employment legislation. Following the 'closed shop' scale of compensation introduced by EA 1982, however, this justification can no longer apply.

Considering that the Acts stress monetary compensation rather than the remedies of reinstatement or re-engagement, it is unfortunate that, in relation to claims of indirect discrimination, they provide that no award of damages shall be made if the respondent proves that the requirement or condition impugned was not applied with the intention of discriminating. Likewise, where a recommendation for remedial action in a case involving indirect discrimination has not been complied with, no award of compensation can be made in the absence of an intention to discriminate.[81]

---

75 *Habib v Elkington & Co. Ltd* [1981] IRLR 344.
76 SDA s.65; RRA s.56. *Irvine v Prestcold Ltd* [1981] IRLR 281; *Price v Civil Service Commission (No.2)* [1978] IRLR 3; *Eke* note 68 above.
77 SDA s.66(1); RRA s.57. Because of this rule, the Law Reform (Contributory Negligence) Act 1945 apparently applies.
78 SDA s.66(4); RRA s.57(4).
79 *Skyrail Oceanic Ltd v Coleman* [1980] ICR 596, at 601.
80 SDA s.65(3); RRA s.56(3).
81 SDA s.66(3); RRA s.57(3). *Bayoomi v British Railways Board* [1981] IRLR 431.

Provided he has the requisite continuity of service, a complainant alleging unlawful discriminatory dismissal is more likely to proceed under the separate unfair dismissal provisions of the EPCA than under the SDA or RRA. The two main advantages to so doing are that the EPCA places the burden of proving the reason for dismissal on the employer and that the level of compensation may be higher. Although infrequently awarded in practice, a further advantage is that reinstatement or re-engagement may be ordered under the EPCA. Section 76 of the EPCA prohibits a double or, as appropriate, a treble award in respect of any 'loss or other matter' if compensation is awarded under its provisions as well as those of the SDA and RRA. Compensation awarded under any two or, as the case may be, three Acts is subject to the maximum for the time being in respect of unfair dismissal. However, if an order of reinstatement or re-engagement is not implemented, then unless the employer shows it was not practicable to comply, the tribunal must award compensation in the ordinary way plus an *additional* award in cases of a 'discriminatory' dismissal of between 26 and 52 weeks' pay (EPCA s.71).

EQUAL PAY

Many women are paid less than their skills and job levels merit and less than a comparable man would be paid. The EqPA[82] aims to bring about equality in pay and also in other terms and conditions of employment such as holidays, hours and provision of clothing.[83] The Act refers to women but its provisions apply equally in a converse case to men and their treatment relative to women. It did not become fully operative until 1976, along with the SDA. The two Acts are regarded as part of a single legislative code of equality.[84]

The scheme of the 1970 Act for assuring parity in pay and terms of employment is threefold. First, the Secretary of State has power to refer a question under s.2(2) of the Act to an industrial tribunal where it is 'not reasonable' to expect the parties to take steps to determine the question. Second, and this is much more important in practice, s.1 provides for individual enforcement before an industrial tribunal. Third, collective agreements, pay structures, and wages regulation orders may be referred to the CAC if they contain provisions applying specifically to men only or to women only (ss.3–5).

In relation to individual complaints and to the amendments to be made to collective agreements, the Act (s.6) excepts terms affected by compliance with the law regulating the employment of women affording special treatment to women in connection with pregnancy or childbirth, and terms related to death or retirement. The question of equality under pension schemes is discussed in Chapter 14 above.

---

[82] See Creighton (1979); Phelps Brown (1977); Hepple (1984).
[83] *Maidment and Hardacre v Cooper* [1978] IRLR 462.
[84] *E Coomes (Holdings) Ltd v Shields* [1978] ICR 1159, at 1168 (per Lord Denning).

Individual Complaints

In 1976 1,742 applications for equal pay were made to industrial tribunals. This number has sharply and steadily declined since then, from 751 in 1977 to 26 in 1983 (EOC, 1984:43). The implication is not that equal pay has been achieved – for full-time workers aged 18 or over, the ratio of women's gross hourly earnings to those of men appears to have settled in the range of 73–75 per cent – but that the Act is much in need of amendment. The principle of equal treatment under the Act (s.1(2)) applies to men and women workers only 'when employed'. This limitation is defined (s.1(6)(a)) as 'employed under a contract of service or of apprenticeship or a contract personally to execute any work or labour'. The Act has been expressly extended (s.1(8)) to those in Crown employment.

The device used by Parliament to implement equal pay is that of an 'equality clause', that is, a statutory term of equality is implied into every woman's contract of employment to ensure that it is not less favourable than that of a comparable man, or the existing terms of her contract are modified if they are less favourable. The equality clause is enforceable before an industrial tribunal following a reference either by the woman herself or by her employer or by the Secretary of State. If proceedings are pending before an ordinary civil court in respect of the operation of an equality clause, the court may refer the matter to an industrial tribunal (s.2(3)). The maximum amount a successful claimant may receive is two years' back pay (s.2(5)). A claimant must have been employed in the employment concerned within six months preceding the date of the reference (s.2(4)).

Equality Clause

Equal pay for work of equal value is the core concept. It was not espoused by the legislature in 1970 when equal pay for work of 'the same or a broadly similar' nature (s.1(2)(a)) and equal pay 'for work rated as equivalent' (s.1(2)(b)) were the preferred and weaker choices. In 1981 the UK government was proceeded against by the Commission of the EC for failure to implement the Treaty of Rome, and specifically Art. 1 of the 1975 EC Directive on Equal Pay, by not providing in its national legislation for individuals to pursue claims for equal pay where they were engaged in work of equal value compared with other workers.[85] As a result the UK government was forced to introduce amending regulations in 1983 concerning equal pay for work of equal value,[86] but, as will be seen, the concept of equal pay for work of equal value is still not installed at the centre of the Act.

A woman must compare herself to a man 'in the same employment' (s.1(6)). This operates to the disadvantage of women in segregated employment. Comparisons with men in another establishment of a multi-plant

---

[85] *Commission of the EC v United Kingdom* [1982] ICR 578. See Crisham (1981).
[86] Equal Pay (Amendment) Regulations SI 1983 No. 1794. See McCrudden (1983); Rubenstein (1984); Szyszczak (1985).

employer are permitted only if 'common terms and conditions of employment are observed' at the two plants; and comparisons with employees at establishments of other employers can be made only if there are such common terms and the employers are 'associated' (a concept discussed in Chapter 5 above). An inquiry will be necessary to find out whether establishments act autonomously in agreeing terms of employment. As regards the person with whom a woman compares her work, the choice is entirely a personal one: it is not open to an industrial tribunal to substitute another employee-comparator.[87] Need the man and the woman be employed contemporaneously? Although that was the construction placed on the Act by the Court of Appeal,[88] the ECJ has ruled that such a restrictive interpretation would be contrary to Art. 119 of the Treaty of Rome.[89] The European Court acknowledged that a difference in pay between two workers occupying the same post but at different times could sometimes be applicable.

A woman is regarded as employed on like work with men if her work and theirs is of the same or of a broadly similar nature 'and the differences (if any) between the things she does and the things they do are not of practical importance in relation to terms and conditions of employment' (s.1(4)). The 'like work' criterion is in fact a rough and ready instrument. Industrial tribunals adopt a 'broad brush' approach.[90] Job specifications are helpful. Job titles are unlikely to be.[91] The Act also enjoins a tribunal, when comparing a woman's work with that of a man, to have regard to the 'frequency or otherwise with which ... differences occur in practice as well as to the nature and extent of the differences'. The time at which work is done is not of practical importance because work at night or other 'unsocial' hours normally attracts a special premium.[92]

A woman's work is rated as equivalent with that of men's work if her job and their jobs 'have been given an equal value in terms of the demand made on a worker under various headings (for instance, effort, skill, decision)' in a job evaluation study (s.1(5)). Once a study has been completed it may form the basis for comparison, although the employer has not yet applied it in practice.[93] A study will not be regarded as completed, however, until the parties who have agreed to carry it out have accepted its validity.[94] A job evaluation study is conclusive except where an equal value would have been given 'but for a system setting different values for men and women on the same demand under any heading' (s.1(5)). If a claimant challenges an evaluation study an industrial tribunal cannot carry out its own study but is limited to asking whether there was an error on the face of the record or

[87] *Ainsworth v Glass Tubes & Components Ltd* [1977] IRLR 74.
[88] *Macarthys Ltd v Smith* [1979] IRLR 316.
[89] *Macarthys Ltd v Smith* [1980] ICR 672; see too *Albion Shipping Agency v Arnold* [1981] IRLR 525.
[90] *Eaton Ltd v Nuttall* [1977] ICR 272.
[91] *Capper Pass Ltd v Lawton* [1977] ICR 83; *Maidment*, note 83 above.
[92] *Electrolux Ltd v Hutchinson* [1977] ICR 252; *Dugdale v Kraft Foods Ltd* [1977] ICR 48.
[93] *O'Brien v Sim-Chem Ltd* [1978] IRLR 398.
[94] *Arnold v Beecham Group Ltd* [1983] IRLR 307.

some other fundamental error.[95] An industrial tribunal will try to establish whether it is possible to arrive at the position of a particular employee at a particular point of the salary grade without taking into account matters other than the nature of the work – such as merit or seniority. The Act does not make it possible to challenge a job evaluation scheme on the ground that it contains hidden indirect discrimination.

In *Commission of the EC v United Kingdom* the UK government tried to rely on the provisions of the EqPA concerning work rated as equivalent as a sufficient compliance with its obligations to legislate in regard to equal value claims. The ECJ rejected this argument. The EC Directive of 1975 requires a worker to have a remedy in such cases where no evaluation study has been carried out by the employer. As a result of this judgment, the Secretary of State for Employment made the Equal Pay (Amendment) Regulations 1983 (EqPAR) under powers conferred by the European Communities Act 1972. These regulations, which amend the EqPA, came into force on 1 January 1984. The right to equal pay for work of equal value is provided by enabling an equality clause to operate where a woman is employed on work which, *not* being 'like work' or 'work rated as equivalent' is, 'in terms of the demands made on her (for instance under such headings as effort, skill and decision), of equal value to that of a man in the same employment' (EqPA s.1(2)(c)). The claim is available only as a right of last resort, when existing remedies are not available or have been exhausted. The House of Lords when approving the regulations did so subject to an amendment 'that this House believes that the Regulations do not adequately reflect' the 1982 decision of the ECJ and Art. 1 of the EC Equal Pay Directive.[96] This was, to say the least, an unusual reservation.

The procedural rules[97] are, as Davies and Freedland (1984:384) remark, long drawn out and likely to cause delays. Once an applicant registers a claim, ACAS attempts conciliation. Unless this is successful the case proceeds to an industrial tribunal. A pre-hearing assessment may be held in certain cases. The EqPA s.2A(1) requires that the tribunal shall not determine an equal value dispute unless it is satisfied that there are 'no reasonable grounds for determining that the work is of equal value' or it has required a member of a panel of independent experts to prepare a report. Members of the panel of independent experts are designated by ACAS (EqPA s.2A (4)). It may not be necessary for them to use formal job evaluation techniques, but their assessments must consider the various demands made on the employees in the jobs being compared. A major difficulty about the new provisions, and a challenge for the independent expert, is the fact that the legislation gives little specific guidance on what equal value means. McCrudden (1983:201) suggests that there are four methods of ascertaining parity which could have been used: measuring

---

[95] *Green v Boxstowe DC* [1977] IRLR 34; *Eaton Ltd*, note 90 above; *England v Bromley London Borough Council* [1978] ICR 1.
[96] See 445 HL Deb, 5 December 1983, 882–90, 894–930.
[97] EqPAR have been applied by Industrial Tribunals (Rules of Procedure) (Equal Value Amendment) Regulations SI 1983 No. 1807. In general see Hepple (1984).

market value, measuring marginal productivity, formal evaluation-study methods, and informal evaluation of job content on a points method. The legislature opted for informal evaluation, despite the problem inherent in such evaluation of discriminatory factor weightings with the effect of favouring men's jobs.

A variant of the factor comparison method of job evaluation was, in fact, used by the independent expert in the first case decided under EqPAR: *Hayward v Cammell Laird Shipbuilders Ltd.*[98] The industrial tribunal accepted the expert's conclusion that a female cook was employed on work of equal value with a male painter, a joiner and a thermal insulation engineer. The independent expert used five heads – physical demands, environmental demands, planning and decision-making, skill and knowledge, and responsibility – and assessed the demands of the jobs done by the claimant and her three comparators as 'low', 'moderate' or 'high'.

Under the amended EqPA s.2A a tribunal may find there are no reasonable grounds for determining that the work of a woman is of equal value if that work and the work of the male comparator have been given different values on a job evaluation study, and there 'are no reasonable grounds for determining that the evaluation contained in the study was made on a system which discriminates on grounds of sex'. An evaluation is made on a system which discriminates on grounds of sex where 'a difference, or coincidence, between values set by that system on different demands under the same or different headings is not justifiable irrespective of the sex of the person on whom those demands are made'. In the absence of a systematic theory of discrimination for equal pay, it is difficult to see, as Rubenstein (1984:82) points out, how a tribunal will be able to determine whether the values set by a job evaluation study are justifiable.[99]

An expert may be called upon to evaluate work of equal value against pay systems based largely on collective bargaining. A comparison of values across several different pay structures may throw up difficulties of interpretation and application for collective agreements. Yet the CAC has been given no role in the new scheme to enable it, with the parties' consent, to inspect collective agreements affected by an equal pay award and to recommend changes to avoid anomalies.

The Employer's Defence

Under the original s.1(3) of the Act of 1970, an employer had a defence if he could show that a variation between the woman's contract and the man's was 'genuinely due to a material difference (other than the difference of sex) between her case and his'. Section 1(3) as amended by EqPAR, however, distinguishes between 'like work' and 'work rated as equivalent' claims on the one hand, and 'equal value' claims on the other. An equality clause does not operate in relation to a variation between the woman's and the man's

[98] [1984] IRLR 463.
[99] Borne out by *Neil v Ford Motor Co. Ltd* [1984] IRLR 339.

contract if the employer proves that the variation is genuinely due to 'a material factor which is not the difference of sex'. That factor, in relation to 'like work' and 'work rated as equivalent' claims, 'must be a material difference between the woman's case and the man's'. In the case of 'equal value' claims the Act says the material factor *may* be such a material difference though, by implication, it need not be. The nature of a 'material factor' which is not a 'material difference' is not specified but, as Hepple (1984:21) observes, the intention was apparently to include commercial factors such as skill shortages or other 'market forces'. In addition to these external labour market factors, the employer may wish to introduce in his defence such factors as average productivity between men and women workers and the effect of different collective bargaining strengths.

Little scope was afforded to the defence of market forces under the jurisprudence of the old s.1(3). Lord Denning confined the defence to personal differences other than sex arising from the particular characteristics of the persons doing the jobs in question, that is, factors relating to a personal equation between them.[100] Factors relevant to this personal equation have been held to include an employee's particular skill, capacity and experience in the job;[101] qualifications;[102] age and length of service;[103] the fact that wages were fixed by different nationally or widely negotiated wage scales;[104] 'red circling';[105] and productivity.[106]

The EqPA as originally drafted did not contain any express provision for dealing with indirect discrimination where this is present in an employer's defence. Under the influence of EC law, however, the Act has been amended by EqPAR so that this can be taken into account, though it is problematical whether the amendment benefits those in quest of equal pay.

In *Jenkins v Kingsgate (Clothing Productions) Ltd*[107] the ECJ ruled that a difference in pay between full- and part-time workers does not amount to discrimination prohibited by Art. 119 of the Treaty of Rome, unless it is in reality merely an indirect way of reducing the pay of part-time workers on the ground that that group of workers is composed exclusively or predominantly of women. The judgment was unclear as to whether it is sufficient, for the purposes of Art. 119, for an employer to justify a pay differential between men and women doing like work on the ground that he had no

---

100   *Coomes (Holdings) Ltd*, note 84 above. See too *Rainey v Greater Glasgow Health Board* [1984] IRLR 88.
101   *National Vulcan Ltd v Wade* [1978] IRLR 225; *Pointon v University of Sussex* [1979] IRLR 294.
102   *Coomes (Holdings) Ltd*, note 84 above.
103   *Capper Pass Ltd*, note 91 above.
104   *Waddington v Leicester Council for Vol. Service* [1977] ICR 266. But see *BL (UK) Ltd v Powell* [1978] IRLR 57.
105   For example, where a person's job has been downgraded as a result of reorganisation or new production methods or where a person is moved to a lower grade job because of age or ill health, if the employee's old rate of pay is protected, this is often referred to as 'red circling'. See *Snoxell and Davies v Vauxhall Motors* [1977] ICR 700; *Outlook Supplies Ltd v Parry* [1978] IRLR 388; *Farthing v Ministry of Defence* [1980] IRLR 402.
106   *Handley v H Mono Ltd* [1979] ICR 147; *Durrant v N Yorkshire Area HA* [1979] IRLR 401.
107   [1981] ICR 592.

intention of discriminating, or whether the employer must also show that the differential in pay is objectively justified for some other reason.

When the case returned to the EAT,[108] Browne-Wilkinson J assumed, without deciding, that Art. 119 did not apply to cases of *unintentional* indirect discrimination. This did not mean, however, that lack of intention to discriminate is a sufficient defence under s.1(3) of the Act. UK statutes might well be construed, said the EAT, so as to confer greater rights than those conferred by Art. 119. An employer will fall short of the mark if he merely shows an intention to achieve some other legitimate objective. He has to show the pay differential actually achieves that different objective. Thus in the case of part-time women, the specific subject of the decision, the EAT ruled that for s.1(3) to apply, the employer must show the difference in pay between full- and part-time workers is reasonably necessary in order to obtain some result other than cheap female labour which the employer requires for economic or other reasons.

The potential effects of this ruling are far reaching. In relation to a length of service defence, for instance, an employer may have to show that service increments actually have the effect of reducing labour turnover among long-term employees. Qualification requirements may be subjected to the same analysis. On the other side of the coin, the decision of the European Court means that, under EC law, the s.1(3) defence cannot be restricted to the personal equation.

The wider defence for claims concerning 'equal value' in the amended EqPA reflects the European Court's interpretation of Art. 119. Doubtless the legislature wished to recognise that in such claims different job characteristics, not to say skills, are in issue. The new defence arguably enables an employer to adduce factors in his defence which can be justified objectively and which are not related to sex discrimination. In that way the employer's 'material difference' defence may have been substantially strengthened. But the new defence introduced three specific requirements: genuine attributability, that is, the variation in pay or terms of employment must be genuinely due to the factor relied on; the factor must not be the difference of sex; and it must be material. McCrudden (1983:212) suggests that these three limitations on the defence should be objectively judged, so that an employer would have to produce facts and figures to sustain his argument. This would follow the EAT's reasoning in *Jenkins*. Again there must be an absence of direct and indirect discrimination. And an employer must show that his action was necessary rather than merely convenient. External labour market forces will not be able to be cited without let or hindrance. The EAT's decision in *Jenkins* supports this interpretation.

Collective Agreements and Pay Structures

Section 3 of the EqPA allows the CAC to make awards on claims which would lie outside the jurisdiction of industrial tribunals because it does not

---

[108]   [1981] ICR 715.

require comparability on the basis of criteria such as 'like work'. The section enables any party to a collective agreement or the Secretary of State to refer an agreement to the CAC where it contains provisions applying specifically to men only or to women only. The CAC is empowered to declare such amendments, if any, as need to be made in the agreement to extend to both men and women provisions applying specifically to men only or to women only; and to eliminate any resulting duplication in the agreement in such a way as not to make the terms and conditions agreed for men, or those agreed for women, less favourable in any respect than they would have been without the amendments. The amendments cannot extend the operation of the collective agreement to men or to women not previously falling within it.

The CAC has been bold in interpreting its powers under s.3, lifting the veil of pay grades not overtly discriminatory to discover covert discrimination, and in some cases carrying out job evaluation studies or encouraging the parties to do so. The Committee has also been willing to carry out a general wages review, determining pay rates of grades resulting from a job evaluation where the parties disagreed on such rates (see Davies, 1980). Its wide-ranging activities were halted, however, by the Divisional Court in *R v CAC ex parte Hy-Mac Ltd*,[109] where the CAC was held to have acted beyond its statutory powers in amending an agreement which did not contain a provision referring specifically to men only or to women only. Browne LJ suggested that the only other situation in which the CAC could amend a collective agreement was where it 'is a sham in fact containing provisions which applied specifically only to men or women, although on its face it does not'.[110] Few agreements are candidates for such a description. The Court also held that in carrying out a general wages review the CAC was acting beyond its powers. The effect of the *Hy-Mac* decision was that s.3 'rapidly became to all intents and purposes defunct' (Davies and Freedland, 1984:380).

EQUAL OPPORTUNITIES COMMISSION AND COMMISSION FOR RACIAL EQUALITY

The EOC and the CRE[111] have three main duties: to work towards the elimination of discrimination; to promote equality of opportunity; and to keep under review the relevant legislation.[112] Their powers and functions are similar. The EOC and the CRE are each empowered to issue codes of practice containing such practical guidelines as the Commission thinks fit on either or both of the first two statutory duties set out above (SDA s.56A; RRA s.47). Both Commissions have done so. The CRE's Code of Practice for the Elimination of Racial Discrimination and the Promotion of Equality

---

[109] [1979] IRLR 461.
[110] At 464. But see now note 40a above.
[111] Each Commission is similarly composed with a chairman and up to 14 members: SDA ss.53–6; RRA ss.43–6.
[112] SDA s.53(1); RRA s.43(1).

of Opportunity in Employment came into force on 1 April 1984. The EOC's Code of Practice for the Elimination of Discrimination on the Grounds of Sex and Marriage and the Promotion of Equality of Opportunity in Employment came into force on 1 May 1985. Failure on the part of any person to observe any provision of a code of practice does not of itself render him liable to proceedings, but in proceedings brought under the two Acts before an industrial tribunal a code is admissible evidence and 'if any provision of such a code appears to the tribunal to be relevant to any question arising ... it shall be taken into account in determining that question' (SDA s.56A(10); RRA s.47(10)).

The legislation enables the Commissions to institute proceedings concerning discriminatory advertisements[113] and instructions or pressure to discriminate.[114] They may assist individuals,[115] a power which, as the Commissions' annual reports show, has proved to be of great significance. They may also conduct inquiries into areas not specifically covered by the legislation,[116] and undertake or assist research for any purpose connected with the carrying out of their statutory functions.[117] They may also carry out investigations.[118] This is particularly significant in relation to indirect discrimination. Through their investigations the Commissions can encourage positive action to secure equal opportunity and can deal with discriminatory practices over a wide span, in industries, firms and institutions (Appleby and Ellis, 1984). This section concentrates on the Commissions' investigative powers. Reference hereafter, for convenience's sake, is to the CRE.

An investigation may be of a specific or general nature. A specific investigation relates to a particular person or persons where the Commission believes they may have acted in a way which is unlawfully discriminatory. A general investigation is one where there are no allegations of discrimination. Investigations may be instigated by the Commission or ordered by the Secretary of State.[119] During an investigation the Commission may require the production of written information, or the attendance of named individuals for the purpose of obtaining oral evidence, or the production of documents.[120] This power is the same as that possessed by the county and sheriff courts and can ultimately be enforced through these courts as appropriate. It is an offence to alter, suppress, conceal or destroy a document the production of which has been required by the Commission, or knowingly or recklessly to make an untrue statement in pursuance of a notice requiring such production. After a formal investigation, the Commission may make recommendations to the Secretary of State or to such other persons as it thinks necessary in order to promote equality of opportunity. There is a duty to publish a report of the findings and recommendations or at

---

[113] SDA ss.38, 67, 72; RRA ss.30, 31, 58, 63. *EOC v Robertson* [1980] IRLR 44.
[114] SDA ss.39, 40, 57, 72; RRA ss.30, 31, 58, 63.
[115] SDA s.75; RRA s.66.
[116] SDA s.53; RRA s.44.
[117] SDA s.54; RRA s.45.
[118] SDA s.57; RRA s.48.
[119] SDA s.57(1); RRA s.48(1).
[120] RRA s.50; cf. SDA s.59.

least to make them publicly available. Further, if in the course of a formal investigation the Commission becomes 'satisfied' that a person has committed any one of the unlawful acts set out in the relevant legislation,[121] a non-discrimination notice (NDN) may be issued. Due warning and an opportunity to make representations are necessary beforehand. As will be seen, an NDN may be appealed. Contravention of an NDN has no legal effect in itself but the Commission is empowered to apply to a county court for an injunction to prevent the occurrence of further acts of discrimination if, within five years of an NDN becoming final or of a finding by a court or industrial tribunal of unlawful discrimination, it appears to the Commission that the respondent is likely to act unlawfully once more.[122] Where such application is based on a supposed violation of an NDN which has not yet been appealed to an industrial tribunal, the Commission must first obtain a decision from a tribunal that an act of unlawful discrimination has actually occurred.

The statutory machinery is 'so elaborate and so cumbersome that it is in danger of grinding to a halt'.[123] Such jurisprudence as there is on formal investigations comes from the activities of the CRE. It is partly responsible for the delays in many of its investigations and for the scrupulous standards the Commission is now forced to adopt in order to avoid challenge. These standards are necessitated by the abundance of procedural safeguards given an investigatee, particularly in relation to a 'named person' investigation.

To begin with, the Commission's terms of reference can be challenged on the grounds of ultra vires or because they are too wide. The Act provides that where the Commission proposes to investigate an unlawful act which it believes a named person may have done, it must inform him of its belief and of its proposal to investigate and offer him an opportunity of making oral and written representations, with legal or other help if he wishes.[124] In *R v London Borough of Hillingdon ex parte CRE*[125] the House of Lords held that before embarking on a formal investigation the Commission must have actually formed a belief that there have been acts of unlawful discrimination, and that the formal investigation cannot range wider than that which is justified by the Commission's belief as stated in the terms of reference. The Commission cannot 'throw the book' at the subject of an investigation. This means that where it has evidence that a particular employment practice is discriminatory, it cannot investigate the general employment policies of the firm in question without already having formed the belief that they are discriminatory. Although in the later case of *In re Prestige Group Plc*[126] the House of Lords confirmed its ruling in *Hillingdon*, Lord Diplock loosened the rein a little. It should, he said, be a condition precedent to the exercise of their named-person investigative power that the Commission should in fact

---

[121] RRA s.58(2); cf. SDA s.67(2). The rules of procedure are set out in Industrial Tribunals (Non-Discrimination Notices Appeals) Regulations SI 1977 No. 1095.
[122] RRA ss.62–4; cf. SDA ss.71–3.
[123] *CRE v Amari Plastics* [1982] QB 1194, at 1203 (per Lord Denning).
[124] RRA s.49(4); cf. SDA s.5B(3A).
[125] [1982] AC 779.
[126] [1984] IRLR 166.

have formed 'a suspicion' that the persons named might have committed some unlawful act of discrimination, and had at any rate some grounds for so suspecting, albeit that the grounds on which any such suspicion was based might, at that stage, 'be no more than tenuous because they had not yet been tested'.[127] The same case ruled that a preliminary inquiry must be held at any time if the terms of reference confine the investigation to named persons' activities and the Commission proposed in the course of it to investigate any act made unlawful by the legislation.

The report and recommendations following a formal investigation may also be challenged for failure to observe natural justice. In *Hillingdon* Lord Denning described the formal investigation as very like a charge against a person accusing him of an unlawful act. He is therefore 'entitled to all the safeguards of natural justice'.[128] Thus the Commission cannot criticise anyone in its report without affording the person criticised the opportunity of an explanation. In practice it is very careful in both the wording and timing of its report.

A person may appeal within six weeks against 'any requirement' of an NDN.[129] Where the appellate body (industrial tribunal, county court or sheriff, as appropriate) considers a requirement to be 'unreasonable because it is based on an incorrect finding of fact or for any other reason', it 'shall quash the requirement'. On quashing a requirement the tribunal or court may direct that the NDN shall be treated as if, in place of the requirement quashed, it had contained a requirement in terms specified in the direction. The ambit of an appeal was considered in *CRE v Amari Plastics Ltd.*[130] The EAT and the Court of Appeal held that an appeal was not confined to the literal requirements in an NDN. Such requirements are based on the judgment that acts of discrimination have been committed, and the reasonableness of these can be ascertained only by inquiring into whether the facts on which they are based are correct. The net result is that all the facts found by the Commission on their investigative journey can be queried on appeal.

The statutory investigative powers have not effected a significant reduction in employment discrimination, though the record of each Commission is markedly different. The EOC has begun ten investigations to date while the CRE has started just under fifty since its first in 1977. (These figures are not confined to investigations in the employment sphere.) The EOC favours greater emphasis on educational and promotional activities, while the CRE ascribes a primary role to law enforcement. Yet a forceful legal policy is arguably what is needed from both bodies. As Appleby and Ellis (1984:273–4) put it,

the use of formal investigations can amount to a more effective use of legal powers in certain areas such as equal pay than numerous individual claims which

---

[127] At 169.
[128] [1982] QB 276, at 287.
[129] RRA s.59; cf. SDA s.68.
[130] [1982] QB 265, EAT; [1982] 1 QB 1194, CA.

are now assisted through the tribunals by the Commissions. Only the Commissions have the time, resources and expertise to collect and present the kinds of facts, statistics and social patterns which are essential evidence in many discrimination cases.

Once it has been decided to favour a more positive law enforcement policy, then some fairly substantial amendments are necessary if the Acts are to enable the Commissions to function effectively.

CONCLUSION

The enactment of anti-discrimination legislation in the 1970s was a major advance. But an examination of these provisions exposes their severe limitations. Claims of indirect discrimination under the SDA and RRA are particularly noteworthy in this respect. Difficulties besetting such claims are compounded by the claimants having to bear the burden of proof. The norm of equality in the EqPA is also deficient – deficient in its understanding of the scope and nature of the problem it tries to redress (the same can be said for maternity protection legislation) and deficient in its treatment of indirect discrimination and in its ability to cope with the defence of market forces. Its shortcomings are not likely to be redressed by the EqPAR which contain scant guidance as to the meaning of equal value.

Confrontation of those who do not wish to comply with new standards is an important element in changing behaviour through legal intervention. British anti-discrimination laws provide little leeway for uprooting collective and structural sources of discrimination and unequal pay. They nurture no serious threats to the prevailing social order, an order which espouses other values such as economic rationality in the market place. In particular, under the SDA and RRA, industrial tribunals are without effective power to combat indirect discrimination, and, as their recommendations are not ultimately enforceable, their power to ensure change is limited.

Initiation of strategic enforcement by the EOC and CRE is a core element, more wide ranging than the investigation of specific complaints. In equal pay cases, for instance, specific complaints must come from men and women 'in the same employment', a criterion which excludes areas of segregated employment, traditionally bastions of discrimination. Laws will not enforce themselves. Hence it is unfortunate that, conscious of the limitations which grow out of appealing to individuals to set the law in motion, Parliament did not legislate to enable the two enforcement agencies to tackle discrimination with less fear of challenge. Systematic enforcement of the SDA, RRA and EqPA involves not only knowledge of violations, but also power to remedy them. The systematic enforcement of anti-discrimination legislation is hindered by various jurisdictional obstacles strewn in the investigative path of the EOC and CRE. If the legislation is to be a significant instrument of social change these bodies must be given less tramelled power to deal with strategic targets in the social structure.

Bibliography

Appleby, G., and E. Ellis. 1984. 'Formal Investigations: The Commission for Racial Equality and the Equal Opportunities Commission as Law Enforcement Agencies'. *Public Law* (Summer), 236–76.

Bindman, G. 1980. 'Proving Discrimination: Is the Burden too Heavy?' *Law Society Gazette*, 77 (December), 1270.

Commission for Racial Equality (CRE). 1983. *The Race Relations Act 1976 – Time for a Change?* London: CRE.

Creighton, B. 1979. *Working Women and the Law*. London: Mansell.

Crisham, C.A. 1981. 'The Equal Pay Principle – Some Recent Decisions of the European Court of Justice'. *Common Market Law Review*, 18 (December), 601–10.

Davies, P. 1980. 'The Central Arbitration Committee and Equal Pay'. *Current Legal Problems*, vol. 33, 165–90.

——, and M. Freedland. 1984. *Labour Law: Text and Materials*. 2nd edn. London: Weidenfeld & Nicolson.

Department of Employment (DE). Annual. *New Earnings Survey*. London: HMSO.

——. 1981. *Labour Force Survey*. London: HMSO.

——. 1985. *Sex Discrimination Act 1975 and European Community Legislation: A Consultative Document*. London: DE.

Dworkin, R. 1977. *Taking Rights Seriously*. London: Duckworth.

Ellis, E., and P. Morrell. 1982. 'Sex Discrimination in Pension Schemes: Has Community Law Changed the Rules?'. *Industrial Law Journal*, 11 (March), 16–28.

Equal Opportunities Commission (EOC). 1979. *Health and Safety Legislation: Should we Distinguish between Men and Women?* Manchester: EOC.

——. 1982. *Job Evaluation Schemes Free of Sex Bias*. Manchester: EOC.

——. 1984. *Eighth Annual Report*. Manchester: EOC.

Hepple, B. 1970. *Race, Jobs and the Law in Britain*. 2nd edn. Harmondsworth: Penguin.

——. 1971. 'Employment'. *The Prevention of Racial Discrimination in Britain*. Ed. S. Abbott. London: Oxford University Press, 155–74.

——. 1984. *Equal Pay and the Industrial Tribunals*. London: Sweet & Maxwell.

——, and P. O'Higgins. 1981. *Employment Law*. 4th edn. B. A. Hepple. London: Sweet & Maxwell.

Lester, A., and G. Bindman. 1972. *Race and Law*. London: Longman.

Lustgarten, L. 1980. *Legal Control of Racial Discrimination*. London: Macmillan.

McCrudden, C. 1982. 'Institutional Discrimination'. *Oxford Journal of Legal Studies*, 2 (Winter), 303–67.

——. 1983. 'Equal Pay for Work of Equal Value: The Equal Pay (Amendment) Regulations 1983'. *Industrial Law Journal*, 12 (December), 197–219.

McKean, W. 1983. *Equality and Discrimination under International Law*. Oxford: Clarendon Press.

Martin, J., and C. Roberts. 1984. *Women and Employment: A Lifetime Perspective.* London: HMSO.

Office of the Minister without Portfolio (OMWP). 1985. *Lifting the Burden.* Cmnd 9571. London: HMSO.

Phelps Brown, E.H. 1977. *The Inequality of Pay.* Oxford: Oxford University Press.

Pole, J.R. 1978. *The Pursuit of Equality in American History.* Berkeley and Los Angeles: University of California Press.

Rainwater, L., and W.L. Yancey. 1967. *The Moynihan Report and the Politics of Controversy.* Cambridge, Mass.: Harvard University Press.

Rideout, R., with J.C. Dyson. 1983. *Rideout's Principles of Labour Law.* 4th edn. London: Sweet & Maxwell.

Rubenstein, M. 1983: 'The Law of Sexual Harassment at Work'. *Industrial Law Journal,* 12 (March), 1–16.

——. 1984. *Equal Pay for Work of Equal Value.* London: Macmillan.

Rustin, B. 1976. *Strategies for Freedom: The Changing Patterns of Black Protest.* New York: Columbia University Press.

Schlei, B.L., and P. Grossman. 1983. *Employment Discrimination Law.* Washington, D.C.: Bureau of National Affairs.

Szyszczak, E. 1985. 'Pay Inequalities and Equal Value Claims'. *Modern Law Review,* 48 (March), 139–57.

Townsend, P. 1979. *Poverty in the United Kingdom.* Harmondsworth: Penguin.

Williams, D. 1981. Note on *Seide v Gillette Industries Ltd* [1980] IRLR 427. *Industrial Law Journal,* 10 (December), 263–6.

Zubaida, S. 1972. 'Sociologists and Race Relations'. *Problems and Prospects of Socio-Legal Research: Proceedings of the Conference on the Sociology of Law, Nuffield College, Oxford, 1971.* Oxford: Nuffield College, 123–46.

18 Marginal Workers

Patricia Leighton

This chapter, as its title suggests, is concerned with workers who for a variety of reasons fall outside the mainstream of labour law. This might be because they are self-employed, casual, homeworkers or, for example, because they work beyond normal retirement age. They have varying titles. They can be described as 'freelance', 'agents', 'temps', 'trainees' or 'consultants', and constitute a wide heterogeneous section of employment. They are linked by one basic characteristic: they pose particular problems for and are treated differently, and usually disadvantageously, by labour law. The topic of marginal work is thus both hard to define and to present in a coherent way. It has also been largely neglected by labour lawyers.

Two general points need to be made, as they underpin some of the arguments and observations implicit in much of the material. The first is that marginal work, whether it be homeworking, job sharing or some other flexible work pattern, is now of considerable economic and social significance, and every indication suggests this will intensify. The second is that the traditional legal approach to marginals has been to struggle to include them within the normal employee 'net', or to make specific provision for them within statutes. It will be argued that, looking to the future, there has to be a more thorough and open analysis of the nature of marginal work and of the needs and perceptions of both employer and worker. This may imply a reconsideration of some of the basic concepts of employment law, in the context of broad economic and social policies relating to pension provision, the encouragement of new and often small businesses, the impact of new technology on working patterns, and equality of opportunity in training and work.

Labour law provisions tend to assume that the worker has a contract of employment, is full-time, and works for an employer for a reasonable time span. This will be referred to as the 'normal' employment contract. Certain key features of normal employment will be considered in order to identify and analyse the distinctive characteristics of marginality. This exercise will help to highlight the range of problems faced by those whose work does not conform to that normal mode.

THE NORMAL CONTRACT

It is possible to identify three major characteristics of the normal employment contract. First, it has continuity and regularity. The majority of employees are full-time; in other words, they work in excess of thirty hours per week. Their hours of work are usually fixed, and although there has been a shift to 'flexi-hours', especially in the financial and secretarial areas of employment and in government service, the basic pattern remains. Most employees also have a fixed workplace, usually on the premises of the employer. Although some employees, typically the younger ones, move from job to job, there is generally little mobility in the employment market, a situation reinforced by declining job opportunities and, probably, the impact and nature of employment law rights.

Second, the model of the normal employment contract is characterised by mutuality and security. Mutuality of obligations allows certain expectations on the part of both employer and employee. The employer expects the employee to be available for work when required and that such work shall be properly carried out. This model also implies in some circumstances a caring even protective obligation on the employer. Apart from the need to ensure employee safety, over 80 per cent of employees have an entitlement to payment from the employers when ill, there has been a steady increase in the incidence and length of paid holidays, and occupational pension schemes have become widespread. Statute law has reinforced this trend, for example, by providing minimum guaranteed payments to employees when laid off, and the right to know their terms of work and details of pay. Pregnant employees have important legal rights which are frequently extended by employers, and there is even a slight trend towards the introduction of paternity rights. Moreover, a greater sense of job security has been encouraged by the unfair dismissal and redundancy provisions, and the long-service, full-time employee is at much less risk of being selected for redundancy. Another important aspect of security is access to an internal career structure. This provides not only steady increases in pay for the long-service employee but also often targets to aim for in terms of training, promotion, increased responsibility, influence and discretion. Most employees can thus look forward to some form of progress during the continuance of the contract.

Third, the normal employee is increasingly in receipt of 'fringe' benefits. It is true that these benefits may often fall outside the scope of enforceable legal rights. Employers frequently insert terms in contracts describing removal expenses, social or sporting facilities, and educational courses as 'discretionary', or 'subject to withdrawal at any time', or only available upon 'recommendation of X'. Nevertheless, such benefits are often a highly valued aspect of jobs and are used by employers to attract staff. In reality they can effectively cement an employment relationship.

Taken together these features of the normal employment contract add up to a comprehensive and interdependent relationship. Such features are buttressed by social bonds at the workplace. The isolation of the marginal worker who works alone, 'on the road', or as 'a casual' can be contrasted with this situation.

Who has the normal employment contract? The simple answer is, of course, any adult who is economically active. But the worker who is most likely to have the normal, full-time contract is male, and tends not to work in the service sector of employment, where there is the concentration of part-time and various forms of intermittent work, overwhelmingly performed by women. The normal employee, especially if male, is likely to be a member of a trade union and to have certain terms of employment – notably levels of pay – collectively or externally determined. There is both cohesion and continuity in this process, which has tended over the years to bring a higher degree of standardisation to most of the contract. This standardisation has been hastened by the growing use and professionalism of personnel managers, and can be measured by the improved and more consistent level of employment documentation (Leighton and Dumville, 1977; Leighton and Doyle, 1982).

Over the last decade, however, there has been a growing awareness of those whose contracts do not conform to the usual contract of employment model. Initially, most of the interest, research and pressure came through the linking of generally disadvantaged groups, such as the low paid, with the fact that they tended to do marginal work. More specifically, women, especially those with young children, cannot always get or remain in normal, full-time employment (Martin and Roberts, 1984). They turn, typically, to part-time, casual and homework so as to reconcile domestic commitments with the need for earnings. Indeed, probably the most sustained campaign so far to improve the situation of a group of marginal workers has been that surrounding homeworkers. There has been mounting evidence on their pay, conditions, aspirations, and value to businesses, which has perhaps led to recent attempts by the courts to provide a realistic analysis of their employment relationships.

Moreover, most forms of marginal work are on the increase. Even on the roughest of estimates, if the 2.5 million self-employed workers are added to the 4.5 million part-timers, to the upper estimate of 660,000 homeworkers, to several hundred thousand each of agency, casual and temporary staff, the result is that between a quarter and a third of all workers are marginal. This estimate is arrived at by allowing for overlap between the various groups of workers. Robinson (1979), among others, has argued that this is a trend in its own right and not merely a response to recession and unemployment. Leicester (1982) has pointed out the massive increase in part-time work since the 1960s, and an IRRR Survey (1984), has shown arrangements by employers for part-time staff to be more systematic than anticipated. Generally, the evidence suggests that flexible, part-time workers will become more vital to the economy. There is also a feeling that such changes are not welcomed by all, especially some trade unions. Overall, though, it seems that marginal workers will become more important; indeed, it is a matter of speculation that the marginals of today will be the normal workers of the future. It is vital, therefore, that labour law makes an appropriate response to these developments.

It is possible, broadly speaking, to define labour law marginality in two main senses. First, if workers are categorised as being self-employed they are excluded from most employment rights and are treated differently for tax and social security purposes. Second, although the workers are employees, there are characteristics of their jobs such as working abroad, beyond retirement age, part-time or as a youth trainee, which materially affects their entitlement to employment rights. Sometimes they are excluded directly from statutory provisions; sometimes they are technically able to qualify but features of their work connected with lack of continuous employment or irregular or insufficient hours bar them from claiming these rights. This is usually coupled with a low level of knowledge about both their terms and conditions of work and their legal rights.

In examining marginality in labour law terms, the major emphasis will be on employment protection rights and anti-discrimination provisions, with some reference to safety at work. Most of the protection and rights are derived from statute, and there is a discernible if implicit scale of rights. Some rights such as those relating to discrimination at work, freedom of association and safety are seen as fundamental, in the sense that all workers, regardless of length of service and sometimes of employment status, are covered. A middle band of rights, such as those relating to statements of terms and conditions and statutory sick pay, require a relatively short period of up to a year. The final band of rights, which have the toughest eligibility requirements, relates to redundancy and maternity provisions, where the worker needs at least two years' continuous service. The present government has moved unfair dismissal rights into this third band.

MARGINALITY: SELF-EMPLOYMENT

Courts, tribunals and various government departments are daily making decisions as to whether a particular worker is an employee or is self-employed. The reasons for this exercise include problems of vicarious liability, claims to assert statutory employment rights, and disputes over the correct rate of social security contributions. The tests for the identification of a contract of employment are discussed above in Chapter 12. Traditionally the interest of labour lawyers ceased once an adjudicating body decided that a particular worker was self-employed. The conventional legal view of the self-employed is that their appropriate legal context is in commercial or business law. They are taxed differently and are largely outside both the social security system and the employment law. And yet vast numbers of self-employed people work as agents, freelances and the like where they are working for another person or organisation. They are in an ambiguous position, for in many ways their employment relationships are not markedly different from those of normal employees in that they work within the usual business and disciplinary structures. Although their work may sometimes be characterised by a significant element of investment, risk and independence, research (Leighton, 1983a) suggests that working conditions and practices can often differ little, if at all, from those classified as employees. Suffice it to say that the law's attempts to provide guidance, logic or counselling in this vital area have not been impressive.

It must also be acknowledged, however, that self-employment is attractive to many workers in that it may offer not only tax advantages but also independence, job satisfaction and opportunities. Unfortunately, much of the literature on the self-employed has tended to emphasise their links with the 'black economy' or petty crime (for example, Henry, 1979; Mars, 1982). The philosophy or ethos of self-employment merits consideration as well (Bechofer and Elliott, 1978; Russell, 1983), especially when there are proposals to draw various groups of self-employed workers within the 'employee net'. Moreover, a very wide range of occupations include self-employed persons: barristers, taxi drivers, construction and repair workers, journalists, entertainers as well as workers in insurance, selling and computing. Self-employment thus embraces great variations in job content, skill, earnings, training and status.

The overall picture of self-employment is complex and contains many legal ambiguities. But some aspects of self-employment do emerge more clearly. First, self-employment is a significant growth area among the economically active. Since the period 1971–9 when estimates remained fairly constant, there has been a marked increase. In 1979 1,950,000 were estimated to be self-employed, by 1981 2,057,000, by 1983 2,199,000, and by 1984 2,433,000 (DE, 1982; 1984; 1985a). Second, the self-employed are concentrated in the service sector, and third, the number of women becoming self-employed is showing a significant increase. There seems every expectation that all these trends will continue.

Another clear and expected feature of self-employment is that few self-employed persons belong to trade unions, with notable exceptions such as journalists, entertainers and musicians. Over recent years a number of other organisations specifically designed to promote the interests of self-employed people have grown up (King and Nugent, 1976). Consistent with the philosophy of self-employment, however, these organisations are more akin to professional bodies and pressure groups, and are rarely involved in collective bargaining or other formal negotiations.

The self-employed are excluded from virtually all employment protection legislation. The assumption is that self-employed people are able to negotiate their own terms of work and there is no need for intervention by law. If a contract to work for another is ended prematurely the ordinary contractual remedies are open to the self-employed, though realistically they are not in any better position in terms of obtaining legal advice and financing legal action than the normal employee. However, there are some areas of labour law rights which are available to the self-employed. Bearing in mind that most self-employed people work for others as, say, agents, suppliers or in generally providing a service, they are just as likely as normal employees to be affected adversely by discriminatory practices in the labour market. If a self-employed person has a 'contract personally to execute any work or labour', he or she is protected under the sex and race discrimination legislation.[1] The meaning of 'personally to execute' would seem potentially wide and this has proved to be the case. In *Gunning v Mirror Group Newspapers*,[2] the rejection of a woman's application to take over her

[1] EqPA s.1(6); SDA s.82(1); and RRA s.78(1).
[2] [1985] IRLR 60.

father's wholesale distribution agency for a newspaper was held to be unlawful sexual discrimination. The agency contract was one to 'personally execute' work and thus covered by legislation. The clear inference of this decision is that most 'consultants', 'freelances' and the like will be protected from discriminatory practices. Also discrimination by organisations of employers, professional and trade associations is unlawful (SDA ss.11–13, RRA s.4) and, to that extent, the position of the self-employed in terms of training, qualifications, and the obtaining of work, at least if 'personally executed', is comparable to that of the employee.

One area of law which is particularly relevant to self-employed workers is that relating to safety and accidents at work. There are very limited circumstances in which the hirer of self-employed or independently-contracted labour is vicariously liable for the latter's tortious acts. Such firms have no obligation to insure their self-employed workforces against injury, and so the self-employed worker has the obligation to take out his own liability and loss cover. There is no legal requirement on the self-employed to insure against third party injury, let alone injury to themselves. If accidents do occur, especially in the construction industry, the tendency is sometimes to construe the relationship as one of a contract of employment.[3] This can be so despite clear intentions to the contrary by the respective parties and the evidence of tax and social security deductions. Overall, the situation regarding the self-employed and injury compensation is unsatisfactory, with the law having seemingly no overall strategy.

Turning to accident prevention, the HSWA does appear to have both a strategy and a relevance with regard to the self-employed. This statute, based on the philosophy of the Robens Report, which saw safety as a broad concern for all at work, provides a comprehensive and coherent package. The self-employed are included, for the objects of the Act are stated to be 'securing the health, safety, and welfare of persons at work' (s.1) and 'work' includes work as a self-employed person (s.52(1)). They are owed duties by those 'manufacturing articles or substances for use at work' (s.6) but at the same time they themselves owe duties to third parties to ensure 'so far as is reasonably practicable' that they are not 'exposed to risks to their health and safety' (s.3). The 1974 Act has proved flexible, as explained above in Chapter 16, but there have been major problems of enforcement. These problems may be severe for self-employed construction workers and also for other groups of self-employed workers such as those who work at home.

The other overall category of marginality concerns the large group of workers who can be considered marginal to labour law in the sense that characteristics of their work deny them benefits offered to the normal employee. The potential range of work is enormous and could include everyone from the retired, priests, au pairs, office holders, and trainees to homeworkers and casuals. For obvious reasons not all groups can be included, let alone highlighted, but it may be useful to present the selected groups under three headings concerned with specific aspects of their work which, in effect, are the cause of their marginality. The first heading focuses

---

[3] E.g. *Ferguson v John Dawson (Contractors) Ltd* [1976] 1 WLR 1213, CA.

on job location and includes some workers whose workplace is away from the main or business premises of their employer. The second considers workers who have hours of work or working patterns which differ in some respect from the normal full-time and continuous contract. The third considers work which has special features in terms of job content. Put succinctly, the three sections are devoted to characteristics in terms of where you work, when you work and how you work.

MARGINALITY: WHERE YOU WORK

Homeworkers

Homeworkers are one group of workers who, after many years of neglect, have recently come into prominence. Traditionally homeworkers have been used by industry to carry out a range of relatively uncomplicated manufacturing, assembling, and packaging tasks. Typical activities might include putting greeting cards in envelopes, assembling jewellery or electrical goods, typing, or child minding. Often such workers are used selectively, especially at times of high or seasonal demand, and are frequently poorly paid.

Largely in response to concern about low pay and reflecting the growing interest in the position of women workers in the labour market, there have been a number of recent investigations into homeworking (see Ewing, 1982). The strategy during the 1970s was to collate basic data about this 'hidden army' of workers (Crine, 1979), and formulate proposals for reform. As a result of these exercises there is a more developed understanding of the personal issues conditioning homework (Cragg and Dawson, 1981) in the context of economic and business factors (Hakim, 1984a; 1984b; 1985).

Those who work entirely at home are estimated to number 251,000 (Hakim, 1984a), though the number rises to 660,000 if those who use their home as a base are included. Research has shown that there is a considerable range in the work done at home and it is by no means confined to manual or routine activities. Huws (1983; 1984) and Williams (1984), in particular, have demonstrated the significant and increasing use of homeworkers for high technology. It appears that approximately half the homeworkers work for a single employer or client, and there has been a general move away from manufacturing into service occupations. Over 70 per cent of homeworkers are women, virtually all of whom are married and there is a high representation of ethnic minorities. Homeworking is rarely a full-time activity.

The role of wages councils in homeworking is crucial. Historically the councils had appeared to guarantee a relatively higher rate of pay for homeworkers doing comparable jobs to factory workers. But with the drift to service work and the general decline in importance of wages councils, homeworkers have become more vulnerable to crude economic pressures. These pressures have tended to make homeworking in some occupations more unstable and patterns of work irregular or intermittent. There is clear evidence (Hakim, 1984b), however, that, from an employer's perspective, using homeworkers makes sound business sense, as regards costs, flexibility, productivity and off-loading of risk. Yet they are frequently low paid, vulnerable, rarely unionised and socially isolated. The picture seems bleak but some, such as Cragg and Dawson (1981), have identified what might be termed a philosophy of homeworking. Regardless of objective factors of pay and conditions, homeworkers are often shown to be independent, proud and, surprisingly, capable of considerable job satisfaction. Despite this, it is apparent that homeworkers can face major legal problems.

There has been a view that most homeworkers are self-employed because of their job location.[4] However, research (Leighton, 1983a; 1983c) would suggest that the picture is more complex and that many homeworkers are regarded as employees. The issue of homeworkers' employment status has aptly demonstrated the legal tangles which can arise when courts try to apply legal tests to the distinctive economic and social situation of homeworkers The emergence of the 'business test' of employment status (see Chapter 12 above) and the subsequent downgrading of 'control' would tend to suggest that homeworkers are self-employed as they use their own premises, fuel, equipment and often have irregular work. But the reality of the dependence of worker on employer, and an awareness that reliability, punctuality, competence and availability are pre-requisites to obtaining and maintaining work presented the law with a dilemma.

In 1978 the EAT had an opportunity to give consideration to these issues in *Airfix Footwear Ltd v Cope.*[5] Mrs Cope had worked regularly for Airfix for about seven years, virtually full-time, albeit usually in the late afternoon and evenings. Her job was to assemble shoe heels for which she was paid a weekly 'wage' based on the number of heels assembled. After this long standing arrangement was terminated, she claimed she had been unfairly dismissed. In considering her employment status the EAT rejected the argument that she was in 'business on her own account', noting that she had no other source of income and was not able to offer her skill 'in the open market'. The EAT instead directed its attention to her closely supervised relationship with Airfix Ltd and to the fact that there had 'by conduct been established a continuing relationship, a continuing contract of employment'.[6] This contract was 'overriding' and Mrs Cope did not merely have a series of short contracts which would have prevented her establishing continuity of employment. Although this decision was a key one for many homeworkers, it contained the proviso that, had Mrs Cope's employment been 'sporadic', the conclusion would not have been the same. *Cope* recognised the value of giving a reliable service and gave notice to employers that the law would not allow them to dispense with workers without compensation where merited.

The more typical part-time and less regular homeworker, however, may also prove to be an employee, especially after the Court of Appeal decision in *Nethermere (St Neots) Ltd v Taverna and Gardiner.*[7] The two claimants in

---

4 See HC Select Committee on Employment 1981–2, 39.
5 [1978] ICR 1210.
6 At 1213 and 1215.
7 [1984] IRLR 240.

unfair dismissal had worked for Nethermere Ltd sewing pockets in childrens' trousers for about three years. Both had previously worked in the same company's factory and, when working at home, did an average of five to seven hours per day. Most importantly, there were weeks when they did no work at all and Mrs Taverna, who worked the less regularly of the two, had up to twelve weeks 'off' per year. Vital also was the fact that, although they could indicate to the delivery driver how much work they wanted each week, it had to be such as 'to make it worthwhile for the driver to call'. In effect, there was a required minimum amount of work. The Court of Appeal was faced with the problem that not only had it to consider the relevance of *Airfix Footwear Ltd v Cope* but, more crucially, its own recent decision on casual workers in *O'Kelly v Trusthouse Forte Plc*.[8] The latter seemed at first sight very unhelpful to the homeworker in that it stressed that for a contract of employment to exist there had to be 'mutuality of obligation'. But the Court of Appeal, in upholding the decision of the EAT on the matter and finding the homeworkers to be employees, seemed to pull back from the onerous ruling of *O'Kelly*. The Court preferred 'an irreductable minimum of obligation' as being the determining factor. Stephen LJ stated, 'I cannot see why well grounded expectations of continuing homework should not be hardened or refined into enforceable contracts by regular giving and taking of work over periods of a year or more and why outworkers should not thereby become employees under contracts of service like those doing similar work in the factory'.[9]

Taverna and Gardiner seems to have resolved the dilemma regarding homework in the workers' favour by apparently ignoring the 'business test' and playing down the impact of *O'Kelly* in its examination of the practice and expectations of the parties. If *O'Kelly* can be criticised for its narrow and legalistic approach to the concept of 'obligation', the same cannot be said of the instant case. Indeed, in its reaffirmation of the existence of an overriding or 'umbrella' contract between the parties – presumably continuing through 'workless' weeks – continuity is preserved. This one case, therefore, may have overcome major legal barriers to homeworkers benefiting from mainstream labour law. Although to be welcomed this judgment throws into sharp relief many of the anomalies, especially regarding tax and social security in this area of employment status.

Another important area of law for homeworkers is that of safety at work, as many carry out manufacturing processes in their own homes. The problem here is not that homeworkers are outside the legal framework but rather that the de facto protection offered seems so limited. Homeworkers may be using dangerous or poorly maintained machines, and the substances they work with may be harmful or unpleasant. There is rarely back-up by supervisors or reinforcement of instructions, and if accidents do occur they can affect families and neighbours of homeworkers and may go unreported and uninvestigated. The HSWA applies to homeworkers, specifically the s. 2 duties on the employer, which will presumably become more relevant

[8] [1983] ICR 728, CA.
[9] *Nethermere (St Neots) Ltd v Taverna and Gardiner* [1984] IRLR 240, at 246.

after *Taverna and Gardiner*. The major problem, as with safety legislation broadly, is that of inspection of enforcement. The House of Commons Employment Committee[10] has voiced serious concern and considers that for improvement to occur there would have to be more radical reform than the current government proposals requiring employers to register homeworkers with the appropriate inspectorate. It has to be recognised, however, that homeworkers will probably always be relatively neglected in terms of safety, against a background of continuing high levels of injuries in major manufacturing premises and construction sites and the limited resources of the enforcing authorities.

Agency Workers

The 1960s and early 1970s saw a massive increase in the use of workers supplied by agencies to a client, usually for a short period of time and often working at the client's premises. Temporary secretarial staff are typical of a very wide range of workers supplied by agencies. They include medical staff, and also the much criticised labour-only sub-contracted workers in the construction industry. Such workers may be used for short-term cover, for example, during holiday periods to replace workers on various forms of leave. They may be used to meet increased or sudden demand for the employers' services or, as in the case of the construction industry, because of well established methods of organising work. The agency can operate in the interests of the workers in that it can ease the problems of finding work and can often act as a stop-gap between jobs, during career changes, or perhaps during student vacations. Agency workers, therefore, constitute a varied group, who frequently have a reasonable level of income, but who, with a few exceptions, have no commitment to a particular employer and generally have irregular work patterns.

There appears to be no recent or accurate assessment of their numbers, but there is an impression (Leighton, 1983a) that numbers have declined in recent years. Research and writing on agency workers has been limited, although the system of labour-only sub-contracting in the construction industry was the subject of the Phelps Brown Report (1968), and there have been a number of investigations into temporary work which have taken in the use of agencies (for example, Federation of Personnel Services, 1975; Employment Services Agency, 1976; IDS, 1982; Leighton, 1984; and McNally, 1979). The supply of labour by an agency to its clients' premises represents an organised and coherent response to business needs and, as Hepple and Napier (1978) have shown, it is a phenomenon which is even more widespread in Europe. Most countries recognise that such workers need special treatment by law, which can deal with the short-term and generally insecure nature of agency work.

A worker supplied by an agency is normally paid by it and the agency makes appropriate deductions. Wage levels are usually arrived at by

---

[10] See note 4. Ewing (1982) discusses the application to homeworkers of safety provisions in specific industries.

reference to negotiations between agency and client, and there is generally little role for trade unions or collective bargaining. The work itself – whether it be secretarial, medical, computing or other work – is carried on at or from the client's premises, where there are the usual requirements of supervision, discipline, and physical conditions. Unless there is a complaint or dispute the agency will not become involved in the work. There are ample opportunities for ambiguities to arise in respect of, say, job content, fringe benefits and insurance, and there are sometimes problems over communication. The agency worker is thus in a paradoxical position, with the formal and financial relationship being with the agency, but the personal day-to-day relationship with the client.

Since 1973, with the Employment Agencies Act and the subsequent regulations of 1976,[11] there has been statutory intervention. Although the major aim of the legislation was to regulate employment agencies and businesses, it does require agencies supplying workers to clients on a temporary basis to provide them with some written information on conditions of work, including a declaration of their employment status. There is evidence (for example, Leighton, 1983a; 1984) that enforcement of regulations by the DE is rigorous, with the ultimate sanction of removal of an agency's licence, and that the written material provided for workers is of a good standard.

Although the law does not demand it, for a variety of practical reasons many agency workers are accorded employee status by the agency and thus are able to overcome the first hurdle to assertion of employment rights. However, where there is doubt as to status the recent EAT decision in *Wickens v Champion Employment*[12] gives cause for concern, not least because it indicates that the usual 'tests' of employment status are inappropriate for these types of workers. The secretarial agency here provided workers 'on the books' with some basic documentation. This included a statement that workers were employees of the agency, but despite this the EAT decided that the claimant was self-employed. In so doing the EAT did not apply the 'business on your own account' test but rather relied on the lack of a binding obligation on the part of the agency to make bookings for work and the absence of any obligation by the worker to accept them. In addition, there was no continuity or requirement of care on the part of the agency.[13]

In reaching this decision the EAT directed its attention exclusively to the relationship of agency and worker at a point when the latter was simply 'on the books'. It would be difficult to challenge the view that, given the wording of the documents, no binding obligations were in existence. But the facts of the case revealed that such documents were only issued *after* a booking had been made and accepted, and a contract had come into existence. Nevertheless, if that contract is analysed as the normal bipartite contract with elements of care and control at a stage when the worker is actually working on the client's premises, the conclusion will be invariably that the worker is

---

[11] Conduct of Employment Agencies and Businesses Regulations SI 1976 No. 715.
[12] [1984] ICR 365.
[13] At 371.

not the employee of the agency. There has to be legal recognition of delegated or devolved care and control in order that workers who have been assigned to a client and whose work is organised and supervised by the client are accorded their proper legal status and rights. Once attention is directed to the worker/client relationship it will be difficult to argue that many workers have the attributes of independence, risk, chance of profit and flexibility which characterise self-employment.

Even if workers are accorded employee status their problems are not over, for frequently the nature of agency work prevents workers establishing continuity of employment. On the assumption that a worker has an employment contract with the agency (and *Wickens* may threaten this), it is arguable that being 'on the books' for a number of years, even allowing for a few breaks, preserves continuity.[14] As yet the issue is unclear and, to establish continuity, parallels would have to be drawn with the case law on homeworkers.

Another aspect of labour law affecting agency workers is that concerned with accidents and injuries. Although agency workers will have some statutory protection from injury while on clients' premises, they are widely used in driving, repair and construction work where the accident rates are high. Accidents occur not only to workers but also to third parties and so issues of vicarious liability and insurance become paramount. This is a very confused area, often only resolved by agreement between agency and client, but which can leave the worker vulnerable to large claims for compensation. All in all, the tripartite nature of the relationship makes it more difficult and yet more pressing that questions of apportionment of liability and arrangements for insurance cover are clearly resolved. When these problems are combined with those over employment status, continuity and the frequent insecurity of this type of work, it is arguable that despite allegedly higher levels of earnings agency workers are in a very weak legal position.

Three Neglected Groups of Workers

To complete this analysis of workers who are marginal due to their job location, one must note three groups who have often been singled out by legislation for exclusion from certain rights and benefits. The reasons for this exclusion are not often clear, and although the numbers affected are hard to estimate, their legal disabilities are compounded by their generally weak economic position. The first group are those who because they ordinarily work outside Great Britain can claim few rights.[15] Experience has shown that defining those who 'ordinarily' work abroad has proved difficult,[16] despite the growing number involved. The second group are those who work in domestic service and as au pairs. They are also excluded from many

---

¹⁴ EPCA Sch.13, para.1(b); *Ford v Warwickshire County Council* [1983] ICR 273, HL. See further Chapter 12 above.
¹⁵ EPCA s.141 excludes such workers from most statutory provisions.
¹⁶ E.g. *Janata Bank v Ahmed* [1981] IRLR 457.

legislative rights. This group has perhaps always been disadvantaged in terms of low earnings, dependence on their employer through 'tied' accommodation, as well as exclusion from aspects of employment law.

The third group of workers are those employed by small firms (see generally Smith, 1985). Even basic rights, for example, those concerned with sex discrimination are denied those who work in firms employing up to five people,[17] such workers also being denied maternity rights.[18] From 1979 to 1985 employees of firms of up to twenty people had a lengthened qualifying period for unfair dismissal rights,[19] and even measures designed to prevent discriminatory practices in the selection of partners for firms excludes firms of less than six partners.[20] It appears that the reason for the exclusions is the need to protect small firms from the onerous demands of employment legislation which could, it is argued, inhibit such firms from recruiting workers. Daniel and Stilgoe (1978) have argued that there is no empirical data to support this view. With the numbers of small firms rising, it is likely that an increasingly higher proportion of the workforce will fall outside the full range of employment rights. It must be noted that these groups of workers are marginal to labour law not so much because of doubts over employment status, but simply because of where they work or whom they work for.

MARGINALITY: WHEN YOU WORK

Part-Time Workers

Part-time workers constitute the single largest group of marginal workers, and they have become the subject of considerable interest in recent years. Although for the purposes of the DE's compilation of statistics a part-time worker is someone who works less than thirty hours per week, the relevant hours for labour law purposes are sixteen and eight.[21] It has been largely because part-timers are overwhelmingly female and likely to have relatively low earnings that research and campaigns have been conducted by organisations such as the Low Pay Unit, EOC, and the National Council for Civil Liberties. In the last few years interest had broadened to cover the nature and value of part-time work to both employer and worker.

Once again current and precise estimates of numbers are hard to make. Leicester (1982) has noted that of 4.5 million part-timers over 81 per cent are women and approximately 18 per cent are retired people, and that since the mid-1960s there has been a net increase of more than 1.5 million part-time jobs. In her review of part-time employment in the EEC, Robinson (1979) has drawn attention to the facts that Britain is one of the

---

[17] SDA s.6(3)(b), although the RRA does not have a comparable provision. But see now DE (1985b).

[18] EPCA s.56A (no right to return to work by pregnant women in firm employing up to five persons).

[19] EPCA s.64A. See further Chapter 1 above, text to note 40.

[20] SDA s.11; RRA s.10.

[21] EPCA s.146(4)–(7); Sch.13 paras.3–5. See further Chapter 12 above.

highest users of part-time workers in Europe and that they work on average over 22 hours per week. Their contribution to the economy generally is undeniable, especially in the service sector. Research has shown their value to employers in terms of productivity, lower overheads and greater flexibility.[22] But there are many drawbacks of part-time work from the workers' perspective. Their lower earnings are largely accounted for by the unavailability of bonuses, shift premiums and overtime, and the fact that part-time work is female-dominated considerably affects wage levels. This is by no means the full explanation. Part-timers are rarely promoted and often remain on the lowest grades or on specifically part-time rates. They are generally denied training opportunities and, although some 80 per cent receive some holiday pay and an estimated 55 per cent sick pay (Leicester, 1982), they rarely have any of the wider employment benefits accorded to many full-time workers. In many ways, the problems of part-timers are simply a reflection of the problems of women's employment, but despite this most surveys have revealed a surprisingly high level of job satisfaction.

To date, all attempts emanating from the EEC to formulate legislation to improve the position of part-timers by, for example, extending pro rata entitlement to employment benefits have failed.[23] The part-timer has to fall back on the usual labour law provisions. The first and most obvious hurdle to surmount is that of employment status, especially where the worker is described as 'freelance' or 'casual' and has self-employed tax and social security arrangements. Although Humphries (1983) suggests that the majority of part-timers are self-employed, this seems unlikely, particularly when they work alongside full-timers and are subject to the same supervisory and organisational framework (Leighton, 1983a).

If part-timers are employees, Humphries (1983) estimates that over 75 per cent work in excess of sixteen hours per week and thus qualify for a range of employment protection rights. In addition, there is the unquantified number who have worked for eight hours per week for five years or more and who also qualify. Although levels of benefit and compensation will be proportionally lower than for the full-timer, legal marginality for part-timers is thus not generally expressed in terms of unavailability of major statutory rights.

One problem which has been the subject of case law is that of variation in part-time hours, on occasions causing them to fall below the relevant eight or sixteen hours per week. The question arose in *Secretary of State for Employment v Deary*[24] as to whether this broke continuity of employment. In cases where there were variations in working patterns, involving some weeks where no work at all was performed, there has been a tendency to treat such breaks as 'temporary cessations of work' so as to preserve continuity.[25] Where work did not cease but fell below the required hours,

---

22 See Martin and Roberts (1984); Robinson and Wallace (1984); IRRR (1984). But the disadvantages are highlighted by Hurstfield (1978); Humphries (1983); and Leicester (1982).

23 See EEC Draft Directive on Voluntary Part Time Work, amended and republished as COM (1982) 830, Final, in December 1982. See Syrett (1983).

24 [1984] IRLR 180.

25 See note 14 above.

would the interpretation be comparable, or would part-timers in such situations be worse off? In *Deary* the EAT appeared to appreciate the difficulty.

The case involved school dinner ladies who had what were described as 'variable hours contracts', which meant that there were specified hours of work (over eight) which could be adjusted according to the number of meals served. In 1980 or 1981 (the evidence was unclear) their hours were reduced so that at times some of the ladies worked less than eight hours per week. It was argued in 1982 when they were all made redundant that they had insufficient continuity of employment to mount a claim for a redundancy payment. The judgment of the EAT showed that the court was alive to the fact that a narrow approach to the issue, which would have the effect of attaching overwhelming significance to the *first* occasion the hours fell below eight, would cause an injustice. It was held that the reduction in hours was a unilateral variation in breach of contract, and that the hours which they were requested 'normally' to work was always over eight. The fact that, on occasions, the hours actually fell below eight was not thus capable of defeating their claim. The EAT was willing to look at the overall working of the contract and to adopt a flexible approach. Although there are difficulties in the decision, it is encouraging to marginal workers in that it seems to recognise that the essential quality of much marginal work – flexibility to employers' demands – has to have some legal recognition. In the matter of compensation for job loss, legislation (EPCA Sch.14) has always made express provision for fluctuating earnings so that in assessing 'a week's pay' the last twelve weeks earnings are averaged.

If some legal rights are accorded to part-timers, their basic problem remains relatively low earnings, compounded by few opportunities for promotion. In this context the EqPA and the SDA are very relevant to part-timers. Initially it was accepted that proportionally lower earnings for part-timers could be justified because of the higher overheads of employing them as compared to full-time staff. But subsequently the EAT stated that if lower pay was to be legally justified not only must the reasons for such payment be 'genuine' and non-discriminatory but they must also be backed up by convincing, practical evidence.[26] What remains to be seen is whether the introduction of an 'equal value' approach (see Chapter 17 above) will aid part-timers, but even if it does it has to be remembered that vast numbers of women part-timers are in 'women's only' employment. Another issue is the extent to which the SDA can be used to encourage promotion for part-time female workers. The failure to promote women part-timers has not been legally challenged and, even if it were, much would hinge on a tribunal's evaluation of reasons of lack of experience and commitment. On the other hand, where part-timers, all women, were selected for redundancy before any full-time staff the EAT held that it was unlawfully discriminatory, given the composition of the part-time workforce.[27]

---

[26] See *Handley v H Mono Ltd* [1979] ICR 147. Its view was tempered in *Jenkins v Kingsgate (Clothing Productions) Ltd* [1981] ICR 715.
[27] *Clarke v Eley (IMI) Kynoch Ltd* [1983] ICR 165. Cf. *Kidd v DRG* [1985] IRLR 190.

Job Sharers

Job sharing is a novel response to changing employment prospects and life styles. It differs from most other forms of marginal work in that often the initiative comes from the worker, or is a joint employer-employee venture. Although frequently presented as a scheme to 'improve the quality of part-time work' (EOC, 1981), its advocates would claim that it is more than that and represents a totally different way of working. The job sharing schemes which have developed in Britain in recent years have been influenced by experience in the USA, and can take varying forms. Work is shared, usually by two people, so as to accommodate their personal needs and interests. Job sharers are not necessarily women with young children, often working in the service sector, who wish to combine a permanent job with child rearing. Experience shows (Hackney Job Share Project, 1984) that a wide range of work and workers are involved and that men are becoming increasingly attracted by job sharing. Schemes can be small, ad hoc, and based on one work unit, or large scale and subject to considerable planning. Jobs can be shared in different ways, for example, mornings for one partner, afternoons for another, or alternate days or weeks.

From a labour law perspective job sharing is particularly interesting because, at the planning stage, most schemes have made a conscious effort to preserve employment protection rights. But experience of job sharing has brought into sharp relief some notoriously grey areas of employment contracts, such as the definition of job content and the role of implied terms. These matters may well become crucial when cases of unfair and wrongful dismissal eventually come before tribunals and courts.

Some schemes of job sharing, especially in teaching, illustrate both the strengths and problems of this form of employment relationship from a legal perspective. One aspect is that the drafting of the employment documents has to be undertaken with particular thought and care, so as to express unambiguously the relative responsibilities of the partners and to anticipate likely difficulties. Basic employment rights can usually be ensured if continuity is preserved and if each partner works more than sixteen hours per week. There also has to be provision to deal with the resignation of one partner. Nevertheless, major problems persist over job content, and 'promotion, occupational pensions schemes and a tendency for job sharers to work longer hours than they are paid for' (EOC, 1981: 83). Disadvantage in pension entitlement, especially where a job sharer has moved from full-time to this form of part-time employment, is perhaps the most serious problem. Occupational pension schemes are overwhelmingly connected with the normal full-time employment contract and have a symbolic as well as practical role, in that they represent the end to be striven for after many years of service. The typical employment profile is of training, then steady promotion leading to a financial peak, which usually determines the level of pension entitlement. The classic marginal worker, into which the job sharer will inevitably merge if the issues of promotion and pensions are not taken on board, tends to have a flatter profile with relatively little promotion and little to aim for at the end of the employment.

Temporary Workers, and those on Fixed Term Contracts

Temporary workers work for an employer for a limited period of time. They may be required for a day, or a few weeks, or a season in, say, catering or agriculture. Their occupations range from selling and fruit picking, through teaching, to various forms of social work. They supply a short-term or specific need and are united by the fact that they have virtually no job security and limited expectations of work. As recent research has shown (Leighton, 1984), they are generally on the lowest rates of pay, denied sick and holiday pay and given the least attractive work to do. Their numbers are hard to estimate and inevitably fluctuate.

In principle, the mere fact that work is performed for an employer over a short period should not threaten employee status, and thus entitlement to basic rights. The law does not generally attach importance to length of service if the other elements of employee status are present. However, where the temporary work is for a very short period, perhaps an evening or a few days, such workers are likely to be classified as self-employed. Where various musicians were brought in for particular concerts or recording sessions, for example, they were held to be self-employed.[28] It was important that the musicians employed agents to arrange bookings and took on a range of work, all of which suggested that the 'business on your own account' test was appropriate. It has been held, nevertheless, that a seasonal contract where the worker provided much of his own equipment was consistent with employee status.[29]

The situation regarding the employment status of temporary or casual workers is therefore complex, but now subject to the Court of Appeal judgment in *O'Kelly v Trusthouse Forte Plc*.[30] Here, 'regular' casual waiters were denied employee status, despite a long standing and regular relationship with Trusthouse Forte. It was held that a system whereby the waiters could be called in when required, leaving them technically able to refuse such work (though they would be demoted from the 'regulars' list if they did so), lacked the essential element of 'mutuality of obligation' to give them employee status. In attaching importance to the strict wording of the contract, rather than its workings and practice, the court ignored the essential characteristic of much temporary work. As has been noted earlier when discussing the decision on agency workers in *Wickens v Champion Employment*,[31] the concentration on legal formalities and the neglect of the economic and human side of the relationship can lead to unfortunate results. But the homeworkers cases, where some of the more restrictive and legalistic aspects of *O'Kelly* were avoided (see above), suggests that temporary workers might be given more sympathetic treatment in the future.

---

[28] E.g. *Addisson v London Philharmonic Orchestra Ltd* [1981] ICR 281; *Winfield v London Philharmonic Orchestra Ltd* [1979] ICR 726.
[29] *Warner Holidays Ltd v Secretary of State for Social Services* [1983] ICR 440.
[30] [1983] ICR 728, CA.
[31] [1984] ICR 365.

Apart from difficulty in establishing employee status, the short-term nature of much of this work in practice prevents the enforcement of many basic rights. For example, entitlement to a statement of particulars of employment may be delayed for up to thirteen weeks and the major rights regarding unfair dismissal, redundancy and maternity are unattainable by most temporary workers. The nature of their work often involves changes of employer or frequent breaks so that the necessary periods of continuous employment are not built up, a point underlined by the tabulation in Chapter 13 of qualifying periods of continuous service for the range of employment protection rights and by the outline in Chapter 12 of the rules on continuity of employment. The case law does, however, indicate that regular though intermittent work with one employer may suffice. In particular, *Ford v Warwickshire County Council*[32] has proved helpful to certain types of intermittent workers.

This case concerned a long-service part-time lecturer in a further education college. Her work pattern was typical in that she taught from September to the following July, returning to college the next September. She made a claim for unfair dismissal when her contract was not renewed, for which she needed to establish at least fifty-two weeks' continuous service. In deciding that the summer breaks were 'temporary cessations' and that she qualified for the statutory right the House of Lords attached importance to the length of service, the mutual expectations that she would recommence work after the break and the length of the working period vis à vis the relatively short break. The court was careful to stress that its decision was strictly based on the facts and was not authority for preserving continuity generally when work was subject to breaks.

The courts have further indicated that there should be an objective assessment of whether a cessation of work is 'temporary' and that there is no need to enquire into the reasons lying behind the decision to interrupt work.[33] Such decisions are helpful to the regular, temporary worker. In contrast, the truly temporary worker is badly disadvantaged in terms of legal entitlements and also, as research has shown (Leighton, 1984), regarding basic pay, fringe benefits, and working conditions.

The worker on the fixed term contract stands in a different position to both the regularly employed temporary worker and the truly casual one. The major characteristic of the fixed term contract is that throughout its continuance the end is always in sight. The contract's length may be fixed with reference to a set date, maternity leave, or the completion of a specific task in, say, research, consultancy or construction work. Usually these contracts are planned so as to implement the specific needs of an employer. A worker may harbour hopes that at the expiry of the term the employer may have a suitable vacancy or renew the arrangement, but for many such workers the job provides no security.

The employment protection legislation deals specifically with the situation of the fixed term contract by treating expiry and non-renewal of the contract

---

[32] [1983] ICR 273, HL.
[33] *Malik v University of Aston* [1984] ICR 492.

as a dismissal. But an employee may agree in writing during the currency of a fixed term contract to waive any claim for unfair dismissal or redundancy pay, provided the fixed term contract is for a minimum duration.[34] Although fixed term contracts have become much more widely used in the last few years, there is little information on the incidence of such waivers. Without a waiver, the worker whose contract is not renewed on expiry and who claims for unfair dismissal is often faced with defences based on, for example, redundancy, reorganisation, or reductions of funding.[35]

A further difficulty faces many workers who have short contracts. This is the possibility that the contract is not a fixed term contract, but one to carry out a specific task and is discharged by performance. In these circumstances the job security legislation can play no role as the worker has not been dismissed.[36] It appears likely that many 'task' contracts are ones of self-employment and thus not protected anyway, but the possibility of the concept carrying over to short contracts of employment seems to place such workers in an even weaker position.

Working beyond Normal Retirement Age

Many people who have retired from one job carry on working part-time in that or another employment. The position of those who 'stay on' at work merits some consideration. Both the unfair dismissal and redundancy provisions exclude those who have reached normal retiring age in their employment or the state pensionable age (65 for men, 60 for women).[37] *Nothman v Barnet London Borough*[38] decided that 65 and 60 years should be considered as the normal retirement age only where the contract is silent. Therefore, in many – perhaps the majority – of circumstances, the contractual position has to be examined to determine the normal age.

With pressure for early retirement to avoid compulsory redundancies and ease unemployment, the issue of normal retirement age has become more urgent, in particular because the assumption that people will work until 65 or 60 is now seriously under challenge. In effect, explicitly or by custom, many occupations will have a 'normal' retirement age which is lower and workers will inevitably lose rights if they happen to work beyond that 'normal' age.

The judicial approach to the definition of 'normal' is far from clear. This may reflect ambiguous terms in contracts, misleading statements made to employees, and the need on the part of the law to interweave the practice and expectations of the parties with the apparent strict or bald language of the contract. In *Waite v Government Communications Headquarters*,[39] the

---

34 One year for unfair dismissal or two years for redundancy pay: EPCA s.142.
35 E.g. *Terry v East Sussex County Council* [1976] IRLR 332.
36 See *Wiltshire County Council v National Association of Teachers in Further and Higher Education* [1980] ICR 455, CA.
37 EPCA s.64(1)(b), s.82(1).
38 [1979] ICR 111, HL.
39 [1983] ICR 653.

House of Lords held that, although the contract of employment would usually determine retirement age, in some circumstances a higher age would be 'normal' where a worker could reasonably expect to work until that date.

Case law has shown, however, that such reasonable expectations are hard to establish, even when clear evidence of hardship is produced. In *Coy v Department of Health and Social Security*,[40] a verbal assurance that a worker could carry on until 65, which prompted him to take out a mortgage on a property, was unenforceable when he was dismissed at 61 only a few months later. The dismissal had been occasioned by a departmental memorandum informing all staff that the previous age of 65 was to be reduced to 60 to ease staffing problems. The memorandum, which was arguably a unilateral variation and invalid, negated the 'reasonable expectation' of working longer. The test in *Waite* is thus superficially attractive, but experience of its operation suggests that management can easily rebut such expectations.

Finally, having considered the position of those who work beyond retirement age, a brief reference must be made to under-age workers. The problems of child labour and the need to provide protective measures have been part of social history and labour law for almost two centuries. Along with women they were given prominence in early factory legislation. It might be thought that, with the gradual raising of the age of compulsory schooling (still enforced by criminal sanctions), the need to protect the youngest members of the labour market would be a declining one. However, it seems that large numbers of school children work long hours for little pay (Low Pay Unit, 1985). Recent legislation, such as the Children Act 1972 and the Employment of Children Act 1973, has failed to prevent abuses of child workers who are unprotected by trade unions in circumstances where local authority powers are frequently only weakly enforced.

MARGINALITY: HOW YOU WORK

This section covers a wide range of occupations where, due to the nature of the work or job content, the workers are marginal. Some occupations are marginal to labour law because the workers are not considered employees, for example, because they are ministers of religion, or apprentices, or students, or participants in a youth training programme. Other occupations are expressly excluded from some or all legislation for a variety of policy and practical reasons. Into this group fall members of the armed services, the police, share fishermen, registered dock workers and some domestic workers. Sometimes they are excluded because they are subject to particular statutory provisions giving them equivalent or greater rights than the normal employee. This goes to explain the exclusion of registered dock workers from the redundancy provisions. But one group of workers may be thought to be generally treated in a more favourable way than the normal employee. These are the various types of 'office holders' in occupations ranging from chief constables to senior civil servants and judges. The rights of office

[40] [1984] ICR 557. See now *DHSS v Hughes* [1985] ICR 419, HL.

holders, particularly in respect of termination of employment, are discussed above in Chapter 12.

An example of how a particular job content may lead to a finding of self-employment is provided by *Parfitt v Methodist Conference.*[41] A minister was dismissed by the Methodist Conference, the body responsible for laying down the conditions upon which he did his work. His claim for unfair dismissal was turned down by the Court of Appeal, for it held that he was not an employee. In long and not entirely convincing judgments, the court considered that the nature of his work required his major working relationship to be with God, and not the merely human members of the Conference. Few occupations are so unusual as regards job content, though it is perhaps surprising that in the late twentieth century ministers and similar occupations should be considered as not having worldly needs. Before leaving those whose work is connected with religion, it should be borne in mind that they form one of the major exceptions to sex discrimination legislation (SDA s.19).

Those who work while at the same time studying or acting under supervision pose serious problems in many areas of law, including contract, education, tax and social security, as well as labour law. Davies and Freedland (1984: ch.1) have drawn attention to some of the particular legal difficulties which have emerged through the growth of job creation programmes.

Daley v Allied Suppliers Ltd[42] has highlighted a major disadvantage of such workers. This is that they have been affected by the tradition which sees any form of apprenticeship as being ascribed a legal form quite distinct from that of a contract of employment. Daley, a member of the Youth Opportunities Programme (YOP), was unable to make a claim under the RRA because she was not an employee. She had no binding relationship with the Manpower Services Commission (MSC), which organised the scheme, and would have had no employment contract with the sponsor where she hoped to work. The EAT derived support from *Wiltshire Police Authority v Wynne*,[43] where the Court of Appeal had held that a police cadet was not an employee, as the primary purpose of the relationship was to teach a trade, with work itself only secondary. The implications of being denied employee status are grave, not least because such safeguards as do exist have to come from the MSC's own regulations and administration. In addition, in *Daley*, the EAT was not even prepared to accept that YOP work was a contract 'personally to execute any work or labour' so as to gain protection from the anti-discrimination legislation.

With the introduction of the Youth Training Scheme (YTS) in 1983 there has been an even clearer commitment to the concept of training as opposed to work experience. It is likely, therefore, that the reasoning of *Daley* and *Wynne* will be reinforced. However, it is possible for trainees to be given employee status by employers if the latter so wish, though as yet it is not

---

[41] [1984] ICR 176, CA.
[42] [1983] IRLR 14.
[43] [1980] ICR 649.

clear how widespread this practice has become. The YTS has received considerable public criticism from trade unions, employers, trainees and educationalists, as well as from labour lawyers who have pointed out its problems beyond those connected with employment status (Freedland, 1983). It is unlikely that most trainees will qualify for statutory sick pay, or industrial injuries compensation, though the MSC has undertaken to pay equivalent sums. The question of injury at work has given rise to particular concern.[44] Generally, if it is not possible or desirable to assimilate trainees and apprentices into normal employment contracts, or to develop an alternative legal strategy to deal with them, their legal position will remain inadequate.

CONCLUSION

By outlining the nature and increasing importance of marginal work and by matching it against the normal employee contract, some of the legal problems of marginal workers have been identified in this chapter. It can be argued that recent years have seen some improvement in their position, instanced by the case law on continuity of employment and the granting of employee status to some homeworkers. Moreover, the widening of categories of protected employment to include 'personally executed' work may have blurred the distinction between self-employed and employed status for some statutory purposes.[45] But the improvement has been neither coherent nor even. Some workers, such as casual and agency workers, may have been adversely affected by recent case law. What has been seen is an ad hoc recognition, often by the EAT, of the problems and essential injustice in the position of many marginals. This development is indicative of the aim of lawyers to draw the legal position of the marginal worker closer to that of the normal employee, and in this regard they have reflected the views of pressure groups concerned with these workers.

It is possible, however, to argue that such a policy may not be appropriate. It is necessary to examine closely the qualities, needs and aspirations which are represented in marginal work. They can be contrasted with those found in the normal contract. Some marginal workers have drawn up their own 'balance sheet' of advantages and disadvantages. Accepting that many marginals are in such work because domestic and other reasons preclude alternative employment, it is possible that they have put on one side of the balance sheet low pay, vulnerability and frequent lack of trade union support but, on the other, flexibility, discretion and relative lack of control by others.

What legal strategies could be adopted for marginal work? It seems clear that any strategy would have to be set in the context of new thinking on the relationship between work, home, leisure and retirement (see Clutterbuck

[44] For the purposes of the HSWA, YTS workers are covered by special regulations: SI 1983 No. 1919; see Chapter 16, note 10.
[45] *Quinnen v Hovells* [1984] IRLR 227.

and Hill, 1981). Such thinking has implicitly questioned the assumptions upon which labour law is based, which find form in the normal, full-time, long-term employment contract. There will be continuing changes in working patterns, and they will inevitably lead, among other things, to a consideration of the role of pensions and their relationship to work (see Chapter 14 above). Currently, even the most sophisticated schemes of flexible job sharing have experienced major problems of accommodating adequate pension provisions. The trends towards linking pension and other benefits to a specific employment and emphasising the value of long-term employment with one employer will have to be reviewed. It seems appropriate to reconsider concurrently the weight which labour law legislation attaches to lengthy continuity of employment.

Perhaps the most problematic and complex area remains that of employment status. Could the two major worker categories – employed and self-employed – be merged? It has to be admitted that traditions run deep and opposition might be considerable, and that there would have to be major tax and other reforms. With basic tax rates for all, allowances for expenses and a unified administration, the system might be fairer and make it easier to engage in different employment situations consecutively or concurrently. There would need to be adjustments to the concepts of implied terms, assuming contract law were to remain the dominant legal mode. It may be necessary, however, to consider whether contract law should be abandoned in favour of a modern and variable concept of status for workers in differing employments.

Bibliography

Bechhofer, Frank, and Brian Elliott. 1978. 'The Voice of Small Business and the Politics of Survival'. *Sociological Review*, 26 (February), 57–88.

Clutterbuck, D., and R. Hill. 1981. *The Remaking of Work*. London: Grant McIntyre.

Cragg, A., and T. Dawson. 1981. *Qualificative Research among Homeworkers*. Research Paper no. 21. London: Department of Employment.

Crine, S. 1979. *The Hidden Army*. London: Low Pay Unit.

Daniel, W.W., and E. Stilgoe. 1978. *The Impact of Employment Protection Laws*. PSI Report no. 577. London: Policy Studies Institute.

Davies, P., and M. Freedland. 1984. *Labour Law: Text and Materials*. 2nd edn. London: Weidenfeld & Nicolson.

Department of Employment (DE). 1982. 'Numbers of Self-Employed People 1971–1979'. *Employment Gazette*, 90 (January), 15–18.

——. 1984. 'Historical Supplement No. 1: Employment Statistics'. *Employment Gazette*, 92 (August).

——. 1985a. 'Revised Employment Estimates for 1981 to 1984'. *Employment Gazette*, 93 (March), 114–18.

——. 1985b. *Sex Discrimination Act 1975 and European Community Legislation: A Consultative Document*. London: DE.

Employment Services Agency. 1976. *Temporary Workers: A Report of an Inquiry for the Employment Services Agency*. London: The Agency.

Equal Opportunities Commission (EOC). 1981. *Job-Sharing*. Manchester: EOC.

Ewing, K.D. 1982. 'Homeworking: A Framework for Reform'. *Industrial Law Journal*, 11 (June), 94–110.

Federation of Personnel Services (FPS). 1975. *The Temporary: A National Survey of Attitudes, Comments and Regional Statistics*. London: FPS.

Freedland, Mark. 1983. 'Labour Law and Leaflet Law: The Youth Training Scheme of 1983'. *Industrial Law Journal*, 12 (December), 220–35.

Hackney Job Share Project. 1984. *Annual Report 83/84*. London: Hackney Job Share Project.

Hakim, C. 1980. 'Homeworking: Some New Evidence'. *Employment Gazette*, 88 (October), 1105–10.

——. 1984a. 'Homework and Outwork: National Estimates from Two Surveys'. *Employment Gazette*, 92 (January), 7–12.

——. 1984b. 'Employers' Use of Homework, Outwork and Freelances'. *Employment Gazette*, 92 (April), 144–50.

——. 1985. *Employers' Use of Outwork*. Research Paper no. 44. London: DE.

Henry, Stuart. 1979. *The Hidden Economy*. London: Martin Robertson.

Hepple, B.A., and B.W. Napier. 1978. 'Temporary Workers and the Law'. *Industrial Law Journal*, 7 (June), 84–99.

Humphries, Judith. 1983. *Part Time Work*. London: Kogan Page.

Hurstfield, Jennifer. 1978. *The Part-time Trap: Part-Time Workers in Britain Today.* London: Low Pay Unit.

Huws, U. 1983. *The New Homeworkers.* Research Report to Equal Opportunities Commission. Manchester: EOC.

——. 1984. 'New Technology Homeworkers'. *Employment Gazette*, 92 (January), 13–17.

Incomes Data Services (IDS). 1982. *Part Time Workers.* Study 267. London: IDS.

Industrial Relations Review and Report (IRRR). 1984. 'Part Time Work: A Survey'. *Industrial Relations Review and Report*, no. 320 (May), 2–9.

King, Roger, and Neill Nugent. 1976. *Respectable Rebels: Middle Class Campaigns in Britain in the 1970s.* London: Hodder & Stoughton.

Leicester, Colin. 1982. 'Towards a Fully Part Time Britain'. *Personnel Management*, 14 (June), 28–31.

Leighton, Patricia. 1982. 'Employment Contracts: A Choice of Relationships'. *Employment Gazette*, 90 (October), 433–9.

——. 1983a. *Contractual Arrangements within Selected Industries.* Research Paper no. 39. London: Department of Employment.

——. 1983b. 'Employment and Self-Employment: Some Problems of Law and Practice'. *Employment Gazette*, 91 (May), 197–203.

——. 1983c. 'The Legal Researcher as Undercover Agent'. *Topical Law*, 5 (1), 37–45.

——. 1984. 'Observing Employment Contracts'. *Industrial Law Journal*, 13 (June), 86–106.

——, and B. Doyle. 1982. *Making and Varying Contracts of Employment.* London: Polytechnic of North London.

——, and S. Dumville. 1977. 'From Statement to Contract – Some Effects of the Contracts of Employment Act 1972'. *Industrial Law Journal*, 6 (September), 133–48.

Lewis, D., and K. Williams. 1981. *The Aftermath of Tribunal Reinstatement and Re-engagement.* Research Paper no. 23. London: Department of Employment.

Low Pay Unit. 1985. *Working Children.* Low Pay Pamphlet No. 34. London: Low Pay Unit.

McNally, Fiona. 1979. *Women for Hire.* London: Macmillan.

Mars, Gerald. 1982. *Cheats at Work.* London: Allen & Unwin.

Martin, J., and C. Roberts. 1984. *Women and Employment: A Lifetime Perspective.* London: HMSO.

Phelps Brown. 1968. Committee of Inquiry under Professor E.H. Phelps Brown into Certain Matters Concerning Labour in Building and Civil Engineering. *Report.* Cmnd 3714. London: HMSO.

Robinson, Olive. 1979. 'Part-Time Employment in the EEC'. *Three Banks Review*, no. 122 (June), 61–76.

——, and J. Wallace. 1984. *Part Time Employment and Sex Discrimination Legislation in Great Britain.* Research Paper no. 43. London: Department of Employment.

Russell, Raymond. 1983. 'Class Formation in the Workplace: The Role of Sources of Income'. *Work and Occupations*, 10 (August), 349–72.

Smith, I. 1985. 'Employment Laws and the Small Firm'. *Industrial Law Journal*, 14 (March), 18–32.

Syrett, Michael. 1983. *Employing Job-Sharers, Part-Time and Temporary Staff.* London: Institute of Personnel Management.

Williams, Virginia. 1984. Employment Implications of New Technology'. *Employment Gazette*, 92 (May), 210–15.

PART VI
Institutions of Labour Law

19 Dispute Settlement Institutions and the Courts

Linda Dickens and David Cockburn

INTRODUCTION

The relatively limited role of the law until the 1960s, which was focused mainly on removing obstacles to collective bargaining, has important implications for dispute settlement machinery. The courts played an important role in industrial relations at particular historical moments, but their concern has been with the boundaries of lawful action rather than the settlement of industrial relations disputes – but, of course, decisions on the former affect the latter. The preference for collective bargaining between unions and employers rather than legislation as a means of regulating jobs meant that the settlement of disputes over job regulation was also left to voluntary procedures and arrangements.

The state's interest in maintaining industrial peace was pursued by the provision of bargaining assistance, notably in the form of third-party conciliation (aiding the parties to reach their own settlement) and arbitration (handing down awards where the parties wished to have the matter determined for them). In peace-time such assistance has been voluntary and non-coercive. This official third-party intervention is usually traced back to the Conciliation Act 1896 and the Industrial Courts Act 1919, although earlier examples of dispute settlement machinery exist (Sharp, 1949:273–89). These Acts provide the roots of a family tree ending today with the Advisory, Conciliation and Arbitration Service (ACAS) and the Central Arbitration Committee (CAC).

Where, as in Britain, collective agreements are relatively informal, not legally binding (see Chapter 4), and sometimes may not even be in writing, and where disputes are normally settled within voluntary procedures, it is difficult to distinguish clearly between disputes of right (the application or interpretation of existing terms) and disputes of interest (the creation of new terms) (see Wedderburn, 1969). Nor is it very meaningful to talk of individual as opposed to collective disputes. Separate voluntary procedures may exist to deal with different kinds of dispute but whether, for example, dismissal is treated as an individual grievance or a collective dispute will depend largely on how unions and employers decide to treat it (Mellish and Collis-Squires, 1976:175; Concannon, 1980:15). In other countries such distinctions may underpin the choice of dispute settlement or rights enforcement machinery (Aaron, 1980:368–71). Judicial adjudication is usually seen as more appropriate for disputes of right and individual disputes, while conciliation processes are seen as better suited to collective disputes of interest. This has not been the case with the autonomous dispute settlement machinery set up through collective bargaining in Britain (Kahn-Freund, 1954), nor with state provided machinery (Davies, 1979:37).

The move towards a positive framework of legal regulation from the 1960s, however, and the legal machinery which accompanied it, imposed something of this distinction, at least as between individual and collective disputes. The range of individual statutory employment rights was seen to require judicial adjudication and was entrusted to a type of specialist court: the industrial tribunals which were set up in 1964. The Donovan Commission (1968:para.576) had tried to distinguish between individual and collective conflicts, wishing only the former to come within the ambit of the tribunals, but, as will be argued, the distinction in practice proved difficult to draw.

Other statutory provisions, under the EPA for example, were viewed as giving rise to collective issues. These included the granting to trade unions of the right to seek recognition (ss.11–16), to disclosure of information (ss.17–21) and to the recognised or 'general level' terms and conditions (Sch.11). Their enforcement was entrusted not to courts or quasi-courts but to a variant of the third-party intervention processes, in particular arbitration by the CAC (see Chapters 3 and 4 above). For a brief period, during the legislative life of the IRA, there was a specialist court, the National Industrial Relations Court (NIRC), empowered to hear complaints from individuals, unions and employers on a range of issues, but this was abolished in 1974. Its function of hearing appeals from industrial tribunals was taken over in due course by the Employment Appeal Tribunal (EAT).

A major factor underlying this allocation of jurisdictions in the 1970s was a view that the ordinary courts and the process of judicial adjudication were inappropriate for the resolution of disputes arising out of the new rights then being created. Following Schmidt (1969:47), a distinction may be drawn between 'administration', including voluntary arbitration, and 'adjudication', the judicial method. Administration 'does not make vested rights a matter of principal concern but aims at the adjustment of the relations of the parties with a view to the future'. Giving certain matters to an arbitral body rather than a court thus implies that something more than a declaration of 'who is right' is being sought. The arbitrator's decision has a 'political' as well as a 'judicial' dimension (Lockwood, 1955:336). Even where judicial adjudication seemed appropriate to enforce individual employment rights, however, a quasi-court was used: the industrial tribunal system. This appeared to offer a way of overcoming the problems of delay, expense and formality associated with the ordinary courts and also problems concerning the unfavourable perception which unions and their members have of the courts.

Utilising the industrial tribunals for disputes involving the adjudication of individual rights and relying on non-judicial mechanisms such as arbitration for others, appeared to offer a way of bringing more legal regulation into industrial relations while maintaining the 'voluntary principle'. This principle, identified by Flanders (1970:174) as the basis of the British system, prevented 'the conduct of industrial relations – and especially the settlement of disputes – from becoming entangled with legal process'. It did not mean necessarily keeping the law out of industrial relations but it did embrace a desire to keep out the courts.

Although the ordinary courts have not been given a dispute settlement role nor entrusted with first instance jurisdictions concerning statutory individual employment rights, in practice they have not been kept out of industrial relations disputes. The courts have wide and important, original, appellate and supervisory jurisdictions in labour law. Their 'original' jurisdiction covers such areas as the lawfulness of industrial action, contractual disputes, most internal union administration disputes, personal injury litigation and public order. Their principal appellate role is on points of law from decisions of the EAT, and their supervisory role is by way of judicial review of certain decisions taken by public bodies.

This chapter focuses on the three kinds of institutions indicated: the 'third parties', the ordinary courts, and the industrial tribunals. Because its concern is dispute settlement and rights enforcement in the labour law area, not all aspects of these institutions will be considered. For example, a great deal of the activity of the courts falls outside the consideration of this chapter, as does ACAS's advisory work, even though this, together with its code-making functions under EPA s.6, may be seen as an indirect form of dispute prevention (ACAS, 1980:57). There are of course other more specialised institutions concerned with rights enforcement in employment. They are dealt with in other chapters; for example, the Commission for Racial Equality and the Equal Opportunities Commission (Chapter 17), the Health and Safety Executive (Chapter 16) and the Wages Councils (Chapter 3). Chapters 10 and 11 deal with the TUC's internal machinery for handling jurisdictional and other disputes between affiliated unions and with the role of the Certification Officer.

THIRD-PARTY DISPUTE SETTLEMENT

Dispute procedures

The vast majority of industrial disputes are settled without recourse to any external body (Jones et al., 1983:17). They are settled through private procedures and arrangements within companies or industries. A survey of manufacturing establishments with over fifty employees undertaken in the late 1970s (Brown, 1981:44) found most employers reporting the existence of procedures for handling disputes over pay and conditions, discipline and dismissal, and individual grievances at establishment level. In a later survey across all industries (Daniel and Millward, 1983:16) 59 per cent of all establishments reported the existence of procedures for dealing with collective disputes on pay and conditions, 82 per cent reported procedures for handling discipline/dismissal disputes, and 80 per cent reported the existence of individual grievance procedures.

The details of the autonomous dispute settlement machinery vary considerably (Singleton, 1975; Davies, 1979; Marsh, 1968). Differences between and within industries exist, for instance, on status quo provisions, that is, whether while the dispute is in procedure the working arrangements that are the subject of the dispute revert to what they were before the dispute arose. Certain outline similarities in procedures, however, can be seen, for example, in the existence of a number of hierarchical stages, normally with time limits, and in the banning of industrial action until a procedure is exhausted (Kessler, 1980:16).

Where a matter cannot be settled in procedure, resort may be made to a third party. In the manufacturing industry survey, for example, 37 per cent of the pay and conditions disputes procedures provided for conciliation, mediation or arbitration by an outside body, other than the employer's association or trade union, as did 21 per cent of both discipline/dismissal and individual grievance procedures. Most procedural arrangements on arbitration envisage a joint rather than unilateral reference. Traditionally provision for, and the use of, arbitration has been more common in the public sector where there are various standing arbitral bodies or specialist tribunals; for example, the Railway Staff National Tribunal and the Civil Service Arbitration Tribunal (Leopold and Beaumont, 1983). Recently there has been renewed interest in arbitration in the private sector, with the EETPU and other unions signing single union agreements some of which provide for 'pendulum' or 'final offer' arbitration as the last stage of the disputes procedure (IRRR, 1984). In such cases the arbitrator can opt only for the final position of either the union or the employer. This lack of flexibility raises doubts about the appropriateness of such arbitration for certain disputes (ACAS, 1985; CAC, 1985).

Third-party intervention may be used even where the disputes procedure does not make provision for it. A survey of parties who had used ACAS collective conciliation (Jones et al., 1983:12) found that in only a minority of cases was ACAS involved directly as a result of the operation of a dispute settlement procedure. When resort is made to a 'third party', it need not be to the state provided service, as shown by the various standing bodies referred to above. ACAS responded to twenty-three requests for nomination of arbitrators for private arbitrations in 1984 (ACAS, 1985:38), but the extent of privately provided ad hoc third-party assistance is unknown. Private provision is unlikely to be widespread, however, not least because the parties would have to meet the costs. Procedures nearly always name ACAS where third-party provision is made, and most reported ad hoc use of outsiders also concerned the publicly funded machinery (Brown, 1981:49; Daniel and Millward, 1983:169).

State Provision

Until they were transferred to ACAS in 1974, the third-party dispute settlement services had been provided by the DE. The transfer of functions reflected the demand for a dispute settlement service independent of government. It was noted earlier that the free provision of third-party services reflects the state's interest in maintaining industrial peace. This interest, however, is not in peace at any price but peace at the right price (Clegg, 1970:305) and to varying degrees governments sought to use or influence third-party dispute settlement mechanisms to control or affect the bargains being struck between unions and·employers. In 1971, for example, the DE refused its conciliation services to parties who appeared likely to reach agreement at a level considered inflationary (Paynter, 1972). The TUC and CBI reacted by moving to establish their own conciliation and arbitration service, the stimulus for setting up in 1974 the body which later became known as ACAS. The Secretary of State pledged 'so far as the government is concerned it will not seek to interfere with the activities of the Service' (Weekes, 1979:150).

ACAS is controlled by a Council which is expressly stated not to be subject to ministerial direction (para.11(1) of EPA Sch.1, in which ACAS's constitution is set out). Although the Council may have as many as fifteen members, it has so far had only nine, in addition to the full-time chair. The nine members are appointed by the Secretary of State for Employment, three after consultation with the TUC, three after consultation with the CBI and three are independent members, to date all academics. The Council is a symbol of ACAS's independence from government interference. There are, of course, various ways in which subtle government influence might be exerted: the ACAS staff are all civil servants within the DE group, the government holds the ACAS purse strings and the Secretary of State appoints the Council. There is, however, no evidence to suggest that any government has sought to inferfere in ACAS's operation and it certainly passed the 'incomes policy test' in the late 1970s (Weekes, 1979:153). The presence of TUC and CBI representatives on the Council symbolises too ACAS's impartiality as between the parties in industrial relations.

Where a trade dispute exists or is apprehended ACAS is empowered under EPA s.2 to provide assistance by way of conciliation 'or by other means', including mediation, and can, under EPA s.3, arrange arbitration. It also has power, under EPA s.5, to hold an inquiry into industrial relations generally, or in a particular firm. This function supplements the power of the Secretary of State to set up a court of enquiry under the Industrial Courts Act 1919 s.4. Courts of enquiry result in a report being laid before Parliament and published but are now used only exceptionally, as in the Grunwick recognition dispute (Scarman, 1977).

Third-party services may be ranged on a continuum according to the extent to which the disputing parties themselves retain control over the outcome of the dispute. Conciliation aims to assist the parties reach their own settlement. The conciliator performs various roles – for example, catalyst, conveyor of information or sounding-board (Dickens, 1979:301; Jones et al., 1983:13–14) – but normally does not suggest or advocate independent solutions in the way a mediator does. Mediation is a more positive form of conciliation although in practice the line between the two processes is fluid. In terms of personnel, ACAS draws a distinction, using its own staff for conciliation but appointing outsiders to perform mediation and arbitration. In arbitration, the parties hand over determination of the dispute to a third party. Whereas they may accept, reject or modify the mediator's suggestions or recommendations, it is normal for the parties to agree beforehand to accept the arbitrator's award.

Because arbitration involves loss of control over the final outcome of the dispute, parties are less likely to resort to it than to conciliation. Hunter (1977:239–40) argues that disputes on issues such as recognition and redundancy are less amenable to arbitration than, say, pay disputes since there is a higher chance of an award which will be unacceptable to one party. Arbitration, he argues, becomes acceptable where the parties have been able to narrow their differences within mutually tolerable limits. This does not mean, of course, that it necessarily will be used since there are a range of political and bargaining considerations which influence the decision to submit to a third party (Dickens, 1979:297–300).

Where arbitration is arranged by ACAS under EPA s.3 it may appoint someone from a list it maintains or it may refer the dispute to the CAC. In practice the former option is normally adopted and the CAC's annual voluntary case load hardly reaches double figures. The ACAS list is made up of academics, a few retired civil servants, and certain retired employer and trade union officials (Jones et al., 1983:14; Lockyer, 1979:59).

The CAC is a standing body, the successor to the Industrial Court set up in 1919, more appropriately named the Industrial Arbitration Board during the currency of the IRA. Cases are normally heard by a committee of three consisting of the chair or one of the several deputy chairs and two members drawn from two panels consisting of people who have experience as representatives respectively of employers and employees.[1] A similar arrangement, a board of arbitration, can be provided by ACAS where the appointed arbitrator sits with an equal number of members, normally one from each side, appointed to represent the respective general interests of the parties to the dispute. This arrangement is normally reserved for the 'more important issues' (ACAS, 1981:3) such as a national, industry-wide pay dispute or where a dispute is unusually complex.

An essential feature of these state provided third-party services is that they are voluntary and non-coercive. If the parties to the dispute do not agree then no conciliation, mediation or arbitration occurs. ACAS is, moreover, under a statutory duty 'to have regard to the desirability of encouraging the parties to use appropriate agreed procedures' (EPA ss.2(3) and 3(2)). Even following ACAS's intervention, there are no legal sanctions to enforce any agreements reached.

As noted in the introduction, however, the EPA gave statutory rights to trade unions which involved the use of third-party services other than on a voluntary basis. The CAC was the adjudication and enforcement body for

---

[1] The constitution of the CAC is set out in EPA Sch.1. Technically the CAC is part of ACAS which has a consultative role regarding the appointments made by the Secretary of State. In practice this means little more than the CAC making its annual report to the Secretary of State via ACAS.

various rights and ACAS was required to offer conciliation where references were made. Most of these provisions – like Sch.11 and the recognition procedure – have been repealed, although a similar example of this use of arbitration remains as part of the disclosure provisions (see Chapter 3). Before examining this aspect of arbitration, the voluntary services are evaluated.

Use and Evaluation of Voluntary Third-Party Services

The workloads of both the CAC and ACAS have been affected by the repeals mentioned in the previous paragraph. While ACAS can point to its continuing role in conciliating industrial tribunal claims (see below), which engages the majority of the Service's operational staff (ACAS, 1984:22), and can emphasise its advisory services, the CAC lacks this ability to compensate for its declining dispute settlement activity. This must raise a question mark over the future of the CAC. The number of non-voluntary references to it fell from a peak of 1,059 in 1978 to a mere 26 in 1984, including 8 cases brought under the Fair Wages Resolution, since rescinded (CAC, 1985:21).

In 1984 ACAS set up 20 boards of arbitration and 158 single arbitrations. Over the period 1974–84 the annual average was 30 boards and 222 single arbitrations. Mediation was much less common with an annual average over the same period of two boards and eighteen single mediations. While use of ACAS's voluntary collective dispute settlement services has declined, partly reflecting the impact of economic recession on the number of disputes, it remains higher than the use made of the third-party services when they were provided by the DE (Goodman and Krislov, 1974:334; ACAS, 1983:39). Research (Jones et al., 1983) has shown that, contrary to popular perception, most ACAS involvement is in relatively minor, small-scale disputes occurring in the regions, rather than with national or industry-wide confrontations. It does of course play a role in such disputes, recent notable examples in the public sector being the coal dispute in 1984–5, the water industry in 1983, and the National Health Service in 1982.

The largest category of disputes handled by ACAS conciliators concerns pay and terms and conditions of employment, accounting for 59 per cent of the collective conciliation case load of 1,448 in 1984 (ACAS, 1985:72). General pay claims are only a small proportion of this category, however, which includes a range 'of minor and subsidiary issues concerning bonus payments, grading, overtime payments and other disputes, mainly affecting small groups of workers, usually at plant level' (Lockyer, 1979:20). Fifteen per cent of collective conciliation cases in 1984 concerned recognition; 13 per cent discipline and dismissal and 5 per cent redundancy disputes. Disputes referred to ACAS for mediation and arbitration that year also predominantly concerned pay and other terms and conditions. This category constituted two-thirds of the mediation and arbitration cases, with dismissal and discipline disputes accounting for 31 per cent (ACAS, 1985:78).

Despite ACAS having the power to intervene in disputes on its own initiative, only 4 per cent of its annual case load arose in this way in 1984 (ACAS, 1985:73). The proportion of collective conciliation requests recorded as being made by the parties jointly has been increasing and accounted for 48 per cent in the same year. Thirty-nine per cent of cases were the result of a union request and 12 per cent arose from employer initiative (ACAS, 1985:73).

Having requested the third-party service, most parties report that the intervention was helpful (Jones et al., 1983:16) and are satisied with the conciliators' neutrality, comprehension of the issues and awareness of collective bargaining intricacies. Apart from consumer satisfaction, however, the effectiveness of third-party dispute settlement machinery is difficult to evaluate. For example, although the use of it may contribute to industrial peace, the vast majority of ACAS's collective conciliation occurs in disputes where no industrial action is being taken (ACAS, 1984:24). Any assessment of its contribution to reducing strikes, therefore, must rest on guesses as to the likelihood of industrial action in the absence of conciliation, taking into account factors such as the number of workers involved and the parties and issues in dispute (see Jones et al., 1983:9–11). ACAS itself claims a high and increasing rate of success in its collective conciliation: 79 per cent in 1982, 85 per cent in 1983 and 86 per cent in 1984 (1984:24; 1985:72). But ACAS's definition of success is extremely wide covering progress towards a settlement (including onward reference to arbitration) as well as actual settlement. In the cases surveyed by Jones et al. (1983:16) about half the disputes were actually resolved by conciliation.

Third-Party Rights Enforcement

As stated earlier, industrial arbitration in Britain can be distinguished from judicial decision-making in that the object is to achieve a workable and acceptable solution, not a determination as to who is 'right' in the technical legal sense. Where arbitration is located within a statutory framework of rules, however, as with the mainly repealed non-voluntary aspects of the CAC's work, the arbitral process may bear some resemblance to the judicial. Rideout (1982:51) has suggested the term 'regulated' arbitration to distinguish this kind of arbitration from voluntary or 'equitable' arbitration, where the parties determine the terms of reference.

The main distinguishing characteristic between this regulated arbitration and traditional arbitration was the compulsory nature of the former. The compulsion lay not, as in the wartime orders,[2] in the arbitration procedure having to be used by parties in dispute, but in the fact that it could be invoked unilaterally by the aggrieved party and in the enforceability of the awards, through incorporation of terms into individual contracts of employment (see Chapter 3). Arbitration under EPA s.3, in common with the other forms of ACAS third-party intervention, has no sanctions attached to it,

---

[2] Conditions of Employment and National Arbitration Order SR & O 1940 No. 1305 and Industrial Disputes Order SI 1951 No. 1376.

although the parties may agree to be bound by awards. Although in both cases the arbitration is provided by a state-funded body, the authority of the arbitrator under s.3 derives from the parties in dispute while under regulated arbitration (as in EPA s.16 or Sch.11) it derived from the state.

Although its special nature may call for a distinguishing label, 'regulated' arbitration was seen by the CAC (Wood, 1979:10) to demand fundamentally the same qualities and approach as voluntary arbitration and, within the legal procedural constraints, the CAC adopted 'an approach in marked contrast to that of a court or tribunal'. The procedure, based on written submissions, differed from legal hearings and its emphasis centred on problem-solving not rule-application. The CAC avoided building up precedents and demanded that the words of statutes be interpreted 'in a common sense way with industrial and industrial relations practice in mind' (CAC, 1978:23). This approach, however, brought it into conflict with the courts exercising their judicial review function.[3] Although judicial supervision operated to minimise some of the distinctions between the arbitral and judicial processes, 'regulated' arbitration by the CAC more closely resembled voluntary dispute settlement processes than the decision-making found in the ordinary court.

THE COURTS

Although specialised courts such as the Companies Court, the Commercial Court, the Restrictive Practices Court and the Patent Court have an important role in the legal system, there is no specialist labour court in the UK with a general jurisdiction over employment-related issues. Instead there has developed alongside the courts an uncoordinated network of specialised institutions through which different aspects of labour legislation are administered and enforced. The industrial tribunal system, with its appellate body the EAT being classified as a superior court of record (EPCA Sch.11, para.12), is the nearest to the model of a labour court, but its jurisdiction is strictly limited. The NIRC was a court with a more extensive jurisdiction over both individual and collective labour law issues but, being created by the IRA, was very much identified with that Act and failed to survive its repeal in 1974.

Even though Parliament has limited the jurisdiction of the ordinary courts over certain labour law issues, they nevertheless retain, as suggested in the introduction to this chapter, wide original, appellate, and supervisory jurisdictions and have a direct influence on the development of the substantive law. The theory that courts have no creative law-making role but merely apply existing common law principles and statutory provisions is a myth. The common law develops and adapts to new social and economic

---

[3]   E.g. *R v CAC ex parte Deltaflow* [1977] IRLR 486; *R v CAC ex parte Hy-Mac* [1979] IRLR 461. But see also *R v CAC ex parte T I Tube Division Services Ltd* [1978] IRLR 183 where a 'common sense' approach to statutory interpretation by the CAC was endorsed. See Chapter 3 above for further examples of judicial review of CAC and ACAS.

conditions through the evolution of judicial decision-making, while complex statutes often await judicial interpretation before the precise manner of their application can be predicted. As a member of the Donovan Commission, Eric Wigham wrote at the time its Report was published: 'supposing we made all the right recommendations and supposing the government gave effect to them all in legislation, how long would it be before the judges turned everything upside down? ... the ingenuity of lawyers is endless' (quoted in Wedderburn, 1971:8).

Labour law disputes are heard by whichever court is appropriate for that particular type of legal problem. They are, accordingly, heard by a wide variety of civil and criminal courts, the structure and composition of which is merely outlined here (see generally Walker and Walker, 1985; Radcliffe and Cross, 1977; Zander, 1980). The distinction between the civil and criminal law is fundamental. It is one which is reflected not only in the different types of court but also in the different judicial principles and procedures applied by those courts. The rationale of the distinction is of course that criminal acts are regarded as harmful to, and therefore actionable on behalf of, the whole community, whereas breaches of the civil law involve the breach of an individual's legal rights and are therefore actionable only by the injured party. Criminal acts are described as illegal whereas breaches of the civil law are described as unlawful. The sanctions imposed by a criminal court are intended to punish, usually by the deprivation of liberty or the imposition of fines, whereas the orders of a civil court are usually intended to compensate. These distinctions have led to stricter standards of proof being adopted in the criminal courts. Whereas plaintiffs in civil litigation can succeed if they establish their cases 'on the balance of probabilities', this is not sufficient to secure a conviction in criminal law where the prosecution must establish its case 'beyond reasonable doubt'.

This crucial distinction has sometimes caused difficulties where a person found to have been fairly dismissed for suspected dishonesty is later acquitted by the criminal courts.[4] Such an apparently contradictory result is explained partly by the different questions the tribunal and courts must ask themselves and partly by the different standards of proof that they apply. The criminal courts also apply much stricter standards of statutory interpretation. Whereas the civil courts sometimes tend to be adventurous in seeking the intention of Parliament, the criminal courts apply the principle that no one should be subject to criminal sanctions, especially loss of liberty, without Parliament having made its intention clear beyond ambiguity. Thus, while it may be relatively easy for an employer to get an injunction against a trade union on the appropriate civil test, the court must be much stricter should there be a later allegation of contempt as this could result in imprisonment. Not only must there be sufficient evidence to establish contempt 'beyond reasonable doubt' but the necessary procedural requirements must have been meticulously followed.[5]

---

[4] E.g. *Harris (Ipswich) Ltd v Harrison* [1978] IRLR 382.
[5] Rules of the Supreme Court Order 45 Rule 7. *Chanel Ltd v FGM Cosmetics* [1981] FSR 471; *Chiltern District Council v Keane* [1985] 2 All ER 118; *Austin Rover v AUEW (TASS)*

Criminal Courts

Although there is a long history of the criminal law being used against both the organisation and activities of trade unions, many of these liabilities had been removed by 1875 (Wedderburn, 1971:305–13, 326; Hedges and Winterbottom, 1930). There are, however, different ways in which the criminal law can still influence trade union activity. Certain occupations and services remain subject to direct criminal penalties for taking industrial action, for example, merchant seamen, the police, the armed services and even postal and telecommunication workers. Offences of more general application include criminal conspiracy and, in certain circumstances, criminal breach of contract contrary to s.5 of the Conspiracy and Protection of Property Act 1875 (see Chapter 8). In recent times, however, public order offences have led to the involvement of the criminal law in industrial disputes, especially picketing; such offences include obstruction, breach of the peace, unlawful assembly, affray and even riot (see Chapter 7).

There are two types of criminal court which hear cases at first instance in England: the magistrates' court and the Crown Court, and in Scotland the magistrates' court and the sheriff's court.[6] Magistrates' courts in England have a summary jurisdiction to adjudicate on relatively minor criminal offences involving terms of imprisonment of six months or less. They also conduct committal proceedings in the more serious offences which are to be later tried on indictment in the Crown Court. Magistrates are appointed by the Lord Chancellor, usually following consultation with local interest groups such as trade unions, trades councils, employers' associations and chambers of commerce. The lay magistrates, who normally sit as a bench of three without a jury, are guided on points of law by a legally qualified justices' clerk. In certain large inner city areas the lay magistrates have been replaced by full-time, legally qualified stipendiary magistrates. Appeal from the magistrates' court is to either the Divisional Court of the Queen's Bench Division, where the appeal is conducted on the papers, or to the Crown Court by way of re-hearing. The Crown Court has exclusive jurisdiction over serious offences in addition to its appellate and sentencing roles. Appeal from the Crown Court is to the Criminal Division of the Court of Appeal and in Scotland from the sheriff's court to the Inner House of the Court of Session. Leave to appeal must be obtained in order to appeal on the facts or on the sentence, but an appeal lies as of right on a point of law against conviction. The final appeal is to the House of Lords where it is necessary to have not only leave to appeal but a certificate that the case involves a point of general public importance.

During the twentieth century the criminal courts have largely escaped the criticisms poured upon the civil courts by the trade union movement, but, in their defence of public order, they have shown firmness and flexibility. When the magistrates' courts looked like being overwhelmed by the huge

---

[1985] IRLR 162. In the Austin Rover case the National Society of Metal Mechanics was found not to be in contempt as the court order they allegedly disobeyed had been served late.

6 See generally on the Scottish legal system, Walker (1981:ch.8).

numbers of prosecutions brought against pickets in the 1984–5 miners' dispute, a range of administrative steps was taken to ensure the system would not break down. These included evening and weekend sittings of the lay magistrates, the use of stipendiaries brought in from the cities, and the use of pro forma bail conditions.[7] The courts were also able to deal with the problems caused by the flying pickets in that dispute by an interpretation of the law which enabled the police lawfully to turn back such pickets miles from their destination,[8] and the police power to regulate street collections in London was confirmed.[9] As to the future, there is no doubt that the criminal courts will continue to be used to maintain public order during industrial disputes but any wider role in the regulation of trade union activities would be extremely contentious.

Civil Courts

County courts. Just as industrial tribunals were set up to be relatively informal bodies where a restricted type of claim could be settled quickly and inexpensively, the county court system was established under the County Courts Act 1846 to provide a similar service for traders with small civil claims that were not worth pursuing in the higher courts (Radcliffe and Cross, 1977:282–4). In Scotland the court with an equivalent jurisdiction is the sheriff's court. The present limit on the jurisdiction of the county court in contract and tort is £5,000, which is less than the maximum that industrial tribunals can award. In view of the considerable number of small claims, an arbitration scheme was introduced by the Administration of Justice Act 1973, which allows a county court registrar to deal with claims of under £500 in a way which is intended to be quicker, cheaper and more informal than appearing before a judge.

County courts have not so far had a significant involvement in labour law, outside the important field of personal injury litigation. They can grant injunctions but only if the application is accepted by a judge as being ancillary to the major remedy being sought, usually damages.[10] As the object of most legal proceedings in industrial dispute cases has been to obtain an injunction, it has seldom been seen as appropriate for such cases to be brought in the county court, despite the obvious advantages in terms of cost and convenience. Whether this will change now that it is possible to claim damages from trade unions (EA 1982 s.15) is a matter of speculation.

As individuals, their trade unions, and legal advisers become more accustomed to pursuing employment rights through legal machinery, it is probable that they will become more aware of the right to bring actions against employers for breach of contract in the county court.[11] Such a case

---

[7] *R v Mansfield Justices ex parte Sharkey* [1984] IRLR 496.
[8] *Moss v McLachlan* [1985] IRLR 76.
[9] *Meaden v Wood* (1985) The Times, 30 April.
[10] County Court Rules 1981, Order 13 Rule 6; County Courts Act 1984 s.38; *Byrne v Herbert* [1966] 2 QB 121.
[11] E.g. *Henthorn v CEGB* [1980] IRLR 361.

might typically arise out of the employer's failure to pay proper sick pay, or holiday pay or give proper notice but it may only emerge after dismissal when the employee commences a claim for unfair dismissal and is informed by the industrial tribunal that it has no jurisdiction over breaches of contract. In some circumstances it would then be necessary to pursue two legal actions, one in the industrial tribunal and the other in the county court. This unsatisfactory position was recognised by the EPA s.109 which gave the Lord Chancellor the power to confer upon industrial tribunals the jurisdiction to entertain complaints of breach of contract of employment. This provision was re-enacted in EPCA s.131 and a draft order was even prepared in 1978. Taking note of the TUC's objections, the then Labour Government decided not to lay the draft order before Parliament. The TUC's objections (see TUC, 1976:97) were to the effect that to introduce contractual issues would further remove industrial tribunals from their primary task of acting as an industrial jury, that industrial tribunals would inevitably become more legalistic, that they could become involved in the interpretation of collective agreements, that they might be led into ruling upon the merits of industrial disputes, and that employers would be able to counter-claim that their losses caused by the employee's conduct, particularly in an industrial dispute, should be set off against the employee's claim. Formidable though these arguments appeared at the time, it is strongly arguable that the average case involving a breach of contract of employment could be better dealt with by an industrial tribunal, using both its industrial and legal experience, than by a county court registrar or judge.

High Court. All substantial civil cases in Scotland start in the Outer House of the Court of Session and in England and Wales in one of the three divisions of the High Court: the Family, Chancery or Queen's Bench Division (QBD). Although the Chancery Division normally deals with disputes over land, mortgages, trusts, patents, bankruptcy and company law, it is the division in which injunctions against unions are often sought. In deciding whether to bring such proceedings in the Chancery Division or QBD, the usual criteria include the speed with which a case can be brought on, having regard to the lists in both divisions, the greater experience of labour law matters that some Chancery judges are believed to have, and the fact that Chancery motions are in open court whereas QBD interlocutory applications are in chambers. The QBD is the largest of the three divisions, employing 60 per cent of the judges and including within it the commercial, admiralty and electoral courts as well as the Divisional Court, which exercises the very important function of judicial review. This is the supervisory jurisdiction under which the quasi-judicial activities of such statutory bodies as the CAC and ACAS can be challenged. The work of the QBD is, however, dominated by personal injury cases which account for some 69 per cent of the 7,000 cases tried there in 1983 (Lord Chancellor's Department, 1984:37).

The whole range of employment-related issues comes before the High Court. First, there are the personal injury cases. Second, there are those cases alleging breaches of contract of employment and involving sums of money in excess of £5,000. Such cases often involve the premature termination of fixed term contracts.[12] More unusually, an employee might go to the High Court to stop the employer unilaterally changing his or her terms and conditions of employment.[13] Employers seldom find it worthwhile taking legal action against their employees for breach of contract, except when they need an injunction to restrain the employee breaking a restrictive covenant (see Chapter 12). Third, there are those cases which union members or former members might bring against their union. These cases will largely be contractual in nature, being based upon the rule book and will involve an examination of whether the union has acted in breach of its constitution. This might happen if the union has, for example, spent money or called industrial action where it is not entitled to do so or if it has disciplined its members in ways not provided for in the rules (see Chapter 10). Union members may also sue the union in the High Court for negligence, alleging, for example, that a union official has negligently failed to submit a personal injury or unfair dismissal claim within the statutory limitation period.[14] Fourth, there are those cases usually based on tortious liabilities brought against the union or its representatives arising out of an industrial dispute (see Chapters 6 and 7).

Court of Appeal (Civil Division). While not the highest court in the land, the Court of Appeal – and in Scotland the Inner House of the Court of Session – is arguably the most important as it deals with many more cases than the House of Lords and, unless there is a further appeal, it is the view of the Court of Appeal which becomes the binding authority on all the lower courts and even itself.[15] In 1983, for example, the House of Lords determined 76 cases compared to 469 determined by the Court of Appeal (Lord Chancellor's Department, 1984:10 and 15). The Civil Division is presided over by the Master of the Rolls and consists of up to eighteen Lord Justices of Appeal. Its influence on the development of labour law is indisputable. The precise nature of this influence has of course changed as differently constituted courts have decided different cases but, as will have been observed in the preceding chapters, both case law and statutory developments were decisively influenced by Lord Denning, Master of the Rolls between 1962 and 1982 (Miller, 1981; Davies and Freedland, 1984).

House of Lords. Subject to certain international obligations and the decisions of the Court of Justice of the European Communities (see Chapter 20), the House of Lords is the supreme civil and criminal court in Great Britain and Northern Ireland. Its decisions can only be overriden by statute or by a change of mind by the House of Lords itself in a later case.[16] Cases are heard not by the full chamber of the House of Lords but by a judicial

12   E.g. *Shove v Downs Surgical Plc* [1985] ICR 532.
13   E.g. *Burdett-Coutts v Hertfordshire CC* [1984] IRLR 91; *Gilham v Kent CC* [1985] IRLR 18.
14   E.g. *Buckley v NUGMW* [1967] 3 All ER 767; *Cross v BISKTA* [1968] 1 All ER 250; see Nock (1968).
15   *Young v Bristol Aeroplane Co.* [1944] KB 718.
16   Practice statement of the Lord Chancellor [1966] 3 All ER 77.

committee which usually consists of five Lords of Appeal in Ordinary, known as 'Law Lords'. In order to bring a civil appeal to the House of Lords it is necessary to obtain the leave of either the Court of Appeal or the House of Lords.

CIVIL REMEDIES AND ENFORCEMENT

The civil law provides a wide range of remedies.[17] Other parts of this book touch on the remedies for breach of the union rule book (Chapter 10), breach of the contract of employment (Chapter 12) and unfair dismissal (Chapter 15). In this section the emphasis will be on the remedies available to plaintiffs in litigation arising from strikes or other industrial action, namely, injunctions and damages.

Injunctions[18]

An injunction is an order to a person either to cease doing something or, in its mandatory form (which in labour disputes is rare), to do something. Injunctions are sometimes granted in cases arising out of internal trade union disputes where the plaintiff is, for example, seeking the restoration of the status quo by way of an injunction, and a ruling as to the lawful limits of the union's power by way of a declaration of the legal position. Its typical application in labour law, however, is by employers who are seeking a quick legal remedy to halt a strike or other industrial action. The rules of legal procedure enable the courts to make temporary or interlocutory orders which effectively require the organisers to call off the action until the case is heard at a full trial.[19] At full trial, the court must decide whether to discharge its original order or grant a permanent injunction, for example, where the dispute has still not been finally settled.

While the granting of a 'labour' injunction will not resolve the underlying dispute, it can have a profound tactical effect on the industrial action and thereby on the balance of bargaining power. The speed and ease with which a labour injunction can be obtained is therefore crucial. Usually an application for such an injunction is made soon after the industrial action has started, although it is possible to seek an order, known as a quia timet injunction, that threatened industrial action should be called off before it has even started. Moreover, in an urgent case an injunction can be granted on an application made ex parte, that is, without giving the person against whom it is made an opportunity to be heard. Such snap labour injunctions were not uncommon in the period before the IRA came into effect (Davies and Anderman, 1973). In order to prevent a recurrence of this practice after the IRA was repealed, TULRA s.17 (1) provides that where in the opinion

[17] See generally McGregor (1980) and Snell (1982).
[18] The assistance of Bob Simpson in the preparation of this section is gratefully acknowledged.
[19] Supreme Court Act 1981 s.37 and Rules of the Supreme Court Order 29 Rule 1.

of the court the party against whom an injunction is sought would be likely to claim that he acted in contemplation or furtherance of a trade dispute it must not grant an injunction unless satisfied that all steps which were reasonable in the circumstances were taken with a view to seeing that he had notice of the application and an opportunity to be heard. In theory sufficient notice should be given to permit the defendant the opportunity of instructing lawyers to make representations about the trade dispute defence; in practice notice of less than twenty-four hours has been accepted.[20]

Ex parte injunctions normally only last for a few days until an inter partes hearing, with both sides either present or given an opportunity to be present. The legal proceedings at this stage are known as 'interlocutory' because, in theory, the rights and wrongs of the case will only be properly determined at a full trial when witnesses will be called and cross-examined and considered legal arguments put to the court. Interlocutory proceedings are usually decided on the basis of legal argument and hurriedly prepared 'affidavits', that is, sworn statements which are treated as evidence without the person concerned being subject to cross-examination. In *American Cyanamid Co. v Ethicon Ltd*,[21] the House of Lords decided that if, on an application for an interlocutory injunction, the plaintiff could show that he had an arguable case in the sense that there was 'a serious question to be tried' – a relatively low hurdle, given the complexity of the law in this area – the grant or a refusal of an injunction should depend on the 'balance of convenience'. In labour disputes this almost invariably weighs heavily in favour of the plaintiff employers who can usually point to mounting economic loss if the industrial action continues (Davies and Anderman, 1973). Against this defendant unions, officials or workers can put only the loss of a bargaining tactic. These judicial criteria left it unclear what, if any, weight should be given to the statutory immunities. Section 17(2) was therefore added to TULRA by the EPA 'for the avoidance of doubt'. It provides that where a party against whom an interlocutory injunction is sought claims that he acted in contemplation or furtherance of a trade dispute, the court shall have regard to the likelihood of that party succeeding in establishing a trade dispute defence under ss.13 or 15 of TULRA.

In *NWL v Woods*,[22] the Law Lords concluded that TULRA s.17(2) was intended to restore the pre-*Cyanamid* law in labour injunction cases. Thus, in addition to seeing whether there is a serious question to be tried and where the balance of convenience lies, the court must also consider the 'likelihood' of a trade dispute defence being established either as part of the balance of convenience or as a separate factor. This conclusion was based on judicial recognition of the 'practical realities' which lie behind applications for labour injunctions, namely, that interlocutory proceedings almost invariably dispose of the case because industrial action can only be pursued

---

[20] In some actions, which received little publicity, it appears that far less notice was accepted as reasonable, if indeed compliance with TULRA s.17(1) was considered. See *United Biscuits (UK) Ltd v Fall* [1979] IRLR 110; *Express Newspapers v Mitchell* [1982] IRLR 465.

[21] [1975] AC 396.

[22] [1979] ICR 867.

effectively by 'striking while the iron is hot'. In *Dimbleby and Sons Ltd v NUJ*,[23] however, the House of Lords revised its appraisal of these practical realities on the grounds that the EA 1982 had since made it possible to pursue unions in damages. Thus it could no longer be assumed that the interlocutory proceedings would dispose of the case and the *Cyanamid* test was once more considered to be the appropriate one. It is nevertheless arguable that now the right to claim damages from unions should lessen the prospect of injunctions being awarded against them as, if the employer can be fully compensated by damages, this must surely influence the court's consideration of the balance of convenience. The plaintiff employers would probably counter this argument by submitting that in a dispute they not only lose calculable profits but incalculable goodwill and potential clients and that in any event there is an upper limit on the damages that a court can order a union to pay (see Chapter 6). Despite these possible arguments both the parties and the court remain aware that the crucial 'practical reality' is that in most situations the granting of a labour injunction will be a decisive blow to the use of industrial action as a tactic in the dispute,[24] a point which is confirmed by research (Evans, 1985).

One effect of the changes in the law made by the Acts of 1980, 1982 and 1984 is to create large areas of industrial action to which no trade dispute defence applies (see Chapter 6). Applications for labour injunctions in these cases are not affected by TULRA s.17(2). Moreover, in the *NWL*, *MacShane* and *Sirs* cases,[25] the Law Lords commented that the courts have a residual discretion to grant a labour injunction. It is not clear when this discretion can properly be exercised in cases where there is a high probability that the action is covered by the remaining immunities, though it is said to cover circumstances when industrial action has particularly serious consequences for the employer or the public at large (Lewis and Simpson, 1981:219). After the substantial dilution of the immunities by the 1980s legislation, it is less likely that this residual discretion to order labour injunctions will be needed by the courts.

One final problem concerning labour injunctions is identifying who is bound to obey them. This may present special problems where injunctions are sought against named pickets (see Chapter 7). Generally, where injunctions are directed against the organisers of industrial action rather than the participants, the scope for avoiding their impact is reduced. This is particularly so now that injunctions can be given against unions as such, even though the extent of their responsibility for the acts of their officials may be unclear.[26]

---

23 [1984] IRLR 67.
24 E.g. the injunction in *Mercury Communications Ltd v Scott-Garner* [1984] ICR 74 was decisive in ending the POEU's campaign against connecting Mercury's private service with British Telecom's system, notwithstanding the protestations of both sides at the time that they intended the case to go to a speedy full trial.
25 *NWL v Woods* [1979] ICR 867; *Express Newspapers v MacShane* [1980] ICR 42; *Duport Steels Ltd v Sirs* [1980] ICR 161.
26 It may now also be possible to enjoin all union members by a representative action against one of its officials. *Michaels (Furriers) Ltd v Askey* (1983) The Times, 25 June.

Damages

Whereas an injunction is an equitable remedy obtainable only at the discretion of the court, damages is a common law remedy available as of right to the successful plaintiff who can prove loss. In actions for breach of contract, the object of damages is to place the plaintiff in the same position, as far as it is possible, as if the contract had been properly performed, and in actions in tort the object is similarly to place the plaintiff in the same position as if the tort had not been committed. The primary object is therefore to compensate and not to punish.

The assessment of damages is the responsibility of the judge, except in defamation cases where a jury makes the award. The judge attempts to calculate the loss as arithmetically as possible but there is often a large discretionary element in his final award where, for example, he has to assess compensation for pain and suffering or lost business opportunities. The forensic examination of an employer's losses during an industrial dispute could prove a most revealing exercise, given the widely-held belief that companies often claim inflated losses arising out of trade disputes.[27]

Damages are of course the principal remedy sought in personal injury and most wrongful dismissal cases and have exceptionally been sought against individual employees in industrial dispute cases in the past.[28] The ability under the EA 1982 to claim damages up to a statutory maximum from the unions is a departure of the greatest significance (see Chapter 6). Whereas individuals could often not satisfy any award and actions against them might produce 'martyrs' in industrial disputes, unions are in a very exposed financial position should a number of claims for damages be successful. This adds a further weapon to the potential bargaining armoury of employers, for they are now unlikely to omit such a claim from any legal action they commence arising out of an industrial dispute, whether or not the claim is pursued to trial. The vulnerability of union funds is intended to engender more control by senior union officials over the calling and conduct of industrial action or to weaken such action through official repudiation (see Chapter 6).

At the full trial arising out of the Stockport Messenger dispute in 1983,[29] the judge awarded compensatory damages not only for lost revenue but also, on grounds which are largely unexplained, for expenditure incurred by the company to protect its property and business in anticipation of industrial action but before any tort had been committed. An additional £10,000 'aggravated' damages was awarded as compensation for the union's reckless pursuit of its intention to close the plaintiff's business down, knowing that its conduct was unlawful and in open defiance of a labour injunction.

---

27 See generally Hyman (1984:36, 38). For example, car manufacturers often refer to their losses by reference to the number of cars lost and their show-room prices. In the 1984 Austin Rover dispute it was claimed that 25,000 cars at a show-room price of 125 million pounds were lost (*Financial Times*, 23 January 1985). The actual losses that could be claimed as damages would be much less than this figure.
28 E.g. *NCB v Galley* [1958] 1 All ER 91.
29 *Messenger Newspapers Group Ltd v NGA* [1984] IRLR 397.

Moreover, £25,000 'exemplary' damages were added to punish the union and teach it that wrongdoing does not pay, bringing the total award to just over £125,000. This is at least a questionable interpretation of the principles governing the award of exemplary damages which, it was generally understood, could only be awarded in such cases where defendants calculate that they will make a profit out of their action, even after paying compensatory damages.[30]

Enforcement

Elaborate legal machinery exists whereby the courts can enforce their orders. It is based partly on legislation, partly on the rules of court and partly on the inherent powers of the courts. It has been used where unions, their officials or members have refused to pay damages and fines or to obey the terms of injunctions.

Disobedience of a court order is a contempt of court and an issue of the utmost seriousness (see Borrie and Lowe, 1983). It leaves the contemnor very much at the mercy of the court which can, at its discretion, impose a wide range of penalties, all aimed at coercing the contemnors to purge their contempt and accept the court's authority. There is even a rule that, once in contempt, a person has no right to be heard by the court or pursue any proceedings without the leave of the court.[31] Penalties have not normally been imposed unless the contempt has been brought to the court's attention by the party who initiated the legal proceedings in the first place. Because of the seriousness of the allegation all applications in contempt proceedings must be strictly proved, any time limits for service carefully observed and the order must contain a penal notice stating that disobedience will render the defendant liable to 'process of execution to compel obedience'.[32] The two sanctions for civil contempt which are specifically referred to in the Rules of the Supreme Court are sequestration and committal (Order 45 Rule 5). In labour law cases, however, the courts have quite frequently used their inherent jurisdiction to impose fines as a lesser penalty with a view to inducing compliance.[33] Where fines go unpaid, there is provision in s.140 of the Supreme Court Act 1981 and s.16 of the Contempt of Court Act 1981 for the moneys to be collected 'in like manner as a judgment of the High Court for the payment of money', and for the court official responsible for enforcing payment to be the Queen's Remembrancer – the senior Queen's Bench Master who normally adjudicates upon pre-hearing procedural matters.

---

[30] See *Rookes v Barnard* [1964] AC 1129, 1221–30 and *Cassell and Co. Ltd v Broome* [1972] AC 1027.
[31] *Hadkinson v Hadkinson* [1952] P 285.
[32] See note 5.
[33] See, for example, *Heatons Transport v TGWU* [1972] ICR 285 (initial fine of £5,000 increased to £50,000); *Goad v AUEW (No. 2 and No. 3)* [1973] ICR 42 and 108 (fines of £5,000 and £50,000); *Express Newspapers v Mitchell* [1982] IRLR 465 (fine of £350 on a lay official of the EETPU).

The methods of enforcing payment are known as processes of execution and are set out in Order 45 Rule 1 of the Rules of the Supreme Court.[34] They are sequestration (Order 45 Rule 5), the sending of a bailiff or sheriff to seize goods of appropriate value (Order 47), garnishee proceedings (Order 49), charging orders (Order 50), the appointment of a receiver (Order 51) and committal to prison (Order 52). The court may direct which of these procedures the Queen's Remembrancer is to use, as in the case of *Austin Rover v TGWU*[35] where the use of garnishee proceedings was directed. This involves identifying someone who owes the union money, usually a bank, and enforcing that person to hand over sufficient of the union's money to cover the fine and legal costs.

Orders committing people in contempt to prison are normally used with great caution and as a matter of last resort. As Donaldson J said in *Howitt Transport Ltd v TGWU*,[36] non-compliance with a court order can vary from a flat defiance of the court's authority at the top end of the scale to a genuine but unsuccessful use of best endeavours to secure compliance at the bottom end. It is only at the top end of the scale that committal orders should be made. At one time contemnors were committed to prison indefinitely until they were prepared to apologise or otherwise purge their contempt, but by s.14(1) of the Contempt of Court Act 1981 a High Court committal order must be for a fixed term of no more than two years. The wisdom of committing those involved in industrial action to prison has long been questioned on the ground that, even if the numbers make it a practical proposition,[37] it is more likely to create martyrs and intransigence than a settlement of the dispute. The Donovan Report (1968:para.486) talks of 'the fruitlessness of the use of penal sanctions for the purposes of enforcing industrial peace'. Their use by the NIRC against the 'Pentonville Five' shop stewards in the 1972 docks dispute[38] only served to confirm this view and hence turned attention to making unions themselves liable. Nevertheless, the power to imprison may have greater efficacy in a changed economic and political climate as shown by the committal of Cammell Laird workers in 1984, who were imprisoned for up to twenty-one days for their contempt in defying a court order arising out of their occupation of an oil rig in Birkenhead.[39]

The release from prison of the unrepentant 'Pentonville Five' was secured following the intervention of the Official Solicitor, an officer of the court who had seldom if ever featured previously in labour law cases. In fact, the department of the Official Solicitor of the Supreme Court has existed since 1875[40] and his duty to review all cases of persons committed to prison for

---

34 These are usefully summarised in *Con Mech v AUEW (No. 2)* [1974] ICR 332, at 344.
35 (1984) The Times, 12 December.
36 [1973] ICR 1, at 11.
37 See the account of the Betteshanger prosecutions in Donovan (1968:app.6).
38 *Churchman v Joint Shop Stewards' Committee of the Workers of the Port of London* [1972] 3 All ER 603; *Midland Cold Storage v Steer* [1972] 3 All ER 773; Griffith (1985:65); Weekes et al. (1975:202).
39 *The Times*, 4 October, 1984.
40 By Order of Lord Chancellor Cairns, 6 November 1875.

contempt dates from a Lord Chancellor's standing direction in 1963. The curious aspect of his involvement in the 'Pentonville Five' case, therefore, was not that he intervened but rather the political convenience of his doing so and the dubious grounds upon which the release was justified; namely, that the enforcement of the law should be against unions rather than individuals, following the expedited decision of the House of Lords in the *Heatons* case (Griffith, 1985:66).

Sequestration can be used as an alternative to or in addition to committal. It was originally a means of coercing the defendants to purge their contempt by depriving them of possession of their property. But during this century, the courts have adopted the practice of applying the money received by the sequestrators in satisfaction of the outstanding debt due under the court order.[41] Upon application by the plaintiff, the court may issue a writ of sequestration. The writ names not fewer than four commissioners in sequestration who are authorised and commanded to take possession of all the contemnor's property. They in effect freeze this property so it cannot be used without their consent. In labour law cases the courts have frequently restricted the scope of the sequestration both as to the total amount and the types of funds to be seized.[42] Anyone who knows of the writ is under a duty not take any action which would frustrate its object. This means that anyone holding the union's property must account for it to the sequestrators and persons approached by the sequestrators for information about the whereabouts of the union's property must report fully and truthfully at the risk of themselves being in contempt.[43]

Even after the fine and costs have been paid out of the funds that have been seized the court still has a discretion as to the discharge of the writ and may, as in the Stockport Messenger dispute, refuse to do so until the union has apologised for its contempt. On the other hand, the court can exercise its discretion to clear a contempt order even without an apology. This was done in the case of the South Wales Area of the NUM after the 1984–5 dispute on the basis that the dispute had ended, the fines for contempt had been paid out of sequestrated funds, no further reports of breaches of the court order had been made after sequestration, and that by applying for their contempt to be cleared the union had demonstrated their recognition of the court's authority. In these circumstances, Scott J said that he was not troubled by the absence of a formal apology. In his view, 'the court's dignity did not depend upon or require an expressed public recantation the sincerity of which, if offered, might be open to question. It was of importance that the rule of law should prevail and that object had been achieved'.[44]

---

[41] For a summary of sequestration as applied to trade unions, see *Con Mech Ltd v AUEW (No. 3)* [1974] ICR 464, at 467.

[42] In *Heatons Transport v TGWU* (note 33) it was said that the court would ensure that pensioners of the union and other innocent third parties would not suffer. In *Con Mech v AUEW (No. 2)* (note 34) it was said that directions would be given to pay the salaries and wages of the ordinary staff of the union.

[43] *Bucknell v Bucknell* [1969] 2 All ER 998; *Eckman v Midland Bank* [1973] 1 QB 519; *Messenger Newspapers Group v NGA* [1984] ICR 345.

[44] *Richard Read (Transport) Ltd v NUM (South Wales) Area* (1985) The Times, 19 March.

The process of sequestration is one to which trade unions are particularly vulnerable. The nature and extent of their assets is reported annually to the CO and any attempt to transfer them out of the jurisdiction of British courts, as occurred in the miners' dispute of 1984–5, is unlikely to be successful in the long term. Such tactics may make the sequestrators' task more difficult and lengthy but their costs will eventually be taken from the assets of the union. In the miners' case, for example, the original fine on the national union was £200,000 but the anticipated fees for its collection were in excess of £800,000.[45]

The appointment of a receiver is not one of the means by which a court deals with contempt. It is a quite separate equitable remedy for which members of a union or other bodies can apply on the ground, among others, that those responsible for managing the organisation are dissipating its funds in breach of their express or implied duties. The remedy is a discretionary one which is normally only granted if it is thought that a declaration would not be obeyed. One of the cases brought against the NUM in the 1984–5 dispute was by working miners who claimed that the executive and trustees were wrongfully dissipating the union's funds by continuing to act in contempt of court. They applied for an order that the executive should be made personally liable for the fine of £200,000 and that the trustees should be replaced by a receiver.[46]

The duties of the receiver are quite different to those of the sequestrator. Whereas the sequestrator only takes possession of the union's property, the receiver becomes in effect its legal owner. The duty of the sequestrator is limited by the terms on the writ of sequestration to merely seizing the property. The receiver's duty is to take over the management of the union and act in its best interests. It is this fundamental difference which was instrumental in enabling the receiver to negotiate the recovery of the NUM's funds from Luxembourg after the sequestrators' many unsuccessful attempts to do so.[47] But it is not only in such extreme cases that receivers are appointed over the assets of trade unions. A receiver has, for example, been appointed at the application of an employer where a union was found to be in breach of duty in refusing to pay the costs that one of their members had been ordered to pay after bringing an unsuccessful personal injury case.[48]

It is clear from this discussion and the preceding chapters that not only can the courts influence the development of the law through their interpretation and application but that the procedures, remedies and enforcement mechanisms exist to ensure that the courts are not brought into disrepute. But by the very nature of the labour law system the intervention of the courts in industrial disputes generally favours the employer and it is therefore not surprising that the issue of 'judicial bias' has been raised.

45 (1985) The Times, 18 February. When the contempt of the South Wales Area of the NUM was cleared the court ordered that £100,000 of the sequestrated money be retained by the sequestrators as security for costs and expenses.
46 (1984) The Times, 1 December. The order to appoint a receiver was upheld by the Court of Appeal: (1984) The Times, 3 December.
47 *Financial Times*, 31 January 1985.
48 *Bourne v Colodense Ltd* [1985] ICR 291.

JUDICIAL BIAS?

Winston Churchill took the view in 1911 that the courts in this country generally commanded the respect and admiration of all sections of the community but that 'where class issues are involved it is impossible to pretend that the courts command the same degree of general confidence. On the contrary they do not, and a very large number of our population have been led to the opinion that they are, unconsciously, no doubt, biased.'[49] A similar view was expressed by an eminent judge a decade later. Scrutton LJ recognised that a 'labour man or trade unionist would have reason to question whether he could get impartial justice', and went on to explain (1921:8) that 'it is very difficult sometimes to be sure that you have put yourself into a thoroughly impartial position between two disputants, one of your own class and one not of your class'.

The trade union movement for its part has made no secret of its distrust of the judiciary. This is partly an emotional response to such cases as the Tolpuddle Martyrs and Taff Vale (Wedderburn, 1971:317). But it is also to be explained by reference to a whole series of cases which have had an adverse impact on trade union organisation and activity (O'Higgins and Partington, 1969; Griffith, 1985:53). Indeed, a major element in the development of British labour law has been the need for legislation to reverse judicial decisions which were regarded by Parliament as fundamentally undermining trade unionism; hence the pattern of judge-made liabilities and statutory immunities. A further factor is the clearly unsympathetic attitude that senior judicial figures have in the past expressed regarding certain trade union activities, among them Lord Halsbury as Lord Chancellor in the period between 1885 and 1905 (Heuston, 1964:118–22, 164–5; Stevens, 1979:91–7) and Lord Denning as Master of the Rolls between 1962 and 1968 (Miller, 1981:126; Davies and Freedland, 1984:367). Against this background it is argued that trade unions cannot expect the judiciary to adopt an approach which is neutral, let alone sympathetic, to their objectives (Griffith, 1985:195).

In assessing the attitudes of the judiciary to labour law it is all too easy to make broad political generalisations and overlook the way that decisions are reached in practice. Very few judges had a labour law practice while at the bar and at best deal irregularly with labour law cases at the bench, such cases being allocated randomly between the thirteen judges of the Chancery Division and the forty-nine judges of the QBD. Not being experts in labour law, most judges must approach each case on the basis of its merits and general legal principles. They will also probably be called upon to absorb a very complicated factual situation and an even more complicated legal situation and give judgment the same day or shortly thereafter. In these circumstances it is hardly surprising that the quality and consistency of some labour law decisions has been mixed.

The application of general legal principles to questions of labour law is in itself likely to give rise to suspicions of bias for such principles are primarily

[49]   26 HC Deb, 30 May 1911, 1022.

based on individual rather than collective rights. With very few exceptions (see Chapter 12), the contract of employment is analysed in accordance with the same general contractual principles as were developed in dealing with commercial contracts. A failure to acknowledge the subordination inherent in the employment contract (Kahn-Freund, 1983:15 and 18) leads, for example, to collective bargaining being viewed as an interference with individual liberty and freedom of contract. As Pain J (1981:143) has commented, 'historically, the law of contract has never come to terms with the reality of industrial life'. It is clearly difficult for judges to suppress a lifetime's training and adopt a different approach when dealing with labour law issues, even if they wanted to. But the central question remains as to whether the judiciary's failure to develop a coherent set of labour law principles is a by-product of the judicial system itself or the result of a tacit consensus among the judiciary that to do so would not be in the public interest, as they perceive it to be. This raises the question of how judges perceive the public interest.

In a review of the published surveys, Griffith (1985:25) indicates that probably over 80 per cent of judges come from the upper and upper middle classes, that about 75 per cent of them attended a major public school and that about 70 per cent went to Oxford or Cambridge. Upon appointment to the bench, the judges will have spent an average of twenty or thirty years working hard in the cloistered atmosphere of the bar and will have been selected for elevation by a process which does not usually reward the unconventional. It is not therefore surprising that Griffith was able to conclude (1985:198) that 'judges have by their education and training and pursuit of their profession as barristers acquired a strikingly homogeneous collection of attitudes, beliefs and principles which to them represent the public interest' (see also Blom-Cooper and Drewrey, 1972:169).

In an article politely critical of Griffith's book, Lord Devlin, a former Law Lord, accepted the generalised premise that judges tend to have a common outlook on many issues but questioned the conclusions that can be drawn from this (1978:505). Devlin argues that the courts are not anti-worker as they have often preceded Parliament in the provision of satisfactory remedies against employers for those injured at work.[50] Indeed in 1983 injured plaintiffs succeeded in 80 per cent of the cases that went to judgment in the High Court.[51] But such cases are consistent with the individualist tradition of the law. The courts are less well-equipped and less eager to defend the collective interests of trade union members. It has been said that the minds of many judges 'will turn naturally to the needs of management, of property, of capital and of the hypothetical "individual" long before they consider those of trade unionists' (Wedderburn, 1985:523). Even some of the exceptional union successes in the courts, as in the 1979–80 trilogy of cases which gave the widest possible interpretation of the trade dispute formula support this argument.[52] In those cases the immunities were

[50] Tracing the cases from *Smith v Baker* [1891] AC 325 to *Wilson v English* [1938] AC 57.
[51] Lord Chancellor's Department (1984); these statistics include all personal injury cases, both at the place of work and elsewhere.
[52] Note 25 above; see Wedderburn (1980:89–93) and Lewis and Simpson (1981:184–95).

variously described as 'intrinsically repugnant'[53] and tending 'to stick in judicial gorges',[54] and the view was expressed that 'if this is the law, surely the time has come for it to be altered'.[55] Amending legislation likely to be more palatable to their lordships soon followed in the EA 1980 and 1982.

As described in the introduction to this chapter, Parliament was not inclined to enlarge the jurisdiction of the ordinary courts when extending trade union rights in the EPA and accordingly entrusted the enforcement of such rights to the CAC and ACAS. Similarly, in the absence of 'a new generation of lawyers' who were 'not insulated from any knowledge of the facts of industrial life' (Kahn-Freund, 1969:301–6), the new individual employment rights were entrusted to tripartite industrial tribunals.

INDUSTRIAL TRIBUNALS

The period after the end of World War II saw a great increase in administrative, social and financial legislation generally conferring rights on individuals as tenants, consumers or users of welfare services. This had been accompanied by the development of tribunals other than courts. These tribunals were seen as a way of providing effective rather than merely formal access to justice (Whelan, 1981:169). They were also thought to be able to pay attention to the social policy intentions underlying legislation in a way the courts had failed to do (Bell, 1969:17). In the employment field too, as noted earlier, the development of a positive framework of employment rights made the use of alternatives to the courts appear necessary and the industrial tribunals were seen to be the answer.

Origin and Composition

The industrial tribunals were set up under the Industrial Training Act 1964 to adjudicate in disputes arising out of the imposition of levies on employers by Industrial Training Boards. Other jurisdictions of this 'administrative tribunal' kind followed under the Selective Employment Payments Act 1966 and the Docks and Harbours Act of the same year. But in 1965 the Redundancy Payments Act conferred on them jurisdiction in certain disputes between employee and employer. This was to become the growth area; the industrial tribunals came to be seen less as administrative tribunals in the traditional sense and more as potential labour courts. This was certainly the view within the civil service and was reflected in the Ministry of Labour's evidence to the Donovan Commission (Clark and Wedderburn, 1983:176).

An important feature of industrial tribunals, distinguishing them from the ordinary courts, is their composition: a legally qualified chairperson (a

---

53 [1980] ICR 161, 177 (Lord Diplock).
54 [1980] ICR 42, 57 (Lord Diplock).
55 [1980] ICR 42, 61 (Lord Salmon).

barrister or solicitor of at least seven years' standing) sits with two lay members, experienced in industry or commerce, drawn from two panels, composed of people nominated by employer organisations and employee organisations. In October 1983 there were 64 full-time and 129 part-time chairpersons in England and Wales appointed by the Lord Chancellor. In Scotland in February 1984 there were, in addition to the President, nine full-time and sixteen part-time chairpersons appointed by the Lord President of the Court of Session. At the end of 1984 there were 2,135 lay members on the England and Wales panels and 230 in Scotland. Lay members are fee-paid and sit as requested.

This tripartite composition is also a feature of the EAT which hears appeals on points of law from the tribunals (EPCA s.136 and Sch.11). A High Court judge (or judge of the Court of Session) sits with lay members who have industrial relations knowledge or experience either as representatives of employers or as representatives of workers. There are some forty lay members appointed by the Queen on the joint recommendation of the Lord Chancellor and the Secretary of State for Employment. In contrast to tribunal lay members, there is no statutory requirement that organisations of employers and employees are consulted before EAT lay member appointments are made but in practice the CBI and TUC are consulted.

The rationale for lay members is to temper judicial decision-making with industrial relations considerations, to help ward off legalism, and to make tribunal and EAT decisions more acceptable to those affected by them (Dickens, 1983:28). They are formally equal judges with the legal member and are expected to exercise impartiality in decision-making.

Jurisdictions

The Donovan Report proposed (1968:para.573) that the jurisdiction of the industrial tribunals 'should be defined so as to comprise all disputes arising between employers and employees from their contracts of employment or from any statutory claims they may have against each other in their capacity as employer and employee'. But it sought to make a distinction between individual and collective conflicts, wishing only the former to come within the ambit of the tribunals (para.576). In practice the tribunals cannot hear all disputes which may arise from the individual employment relation. The Lord Chancellor (and Secretary of State for Sctoland) have the power under the EPCA s.131 to confer jurisdiction upon tribunals in respect of claims for breach of contract but this power has not been exercised (see above). Also, although most jurisdictions concern rights given to individuals to be exercised against employers, tribunals do hear disputes which clearly arise from and affect collective relations (Dickens et al., 1985:5). In such cases, however, the approach and remedy are centred on the individual even if the claimant is a trade union. For example, industrial tribunals may hear claims by trade unions against employers concerning consultation over redundancies (EPA s.101), but the remedy is an award to individual employees (see Chapter 15 above). The tribunals' jurisdiction now also includes, under EA 1980 s.4, disputes between unions and employees over alleged unreasonable exclusion or expulsion from membership.

There is no doubting the importance of the industrial tribunal system. This is shown both by the range of its jurisdictions under eleven different Acts and various statutory regulations and by the number of cases handled each year. Table 19.1 provides information on these two aspects. Unfair dismissal cases account for the vast majority of applications to industrial tribunals with all the other jurisdictions together making up less than 30 per cent.

Appeal from the industrial tribunals generally is to the EAT on points of law only (except in unreasonable exclusion and expulsion claims under EA 1980 s.4, where it is on fact and law) and thence, with leave, to the Court of Appeal (Court of Session in Scotland) and the House of Lords. Appeal must be made to the EAT within forty-two days. The EAT also has appellate jurisdiction over certain decisions of the Certification Officer.[56] In 1983 the EAT registered 377 appeals by employers, and 574 by employees from decisions of industrial tribunals (DE, 1984a:492).

Use and Outcome Patterns

The number of applications registered by tribunals more than trebled between 1972 and 1976, going from almost 15,000 to almost 48,000 as the number and scope of tribunal jurisdictions increased. Thereafter there was a decline, broken in 1981, when 44,852 applications were registered. In 1983 there were 39,959 applications.

The actual use of industrial tribunals however appears small compared with the potential caseload. Table 19.1 shows the unfair dismissal jurisdiction providing around three-quarters of the tribunals' cases, yet research has found that applying to an industrial tribunal is not the usual response of a dismissed worker and suggests an application rate of around 12 per cent (Dickens et al., 1985:31). The same research (1985:35) found the typical unfair dismissal applicant to be a manual worker dismissed from a small firm in the private sector who was not a member of a trade union. Individual legal rights are often seen as providing a safety net for the unorganised and it would appear that applications to industrial tribunals come particularly from such workers.

The existence of collective bargaining protection as an alternative, however, cannot be the only explanation for relatively low tribunal application rates as indicated by the low tribunal caseload in the discrimination jurisdiction. The number of claims under the RRA and SDA is minute when viewed in the context of evidence of widespread and continuing discrimination in employment and the relatively poor record of collective bargaining as a way of combatting it (see Chapter 17; Snell et al., 1981; Smith, 1977). In

---

[56] EPCA 1978 s.136. The EAT also has appellate jurisdiction on points of law under the Trade Union Act 1913 and Trade Union (Amalgamations) Act 1964 and on fact and law under TULRA s.8 and EPA s.8 (see Chapter 10 above).

TABLE 19.1
TRIBUNAL JURISDICTION AND CASELOAD, 1983

Jurisdiction	Main Source	Caseload (%)
Unfair dismissal	EPCA s.67	73.4
Redundancy payments	EPCA s.91(1); s.108; s.112	9.4
Unfair dismissal/red. payment		5.5
Employment protection (contracts of employment; time off for union or public duties; action short of dismissal; maternity pay etc.)	EPCA s.11; s.17; s.23; s.27(7); s.28(4); s.29(6); s.31(6); s.36(1); s.53(4); s.103(1)	5.5
Equal pay	EqPA s.2 as amended	3.2
Sex discrimination	SDA s.63	0.8
Health and safety	HSWA s.24; Safety Rep. and Safety Cttee Regs. 1977	0.4
Industrial training levy	Ind. Training Act 1964 s.12	0.3
Race relations	RRA 1976 s.54	1.3
Miscellaneous[a]		0.2

Source: Caseload from DE (1984a:488).
Note
[a]Among the remaining jurisdictions are complaints under the Transfer of Undertakings (Protection of Employment) Regulations 1981; complaints of exclusion or expulsion from a trade union under EA 1980 s.4; references concerning occupational pension schemes and the determination of questions delegated to tribunals under a variety of compensation regulations. For complete list see Hepple and O'Higgins (1981:362).

1983 there were only 265 SDA and 310 RRA applications. Equal pay claims had dwindled from 1,742 in 1976 to 35 in 1983.

Among the various factors influencing the use of the industrial tribunals by aggrieved employees will be their perceptions of the remedies available and the ease and likelihood of obtaining them. From this point of view the outcome statistics are not very encouraging. A high proportion of cases do not reach a tribunal hearing but are disposed of through conciliation by ACAS. Some two-thirds of unfair dismissal cases do not reach a hearing and about half of the cases brought under the discrimination jurisdictions are also withdrawn. The unfair dismissal cases which are withdrawn are divided fairly equally between those which are settled and those where the case is simply abandoned. In the discrimination jurisdiction it is more likely that a case will be withdrawn without any settlement having been agreed. In over two-thirds of the race relations applications withdrawn without a hearing from 1977 to the end of 1983, no settlement was recorded. Similarly, in the years 1976 to 1983 less than half the sex discrimination cases which were not heard by tribunals were withdrawn in return for a settlement agreed privately or through ACAS.

In unfair dismissal cases the remedy normally awarded to successful applicants is compensation. The median compensation award in 1983 was £1,345; compensation amounted to less than £500 in about one-fifth of awards. Reinstatement and re-engagement are rare; in 1983 they constituted only 3 per cent of tribunal awards. This pattern is reflected in conciliated settlements: re-employment also constituted 3 per cent of conciliated settlements in 1983. Most settlements were on the basis of a money payment, at an average level of about half the amount of tribunal awards (DE, 1984a: 490–91).

Those found to have been discriminated against unlawfully also generally receive financial compensation as a remedy. Tribunals may also make a declaration of rights and a recommendation of action to remove the effects of discrimination. Failure to comply with a recommendation leads to increased compensation award, subject to a maximum figure. The level of awards in discrimination cases has been described as 'derisory' (Hepple, 1983:73). In 1983 ten out of twenty-six (38 per cent) SDA applicants and three out of twenty-four (12.5 per cent) RRA applicants who received compensation obtained awards of £1,000 and over (DE, 1984b:542–4). Forty-six per cent under the SDA and 62 per cent under RRA received less than £500. Compensation is based on economic loss but in discrimination cases an award may be made also for 'injury to feelings' (see Chapter 17). The 'going rate' under this head in 1984 was less than £200.

In seeking to explain the pattern of outcomes much depends of course on the provisions in the statutes which the tribunals operate – both in deciding the case and in the remedial powers open to them. For instance, regarding remedies, unfair dismissal compensation generally consists of a basic award, which is related to length of service and compensates for loss of accrued rights, and a compensatory award, concerned with the loss sustained by the employee because of the dismissal (see Chapter 15 above). The compensatory provisions show no awareness that awarding damages over and above the compensation for demonstrable financial loss could have a broader function in providing a stimulus for change in keeping with the reform intention of the legislation (Dickens et al., 1985:125). This 'deterrent-regulatory' view of compensation is similarly absent from the discrimination provisions (Lustgarten, 1980:226) since there is no penal element in the awards against employers who have acted unlawfully. In a similar way, the post hoc nature of the general unfair dismissal provisions (in contrast to a situation where the contract continues in existence until the dispute is determined), and the presence of the common law duty to mitigate, influences the outcome pattern by making re-employment less likely and helping keep compensation awards low.

But explanations do not lie only in the inherent limitations of the statutory provisions. In those areas where the tribunals and courts have discretion, it generally has not been exercised to the benefit of applicants. For instance, in unfair dismissal cases industrial tribunals and the higher courts have exercised their discretion in ways generally supportive of managerial prerogative.[57] Nor has the individualist, common law bias of judicial decision-making appeared well-suited to deal with disputes such as those concerning dismissal of trade unionists or sexual or racial discrimination where, it is argued, a focus wider than the individual is required.[58] The exercise of discretion in relation to remedies has also resulted in minimising the potential impact of the legislation. This can be seen, for instance, in the tribunals' approach to unfair dismissal remedies, both in calculating what is 'just and equitable' in awarding compensation (see Dickens et al., 1985:126–35) and in deciding whether to award reinstatement (Williams and Lewis, 1981:28–31; Dickens et al., 1981). It can also be seen in the remedies for discrimination on grounds of sex or race. Attempts by some industrial tribunals to be generous in 'injury to feelings' awards[59] and to use imaginatively their power to make recommendations[60] have been thwarted by the Court of Appeal.

Tribunals were meant to enable unrepresented parties to bring and defend cases without prejudicing their chance of success and to overcome problems which arise because of the ordinary courts' approach to employment issues. Whether they have done so can be examined by reference to the characteristics identified by the Franks Report (1957:para.406) for administrative tribunals generally, namely, 'cheapness, accessibility, freedom from technicality, expedition and expert knowledge of a particular subject'.

The Tribunal System: An Evaluation[61]

The tribunal system was designed to be an accessible system – geographically, procedurally and financially. Regional tribunal offices provide geographic accessibility; there is a relatively straightforward application procedure and no application or court fees are payable. Travelling and subsistence costs incurred by the parties and their witnesses in attending hearings are reimbursed and actual loss of earnings is recoverable up to a daily maximum. The parties may represent themselves at a tribunal hearing and thereby avoid legal fees, and the losing party generally does not have to bear the other party's costs.

Employer fears that the tribunals were 'too accessible' have, however, resulted in some changes. The scope for awarding costs was widened in 1980 and now covers cases brought or conducted 'frivolously, vexatiously or otherwise unreasonably'.[62] At the same time a new stage was introduced

---

57 See Chapter 15; Bowers and Clarke (1981:39,43); Collins (1982:177); Dickens et al. (1985:97).
58 See Chapters 2 and 17; Dickens et al. (1985:295); Hepple (1983:84) and Lustgarten (1980:224–36).
59 See *Coleman v Skyrail Oceanic Ltd* [1981] IRLR 398 where a tribunal award of £1,000 for injury to feelings was reduced to £100 by the Court of Appeal.
60 See *Prestcold Ltd v Irvine* [1980] IRLR 267; discussed by Hepple (1983:73).
61 What follows draws freely on Dickens et al. (1985:ch.7).
62 Industrial Tribunals (Rules of Procedure) Regulations SI 1985 No. 16 para. 11.

into the tribunal system – pre-hearing assessment (PHA) – to enable parties with prima facie weak cases to be warned that a costs award against them might be made if they were to lose at the full hearing.[63] The operation of this stage deters a number of applicants from continuing. From the beginning of the PHA's operation in October 1980 to the end of December 1983, 8,854 PHAs were held. Costs warnings were issued against 3,240 applicants, over 80 per cent of whom subsequently did not pursue their cases to full hearing. Those warned applicants who proceeded to tribunal hearing were less likely than other applicants to succeed but 13 per cent of warned applicants did win in 1983, leading to criticism by the Council on Tribunals (1984) of the inaccuracy of PHA forecasts.

The procedure is designed to be speedy. The tribunal regulations contain some time requirements (for example, the parties have to be given fourteen days' notice of the date of the hearing) which, adding on time for processing forms, gives a practical base line of around six weeks. The research by Dickens et al. (1985:201) found a fifth of the unfair dismissal cases not disposed of by ACAS came to hearing within this time and 39 per cent reached a hearing within eight weeks of application. Under a third took more than three months. Although shorter than for the ordinary courts, this time lapse between application and hearing may appear too long in the context of certain disputes, particularly those where collective action may be expected. This problem is recognised by the provision of the expedited interim relief procedure (EPCA s.77) first introduced for cases where dismissal is alleged on grounds of trade union membership or activity, and now also covering cases where dismissal is alleged on grounds of non-membership of a union (see Chapter 2).

Cases are disposed of relatively quickly once they reach a hearing. Only about one in ten unfair dismissal cases takes longer than a day to be heard. Several weeks may elapse, however, after the hearing before a copy of the decision is received. Changes to the tribunal regulations with effect from 1 March 1985 allow the tribunal to give its reasons in summary form in most unfair dismissal cases.[64] The parties may then request full reasons if desired. This should mean that summary reasons for the decisions should be available more speedily but may pose problems for parties contemplating appeal. Successful applicants generally wait several weeks before receiving their compensation awards. Where an award is not paid it has to be enforced in England and Wales via the county court. In Scotland tribunal awards are recoverable by sheriff's officers. When a tribunal decision is appealed of course the time between application and final decision is lengthened considerably.

The regulations governing tribunal hearings emphasise informality and flexibility of procedure, and the tribunal members, particularly the chair, often play a more active role than does the judge in an ordinary court, intervening where necessary to help the parties, particularly when not represented, present their cases. Certain characteristics associated with

63 SI 1985 No.16 para.6.
64 SI 1985 No.16 para.9.

court hearings, such as wigs and gowns, are missing from tribunals although some others, such as oath-taking, remain. Various features of the industrial tribunal system, however, pull against the attainment of the ideal of 'simple informal justice' (Conroy, 1971:4), in particular the underlying accusatorial model of tribunal hearings embodied in the regulations.

The expectation of the accusatorial or adversarial model, as opposed to that of an inquiry, is that the parties, normally through representatives, will give evidence, call witnesses, cross-examine and make submissions to the tribunal. That is to say, they take the intiative in the presentation of the case. Thus the tribunal, except on application of a party, cannot compel the attendance of witnesses, or join additional parties, or order the production of documents. What material is presented and what evidence is produced is up to the parties. This adversarial approach has implications in terms of the knowledge, ability and expertise needed by lay people seeking to prepare and present their own cases and in practice places a premium on specialist representation. The view of the Royal Commission on Legal Services (Benson, 1979:para.2:17) that 'whatever the tribunal and however informal its procedure, representation, whether by a lawyer or skilled layman, in the majority of cases confers an advantage on the represented party' is borne out by research into unfair dismissal applications to industrial tribunals (Dickens et al., 1985:88–93; Dickens, 1985). Representation, particularly by lawyers, was seen to confer advantage in both case preparation and presentation. This was particularly true for applicants, who generally felt at a disadvantage vis à vis the employers at their hearings. This perception was one shared by many employers and was not simply a reflection of how the case was decided. The view that representation is advantageous was held not only by the parties but also by tribunal members who generally felt that self-representation should not be encouraged.

Unfair dismissal applicants represented by solicitors consistently win a higher proportion of their cases than those represented by trade union officers or those representing themselves. The overall success rate for each group between 1979 and 1982 was 31, 26 and 25 per cent (Dickens, 1985: 30). Similarly, in the discrimination jurisdictions, where the applicant is disadvantaged further by bearing the burden of proof, representation by lawyers increases the likelihood of success. As Hepple notes (1983:79–81), in these cases evidence of discrimination is rarely direct and success or failure may crucially depend upon the quality of circumstantial evidence from which the tribunal is asked to draw an inference of discrimination. This evidence has to be produced by the parties. A decisive factor in winning or losing may be the skills of those who cross-examine the employer's witnesses.

The lack of representation is also a disadvantage to applicants in the stages prior to hearing. They are less likely to be aware of, and use, provisions providing for discovery, further and better particulars of the employer's case or witness orders (Dickens, 1985) or the questionnaire form in discrimination claims. Some unrepresented applicants expect ACAS individual conciliation officers to help and advise them. In particular, such applicants are seeking advice on how good their case is and how the law or the tribunal system operates (Dickens et al., 1985:153). ACAS's failure to give support or certain advice to applicants has been a feature of criticism of this aspect of the tribunal system (see Gregory, 1982:81–2; McIlroy, 1980; Lewis, 1982:54). This criticism, however, is more appropriately directed at the statutory duty under EPCA s.134, which provides, not that ACAS is to help applicants enforce their rights, but rather is to act neutrally as between the parties in an endeavour to dispose of the case without a tribunal hearing. The nature of any settlement is for the parties themselves to determine; only when considering re-employment in an unfair dismissal case is ACAS required to take a view as to the equity of the settlement. This requirement does not apply to the terms of any monetary settlement. In practice this means that applicants, because of their disadvantaged position in the tribunal system (often conveyed to them through information given by ACAS), generally accept the employers' first offers of settlement and, in many cases where no offer is made, abandon their cases (Dickens et al., 1985:ch.6; Gregory, 1982).

Despite the self-help ideology of the tribunal system, and the absence of legal aid for representation at hearings, the use of legal representation has been increasing over the years. In 1983, 36 per cent of applicants and 49 per cent of respondents in all jurisdictions had legal representation. This compares with 20 per cent and 37 per cent respectively in 1973 (Dickens, 1985). It is not just the adversarial nature of hearings but also the importance, complexity and volume of statute and case law which the tribunals have to apply which makes legal representation appear appropriate and beneficial. As Munday notes (1981:149), the 'belief that industrial law is fundamentally layman's law' is a mistaken one. If legal representation is to some extent a consequence of legalism in the tribunals, it is also in part a cause. Increased legal representation was found (Dickens et al., 1985:ch.7) to reduce the extent to which the tribunals could display the cheapness, speed, accessibility and informality desired of them. In their operation, therefore, the tribunals have become more court-like than originally intended – a development which, to a large extent, can be seen as inevitable (see Munday, 1981).

What then of the second strand of expectations: that the tribunals would differ from the ordinary courts in their expert decision-making, reflecting social policy and displaying a sensitivity to the wider, notably industrial relations, aspects of disputes? Again the picture is of largely misplaced and, therefore, largely unfulfilled expectations. Some of these expectations rested on the presence of lay members on tribunals as equal judges with the legal chairperson. Lay members bring a general experience of industrial or commercial life. In discrimination cases efforts are made to have at least one tribunal member with a more particular background. Thus when sex discrimination or equal pay cases are heard one member at least is usually female and in race relations cases one person should have special experience or knowledge in this area (see Chapter 17). An applicant does not have the right, however, to insist on this.[65] Where equal pay for equal value work is

---

[65] *Habib v Elkington Ltd* [1981] IRLR 344.

claimed, the Industrial Tribunal Rules now provide for another source of expertise, an independent expert appointed by the tribunal (see Chapter 17).

The value and importance of lay members in tribunal decision-making has often been acknowledged (Browne-Wilkinson, 1982:70; Jukes, 1978:5) and there have been notable, although very rare, occasions when the two lay members have outvoted the chair.[66] The scope for lay members to make an expert contribution and to influence decision-making, however, is constrained by such factors as their backgrounds and training, their allocation to hearings, and the quasi-court nature of the tribunal system itself (Dickens, 1983; Hepple, 1983:78). Although formally the three members of the tribunal are equal judges, in practice the chairperson is *primus inter pares*, a position arising from the combination of a number of factors including the importance which necessarily attaches to the law within a judicial system. Should what is legally 'right' conflict with what seems to make industrial relations sense, or with what conforms to the underlying social policy of the legislation, then the system usually ensures the solution argued to be legally right is applied. And, of course, what is legally 'right' owes much to the way in which the appeal courts have interpreted the statutory provisions.

In its early years, from 1976, the EAT adopted an interventionist stance, taking a wide view of what constituted an error of law in order to lay down precedent and provide guidelines to amplify the statutory provisions. This contributed to legalism in the industrial tribunals but was argued by EAT Presidents to be necessary to introduce consistency into their decisions (Phillips, 1978:139), and to provide uniform principles of good industrial relations practice 'by reference to which employers and employees can regulate their conduct' (Browne-Wilkinson, 1982:75).

The early interventionism of the EAT was curbed by the Court of Appeal which, in 1978, began a series of judgments restricting the ability of the EAT to interfere with tribunal decisions.[67] The Court of Appeal also held it was 'unwise' to set out guidelines and 'wrong to make rules and establish presumptions for industrial tribunals to follow'.[68] The EAT's scope for interfering with a tribunal decision is restricted to cases where the tribunal has erred in law.[69] In a number of recent decisions issues have been declared to be questions of fact, not law, and thus for tribunals to decide free from appellate interference.[70] The Court of Appeal's restrictive view of the EAT's role now appears to have been adopted by the EAT itself under its President, Waite, J.[71] The recent procedural changes concerning reasoned

---

[66] E.g. *Midland Plastics v Till* [1983] IRLR 9 on whether the threat of industrial action itself constituted industrial action, and *Nethermere (St Neots) Ltd v Gardiner and Taverna* [1983] IRLR 103, on whether homeworkers in the case were 'employees'.

[67] *Retarded Children's Aid Society v Day* [1978] ICR 437 was the first of a number of cases.

[68] *Bailey v BP Oil (Kent Refinery) Ltd* [1980] ICR 642, 648.

[69] On errors of law through legal perversity see *Edwards v Bairstow* [1956] AC 14.

[70] E.g. *O'Kelly v Trusthouse Forte Plc* [1983] IRLR 369 (whether someone is an employee); *Martin v MBS Fastenings (Glynwed) Distribution Ltd* [1983] IRLR 198 (whether constructive dismissal occurred); *Hollier v Plysu Ltd* [1983] IRLR 260 (on the degree of contributory fault). See further Chapter 15.

[71] *Anandarajah v Lord Chancellor's Department* [1983] IRLR 131.

decisions (see above) may also be seen as in keeping with a reduced appellate role and indeed were foreshadowed in a decision of the Court of Appeal, which pointed out that since there is no right of appeal on a question of fact there is no use having a detailed recitation of the evidence in the decision.[72]

On the face of it, the Court of Appeal, in seeking to curb the EAT's guidance activity, appeared as defender of industrial tribunal autonomy. It is the Court of Appeal itself, however, which has placed perhaps the greatest constraint on the ability of an industrial tribunal to operate as an expert body in deciding unfair dismissal cases by laying down the 'reasonable employer' test (see Chapter 15). The tribunal is to judge an employer's action in dismissing not by its own view of what would have been reasonable in the circumstances but by the standards of the 'reasonable employer'. Tribunals must be norm reflecting not norm setting. The tribunal is not allowed to act as an expert body and impose its own independent solution in the way an industrial arbitration body would: to do so is to err in law. The appellate courts have thus played a crucial role in giving meaning to the concepts of the statutes, imposing their own views on the expert tribunals, and restricting their ability to display 'doctrinal flexibility' or 'policy consciousness' (Abel Smith and Stevens, 1968:220). This development was one which might have been foreseen from the early operation of the redundancy payments legislation (Wedderburn and Davies, 1969:267).

The conciliation stage, the presence of lay people as equal tribunal members and the emphasis on procedural flexibility can be seen as part of an attempt to bring elements of the voluntary dispute resolution process into the adjudication and enforcement of statutory rights and to ensure attention was paid to considerations wider than the black letter of the law. But the structure within which the tribunals operate and their quasi-court nature have helped bear out the contention (Abel-Smith and Stevens, 1968:224) that the differences between tribunals and courts are differences of degree and not of kind.

CONCLUSION

The narrowing of trade dispute immunities in recent years has increased the potential for judicial intervention in industrial disputes by the traditional method of determining the boundaries of lawful action. The legislative changes have not given the courts a dispute settlement role. Such a role, however, has been advocated. In 1975 Sir John Donaldson, as he then was, queried the self-help tradition of industrial dispute settlement, arguing that industrial disputes were justiciable and declared 'there is nothing that an arbitrator can do that a specialised labour court cannot do better' (1975a:67–8). It has further been argued (Browne-Wilkinson, 1982:77) that the tripartite industrial tribunals and particularly the EAT provide a working

---

[72] *Kearney and Trecker Marwin Ltd v Varndell* [1983] IRLR 35.

model which 'may well point the way to the best method of bringing the law into other sectors of labour relations where the law may have a role to play'.

The discussion in this chapter, however, has indicated that the tribunal system, despite its best attempts, shares with the courts various features which are problematic in the context of industrial relations dispute settlement. Indeed, rather than seeing the tribunal system as a pointer to the future some (Dickens et al., 1985:ch.9; Hepple, 1983:84) have suggested that an arbitral system would be a preferable alternative for disputes currently within the tribunals' jurisdiction.

As argued in this chapter, the legalistic and individualistic approach of a conservative judiciary steeped in a common law 'which knows nothing of a balance of collective forces' (Kahn-Freund, 1983:12) is inappropriate for disputes arising between employers and trade unions. But the main flaw in the Donaldson argument is the assumption that there is a 'right' answer to such disputes which proper examination will reveal (Donaldson, 1975b:191–2). There are no right answers to questions such as what is a 'fair day's work' or a 'fair wage' or the proper scope of management prerogative. Such issues 'are determined by economic and political strength not by the application of legal principles or guidelines' (Griffith, 1985:70). The judicial and political mix in arbitral decision-making recognises this.

It is suggested that the judicial approach can be typified by a focus on who is legally right and on the reasonableness of action while the arbitral approach is typified by problem-solving focused on finding a workable and acceptable solution which takes account of the wider context. Arbitration awards have to be flexible and often share some of the features of the collective bargaining system which arbitration assists – a system which rests ultimately on compromise (Wood, 1980:55).

In making the contrast with the courts, it is not being argued that arbitration is appropriate for all industrial relations disputes. It has limitations, for example, where there is an absence of normative consensus concerning collective bargaining itself. In such cases conciliation and mediation may be more appropriate. Nor is it argued that the courts have no role whatsoever in regulating any aspect of the employment relationship. Rather it is suggested that the third-party processes of conciliation, mediation and arbitration are more suited to the realities of industrial relations dispute settlement whenever negotiation – in practice the prime method – fails.

Bibliography

Aaron, Benjamin. 1980. 'The Administration of Justice in Labor Law: Arbitration and the Role of the Courts: An International Survey'. *International Collection of Essays in Memoriam Sir Otto Kahn-Freund*. Eds. F. Gamillscheg et al. Munich: C.H. Beck, 363–84.

Abel-Smith, B., and R. Stevens. 1968. *In Search of Justice*. London: Allen Lane.

Advisory, Conciliation and Arbitration Service (ACAS). 1979. *Annual Report 1978*. London: HMSO.

——. 1980. *Annual Report 1979*. London: HMSO.

——. 1981. *Annual Report 1980*. London: HMSO.

——. 1984. *Annual Report 1983*. London: HMSO.

——. 1985. *Annual Report 1984*. London: HMSO.

Bell, Kathleen. 1969. *Tribunals in the Social Services*. London: Routledge & Kegan Paul.

Benson. 1979. Royal Commission on Legal Services. *Final Report*. Cmnd 7648. London: HMSO.

Blom-Cooper, L., and G. Drewrey. 1972. *Final Appeal: A Study of the House of Lords in Its Judicial Capacity*. Oxford: Clarendon Press.

Borrie, G., and N. Lowe. 1983. *The Law of Contempt*. 2nd edn. London: Butterworths.

Bowers, J., and A. Clarke. 1981. 'Unfair Dismissal and Managerial Prerogative: A Study of "Other Substantial Reason"'. *Industrial Law Journal*, 10 (March), 34–44.

Brown, W.A. (ed.). 1981. *The Changing Contours of British Industrial Relations: A Survey of Manufacturing Industry*. Oxford: Blackwell.

Browne-Wilkinson, The Hon. Mr Justice. 1982. 'The Role of the Employment Appeal Tribunal in the 1980s'. *Industrial Law Journal*, 11 (June), 69–77.

Central Arbitration Committee (CAC). 1978. *Annual Report 1977*. London: HMSO.

——. 1984. *Annual Report 1983*. London: HMSO.

——. 1985. *Annual Report 1984*. London: HMSO.

Clark, Jon, and *Lord* Wedderburn. 1983. 'Modern Labour Law: Problems, Functions and Policies'. *Labour Law and Industrial Relations: Building on Kahn-Freund*. Eds. *Lord* Wedderburn, R. Lewis and J. Clark. Oxford: Clarendon Press, 127–242.

Clegg, H.A. 1970. 'The Role of Government Agencies'. *Scottish Journal of Political Economy*, 17 (June), 305–18.

Collins, Hugh. 1982. 'Capitalist Discipline and Corporatist Law – Part II'. *Industrial Law Journal*, 11 (September), 170–77.

Concannon, H. 1980. 'Handling Dismissal Disputes by Arbitration'. *Industrial Relations Journal*, 11 (May-June), 13–23.

Conroy, Diarmaid. 1971. 'Do Applicants Need Advice or Representation?' *The Future of Administrative Tribunals*. Edited transcript of proceedings of a conference held at Institute of Judicial Administration, University of Birmingham, April 1971. Birmingham: Institute of Judicial Administration.

Council on Tribunals. 1984. *Annual Report 1983–84*. London: HMSO.

Daniel, W.W., and Neil Millward. 1983. *Workplace Industrial Relations in Britain: The DE/PSI/SSRC Survey*. London: Heinemann.

Davies, Paul L. 1979. 'Arbitration and the Role of Courts in the United Kingdom'. *Comparative Labor Law*, 3 (Fall), 31–51.

——, and S. Anderman. 1973. 'Injunction Procedure in Labour Disputes – I'. *Industrial Law Journal*, 2 (December), 213–28.

——, and M. Freedland. 1984. 'Labour Law'. *Lord Denning: The Judge and the Law*. Eds. J.L. Jowell and J.P.W.B. McAuslan. London: Sweet & Maxwell, 367–438.

Department of Employment (DE). 1984a. 'Industrial Tribunals and the Employment Appeal Tribunal'. *Employment Gazette*, 92 (November), 487–92.

——. 1984b. 'Industrial Tribunals and the Employment Appeal Tribunal (Discrimination Cases)'. *Employment Gazette*, 92 (December), 540–44.

Devlin, Patrick. 1978. 'Judges, Government and Politics'. *Modern Law Review*, 41 (September), 501–11.

Dickens, Linda. 1979. 'Conciliation, Mediation and Arbitration in British Industrial Relations'. *Industrial Relations: A Social Psychological Approach*. Eds. G. Stephenson and C. Brotherton. Chichester: Wiley & Sons, 289–307.

——. 1983. 'Do Lay Members Influence Tribunal Decisions?'. *Personnel Management* (November), 28–31.

——. 1985. 'Industrial Tribunals – The People's Courts?'. *Employee Relations*, 7(1), 27–32.

——, M. Hart, M. Jones and B. Weekes. 1981. 'Re-employment of Unfairly Dismissed Workers: The Lost Remedy'. *Industrial Law Journal*, 10 (September), 160–75.

——, M. Jones, B. Weekes and M. Hart. 1985. *Dismissed: A Study of Unfair Dismissal and the Industrial Tribunal System*. Oxford: Blackwell.

Donaldson, John. 1975a. 'The Role of Labour Courts'. *Industrial Law Journal*, 4 (June), 63–8.

——. 1975b. 'Lessons from the Industrial Court'. *Law Quarterly Review*, 91 (April), 181–92.

Donovan. 1968. Royal Commission on Trade Unions and Employers' Associations 1965–1968. *Report*. Cmnd 3623. London: HMSO.

Evans, Stephen. 1985. 'The Use of Injunctions in Industrial Disputes'. *British Journal of Industrial Relations*, 23 (March), 133–7.

Flanders, Allan. 1970. *Management and Unions*. London: Faber.

Franks. 1957. Committee on Administrative Tribunals and Enquiries. *Report*. Cmnd 218. London: HMSO.

Goodman, J., and J. Krislov. 1974. 'Conciliation in Industrial Disputes in Great Britain: A Survey of the Attitudes of the Parties'. *British Journal of Industrial Relations*, 12 (November), 327–51.

Gregory, J. 1982. 'Equal Pay and Sex Discrimination: Why Women are Giving Up the Fight'. *Feminist Review*, 10 (Spring), 75–89.

Griffith, J.A.G. 1985. *The Politics of the Judiciary*. 3rd edn. Glasgow: Fontana.

Hedges, R.V., and A. Winterbottom. 1930. *The Legal History of Trade Unions*. London: Longman.

Hepple, B.A. 1983. 'Judging Equal Rights'. *Current Legal Problems*, vol. 36, 71–90.

——, and P. O'Higgins. 1981. *Employment Law*. 4th edn. B. A. Hepple. London: Sweet & Maxwell.

Heuston, R.F.V. 1964. *The Lives of Lord Chancellors 1885–1945*. London: Oxford University Press.

Hunter, L.C. 1977. 'Economic Issues in Conciliation and Arbitration'. *British Journal of Industrial Relations*, 15 (July), 226–45.

Hyman, R. 1984. *Strikes*. 3rd edn. London: Fontana.

Industrial Relations Review and Report (IRRR). 1984. 'No-Strike Deals in Perspective'. *Industrial Relations Review and Report*, no. 304 (July), 8–11.

Jones, M., L. Dickens, B. Weekes and M. Hart. 1983. 'Resolving Industrial Disputes: The Role of ACAS Conciliation'. *Industrial Relations Journal*, 14 (Summer), 6–17.

Jukes, M. 1978. 'Reply: Tribunals – Justice for All?'. *Industrial Society*, 60 (September/October), 5–6.

Kahn-Freund, Otto. 1954. 'Intergroup Conflicts and their Settlement'. *British Journal of Sociology*, 5 (September), 193–227.

——. 1969. 'Industrial Relations and the Law – Retrospect and Prospect'. *British Journal of Industrial Relations*, 7 (November), 301–16.

——. 1983. *Labour and the Law*. 3rd edn. Ed. and intr. by P. Davies and M. Freedland. London: Stevens.

Kessler, S. 1980. 'The Prevention and Settlement of Collective Labour Disputes in the United Kingdom'. *Industrial Relations Journal*, 11 (March-April), 5–31.

Leopold, J.W., and P.B. Beaumont. 1983. 'Arbitration Arrangements in the Public Sector in Britain'. *Arbitration Journal*, 38 (June), 52–9.

Lewis, P. 1982. 'The Role of ACAS Conciliators in Unfair Dismissal Cases'. *Industrial Relations Journal*, 13 (Autumn), 50–56.

Lewis, R., and R. Simpson. 1981. *Striking a Balance? Employment Law After the 1980 Act*. Oxford: Martin Robertson.

Lockwood, D. 1955. 'Arbitration and Industrial Conflict'. *British Journal of Sociology*, 6 (December), 335–47.

Lockyer, John. 1979. *Industrial Arbitration in Great Britain – Everyman's Guide*. London: IPM.

Lord Chancellor's Department. 1984. *Judicial Statistics England and Wales for the Year 1983*. Cmnd 9370. London: HMSO.

Lustgarten, Laurence. 1980. *Legal Control of Racial Discrimination*. London: Macmillan.

McGregor, Harvey. 1980. *McGregor on Damages*. 14th edn. London: Sweet & Maxwell.

McIlroy, J. 1980. 'Conciliation'. *Industrial Law Journal*, 9 (September), 179–83.

Marsh, A. 1968. *Disputes Procedures in Britain*. Research Paper 2, Royal Commission on Trade Unions and Employers' Associations. London: HMSO.

Mellish, M., and N. Collis-Squires. 1976. 'Legal and Social Norms in Discipline and Dismissal'. *Industrial Law Journal*, 5 (September), 164–77.

Miller, K. 1981. 'The Labours of Lord Denning'. *Justice, Lord Denning and the Constitution*. Eds. P. Robson and P. Watchman. Farnborough: Gower, 126–57.

Munday, Roderick. 1981. 'Tribunal Lore: Legalism and the Industrial Tribunals'. *Industrial Law Journal*, 10 (September), 146–59.

Nock, R.S. 1968. 'Trade Unions, Advice and Limitation'. *Modern Law Review*, 3 (July), 456–9.

O'Higgins, P., and M. Partington. 1969. 'Industrial Conflict: Judicial Attitudes'. *Modern Law Review*, 32 (January), 53–8.

Pain, The Hon. Mr Justice Peter. 1981. 'Contract and Contact: The Trade Unionist and the Lawyer'. *Industrial Law Journal*, 10 (September 7, 137–45.

Paynter, W. 1972. 'Is There a Future for Conciliation and Arbitration?'. *Personnel Management* (December), 18–21.

Phillips, The Hon Mr. Justice. 1978. 'Some Notes on the Employment Appeal Tribunal'. *Industrial Law Journal*, 7 (September), 137–42.

Radcliffe and Cross. 1977. *The English Legal System*. 6th edn. Edited by A.J. Hand and D.J. Bentley. London: Butterworths.

Rideout, R.W. 1982. 'Arbitration and the Public Interest: Regulation Arbitration'. *Labour Law and the Community: Perspectives for the 1980s*. Eds. *Lord* Wedderburn and W.T. Murphy. London: Institute of Advanced Legal Studies, 49–60.

Scarman. 1977. *Report of a Court of Inquiry under the Rt Hon Lord Justice Scarman, OBE into a Dispute between Grunwick Processing Laboratories Limited and Members of the Association of Professional, Executive, Clerical and Computer Staff*. Cmnd 6922. London: HMSO.

Schmidt, Folke. 1969. 'Conciliation, Adjudication and Administration: Three Methods of Decision-Making in Labor Disputes'. *Dispute Settlement Procedures in Five Western European Countries*. Ed. B. Aaron. Los Angeles: Institute of Industrial Relations, University of California, 45–64.

Scrutton, Lord Justice. 1921. 'The Work of the Commercial Courts'. *Cambridge Law Journal*, 1(1), 6–20.

Sharp, Ian G. 1949. *Industrial Conciliation and Arbitration in Britain*. London: Allen & Unwin.

Singleton, N. 1975. *Industrial Relations Procedures*. Department of Employment, Manpower Papers 14. London: HMSO.

Smith, D.J. 1977. *Racial Disadvantage in Britain*. Harmondsworth: Penguin.

Snell, E. 1982. *The Principles of Equity*. 28th edn. London: Sweet & Maxwell.

Snell, M.W., P. Glucklich and M. Povall. 1981. *Equal Pay and Opportunities: A Study of the Implementation and Effects of the Equal Pay and Sex Discrimination Acts in 26 Organisations*. Research Paper no. 20. London: Department of Employment.

Stevens, R. 1979. *Law and Politics: The House of Lords as a Judicial Body 1800–1976*. London: Weidenfeld & Nicolson.

Trades Union Congress (TUC). 1976. *Annual Report 1975*. London: TUC.

Walker and Walker. 1985. *The English Legal System*. 5th edn. by R.J. Walker. London: Butterworths.

Walker, D.M. 1981. *The Scottish Legal System: An Introduction to the Study of Scots Law*. 5th edn. Edinburgh: W. Green & Sons.

Wedderburn, K.W. (*Lord*). 1969. 'Conflicts of "Rights" and Conflicts of "Interests" in Labor Disputes'. *Dispute Settlement Procedures in Five Western European Countries*. Ed. B. Aaron. Los Angeles: Institute of Industrial Relations, University of California, 65–90.

——. 1971. *The Worker and the Law*. 2nd edn. Harmondsworth: Penguin.

——. 1980. 'Industrial Relations and the Courts'. *Industrial Law Journal*, 9 (June), 65–94.

——. 1985. 'The New Politics of Labour Law'. *Trade Unions*. Ed. W.E.J. McCarthy. 2nd edn. Harmondsworth: Penguin, 497–532.

——, and P.L. Davies. 1969. *Employment Grievances and Disputes Procedures in Britain*. Berkeley and Los Angeles: University of California Press.

Weekes, B.C.M. 1979. 'ACAS – An Alternative to Law?'. *Industrial Law Journal*, 9 (September), 147–59.

——, M. Mellish, L. Dickens and J. Lloyd. 1975. *Industrial Relations and the Limits of Law: The Industrial Effects of the Industrial Relations Act 1971*. Oxford: Blackwell.

Whelan, C.J. 1981. 'Informalising Judicial Procedures'. *Informal Institutions*. Ed. S. Henry. New York: St Martin's Press, 166–75.

Williams, K., and D. Lewis. 1981. *The Aftermath of Tribunal Reinstatement and Re-engagement*. Research Paper no. 23. London: Department of Employment.

Wood, John. 1979. 'The Central Arbitration Committee: A Consideration of Its Role and Approach'. *Employment Gazette*, 87 (January), 9–17.

——. 1980. 'The Case for Arbitration'. *Personnel Management* (October), 52–5.

Zander, Michael. 1980. *Cases and Materials on the English Legal System*. 3rd edn. London: Weidenfeld & Nicolson.

20 International Standards and British Labour Law

Paul O'Higgins

The relationship of the United Kingdom to international labour standards is full of strange paradoxes. For many years the UK was one of a number of advanced industrial countries most active in promoting the concept of international labour standards.[1] Now the UK is slow and reluctant to implement obligatory international standards and shows no enthusiasm for the maintenance of existing standards let alone their improvement and development in new areas. Enforcement proceedings by the Commission of the European Communities against the UK are now a regular feature over such issues as the tachograph, equal pay and sex discrimination.[2]

In the past many of the advances in social and industrial relations pioneered by the UK came to provide the basic core of international labour standards. One of the most important administrative reforms of nineteenth century Britain was the establishment of the factory inspectorate. This, in turn, was the model for labour inspectorates adopted in many other countries. One of the first Recommendations adopted by the ILO in 1923 was that there should be a general inspection for safety purposes of all establishments not less than once every year. This was replaced in 1947 by the Labour Inspection Convention No. 81, which toughened the standard by requiring that workplaces should be inspected as often and as thoroughly as was necessary to ensure safe and healthy working conditions. Paradoxically, the UK has never fully implemented either the Recommendation or the current Convention (Williams, 1960:135–6).

Another British device designed to protect and improve working conditions was the Fair Wages Resolution of the House of Commons first adopted

---

[1] There is surprisingly no adequate, detailed and comprehensive account of international labour standards. The closest we have are contributions on aspects of the subject in Blanpain (1970 and 1982). In addition, there is Valticos (1979). The best work on the subject is in French by Valticos (1983). The only British textbook which devotes specific attention to international labour standards is Hepple and O'Higgins (1981). The text of the various international instruments referred to in this chapter can be found in Brownlie (1980); ILO (1982) and Robinson (1983). A full listing of British and Irish publications dealing with international labour standards can be found in Hepple et al. (1975:81, 175–7); Hepple et al. (1981:39–42, 64–5); O'Higgins (1985); and O'Higgins and Partington (1986: Part III).

[2] E.g. *Commission of the EC v UK* [1982] ICR 578, ECJ and *Commission of the EC v UK* [1984] ICR 192, ECJ.

in 1891 and in its final form in 1946. In effect this required people providing goods or services to government to be subjected to contractual requirements by the department concerned to maintain reasonable terms and conditions of employment. This technique of using the state's bargaining power to ensure decent conditions for workers is the historical root of the ILO Convention No. 94 on Labour Clauses (Public Contracts), adopted in 1949. The UK has now denounced the Convention and abrogated the Fair Wages Resolution (see Chapter 4 above).

United Kingdom practice was often the source of international labour standards in the past because the UK was a socially advanced country. Now that Britain lags behind many advanced industrial countries in social standards, measured by such conventional factors as the proportion of the Gross National Product spent on health care and social security, the proportion of young people in third-level education or the level of real wages, British practice is no longer the model for international labour standards. On the contrary, many of the most progressive legislative changes in the field of British labour legislation – for example, legislation against sex discrimination and in favour of equal pay, the protection of pregnant workers and the prohibition of anti-union discrimination by employers in the workplace – have as their primary source the legal obligations imposed upon the UK through its membership of international standard-setting organisations, whatever may have been the indigenous pressures for such changes.

Historically, one of the prime motivating reasons for advanced industrial countries to press for the adoption of international labour standards has been the need to reduce the impact on these countries of unfair foreign competition based on low pay and working conditions. But one of the principal arguments now used on behalf of the UK against the adoption of further and better international standards is that to do so would reduce Britain's competitiveness. Thus, in commenting on the EEC's Draft Directive on Temporary Work, intended to give temporary workers the same kind of rights as permanent employees, the government stated (DE, 1984a) its total opposition to

> unnecessary proposals for legislation [which] have nothing to do with the creation of a common market and are, frankly, seen by a great many people in this country as an irrelevant piece of European busybodying ... By imposing new obligations on employers, by restricting the use of temporary labour, it would probably introduce rigidities into the labour market, undermine competitiveness and actually reduce the number of jobs on offer.

Another reason for the fundamental alteration in the UK's attitude towards international labour standards is that the government believes that market forces, and, in particular, deregulation of the labour market, are generally in the public interest: employment prospects will be improved by removing barriers to the free operation of the labour market, whether these barriers are represented by the closed shop, the Fair Wages Resolution, statutory controls in the form of employment protection legislation, or trade union action. According to this theory, workers have priced themselves out of jobs – and price here includes not merely wages but also the costs necessarily imposed upon employers by legal obligations to pay above the market rate – and therefore job prospects may be improved by weakening those rules, factors or institutions which have a tendency to push up wages. One of the reasons given by the government for recently reducing some of the safeguards in employment protection legislation has been to lessen the disincentive this legislation represents to employers to offer employment.[3]

Many employers share the government's hostility to the improvement of international labour standards. Evidence for this can be found in the resolution unanimously adopted in 1984 by the national conference of the CBI. This called upon the European Commission to concentrate on promoting the economic strength of the Community, and warned the Commission that the pursuit of 'costly social engineering ambitions' would weaken European industry and damage employment prospects. In moving this resolution, the Director-General of the EEF said:

> Employment will not be improved in Europe if all we can do is burden employers with additional obligations and costs. The flood of draft directives and recommendations that the Commission has sponsored would have done credit to the 1974 Labour Government, when it was still totally in thrall to the unions ... Looked at on their own, by somebody who lived in Utopia rather than in Europe, nearly all these ideas may seem well-intentioned. Social engineering always does. They have something else in common – they all cost money and they all make additional problems for the running of a business. The one thing that they have nothing at all to do with is making and selling the products on which our lives depend. It seems to me that they are inspired by people who think European industry is still so large and prosperous that it can bear any burden put upon it. So we should look at the Commission's proposals in this light. Do they help us to compete or do they hinder us? The answer is obvious. They hinder us. And in hindering us, they damage employment prospects.[3a]

By international labour standards is meant rules adopted internationally by states laying down minimum standards in the fields of employment and social security for those who work. Such rules may be legally enforceable, either internationally or within national legal systems, or they may lack legal enforceability. The rules may represent legally obligatory standards or standards which states are under a legal or even merely a moral obligation to seek to attain. Enforcement ranges from judicial proceedings at the one extreme to reports by independent experts who examine a state's performance at the other extreme, where the only sanction for non-compliance is the publicity that may be given to the experts' report. The agencies developing such rules may be bilateral treaties between states, the activities of regional organisations, the United Nations organisation, the ILO, the Council of Europe, the European Communities and the Organisation for Economic Co-operation and Development (OECD). The most important from the

---

[3] Empirical evidence suggests, however, that the legislation does not have the alleged disincentive effect: see Chapters 1, 13 and 15 above.
[3a] *EEF Director General's Speech to CBI* (1984).

point of view of labour standards are the ILO, the Council of Europe, the European Communities and the OECD.

ILO

The ILO was established by the victorious powers at the end of World War I. Its first constitution forms part of the 1919 Treaty of Versailles, Arts.387–427. The preamble explains the motivation, or at least the ostensible motivation, for the establishment of the organisation. The considerations were that social injustice was a threat to the peace of the world, that sentiments of justice and humanity required an improvement in the condition of workers, and that the failure 'of any nation to adopt humane conditions of labour is an obstacle in the way of other nations which desire to improve conditions in their own countries'. The last is, of course, the old argument that advanced nations cannot afford to improve their working conditions in the face of competition from backward countries whose workers experience lower labour standards. Article 427 went on to lay down the basic principles which were to infuse all activities of the ILO:

> The High Contracting Parties ... recognise that differences of climate, habits and customs, of economic opportunity and industrial tradition make strict uniformity in the conditions of labour difficult of immediate attainment. But, holding as they do that labour should not be regarded merely as an article of commerce, they think that there are methods and principles for regulating labour conditions which all industrial communities should endeavour to apply, so far as their special circumstances will permit.
>
> Among these methods and principles, the following seem to the High Contracting Parties to be of special and urgent importance: *First*. The guiding principle above enunciated that labour should not be regarded merely as a commodity or article of commerce ... *Third*. The payment to the employed of a wage adequate to maintain a reasonable standard of life as this is understood in their time and country (Shotwell, 1934:424).

In 1944 at Philadelphia the ILO adopted a revised Constitution attached to which is a Declaration concerning the Aims and Purposes of the ILO. Article 1 provides that the ILO 'reaffirms the fundamental principles on which the Organisation is based and, in particular, that ... labour is not a commodity' (Johnston, 1976:302).

The notion that labour is not a commodity has to be understood as meaning two things. First, the price of labour must not be regulated primarily by market forces but rather by the human needs of the worker for a reasonable standard of living. Second, the labouring power of workers should not be transferred from one employer to another without the consent of the worker concerned.

Standard Setting by the ILO

Practically every state in the world is a member of the ILO. It is the oldest and most experienced of the international institutions concerned with the formulation of international labour standards. The standards developed by the ILO in turn are one of the prime sources of the standards elaborated by other organisations such as the Council of Europe and the European Communities. As a result, it is common, although not invariable, practice for representatives of the International Labour Office to be invited to participate as advisors or observers when international organisations with a more limited membership than the ILO are drawing up instruments proposing minimum labour standards. The purpose and intent behind this practice is that member states of the ILO, when adopting international labour standards on a limited or regional basis, should be careful to ensure that the standards they formulate take account of, develop and are compatible with the obligations accepted by those states as members of the ILO. Thus the international labour standards adopted by the Council of Europe and by the European Communities must be understood and interpreted in the light of the basic principles of the ILO.

The most distinctive feature of the ILO is its tripartite character. Each national delegation at the International Labour Conference, which meets annually in Geneva, consists of two government delegates, one employer delegate and one worker delegate. The latter pair are appointed after consultation with representative organisations of workers and employers in the state concerned. Each delegate has one vote and the voting rules are such that no one group can get its way without the support of members of at least one of the other groups. The tripartite character of representation runs throughout the structure of the ILO, including its Governing Body.

The principal means whereby the ILO establishes international standards is by the International Labour Conference adopting the texts of Conventions and Recommendations. Conventions are treaties to which member states may become party; Recommendations are standards to be aimed at by member states. Member governments must report regularly to the ILO on a range of matters including the measures taken to submit newly adopted standards to the competent authorities, usually the legislature of the state concerned; the position of their national law and practice with regard to unratified Conventions and Recommendations; and the measures taken to give effect to ratified Conventions.

These reports are submitted for scrutiny by a Committee of Experts on the Application of Conventions and Recommendations. The Experts' Reports are then examined further at the annual session of the International Labour Conference. This process of examination is intended to have the effect of bringing governments into line with the obligations they have accepted through ratifying Conventions, and of subjecting them to some pressure to extend the range of Conventions ratified by them and to implement Recommendations. While it is usual for Conventions to allow for denunciation by a member state, where a Convention has been ratified there is a system of representations and complaints which may lead to a member state being found to be in breach of its obligations, particularly in regard to ratified Conventions. Complaints relating to breaches of the Conventions dealing with freedom of association are processed through a separate procedure.

In 1951 the ILO's Governing Body set up a Committee on Freedom of Association, whose function initially was merely to carry out a preliminary examination to determine whether a complaint presented by a worker's or employer's organisation or by a government alleging violation of any of the ILO Conventions on Freedom of Association was sufficiently well founded to merit further investigation. In practice, the Governing Body's Committee on Freedom of Association came to perform a quasi-judicial function, by examining the substance of the complaint, recommending remedial action where appropriate to the government of the state complained against, and submitting its findings to the Governing Body. Over the years more than a thousand complaints have been investigated by the Committee. According to the ILO's account (1978:76):

> In many instances, as a result of recommendations made by the Committee, legislation criticised has been repealed or amended, practices incompatible with the principle of freedom of association have been discontinued, situations giving rise to complaints have been remedied ... Experience has shown that the mere possibility of recourse to the complaints procedure has sometimes led the parties concerned to remedy an existing situation merely in order to avoid having it investigated at the international level. In other cases, the fact that a complaint has been lodged has acted as a spur to negotiations between the government and the trade union concerned, and has finally led to a settlement and a withdrawal of the complaint.

The reports of the Committee on Freedom of Association have built up over the years an authoritative body of case law on the proper interpretation of the ILO Conventions dealing with freedom of association (see Pankert, 1982). It may indeed be claimed that the case law of the Committee has in many cases become part of customary international law. The most important illustration of this last point is the Committee's establishment, even in the absence of any express provision on the point in the Conventions, of a right to strike (ILO, 1976:109).

ILO Standards and the United Kingdom

Over the years, the UK has ratified a number of International Labour Conventions, which have in turn led to modification of British labour legislation (see Johnston, 1968). Two examples will suffice. The Baking Industry (Hours of Work) Act 1954 was enacted to give effect to ILO Convention No. 20 on Night Work (Bakeries) of 1925. The provisions of EPCA ss.23 and 58, which have the effect obliquely and indirectly of conferring a 'right' upon a trade union to conduct activities on the employer's premises, were enacted to give effect to ILO Convention No. 135 on Workers' Representatives (see Chapter 2).

A state may be free to give effect to a Convention not only by means of legislation but alternatively by practice or by collective bargaining. It is however a myth constantly reiterated – for example, by Johnston (1968) – that the UK only ratifies an International Labour Convention if British law or practice has already attained a standard prescribed by the Convention. Thus Convention No. 98 Concerning the Application of the Principles of the Right to Organise and to Bargain Collectively of 1949 was ratified by the UK in 1951. Article 1(1) provides that 'workers shall enjoy adequate protection against acts of anti-union discrimination in respect of their employment'. But it was not until the Industrial Relations Act 1971 that British workers were first given some legal protection against dismissal on the grounds of trade union membership. Even now, in breach of Convention No. 98, a British employer may refuse to offer employment to workers on the ground that they belong to a trade union.

The future impact of ILO standards in the UK appears to be likely to decline. The government has indicated (DE, 1983) that it will not ratify Convention No. 158 on Termination of Employment (1982).This Convention strengthens the standards already laid down in Recommendation No. 119 on Termination of Employment at the Initiative of the Employer (1963), which is of course the source from which the concept of 'unfair dismissal' in British law is derived (see Napier (1983) and Chapter 15 above). In addition to the denunciation of Convention No. 94 on Labour Clauses (Public Contracts) 1949, the UK has also denounced Convention No. 95 on Protection of Wages 1949 preparatory to the repeal of truck legislation (see DE, 1984b). While purporting to consult over the future of the wages council system, the government has announced that it will in any event denounce shortly Convention No. 26 on Minimum Wage-Fixing Machinery (1929), which ironically is largely based upon British practice (DE, 1985:paras. 21–3).

The supreme example of the government's attitude towards ILO standards arose from the banning of trade unions at GCHQ (for details of the litigation and judgments in the British courts see Chapters 2 and 8 above). The relevant ILO conventions were Nos. 87, 98 and 151. Since the government's action withdrew the right of civil servants in GCHQ to belong to trade unions of their own choosing on pain of being dismissed, and permitted them only to belong to officially approved employees' organisations, the issue arose of the compatibility of the government's action with these Conventions, which have been ratified by the UK. Convention No. 87 on Freedom of Association and Protection of the Right to Organise provides in Art.2 that 'workers ... *without distinction whatsoever*, shall have the right ... to join organisations of their own choosing without previous authorisation' (italics added). Convention No. 98 on the Right to Organise and to Bargain Collectively provides in Art.1 that

> Workers shall enjoy adequate protection against acts of anti-union discrimination ... such protection shall apply more particularly in respect of acts calculated to (a)

make the employment of a worker subject to the condition that he shall not join a union or shall relinquish trade union membership; (b) cause the dismissal of or otherwise prejudice a worker by reason of union membership.

Convention No. 87 applies to public servants but No. 98 provides in Art.6 that, although the Convention does not deal with the position of public servants, it is not to be construed 'as prejudicing their rights or status in any way'. Convention No. 151 on the Protection of the Right to Organise and Procedures for Determining Conditions of Employment in the Public Service (1978):

> applies to all persons employed by public authorities, to the extent that more favourable provisions in other international labour Conventions are not applicable to them. The extent to which the guarantees provided for in this Convention shall apply ... to employees of a highly confidential nature, shall be determined by national laws or regulation.

Article 4 of the same Convention provides public employees with protection from acts of anti-union discrimination in terms similar to Convention No. 98. Article 5(1) further provides that public employees' organisations should 'enjoy complete independence from public authorities'.

In 1984 the TUC presented a complaint to the Governing Body's Committee on Freedom of Association alleging violation of trade union rights against the UK. The International Confederation of Free Trade Unions and the Public Services International also formally associated themselves with the complaint. In proceedings before the Committee, the government's essential contention was that Convention No. 151 modified and reduced the guarantee to all workers of the right to freedom of association under Convention No. 87. With somewhat unnecessary pomposity, not to say inaccuracy, the government confirmed 'its continued adherence to its long-established policy of strictly respecting its obligations under all ILO Conventions that it has ratified and its commitment to the principles enshrined in these Conventions'. The Committee summarised the issue before it as being whether the British government had the right 'to deprive a particular category of public servants of their basic right to form or join a trade union of their choice or ... to maintain their membership of the union of their choice'. The Committee found that Convention No. 151 was intended to complement and not in any way to contradict or dilute 'the basic rights of association guaranteed to all workers by virtue of Convention No. 87'. The Committee's inevitable conclusion was that the unilateral action taken by the British government to deprive civil servants at GCHQ of their right to belong to a trade union of their choice was a breach of Convention No. 87.[4]

The government's reaction to the Governing Body's Committee established a precedent unique among democratic countries: it rejected the findings of the Committee. The government insisted that its interpretation of

---

[4] Report of Committee on Freedom of Association, Case No. 1261, *ILO Official Bulletin*, vol. 67 (1984), Series B, No. 2, pp. 112–20; endorsed by Committee of Experts (1985).

the relevant Conventions was correct and that in any case the Governing Body's Committee was not a judicial body.

The government decision over GCHQ was legally challenged, but the British courts did not and could not take account of either the ILO Conventions or the decision of the Governing Body's Committee.[5] This is because of the rule governing relations between British law and the UK's international legal obligations: treaties do not become part of British law unless an Act of Parliament provides that they should. In case of conflict between an ILO Convention and British law, the judges must allow the British law to prevail even if it involves a violation by the UK of its international legal obligations. But where a British statute or statutory instrument has been adopted to give effect to an international obligation, then a different consideration applies. Given that the UK – like all other members of the European Communities – is a member of the ILO, any instrument adopted by the European Communities and given effect as part of British law must be interpreted in the light of the basic principles of the ILO. So far as British practice is concerned, however, this basic proposition has been lost sight of. A single example will suffice; it concerns the proper interpretation of the EEC Directive on Acquired Rights of Workers on Transfers of Undertakings.[6]

The issue is a very simple one: does the Directive have the effect of transferring employees from one employer to another without or even against their agreement, or does it give, in certain circumstances, a guarantee that if the workers so desire the new owner of the enterprise must retain the old labour force in employment on the same terms as with the previous employer? Admittedly, the Directive is not specific on this point. Even less specific is the Transfer of Undertakings (Protection of Employment) Regulations[7] adopted reluctantly and with ill grace by the British government to give effect to the Directive (see Davies and Freedland, 1982).

The statutory instrument was made under the European Communities Act 1972 as delegated legislation to give effect to the terms of the Directive, and it clearly must be interpreted in the light of the meaning of the Directive, which should in turn be consistent with ILO principles. The practice of the courts has, it appears, been to consider almost exclusively only the terms of the statutory instrument rather than reading it through the provisions of the Directive.[7a] Even so, the question should have arisen of whether the new measures overrode the earlier fundamental principle of English law, as established in *Nokes v Doncaster Amalgamated Collieries Ltd*,[8] that a worker cannot be transferred without his or her consent from one employer to another. When the draft Directive was discussed by members of the panel of experts in labour law of the European Communities, the question was asked whether its terms, which did not differ significantly from the final Directive, were to be interpreted as providing for the transfer of workers

---

5   *Council of Civil Service Unions v Minister for the Civil Service* [1985] ICR 14, HL.
6   OJ 1977, L61/26.
7   SI 1981 No. 1794.
7a But cf. *McGrath v Rank Leisure Ltd* [1985] IRLR 323.
8   [1940] AC 1014.

without or against their will from one employer to another. The answer was an unanimous 'No'. This answer was inevitable given two things: the democratic legal conditions of the states from which the experts came, and the fundamental principle that 'labour is not a commodity', to which all member states of the European Communities have subscribed by virtue of their also being members of the ILO.

Yet judicial decisions on the interpretation of the UK regulations have not even discussed the difficulties involved in ignoring these basic principles. For example, in one case the EAT stated:

> The new Regulations were made to implement [the] Directive ... The general scheme of the Regulations is directly contrary to the pre-existing law. The general rule is that on the transfer of a business the employees of that business are transferred with it, that is, the employees' contract of employment with A undergoes a statutory novation and becomes a contract of employment with B ... In our judgment in the ordinary case the effect of the Regulations is that, if a business is transferred, the *employees are automatically transferred with it irrespective of the wishes of the transferee or of the employees* (italics added).[9]

The implications of this kind of approach to the interpretation of the European rules intended to protect employees in case of a transfer of an undertaking must be underlined. It means that the seller of a business may not only charge the purchaser a price for the business but, particularly where the labour force possesses a unique skill, the purchaser can add a charge for the transfer of the labour force. Furthermore, if members of such a transferred labour force refuse to work for the purchaser of the business, they could in certain circumstances, by no means far-fetched, face a claim for damages for breach of contract from the new purchaser. This would apply to skilled workers on fixed-term contracts. That, patently, cannot have been the intention behind a Directive intended to protect the rights of the employees.

COUNCIL OF EUROPE

European Convention on Human Rights

The Council of Europe has drawn up a number of treaties embodying international labour standards. Although the European Convention on Human Rights and Fundamental Freedoms is primarily concerned with political rights, it also contains provisions that are relevant to industrial relations. In particular, Art.8 guarantees a right to privacy, Art.10 guarantees a right to freedom of expression, and Art.11 guarantees a right both to freedom of assembly and to freedom of association.

The British law on picketing, as illustrated by such decisions as *Piddington v Bates*,[10] is patently a violation of Arts.10 and 11 of the European

---

[9] *Premier Motors (Medway) Ltd v Total Oil Great Britain Ltd* [1984] ICR 58, 61, 63.
[10] [1961] 1 WLR 162.

Convention. *Piddington v Bates* allows a policeman, when faced with two pickets in an entirely peaceful situation, to refuse to allow a third picket to join the picket line, provided the policeman reasonably believes that a breach of the peace may possibly occur. If the third would-be picket disobeys the policeman's instruction, not only does he run the risk of being arrested unlawfully – there being no power to arrest without warrant in this situation – but he may be charged with the offence of obstructing a policeman in the execution of his duty. To establish liability for this offence, it is not necessary for the prosecution to prove that there was a probability of a breach of the peace occurring. It is only necessary to prove a possibility and it is arguably always possible for a breach of the peace to occur wherever there is a difference of opinion, as in any industrial dispute. The policeman does not have to inferfere with picketing in this situation. He is under no legal obligation to do so. He merely has a discretion to interfere. Articles 10 and 11 of the Convention permit interference with picketing by the police if two conditions are satisfied. The first is that the restriction imposed by the policeman is prescribed by law. This means that it must be ascertainable in advance that the restriction will be imposed by the policeman. This is clearly not so in factual situations as exemplified by *Piddington v Bates*. The second is that the policeman's action must be 'necessary' to preserve, among other things, public order. In *Piddington v Bates* there was no compelling reason for the policeman's action; it was merely convenient for the police.

The machinery for the enforcement of the European Convention on Human Rights, after what are essentially mediation proceedings before the European Commission on Human Rights, admits of a reference by a state or by the Commission of an alleged violation of the European Convention to a court, the European Court of Human Rights. The Court can grant appropriate remedies to deal with the violation of the Convention. It has, as was illustrated by the case of *Young, James and Webster v UK*,[11] the power to award damages to individuals whose rights have not been respected. In that case, the Court awarded the complainants £65,000 damages in respect of loss suffered and £11,000 by way of just satisfaction in addition to legal costs.

A number of cases involving freedom of association have been considered by the European Court of Human Rights (Forde, 1983). The decision of most significance so far as the UK is concerned is *Young, James and Webster v UK*[12] (for the factual background to this case and its implications for British law see Chapter 2). In a somewhat confused majority judgment, the Court declined to read into Art.11 of the Convention an unqualified right not to belong to a trade union but none the less found that there had been a violation of the right of freedom of association of the complainants. Whether the Court's finding turned primarily upon the complainants' having become employees of British Rail prior to the establishment of a closed shop or upon the Court's view that loss of employment was a disproportionately severe sanction for refusing to join a trade union is not clear. Three

[11]   [1983] IRLR 35.
[12]   [1981] IRLR 408.

members of the Court dissented from the judgment. They did so on the basis that the *travaux préparatoires* to the Convention showed clearly that the states who drew up the Convention, including the UK, did not intend any negative right not to belong to a trade union to be implicit in Article 11. This is consonant with the tradition of the ILO's Conventions on freedom of association, which are designed to protect the right to join or form a trade union and leave the question of protecting a right not to join to be dealt with by national legislation if so desired. In the light of these considerations, it may be that later decisions of the European Court of Human Rights on freedom of association issues will see the *Young, James and Webster* case as being based, albeit somewhat unrealistically, upon a denial to the complainants of a right to form their own trade union. The British government carefully refrained from arguing, as was open to it, the defence that the provisions on dismissal in connection with the closed shop were necessary to protect the rights of others, that is, the other members of the trade union concerned. The Court, perhaps improperly, chose to consider the possibility that this defence might have been advanced and decided that it would not have succeeded. This expression of opinion was certainly obiter. In any event the British government heartily welcomed the decision and made arrangements in EA 1982 Sch.1 for the payment of compensation to people who had been dismissed between 1974 and 1980 on account of the closed shop. This of course was not necessitated by the decision of the Court.

European Social Charter

More important for employment practices in general is the European Social Charter (see Kahn-Freund, 1976). This treaty is unusual in that it allows adherent states to become parties to the treaty subject to their accepting a minimum number of the obligations contained in the Charter. The machinery for enforcement of the obligations under the Charter is very limited. Governments are required to make biennial reports in which they summarise their law and practice in relation to the obligations they have promised to fulfil under the Charter. These reports are sent to representative organisations of workers and employers in the states concerned inviting their comments. Such comments have rarely been forthcoming. This has led to the Committee of Independent Experts, to whom the governments' reports are submitted, being unable to form a judgment as to a particular state's compliance with its obligations on any other evidence than that submitted by the relevant state. The absence of comment from trade unions has enabled governments to make claims to conformity with the Charter where such claims may lack any substantial foundation in fact. But, so far as formal findings by the Committee of Experts of Britain's failure to comply with its obligations under the Charter are concerned, the British record is not significantly worse or better than that of other states party to the Charter.

The Social Charter is a direct source of a number of important changes in British labour legislation. For example, Art.8 (1) on paid leave for women employees before and after childbirth is the source of EPCA ss.33–5. The recent abandonment of arrangements with Denmark, the Federal Republic of Germany, the Netherlands and Greece for the surrender of merchant seamen deserters, under the Merchant Shipping Act 1970 s.89, was due to pressure from the Committee of Experts that Britain should come into line with its obligations under Art.1 (2) of the Charter to remove the taint of forced labour involved in this specialised form of extradition.

The Eighth Report of the Committee of Experts, which covers 1979 to 1981, found Britain to be in breach of a number of obligations under the Charter (Council of Europe, 1983). These included the failure to provide for adequate minimum periods of notice for workers dismissed with under two years' service (cf. EPCA s.64A). The period of maternity pay for women under EPCA ss.33–5 was for six weeks only, whereas Art.8(1) of the Charter required that it should last for at least twelve weeks; also the qualifying period of two years' employment for maternity pay was excessive. Most surprisingly, Britain was found in breach because it has not removed various discriminatory barriers to free movement of labour between member states signatory to the Social Charter.

Apart from sponsoring inquiries and making recommendations in the field of worker protection and equality for women, the Council of Europe has drawn up a series of important provisions: an agreement laying down terms for the employment of 'au pair' girls (1969), a European Code of Social Security including a system of international control similar to that of the Social Charter, a European Convention on Social Security (1977), and a European Convention on the Legal Status of Migrant Workers (1977). Of most significance, if it were to come to pass, would be the proposal to draw up a Protocol to the European Convention on Human Rights to include many of the rights embodied in the Social Charter. This would have the inestimable advantage of enabling individuals to petition the European Commission of Human Rights in cases involving alleged violation of their social rights, with the possibility of the ultimate reference of such complaints to the European Court of Human Rights.

Three of Britain's obligations under the Social Charter deserve special attention: the right to adequate remuneration, the prohibition of deductions from wages, and the right to strike. Article 4(1) of the Charter requires the UK 'to recognise the right of workers to a remuneration such as will give them and their families a decent standard of living'. This is, of course, based upon the fundamental principles of the ILO and is incompatible with allowing the price of labour to be determined exclusively by market forces. Thus, when the government abandoned the basic 'Priestley principle' of fair comparability for the determination of civil service pay and replaced it in 1982 with the principle that lower ranks of civil servants should be paid only sufficient 'to recruit, retain and motivate them', it would appear to have breached Art.4(1). The Committee of Experts had already found that, since over 10 per cent of men, 50 per cent of female manual workers and 25 per cent of non-manual female workers had earnings below two-thirds of national average wages (£78.20 in 1981), 'the situation could not be considered in conformity with the Charter' (Council of Europe, 1983).

Article 4(5) requires the UK 'to permit deductions from wages only under conditions and to the extent prescribed by national laws or regulations or fixed by collective agreements or arbitration awards'. The Committee of Experts found the UK to be in breach of its obligations under this provision because the truck legislation, being confined to workers engaged in manual labour, imposed no restriction upon deductions from the wages of non-manual workers. This led to a vigorous retort from the British government that it had no intention of altering British law 'since no deductions were in fact made from non-manual workers' wages and their interest (*sic*) were well protected by the practice and activities of a powerful workers' association' (Council of Europe, 1971). In a later report, the Committee of Experts clarified the obligation of Art.4(5) and declared 'that a state must be regarded as acting in conformity with this provision when deductions from wages are permitted for the large majority of workers only when they are expressly authorised by laws, regulations, collective agreements or arbitration awards'. The UK was apparently able to satisfy the Committee that this aptly described the situation in Britain (Council of Europe, 1977).

As indicated above, preparatory to ridding itself of the Truck Acts, the UK has denounced ILO Convention No. 95. There remains the difficult hurdle of Art.4(5) of the Social Charter which cannot be denounced. In the government's consultative paper (DE, 1984b), there is no mention of either ILO Convention No. 95 or of Art.4(5) of the Social Charter. Yet the proposed legislation would permit deductions from wages by an employer if they were authorised under statute, or expressly provided for in an individual's contract of employment, or provided for impliedly by any means such as collective agreements or custom and practice in the trade or industry concerned, or otherwise agreed to by the individual in writing. Individual agreements are arguably in breach of Art.4(5) of the Charter.

In the UK there is no right to strike, only a series of limited immunities that in certain circumstances prevent claims from being brought against trade unions or the organisers of strikes. While there may be debate about the respective merits of a system of immunities as against a legal right to strike, Britain is bound by international treaty to give effect to a right to strike. Such a right would imply a definition of the line to be drawn between unlawful and lawful strikes, and a ban on action taken by an employer to penalise workers who exercise their legal right to strike (see O'Higgins, 1976). How far it might be possible to modify the British system based upon immunities so that it could provide virtually the same protection to strikers as would be theirs in a system with the legal right to strike is open to debate (see further Chapters 6 and 9 above). What is quite clear, however, is that cases like *Cruikshank v Hobbs*,[13] where an employer was found lawfully able to select workers for dismissal for redundancy on the basis of their having participated in an official strike, are incompatible with any notion of a right to strike. Article 6(4) of the Social Charter requires the UK to recognise 'the right for workers and employers to collective action in cases of conflicts of interest, including the right to strike, subject to obligations that might arise out of collective agreements previously entered into'. Although

---

[13] [1977] ICR 725.

the Committee of Experts have had some difficulty in coping with the British concept of immunities for strike action, they have stated repeatedly (for example, Council of Europe, 1973:38) that there is no right to strike within the meaning of Art.6(4) where the employer is free not to re-employ all the strikers at the end of the strike and where, if he does re-employ them he does so on terms that do not preserve all the rights and advantages attached to their previous employment contracts. The significance of this point can only be reinforced by the amendment to EPCA s.62 (discussed in Chapter 9), which make it easier for employers to dismiss and selectively to re-engage strikers.

EUROPEAN COMMUNITIES

The Treaty of Rome 1957 establishing the European Economic Community always had as a necessary part the achievement of certain social aims, the most fundamental being the improvement of conditions of workers (Art.117 of the Treaty). The Treaty contains numerous provisions relevant to employment. Articles 48 onwards deal with freedom of movement on a non-discriminatory basis for workers seeking employment. Article 117 provides for the harmonisation of social security and of working conditions. Article 118 provides for co-operation between members states in fields such as labour law and social security. Article 119 deals with equal pay between men and women. Perhaps the most significant of all, Art.100 requires action to be taken to remove any institution or rule which distorts the proper functioning of the Community. The Council Directives on Equal Pay for Men and Women,[14] Collective Redundancies,[15] and Transfer of Undertakings[16] derive their legal authority wholly or in part from this Article.

The rationale is that the disparity between the labour costs imposed upon employers by national legislation in the different member states as regards, for example, reducing the size of the labour force or taking over of another employer's business had the effect of distorting competition between employers in different member states. When the CBI tried to persuade the government not to give effect to the Directive on Collective Redundancies (in the form of EPA ss.99–107) on the grounds that it would add to British labour costs, they missed the point. Its purpose was to add to labour costs of employers in countries with low levels of labour protection who were seen as competing unfairly with the more socially advanced member states of the Community. As a former EEC Commissioner for Employment and Social Affairs explained (Richard, 1984:5), 'support for Community action often derives in practice from an anxiety on the part of some member states to ensure that all member states are competing equally on an economic front and should therefore shoulder a similar burden as regards social policy'. This

[14]   OJ 1975, L45/19.
[15]   OJ 1975, L48/29.
[16]   OJ 1977, L61/26.

is the old competition argument which is one of the foundations of all international labour standards: socially advanced industrial states seek to impose labour standards on the less advanced in order to lessen the competitive advantage of countries with poor working conditions.

A critical element in the Community's concern with employment issues is represented by the Social Action Programme, which the Commission produced in 1973. There were three principal parts to the programme. The first called for action to attain full and better employment. The second aimed at the improvement of living and working conditions, so as to make possible their harmonisation. The third was aimed at increased involvement of management and labour in the economic and social decisions of the Community, and of workers, or their representatives, in the management of undertakings. The European Social Fund was given a wider mandate to cope with economic and social problems arising out of restructuring, unemployment and lack of adequate training or re-training facilities. Since 1973, the Community has produced many important standards in the field of labour relations and social security. Particularly significant has been the action of the Community in promoting equality for men and women in working life (see Chapter 17), improving occupational safety (see Chapter 16), encouraging greater worker participation (see Chapter 5) and improving the basic rights of workers, for example, in the case of the bankruptcy of an employer (cf. EPCA s.106).

Of all the international organisations that lay down labour standards, the European Communities have the most effective means of enforcement. The Commission, which may act on its own initiative or as the result of a complaint from an organisation or individual, may take proceedings against a member state that has failed to fulfil its obligations under the Rome Treaty. It is a lengthy procedure and there is currently a substantial backlog of work, but ultimately the Commission may refer an issue to the European Court of Justice (ECJ). A member state which considers that another member is failing to fulfil its obligations may also refer the matter to the ECJ. The Court has limited powers and the usual outcome is a ruling on whether or not the member state concerned is fulfilling or is in breach of its obligations. If found to be in breach, the member state is bound to take the necessary remedial steps.

As for individuals who have been denied rights given them by the Rome Treaty or by regulations made under the Treaty, they may either initiate proceedings in a national court or make a complaint to the Commission, which may or may not take the matter further. As regards proceedings by individuals before British courts, the terms of the Treaty article or regulation must be directly effective, that is, they must form part of the British legal system, which they will do under the European Communities Act 1972, and also their terms must be such as to be appropriate to confer rights on individuals. It used to be considered that the terms of Directives could not be directly enforced but, as a result of judicial interpretation by the ECJ, a Directive subject to the same conditions as apply to Treaty articles and regulations may occasionally be directly effective (Hartley, 1981:185).

Implementation in UK of Community Standards

The UK's failure to give full implementation to Community law is well illustrated by its response to the Collective Redundancies Directive in the form of Part IV of the EPA on redundancy consultation. The Directive is intended to lay down certain standards and procedures to be applied by employers in cases of 'collective redundancies', which are defined in Art.1 as 'dismissals effected by an employer for one or more reasons not related to the individual worker concerned'. This is a much broader concept than the one used in Part IV of the EPA, which utilises the definition of 'redundancy' in EPCA s.81(2), where it is restricted to a cessation or reduction of business or a decline in demand for work of a particular kind (see Chapter 15 above). It is easy enough to give examples of situations which would be covered by the Directive, but which are not covered by the redundancy consultation provisions of the EPA. In *Chapman v Goonvean and Rostowrack China Clay Co. Ltd*[17] workers lost their employment after their employer withdrew a free bus which had taken them to and from their work. The employer's reason for withdrawing the bus was economic. The employees concerned were held not to have lost their employment due to redundancy. In *Johnson v Nottinghamshire Combined Police Authority*,[18] two clerks lost their employment because they were unable to continue to do the same number of hours' work per week when their employer radically altered the working arrangements by introducing a new shift system. Again it was held that this was not a redundancy situation. In both these kinds of cases the EPA's consultation duty would have no application, although clearly dismissal for these kinds of reasons are within the coverage of the Directive.

Article 2 of the Directive requires the employer to consult workers' representatives 'with a view to reaching agreement'. This may involve a duty close to the North American duty of bargaining in good faith. The provisions in the EPA, however, do not require the employer to consult with the aim of reaching agreement. It is sufficient that he should consider representations made to him on behalf of the workers and state why he chooses to reject any of these representations. Furthermore, Art.2 of the Directive indicates that consultations are to cover 'ways and means of avoiding collective redundancies or reducing the number of workers affected'. There is no equivalent obligation in the EPA. Under the Act, as under the Directive, a public authority has to be notified of the impending redundancies. The Directive states that 'the workers' representatives may send any comments they may have to the competent public authority', but there is no equivalent provision in the Act. The Act obliges the employer to consult only the representatives of 'recognised' trade unions. Where he does not recognise any union, in apparent contrast to the Directive, he does not have to consult anyone.

Another example of defective implementation is the Transfer of Undertakings (Protection of Employment) Regulations 1981 as compared with the

---

[17] [1973] ICR 50.
[18] [1974] ICR 170.

Transfer of Undertakings Directive. As explained above, difficult problems of interpretation have arisen here. British courts and commentators seem unaware of the fundamental principles of international labour law as established by the ILO, which must inform the interpretation of international labour standards drawn up by organisations such as the European Communities all of whose members subscribe to the principles of the ILO. There is another relevant principle, particularly having regard to Art.100 of the Rome Treaty, which must also inform the proper interpretation of Community labour standards, namely, the aim of harmonising standards between member states of the Communities.

Article 3(2) of the Transfer of Undertakings Directive provides that the new owner of an undertaking 'shall continue to observe the terms and conditions agreed in any collective agreement on the same terms applicable to the transferor under that agreement, until the date of termination or expiry of the collective agreement or the entry into force or application of another collective agreement'. The issue of interpretation is whether it was intended that the acquirors of businesses in all member states should be under an identical obligation to respect collective agreements, or whether countries like Britain should be exempt from common standards. Posed in that way, the answer must surely be that it was the intention that the obligation should be the same in all member countries. It may be objected that Art.3(2) has no application to a British transferor since in Britain collective agreements, save where incorporated in contracts of employment, are not a source of legal obligation. But only a lawyer could make a point like that. Even in Britain employers observe and, in practice though not in law, are obliged to observe the terms of collective agreements. The intention of Art.3(2) is to impose a legal obligation upon the transferee to continue to respect the terms of a collective agreement which were binding on the transferor, whether or not the binding force derives from law.

There is nothing novel in a legal duty to respect obligations which are themselves not legally enforceable. An illustration of this is the legislation on the restoration of pre-war trade practices of 1919, 1942 and 1950, which subjected British employers to a statutory obligation to respect collective agreements and custom and practice even where these were not contractually binding. There is no recognisable equivalent of Art.3(2) in the Transfer of Undertakings (Protection of Employment) Regulations 1981. There is reg.6, however, which provides:

> Where at the time of a relevant transfer there exists a collective agreement made by or on behalf of the transferor ... without prejudice to [TULRA s.18 – collective agreements presumed to be unenforceable] that agreement, in its application in relation to the employee, shall, after the transfer, have effect as if made by or on behalf of the transferee with that trade union, and accordingly anything done under or in connection with it, in its application as aforesaid, by or in relation to the transferor before the transfer, shall, after the transfer, be deemed to have been done by or in relation to the transferee.

This gobbledegook is virtually impossible to interpret. Davies and Freedland (1982) believe that it may have no legal effect. But this may be because they are over-impressed by the lack of legal enforceability of collective agreements in British law. If it is possible to read the provisions of Art.3(2) into reg.6, then the latter, being intended to subject transferees of undertakings in Britain to the same obligations as transferees of undertakings in France or Germany, has a clear legally enforceable content, without prejudice to the ordinary British rule that collective agreements are not part of contracts of employment of the workers concerned unless expressly or impliedly incorporated.

Multinational Companies and the European Communities

Concern about the activities of multi-national companies and in particular their impact on developing countries has led to the principal international organisations laying down standards. In 1977 the ILO adopted a Tripartite Declaration of Principles Concerning Multinational Enterprises and Social Policy. The European Communities, in addition to the obligatory legal standards laid down in various instruments concerning taxation and competition, have also sought to draw up a series of further legally binding standards which would help to control the activities of multinationals as regards employment relations, for example, the 'Vredeling' draft directive[19] and the draft Fifth Directive concerning the structure of public companies.[20] Vigorous lobbying campaigns have been conducted, in the interests in particular of American corporations, to delay, water down, and frustrate the adoption of such standards, which are discussed in more detail in Chapter 5.

In September 1977 the foreign ministers of the member states of the European Communities adopted a Code of Conduct for Companies with Subsidiaries, Branches or Representation in South Africa. Among other provisions designed to improve labour conditions for black workers was paragraph 3, which provided that companies 'should formulate specific policies aimed at improving their terms of employment. Pay, based on the absolute minimum necessary for a family to survive, cannot be considered as being sufficient. The minimum wages should initially exceed by at least 50 per cent the minimum level required to satisfy the basic needs of an employee and his family'. Policing of this Code was left to member states. British companies operating in South Africa were requested to report annually to the Department of Trade, to provide information on the number of Africans they employed, the facilities for consultation and management attitudes to trade unions, wages, fringe benefits and other matters. The British labour attaché in South Africa was required to monitor the labour practices in British companies there, recording any discrepancies between what they reported to the Department and what happened in practice. The British government initially published a list of all companies paying wages below the level required by the Code, but in 1979 the new Conservative Government ceased publishing a list of defaulting companies and withdrew the labour attaché from South Africa (LRD, 1983).

[19] OJ No. C 217/3 12.8.1983.
[20] OJ No. C 240/2 9.9.1983.

The European Communities have also sought to encourage transnational collective bargaining as a means of providing a countervailing power to the activities of multinationals. This has been unsuccessful. For the transnational power of trade unions to be effective, it needs not only transnational collective bargaining but also freedom to take trans-national industrial action. Unions in one country must be able lawfully to take industrial action in support of workers in other countries. A particular instance of the need for such freedom is the long campaign by the International Transport Workers' Federation against flags of convenience (see Northrup and Rowan, 1983). The amendment of the definition of 'trade dispute' by EA 1982 s.18(4) makes it practically impossible for any form of international sympathy action to be lawful (see Chapter 6 above). This is arguably a breach of both ILO standards and Art.6(4) of the European Social Charter.

OECD

The OECD, whose members are the twenty-four most advanced Western industrial states, is primarily concerned to protect the economic interests of these states. During the late 1960s and early 1970s, a number of states including many in the Third World criticised the activities of multinational companies with allegations of transfer pricing, tax evasion and the provision of poor working conditions. With what might be regarded as indecent haste and in order to head off proposed legal controls on multinationals emanating from organisations such as the United Nations, the ILO and the European Communities, the governments of the OECD states adopted a Declaration on International Investment and Multinational Enterprises, which was later revised in 1979 and 1984.

The Declaration includes nine short paragraphs dealing with employment and industrial relations. These provide that, within the framework of local laws and practices governing industrial relations, multinationals should respect the right of employees to be represented by trade unions and engage in constructive negotiations with a view to reaching agreement on employment conditions; give workers' representatives adequate facilities to assist in collective bargaining and information necessary for meaningful negotiations; provide them with information on the performance of the local subsidiary, or 'where appropriate', the multinational as a whole; observe labour standards not less favourable than those followed by comparable employers in the host country; provide training for, and opportunities for promotion to, their employees; provide reasonable notice to workers' representatives of changes in their operations likely to have major effects upon the livelihood of their employees and to co-operate to mitigate adverse effects of such changes; promote greater equality of employment opportunity between different groups of employees; not threaten to transfer operating units or employees from one country to another in order to influence unfairly negotiations or the right to organise; and, enable workers' representatives to negotiate with managers 'authorised to take decisions on the matters under negotiation'.

These guideline are voluntary and are not legally enforceable. The publicity that may accompany violation of the guidelines is, however, sufficient in certain cases to persuade some companies, for the sake of their public image, to be seen to act in conformity with them. Given the vagueness and uncertainty of the meaning of the guidelines, considerable importance is attached to their clarification by the OECD Committee on International Investment and Multinational Enterprises (IME Committee). The IME Committee has had a number of cases referred to it by governments or by the Trade Union Advisory Committee (TUAC) to the OECD.

The well-known *Badger* case (see Campbell and Rowan, 1983:124), referred to the IME Committee both by the Belgian government and by TUAC in 1977, demonstrated that though the guidelines lacked any effective teeth 'they may operate as an important pressure point on a multinational corporation to go beyond what is strictly required by law' (Hepple and O'Higgins, 1981:349). The background was that a Belgian subsidiary of the Badger Co. Inc., an American multinational, closed its Antwerp office and became bankrupt, leaving insufficient funds to pay the required compensation to the dismissed employees. Under pressure the Badger Co. finally undertook, having particular regard to the guidelines requiring co-operation to mitigate the adverse effects of major changes, to supplement the assets of the local Belgian subsidiary by the amount necessary to pay proper compensation to the dismissed employees. The view has been expressed, in the light of this case, that 'in the course of time, sections of the guidelines, although voluntary in origin and not being sanctioned by law, may pass, by virtue of their general acceptance and frequent application, into the general course of customary international law, even for those international enterprises that have never explicitly accepted them'. This view, expressed in an IME Committee internal memorandum cited by Robinson (1983:128), may be over-optimistic.

CONCLUSION

In the early stages of the evolution of international labour standards, the British state, civil servants and politicians played a pioneering role. In the middle stage of this history, from the establishment of the ILO up to the late 1960s, the UK frequently improved its own labour legislation to take account of international labour standards. From the middle or late 1970s onwards, the UK has largely played a negative role in relation to the improvement of international labour standards. This is a vital issue for Britain's relationship with the European Community, which has a lengthy agenda of proposed new labour standards ranging from noise levels and parental leave to disclosure, consultation and employee participation in management. If the UK is in future able to prevent the adoption of new labour standards, not only will the Community cease to be a prime source of changes in British labour legislation but also the future development of the Community itself will be impaired.

Bibliography

Blanpain, Roget (ed.). 1970. *International Encyclopaedia for Labour Law and Industrial Relations*. Deventer: Kluwer.
—— (ed.). 1982. *Comparative Labour Law and Industrial Relations*. Deventer: Kluwer.
Brownlie, Ian. 1980. *Basic Documents on Human Rights*. Oxford: Clarendon Press.
Campbell, Duncan C., and Richard L. Rowan. 1983. *Multinational Enterprises and the OECD: Industrial Relations Guidelines*. Philadelphia: University of Pennsylvania.
Council of Europe. 1971. Committee of Independent Experts on the European Social Charter. *Conclusions II*. Strasbourg: Council of Europe.
——. 1973. Committee of Independent Experts on the European Social Charter. *Conclusions III*. Strasbourg: Council of Europe.
——. 1977. Committee of Independent Experts on the European Social Charter. *Conclusions V*. Strasbourg: Council of Europe.
——. 1983. Committee of Independent Experts on the European Social Charter. *Conclusions VIII*. Strasbourg: Council of Europe.
Davies, P., and M. Freedland. 1982. *Transfer of Employment*. London: Sweet & Maxwell.
Department of Employment (DE). 1983. *International Labour Conference*. Cmnd 9078. London: HMSO.
——. 1984a. Press Notice, 15 November.
——. 1984b. *Protection of Wages: Legislative Proposals*. London: DE.
——. 1985. *Consultative Paper on Wages Councils*. London: DE.
Forde, M. 1983. 'The European Convention on Human Rights and Labor Law'. *American Journal of Comparative Law*, 31 (Spring), 301–32.
Hartley, T.C. 1981. *The Foundations of European Community Law*. Oxford: Clarendon Press.
Hepple, B.A., J. Hepple, Paul O'Higgins and Paula Stirling. 1981. *Labour Law in Great Britain and Ireland to 1978*. London: Sweet & Maxwell.
——, J.M. Neeson and Paul O'Higgins. 1975. *A Bibliography of the Literature on British and Irish Labour Law*. London: Mansell.
——, and P. O'Higgins. 1981. *Employment Law*. 4th edn. B. A. Hepple. London: Sweet & Maxwell.
International Labour Organisation (ILO). 1976. *Freedom of Association: Digest of Decisions of the Freedom of Association Committee of the Governing Body of the ILO*. 2nd edn. Geneva: ILO.
——. 1978. *International Labour Standards: A Workers' Educational Manual*. Geneva: ILO.
——. 1982. *ILO Conventions and Recommendations 1919–1981*. Geneva: ILO.
Johnston, G.A. 1968. 'The Influence of International Labour Standards on Legislation and Practice in the United Kingdom'. *International Labour Review*, 97 (May), 465–87.

——. 1976. *The International Labour Organisation*. London: Europa Publications.

Kahn-Freund, Otto. 1976. 'European Social Charter'. *European Law and the Individual*. Ed. F.G. Jacobs. Amsterdam: North-Holland, 181–211.

Labour Research Department (LRD). 1983. 'South Africa: British Companies Aid Apartheid'. *Labour Research*, 72 (August), 214–15.

Napier, Brian. 1983. 'Dismissals – The New ILO Standards'. *Industrial Law Journal*, 12 (March), 17–27.

Northrup, Herbert R., and Richard L. Rowan. 1983. *The International Transport Workers' Federation and Flag of Convenience Shipping*. Philadelphia: University of Pennsylvania.

O'Higgins, P. 1976. 'The Right to Strike – Some International Reflections'. *Studies in Labour Law*. Ed. J.R. Carby-Hall. Bradford: MCB Books, 110–18.

——. 1986. *Labour Law in Great Britian and Ireland 1979–84*. London: Mansell.

——, and Martin Partington. 1986. *Bibliography of British and Irish Social Security Law*. London: Mansell.

Pankert, A. 1982. 'Freedom of Association'. *Comparative Labour Law and Industrial Relations*. Ed. R. Blanpain. Deventer: Kluwer, 146–65.

Richard, Ivor. 1984. *The Future of Community Social Legislation*. Exeter: University of Exeter.

Robinson, John. 1983. *Multinationals and Political Control*. Aldershot: Gower.

Shotwell, J.T. 1934. *The Origins of the International Labour Organisation*. 2 vols. New York: Columbia University Press.

Valticos, N. 1979. *International Labour Law*. Deventer: Kluwer.

——. 1983. *Droit international du travail*. 2me Ed. Paris: Dalloz.

Williams, J.L. 1960. *Accidents and Ill-Health at Work*. London: Staple Press.

Index